The Holy Qur'an

English Translation of the Meanings of the Qur'an with Notes

Abdullah Yusuf Ali

Published by

H & C
INTERNATIONAL

IMPORTANT NOTE: This is only the translation of the meanings of the Qur'an, and it by no means replaces the need for the original Arabic which is the only revealed message of God verbatim.

Copyright © 1992, H &C International, P.O. Box 51841, Indianapolis, IN 46251, USA.

Library of Congress Cataloging in Publication Data
            92-73241
                CIP

ISBN   0-9633850-0-3

Typesetting and cover design by A-Ztype

بسم الله الرحمن الرحيم

In The Name Of Allah, The Merciful, The Gracious

CONTENTS

Publisher's Note vi

From the Preface to the First Edition viii

Chapter 1: Al-Fātihah   - The Opening 1

Chapter 2: Al-Baqarah   - The Cow 2

Chapter 3: Āl-i-'Imran   - The Family of Imran 37

Chapter 4: An-Nisā'   - The Women 57

Chapter 5: Al-Mā'ida   - The Table Spread 76

Chapter 6: Al-An'ām   - The Cattle 91

Chapter 7: Al-A'rāf   - The Heights 109

Chapter 8: Al-Anfāl   - The Spoils of War 128

Chapter 9: At-Tawbah   - The Repentance 135

Chapter 10: Yūnus   - Jonah 149

Chapter 11: Hūd   - The Prophet Hud 160

Chapter 12: Yūsuf   - Joseph 171

Chapter 13: Ar-Ra'd   - The Thunder 182

Chapter 14: Ibrahim   - Abraham 187

Chapter 15: Al-Hijr   - The Rocky Tract 192

Chapter 16: Al-Nahl   - Bees 197

Chapter 17: Al-Isra'   - The Night Journey 209

Chapter 18: Al-Kahf   - The Cave 219

Chapter 19: Maryam   - Mary 229

Chapter 20: Tā-Hā   - Tā-Hā 235

Chapter 21: Al-Anbiyā   - The Prophets 245

Chapter 22: Al-Hajj   - The Pilgrimage 253

Chapter 23: Al-Mu'minūn   - The Believers 261

Chapter 24: An-Nūr   - The Light 268

Chapter 25: Al-Furqān   - The Criterion 276

Chapter 26: Ash-Shu'arā   - The Poets 282

Chapter 27: Al-Naml   - The Ants 292

Chapter 28: Al-Qasas   - The Narrations 299

Chapter 29: Al-'Ankabūt   - The Spider 308

Chapter 30: Ar-Rūm   - The Romans 314

Chapter 31: Luqmān   - Luqman The Wise 320

ii

Chapter 32: As-Sajdah - The Prostration 324

Chapter 33: Al-Ahzāb - The Confederates 326

Chapter 34: Saba - Sheba 334

Chapter 35: Fatir - The Originator of Creation 340

Chapter 36: Yā-Sïn - Yā Sïn 345

Chapter 37: As-Safat - Those Ranged in Ranks 351

Chapter 38: Sād - Sād 358

Chapter 39: Az-Zumar - Crowds 364

Chapter 40: Ghāfir[1] - The Forgiver 372

Chapter 41: Fussilat[2] - Explained 380

Chapter 42: Ash-Shura - Consultation 385

Chapter 43: Az-Zukhruf - Ornaments of Gold 390

Chapter 44: Ad-Dukhān - The Smoke 396

Chapter 45: Al-Jathiyah - The Kneeling Down 399

Chapter 46: Al-Ahqāf - Winding Sand-tracts 403

Chapter 47: Muhammad - Muhammad The Prophet 407

Chapter 48: Al-Fath - The Victory 412

Chapter 49: Al-Hujurāt - The Inner Apartments 416

Chapter 50: Qāf - Qāf 418

Chapter 51: Adh-Dhāriyāt - The Winds That Scatter 422

Chapter 52: At-Tür - The Mount 425

Chapter 53: An-Najm - The Star 428

Chapter 54: Al-Qamar - The Moon 431

Chapter 55: Ar-Rahmān - The Most Gracious 434

Chapter 56: Al-Waqi'ah - The Inevitable Event 437

Chapter 57: Al-Hadïd - Iron 442

Chapter 58: Al-Mujādilah - The Woman Who Pleads 446

Chapter 59: Al-Hashr - The Gathering 449

Chapter 60: Al-Mumtahinah - The Woman To Be Examined 452

Chapter 61: As-Saff - The Battle Array 454

Chapter 62: Al-Jumu'ah - Friday 455

Chapter 63: Al-Munāfiqün - The Hypocrites 457

Chapter 64: At-Taghābun - The Mutual Loss And Gain 458

Chapter 65: At-Talāq - Divorce 460

---

[1] Also called Surah Al-Mu'min (The Believer).

[2] Or Surah Hā Mïm.

iii

Chapter 66: At-Tahrim - Prohibition 461
Chapter 67: Al-Mulk - The Dominion 463
Chapter 68: Al-Qalam[3] - The Pen 466
Chapter 69: Al-Haqqah - The Sure Reality 468
Chapter 70: Al-Ma'arij - The Ways of Ascent 471
Chapter 71: Nüh - Noah 472
Chapter 72: Al-Jinn - The Spirits 474
Chapter 73: Al-Muzzammil - The Folded in Garments 476
Chapter 74: Al-Muddaththir - The One Wrapped Up 478
Chapter 75: Al-Qiyamah - The Resurrection 480
Chapter 76: Al-Insan[4] - Man 482
Chapter 77: Al-Mursalat - Those Sent Forth 484
Chapter 78: An-Naba' - The Great News 486
Chapter 79: An-Nazi'at - Those Who Tear Out 488
Chapter 80: 'Abasa - He Frowned 490
Chapter 81: At-Takwir - The Folding Up 491
Chapter 82: Al-Infitar - The Cleaving Asunder 493
Chapter 83: Al-Mutaffifin - The Dealers in Fraud 494
Chapter 84: Al-Inshiqaq - The Rending Asunder 495
Chapter 85: Al-Buruj - The Zodiacal Signs 497
Chapter 86: At-Tariq - The Night Star 498
Chapter 87: Al-A'la - The Most High 498
Chapter 88: Al-Ghashiyah - The Overwhelming Event 499
Chapter 89: Al-Fajr - The Dawn 500
Chapter 90: Al-Balad - The City 502
Chapter 91: Ash-Shams - The Sun 503
Chapter 92: Al-Layl - The Night 503
Chapter 93: Ad-Duha - The Glorious Morning Light 504
Chapter 94: Al-Inshrah[5] - The Expansion of the Breast 505
Chapter 95: At-Tin - The Fig 505
Chapter 96: Al-'Alaq[6] - The Clinging Clot 506
Chapter 97: Al-Qadr - The Night of Power 507

---

[3] Or Surah Nun.
[4] Or Ad-Dahr (The Time).
[5] Or Surah Al-Sharh.
[6] Or Surah Iqra' (Read!)

Chapter 98: Al-Bayyinah   - The Clear Evidence 507

Chapter 99: Al-Zalzalah   - The Earthquake 508

Chapter 100: Al-'Adiyat   - Those That Run 508

Chapter 101: Al-Qāri'ah   - The Great Calamity 509

Chapter 102: At-Takāthur   - The Piling Up 510

Chapter 103: Al-'Asr   - Time Through the Ages 510

Chapter 104: Al-Humaza   - The Scandalmonger 510

Chapter 105: Al-Fīl   - The Elephant 511

Chapter 106: Quraysh   - The Tribe of Quraysh 511

Chapter 107: Al-Ma'ūn   - The Neighbouly Needs 512

Chapter 108: Al-Kauthar   - The Abundance 512

Chapter 109: Al-Kāfirūn   - The Disbelievers 512

Chapter 110: An-Nasr   - The Help 513

Chapter 111: Abu Lahab[7]   - The Father of Flame 513

Chapter 112: Al-Ikhlas   - The Purity of Faith 513

Chapter 113: Al-Falaq   - The Daybreak 514

Chapter 114: An-Nās   - The Mankind 514

Index 515

---

[7] Or Surah Al-Masad (The Plaited Rope).

v

Publisher's Note

Abdullah Yusuf Ali's translation of the Qur'an is the most popular one today. It is his approach and intellectual honesty that makes his work so appealing and of enduring interest to Muslims all over the world. "In translating the Text," he says, "I have aired no views of my own, but followed the received Commentators." His masterly skill with which he tried to reflect in his translation the rhythm, music, and exalted tone of the original has given it a special status, and endeared it to so many readers. Here we have a faithful rendition of the Word of God and in a garb befitting its beauty, majesty, and grandeur, if any human effort can ever hope to weave such a garb. True, it is impossible to translate the Qur'an; nor can its eloquence and beauty be adequately captured by any man in any other human language. Among the few who were fortunate enough to capture a glimpse, "a faint reflection," at least of the original, Abdullah Yusuf Ali's work stands out prominently.

Ever since its first publication Abdullah Yusuf Ali's interpretation of the Qur'an has guided and comforted millions in all parts of the globe, and it still remains popular among students of the Qur'an. Considering its popularity there have been in recent years some efforts to update its language, but even the strongest critics have not been able to suggest any substantive changes in the translation of the Text, excepting a few minor ones.

We, at H & C International, decided to launch our new venture by publishing the original translation of Abdullah Yusuf Ali because we believe it better meets the intellectual needs of both the Muslims and the non-Muslims in the West. Secondly, we could think of nothing better than the propagation of the Word of Allah at the threshold of our long journey ahead. We are a small group and are, as such, rival to none, but we are big enough to cooperate and help in promoting the cause of goodness and Truth.

The strongest criticism of this translation has been directed toward its use of old English, archaic and obsolete words. By providing footnotes and definitions to all such terms and words, we have tried to preserve the beauty of the original while making it easy to comprehend and follow.

The publication of this annotated edition marks an important step in the Islamic education of the new generation in this country. We dedicate this to all Muslim parents — in this country and abroad where English language is spoken and read — who are concerned with the moral and spiritual welfare of their children, and non-Muslims interested in learning about Islam. This translation may be easily used by children and parents at home, as well as in weekend and full time Islamic schools for Quranic classes. We hope to publish an enlarged edition with English translation, footnotes and commentary very soon. Any criticism, suggestions and comments are most welcome and should be directed to the address given below.

H&C International
May 6, 1992

P.O. Box 51841 • Indianapolis, IN 46251 • U.S.A.

From the Preface to the First Edition

It is the duty of every Muslim, man, woman, or child, to read the Qur'an and understand it according to his own capacity. If any one of us attains some knowledge or understanding of it by study, contemplation, and the test of life, both outward and inward, it is his duty, according to his capacity, to instruct others, and share with them the joy and peace which result from contact with the spiritual world. The Qur'an — indeed every religious book — has to be read, not only with the tongue and voice and eyes, but with the best light that our intellect can supply, and even more, with the truest and purest light which our heart and conscience can give us. It is in this spirit that I would have my readers approach the Qur'an.

It was between the ages of four and five that I first learned to read its Arabic words, to revel in its rhythm and music, and wonder at its meaning. I have a dim recollection of the Khatam ceremony which closed that stage. It was called "completion"; it really just began a spiritual awakening that has gone on ever since my revered father taught me Arabic, but I must have imbibed from him into my innermost being something more, — something which told me that all the world's thoughts, all the world's most beautiful languages and literatures are but vehicles for that ineffable message which comes to the heart in rare moments of ecstasy. The soul of mysticism and ecstasy is in the Qur'an, as well as the plain guidance for the plain man which a world in a hurry affects to consider as sufficient. It is good to make this personal confession, to an age in which it is in the highest degree unfashionable to speak of religion or spiritual peace or consolation, an age in which words like these draw forth only derision, pity, or contempt.

1 have explored Western lands, Western manners, and the depths of Western thought and Western learning, to an extent which has rarely fallen to the lot of an Eastern mortal. But I have never lost touch with Eastern heritage. Through all my successes and failures I have learned to rely more and more upon the one true thing in all life — the voice that speaks in a tongue above that of mortal man. For me

the embodiment of that voice has been in the noble words of the Arabic Qur'an, which I have tried to translate for myself and apply to my experience again and again. The service of the Qur'an has been the pride and the privilege of many Muslims. 1 felt that with such life-experience as has fallen to my lot, my service to the Qur'an should be to present it in a fitting garb in English. That ambition I have cherished in my mind for more than forty years. I have collected books and materials for it. I have visited places, undertaken journeys, taken notes, sought the society of men, and tried to explore their thoughts and hearts, in order to equip myself for the task. Sometimes I have considered it too stupendous for me — the double task of understanding the original, and reproducing its nobility, its beauty, its poetry, its grandeur, and its sweet practical reasonable application to everyday experience. Then I have blamed myself for lack of courage — the spiritual courage of men who dared all in the Cause which was so dear to them.

Two sets of apparently accidental circumstances at last decided me. A man's life is subject to inner storms far more devastating than those in the physical world around him. In such a storm , in the bitter anguish of a personal sorrow which nearly unseated my reason and made life seem meaningless, a new hope was born out of a systematic pursuit of my long cherished project. Watered by tears, my manuscript began to grow in depth and earnestness if not in bulk. I guarded it like a secret treasure. Wanderer that I am, I carried it about, thousands of miles, to all sorts of countries and among all sorts of people. At length, in the city of Lahore, I happened to mention the matter to some young people who held me in respect and affection. They showed an enthusiasm and an eagerness which surprised me. They almost took the matter out of my hands. They asked for immediate publication. I had various bits ready, but not even one Sipara. They made me promise to complete at least one Sipara before I left Lahore. As if by magic, a publisher, a Katib (calligraphist, to write the Arabic Text), an engraver of blocks for such text, and a printer were found, all equally anxious to push forward the scheme. Blessed be youth, for its energy and determination! "Where others flinch, rash youth will dare!"

Gentle and discerning reader! what I wish to present to you is an English Interpretation. The English shall be, not a mere substitution of one word for another but the best expression I can give to the fullest meaning which I can understand from the Arabic Text. The rhythm, music, and exalted tone of the original should be reflected in the English Interpretation. It may be but a faint reflection, but such beauty and power as my pen can command shall be brought to its service. I want to make English itself an Islamic language, if such a person as I can do it, and I must give you all the accessory aid which I can. .. Each Sura and the verse of each Sura is separately numbered, and the numbers are shown page by page. ....

In translating the Text I have aired no views of my own, but followed the received Commentators. Where they differ among themselves, I have had to choose what appeared to me to be the most reasonable opinion from all points of view. .. In choosing an English word for an Arabic word, a translator necessarily exercises his own judgement and may be unconsciously expressing a point of view, but that is inevitable. ... It will be found that every verse revealed for a particular occasion has also a general meaning. The particular occasion and the particular people concerned have passed away, but the general meaning and its application remain true for all time. What we are concerned now is: what guidance can we draw for ourselves from the message of God?

I spoke of the general meaning of the verses. Every earnest and reverent student of the Qur'an, as he proceeds with his study, will find, with an inward joy difficult to describe, how this general meaning also enlarges as his own capacity for understanding increases. It is like a traveller climbing a mountain: the higher he goes, the farther he sees.

How much greater is the joy and sense of wonder and miracle when the Qur'an opens our spiritual eyes! The meaning which we thought we had grasped expands. New worlds are opened out. As we progress, still newer, and again newer worlds, "swim into our ken." The miracle deepens and deepens, and almost completely absorbs us. And yet we know that the "face of God" — our final goal — has not yet been reached. Such meaning it is most difficult to express. But where I can, I have indicated it in the notes, in the Commentary, and with the help of the rhythm and the elevated language of the Text.[1] ...

One final word to my readers. Read, study, and digest the Holy Book. Read slowly, and let it sink into your heart and soul. Such study will, like virtue, be its own reward.

Lahore A. Yusuf 'Ali
4th April, 1934
== 18th of the month
of Pilgrimage, 1352 H.

---

[1] For the notes and commentary please refer to our forthcoming enlarged edition of A. Yusuf Ali's work.

xi

Chapter 1
Sūrah Al-Fatihāh (The Opening)
Revealed at Makkah, 7 verses.

1. In the name of God, Most Gracious, Most Merciful.
2. Praise be to God, the Cherisher and Sustainer of the Worlds;
3. Most Gracious, Most Merciful.
4. Master of the Day of Judgement.
5. Thee do we worship, and Thine aid we seek.[1]
6. Show us the straight way.
7. The way of those on whom Thou hast bestowed Thy Grace, Those whose (portion) is not wrath[2], and who go not astray.

---

[1] The translator frequently uses some old forms of pronouns: 'thou' for you (singular), 'thee' for you (objective case), 'thy' for your, and 'thine' for yours.
[2] Anger

Chapter 2
Sürah Al-Baqarah (The Cow)
Revealed at Madinah, 286 verses.

In the name of God, Most Gracious, Most Merciful.

1. Alif Lãm Mïm.

2. This is the Book; in it is guidance sure, without doubt, to those who fear God;

3. Who believe in the Unseen, are steadfast[3] in prayer, and spend out of what We have provided for them;

4. And who believe in the Revelation sent to thee, and sent before thy time, and (in their hearts) have the assurance of the Hereafter[4].

5. They are on (true) guidance, from their Lord, and it is these who will prosper.

6. As to those who reject Faith, it is the same to them whether thou warn them or do not warn them; they will not believe.

7. God hath set a seal on their hearts and on their hearing, and on their eyes is a veil; great is the penalty they (incur).

8. Of the people there are some who say: "We believe in God and the Last Day," but they do not (really) believe.

9. Fain[5] would they deceive God and those who believe, but they only deceive themselves and realize (it) not!

10. In their hearts is a disease; and God has increased their disease, and grievous[6] is the penalty[7] they (incur), because they are false (to themselves).

11. When it is said to them: "Make not mischief on the earth," they say: "Why, we only want to make peace!"

12. Of a surety, they are the ones who make mischief, but they realize (it) not.

13. When it is said to them: "Believe as the others believe" they say: "Shall we believe as the fools believe?" — nay, of a surety they

---

[3] Constant, firm
[4] Life after death
[5] Gladly or willingly
[6] Causing great harm and sorrow.
[7] A punishment imposed for a violation of law.

are the fools, but they do not know.

14. When they meet those who believe, they say: "We believe," but when they are alone with their evil ones, they say: "We are really with you; we (were) only jesting."

15. God will throw back their mockery[8] on them, and give them rope in their trespasses[9]; so they will wander like blind ones (to and fro).

16. These are they who have bartered[10] guidance for error: but their traffic[11] is profitless, and they have lost true direction.

17. Their similitude[12] is that of a man who kindled[13] a fire; when it lighted all around him, God took away their light and left them in utter[14] darkness, so they could not see.

18. Deaf, dumb, and blind, they will not return (to the path).

19. Or (another similitude) is that of a rain-laden cloud from the sky; in it are zones of darkness, and thunder and lightning: they press their fingers in their ears to keep out the stunning[15] thunderclap, the while they are in terror of death. But God is ever round the rejecters of Faith!

20. The lightning all but snatches away their sight; every time the light (helps) them, they walk therein, and when the darkness grows on them, they stand still. And if God willed, He could take away their faculty of hearing and seeing; for God hath power over all things.

21. O ye people! adore[16] your Guardian-Lord, who created you and those who came before you, that ye may have the chance to learn righteousness,

22. Who has made the earth your couch, and the heaven your canopy; and sent down rain from the heavens; and brought forth

---

8 Ridicule
9 Offense, sins, or wrongs.
10 Exchanged
11 Commerce or business
12 Likeness, parable
13 Lighted
14 Complete, total
15 Startling
16 Worship and love

3

therewith fruits for your sustenance[17]; then set not up rivals unto God when ye know (the truth).

23. And if ye are in doubt as to what We have revealed from time to time to Our servant, then produce a Sūrah like thereunto; and call your witnesses or helpers (if there are any) besides God, if your (doubts) are true.

24. But if ye cannot, and of a surety ye cannot, then fear the fire whose fuel is Men and Stones, which is prepared for those who reject Faith.

25. But give glad tidings[18] to those who believe and work righteousness, that their portion is Gardens, beneath which rivers flow. Every time they are fed with fruits therefrom, they say: "Why, this is what we were fed with before," for they are given things in similitude; and they have therein Companions (pure and holy); and they abide[19] therein (forever).

26. God disdains[20] not to use the similitude of things, lowest as well as highest. Those who believe know that it is truth from their Lord; but those who reject Faith say: "What means God by this similitude?" By it He causes many to stray, and many He leads into the right path, but He causes not to stray, except those who forsake (the path).

27. Those who break God's Covenant[21] after it is ratified[22], and who sunder[23] what God has ordered to be joined, and do mischief on earth: These cause loss (only) to themselves.

28. How can ye reject the faith in God? Seeing that ye were without life, and He gave you life; then will He cause you to die, and will again bring you to life; and again to Him will ye return.

29. It is He who hath created for you all things that are on earth; moreover His design comprehended the heavens, for He gave order

---

[17] Means of livelihood.
[18] News
[19] Dwell, live.
[20] To consider unworthy of notice or response.
[21] A solemn pledge.
[22] Confirmed, approved
[23] Divide, separate

and perfection to seven firmaments [24]; and of all things he hath perfect knowledge.

30. Behold, thy Lord said to the angels: "I will create a vicegerent[25] on earth." They said, "Wilt thou place therein one who will make mischief therein and shed blood? Whilst we do celebrate Thy praises and glorify[26] Thy holy (name)?" He said: "I know what ye know not."

31. And He taught Adam the nature of all things; then He placed them before the angels, and said: "Tell Me the nature of these if ye are right."

32. They said: "Glory to Thee, of knowledge we have none, save that Thou hast taught us: in truth it is Thou who art perfect in knowledge and wisdom."

33. He said: "O Adam! tell them their natures." When he had told them, God said: "Did I not tell you that I know the secrets of heaven and earth, and I know what ye reveal and what ye conceal?"

34. And behold, We said to the angels: "Bow down to Adam;" and they bowed down, not so Iblis, he refused and was haughty,[27] he was of those who reject Faith.

35. We said: "O Adam! dwell thou and thy wife in the garden, and eat of the bountiful[28] things therein as (where and when) ye will, but approach not this tree, or ye run into harm and transgression."[29]

36. Then did Satan make them slip from the (garden), and get them out of the state (of felicity[30]) in which they had been. We said: "Get ye down, all (ye people), with enmity between yourselves. On earth will be your dwelling place and your means of livelihood for a time."

37. Then learnt Adam from his Lord words of inspiration, and his Lord turned toward him; for He is Oft-Returning, Most Merciful.

38. We said: "Get ye down all from here; and if, as is sure, there

---

[24] The arch or vault of heaven, sky.

[25] A deputy

[26] Adore, praise, extol

[27] Proud, arrogant

[28] Ample, abundant

[29] Offense, sin, violation.

[30] Bliss, delight

comes to you guidance from Me," whosoever follows My guidance on them shall be no fear, nor shall they grieve.

39. "But those who reject Faith and belie[31] Our Signs, they shall be Companions of the Fire; they shall abide therein."

40. O Children of Israel! call to mind the (special) favor which I bestowed upon you, and fulfil your covenant with Me as I fulfil My covenant with you and fear none but Me.

41. And believe in what I reveal, confirming the revelation which is with you, and be not the first to reject faith therein, nor sell My Signs for a small price; and fear Me, and Me alone.

42. And cover not Truth with falsehood, nor conceal the Truth when ye know (what it is).

43. And be steadfast in prayer; practice regular charity; and bow down your heads with those who bow down (in worship).

44. Do ye enjoin[32] right conduct on the people, and forget (to practice it) yourselves, and yet ye study the Scripture?[33] Will ye not understand?

45. Nay, seek (God's) help with patient perseverance[34] and prayer: it is indeed hard, except to those who bring a lowly[35] spirit.

46. Who bear in mind the certainty that they are to meet their Lord, and that they are to return to Him.

47. O Children of Israel! call to mind the (special) favor which I bestowed upon You, and that I preferred you to all others (for My message).

48. Then guard yourselves against a day when one soul shall not avail another nor shall intercession[36] be accepted for her, nor shall compensation[37] be taken from her, nor shall anyone be helped (from outside).

---

[31] To be false to, to contradict, to misrepresent.

[32] Direct, order

[33] Torah or Injil or both.

[34] Endurance, steadfastness

[35] Humble

[36] Pleading to God on behalf of another person.

[37] Something given or received for a loss or injury — a payment to escape punishment for their sins.

49. And remember, We delivered[38] you from the people of Pharaoh[39]: they set you hard tasks and punishments, slaughtered your sons and let your womenfolk live; therein was a tremendous[40] trial from your Lord.

50. And remember We divided the sea for you and saved you and drowned Pharaoh's people within your very sight.

51. And remember We appointed forty nights for Moses, and in his absence you took the calf (for worship), and ye did grievous wrong.

52. Even then We did forgive you; there was a chance for you to be grateful.

53. And remember We gave Moses the Scripture and the Criterion[41] (between right and wrong), there was a chance for you to be guided aright.

54. And remember Moses said to his people: "O my people! Ye have indeed wronged yourselves by your worship of the calf, so turn (in repentance) to your Maker, and slay yourselves (the wrongdoers); that will be better for you in the sight of your Maker." Then He turned toward you (in forgiveness); for He is Oft-returning, Most Merciful.

55. And remember ye said: "O Moses! we shall never believe in thee until we see God manifestly," but ye were dazed[42] with thunder and lightning even as ye looked on.

56. Then We raised you up after your death; ye had the chance to be grateful.

57. And We gave You the shade of clouds and sent down to you manna[43] and quails[44], saying: "Eat of the good things We have provided for you"; (but they rebelled); to Us they did no harm, but they harmed their own souls.

58. And remember We said: "Enter this town, and eat of the plenty therein as ye wish; but enter the gate with humility, in posture

---

[38] Freed, saved

[39] Title of an old Egyptian king.

[40] Enormous, dreadful.

[41] Standard, yardstick

[42] Stupefied, dazzled.

[43] The food supplied by God miraculously to the Children of Israel in the wilderness,

[44] A small bird of the pheasant family.

7

and in words, and We shall forgive you your faults and increase (the portion of) those who do good."

59. But the transgressors changed the word from that which had been given them; so We sent on the transgressors a plague from heaven, for that they infringed[45] (our command) repeatedly.

60. And remember Moses prayed for water for his people; We said: "Strike the rock with thy staff." Then gushed[46] forth therefrom twelve springs. Each group knew its own place for water. So eat and drink of the sustenance[47] provided by God and do no evil nor mischief on the (face of the) earth.

61. And remember ye said: "O Moses! we cannot endure one kind of food (always); so beseech thy Lord for us to produce for us of what the earth groweth, its pot-herbs, and cucumbers, its garlic, lentils, and onions." He said: "will ye exchange the better for the worse? Go ye down to any town, and ye shall find what ye want!" They were covered with humiliation and misery; they drew on themselves the wrath of God. This because they went on rejecting the Signs of God and slaying His messengers without just cause. This because They rebelled and went on transgressing.

62. Those who believe (in the Qur'an) and those who follow the Jewish (Scriptures), and the Christians and the Sabians, and who believe in God and the last day, and work righteousness, shall have their reward with their Lord; on them shall be no fear, nor shall they grieve.

63. And remember We took your covenant and We raised above you (the towering height) of Mount (Sinai) (saying): "Hold firmly to what We have given you and bring (ever) to remembrance what is therein, perchance[48] ye may fear God."

64. But ye turned back thereafter, had it not been for the Grace and Mercy of God to you, ye had surely been among the lost.

65. And well ye knew those amongst you who transgressed in the matter of the Sabbath; We said to them: "Be ye apes, despised

---

[45] Violated, trespassed
[46] Gush = A sudden copious outflow of water.
[47] Means of livelihood.
[48] Perhaps, maybe.

8

and rejected."

66. So We made it an example to their own time, and to their posterity,[49] and a lesson to those who fear God.

67. And remember Moses said to his people: "God commands that ye sacrifice a heifer."[50] They said: "Makest thou a laughing-stock of us?" He said: "God save me from being an ignorant (fool)!"

68. They said: "Beseech[51] on our behalf thy Lord to make plain to us what (heifer) it is! He said: "He says: The heifer should be neither too old nor too young, but of middling age; now do what ye are commanded!

69. They said: "Beseech on our behalf thy Lord to make plain to us her color." He said: " He says: A fawn-colored[52] heifer, pure and rich in tone, the admiration of beholders!"

70. They said, "Beseech on our behalf thy Lord to make plain to us what she is, to us are all heifers alike; we wish indeed for guidance, if God wills."

71. He said: "He says: A heifer not trained to till the soil or water the fields; sound and without blemish."[53] They said: "Now hast thou brought the truth." Then they offered her in sacrifice, but not with goodwill.

72. Remember ye slew a man and fell into a dispute among yourselves as to the crime, but God was to bring forth what ye did hide.

73. So We said: "Strike the (body) with a piece of the (heifer)." Thus God bringeth the dead to life and showeth you His Signs, perchance ye may understand.

74. Thenceforth were your hearts hardened; they became like a rock and even worse in hardness. For among rocks there are some from which rivers gush forth; others there are which when split asunder send forth water; and others which sink for fear of God. And God is not unmindful of what ye do.

---

[49] Their future generations.

[50] A young cow.

[51] Beg or request eagerly.

[52] Light yellowish brown color.

[53] Flaw or defect.

75. Can ye (O ye men of Faith) entertain the hope that they will believe in you? Seeing that a party of them heard the word of God, and perverted[54] it knowingly after they understood it.

76. Behold! when they meet the men of Faith, they say: "We believe," but when they meet each other in private, they say: "Shall you tell them what God hath revealed to you, that they may engage you in argument about it before your Lord?" Do ye not understand (their aim)?

77. Know they not that God knoweth what they conceal and what they reveal?

78. And there are among them illiterates, who know not the Book but (see therein their own) desires, and they do nothing but conjecture.[55]

79. Then woe to those who write the Book with their own hands and then say: "This is from God," to traffic with it for a miserable price! Woe to them for what their hands do write, and for the gain they make thereby.

80. And they say: "The Fire shall not touch us but for a few numbered days"; Say: "Have ye taken a promise from God for He never breaks His promise? Or is it that ye say of God what ye do not know?"

81. Nay, those who seek gain in Evil, and are girt[56] round by their sins, they are Companions of the Fire, therein shall they abide (forever).

82. But those who have faith and work righteousness, they are Companions of the Garden, therein shall they abide (forever).

83. And remember We took a Covenant from the Children of Israel (to this effect): worship none but God; treat with kindness your parents and kindred, and orphans and those in need; speak fair to the people; be steadfast in prayer; and practice regular charity. Then did ye turn back, except a few among you, and ye backslide[57] (even now).

---

[54] Misinterpreted, distorted or misapplied

[55] Form an opinion or theory without sufficient proof, guesswork.

[56] Encircled

[57] Relapse into sinful behavior.

84. And remember We took your Covenant (to this effect): shed no blood amongst you, nor turn out your own people from your homes; and this ye solemnly ratified, and to this ye can bear witness.

85. After this it is ye, the same people, who slay among yourselves, and banish a party of you from their homes; assist (their enemies) against them, in guilt and rancor[58]; and if they come to you as captives, ye ransom[59] them, though it was not lawful for you to banish them. Then is it only a part of the Book that ye believe in, and do ye reject the rest? But what is the reward for those among you who behave like this, but disgrace in this life? and on the Day of Judgement they shall be consigned[60] to the most grievous penalty. For God is not unmindful of what ye do.

86. These are the people who buy the life of this world at the price of the Hereafter; their penalty shall not be lightened, nor shall they be helped.

87. We gave Moses the Book and followed him up with a succession of Apostles[61]; We gave Jesus the son of Mary clear (Signs) and strengthened him with the Holy Spirit. Is it that whenever there comes to you an Apostle with what ye yourselves desire not, ye are puffed up with pride? Some ye called impostors,[62] and others ye slay!

88. They say, "Our hearts are the wrappings[63] (which preserve God's word, we need no more)." Nay, God's curse is on them for their blasphemy; little is it they believe.

89. And when there comes to them a Book from God, confirming what is with them, although from of old they had prayed for victory against those without faith, when there comes to them that which they (should) have recognized, they refused to believe in it, but the curse of God is on those without Faith.

90. Miserable is the price for which they have sold their souls, in that they deny (the revelation) which God has sent down, in insolent

---

58 Bitter resentment or ill will.
59 Rescue them from captivity by paying a demanded price.
60 Handed over, entrusted.
61 Messengers
62 Liars or deceivers.
63 The covering in which something is wrapped.

11

envy that God of His Grace should send it to any of His servants He pleases; thus have they drawn on themselves wrath upon wrath. And humiliating is the punishment of those who reject Faith.

91. When it is said to them: "Believe in what God hath sent down," they say, "We believe in what was sent down to us;" yet they reject all besides, even if it be truth confirming what is with them. Say: "Why then have ye slain the prophets of God in times gone by, if ye did indeed believe?"

92. There came to you Moses with clear (Signs); yet ye worshipped the Calf (even) after that, and ye did behave wrongfully.

93. And remember We took your Covenant and We raised above you (the towering height) of Mount (Sinai), (saying): "Hold firmly to what We have given you and hearken (to the Law)"; they said: "We hear, and we disobey": and they had to drink into their hearts (of the taint[64]) of the calf because of their faithlessness. Say: "Vile[65] indeed are the behests[66] of your faith if ye have any faith!"

94. Say: "If the last Home, with God, be for you specially, and not for anyone else, then seek ye for death, if ye are sincere."

95. But they will never seek for death, on account of the (sins) which their hands have sent on before them. And God is well acquainted with the wrongdoers.

96. Thou wilt indeed find them, of all people, most greedy of life, even more than the idolaters; each one of them wishes he could be given a life of a thousand years; but the grant of such life will not save him from (due) punishment, for God sees well all that they do.

97. Say: Whoever is an enemy to Gabriel, for he brings down the (revelation) to thy heart by God's will, a confirmation of what went before, and guidance and glad tidings for those who believe.

98. Whoever is an enemy to God and His angels and apostles, to Gabriel and Michael, Lo! God is an enemy to those who reject faith.

99. We have sent down to thee manifest Signs; and none reject

---

64 Evil trace of calf-worship.
65 Morally despicable
66 Commands, directives

them, but those who are perverse.

100. Is it not (the case) that every time they make a Covenant, some party among them throw it aside? - Nay, most of them are faithless.

101. And when came to them an Apostle from God, confirming what was with them, a party of the People of the Book threw away the Book of God behind their backs, as if (it had been something) they did not know!

102. They followed what the evil ones gave out (falsely) against the power of Solomon; the blasphemers were, not Solomon, but the evil ones, teaching men magic, and such things as came down at Babylon to the angels Harut and Marut. But neither of these taught anyone (such things) without saying: "We are only for trial, so do not blaspheme[67]." They learned from them the means to sow discord[68] between man and wife. But they could not thus harm anyone except by God's permission. And they learned what harmed them, not what profited them. And they knew that the buyers of (magic) would have no share in the happiness of the Hereafter. And vile was the price for which they did sell their souls, if they but knew!

103. If they had kept their faith and guarded themselves from evil, far better had been the reward from their Lord, if they but knew!

104. O ye of Faith! say not (to the Apostle) words of ambiguous import[69], but words of respect; and hearken[70] (to him): to those without faith is a grievous punishment.

105. It is never the wish of those without faith among the people of the Book, nor of the Pagans, that anything good should come down to you from your Lord. But God will choose for His special Mercy whom He will, for God is Lord of grace abounding.

106. None of Our revelations do We abrogate or cause to be forgotten, but We substitute something better or similar; knowest thou not that God hath power over all things?

107. Knowest thou not that to God belongeth the dominion of

---

[67] To speak impiously of God or sacred things.
[68] Disagreement, strife
[69] Significance, meaning.
[70] Listen attentively.

the heavens and the earth! And besides Him ye have neither patron nor helper.

108. Would ye question your Apostle as Moses was questioned of old? But whoever changeth from faith to unbelief, hath strayed without doubt from the even way.

109. Quite a number of the People of the Book wish they could turn you (people) back to infidelity after ye have believed. From selfish envy, after the truth hath become manifest unto them; but forgive and overlook, till God accomplish His purpose; for God hath power over all things.

110. And be steadfast in prayer and regular in charity: and whatever good ye send forth for your souls before you, ye shall find it with God; for God sees well all that ye do.

111. And they say: "None shall enter Paradise unless he be a Jew or a Christian." Those are their (vain) desires. Say: "Produce your proof if ye are truthful."

112. Nay, whoever submits his whole self to God and is a doer of good, he will get his reward with his Lord; on such shall be no fear, nor shall they grieve.

113. The Jews say: "The Christians have naught[71] (to stand) upon"; and the Christians say: "The Jews have naught (to stand) upon." Yet they (profess to) study the (same) Book. Like unto their word is what those say who know not, but God will judge between them in their quarrel on the Day of Judgement.

114. And who is more unjust than he who forbids that in places for the worship of God, God's name should be celebrated? Whose zeal is (in fact) to ruin them? It was not fitting that such should themselves enter them except in fear. For them there is nothing but disgrace in this world, and in the world to come, an exceeding torment.

115. To God belong the East and the West; whithersoever[72] ye turn, there is the presence of God. For God is All-Pervading, All-Knowing.

116. They say: "God hath begotten a son"; Glory be to Him. Nay,

---

[71] Nothing (no basis)
[72] Whichever direction

to Him belongs all that is in the heavens and on earth; everything renders worship to Him.

117. To Him is due the primal[73] origin of the heavens and the earth; when He decreeth a matter He saith to it: "Be"; and it is.

118. Say those without knowledge: "Why speaketh not God unto us? Or why cometh not unto us a Sign?" So said the people before them, words of similar import. Their hearts are alike. We have indeed made clear the Signs unto any people who hold firmly to faith (in their hearts).

119. Verily, We have sent thee in truth as a bearer of glad tidings and a warner. But of thee no question shall be asked of the Companions of the Blazing Fire.

120. Never will the Jews or the Christians be satisfied with thee unless thou follow their form of religion. Say: "The guidance of God, that is the (only) guidance." Wert thou to follow their desires after the knowledge which hath reached thee, then wouldst thou find neither protector nor helper against God.

121. Those to whom We have sent the book study it as it should be studied; they are the ones that believe therein; those who reject faith therein, the loss is their own.

122. O Children of Israel! call to mind the special favor which I bestowed upon you, and that I preferred you to all others (for my message).

123. Then guard yourselves against a day when one soul shall not avail another, nor shall compensation be accepted from her, nor shall intercession profit her, nor shall anyone be helped (from outside).

124. And remember that Abraham was tried by his Lord, with certain commands, which he fulfilled; He said: "I will make thee an Imam[74] to the Nations." He pleaded: "And also (Imams) from my offspring!" He answered: "But my promise is not within the reach of evildoers."

125. Remember We made the House a place of assembly for men and a place of safety; and take ye the station of Abraham as a place of prayer; and We covenanted with Abraham and Isma'il, that they

---

[73] First, original

[74] Leader

15

should sanctify[75] My House for those who compass it round, or use it as a retreat, or bow, or prostrate themselves (therein in prayer).

126. And remember Abraham said: "My Lord, make this a City of Peace, and feed its people with fruits, such of them as believe in God and the Last Day." He said: "(Yea), and such as reject faith, for a while will I grant them their pleasure, but will soon drive them to the torment of Fire, an evil destination (indeed)!"

127. And remember Abraham and Isma'il raised the foundations of the House (with this prayer): "Our Lord! accept (this service) from us, for thou art the All-Hearing, the All-Knowing.

128. "Our Lord! make of us Muslims, bowing to Thy (Will), and of our progeny[76] a people Muslim, bowing to Thy (Will), and show us our places for the celebration of (due) rites; and turn unto us (in mercy); for Thou art the Oft-Returning, Most-Merciful.

129. "Our Lord! send amongst them an Apostle of their own, who shall rehearse[77] Thy Signs to them and instruct them in Scripture[78] and Wisdom, and sanctify them; for Thou art the Exalted in Might, the Wise."

130. And who turns away from the religion of Abraham but such as debase their souls with folly? Him We chose and rendered pure in this world: and he will be in the Hereafter in the ranks of the righteous.

131. Behold! his Lord said to him: "Bow (thy will to Me)" He said: "I bow (my Will) to the Lord and Cherisher of the universe."

132. And this was the legacy[79] that Abraham left to his sons, and so did Jacob; "O my sons! God hath chosen the faith for you; then die not except in the faith of Islam."

133. Were ye witnesses when death appeared before Jacob? Behold, he said to his sons: "What will ye worship after me?" They said: "We shall worship thy God and the God of thy fathers, of

---

[75] Clean, purify
[76] Offspring
[77] Convey, repeat
[78] The Book
[79] Heritage, tradition

Abraham, Isma'il, and Isaac, the one (true) God, to Him we bow (in Islam)."

134. That was a People that hath passed away. They shall reap the fruit of what they did, and ye of what ye do! Of their merits there is no question in your case!

135. They say: "Become Jews or Christians if ye would be guided (to salvation)." Say thou: "Nay! (I would rather) the religion of Abraham the true, and he joined not gods with God."

136. Say ye: "We believe in God, and the revelation given to us, and to Abraham, Isma'il, Isaac, Jacob, and the Tribes, and that given to Moses and Jesus and that given to (all) Prophets from their Lord, we make no difference between one and another of them, and we bow to God (in Islam)."

137. So if they believe as ye believe, they are indeed on the right path; but if they turn back, it is they who are in schism[80]; but God will suffice thee as against them, and He is the All-Hearing, the All-Knowing.

138. (Our religion is) the baptism of God; and who can baptize better than God? and it is He whom we worship.

139. Say: Will ye dispute with us about God, seeing that He is our Lord and your Lord; that we are responsible for our doings and ye for yours; and that we are sincere (in our faith) in Him?

140. Or do ye say that Abraham, Isma'il, Isaac, Jacob and the Tribes were Jews or Christians? Say: Do ye know better than God? Ah! who is more unjust than those who conceal the testimony they have from God? But God is not unmindful of what ye do!

141. That was a people that hath passed away. They shall reap the fruit of what they did, and ye of what ye do! Of their merits there is no question in your case.

142. The fools among the people will say: "What hath turned them from the Qiblah[81] to which they were used?" Say: To God belong both East and West; He guideth whom He will to a Way that is straight.

143. Thus have We made of you an *Ummah* justly balanced, that

---

[80] Division or disunion into mutually opposed parties, hostility.
[81] Direction faced in prayer.

ye might be witnesses over the nations, and the Apostle a witness over yourselves; and We appointed the *Qiblah*[82] to which thou wast used, only to test those who followed the Apostle from those who would turn on their heels (from the faith). Indeed it was (a change) momentous, except to those guided by God. And never would God make your faith of no effect. For God is to all people most surely full of kindness, Most Merciful.

144. We see the turning of thy face (for guidance) to the heavens; now shall We turn thee to a *Qiblah* that shall please thee. Turn then thy face in the direction of the Sacred Mosque; wherever ye are, turn your faces in that direction. The People of the Book know well that that is the truth from their Lord, nor is God unmindful of what they do.

145. Even if thou wert to bring to the People of the Book all the Signs (together), they would not follow thy *Qiblah*; nor art thou going to follow their *Qiblah*; nor indeed will they follow each other's *Qiblah*. If thou, after the knowledge hath reached thee, wert to follow their (vain) desires, then wert thou indeed (clearly) in the wrong.

146. The People of the Book know this as they know their own sons; but some of them conceal the truth which they themselves know.

147. The truth is from thy Lord, so be not at all in doubt.

148. To each is a goal to which God turns him; then strive together (as in a race) toward all that is good. Wheresoever ye are, God will bring you together. For God hath power over all things.

149. From whencesoever thou startest forth, turn thy face in the direction of the Sacred Mosque; that is indeed the truth from thy Lord. And God is not unmindful of what ye do.

150. So from whencesoever thou startest forth, turn thy face in the direction of the Sacred Mosque; and wheresoever ye are turn your face thither: that there be no ground of dispute against you among the people, except those of them that are bent on wickedness; so fear them not, but fear Me; and that I may complete My favors on you, and ye may (consent to) be guided.

151. A similar (favor have ye already received) in that We have

---

[82] Direction of Ka'abah (Makkah).

sent among you an Apostle of your own, rehearsing to you Our Signs, and sanctifying you, and instructing you in Scripture and Wisdom, and in new Knowledge.

152. Then do ye remember Me; I will remember you. Be grateful to Me, and reject not faith.

153. O ye who believe! seek help with patient perseverance and prayer: for God is with those who patiently persevere.[83]

154. And say not of those who are slain in the way of God: "They are dead." Nay, they are living, though ye perceive (it) not.

155. Be sure We shall test you with something of fear and hunger, some loss in goods or lives or the fruits (of your toil[84]), but give glad tidings to those who patiently persevere.

156. Who say, when afflicted with calamity: " To God we belong, and to Him is our return."

157. They are those on whom (descend) blessings from God, and Mercy, and they are the ones that receive guidance.

158. Behold! Safā and Marwah are among the Symbols of God. So if those who visit the House in the season or at other times, should compass them round, it is no sin in them. And if anyone obeyeth his own impulse to good, be sure that God is He Who recogniseth and knoweth.

159. Those who conceal the clear (Signs) We have sent down, and the guidance, after We have made it clear for the people in the book, on them shall be God's curse, and the curse of those entitled to curse.

160. Except those who repent and make amends and openly declare (the truth), to them I turn; for I am Oft-Returning, Most Merciful.

161. Those who reject faith, and die rejecting, on them is God's curse, and the curse of angels, and of all mankind.

162. They will abide therein: Their penalty will not be lightened, nor will respite be their (lot).

163. And your God is one God; there is no god but He, Most Gracious, Most Merciful.

---

[83] Endure
[84] Labor, work.

164. Behold! In the creation of the heavens and the earth; in the alternation of the Night and the Day; in the sailing of the ships through the ocean for the profit of mankind; in the rain which God sends down from the skies, and the life which He gives therewith to an earth that is dead; in the beasts of all kinds that He scatters through the earth; in the change of the winds, and the clouds which they trail like their slaves between the sky and the earth; (here) indeed are Signs for a people that are wise.

165. Yet there are men who take (for worship) others besides God as equal (with God); they love them as they should love God. But those of faith are overflowing in their love for God. If only the unrighteous could see, behold, they would see the penalty, that to God belongs all power, and God will strongly enforce the penalty.

166. Then would those who are followed clear themselves of those who follow (them); they would see the penalty, and all relations between them would be cut off.

167. And those who followed would say: "If only we had one more chance, we would clear ourselves of them, as they have cleared themselves of us." Thus will God show them (the fruits of) their deeds as (nothing but) regrets, nor will there be a way for them out of the fire.

168. O ye people! eat of what is on earth, lawful and good; and do not follow the footsteps of the evil one, for he is to you an avowed enemy.

169. For he commands you what is evil and shameful, and that ye should say of God that of which ye have no knowledge.

170. When it is said to them: "Follow what God hath revealed," they say: "Nay! we shall follow the ways of our fathers." What! even though their fathers were void[85] of wisdom and guidance?.

171. The parable of those who reject faith is as if one were to shout like a goat-herd, to things that listen to nothing but calls and cries: deaf, dumb, and blind, they are void of wisdom.

172. O ye who believe! eat of the good things that We have provided for you, and be grateful to God, if it is Him ye worship.

---

[85] Empty, lacking in

173. He hath only forbidden you dead meat, and blood, and the flesh of swine[86], and that on which any other name hath been invoked besides that of God, but if one is forced by necessity, without wilful disobedience, nor transgressing due limits, then is he guiltless. For God is Oft-Forgiving, Most Merciful.

174. Those who conceal God's revelations in the Book, and purchase for them a miserable profit, they swallow into themselves naught but Fire; God will not address them on the Day of Resurrection, nor purify them; grievous will be their Penalty.

175. They are the ones who buy Error in place of guidance and torment in place of forgiveness. Ah! what boldness (they show) for the Fire!.

176. (Their doom is) because God sent down the Book in truth, but those who seek causes of dispute in the Book are in a schism far (from the purpose).

177. It is not righteousness that ye turn your faces toward East or West; but it is righteousness to believe in God and the Last Day, and the Angels, and the Book, and the Messengers; to spend of your substance,[87] out of love for Him, for your kin, for orphans, for the needy, for the wayfarer, for those who ask, and for the ransom of slaves; to be steadfast in prayer, and practice regular charity; to fulfil the contracts which ye have made; and to be firm and patient, in pain (or suffering) and adversity, and throughout all periods of panic. Such are the people of truth, the God-fearing.

178. O ye who believe! the law of equality is prescribed to you in cases of murder; the free for the free, the slave for the slave, the woman for the woman. But if any remission[88] is made by the brother of the slain, then grant any reasonable demand, and compensate him with handsome gratitude; this is a concession and a mercy from your Lord. After this whoever exceeds the limits shall be in grave penalty.

179. In the law of equality there is (saving of) life to you, O ye men of understanding! that ye may restrain yourselves.

---

[86] Pork or meat of pig.

[87] Wealth or property.

[88] Decrease (in blood money).

180. It is prescribed, when death approaches any of you, if he leave any goods, that he make a bequest to parents and next of kin, according to reasonable usage; this is due from the God-fearing.

181. If anyone changes the bequest after hearing it, the guilt shall be on those who make the change. For God hears and knows all things.

182. But if anyone fears partiality or wrongdoing on the part of the testator, and makes peace between (the parties concerned), there is no wrong in him; for God is Oft-Forgiving, Most Merciful.

183. O ye who believe! fasting is prescribed[89] to you as it was prescribed to those before you, that ye may (learn) self-restraint—

184. (Fasting) for a fixed number of days; but if any of you is ill, or on a journey, the prescribed number (should be made up) from days later. For those who can do it (with hardship), is a ransom, the feeding of one that is indigent.[90] But he that will give more, of his own free will, it is better for him, and it is better for you, that ye fast, if ye only knew.

185. Ramadan is the (month) in which was sent down the Qur'an, as a guide to mankind, also clear (Signs) for guidance and judgement (between right and wrong). So everyone of you who is present (at his home) during that month should spend it in fasting, but if anyone is ill or on a journey, the prescribed period, (should be made up) by days later. God intends every facility for you, He does not want to put you to difficulties. (He wants you) to complete the prescribed period, and to glorify Him in that He has guided you; and perchance ye shall be grateful.

186. When my servants ask thee concerning Me, I am indeed close (to them); I listen to the prayer of every suppliant when he calleth on Me; let them also, with a will, listen to My call, and believe in Me; that they may walk in the right way.

187. Permitted to you, on the night of the fasts, is the approach to your wives. They are your garments. And ye are their garments. God knoweth what ye used to do secretly among yourselves; but He turned to you and forgave you; so now associate with them, and seek

---

[89] Laid down, decreed
[90] Needy poor

what God hath ordained for you, and eat and drink, until the white thread of dawn appear to you distinct from its black thread; then complete your fast till the night appears; but do not associate with your wives while ye are in retreat in the mosques. Those are limits (set by) God; approach not nigh thereto. Thus doth God make clear His Signs to men, that they may learn self-restraint.

188. And do not eat up your property among yourselves for vanities, nor use it as bait for the judges, with intent that ye may eat up wrongfully and knowingly a little of (other) people's property.

189. They ask thee concerning the new moons. Say: they are but signs to mark fixed periods of time in (the affairs of) men, and for pilgrimage. It is no virtue if ye enter your houses from the back; it is virtue if ye fear God. Enter houses through the proper doors, and fear God, that ye may prosper.

190. Fight in the cause of God, those who fight you, but do not transgress limits; for God loveth not transgressors.

191. And slay them wherever ye catch them, and turn them out from where they have turned you out; for tumult and oppression are worse than slaughter; but fight them not at the Sacred Mosque, unless they (first) fight you there; but if they fight you, slay them. Such is the reward of those who suppress faith.

192. But if they cease, God is Oft-Forgiving, Most Merciful.

193. And fight them on until there is no more tumult or oppression, and there prevail justice and faith in God; but if they cease, let there be no hostility except to those who practice oppression.

194. The prohibited month for the prohibited month, and so for all things prohibited, there is the law of equality. If then anyone transgresses the prohibition against you, transgress ye likewise against him. But fear God, and know that God is with those who restrain themselves.

195. And spend of your substance in the cause of God, and make not your own hands contribute to your destruction, but do good; for God loveth those who do good.

196. And complete the Hajj or 'Umra in the service of God. But if ye are prevented (from completing it), send an offering for sacrifice, such as ye may find, and do not shave your heads until the offering reaches the place of sacrifice. And if any of you is ill, or has an ailment

in his scalp, (necessitating shaving), (he should) in compensation either fast, or feed the poor, or offer sacrifice; and, when ye are in peaceful conditions (again), if anyone wishes to continue the 'Umra on to the Hajj, he must make an offering, such as he can afford it, he should fast three days during the Hajj and seven days on his return, making ten days in all. This is for those whose household is not in (the precincts of) the Sacred Mosque. And fear God, and know that God is strict in punishment.

197. For Hajj are the months well known. If anyone undertakes that duty therein, let there be no obscenity nor wickedness, nor wrangling in the Hajj. And whatever good ye do, (be sure) God knoweth it. And take a provision (with you) for the journey, but the best of provisions is right conduct. So fear Me, o ye that are wise.

198. It is no crime in you if ye seek of the bounty of your Lord (during pilgrimage). Then when ye pour down from (Mount) Arafat, celebrate the praises of God at the Sacred Monument, and celebrate His praises as He has directed you, even though, before this, ye went astray.

199. Then pass on at a quick pace from the place whence it is usual for the multitude so to do, and ask for God's forgiveness. For God is Oft-Forgiving, Most Merciful.

200. So when ye have accomplished your holy rites, celebrate the praises of God, as ye used to celebrate the praises of your fathers — Yea, with far more heart and soul. There are men who say: "Our Lord! give us (thy bounties) in this world!" but they will have no portion in the Hereafter.

201. And there are men who say: "Our Lord! give us good in this world and good in the Hereafter, and defend us from the torment of the Fire!"

202. To these will be allotted what they have earned, and God is quick in account.

203. Celebrate the praises of God during the Appointed Days, but if anyone hastens to leave in two days, there is no blame on him, and if anyone stays on, there is no blame on him, if his aim is to do right. Then fear God, and know that ye will surely be gathered unto Him.

204. There is the type of man whose speech about this world's

life may dazzle thee, and he calls God to witness about what is in his heart; yet is he the most contentious of enemies.

205. When he turns his back, his aim everywhere is to spread mischief through the earth and destroy crops and cattle. But God loveth not mischief.

206. When it is said to him, "Fear God," he is led by arrogance to (more) crime. Enough for him is Hell; an evil bed indeed (to lie on)!

207. And there is the type of man who gives his life to earn the pleasure of God; and God is full of kindness to (His) devotees.

208. O ye who believe! enter into Islam wholeheartedly; and follow not the footsteps of the Evil One; for he is to you an avowed enemy.

209. If ye backslide after the Clear (Signs) have come to you, then know that God is Exalted in Power, Wise.

210. Will they wait until God comes to them in canopies of clouds, with angels (in His train) and the question is (thus) settled? But to God do all questions go back (for decision).

211. Ask the Children of Israel how many Clear (Signs) We have sent them. But if anyone, after God's favor has come to him, substitutes (something else), God is strict in punishment.

212. The life of this world is alluring to those who reject faith, and they scoff at those who believe. But the righteous will be above them on the Day of Resurrection; for God bestows His abundance without measures on whom He will.

213. Mankind was one single nation, and God sent Messengers with glad tidings and warnings; and with them He sent the Book in truth, to judge between people in matters wherein they differed; but the People of the Book, after the Clear Signs came to them, did not differ among themselves, except through selfish contumacy.[91] God by His Grace guided the Believers to the truth, concerning that wherein they differed. For God guides whom He will to a path that is straight.

214. Or do ye think that ye shall enter the Garden (of Bliss[92]) without such (trials) as came to those who passed away before you? They encountered suffering and adversity, and were so shaken in spirit that

---

91 Wilful disobedience to God.
92 Supreme joy, utter contentment

even the Apostle and those of faith who were with him cried: "When (will come) the help of God?" Ah! verily, the help of God is (always) near!

215. They ask thee what they should spend (in charity). Say: Whatever ye spend that is good, is for parents and kindred and orphans and those in want and for wayfarers. And whatever ye do that is good, God knoweth it well.

216. Fighting is prescribed for you, and ye dislike it. But it is possible that ye dislike a thing which is good for you and that ye love a thing which is bad for you. But God knoweth, and ye know not.

217. They ask thee concerning fighting in the Prohibited Month. Say: "Fighting therein is a grave (offence); but graver is it in the sight of God to prevent access to the path of God, to deny Him, to prevent access to the Sacred Mosque, and drive out its members. Tumult and oppression are worse than slaughter. Nor will they cease fighting you until they turn you back from your faith if they can. And if any of you turn back from their faith and die in unbelief, their works will bear no fruit in this life and in the Hereafter; they will be Companions of the Fire and will abide therein.

218. Those who believed and those who suffered exile and fought (and strove and struggled) in the path of God, they have the hope of the Mercy of God; and God is Oft-Forgiving, Most Merciful.

219. They ask thee concerning wine and gambling. Say: "In them is great sin, and some profit, for men; but the sin is greater than the profit." They ask thee how much they are to spend; Say: "What is beyond your needs." Thus doth God make clear to you His Signs: in order that ye may consider —

220. (Their bearings) on this life and the Hereafter. They ask thee concerning orphans. Say: "The best thing to do is what is for their good; if ye mix their affairs with yours, they are your brethren; but God knows the man who means mischief from the man who means good. And if God had wished, He could have put you into difficulties: He is indeed Exalted in Power, Wise."

221. Do not marry unbelieving women (idolaters), until they believe; a slave woman who believes is better than an unbelieving woman, even though she allure you. Nor marry (your girls) to Un-

believers until they believe: a man slave who believes is better than an unbeliever, even though he allure you. Unbelievers do (but) beckon[93] you to the Fire. But God beckons by His Grace to the Garden (of Bliss) and forgiveness, and makes His Signs clear to mankind: that they may celebrate His praise.

222. They ask thee concerning women's courses. Say: They are a hurt and a polLution; so keep away from women in their courses, and do not approach them until they are clean. But when they have purified themselves ye may approach them in any manner, time, or place ordained for you by God. For God loves those who turn to Him constantly and He loves those who keep themselves pure and clean.

223. Your wives are as a tilth[94] unto you; so approach your tilth when or how ye will. But do some good act for your souls beforehand; and fear God, and know that ye are to meet Him (in the Hereafter), and give (these) good tidings to those who believe.

224. And make not God's (name) an excuse in your oaths against doing good, or acting rightly, or making peace between persons; for God is one who heareth and knoweth all things.

225. God will not call you to account for thoughtlessness in your oaths, but for the intention in your hearts; and He is Oft-Forgiving, Most Forbearing.

226. For those who take an oath for abstention from their wives, a waiting for four months is ordained; if then they return, God is Oft-Forgiving, Most Merciful.

227. But if their intention is firm for divorce, God heareth and knoweth all things.

228. Divorced women shall wait concerning themselves for three monthly periods, nor is it lawful for them, to hide what God hath created in their wombs, if they have faith in God and the Last Day. And their husbands have the better right to take them back in that period, if they wish for reconciliation. And women shall have rights similar to the rights against them, according to what is equitable; but men have a degree (of advantage) over them and God is Exalted in Power, Wise.

---

[93] Lure to, summon to

[94] A cultivation, tillage

229. A divorce is only permissible twice: after that, the parties should either hold together on equitable terms or separate with kindness. It is not lawful for you, (men), to take back any of your gifts (from your wives), except when both parties fear that they would be unable to keep the limits ordained by God. If ye (judges) do indeed fear that they would be unable to keep the limits ordained by God, there is no blame on either of them if she give something for her freedom. These are the limits ordained by God; so do not transgress them. If any do transgress the limits ordained by God, such persons wrong (themselves as well as others).

230. So if a husband divorces his wife (irrevocably), he cannot, after that, remarry her until after she has married another husband and he has divorced her. In that case there is no blame on either of them if they reunite, provided they feel that they can keep the limits ordained[95] by God. Such are the limits ordained by God, which He makes plain to those who understand.

231. When ye divorce women, and they fulfil the term of their ('Iddah[96]), either take them back on equitable terms or set them free on equitable terms; but do not take them back to injure them or to take undue advantage; if anyone does that, He wrongs his own soul. Do not treat God's Signs as a jest, but solemnly rehearse God's favors on you, and the fact that He sent down to you the Book and Wisdom, for your instruction. And fear God, and know that God is well acquainted with all things.

232. When ye divorce women, and they fulfil the term of their ('Iddah), do not prevent them from marrying their (former) husbands, if they mutually agree on equitable terms. This instruction is for all amongst you, who believe in God and the Last Day. That is (the course making for) most virtue and purity amongst you, and God knows, and ye know not.

233. The mothers shall give suck to their offspring for two whole years, if the father desires to complete the term. But he shall bear the cost of their food and clothing on equitable terms. No soul shall

---

[95] Decreed, commanded or ordered
[96] The prescribed period of waiting during which a woman may not remarry after being widowed or divorced.

have a burden laid on it greater than it can bear. No mother shall be treated unfairly on account of her child, nor father on account of his child. An heir shall be chargeable in the same way, if they both decide on weaning, by mutual consent, and after due consultation, there is no blame on them. If ye decide on a foster-mother for your offspring, there is no blame on you, provided ye pay (the mother) what ye offered, on equitable terms. But fear God and know that God sees well what ye do.

234. If any of you die and leave widows behind, they shall wait concerning themselves four months and ten days: when they have fulfilled their term, there is no blame on you if they dispose of themselves in a just and reasonable manner. And God is well acquainted with what ye do.

235. There is no blame on you if ye make an offer of betrothal[97] or hold it in your hearts. God knows that ye cherish them in your hearts: but do not make a secret contract with them except in terms honourable, nor resolve on the tie of marriage till the term prescribed is fulfilled. And know that God knoweth what is in your hearts and take heed of Him; and know that God is Oft Forgiving, Most Forbearing.

236. There is no blame on you if ye divorce women before consummation or the fixation of their dower; but bestow on them (a suitable gift), the wealthy according to his means, and the poor according to his means; a gift of a reasonable amount is due from those who wish to do the right thing.

237. And if ye divorce them before consummation, but after the fixation of a dower for them, then the half of the dower (is due to them), unless they remit it. Or (the man's half) is remitted by him in whose hands is the marriage tie; and the remission (of the man's half) is the nearest to righteousness. And do not forget liberality between yourselves. For God sees well all that ye do.

238. Guard strictly your (habit of) prayers, especially the middle prayer, and stand before God in a devout (frame of mind).

239. If ye fear (an enemy), pray on foot, or riding (as may be most convenient), but when ye are in security, celebrate God's praises

---

[97] Engagement

in the manner He has taught you, which ye knew not (before).

240. Those of you who die and leave widows should bequeath for their widows a year's maintenance and residence; but if they leave (the residence), there is no blame on you for what they do with themselves, provided it is reasonable, and God is Exalted in Power, Wise.

241. For divorced women maintenance (should be provided) on a reasonable (scale). This is a duty on the righteous.

242. Thus doth God make clear His Signs to you: in order that ye may understand.

243. Didst thou not turn thy vision to those who abandoned their homes, though they were thousands (in number), for fear of death? God said to them: "Die." Then He restored them to life. For God is full of bounty[98] to mankind, but most of them are ungrateful.

244. Then fight in the cause of God, and know that God heareth and knoweth all things.

245. Who is he that will loan to God a beautiful loan, which God will double unto his credit and multiply many times? It is God that giveth (you) want or plenty, and to Him shall be your return.

246. Hast thou not turned thy vision to the chiefs of the children of Israel after (the time of) Moses? They said to a Prophet (that was) among them: "Appoint for us a king, that we may fight in the cause of God." He said: "Is it not possible if ye were commanded to fight, that ye will not fight?" They said: "How could we refuse to fight in the cause of God, seeing that we were turned out of our homes and our families?" But when they were commanded to fight, they turned back, except a small band among them. But God has full knowledge of those who do wrong.

247. Their Prophet said to them: "God hath appointed Talüt as king over you." They say: "How can he exercise authority over us when we are better fitted than he to exercise authority, and he is not even gifted with wealth in abundance?" He said: "God hath chosen him above you, and hath gifted him abundantly with knowledge and bodily prowess[99]; God granteth His authority to whom He pleaseth.

---

[98] Generosity, mercy or grace

[99] Exceptional ability, skill or strength.

God careth for all, and He knoweth all things."

248. And (further) their Prophet said to them: "A Sign of his authority is that there shall come to you the Ark of the Covenant, with (an assurance) therein of security from your Lord, and the relics[100] left by the family of Moses and the family of Aaron, carried by angels. In this is a Symbol for you if ye indeed have faith."

249. When Talüt set forth with the armies, he said: "God will test you at the stream; if any drinks of its water, he goes not with my army; only those who taste not of it go with me; a mere sip out of the hand is excused." But they all drank of it, except a few. When they crossed the river, he and the faithful ones with him, they said: "This day we cannot cope with Goliath and his forces." But those who were convinced that they must meet God, said: "How oft, by God's will, hath a small force vanquished a big one? God is with those who steadfastly persevere."

250. When they advanced to meet Goliath and his forces, they prayed: "Our Lord! pour out constancy on us and make our steps firm; help us against those that reject faith."

251. By God's will they routed them: and David slew Goliath; and God gave him power and wisdom and taught him whatever (else) He willed. And did not God check one set of people by means of another, the earth would indeed be full of mischief, but God is full of bounty to all the Worlds.

252. These are the Signs of God; We rehearse them to thee in truth: verily thou art one of the apostles.

253. Those apostles We endowed with gifts, some above others: to one of them God spoke; others He raised to degrees (of honour); to Jesus the son of Mary, We gave clear (Signs), and strengthened him with the Holy Spirit. If God had so willed, succeeding generations would not have fought among each other, after clear (Signs) had come to them, but they (chose) to wrangle, some believing and others rejecting. If God had so willed, they would not have fought each other; but God fulfilleth His plan.

254. O ye who believe! spend out of (the bounties) We have

---

[100] Surviving memorials

provided for you, before the day comes when no bargaining (will avail), nor friendship, nor intercession. Those who reject faith — they are the wrongdoers.

255. God! there is no God but He, the Living, the Self-subsisting, Eternal. No slumber can seize him nor sleep. His are all things in the heavens and on earth. Who is there can intercede in His presence except as He permitteth? He knoweth what (appeareth to His creatures as) before or after or behind them. Nor shall they compass aught of His knowledge except as He willeth. His throne doth extend over the heavens and the earth, and He feeleth no fatigue in guarding and preserving them. For He is the Most High, the Supreme (in glory).

256. Let there be no compulsion in religion. Truth stands out clear from error; whoever rejects evil and believes in God hath grasped the most trustworthy hand-hold, that never breaks. And God heareth and knoweth all things.

257. God is the Protector of those who have faith: from the depths of darkness He will lead them forth into light. Of those who reject faith, the patrons are the Evil Ones: from light they will lead them forth into the depths of darkness. They will be Companions of the Fire, to dwell therein (forever).

258. Hast thou not turned thy vision to one who disputed with Abraham about his Lord, because God had granted him power? Abraham said: "My Lord is He Who Giveth life and death." He said: "I give life and death." Said Abraham: "But it is God that causeth the sun to rise from the East, do thou then cause him to rise from the West?" Thus was he confounded who (in arrogance) rejected faith. Nor doth God give guidance to a people unjust.

259. Or (take) the similitude of one who passed by a hamlet[101], all in ruins to its roofs. He said: "Oh! how shall God bring it (ever) to life, after (this) its death?" But God caused him to die for a hundred years, then raised him up (again). He said: "How long didst thou tarry[102] (thus)?" He said: "(Perhaps) a day or part of a day." He said: "Nay, thou hast tarried thus a hundred years; but look at thy food and thy drink; they show no signs of age; and look at thy donkey: and that

---

[101] A small village.
[102] Stay

We may make of thee a Sign unto the people, look further at the bones, how We bring them together and clothe them with flesh! When this was shown clearly to him he said: "I know that God hath power over all things."

260. Behold! Abraham said: "My Lord! show me how thou givest life to the dead." He said: "Dost thou not then believe?" He said: "Yea! but to satisfy my own understanding." He said: "Take four birds; tame them to turn to thee; put a portion of them on every hill, and call to them; they will come to thee (flying) with speed. Then know that God is Exalted in Power, Wise."

261. The parable of those who spend their substance in the way of God is that of a grain of corn: it groweth seven ears, and each ear hath a hundred grains. God giveth manifold increase to whom He pleaseth; and God careth for all and He knoweth all things.

262. Those who spend their substance in the cause of God, and follow not up their gifts with reminders of their generosity or with injury, for them their reward is with their Lord; on them shall be no fear, nor shall they grieve.

263. Kind words and the covering of faults are better than charity followed by injury. God is free of all wants, and He is Most Forbearing.

264. O ye who believe! cancel not your charity by reminders of your generosity or by injury, like those who spend their substance to be seen of men, but believe neither in God nor in the last day. They are in Parable like a hard, barren rock, on which is a little soil; on it falls heavy rain, which leaves it (just) a bare stone. They will be able to do nothing with aught they have earned. And God guideth not those who reject faith.

265. And the likeness of those who spend their substance, seeking to please God and to strengthen their souls, is as a garden, high and fertile: heavy rain falls on it but makes it yield a double increase of harvest, and if it receives not heavy rain, light moisture sufficeth it. God seeth well whatever ye do.

266. Does any of you wish that he should have a garden with date-palms and vines and streams flowing underneath, and all kinds of fruit, while he is stricken with old age, and his children are not strong (enough to look after themselves) that it should be caught in a whirlwind, with fire therein and be burnt up? Thus doth God make

clear to you (His) Signs; that ye may consider.

267. O ye who believe! give of the good things which ye have (honourably) earned, and of the fruits of the earth which We have produced for you, and do not even aim at getting anything which is bad, in order that out of it ye may give away something,when ye yourselves would not receive it except with closed eyes. And know that God is free of all wants, and worthy of all praise.

268. The Evil One threatens you with poverty and bids you to conduct unseemly. God promiseth you His forgiveness and bounties and God careth for all and He knoweth all things.

269. He granteth wisdom to whom He pleaseth; and he to whom wisdom is granted receiveth indeed a benefit overflowing; but none will grasp the message but men of understanding.

270. And whatever ye spend in charity or devotion, be sure God knows it all. But the wrongdoers have no helpers.

271. If ye disclose (acts of) charity, even so it is well, but if ye conceal them, and make them reach those (really) in need, that is best for you: it will remove from you some of your (stains of) evil. And God is well acquainted with what ye do.

272. It is not required of thee (O Apostle), to set them on the right path, but God sets on the right path whom He pleaseth. Whatever of good ye give benefits your own souls, and ye shall only do so seeking the "Face" of God. Whatever good ye give, shall be rendered back to you, and ye shall not be dealt with unjustly.

273. (Charity is) for those in need, who, in God's cause, are restricted (from travel), and cannot move about in the land, seeking (for trade or work). The ignorant man thinks, because of their modesty, that they are free from want. Thou shalt know them by their (unfailing) mark: they beg not importunately[103] from all and sundry[104]. And whatever of good ye give, be assured God knoweth it well.

274. Those who (in charity) spend of their goods by night and by day, in secret and in public, have their reward with their Lord: on them shall be no fear, nor shall they grieve.

---

[103] Persistently
[104] All individually and collectively.

275. Those who devour usury[105] will not stand except as stands one whom the Evil One by his touch hath driven to madness. That is because they say: "Trade is like usury, but God hath permitted trade and forbidden usury. Those who, after receiving direction from their Lord, desist, shall be pardoned for the past; their case is for God (to judge); but those who repeat (the offence) are Companions of the Fire: they will abide therein (forever).

276. God will deprive usury of all blessing, but will give increase for deeds of charity: for He loveth not creatures ungrateful and wicked.

277. Those who believe, and do deeds of righteousness, and establish regular prayers and regular charity, will have their reward with their Lord: on them shall be no fear, nor shall they grieve.

278. O ye who believe! fear God, and give up what remains of your demand for usury, if ye are indeed Believers.

279. If ye do it not, take notice of war from God and his Apostle: but if ye turn back, ye shall have your capital sums; deal not unjustly, and ye shall not be dealt with unjustly.

280. If the debtor is in a difficulty, grant him time till it is easy for him to repay, but if ye remit it by way of charity, that is best for you if ye only knew.

281. And fear the day when ye shall be brought back to God. Then shall every soul be paid what it earned, and none shall be dealt with unjustly.

282. O ye who believe! when ye deal with each other, in trans-actions involving future obligations in a fixed period of time, reduce them to writing. Let a scribe[106] write down faithfully as between the parties; let not the scribe refuse to write, as God has taught him, so let him write. Let him who incurs the liability dictate, but let him fear his Lord God, and not diminish aught[107] of what he owes. If the party liable is mentally deficient, or weak, or unable himself to dictate, let his guardian dictate faithfully. And get two witnesses, out of your own men, and if there are not two men, then a man and two women, such as ye choose, for witnesses, so that if one of them errs, the other

---

[105] Receiving interest on money lent to others.
[106] One who writes down.
[107] Anything whatever, any part

35

can remind her. The witnesses should not refuse when they are called on (for evidence). Disdain not to reduce to writing (your contract) for a future period, whether it be small or big: it is juster[108] in the sight of God, more suitable as evidence, and more convenient to prevent doubts among yourselves; but if it be a transaction which ye carry out on the spot among yourselves, there is no blame on you if ye reduce it not to writing. But take witnesses whenever ye make a commercial contract; and let neither scribe nor witness suffer harm. If ye do (such harm), it would be wickedness in you. So fear God; for it is God that teaches you. And God is well acquainted with all things.

283. If ye are on a journey, and cannot find a scribe, a pledge[109] with possession (may serve the purpose). And if one of you deposits a thing on trust with another, let the trustee (faithfully) discharge his trust, and let him fear his Lord. Conceal not evidence; for whoever conceals it, his heart is tainted with sin. And God knoweth all that ye do.

284. To God belongeth all that is in the heavens and on earth. Whether ye show what is in your minds or conceal it, God calleth you to account for it. He forgiveth whom He pleaseth, and punisheth whom He pleaseth. For God hath power over all things.

285. The Apostle believeth in what hath been revealed to him from his Lord, as do the men of faith. Each one (of them) believeth in God, His angels, His books, and His Apostles "We make no distinction (they say) between one and another of His Apostles." And they say: "We hear, and we obey; (We seek) Thy forgiveness, Our Lord, and to Thee is the end of all journeys."

286. On no soul doth God place a burden greater than it can bear. It gets every good that it earns, and it suffers every ill that it earns. (Pray): "Our Lord! condemn us not if we forget or fall into error; Our Lord! Lay not on us a burden like that which Thou didst lay on those before us; Our Lord! lay not on us a burden greater than we have strength to bear. Blot out our sins, and grant us forgiveness. Have mercy on us. Thou art our Protector; help us against those who stand against faith."

---

[108] More just

[109] Something given as security for the payment of a debt or fulfillment of a promise.

Chapter 3
Al-i-'Imran (The Family of 'Imran)
Revealed at Madinah, 200 verses.

In the name of God, Most Gracious, Most Merciful.

1. Alif Lãm Mïm.

2. God! there is no god but He — the Living, the Self-Subsisting,[1] Eternal.

3. It is He Who sent down to thee (step by step), in truth, the Book, confirming what went before it; and He sent down the Law (of Moses) and the Gospel (of Jesus) before this, as a guide to mankind, and He sent down the Criterion (of judgment between right and wrong).

4. Then those who reject Faith in the Signs of God will suffer the severest penalty, and God is Exalted in Might, Lord of Retribution.[2]

5. From God, verily nothing is hidden on earth or in the heavens.

6. He it is Who shapes you in the wombs as He pleases. There is no god but He, the Exalted in Might, the Wise.

7. He it is Who has sent down to thee the Book: in it are verses basic or fundamental (of established meaning); they are the foundation of the Book: others are allegorical[3]. But those in whose hearts is perversity follow the part thereof that is allegorical, seeking discord, and searching for its hidden meanings, but no one knows its hidden meanings except God and those who are firmly grounded in knowledge say: "We believe in the Book; the whole of it is from our Lord"; and none will grasp the Message except men of understanding.

8. "Our Lord!" (they say), "Let not our hearts deviate now after Thou hast guided us, but grant us mercy from Thine own Presence; for Thou art the Grantor of bounties without measure.

9. "Our Lord! Thou art He that will gather mankind together against a day about which there is no doubt: for God never fails in His promise."

10. Those who reject faith, neither their possessions nor their

---

[1] Existing by Himself and does not depend on any one else.

[2] Distribution of reward and punishment.

[3] Representing moral, spiritual and abstract meanings figuratively or through symbols.

(numerous) progeny will avail them aught against God: they are themselves but fuel for the Fire.

11. (Their plight will be) no better than that of the people of Pharaoh, and their predecessors: they denied Our Signs, and God called them to account for their sins. For God is strict in punishment.

12. Say to those who reject Faith: "Soon will ye be vanquished[4] and gathered together to Hell, an evil bed indeed (to lie on)!

13. "There has already been for you a Sign in the two armies that met (in combat): one was fighting in the cause of God, the other resisting God; these saw with their own eyes twice their number. But God doth support with His aid whom He pleaseth. In this is a warning for such as have eyes to see."

14. Fair in the eyes of men is the love of things they covet: women and sons; heaped-up hoards of gold and silver; horses branded (for blood and excellence); and (wealth of) cattle and well-tilled land. Such are the possessions of this world's life; but in nearness to God is the best of the goals (to return to).

15. Say: Shall I give you glad tidings of things far better than those? For the righteous are Gardens in nearness to their Lord, with rivers flowing beneath; therein is their eternal home; with Companions pure (and holy), and the good pleasure of God. For in God's sight are (all) His servants —

16. (Namely), those who say: "Our Lord! we have indeed believed: forgive us, then, our sins, and save us from the agony of the Fire."

17. Those who show patience, firmness and self-control; who are true (in word and deed); who worship devoutly; who spend (in the way of God); and who pray for forgiveness in the early hours of the morning.

18. There is no god but He: that is the witness of God, His angels, and those endued with knowledge, standing firm on justice. There is no god but He, the Exalted in Power, the Wise.

19. The Religion before God is Islam (submission to His Will): nor did the people of the Book dissent therefrom except through envy of each other, after knowledge had come to them. But if any deny

---

4 Defeated

the Signs of God, God is swift in calling to account.

20. So if they dispute with thee, say: "I have submitted my whole self to God and so have those who follow me." And say to the people of the Book and to those who are unlearned: "Do ye (also) submit yourselves?" If they do, they are in right guidance, but if they turn back, thy duty is to convey the Message; and in God's sight are (all) His servants.

21. As to those who deny the Signs of God, and in defiance of right, slay the Prophets, and slay those who teach just dealing with mankind, announce to them a grievous penalty.

22. They are those whose works will bear no fruit in this world and in the Hereafter, nor will they have anyone to help.

23. Hast thou not turned thy vision to those who have been given a portion of the Book? They are invited to the Book of God, to settle their dispute, but a party of them turn back and decline (the arbitration).

24. This because they say: "The Fire shall not touch us but for a few numbered days"; for their forgeries deceive them as to their own religion.

25. But how (will they fare) when We gather them together against a day about which there is no doubt, and each soul will be paid out just what it has earned, without (favor or injustice)?

26. Say: "O God! Lord of Power (and Rule), thou givest Power to whom Thou pleasest, and Thou strippest off power from whom Thou pleasest, thou enduest with honour whom thou pleasest, and thou bringest low whom Thou pleasest; in Thy hand is all Good. Verily, over all things thou hast power.

27. "Thou causest the Night to gain on the Day, and Thou causest the Day to gain on the Night; Thou bringest the Living out of the Dead, and thou bringest the Dead out of the Living; and Thou givest sustenance to whom Thou pleasest without measure."

28. Let not the believers take for friends or helpers unbelievers rather than believers; if any do that, in nothing will there be help from God; except by way of precaution, that ye may guard yourselves from them. But God cautions you (to remember) Himself, for the final goal is to God.

29. Say: "Whether ye hide what is in your hearts or reveal it, God knows it all. He knows what is in the heavens, and what is on earth.

And God has power over all things.

30. "On the day when every soul will be confronted with all the good it has done, and all the evil it has done, it will wish there were a great distance between it and its evil. But God cautions you (to remember) Himself. And God is full of kindness to those that serve Him.

31. Say: "If ye do love God, follow me: God will love you, and forgive you your sins, for God is Oft-Forgiving, Most Merciful."

32. Say: "Obey God and His Apostle": but if they turn back, God loveth not those who reject Faith.

33. God did choose Adam and Noah, the family of Abraham and the family of 'Imran above all people —

34. Offspring, one of the other; and God heareth and knoweth all things.

35. Behold! a woman of 'Imran said: "O my Lord! I do dedicate unto thee what is in my womb for Thy special service, so accept this of me, for Thou hearest and knowest all things."

36. When she was delivered, she said: "O my Lord! behold! I am delivered of a female child!" And God knew best what she brought forth — "and no wise is the male like the female. I have named her Mary, and I commend her and her offspring to Thy protection from the Evil One, the Rejected."

37. Right graciously did her Lord accept her: He made her grow in purity and beauty; to the care of Zakariya was she assigned. Every time that he entered (her) chamber to see her, he found her supplied with sustenance. He said: "O Mary! whence (comes) this to you?" She said: "From God: for God provides sustenance to whom He pleases, without measure."

38. There did Zakariya pray to his Lord, saying: "O my Lord! grant unto me from Thee a progeny that is pure; for Thou art He that heareth prayer!"

39. While he was standing in prayer in the chamber, the angels called unto him: "God doth give thee glad tidings of Yahya, witnessing the truth of a Word from God, and (be besides) noble, chaste, and a Prophet, of the (goodly) company of the righteous."

40. He said: "O my Lord! how shall I have a son, seeing I am very old, and my wife is barren?" "Thus," was the answer, "doth God

accomplish what He willeth."

41. He said: "O my Lord! give me a Sign!" "Thy Sign," was the answer, "shall be that thou shalt speak to no man for three days but with signals. Then celebrate the praises of thy Lord again and again, and glorify Him in the evening and in the morning."

42. Behold! the angels said: "O Mary! God hath chosen thee and purified thee; chosen thee above the women of all nations.

43. "O Mary! worship thy Lord devoutly; prostrate thyself, and bow down (in prayer) with those who bow down."

44. This is part of the tidings of the things unseen, which We reveal unto thee (O Apostle!) by inspiration; thou wast not with them when they cast lots with arrows, as to which of them should be charged with the care of Mary; nor wast thou with them when they disputed (the point).

45. Behold! the angels said "O Mary! God giveth thee glad tidings of a Word from Him: his name will be Christ Jesus, the son of Mary, held in honour in this world and the Hereafter and of (the company of) those nearest to God.

46. "He shall speak to the people in childhood and in maturity, and he shall be (of the company) of the righteous."

47. She said: "O my Lord! how shall I have a son when no man hath touched me?" He said: "Even so: God createth what He willeth; when He hath decreed a plan, He but saith to it 'Be', and it is!

48. "And God will teach him the Book and Wisdom, the Law and the Gospel.

49. "And (appoint him) an Apostle to the Children of Israel, (with this message): I have come to you, with a Sign from your Lord, in that I make for you out of clay, as it were, the figure of a bird, and breathe into it, and it becomes a bird by God's leave; and I heal those born blind, and the lepers, and I quicken[5] the dead, by God's leave; and I declare to you what ye eat, and what ye store in your houses. Surely therein is a Sign for you if ye did believe.

50. "(I have come to you), to attest the Law which was before me, and to make lawful to you part of what was (before) forbidden

---

[5] To restore life to

41

to you; I have come to you with a Sign from your Lord. So fear God, and obey me.

51. "It is God who is my Lord and your Lord; then worship Him. This is a way that is straight."

52. When Jesus found unbelief on their part he said: "Who will be my helpers to (the work of) God?" Said the Disciples: "We are God's helpers, we believe in God, and do thou bear witness that we are Muslims.

53. "Our Lord! we believe in what thou hast revealed, and we follow the Apostle; then write us down among those who bear witness."

54. And (then unbelievers) plotted and planned, and God too planned, and the best of planners is God.

55. Behold! God said: "O Jesus! I will take thee and raise thee to Myself and clear thee (of the falsehoods) of those who blaspheme; I will make those who follow thee superior to those who reject Faith, to the Day of Resurrection; then shall ye all return unto Me, and I will judge between you of the matters wherein ye dispute.

56. "As to those who reject faith, I will punish them with terrible agony in this world and in the Hereafter, nor will they have anyone to help.

57. "As to those who believe and work righteousness, God will pay them (in full) their reward; but God loveth not those who do wrong.

58. "This is what We rehearse[6] unto thee of the Signs and the Message of Wisdom."

59. The similitude of Jesus before God is as that of Adam: He created him from dust, then said to him: "Be," and he was.

60. The truth (comes) from God alone; so be not of those who doubt.

61. If anyone disputes in this matter with thee, now after (full) knowledge hath come to thee, say: "Come! let us gather together, our sons and your sons, our women and your women, ourselves and yourselves: then let us earnestly pray, and invoke the curse of God on those who lie!"

---

[6] Repeat

62. This is the true account: there is no god except God; and God — He is indeed the Exalted in Power, the Wise.

63. But if they turn back, God hath full knowledge of those who do mischief.

64. Say: "O people of the Book! come to common terms as between us and you: that we worship none but God; that we associate no partners with Him; that we erect not, from among ourselves, Lords and patrons other than God." If then they turn back, say: "Bear witness that we (at least) are Muslims (bowing to God's will)."

65. Ye people of the Book! why dispute ye about Abraham, when the Law[7] and the Gospel[8] were not revealed till after him? Have ye no understanding?

66. Ah! ye are those who fell to disputing (even) in matters of which ye had some knowledge! but why dispute ye in matters of which ye have no knowledge? It is God Who knows, and ye who know not!

67. Abraham was not a Jew nor yet a Christian, but he was true in faith, and bowed his will to God's (which is Islam), and he joined not gods with God.

68. Without doubt, among men the nearest of kin to Abraham are those who follow him, as are also this Apostle and those who believe; and God is the Protector of those who have faith.

69. It is the wish of a section of the People of the Book to lead you astray. But they shall lead astray (not you), but themselves and they do not perceive!

70. Ye People of the Book! Why reject ye the Signs of God, of which ye are (yourselves) witnesses?

71. Ye People of the Book! Why do ye clothe truth with falsehood, and conceal the truth, while ye have knowledge?

72. A section of the People of the Book say: "Believe in the morning what is revealed to the believers, but reject it at the end of the day; perchance they may (themselves) turn back.

73. "And believe no one unless he follows your religion." Say: "True guidance is the guidance of God; (fear ye) lest a revelation

---

[7] Torah.

[8] Injil.

be sent to someone (else) like unto that which was sent unto you. Or that those (receiving such revelation) should engage you in argument before your Lord." Say: "All bounties are in the hand of God: He granteth them to whom He pleaseth; and God careth for all, and He knoweth all things."

74. For His Mercy He specially chooseth whom He pleaseth: for God is the Lord of bounties unbounded.

75. Among the People of the Book are some who, if entrusted with a hoard of gold, will (readily) pay it back; others, who, if entrusted with a single silver coin, will not repay it unless thou constantly stoodest demanding, because, they say, "There is no call on us (to keep faith) with these ignorant (pagans)." But they tell a lie against God, and (well) they know it.

76. Nay, — Those that keep their plighted faith[9] and act aright, verily God loves those who act aright.

77. As for those who sell the faith they owe to God and their own plighted word for a small price, they shall have no portion in the Hereafter: nor will God (deign[10] to) speak to them or look at them on the Day of Judgment, nor will He cleanse them (of sin); they shall have a grievous penalty.

78. There is among them a section who distort the Book with their tongues; (as they read) you would think it is a part of the Book, but it is no part of the Book; and they say, "That is from God," but it is not from God: it is they who tell a lie against God, and (well) they know it!

79. It is not (possible) that a man, to whom is given the Book, and Wisdom, and the prophetic office, should say to people: "Be ye my worshippers rather than God's; on the contrary (he would say): "Be ye worshippers of Him Who is truly the Cherisher of all, for ye have taught the Book and ye have studied it earnestly."

80. Nor would he instruct you to take angels and prophets for Lords and Patrons. What! Would he bid you to unbelief after ye have bowed your will (to God in Islam)?

---

[9] Pledge, bond or covenant.
[10] To think fit, to condescend to.

81. Behold! God took the covenant of the Prophets, saying: "I give you a Book and Wisdom; then comes to you an Apostle confirming what is with you; do ye believe him and render him help." God said: "Do ye agree, and take this My Covenant as binding on you?" They said: "We agree." He said: "Then bear witness, and I am with you among the witnesses."

82. If any turn back after this, they are perverted[11] transgressors.

83. Do they seek for other than the Religion of God? — while all creatures in the heavens and on earth have, willing or unwilling, bowed to His Will (accepted Islam), and to Him shall they all be brought back.

84. Say: "We believe in God, and in what has been revealed to us and what was revealed to Abraham, Isma'il, Isaac, Jacob, and the Tribes, and in (Books) given to Moses, Jesus, and the Prophets, from their Lord; we make no distinction between one and another among them, and to God do we bow our will (in Islam)."

85. If anyone desires a religion other than Islam (submission to God), never will it be accepted of him; and in the Hereafter he will be in the ranks of those who have lost (all spiritual good).

86. How shall God guide those who reject faith after they accepted it and bore witness that the Apostle was true and that clear Signs had come unto them? But God guides not a people unjust.

87. Of such the reward is that on them (rests) the curse of God, of His angels, and of all mankind.

88. In that will they dwell; nor will their penalty be lightened, nor respite be their (lot).

89. Except for those that repent (even) after that, and make amends: for verily God is Oft-Forgiving, Most Merciful.

90. But those who reject faith after they accepted it, and then go on adding to their defiance of faith — never will their repentance be accepted; for they are those who have (of set purpose) gone astray.

91. As to those who reject faith, and die rejecting, never would be accepted from any such as much gold as the earth contains, though they should offer it for ransom. For such is (in store) a penalty

---

[11] Morally stray

grievous, and they will find no helpers.

92. By no means shall ye attain righteousness unless ye give (freely) of that which ye love; and whatever ye give, of a truth God knoweth it well.

93. All food was lawful to the Children of Israel, except what Israel made unlawful for itself, before the Law (of Moses) was revealed. Say: "Bring ye the Law and study it, if ye be men of truth."

94. If any, after this, invent a lie and attribute it to God, they are indeed unjust wrongdoers.

95. Say: "God speaketh the truth: follow the religion of Abraham, the sane in faith; he was not of the pagans."

96. The first House (of worship) appointed for men was that at Bakka full of blessing and of guidance for all kinds of beings:

97. In it are Signs manifest; (for example), the Station of Abraham; whoever enters it attains security; pilgrimage thereto is a duty men owe to God, those who can afford the journey; but if any deny faith, God stands not in need of any of his creatures.

98. Say: "O people of the Book! why reject ye the Signs of God, when God is Himself witness to all ye do?

99. Say: "O ye People of the Book! why obstruct ye those who believe, from the path of God, seeking to make it crooked, while ye were yourselves witnesses (to God's Covenant)? But God is not unmindful of all that ye do."

100. O ye who believe! if ye listen to a faction among the People of the Book, they would (indeed) render you apostates[12] after ye have believed!

101. And how would ye deny faith while unto you are rehearsed the Signs of God, and among you lives the Apostle? Whoever holds firmly to God will be shown a way that is straight.

102. O ye who believe! fear God as He should be feared, and die not except in a state of Islam.

103. And hold fast, all together, by the rope which God (stretches out for you), and be not divided among yourselves; and remember with gratitude God's favor on you; for ye were enemies and He joined your hearts in love, so that by His grace, ye became brethren; and

---

[12] Those who abandon their religious faith.

ye were on the brink of the Pit of Fire, and He saved you from it. Thus doth God make His Signs clear to you: that ye may be guided.

104. Let there arise out of you a band of people inviting to all that is good, enjoining what is right, and forbidding what is wrong; they are the ones to attain felicity.[13]

105. Be not like those who are divided amongst themselves and fall into disputations[14] after receiving clear Signs; for them is a dreadful penalty.

106. On the day when some faces will be (lit up with) white, and some faces will be (in the gloom of) black; to those whose faces will be black, (will be said): "Did ye reject faith after accepting it? Taste then the penalty for rejecting faith."

107. But those whose faces will be (lit with) white, they will be in (the light of) God's Mercy; therein to dwell (forever).

108. These are the Signs of God: We rehearse them to thee in truth: and God means no injustice to any of His creatures.

109. To God belongs all that is in the heavens and on earth; to Him do all questions go back (for decision).

110. Ye are the best of peoples, evolved for mankind, enjoining what is right, forbidding what is wrong, and believing in God. If only the People of the Book had faith, it were best for them; among them are some who have faith, but most of them are perverted transgressors.

111. They will do you no harm, barring a trifling annoyance[15]; if they come out to fight you, they will show you their backs, and no help shall they get.

112. Shame is pitched[16] over them (like a tent) wherever they are found, except when under a covenant (of protection) from God and from men; they draw on themselves wrath from God, and pitched over them is (the tent of) destitution. This because they rejected the Signs of God, and slew the prophets in defiance[17] of right; this because they rebelled and transgressed beyond bounds.

---

[13] Bliss, supreme joy.
[14] Controversies, wrangling or bickerings.
[15] A small nuisance.
[16] Set up, or hurled at them.
[17] Open disregard.

113. Not all of them are alike: of the People of the Book are a portion that stand (for the right); they rehearse the Signs of God all night long, and then prostrate themselves in adoration.

114. They believe in God and the Last Day; they enjoin what is right, and forbid what is wrong; and they (hasten in emulation[18]) in (all) good works; they are in the ranks of the righteous.

115. Of the good that they do, nothing will be rejected of them; for God knoweth well those that do right.

116. Those who reject faith, neither their possessions nor their (numerous) progeny will avail them aught against God; they will be Companions of the Fire, dwelling therein (forever).

117. What they spend in the life of this (material) world may be likened to a wind which brings a nipping[19] frost: it strikes and destroys the harvest of men who have wronged their own souls; it is not God that hath wronged them, but they wrong themselves.

118. O ye who believe! take not into your intimacy those outside your ranks; they will not fail to corrupt you. They only desire your ruin: rank[20] hatred has already appeared from their mouths; what their hearts conceal is far worse. We have made plain to you the Signs, if ye have wisdom.

119. Ah! ye are those who love them, but they love you not, though ye believe in the whole of the Book. When they meet you, they say, "We believe"; but when they are alone, they bite off the very tips of their fingers at you in their rage. Say: "Perish in your rage; God knoweth well all the secrets of the heart."

120. If aught that is good befalls you, it grieves them; but if some misfortune overtakes you, they rejoice at it. But if ye are constant and do right, not the least harm will their cunning do to you, for God compasseth round about all that they do.

121. Remember that morning thou didst leave the household (early) to post the faithful at their stations for battle: and God heareth and knoweth all things.

122. Remember two of your parties meditated cowardice; but God

---

[18] In an effort to excel others.
[19] Sharp and painful.
[20] Bitter and virulent.

was their Protector, and in God should the faithful (ever) put their trust.

123. God had helped you at Badr, when ye were a contemptible little force; then fear God; thus may ye show your gratitude.

124. Remember thou saidst to the faithful: is it not enough for you that God should help you with three thousand angels (specially) sent down?.

125. "Yea," if ye remain firm, and act aright, even if the enemy should rush here on you in hot haste, your Lord would help you with five thousand angels making a terrific onslaught.

126. God made it but a message of hope for you; and an assurance to your hearts: (in any case) there is no help except from God the Exalted, the Wise:

127. That he might cut off a fringe of the unbelievers or expose them to infamy, and they should then be turned back, frustrated of their purpose.

128. Not for thee, (but for God), is the decision: whether He turn in mercy to them, or punish them; for they are indeed wrongdoers.

129. To God belongeth all that is in the heavens and on earth. He forgiveth whom He pleaseth and punisheth whom He pleaseth: but God is Oft-Forgiving, Most Merciful.

130. O ye who believe! devour not usury[21], doubled and multiplied; but fear God; that ye may (really) prosper.

131. Fear the Fire, which is prepared for those who reject faith.

132. And obey God and the Apostle; that ye may obtain mercy.

133. Be quick in the race for forgiveness from your Lord, and for a Garden whose width is that (of the whole) of the heavens and of the earth, prepared for the righteous.

134. Those who spend (freely), whether in prosperity, or in adversity; who restrain anger, and pardon (all) men; for God loves those who do good.

135. And those who, having done something to be ashamed of, or wronged their own souls, earnestly bring God to mind, and ask for forgiveness for their sins — and who can forgive sins except God?

---

[21] Income received from lending money to others.

— And are never obstinate in persisting knowingly in (the wrong) they have done.

136. For such the reward is forgiveness from their Lord, and Gardens with rivers flowing underneath, an eternal dwelling; how excellent a recompense for those who work (and strive)!

137. Many were the Ways of Life that have passed away before you: travel through the earth, and see what was the end of those who rejected truth.

138. Here is a plain statement to men, a guidance and instruction to those who fear God!

139. So lose not heart, nor fall into despair: for ye must gain mastery if ye are true in faith.

140. If a wound hath touched you, be sure a similar wound hath touched the others. Such days (of varying fortunes) We give to men and men by turns: that God may know those that believe, and that He may take to Himself from your ranks martyr-witnesses (to Truth). And God loveth not those that do wrong.

141. God's object also is to purge those that are true in faith and to deprive of blessing those that resist faith.

142. Did ye think that ye would enter heaven without God testing those of you who fought hard (in His cause) and remained steadfast?

143. Ye did indeed wish for death before ye met him: now ye have seen him with your own eyes (and ye flinch[22]!).

144. Muhammad is no more than an Apostle: many were the Apostles that passed away before him. If he died or were slain, will ye then turn back on your heels? If any did turn back on his heels, not the least harm will he do to God; but God (on the other hand) will swiftly reward those who (serve him) with gratitude.

145. Nor can a soul die except by God's leave, the term being fixed as by writing. If any do desire a reward in this life, We shall give it to him; and if any do desire a reward in the Hereafter, We shall give it to him. And swiftly shall We reward those that (serve Us with) gratitude.

146. How many of the Prophets fought (in God's way), and with

---

[22] Shrink or draw back.

them (fought) large bands of godly men? But they never lost heart if they met with disaster in God's way, nor did they weaken (in will) nor give in. And God loves those who are firm and steadfast.

147. All that they said was: "Our Lord! forgive us our sins and anything we may have done that transgressed our duty: establish our feet firmly, and help us against those that resist faith."

148. And God gave them a reward in this world, and the excellent reward of the Hereafter. For God loveth those who do good.

149. O ye who believe! if ye obey the unbelievers, they will drive you back on your heels, and ye will turn back (from faith) to your own loss.

150. Nay, God is your Protector, and He is the best of helpers.

151. Soon shall We cast terror into the hearts of the unbelievers, for that they joined companions with God, for which He had sent no authority: their abode will be the Fire; and evil is the home of the wrongdoers!

152. God did indeed fulfil His promise to you when ye with His permission were about to annihilate your enemy — until ye flinched and fell to disputing about the order and disobeyed it after He brought you in sight (of the Booty) which ye covet. Among you are some that hanker[23] after this world and some that desire the Hereafter. Then did He divert you from your foes in order to test you, but He forgave you: for God is full of grace to those who believe.

153. Behold! ye were climbing up the high ground, without even casting a side glance at anyone, and the Apostle in your rear was calling you back. There did God give you one distress after another by way of requital[24], to teach you not to grieve for (the booty) that had escaped you and for (the ill) that had befallen you. For God is well aware of all that ye do.

154. After (the excitement) of the distress, He sent down calm on a band of you overcome with slumber, while another band was stirred to anxiety by their own feelings, moved by wrong suspicions of God — suspicions due to ignorance. They said: "What affair is this of ours?" Say thou: "Indeed, this affair is wholly God's." They

---

[23] Greatly desire
[24] Retaliation or punishment.

hide in their minds what they dare not reveal to thee. They say (to themselves): "If we had had anything to do with this affair, we should not have been in the slaughter here." Say: "Even if you had remained in your homes, those for whom death was decreed would certainly have gone forth to the place of their death"; but (all this was) that God might test what is in your breasts and purge what is in your hearts: for God knoweth well the secrets of your hearts.

155. Those of you who turned back on the day the two hosts met, it was Satan who caused them to fail, because of some (evil) they had done. But God has blotted out (their fault): for God is Oft-Forgiving, Most Forbearing.

156. O ye who believe! be not like the unbelievers, who say of their brethren, when they are travelling through the earth or engaged in fighting: "If they had stayed with us, they would not have died, or been slain." This that God may make it a cause of sighs and regrets in their hearts. It is God that gives life and death, and God sees well all that ye do.

157. And if ye are slain, or die, in the way of God, forgiveness and mercy from God are far better than all they could amass.

158. And if ye die, or are slain, Lo! it is unto God that ye are brought together.

159. It is part of the Mercy of God that thou dost deal gently with them. Wert thou severe or harsh-hearted, they would have broken away from about thee; so pass over (their faults), and ask for (God's) forgiveness for them; and consult them in affairs (of moment). Then, when thou hast taken a decision, put thy trust in God. For God loves those who put their trust (in Him).

160. If God helps you, none can overcome you: if He forsakes you, who is there, after that, that can help you? In God, then, let believers put their trust.

161. No prophet could (ever) be false to his trust. If any person is so false, he shall, on the Day of Judgment, restore what he misappropriated[25]; then shall every soul receive its due, whatever it earned — and none shall be dealt with unjustly.

---

[25] To take something wrongfully or dishonestly.

162. Is the man who follows the good pleasure of God like the man who draws on himself the wrath of God, and whose abode is in Hell? — A woeful refuge!

163. They are in varying grades in the sight of God; and God sees well all that they do.

164. God did confer a great favor on the Believers when He sent among them an Apostle from among themselves, rehearsing unto them the Signs of God, sanctifying them, and instructing them in Scripture and Wisdom, while, before that, they had been in manifest error.

165. What! when a single disaster smites you, although ye smote (your enemies) with one twice as great, do ye say? "Whence is this?" Say (to them): "It is from yourselves: for God hath power over all things."

166. What ye suffered on the day the two armies met, was with the leave of God, in order that He might test the Believers—

167. And the Hypocrites also. These were told: "Come, fight in the way of God, or (at least) drive (the foe from your city)." They say: "Had we known how to fight, we should certainly have followed you." They were that day nearer to unbelief than to faith, saying with their lips what was not in their hearts. But God hath full knowledge of all they conceal.

168. (They are) the ones that say, (of their brethren slain), while they themselves sit (at ease): "If only they had listened to us, they would not have been slain." Say: "Avert death from your own selves, if ye speak the truth."

169. Think not of those who are slain in God's way as dead. Nay, they live, finding their sustenance in the presence of their Lord.

170. They rejoice in the bounty provided by God: and with regard to those left behind, who have not yet joined them (in their bliss), the (Martyrs) glory in the fact that on them is no fear, nor have they (cause to) grieve.

171. They glory in the Grace and the Bounty from God, and in the fact that God suffereth not the reward of the faithful to be lost (in the least).

172. Of those who answered the call of God and the Apostle, even after being wounded, those who do right and refrain from wrong have a great reward—

173. Men said to them: "A great army is gathering against you": and frightened them: but it (only) increased their faith. They said: "For us God sufficeth, and He is the best disposer of affairs."

174. And they returned with Grace and Bounty from God: no harm ever touched them; for they followed the good pleasure of God: and God is the Lord of bounties unbounded.

175. It is only the Evil One that suggests to you the fear of his votaries[26]: be ye not afraid of them, but fear Me, if ye have faith.

176. Let not those grieve thee who rush headlong into unbelief: not the least harm will they do to God: God's plan is that He will give them no portion in the Hereafter, but a severe punishment.

177. Those who purchase unbelief at the price of faith, not the least harm will they do to God, but they will have a grievous punishment.

178. Let not the Unbelievers think that our respite to them is good for themselves: We grant them respite that they may grow in their iniquity[27]: but they will have a shameful punishment.

179. God will not leave the believers in the state in which ye are now, until He separates what is evil from what is good. Nor will He disclose to you the secrets of the Unseen. But He chooses of His Apostles (for the purpose) whom He pleases. So believe in God and His Apostles: and if ye believe and do right, ye have a reward without measure.

180. And let not those who covetously withhold of the gifts which God hath given them of His Grace, think that it is good for them: nay, it will be the worse for them: soon shall the things which they covetously withheld be tied to their necks like a twisted collar[28], on the Day of Judgment. To God belongs the heritage of the heavens and the earth; and God is well acquainted with all that ye do.

181. God hath heard the taunt[29] of those who say: "Truly, God is indigent[30] and we are rich!." We shall certainly record their word and (their act) of slaying the Prophets in defiance of right, and We shall say: "Taste ye the penalty of the Scorching Fire!.

---

[26] Devoted followers.

[27] Unfairness, injustice.

[28] A leather or metal band fastened around the neck of an animal.

[29] A scornful reproach.

[30] Destitute, poor.

182. "This is because of the (unrighteous deeds) which your hands sent on before ye: for God never harms those who serve Him."

183. They (also) said: "God took our promise not to believe in an Apostle unless He showed us a sacrifice consumed by fire (from heaven)." Say: "There came to you Apostles before me, with clear Signs and even with what ye ask for: why then did ye slay them, if ye speak the truth?.

184. Then if they reject thee, so were rejected Apostles before thee, who came with clear Signs, Books of dark prophecies, and the Book of enlightenment.

185. Every soul shall have a taste of death: and only on the Day of Judgment shall you be paid your full recompense. Only he who is saved far from the fire and admitted to the Garden will have attained the object (of life): for the life of this world is but goods and chattels[31] of deception.

186. Ye shall certainly be tried and tested in your possessions and in your personal selves; and ye shall certainly hear much that will grieve you, from those who received the Book before you and from those who worship many gods. But if ye persevere patiently, and guard against evil — then that will be a determining factor in all affairs.

187. And remember God took a Covenant from the People of the Book, to make it known and clear to mankind, and not to hide it; but they threw it away behind their backs, and purchased with it some miserable gain! and vile was the bargain they made!

188. Think not that those who exult in what they have brought about, and love to be praised for what they have not done — think not that they can escape the penalty. For them is a penalty grievous indeed.

189. To God belongeth the dominion of the heavens and the earth; and God hath power over all things.

190. Behold! in the creation of the heavens and the earth, and the alternation of Night and Day, there are indeed Signs for men of understanding —

191. Men who celebrate the praises of God, standing, sitting, and lying down on their sides, and contemplate the (wonders of) creation

---

[31] Movable articles of personal property.

55

in the heavens and the earth, (with the thought): "Our Lord! not for naught hast thou created (all) this! Glory to thee! give us salvation from the penalty of the Fire.

192. "Our Lord! any whom thou dost admit to the Fire, truly thou coverest with shame, and never will wrongdoers find any helpers!

193. "Our Lord! we have heard the call of one calling (us) to faith, 'Believe ye in the Lord', and we have believed. Our Lord! forgive us our sins, blot out from us our iniquities, and take to thyself our souls in the company of the righteous.

194. "Our Lord! grant us what Thou didst promise unto us through thine Apostles, and save us from shame on the Day of Judgment: for thou never breakest Thy promise."

195. And their Lord hath accepted of them, and answered them: "Never will I suffer to be lost the work of any of you, be he male or female: ye are members, one of another; those who have left their homes, or been driven out therefrom, or suffered harm in My cause, or fought or been slain, verily, I will blot out from them their iniquities, and admit them into Gardens with rivers flowing beneath; a reward from the presence of God, and from His presence is the best of rewards."

196. Let not the strutting[32] about of the Unbelievers through the land deceive thee:

197. Little is it for enjoyment; their ultimate abode is Hell: what an evil bed (to lie on)!

198. On the other hand, for those who fear their Lord, are Gardens, with rivers flowing beneath, therein are they to dwell (forever), a gift from the presence of God, and that which is in the presence of God is the best (bliss) for the righteous.

199. And there are, certainly, among the people of the Book, those who believe in God, in the revelation to you, and in the revelation to them, bowing in humility to God: they will not sell the Signs of God for a miserable gain! For them is a reward with their Lord, and God is swift in account.

200. O ye who believe! persevere in patience and constancy: vie in such perseverance; strengthen each other; and fear God; that ye may prosper.

---

[32] Walking with a vain, pompous bearing.

Chapter 4
Sürah An-Nisa, (The Women)
Revealed at Madinah, 176 verses.

In the name of God, Most Gracious, Most Merciful.

1. O mankind! reverence[1] your Guardian-Lord, Who created you from a single person, created, of like nature, his mate, and from them twain[2] scattered (like seeds) countless men and women; reverence God, through Whom ye demand your mutual (rights), and (reverence) the wombs (that bore you): for God ever watches over you.

2. To orphans restore their property (when they reach their age), nor substitute (your) worthless things for (their) good ones; and devour not their substance (by mixing it up) with your own. For this is indeed a great sin.

3. If ye fear that ye shall not be able to deal justly with the orphans, marry women of your choice, two, or three, or four; but if ye fear that ye shall not be able to deal justly (with them), then only one, or (a captive) that your right hands possess. That will be more suitable, to prevent you from doing injustice.

4. And give the women (on marriage) their dower as a free gift; but if they, of their own good pleasure, remit any part of it to you, take it and enjoy it with right good cheer.

5. To those weak of understanding make not over your property, which God hath made a means of support for you, but feed and clothe them therewith, and speak to them words of kindness and justice.

6. Make trial of orphans until they reach the age of marriage; if then ye find sound judgment in them, release their property to them; but consume it not wastefully, nor in haste against their growing up. If the guardian is well-off, let him claim no remuneration, but if he is poor, let him have for himself what is just and reasonable. When ye release their property to them, take witnesses in their presence: but All-Sufficient is God in taking account.

7. From what is left by parents and those nearest related there is a share for men and a share for women, whether the property be small

---

[1] Feeling of deep respect tinged with awe.
[2] From them two

or large, a determinate[3] share.

8. But if at the time of division other relatives, or orphans, or poor, are present, feed them out of the (property), and speak to them words of kindness and justice.

9. Let those (disposing of an estate) have the same fear in their minds as they would have for their own if they had left a helpless family behind: let them fear God, and speak words of appropriate (comfort).

10. Those who unjustly eat up the property of orphans, eat up a Fire into their own bodies: they will soon be enduring a Blazing Fire!

11. God (thus) directs you as regards your children's (inheritance): to the male, a portion equal to that of two females: if only daughters, two or more, their share is two-thirds of the inheritance; if only one, her share is a half. For parents, a sixth share of the inheritance to each, if the deceased left children; if no children, and the parents are the (only) heirs, the mother has a third; if the deceased left brothers (or sisters), the mother has a sixth. (The distribution in all cases is) after the payment of legacies and debts. Ye know not whether your parents or your children are nearest to you in benefit. These are settled portions ordained by God and God is All-Knowing, All-Wise.

12. In what your wives leave, your share is a half, if they leave no child; but if they leave a child, ye get a fourth; after payment of legacies and debts. In what ye leave, their share is a fourth, if ye leave no child; but if ye leave a child, they get an eighth; after payment of legacies and debts. If the man or woman whose inheritance is in question, has left neither ascendants[4] nor descendants, but has left a brother or a sister, each one of the two gets a sixth; but if more than two, they share in a third; after payment of legacies and debts; so that no loss is caused (to anyone). Thus is it ordained by God, and God is All-Knowing, Most Forbearing.

13. Those are limits set by God: those who obey God and His Apostle will be admitted to Gardens with rivers flowing beneath, to abide therein (forever) and that will be the Supreme achievement.

14. But those who disobey God and His Apostle and transgress

---

[3] Definite or distinct
[4] Ancestors

His limits will be admitted to a Fire, to abide therein: and they shall have a humiliating punishment.

15. If any of your women are guilty of lewdness,[5] take the evidence of four (reliable) witnesses from amongst you against them; and if they testify, confine them to houses until death do claim them, or God ordain for them some (other) way.

16. If two men among you are guilty of lewdness, punish them both. If they repent and amend, leave them alone; for God is Oft-Returning, Most Merciful.

17. God accepts the repentance of those who do evil in ignorance and repent soon afterwards; to them will God turn in mercy; for God is full of knowledge and wisdom.

18. Of no effect is the repentance of those who continue to do evil, until death faces one of them, and he says, "Now have I repented indeed;" nor of those who die rejecting faith; for them have We prepared a punishment most grievous.

19. O ye who believe! ye are forbidden to inherit women against their will. Nor should ye treat them with harshness, that ye may take away part of the dower ye have given them, except where they have been guilty of open lewdness; on the contrary live with them on a footing of kindness and equity. If ye take a dislike to them it may be that ye dislike a thing, and God brings about through it a great deal of good.

20. But if ye decide to take one wife in place of another, even if ye had given the latter a whole treasure for dower, take not the least bit of it back: would ye take it by slander and a manifest wrong?

21. And how could ye take it when ye have gone in unto each other, and they have taken from you a solemn covenant?

22. And marry not women whom your fathers married, except what is past: it was shameful and odious, an abominable custom indeed.

23. Prohibited to you (for marriage) are — your mothers, daughters, sisters, father's sisters, mother's sisters; brother's daughters, sister's daughters, foster-mothers (who gave you suck), foster-sisters; your wives' mothers; your step-daughters under your

---

[5] Indecency, obscenity

guardianship, born of your wives to whom ye have gone in, no prohibition if ye have not gone in; (those who have been) wives of your sons proceeding from your loins[6]; and two sisters in wedlock at one and the same time, except for what is past; for God is Oft-Forgiving, Most Merciful.

24. Also (prohibited are) women already married, except those whom your right hands possess. Thus hath God ordained (prohibitions) against you: except for these, all others are lawful, provided ye seek (them in marriage) with gifts from your property, desiring chastity, not lust. Seeing that ye derive benefit from them, give them their dowers (at least) as prescribed; but if after a dower is prescribed, ye agree mutually (to vary it), there is no blame on you, and God is All-Knowing, All-Wise.

25. If any of you have not the means wherewith to wed free believing women, they may wed believing girls from among those whom your right hands possess: and God hath full knowledge about your faith. Ye are one from another: wed them with the leave of their owners, and give them their dowers, according to what is reasonable: they should be chaste, not lustful, nor taking paramours[7]: when they are taken in wedlock, if they fall into shame, their punishment is half that for free women. This (permission) is for those among you who fear sin; but it is better for you that ye practice self-restraint: and God is Oft-Forgiving, Most Merciful.

26. God doth wish to make clear to you and to show you the ordinances of those before you; and (He doth wish to) turn to you (in Mercy): and God is All-Knowing, All-Wise.

27. God doth wish to turn to you, but the wish of those who follow their lusts is that ye should turn away (from Him) — far, far away.

28. God doth wish to lighten your (difficulties): for man was created weak (in flesh).

29. O ye who believe! eat not up your property among yourselves in vanities: but let there be amongst you traffic and trade by mutual goodwill: nor kill (or destroy) yourselves: for verily God hath been to you Most Merciful.

---

[6] That is, your begotten offspring.
[7] Illicit lovers

30. If any do that in rancor and injustice, soon shall We cast them into the Fire: and easy it is for God.

31. If ye (but) eschew the most heinous of the things which ye are forbidden to do, We shall expel out of you all the evil in you, and admit you to a Gate of great honour.

32. And in no wise covet those things in which God hath bestowed His gifts more freely on some of you than on others: to men is allotted what they earn, and to women what they earn: but ask God of His bounty: for God hath full knowledge of all things.

33. To (benefit) everyone, We have appointed sharers and heirs to property left by parents and relatives. To those also, to whom your right hand was pledged, give their due portion: for truly God is witness to all things.

34. Men are the protectors and maintainers of women, because God has given the one more (strength) than the other, and because they support them from their means. Therefore the righteous women are devoutly obedient, and guard in (the husband's) absence what God would have them guard. As to those women on whose part ye fear disloyalty and ill-conduct, admonish them (first), (next), refuse to share their beds, (and last) beat them (lightly); but if they return to obedience, seek not against them means (of annoyance): for God is Most High, Great (above you all).

35. If ye fear a breach between them twain, appoint (two) arbiters, one from his family, and the other from hers; if they wish for peace, God will cause their reconciliation: for God hath full knowledge, and is acquainted with all things.

36. Serve God, and join not any partners with Him: and do good — to parents, kinsfolk, orphans, those in need, neighbors who are near, neighbors who are strangers, the companion by your side, the wayfarer (ye meet), and what your right hands possess: for God loveth not the arrogant, the vainglorious[8];

37. (Nor) those who are niggardly or enjoin niggardliness on others, or hide the bounties which God hath bestowed on them; for We have prepared, for those who resist faith, a punishment that steeps them in contempt—

---

[8] Boastful, arrogant

38. (Nor) those who spend of their substance[9], to be seen of men, but have no faith in God and the Last Day: if any take the Evil One for their intimate, what a dreadful intimate he is!

39. And what burden were it on them if they had faith in God and in the Last Day, and they spent out of what God hath given them for sustenance? For God hath full Knowledge of them.

40. God is never unjust in the least degree: if there is any good (done), He doubleth it, and giveth from His own presence a great reward.

41. How then if We brought from each people a witness, and We brought thee as a witness against these people!

42. On that day those who reject faith and disobey the Apostle will wish that the earth were made one with them: but never will they hide a single fact from God!

43. O ye who believe! approach not prayers with a mind befogged, until ye can understand all that ye say, nor in a state of ceremonial impurity (except when travelling on the road), until after washing your whole body. If ye are ill, or on a journey, or one of you cometh from offices of nature, or ye have been in contact with women, and ye find no water, then take for yourselves clean sand or earth, and rub therewith your faces and hands. For God doth blot out sins and forgive again and again.

44. Hast thou not turned thy vision to those who were given a portion of the Book? They traffic[10] in error, and wish that ye should lose the right path.

45. But God hath full knowledge of your enemies: God is enough for a Protector, and God is enough for a Helper.

46. Of the Jews there are those who displace words from their (right) places, and say: "We hear and we disobey"; and "Hear what is not heard"; and "*Ra'ina*[11]"; with a twist of their tongues and a slander to faith. If only they had said: "We hear and we obey"; and "Do hear";

---

[9] Wealth

[10] Trade, bargain

[11] *Ra'ina* in Arabic means "Please attend to us." With a twist of their tongues, they suggested an insulting meaning, such as "O you that take us to pasture!" or in Hebrew, "Our bad one!"

and "Do look at us": it would have been better for them, and more proper; but God hath cursed them, for their unbelief; and but few of them will believe.

47. O ye people of the Book! believe in what We have (now) revealed, confirming what was (already) with you, before We change the face and fame of some (of you) beyond all recognition, and turn them hindwards, or curse them as We cursed the Sabbath-breakers: for the decision of God must be carried out.

48. God forgiveth not that partners should be set up with Him; but He forgiveth anything else, to whom He pleaseth; to set up partners with God is to devise a sin most heinous[12] indeed.

49. Hast thou not turned thy vision to those who claim sanctity for themselves? Nay, but God doth sanctify whom He pleaseth but never will they fail to receive justice in the least little thing.

50. Behold! how they invent a lie against God! but that by itself is a manifest sin!.

51. Hast thou not turned thy vision to those who were given a portion of the Book? They believe in sorcery[13] and evil, and say to the Unbelievers that they are better guided in the (right) way than the Believers!.

52. They are (men) whom God hath cursed: and those whom God hath cursed, thou wilt find, have no one to help.

53. Have they a share in dominion or power? Behold, they give not a farthing to their fellow-men!.

54. Or do they envy mankind for what God hath given them of His bounty? But We had already given the people of Abraham the Book and Wisdom, and conferred upon them a great kingdom.

55. Some of them believed and some of them averted their faces from him; and enough is Hell for a burning Fire.

56. Those who reject Our Signs, We shall soon cast into the Fire: as often as their skins are roasted through, We shall change them for fresh skins, that they may taste the Penalty: for God is Exalted in Power, Wise.

57. But those who believe and do deeds of righteousness, We shall

---

12 Monstrous, abominable
13 Magic

63

soon admit to Gardens, with rivers flowing beneath, their eternal home; therein shall they have Companions pure and holy: We shall admit them to shades, cool and ever deepening.

58. God doth command you to render back your trusts to those to whom they are due; and when ye judge between man and man, that ye judge with justice: verily how excellent is the teaching which He giveth you! for God is He who heareth and seeth all things.

59. O ye who believe! obey God, and obey the Apostle, and those charged with authority among you. If ye differ in anything among yourselves, refer it to God and His Apostle, if ye do believe in God and the Last Day: that is best, and most suitable for final determination.

60. Hast thou not turned thy vision to those who declare that they believe in the revelations that have come to thee and to those before thee? Their (real) wish is to resort together for judgment (in their disputes) to the Evil One, though they were ordered to reject him. But Satan's wish is to lead them astray far away (from the Right).

61. When it is said to them: "Come to what God hath revealed, and to the Apostle": thou seest the Hypocrites avert their faces from thee in disgust.

62. How then, when they are seized by misfortune, because of the deeds which their hands have sent forth? Then they come to thee, swearing by God: "We meant no more than goodwill and conciliation!"

63. Those men, God knows what is in their hearts; so keep clear of them, but admonish them, and speak to them a word to reach their very souls.

64. We sent not an Apostle, but to be obeyed, in accordance with the Will of God. If they had only, when they were unjust to themselves, come unto thee and asked God's forgiveness, and the Apostle had asked forgiveness for them, they would have found God indeed Oft-Returning, Most Merciful.

65. But no, by thy Lord, they can have no (real) Faith, until they make thee judge in all disputes between them, and find in their souls no resistance against thy decisions, but accept them with the fullest conviction.

66. If We had ordered them to sacrifice their lives or to leave their homes, very few of them would have done it: but if they had done

what they were (actually) told, it would have been best for them, and would have gone farthest to strengthen their (faith).

67. And We should then have given them from Our Presence a great reward.

68. And We should have shown them the Straight Way.

69. All who obey God and the Apostle are in the company of those on whom is the Grace of God, of the Prophets (who teach), the sincere (lovers of truth), the witnesses (who testify), and the righteous (who do good): Ah! what a beautiful fellowship!

70. Such is the Bounty from God: and sufficient is it that God knoweth all.

71. O ye who believe! take your precautions, and either go forth in parties or go forth all together.

72. There are certainly among you men who would tarry behind: if a misfortune befalls you. They say: "God did favor us in that we were not present among them."

73. But if good fortune comes to you from God, they would be sure to say, as if there had never been ties of affection between you and them, "Oh! I wish I had been with them; a fine thing should I then have made of it!"

74. Let those fight in the cause of God who sell the life of this world for the Hereafter, to him who fighteth in the cause of God, whether he is slain or gets victory, soon shall We give him a reward of great (value).

75. And why should ye not fight in the cause of God and of those who, being weak, are ill-treated (and oppressed)? Men, women, and children whose cry is: "Our Lord! rescue us from this town, whose people are oppressors; and raise for us from Thee one who will protect; and raise for us from Thee one who will help!"

76. Those who believe fight in the cause of God, and those who reject faith fight in the cause of evil: so fight ye against the friends of Satan: feeble indeed is the cunning of Satan.

77. Hast thou not turned thy vision to those who were told to hold back their hands (from fight), but establish regular prayers and spend in regular charity? When (at length) the order for fighting was issued to them, Behold! a section of them feared men as, or even more than, they should have feared God: they say: "Our Lord! why hast Thou

ordered us to fight? Wouldst Thou not grant us respite to our (natural) term, near (enough)?" Say: "Short is the enjoyment of this world: the Hereafter is the best for those who do right: never will ye be dealt with unjustly in the very least!

78. "Wherever ye are, death will find you out, even if ye are in towers built up strong and high!" If some good befalls them, they say, "This is from God"; but if evil, they say, "This is from thee" (O Prophet). "Say: "All things are from God. But what hath come to these people, that they fail to understand a single fact?

79. Whatever good, (O man!) happens to thee, is from God; but whatever evil happens to thee, is from thy (own) soul. And We have sent thee as an Apostle to (instruct) mankind: and enough is God for a witness.

80. He who obeys the Apostle, obeys God: but if any turn away, We have not sent thee to watch over their (evil deeds).

81. They have "Obedience" on their lips; but when they leave thee, a section of them meditate all night on things very different from what thou tellest them, but God records their nightly (plots): so keep clear of them, and put thy trust in God; and enough is God as a disposer of affairs.

82. Do they not consider the Qur'an (with care)? Had it been from other than God, they would surely have found therein much discrepancy.

83. When there comes to them some matter touching (public) safety or fear, they divulge[14] it. If they had only referred it to the Apostle, or to those charged with authority among them, the proper investigators would have tested it from them (direct). Were it not for the Grace and Mercy of God unto you, all but a few of you would have fallen into the cLütches of Satan.

84. Then fight in God's cause, thou art held responsible only for thyself, and rouse the Believers. It may be that God will restrain the fury of the Unbelievers: for God is the strongest in might and in punishment.

85. Whoever recommends and helps a good cause becomes a

---

[14] Disclose

66

partner therein: and whoever recommends and helps an evil cause, shares in its burden: and God hath power over all things.

86. When a (courteous) greeting is offered you, meet it with a greeting still more courteous, (at least) of equal courtesy. God takes careful account of all things.

87. God! there is no god but He: of a surety He will gather you together against the Day of Judgment, about which there is no doubt. And whose word can be truer than God's?

88. Why should ye be divided into two parties about the Hypocrites? God hath upset them for their (evil) deeds. Would ye guide those whom God hath thrown out of the way? For those whom God hath thrown out of the way, never shalt thou find the way.

89. They but wish that ye should reject faith, as they do, and thus be on the same footing (as they): but take not friends from their ranks until they flee in the way of God (from what is forbidden). But if they turn renegades,[15] seize them and slay them wherever ye find them; and (in any case) take no friends or helpers from their ranks.

90. Except those who join a group between whom and you there is a treaty (of peace), or those who approach you with hearts restraining them from fighting you as well as fighting their own people. If God had pleased, He could have given them power over you, and they would have fought you: therefore if they withdraw from you but fight you not, and (instead) send you (guarantees of) peace, then God hath opened no way for you (to war against them).

91. Others you will find that wish to gain your confidence as well as that of their people: every time they are sent back to temptation, they succumb thereto: if they withdraw not from you nor give you (guarantees) of peace besides restraining their hands, seize them and slay them wherever ye get them; in their case We have provided you with a clear argument against them.

92. Never should a Believer kill a Believer; but (if it so happens) by mistake, (compensation is due): if one (so) kills a Believer, it is ordained that he should free a believing slave, and pay compensation to the deceased's family, unless they remit it freely. If the deceased

---

[15] Apostate

belonged to a people at war with you, and he was a Believer, the freeing of a believing slave (is enough). If he belonged to a people with whom ye have a treaty of mutual alliance, compensation should be paid to his family, and a believing slave be freed. For those who find this beyond their means, (is prescribed) a fast for two months running: by way of repentance to God: for God hath all knowledge and all wisdom.

93. If a man kills a Believer intentionally, his recompense is Hell, to abide therein (forever): and the wrath and the curse of God are upon him, and a dreadful penalty is prepared for him.

94. O ye who believe! when ye go abroad in the cause of God, investigate carefully, and say not to anyone who offers you a saLütation: "Thou art none of a Believer!" Coveting the perishable goods of this life: with God are profits and spoils abundant. Even thus were ye yourselves before, till God conferred on you His favors: therefore carefully investigate, for God is well aware of all that ye do.

95. Not equal are those Believers who sit (at home) and receive no hurt, and those who strive and fight in the cause of God with their goods and their persons. God hath granted a grade higher to those who strive and fight with their goods and persons than to those who sit (at home): unto all (in faith) hath God promised good: but those who strive and fight hath He distinguished above those who sit (at home) by a special reward —

96. Ranks specially bestowed by Him, and Forgiveness and Mercy. For God is Oft-Forgiving, Most Merciful.

97. When angels take the souls of those who die in sin against their souls, they say: "In what (plight) were ye?" They reply: "Weak and oppressed were we in the earth." They say: "Was not the earth of God spacious enough for you to move yourselves away (from evil)?" Such men will find their abode in Hell — what an evil refuge! —

98. Except those who are (really) weak and oppressed, men, women, and children who have no means in their power, nor (a guide-post) to direct their way.

99. For these, there is hope that God will forgive: for God doth blot out (sins) and forgive again and again.

100. He who forsakes his home in the cause of God, finds in the

earth many a refuge, wide and spacious: should he die as a refugee from home for God and his Apostle, his reward becomes due and sure with God: and God is Oft-Forgiving, Most Merciful.

101. When ye travel through the earth, there is no blame on you if ye shorten your prayers, for fear the Unbelievers may attack you: for the Unbelievers are unto you open enemies.

102. When thou (O Apostle) art with them, and standest to lead them in prayer, let one party of them stand up (in prayer) with thee, taking their arms with them: when they finish their prostrations, let them take their positions in the rear, and let the other party come up, which hath not yet prayed — and let them pray with thee, taking all precautions, and bearing arms: the Unbelievers wish, if ye were negligent of your arms and your baggage, to assault you in a single rush, but there is no blame on you if ye put away your arms because of the inconvenience of rain or because ye are ill; but take (every) precaution for yourselves. For the Unbelievers God hath prepared a humiliating punishment.

103. When ye pass (congregational) prayers, celebrate God's praises, standing, sitting down, or lying down on your sides; but when ye are free from danger, set up regular prayers: for such prayers are enjoined on Believers at stated times.

104. And slacken not in following up the enemy: if ye are suffering hardships, they are suffering similar hardships; but ye have hope from God, while they have none. And God is full of knowledge and wisdom.

105. We have sent down to thee the Book in truth, that thou mightest judge between men, as guided by God: so be not (used) as an advocate by those who betray their trust.

106. But seek the forgiveness of God; for God is Oft-Forgiving, Most Merciful.

107. Contend not on behalf of such as betray their own souls: for God loveth not one given to perfidy[16] and crime.

108. They may hide (their crimes) from men, but they cannot hide (them) from God, seeing that He is in their midst when they plot by night, in words that He cannot approve: and God doth compass round

---

[16] Breach of faith, treachery.

all that they do.

109. Ah! these are the sort of men on whose behalf ye may contend in this world; but who will contend with God on their behalf on the Day of Judgment, or who will carry their affairs through?

110. If anyone does evil or wrongs his own soul, but afterwards seeks God's forgiveness, he will find God Oft-Forgiving, Most Merciful.

111. And if anyone earns sin, he earns it against his own soul: for God is full of knowledge and wisdom.

112. But if anyone earns a fault or a sin and throws it on to one that is innocent, He carries (on himself) (both) a falsehood and a flagrant sin.

113. But for the Grace of God to thee and His Mercy, a party of them would certainly have plotted to lead thee astray. But (in fact) they will only lead their own souls astray, and to thee they can do no harm in the least. For God hath sent down to thee the Book and wisdom and taught thee what thou knewest not (before); and great is the grace of God unto thee.

114. In most of their secret talks there is no good: but if one exhorts to a deed of charity or justice or conciliation between men, (secrecy is permissible): to him who does this, seeking the good pleasure of God, We shall soon give a reward of the highest (value).

115. If anyone contends with the Apostle even after guidance has been plainly conveyed to him, and follows a path other than that becoming to men of faith, We shall leave him in the path he has chosen, and land him in Hell — what an evil refuge?

116. God forgiveth not (the sin of) joining other gods with Him: but He forgiveth whom He pleaseth other sins than this: one who joins other gods with God, hath strayed far, far away (from the right).

117. (The pagans), leaving Him, call but upon female deities: they call but upon Satan the persistent rebel!

118. God did curse him, but he said: "I will take of Thy servants a portion marked off.

119. "I will mislead them, and I will create in them false desires; I will order them to slit the ears of cattle, and to deface the (fair) nature created by God." Whoever, forsaking God, takes Satan for a friend, hath of a surety suffered a loss that is manifest.

120. Satan makes them promises, and creates in them false desires; but Satan's promises are nothing but deception.

121. They (his dupes) will have their dwelling in Hell, and from it they will find no way of escape.

122. But those who believe and do deeds of righteousness, We shall soon admit them to Gardens, with rivers flowing beneath, to dwell therein forever. God's promise is the truth, and whose word can be truer than God's?

123. Not your desires, nor those of the people of the Book (can prevail): whoever works evil, will be requited accordingly. Nor will he find, besides God, any protector or helper.

124. If any do deeds of righteousness, be they male or female, and have faith, they will enter heaven and not the least injustice will be done to them.

125. Who can be better in religion than one who submits his whole self to God, does good, and follows the way of Abraham the true in faith? For God did take Abraham for a friend.

126. But to God belong all things in the heavens and on earth; and He it is that encompasseth all things.

127. They ask thy instruction concerning the women. Say: God doth instruct you about them: and (remember) what hath been re-hearsed unto you in the Book, concerning the orphans of women to whom ye give not the portions prescribed, and yet whom ye desire to marry, as also concerning the children who are weak and oppressed: that ye stand firm for justice to orphans. There is not a good deed which ye do, but God is well-acquainted therewith.

128. If a wife fears cruelty or desertion on her husband's part, there is no blame on them if they arrange an amicable settlement between themselves; and such settlement is best; even though men's souls are swayed by greed. But if ye do good and practice self-restraint, God is well-acquainted with all that ye do.

129. Ye are never able to be fair and just as between women, even if it is your ardent desire: but turn not away (from a woman) altogether so as to leave her (as it were) hanging (in the air). If ye come to a friendly understanding and practice self-restraint, God is Oft-Forgiving, Most Merciful.

130. But if they disagree (and must part), God will provide

abundance for all from His All-Reaching bounty: for God is He that careth for all and is Wise.

131. To God belong all things in the heavens and on earth. Verily We have directed the people of the Book before you, and you (O Muslims) to fear God. But if ye deny Him, lo! unto God belong all things in the heavens and on earth, and God is free of all wants, worthy of all praise.

132. Yea, unto God belong all things in the heavens and on earth, and enough is God to carry through all affairs.

133. If it were His Will, He could destroy you, O mankind, and create another race; for He hath power this to do.

134. If anyone desires a reward in this life, in God's (gift) is the reward (both) of this life and of the Hereafter: for God is He that heareth and seeth (all things).

135. O ye who believe! stand out firmly for justice, as witnesses to God, even as against yourselves, or your parents, or your kin, and whether it be (against) rich or poor: for God can best protect both. Follow not the lusts (of your hearts), lest ye swerve, and if ye distort (justice) or decline to do justice, verily God is well-acquainted with all that ye do.

136. O ye who believe! believe in God and his Apostle, and the scripture which He hath sent to His Apostle and the scripture which He sent to those before (him). And who denieth God, His angels, His Books, His Apostles, and the Day of Judgment, hath gone far, far astray.

137. Those who believe, then reject faith, then believe (again) and (again) reject faith, and go on increasing in unbelief — God will not forgive them nor guide them on the way.

138. To the Hypocrites give the glad tidings that there is for them (but) a grievous penalty.

139. Yea, to those who take for friends Unbelievers rather than Believers: is it honour they seek among them? Nay, all honour is with God.

140. Already has He sent you word in the Book, that when ye hear the Signs of God held in defiance and ridicule, ye are not to sit with them unless they turn to a different theme: if ye did, ye would be like them. For God will collect the Hypocrites and those who defy

faith, all in Hell—

141. (These are) the ones who wait and watch about you: if ye do gain a victory from God, they say: "Were we not with you?" But if the Unbelievers gain a success, they say (to them): "Did we not gain an advantage over you, and did we not guard you from the Believers?" But God will judge betwixt you on the Day of Judgment. And never will God grant to the Unbelievers a way (to triumph) over the Believers.

142. The Hypocrites — they think they are over-reaching[17] God, but He will over-reach them: when they stand up to prayer, they stand without earnestness, to be seen of men, but little do they hold God in remembrance.

143. (They are) distracted in mind even in the midst of it, being (sincerely) for neither one group nor for another. Whom God leaves straying, never wilt thou find for him the way.

144. O ye who believe! take not for friends Unbelievers rather than Believers: do ye wish to offer God an open proof against yourselves?

145. The Hypocrites will be in the lowest depths of the Fire: no helper wilt thou find for them —

146. Except for those who repent, mend (their life), hold fast to God, and purify their religion as in God's sight: if so they will be (numbered) with the Believers. And soon will God grant to the Believers a reward of immense value.

147. What can God gain by your punishment, if ye are grateful and ye believe? Nay, it is God that recogniseth (all good), and knoweth all things.

148. God loveth not that evil should be noised abroad in public speech, except where injustice hath been done; for God is He who heareth and knoweth all things.

149. Whether ye publish a good deed or conceal it or cover evil with pardon, verily God doth blot out (sins) and hath power (in the judgment of values).

150. Those who deny God and his Apostles, and (those who) wish to separate God from His Apostles, saying: "We believe in some but

---

[17] To get better of, especially by trick and deceit.

reject others": and (those who) wish to take a course midway —

151. They are in truth (equally) Unbelievers; and We have prepared for Unbelievers a humiliating punishment.

152. To those who believe in God and His Apostles and make no distinction between any of the Apostles, We shall soon give their (due) rewards: for God is Oft-Forgiving, Most Merciful.

153. The People of the Book ask thee to cause a book to descend to them from heaven: indeed they asked Moses for an even greater (miracle), for they said: "Show us God in public," but they were dazed for their presumption, with thunder and lightning. Yet they worshipped the calf even after clear Signs had come to them; even so We forgave them; and gave Moses manifest proofs of authority.

154. And for their Covenant We raised over them (the towering height) of Mount (Sinai); and (on another occasion) We said: "Enter the gate with humility"; and (once again) We commanded them: "Transgress not in the matter of the Sabbath." And We took from them a solemn Covenant.

155. (They have incurred divine displeasure): in that they broke their Covenant: that they rejected the Signs of God; that they slew the Messengers in defiance of right; that they said, "Our hearts are the wrappings (which preserve God's Word; we need no more)"; nay God hath set the seal on their hearts for their blasphemy, and little is it they believe —

156. That they rejected faith; that they uttered against Mary a grave false charge.

157. That they said (in boast), "We killed Christ Jesus the son of Mary, the Apostle of God"; but they killed him not, nor crucified him, but so it was made to appear to them, and those who differ therein are full of doubts, with no certain) knowledge, but only conjecture to follow, for of a surety they killed him not —

158. Nay, God raised him up unto Himself; and God is Exalted in Power, Wise —

159. And there is none of the People of the Book but must believe in him before his death; and on the Day of Judgment He will be a witness against them —

160. For the iniquity of the Jews We made unlawful for them certain (foods) good and wholesome which had been lawful for them; in that

they hindered many from God's way —

161. That they took usury, though they were forbidden; and that they devoured men's substance wrongfully; We have prepared for those among them who reject faith a grievous punishment.

162. But those among them who are well-grounded in knowledge, and the Believers, believe in what hath been revealed to thee; and (especially) those who establish regular prayer and practice regular charity and believe in God and in the Last Day: to them shall We soon give a great reward.

163. We have sent thee inspiration, as We sent it to Noah and the Messengers after him; We sent inspiration to Abraham, Ismail, Isaac, Jacob, and the Tribes, to Jesus, Job, Jonah, Aaron, and Solomon, and to David We gave the Psalms.

164. Of some Apostles We have already told thee the story; of others We have not — and to Moses God spoke direct —

165. Apostles who gave good news as well as warning, that mankind, after (the coming) of the Apostles, should have no plea against God: for God is Exalted in Power, Wise.

166. But God beareth witness that what He hath sent unto thee He hath sent from His (Own) Knowledge, and the angels bear witness: but enough is God for a Witness.

167. Those who reject faith and keep off (men) from the way of God, have verily strayed far, far away from the path.

168. Those who reject faith and do wrong — God will not forgive them nor guide them to any way —

169. Except the way of Hell, to dwell therein forever: and this to God is easy.

170. O mankind! the Apostle hath come to you in truth from God: believe in him: it is best for you. But if ye reject faith, to God belong all things in the heavens and on earth: and God is All-Knowing, All-Wise.

171. O People of the Book! commit no excesses in your religion: nor say of God aught but truth. Christ Jesus the son of Mary was (no more than) an Apostle of God, and His Word, which He bestowed on Mary, and a Spirit proceeding from Him: so believe in God and His Apostles. Say not "Trinity": desist: it will be better for you: for God is One God: Glory be to Him: (for Exalted is He) above having

a son. To Him belong all things in the heavens and on earth. And enough is God as a disposer of affairs.

172. Christ disdaineth not to serve and worship God, nor do the angels, those nearest (to God): those who disdain His worship and are arrogant — He will gather them all together unto Himself to (answer).

173. But those who believe and do deeds of righteousness, He will give their (due) rewards — and more, out of His bounty: but those who are disdainful and arrogant, He will punish with a grievous penalty; nor will they find, besides God, any to protect or help them.

174. O mankind! verily there hath come to you a convincing proof from your Lord: for We have sent unto you a light (that is) manifest.

175. Then those who believe in God, and hold fast to Him — soon will He admit them to Mercy and Grace from Him, and guide them to Himself by a straight Way.

176. They ask thee for a legal decision. Say: God directs (thus) about those who leave no descendants or ascendants as heirs. If it is a man that dies, leaving a sister but no child, she shall have half the inheritance: if (such a deceased was) a woman, who left no child, her brother takes her inheritance: if there are two sisters, they shall have two-thirds of the inheritance (between them): if there are brothers and sisters, (they share), the male having twice the share of the female. Thus doth God make clear to you (His law), lest ye err. And God hath knowledge of all things.

Chapter 5
Sürah Al-Ma'idah (The Table Spread)
Revealed at Madinah, 120 verses.

In the name of God, Most Gracious, Most Merciful.

1. O ye who believe! fulfil (all) obligations. Lawful unto you (for food) are all four-footed animals, with the exceptions named: but animals of the chase are forbidden while ye are in the Sacred Precincts or in pilgrim garb: for God doth command according to His Will and Plan.

2. O ye who believe! violate not the sanctity of the Symbols of

God, nor of the Sacred Month, nor of the animals brought for sacrifice, nor the garlands that mark out such animals, nor the people resorting to the Sacred House, seeking of the bounty and good pleasure of their Lord. But when ye are clear of the Sacred Precincts and of pilgrim garb, ye may hunt, and let not the hatred of some people in (once) shutting you out of the Sacred Mosque lead you to transgression (and hostility on your part). Help ye one another in righteousness and piety, but help ye not one another in sin and rancor: fear God: for God is strict in punishment.

3. Forbidden to you (for food) are: dead meat, blood, the flesh of swine, and that on which hath been invoked the name of other than God, that which hath been killed by strangling, or by a violent blow, or by a headlong fall, or by being gored[1] to death; that which hath been (partly) eaten by a wild animal; unless ye are able to slaughter it (in due form); that which is sacrificed on stone (altars); (forbidden) also is the division (of meat) by raffling with arrows: that is impiety. This day have those who reject faith given up all hope of your religion: yet fear them not but fear Me. This day have I perfected your religion for you, completed my favor upon you, and have chosen for you Islam as your religion. But if any is forced by hunger, with no inclination to transgression, God is indeed Oft-Forgiving, Most Merciful.

4. They ask thee what is lawful to them (as food). Say: Lawful unto you are (all) things good and pure: and what ye have taught your trained hunting animals (to catch) in the manner directed to you by God; eat what they catch for you, but pronounce the name of God over it: and fear God; for God is swift in taking account.

5. This day are (all) things good and pure made lawful unto you. The food of the People of the Book is lawful unto you and yours is lawful unto them. (Lawful unto you in marriage) are (not only) chaste women who are Believers, but chaste women among the People of the Book, revealed before your time — when ye give them their due dowers, and desire chastity, not lewdness, nor secret intrigues. If anyone rejects faith, fruitless is his work, and in the Hereafter he will be in the ranks of those who have lost (all spiritual good).

---

[1] Pierced with a horn or tusk

6. O ye who believe! when ye prepare for prayer, wash your faces, and your hands (and arms) to the elbows; rub your heads (with water); and (wash) your feet to the ankles. If ye are in a state of ceremonial impurity, bathe your whole body. But if ye are ill, or on a journey, or one of you cometh from offices of nature, or ye have been in contact with women, and ye find no water, then take for yourselves clean sand or earth, and rub therewith your faces and hands. God doth not wish to place you in a difficulty, but to make you clean, and to complete His favor to you, that ye may be grateful.

7. And call in remembrance the favor of God unto you, and His Covenant,which He ratified with you, when ye said: "We hear and we obey": and fear God, for God knoweth well the secrets of your hearts.

8. O ye who believe! stand out firmly for God, as witnesses to fair dealing, and let not the hatred of others to you make you swerve to wrong and depart from justice. Be just: that is next to Piety: and fear God, for God is well-acquainted with all that ye do.

9. To those who believe and do deeds of righteousness hath God promised forgiveness and a great reward.

10. Those who reject faith and deny Our Signs will be Companions of Hell-Fire.

11. O ye who believe! call in remembrance the favor of God unto you when certain men formed the design to stretch out their hands against you, but (God) held back their hands from you: so fear God. And on God let Believers put (all) their trust.

12. God did aforetime take a Covenant from the Children of Israel, and We appointed twelve Captains among them, and God said: "I am with you: if ye (but) establish regular prayers, practice regular charity, believe in My apostles, honour and assist them and loan to God a beautiful loan, verily I will wipe out from you your evils, and admit you to Gardens with rivers flowing beneath; but if any of you, after this, resisteth faith, he hath truly wandered from the path of rectitude[2]."

13. But because of their breach of their Covenant, We cursed them, and made their hearts grow hard: they change the words from their

---

[2] Rightness, righteousness

(right) places and forget a good part of the Message that was sent them, nor wilt thou cease to find them, barring a few, ever bent on (new) deceits: but forgive them and overlook (their misdeeds): for God loveth those who are kind.

14. From those, too, who call themselves Christians, We did take a Covenant, but they forgot a good part of the Message that was sent them: so We estranged them, with enmity and hatred between the one and the other, to the Day of Judgment. And soon will God show them what it is they have done.

15. O People of the Book! there hath come to you Our Apostle, revealing to you much that ye used to hide in the Book, and passing over much (that is now unnecessary): There hath come to you from God a (new) Light and a perspicuous[3] Book—

16. Wherewith God guideth all who seek His good pleasure to ways of peace and safety, and leadeth them out of darkness, by His Will, unto the light, guideth them to a Path that is Straight.

17. In blasphemy indeed are those that say that God is Christ the son of Mary. Say: "Who then hath the least power against God, if His Will were to destroy Christ the son of Mary, his mother, and all, everyone that is on the earth? For to God belongeth the dominion of the heavens and the earth, and all that is between. He createth what He pleaseth. For God hath power over all things."

18. (Both) the Jews and the Christians say: "We are sons of God, and His beloved." Say: "Why then doth He punish you for your sins? Nay, ye are but men — of the men He hath created: He forgiveth whom He pleaseth, and He punisheth whom He pleaseth: and to God belongeth the dominion of the heavens and the earth, and all that is between: and unto Him is the final goal (of all)."

19. O People of the Book! now hath come unto you, making (things) clear unto you, Our Apostle, after the break in (the series of) Our Apostles, lest ye should say: there came unto us no bringer of glad tidings and no warner (from evil): but now hath come unto you a bringer of glad tidings and a warner (from evil): and God hath power over all things.

20. Remember Moses said to his people: "O my people! call in

---

[3] Clearly expressed, easily understood

remembrance the favor of God unto you, when He produced prophets among you, made you kings, and gave you what He had not given to any other among the peoples.

21. "O my people! enter the holy land which God hath assigned unto you and turn not back ignominiously[4], for then will ye be overthrown, to your own ruin."

22. They said: "O Moses! in this land are a people of exceeding strength: never shall we enter it until they leave it: if (once) they leave, then shall we enter."

23. (But) among (their) God-fearing men were two on whom God had bestowed His Grace: they said: "Assault them at the (proper) gate: when once ye are in, victory will be yours; But on God put your trust if ye have faith."

24. They said: "O Moses! while they remain there, never shall we be able to enter, to the end of time. Go thou, and thy Lord, and fight ye two, while we sit here (and watch)."

25. He said: "O my Lord! I have power only over myself and my brother, so separate us from this rebellious people!"

26. God said: "Therefore will the land be out of their reach for forty years; in distraction will they wander through the land: but sorrow thou not over these rebellious people."

27. Recite to them the truth of the story of the two sons of Adam. Behold! they each presented a sacrifice (to God): it was accepted from one, but not from the other. Said the latter: "Be sure I will slay thee." "Surely," said the former, "God doth accept of the sacrifice of those who are righteous.

28. "If thou dost stretch thy hand against me, to slay me, it is not for me to stretch my hand against thee to slay thee: for I do fear God, the Cherisher of the Worlds.

29. "For me, I intend to let thee draw on thyself my sin as well as thine, for thou wilt be among the Companions of the Fire, and that is the reward of those who do wrong."

30. The (selfish) soul of the other led him to the murder of his brother: he murdered him, and became (himself) one of the lost ones.

31. Then God sent a raven, who scratched the ground, to show

---

[4] In a humiliating manner

him how to hide the shame of his brother. "Woe is me!" said he: "Was I not even able to be as this raven, and to hide the shame of my brother?" Then he became full of regrets —

32. On that account: We ordained for the Children of Israel that if anyone slew a person — unless it be for murder or for spreading mischief in the land — it would be as if he slew the whole people: and if anyone saved a life, it would be as if he saved the life of the whole people. Then although there came to them Our Apostles with clear Signs, yet, even after that, many of them continued to commit excesses in the land.

33. The punishment of those who wage war against God and His Apostle, and strive with might and main[5] for mischief through the land is: execution, or crucifixion, or the cutting off of hands and feet from opposite sides, or exile from the land: that is their disgrace in this world, and a heavy punishment is theirs in the Hereafter.

34. Except for those who repent before they fall into your power: in that case, know that God is Oft-Forgiving, Most Merciful.

35. O ye who believe! do your duty to God, seek the means of approach unto Him, and strive with might and main in His cause: that ye may prosper.

36. As to those who reject faith, if they had everything on earth and twice repeated, to give as ransom for the penalty of the Day of Judgment, it would never be accepted of them. Theirs would be a grievous Penalty.

37. Their wish will be to get out of the Fire, but never will they get out therefrom: their penalty will be one that endures.

38. As to the thief, male or female, cut off his or her hands: a punishment by way of example, from God, for their crime: and God is Exalted in Power.

39. But if the thief repents after his crime, and amends his conduct, God turneth to him in forgiveness; for God is Oft-Forgiving, Most Merciful.

40. Knowest thou not that to God (alone) belongeth the dominion of the heavens and the earth? He punisheth whom He pleaseth, and He forgiveth whom He pleaseth: and God hath power over all things.

---

[5] One's utmost power.

41. O Apostle! let not those grieve thee, who race each other into unbelief: (whether it be) among those who say: "We believe" with their lips but whose hearts have no faith; or it be among the Jews — men who will listen to any lie — will listen even to others who have never so much as come to thee. They change the words from their (right) times and places; they say, "If ye are given this, take it, but if not, beware:" If anyone's trial is intended by God, thou hast no authority in the least for him against God. For such — it is not God's will to purify their hearts. For them there is disgrace in this world, and in the Hereafter a heavy punishment.

42. (They are fond of) listening to falsehood, of devouring anything forbidden. If they do come to thee, either judge between them, or decline to interfere. If thou decline, they cannot hurt thee in the least. If thou judge, judge in equity between them; for God loveth those who judge in equity.

43. But why do they come to thee for decision, when they have (their own) laws before them? Therein is the (plain) command of God; yet even after that, they would turn away. For they are not (really) People of Faith.

44. It was We who revealed the law (to Moses); therein was guidance and light. By its standard have been judged the Jews, by the Prophets who bowed (as in Islam) to God's Will, by the Rabbis and the Doctors of Law: for to them was entrusted the protection of God's Book, and they were witnesses thereto: therefore fear not men, but fear Me, and sell not My Signs for a miserable price. If any do fail to judge by (the light of) what God hath revealed, they are (no better than) Unbelievers.

45. We ordained therein for them: "Life for life, eye for eye, nose for nose, ear for ear, tooth for tooth, and wounds equal for equal." But if anyone remits the retaliation by way of charity, it is an act of atonement for himself. And if any fail to judge by (the light of) what God hath revealed, they are (no better than) wrongdoers.

46. And in their footsteps We sent Jesus the son of Mary, confirming the law that had come before him: We sent him the Gospel: therein was guidance and light, and confirmation of the law that had come before him: a guidance and an admonition to those who fear God.

47. Let the People of the Gospel judge by what God hath revealed therein. If any do fail to judge by (the light of) what God hath revealed, they are (no better than) those who rebel.

48. To thee We sent the Scripture in truth, confirming the Scripture that came before it, and guarding it in safety; so judge between them by what God hath revealed, and follow not their vain desires, diverging from the truth that hath come to thee. To each among you have We prescribed a Law and an Open Way. If God had so willed, He would have made you a single people, but (His plan is) to test you in what He hath given you: so strive as in a race in all virtues. The goal of you all is to God; it is He that will show you the truth of the matters in which ye dispute.

49. And this (He commands): Judge thou between them by what God hath revealed, and follow not their vain desires, but beware of them lest they beguile thee from any of that (teaching) which God hath sent down to thee. And if they turn away, be assured that for some of their crimes it is God's purpose to punish them. And truly most men are rebellious.

50. Do they then seek after a judgment of (the Days of) Ignorance? But who, for a people whose faith is assured, can give better judgment than God?

51. O ye who believe! take not the Jews and the Christians for your friends and protectors: they are but friends and protectors to each other. And he amongst you that turns to them (for friendship) is of them. Verily God guideth not a people unjust.

52. Those in whose heart is a disease — thou seest how eagerly they run about amongst them, saying: "We do fear lest a change of fortune bring us disaster." Ah! perhaps God will give (thee) victory, or a decision according to His Will. Then will they repent of the thoughts which they secretly harbored in their hearts.

53. And those who believe will say: "Are these the men who swore their strongest oaths by God, that they were with you?" All that they do will be in vain, and they will fall into (nothing but) ruin.

54. O ye who believe! if any from among you turn back from his faith, soon will God produce a people whom He will love as they will love Him, lowly with the Believers, mighty against the rejecters, fighting in the way of God, and never afraid of the reproaches of

such as find fault. That is the Grace of God, which He will bestow on whom He pleaseth: and God encompasseth all, and He knoweth all things.

55. Your (real) friends are (no less than) God, His Apostle, and the (fellowship of) Believers — those who establish regular prayers and regular charity, and they bow down humbly (in worship).

56. As to those who turn (for friendship) to God, His Apostle, and the (fellowship of) Believers — it is the fellowship of God that must certainly triumph.

57. O ye who believe! take not for friends and protectors those who take your religion for a mockery or sport — whether among those who received the Scripture before you, or among those who reject faith; but fear ye God, if ye have Faith (indeed).

58. When ye proclaim your call to prayer, they take it (but) as mockery and sport; that is because they are a people without understanding.

59. Say: "O People of the Book! do ye disapprove of us for no other reason than that we believe in God, and the revelation that hath come to us and that which came before (us), and (perhaps) that most of you are rebellious and disobedient?"

60. Say: "Shall I point out to you something much worse than this, (as judged) by the treatment it received from God? Those who incurred the curse of God and His wrath, those of whom some He transformed into apes and swine, those who worshipped Evil — these are (many times) worse in rank, and far more astray from the even Path!

61. When they come to thee, they say: "We believe": but in fact they enter with a mind against Faith, and they go out with the same: but God knoweth fully all that they hide.

62. Many of them dost thou see, racing each other in sin and rancor, and their eating of things forbidden. Evil indeed are the things that they do.

63. Why do not the Rabbis and the Doctors of Law forbid them from their (habit of) uttering sinful words and eating things forbidden? Evil indeed are their works.

64. The Jews say: "God's hand is tied up." Be their hands tied up and be they accursed for the (blasphemy) they utter. Nay, both

His hands are widely outstretched: He giveth and spendeth (of His bounty) as He pleaseth. But the revelation that cometh to thee from God increaseth in most of them their obstinate rebellion and blasphemy. Amongst them We have placed enmity and hatred till the Day of Judgment. Every time they kindle the fire of war, God doth extinguish it; but they (ever) strive to do mischief on earth. And God loveth not those who do mischief.

65. If only the People of the Book had believed and been righteous, We should indeed have blotted out their iniquities and admitted them to Gardens of Bliss.

66. If only they had stood fast by the Law, the Gospel, and all the revelation that was sent to them from their Lord, they would have enjoyed happiness from every side. There is from among them a party on the right course; but many of them follow a course that is evil.

67. O Apostle! proclaim the (Message) which hath been sent to thee from thy Lord. If thou didst not, thou wouldst not have fulfilled and proclaimed His mission: and God will defend thee from men (who mean mischief). For God guideth not those who reject faith.

68. Say: "O People of the Book! ye have no ground to stand upon unless ye stand fast by the Law, the Gospel, and all the revelation that has come to you from your Lord." It is the revelation that cometh to thee from thy Lord, that increaseth in most of them their obstinate rebellion and blasphemy. But sorrow thou not over (these) people without Faith.

69. Those who believe (in the Qur'an), those who follow the Jewish (Scriptures), and the Sabians and the Christians — any who believe in God and the Last Day, and work righteousness — on them shall be no fear, nor shall they grieve.

70. We took the Covenant of the Children of Israel and sent them Apostles. Every time there came to them an Apostle with what they themselves desired not — some (of these) they called impostors, and some they (go so far as to) slay.

71. They thought there would be no trial (or punishment); so they became blind and deaf: yet God (in mercy) turned to them: yet again many of them became blind and deaf. But God sees well all that they do.

72. They do blaspheme who say: "God is Christ the son of Mary."

But said Christ: "O Children of Israel! Worship God, my Lord and your Lord." Whoever joins other gods with God — God will forbid him the Garden, and the Fire will be his abode. There will for the wrongdoers be no one to help.

73. They do blaspheme who say: God is one of three in a Trinity: for there is no god except One God. If they desist not from their word (of blasphemy), verily a grievous penalty will befall the blasphemers among them.

74. Why turn they not to God, and seek His forgiveness? For God is Oft-Forgiving, Most Merciful.

75. Christ the son of Mary was no more than an Apostle; many were the Apostles that passed away before him. His mother was a woman of truth. They had both to eat their (daily) food. See how God doth makes His Signs clear to them; yet see in what ways they are deluded away from the truth!

76. Say: Will ye worship, besides God, something which hath no power either to harm or benefit you? But God — He it is that heareth and knoweth all things."

77. Say: "O People of the Book! Exceed not in your religion the bounds (of what is proper), trespassing beyond the truth, nor follow the vain desires of people who went wrong in times gone by, who misled many, and strayed (themselves) from the even way.

78. Curses were pronounced on those among the Children of Israel who rejected faith, by the tongue of David and of Jesus the son of Mary, because they disobeyed and persisted in excesses.

79. Nor did they (usually) forbid one another the iniquities which they committed: evil indeed were the deeds which they did.

80. Thou seest many of them turning in friendship to the Unbelievers. Evil indeed are (the works) which their souls have sent forward before them (with the result), that God's wrath is on them, and in torment will they abide.

81. If only they had believed in God, in the Apostle, and in what hath been revealed to him, never would they have taken them for friends and protectors, but most of them are rebellious wrongdoers.

82. Strongest among men in enmity to the Believers wilt thou find the Jews and Pagans; and nearest among them in love to the believers wilt thou find those who say: "We are Christians": because amongst

these are men devoted to learning and men who have renounced the world, and they are not arrogant.

83. And when they listen to the revelation received by the Apostle, thou wilt see their eyes overflowing with tears, for they recognize the truth: they pray: "Our Lord! we believe; write us down among the witnesses.

84. "What cause can we have not to believe in God and the truth which has come to us, seeing that we long for our Lord to admit us to the Company of the righteous?"

85. And for this their prayer hath God rewarded them with Gardens, with rivers flowing underneath — their eternal home. Such is the recompense of those who do good.

86. But those who reject faith and belie Our Signs — they shall be Companions of Hell-Fire.

87. O ye who believe! make not unlawful the good things which God hath made lawful for you, but commit no excess; for God loveth not those given to excess.

88. Eat of the things which God hath provided for you, lawful and good: but fear God, in Whom ye believe.

89. God will not call you to account for what is futile in your oaths, but He will call you to account for your deliberate oaths: for expiation[6], feed ten indigent persons, on a scale of the average for the food of your families; or clothe them; or give a slave his freedom. If that is beyond your means, fast for three days. That is the expiation for the oaths ye have sworn. But keep to your oaths. Thus doth God make clear to you His Signs, that ye may be grateful.

90. O ye who believe! intoxicants and gambling, (dedication of) stones, and (divination by) arrows, are an abomination, of Satan's handiwork: eschew such (abomination), that ye may prosper.

91. Satan's plan is (but) to excite enmity and hatred between you, with intoxicants and gambling, and hinder you from the remembrance of God, and from prayer: will ye not then abstain?

92. Obey God, and obey the Apostle, and beware (of evil): if ye do turn back, know ye that it is Our Apostle's duty to proclaim (the Message) in the clearest manner.

---

[6] To make amends for

93. On those who believe and do deeds of righteousness there is no blame for what they ate (in the past), when they guard themselves from evil and believe, and do deeds of righteousness — (or) again, guard themselves from evil and believe — (or) again guard themselves from evil and do good. For God loveth those who do good.

94. O ye who believe! God doth but make a trial of you in a little matter of game well within reach of your hands and your lances, that He may test who feareth Him unseen: any who transgress thereafter will have a grievous penalty.

95. O ye who believe! kill not game, while in the Sacred Precincts or in pilgrim garb. If any of you doth so intentionally, the compensation is an offering, brought to the Ka'bah of a domestic animal equivalent to the one he killed, as adjudged by two just men among you; or by way of atonement, the feeding of the indigent; or its equivalent in fasts: that he may taste of the penalty of his deed. God forgives what is past: for repetition God will exact from him the penalty: for God is Exalted, and Lord of Retribution.

96. Lawful to you is the pursuit of water-game and its use for food, for the benefit of yourselves and those who travel; but forbidden is the pursuit of land-game: as long as ye are in the Sacred Precincts or in pilgrim garb. And fear God, to whom ye shall be gathered back.

97. God made the Ka'bah, the Sacred House, an asylum of security for men, as also the Sacred Months, the animals for offerings, and the garlands that mark them: that ye may know that God hath knowledge of what is in the heavens and on earth and that God is well acquainted with all things.

98. Know ye that God is strict in punishment and that God is Oft-Forgiving, Most Merciful.

99. The Apostle's duty is but to proclaim (the Message): but God knoweth all that ye reveal and ye conceal.

100. Say: "Not equal are things that are bad and things that are good, even though the abundance of the bad may dazzle thee; so fear God, O ye that understand! that (so) ye may prosper."

101. O ye who believe! ask not questions about things which, if made plain to you, may cause you trouble. But if ye ask about things when the Qur'an is being revealed, they will be made plain to you: God will forgive those: for God is Oft-Forgiving, Most Forbearing.

102. Some people before you did ask such questions, and on that account lost their faith.

103. It was not God Who instituted (superstitions like those of) a slit-ear she-camel, or a she-camel let loose for free pasture, or idol sacrifices for twin-births in animals, or stallion-camels freed from work; it is blasphemers who invent a lie against God, but most of them lack wisdom.

104. When it is said to them: "Come to what God hath revealed; come to the Apostle": They say: "Enough for us are the ways we found our fathers following." What! even though their fathers were void of knowledge and guidance?

105. O ye who believe! guard your own souls: if ye follow (right) guidance, no hurt can come to you from those who stray. The goal of you all is to God: it is He that will show you the truth of all that ye do.

106. O ye who believe! when death approaches any of you, (take) witnesses among yourselves when making bequests, two just men of your own (brotherhood) or others from outside if ye are journeying through the earth, and the chance of death befalls you (thus). If ye doubt (their truth), detain them both after prayer, and let them both swear by God: "We wish not in this for any worldly gain, even though the (beneficiary) be our near relation: we shall hide not the evidence before God: if we do, then behold! the sin be upon us!"

107. But if it gets known that these two were guilty of the sin (of perjury). Let two others stand forth in their places, nearest in kin from among those who claim a lawful right: let them swear by God: "We affirm that our witness is truer than that of those two, and that we have not trespassed (beyond the truth): if we did, behold! the wrong be upon us!.

108. That is most suitable: that they may give the evidence in its true nature and shape, or else they would fear that other oaths would be taken after their oaths. But fear God, and listen (to His counsel): for God guideth not a rebellious people.

109. One day will God gather the Apostles together, and ask: "What was the response ye received (from men to your teaching)? They will say: "We have no knowledge: it is thou who knowest in full all that is hidden.

110. Then will God say: "O Jesus the son of Mary! recount my favor to thee and to thy mother. Behold! I strengthened thee with the holy spirit, so that thou didst speak to the people in childhood and in maturity. Behold! I taught thee the Book and Wisdom, the Law and the Gospel. And behold! thou makest out of clay, as it were, the figure of a bird, by My leave, and thou breathest into it, and it becometh a bird by My leave, and thou healest those born blind, and the lepers by My leave. And behold! thou bringest forth the dead by My leave. And behold! I did restrain the Children of Israel from (violence to) thee when thou didst show them the clear Signs, and the Unbelievers among them, said: 'This is nothing but evident magic.'

111. "And behold! I inspired the Disciples to have faith in Me and Mine Apostle: they said, 'We have faith, and do thou bear witness that we bow to God as Muslims'."

112. Behold! the Disciples said: "O Jesus the son of Mary! Can thy Lord send down to us a table set (with viands[7]) from heaven?" Said Jesus: "Fear God, if ye have faith.

113. They said: "We only wish to eat thereof and satisfy our hearts, and to know that thou hast indeed told us the truth; and that we ourselves may be witnesses to the miracle.

114. Said Jesus the son of Mary: "O God our Lord! send us from heaven a table set (with viands), that there may be for us — for the first and the last of us — a solemn festival and a Sign from Thee; and provide for our sustenance, for Thou art the best Sustainer (of our needs).

115. God said: "I will send it down unto you: but if any of you after that resisteth faith, I will punish him with a penalty such as I have not inflicted on anyone among all the peoples.

116. And behold! God will say "O Jesus the son of Mary! didst thou say unto men, 'Worship me and my mother as gods in derogation of God'"? He will say: "Glory to Thee! never could I say what I had no right (to say). Had I said such a thing, Thou wouldst indeed have known it. Thou knowest what is in my heart, though I know not what is in Thine. For Thou knowest in full all that is hidden.

---

[7] Articles of food.

117. "Never said I to them aught except what Thou didst command me to say, to wit[8], 'Worship God, my Lord and your Lord'; and I was a witness over them whilst I dwelt amongst them; when Thou didst take me up, thou wast the Watcher over them, and Thou art a Witness to all things.

118. "If Thou dost punish them, they are Thy servants: if Thou dost forgive them, Thou art the Exalted, the Wise.

119. God will say: "This is a day on which the truthful will profit from their truth: theirs are Gardens, with rivers flowing beneath, their eternal home: God well-pleased with them, and they with God: that is the great Salvation, (the fulfillment of all desires).

120. To God doth belong the dominion of the heavens and the earth, and all that is therein, and it is He Who hath power over all things.

Chapter 6
Sürah Al-An'am (The Cattle)
Revealed at Makkah, 165 verses

In the name of God, Most Gracious, Most Merciful.

1. Praise be to God, Who created the heavens and the earth, and made the Darkness and the Light. Yet those who reject Faith hold (others) as equal with their Guardian-Lord.

2. He it is who created you from clay, and then decreed a stated term (for you). And there is in His presence another determined term; yet ye doubt within yourselves!

3. And He is God in the heavens and on earth. He knoweth what ye hide, and what ye reveal, and He knoweth the (recompense) which ye earn (by your deeds).

4. But never did a single one of the Signs of their Lord reach them, but they turned away therefrom.

5. And now they reject the truth when it reaches them: but soon shall they learn the reality of what they used to mock at.

6. See they not how many of those before them We did destroy? Generations We had established on the earth, in strength such as We have not given to you, for whom We poured out rain from the skies

---

8 That is to say, namely.

in abundance, and gave (fertile) streams flowing beneath their (feet): yet for their sins We destroyed them, and raised in their wake fresh generations (to succeed them).

7. If We had sent unto thee a written (Message) on parchment[1], so that they could touch it with their hands, the Unbelievers would have been sure to say: "This is nothing but obvious magic!"

8. They say: "Why is not an angel sent down to him?" If We did send down an angel, the matter would be settled at once, and no respite would be granted them.

9. If We had made it an angel, We should have sent him as a man, and We should certainly have caused them confusion in a matter which they have already covered with confusion.

10. Mocked were (many) Apostles before thee; but the scoffers[2] were hemmed in[3] by the thing that they mocked.

11. Say: "Travel through the earth and see what was the end of those who rejected truth."

12. Say: "To whom belongeth all that is in the heavens and on earth?" Say: "To God. He hath inscribed[4] for Himself (the rule of) Mercy that He will gather you together for the Day of Judgment, there is no doubt whatever. It is they who have lost their own souls, that will not believe.

13. "To Him belongeth all that dwelleth (or lurketh) in the Night and the Day. For He is the One Who heareth and knoweth all things.

14. Say: "Shall I take for my protector any other than God, the Maker of the heavens and the earth? And He is that feedeth but is not fed." Say: "Nay! but I am commanded to be the first of those who bow to God (in Islam), and be not thou of the company of those who join gods with God."

15. Say: "I would, if I disobeyed my Lord, indeed have fear of the Penalty of a Mighty Day.

16. "On that day, if the Penalty is averted from any, it is due to God's Mercy; and that would be (Salvation), the obvious fulfillment

---

[1] Manuscript, scroll
[2] Mockers, those who ridiculed it.
[3] Confined, enclosed
[4] Decreed, decided

of all desire.

17. "If God touch thee with affliction, none can remove it but He; if He touch thee with happiness, He hath power over all things.

18. "He is the Irresistible, (watching) from above over His worshippers; and He is the Wise, acquainted with all things."

19. Say: "What thing is most weighty in evidence?" Say: "God is witness between me and you: this Qur'an hath been revealed to me by inspiration that I may warn you and all whom it reaches. Can ye possibly bear witness that besides God there is another god?" Say: "Nay! I cannot bear witness!" Say: "But in truth He is the One God, and I truly am innocent of (your blasphemy of) joining others with Him.

20. Those to whom We have given the Book know this as they know their own sons. Those who have lost their own souls refuse therefore to believe.

21. Who doth more wrong than he who inventeth a lie against God or rejecteth His Signs? But verily the wrongdoers never shall prosper.

22. One day shall We gather them all together: We shall say to those who ascribed partners (to Us): "Where are the partners whom ye (invented and) talked about?"

23. There will then be (left) no subterfuge[5] for them but to say: "By God, Our Lord, we were not those who joined gods with God."

24. Behold! how they lie against their own souls! But the (lie) which they invented will leave them in the lurch[6].

25. Of them there are some who (pretend to) listen to thee; but We have thrown veils on their hearts, so they understand it not, and deafness in their ears; if they saw every one of the Signs, they will not believe in them; in so much that when they come to thee, they (but) dispute with thee; the Unbelievers say: "These are nothing but tales of the ancients."

26. Others they keep away from it, and themselves they keep away; but they only destroy their own souls, and they perceive it not.

---

[5] Scheme or trick

[6] To desert an ally or friend in difficulties

93

27. If thou couldst but see when they are confronted with the Fire! They will say: "Would that we were but sent back! Then would we not reject the Signs of our Lord, but would be amongst those who believe!.

28. Yea, in their own (eyes) will become manifest what before they concealed, but if they were returned, they would certainly relapse to the things they were forbidden, for they are indeed liars.

29. And they (sometimes) say: "There is nothing except our life on this earth, and never shall we be raised up again."

30. If thou couldst but see when they are confronted with their Lord! He will say: "Is not this the truth?" They will say: "Yea, by our Lord!" He will say: "Taste ye then the penalty, because ye rejected faith."

31. Lost indeed are they who treat it as a falsehood that they must meet God, until on a sudden the Hour is on them, and they say: "Ah! woe unto us that we took no thought of it;" for they bear their burdens on their backs; and evil indeed are the burdens that they bear!

32. What is the life of this world but play and amusement? But best is the home in the Hereafter, for those who are righteous. Will ye not then understand?

33. We know indeed the grief which their words do cause thee: it is not thee they reject: it is the Signs of God, which the wicked contemn[7].

34. Rejected were the Apostles before thee: with patience and constancy they bore their rejection and their wrongs, until Our aid did reach them: there is none that can alter the Words (and Decrees) of God. Already hast thou received some account of those Apostles.

35. If their spurning[8] is hard on thy mind, yet if thou wert able to seek a tunnel in the ground or a ladder to the skies and bring them a Sign — (what good?). If it were God's Will, He could gather them together unto true guidance: so be not thou amongst those who are swayed by ignorance (and impatience)!

36. Those who listen (in truth), be sure, will accept: as to the dead, God will raise them up: then will they be turned unto Him.

---

[7] (Old English) Despise, treat with disregard.

[8] Rejection, disdain

37. They say: "Why is not a Sign sent down to him from his Lord?" Say: "God hath certainly power to send down a Sign: but most of them understand not."

38. There is not an animal (that lives) on the earth, nor a being that flies on its wings, but (forms part of) communities like you. Nothing have We omitted from the Book, and they (all) shall be gathered to their Lord in the end.

39. Those who reject Our Signs are deaf and dumb, in the midst of darkness profound: whom God willeth, He leaveth to wander, whom He willeth, He placeth on the way that is straight.

40. Say: "Think ye to yourselves, if there come upon you the wrath of God, or the Hour (that ye dread), would ye then call upon other than God? (Reply) if ye are truthful!

41. "Nay, On Him would ye call, and if it be His Will, He would remove (the distress) which occasioned your call upon Him, and ye would forget (the false gods) which ye join with Him!"

42. Before thee We sent (Apostles) to many nations and We afflicted the nations with suffering and adversity, that they might learn humility.

43. When the suffering reached them from Us, why then did they not learn humility? On the contrary their hearts became hardened, and Satan made their (sinful) acts seem alluring to them.

44. But when they forgot the warning they had received, We opened to them the gates of all (good) things, until, in the midst of their enjoyment of Our gifts, on a sudden, We called them to account, when lo! they were plunged in despair!

45. Of the wrongdoers the last remnant was cut off. Praise be to God, the Cherisher of the Worlds.

46. Say: "Think ye, if God took away your hearing and your sight, and sealed up your hearts, who — a god other than God — could restore them to you? See how We explain the Signs by various (symbols): Yet they turn aside.

47. Say: "Think ye, if the punishment of God comes to you, whether suddenly or openly, will any be destroyed except those who do wrong?"

48. We send the Apostles only to give good news and to warn: so those who believe and mend (their lives) — upon them shall be

no fear, nor shall they grieve.

49. But those who reject Our Signs — them shall our punishment touch, for that they ceased not from transgressing.

50. Say: "I tell you not that with me are the treasures of God, nor do I know what is hidden, nor do I tell you I am an angel. I but follow what is revealed to me." Say: "Can the blind be held equal to the seeing?" Will ye then consider not?

51. Give the warning to those in whose (hearts) is the fear that they will be brought (to Judgment) before their Lord: except for Him they will have no protector nor intercessor: that they may guard (against evil).

52. Send not away those who call on their Lord morning and evening, seeking His Face. Naught have they to gain from thee, and naught hast thou to gain from them, that thou shouldst turn them away, and thus be (one) of the unjust.

53. Thus did We try some of them by comparison with others, that they should say: Is it these then that God hath favored from amongst us?" Doth not God know best those who are grateful?

54. When those come to thee who believe in Our Signs, say: "Peace be on you: your Lord hath inscribed for Himself (the rule of) Mercy: verily, if any of you did evil in ignorance, and thereafter repented and amended (his conduct), lo! He is Oft-Forgiving, Most Merciful."

55. Thus do We explain the Signs in detail: that the way of the sinners may be shown up.

56. Say: "I am forbidden to worship those — other than God — whom ye call upon." Say: "I will not follow your vain desires: if I did, I would stray from the path, and be not of the company of those who receive guidance."

57. Say: "For me, I (work) on a clear Sign from my Lord, but ye reject Him. What ye would see hastened is not in my power. The Command rests with none but God: He declares the truth, and He is the best of Judges."

58. Say: "If what ye would see hastened were in my power, the matter would be settled at once between you and me. But God knoweth best those who do wrong."

59. With Him are the keys of the Unseen, the treasures that none knoweth but He. He knoweth whatever there is on the earth and in

the sea. Not a leaf doth fall but with His knowledge: there is not a grain in the darkness (or depths) of the earth, nor anything fresh or dry (green or withered), but is (inscribed) in a Record Clear (to those who can read).

60. It is He Who doth take your souls by night, and hath knowledge of all that ye have done by day. By day doth He raise you up again; that a term appointed be fulfilled; in the end unto Him will be your return, then will He show you the truth of all that ye did.

61. He is the Irresistible, (watching) from above over His worshippers, and He sets guardians over you. At length, when death approaches one of you, Our angels take his soul, and they never fail in their duty.

62. Then are men returned unto God, their Protector, the (only) reality: is not His the Command? And He is the swiftest in taking account.

63. Say: "Who is it that delivereth you from the dark recesses of land and sea, when ye call upon Him in humility and silent terror: 'If He only delivers us from these (dangers), (we vow) we shall truly show our gratitude'?"

64. Say: "It is God that delivereth you from these and all (other) distresses: and yet ye worship false gods!"

65. Say: "He hath power to send calamities on you, from above and below, or to cover you with confusion in party strife giving you a taste of mutual vengeance — each from the other." See how We explain the Signs by various (symbols), that they may understand.

66. But thy people reject this, though it is the truth. Say: "Not mine is the responsibility for arranging your affairs;

67. "For every Message is a limit of time and soon shall ye know it."

68. When thou seest men engaged in vain discourse about Our Signs, turn away from them unless they turn to a different theme. If Satan ever makes thee forget, then after recollection, sit not thou in the company of the ungodly.

69. On their account no responsibility falls on the righteous, but (their duty) is to remind them, that they may (learn to) fear God.

70. Leave alone those who take their religion to be mere play and amusement, and are deceived by the life of this world. But proclaim

(to them) this (truth): that every soul delivers itself to ruin by its own acts: it will find for itself no protector or intercessor except God: if it offered every ransom (or reparation), none will be accepted: such is (the end of) those who deliver themselves to ruin by their own acts: they will have for drink (only) boiling water, and for punishment, one most grievous: for they persisted in rejecting God.

71. Say: "Shall we indeed call on others besides God, things that can do us neither good nor harm, and turn on our heels after receiving guidance from God? — like one whom the evil ones have made into a fool, wandering bewildered through the earth, his friends calling 'Come to us', (vainly) guiding him to the Path." Say: "God's guidance is the (only) guidance, and we have been directed to submit ourselves to the Lord of the Worlds —

72. "To establish regular prayers and to fear God; for it is to Him that we shall be gathered together."

73. It is He Who created the heavens and the earth in true (proportions): the day He saith, "Be," Behold! it is. His Word is the truth. His will be the dominion the day the trumpet will be blown. He knoweth the Unseen as well as that which is open. For He is the Wise, well acquainted (with all things).

74. Lo! Abraham said to his father Azar: "Takest thou idols for gods? for I see thee and thy people in manifest error."

75. So also did We show Abraham the power and the laws of the heavens and the earth, that he might (with understanding) have certitude.

76. When the night covered him over, he saw a star: he said: "This is my Lord." But when it set, he said: "I love not those that set."

77. When he saw the moon rising in splendor, He said: "This is my Lord." but when the moon set, he said: "Unless my Lord guide me, I shall surely be among those who go astray."

78. When he saw the sun rising in splendor, he said: "This is my Lord; this is the greatest (of all)." But when the sun set, he said: "O my people! I am (now) free from your (guilt) of giving partners to God.

79. "For me, I have set my face, firmly and truly, toward Him Who created the heavens and the earth, and never shall I give partners to God."

80. His people disputed with him. He said: "(Come) ye to dispute with me, about God, when He (Himself) hath guided me? I fear not (the beings) ye associate with God: unless my Lord willeth, (nothing can happen). My Lord comprehendeth in His knowledge all things: will ye not (yourselves) be admonished?.

81. "How should I fear (the beings) ye associate with God, when ye fear not to give partners to God without any warrant[9] having been given to you? Which of (us) two parties hath more right to security? (tell me) if ye know.

82. "It is those who believe and confuse not their beliefs with wrong — that are (truly) in security, for they are on (right) guidance."

83. That was the reasoning about Us, which We gave to Abraham (to use) against his people: We raise whom We Will, degree after degree: for thy Lord is full of wisdom and knowledge.

84. We gave him Isaac and Jacob: all (three) We guided: and before him, We guided Noah, and among his progeny[10], David, Solomon, Job, Joseph, Moses, and Aaron: thus do We reward those who do good:

85. And Zakariya and John, and Jesus and Elias: all in the ranks of the righteous:

86. And Ismail and Elisha, and Jonah, and Lot: and to all We gave favor above the nations:

87. (To them) and to their fathers, and progeny and brethren: We chose them. And We guided them to a straight way.

88. This is the guidance of God: He giveth that guidance to whom He pleaseth, of His worshippers. If they were to join other gods with Him, all that they did would be vain for them.

89. These were the men to whom We gave the Book, and authority, and prophethood: if these (their descendants) reject them, behold! We shall entrust their charge to a new People who reject them not.

90. Those were the (prophets) who received God's guidance: Copy the guidance they received; Say: "No reward for this do I ask of you: this is no less than a Message for the nations."

91. No just estimate of God do they make when they say: "Nothing

---

[9] Authority
[10] Descendants, offspring

doth God send down to man (by way of revelation)": Say: "Who then sent down the Book which Moses brought? — A light and guidance to man: but ye make it into (separate) sheets for show, while ye conceal much (of its contents): therein were ye taught that which ye knew not — neither ye nor your fathers." Say: "God (sent it down):" then leave them to plunge in vain discourse and trifling[11].

92. And this is a Book which We have revealed, bringing blessings, and confirming (the revelations) which came before it: that thou mayest warn the Mother of Cities[12] and all around her. Those who believe in the Hereafter believe in this (Book), and they are constant in guarding their prayers.

93. Who can be more wicked than one who inventeth a lie against God, or saith, "I have received inspiration," when he hath received none, or (again) who saith, "I can reveal the like of what God hath revealed?" If thou couldst but see how the wicked (do fare) in the flood of confusion at death! — the angels stretch forth their hands, (saying), "Yield up your souls. This day shall ye receive your reward — a penalty of shame, for that ye used to tell lies against God, and scornfully to reject of His Signs!"

94. "And behold! ye come to Us bare and alone as We created you for the first time: Ye have left behind you all (the favors) which We bestowed on you: We see not with you your intercessors whom ye thought to be partners in your affairs: so now all relations between you have been cut off, and your (pet) fancies have left you in the lurch!"

95. It is God Who causeth the seedgrain and the datestone to split and sprout. He causeth the living to issue from the dead, and He is the one to cause the dead to issue from the living. That is God; then how are ye deluded away from the truth?

96. He it is that cleaveth the daybreak (from the dark): He makes the night for rest and tranquillity, and the sun and moon for the reckoning (of time): such is the judgment and ordering of (Him), the Exalted in Power, the Omniscient.

97. It is He Who maketh the stars (as beacons) for you, that ye

---

[11] Worthless

[12] Makkah

may guide yourselves, with their help, through the dark spaces of land and sea: We detail Our Signs for people who know.

98. It is He who hath produced you from a single person: here is a place of sojourn and a place of departure: We detail Our Signs for people who understand.

99. It is He who sendeth down rain from the skies: with it We produce vegetation of all kinds: from some We produce green (crops), out of which We produce grain, heaped up (at harvest); out of the datepalm and its sheaths (or spathes) (come) clusters of dates hanging low and near: and (then there are) gardens of grapes, and olives, and pomegranates, each similar (in kind) yet different (in variety): when they begin to bear fruit, feast your eyes with the fruit and the ripeness thereof. Behold! in these things there are Signs for people who believe.

100. Yet they make the Jinns equals with God, though God did create the Jinns; and they falsely, having no knowledge, attribute to Him sons and daughters. Praise and glory be to Him! (for He is) above what they attribute to Him!

101. To Him is due the primal origin of the heavens and the earth: how can He have a son when He hath no consort? He created all things, and He hath full knowledge of all things.

102. That is God your Lord! There is no god but He, the Creator of all things: then worship ye Him: and He hath power to dispose of all affairs.

103. No vision can grasp Him, but His grasp is over all vision: He is above all comprehension, yet is acquainted with all things.

104. "Now have come to you, from your Lord, proofs to open your eyes: if any will see, it will be for (the good of) his own soul; if any will be blind, it will be to his own (harm): I am not (here) to watch over your doings."

105. Thus do We explain the Signs by various (symbols): that they may say "Thou hast taught us diligently," and that We may make the matter clear to those who know.

106. Follow what thou art taught by inspiration from thy Lord: there is no god but He: and turn aside from those who join gods with God.

107. If it had been God's Plan, they would not have taken false gods: but We made thee not one to watch over their doings, nor art

thou set over them to dispose of their affairs.

108. Revile[13] not ye those whom they call upon besides God, lest they out of spite revile God in their ignorance. Thus have We made alluring to each people its own doings. In the end will they return to their Lord, and We shall then tell them the truth of all that they did.

109. They swear their strongest oaths by God that if a (special) Sign came to them, by it they would believe. Say: "Certainly (all) Signs are in the power of God: but what will make you (Muslims) realize that even if a (special) Sign comes, they will not believe."

110. We (too) shall turn to (confusion) their hearts and their eyes, even as they refused to believe in the first instance: We shall leave them in their trespasses, to wander in distraction.

111. Even if We did send unto them angels, and the dead did speak unto them, and We gathered together all things before their very eyes, they are not the ones to believe, unless it is in God's Plan: but most of them ignore (the truth).

112. Likewise did We make for every Messenger an enemy, evil ones among men and Jinns, inspiring each other with flowery discourses by way of deception. If thy Lord had so planned, they would not have done it: so leave them and their inventions alone.

113. To such (deceit) let the hearts of those incline, who have no faith in the Hereafter: let them delight in it, and let them earn from it what they may.

114. Say: "Shall I seek for judge other than God? When He it is Who hath sent unto you the Book, explained in detail." They know full well, to whom We have given the Book, that it hath been sent down from thy Lord in truth. Never be then of those who doubt.

115. The Word of thy Lord doth find its fulfillment in truth and in justice: none can change His Words: for He is the one who heareth and knoweth all.

116. Wert[14] thou to follow the common run of those on earth, they will lead thee away from the Way of God. They follow nothing but conjecture: they do nothing but lie.

---

[13] Abuse, ridicule

[14] Were

117. Thy Lord knoweth best who strayeth from His Way. He knoweth best who they are that receive His guidance.

118. So eat of (meats) on which God's name hath been pronounced, if ye have faith in His Signs.

119. Why should ye not eat of (meats) on which God's name hath been pronounced, when He hath explained to you in detail what is forbidden to you — except under compulsion of necessity? But many do mislead (men) by their appetites unchecked by knowledge. Thy Lord knoweth best those who transgress.

120. Eschew[15] all sin, open or secret: those who earn sin, will get due recompense for their "earnings."

121. Eat not of (meats) on which God's name hath not been pronounced: that would be impiety. But the evil ones ever inspire their friends to contend with you; if ye were to obey them, ye would indeed be pagans.

122. Can he who was dead, to whom We gave life, and a Light whereby he can walk amongst men, be like him who is in the depths of darkness, from which he can never come out? Thus to those without faith their own deeds seem pleasing.

123. Thus have We placed leaders in every town, its wicked men, to plot (and burrow[16]) therein: but they only plot against their own souls, and they perceive it not.

124. When there comes to them a Sign (from God), they say: "We shall not believe until we receive one (exactly) like those received by God's Apostles." God knoweth best where (and how) to carry out His mission. Soon will the wicked be overtaken by humiliation before God, and a severe punishment, for all their plots.

125. Those whom God (in His Plan) willeth to guide, He openeth their breast to Islam; those whom He willeth to leave straying, He maketh their breast close and constricted[17], as if they had to climb up to the skies: thus doth God (heap) the penalty on those who refuse to believe.

126. This is the way of thy Lord, leading straight: We have detailed

---

[15] Avoid

[16] Dig, hide (in a hole)

[17] Shrunk, compressed

the Signs for those who receive admonition.

127. For them will be a Home of Peace in the presence of their Lord: He will be their Friend, because they practiced (righteousness).

128. One day will He gather them all together, (and say): "O ye assembly of Jinns! much (toll) did ye take of men." Their friends amongst men will say: "Our Lord! we made profit from each other: but (alas!) we reached our term — which Thou didst appoint for us." He will say: "The Fire be your dwelling-place: you will dwell therein forever, except as God willeth." For thy Lord is full of wisdom and knowledge.

129. Thus do We make the wrongdoers turn to each other, because of what they earn.

130. O ye assembly of Jinns and men! came there not unto you apostles from amongst you, setting forth unto you of the meeting of this day of yours?" They will say: "We bear witness against ourselves." It was the life of this world that deceived them. So against themselves will they bear witness that they rejected faith.

131. (The apostles were sent) thus, for thy Lord would not destroy for their wrongdoing men's habitations whilst their occupants were unwarned.

132. To all are degrees (or ranks) according to their deeds: for thy Lord is not unmindful of anything that they do.

133. Thy Lord is Self-sufficient, full of Mercy: if it were His Will, He could destroy you, and in your place appoint whom He will as your successors, even as he raised you up from the posterity[18] of other people.

134. All that hath been promised unto you will come to pass: nor can ye frustrate it (in the least bit).

135. Say: "O my people! do whatever ye can: I will do (my part): soon will ye know who it is whose end will be (best) in the Hereafter: certain it is that the wrongdoers will not prosper."

136. Out of what God hath produced in abundance in tilth and in cattle, they assigned Him a share: they say, according to their fancies: "This is for God, and this for our 'partners'"! But the share of their 'partners' reacheth not God, whilst the share of God reacheth their

---

[18] Offspring, descendants

'partners'! Evil (and unjust) is their assignment!

137. Even so, in the eyes of most of the Pagans, their 'partners' made alluring the slaughter of their children, in order to lead them to their own destruction, and cause confusion in their religion. If God had willed, they would not have done so: but leave alone them and their inventions.

138. And they say that such and such cattle and crops are taboo, and none should eat of them except those whom — so they say — we wish; further, there are cattle forbidden to yoke or burden, and cattle on which (at slaughter), the name of God is not pronounced; inventions against God's name: soon will He requite[19] them for their inventions.

139. They say: "What is in the wombs of such and such cattle is specially reserved (for food) for our men, and forbidden to our women; but if it is stillborn then all have shares therein. For their (false) attribution (of superstitions to God): He will soon punish them: for He is full of Wisdom and Knowledge.

140. Lost are those who slay their children, from folly, without knowledge, and forbid food which God hath provided for them, inventing (lies) against God. They have indeed gone astray and heeded no guidance.

141. It is He who produceth gardens, with trellises[20] and without, and dates, and tilth with produce of all kinds, and olives and pomegranates, similar (in kind) and different (in variety): eat of their fruit in their season, but render the dues that are proper on the day that the harvest is gathered. But waste not by excess: for God loveth not the wasters.

142. Of the cattle are some for burden and some for meat. Eat what God hath provided for you, and follow not the footsteps of Satan: for he is to you an avowed enemy.

143. (Take) eight (head of cattle) in (four) pairs: of sheep a pair, and of goats a pair; say, hath He forbidden the two males, or the two females, or (the young) which the wombs of the two females enclose? Tell me with knowledge if ye are truthful.

---

[19] Repay (for one's good or bad deeds)
[20] Lattice or grating of light wooden crossbars.

144. Of camels a pair, and of oxen a pair; say, hath He forbidden the two males, or the two females, or the (the young) which the wombs of the two females enclose? Were ye present when God ordered you such a thing? But who doth more wrong than one who invents a lie against God, to lead astray men without knowledge? For God guideth not people who do wrong.

145. Say: "I find not in the Message received by me by inspiration any (meat) forbidden to be eaten by one who wishes to eat it, unless it be dead meat, or blood poured forth, or the flesh of swine — for it is an abomination — or, what is impious, (meat) on which a name has been invoked, other than God's." But (even so), if a person is forced by necessity, without wilful disobedience, nor transgressing due limits — thy Lord is Oft-Forgiving, Most Merciful.

146. For those who followed the Jewish Law, We forbade every (animal) with undivided hoof, and We forbade them the fat of the ox and the sheep, except what adheres to their backs or their entrails, or is mixed up with a bone: this in recompense for their wilful disobedience: for We are True (in Our ordinances).

147. If they accuse thee of falsehood, say: "Your Lord is full of Mercy All-Embracing;" but from people in guilt never will His wrath be turned back.

148. Those who give partners to God will say, "If God had wished, we should not have given partners to Him, nor would our fathers; nor should we have had any taboos[21]." So did their ancestors argue falsely, until they tasted of Our wrath. Say: "Have ye any (certain) Knowledge? If so, produce it before us. Ye follow nothing but conjecture: Ye do nothing but lie."

149. Say: "With God is the argument that reaches home: if it had been His Will, He could indeed have guided you all."

150. Say: "Bring forward your witnesses to prove that God did forbid so and so." If they bring such witnesses, be not thou amongst them: nor follow thou the vain desires of such as treat Our Signs as falsehoods, and such as believe not in the Hereafter: for they hold others as equal with their Guardian-Lord.

---

[21] Setting apart a person or thing as accursed or sacred, ban, prohibition

151. Say: "Come, I will rehearse[22] what God hath (really) prohibited you from": join not anything as equal with Him; be good to
your parents: kill not your children on a plea of want; — We provide
sustenance for you and for them; — come not nigh to shameful deeds,
whether open or secret; take not life, which God hath made sacred,
except by way of justice and law: thus doth He command you, that
ye may learn wisdom.

152. And come not nigh to the orphan's property, except to improve
it, until he attains the age of full strength; give measure and weight
with (full) justice — no burden do We place on any soul, but that
which it can bear — whenever ye speak, speak justly, even if a near
relative is concerned; and fulfil the Covenant of God: thus doth He
command you, that ye may remember.

153. Verily, this is My Way, leading straight: follow it: follow
not (other) paths: they will scatter you about from His (great) path:
thus doth He command you that ye may be righteous.

154. Moreover, We gave Moses the Book, completing (Our favor)
to those who would do right, and explaining all things in detail, and
a guide and a mercy, that they might believe in the meeting with their
Lord.

155. And this is a Book which We have revealed as a blessing:
so follow it and be righteous, that ye may receive mercy:

156. Lest ye should say: "The Book was sent down to two peoples
before us, and for our part, we remained unacquainted with all that
they learned by assiduous[23] study."

157. Or lest ye should say: "If the Book had only been sent down
to us, we should have followed its guidance better than they." Now
then hath come unto you a Clear (Sign) from your Lord, and a guide
and a mercy: then who could do more wrong than one who rejecteth
God's Signs, and turneth away therefrom? In good time shall We
requite those who turn away from Our Signs, with a dreadful penalty,
for their turning away.

158. Are they waiting to see if the angels come to them, or thy
Lord (Himself), or certain of the Signs of thy Lord! The day that

---

[22] Recite, recount
[23] Diligent

certain of the Signs of thy Lord do come, no good will it do to a soul to believe in them then, if it believed not before nor earned righteousness through its Faith. Say: "Wait ye: we too are waiting."

159. As for those who divide their religion and break up into sects, thou hast no part in them in the least: their affair is with God: He will in the end tell them the truth of all that they did.

160. He that doeth good shall have ten times as much to his credit: he that doeth evil shall only be recompensed according to his evil. No wrong shall be done unto (any of) them.

161. Say: "Verily, my Lord hath guided me to a way that is straight, a religion of right — the path (trod) by Abraham the true in faith, and he (certainly) joined not gods with God."

162. Say: "Truly, my prayer and my service of sacrifice, my life and my death, are (all) for God, the Cherisher of the Worlds:

163. No partner hath He: this am I commanded, and I am the first of those who bow to His Will.

164. Say: "Shall I seek for (my) Cherisher other than God, when He is the Cherisher of all things (that exist)?" Every soul draws the meed[24] of its acts on none but itself: no bearer of burdens can bear the burden of another. Your goal in the end is toward God: He will tell you the truth of the things wherein ye disputed.

165. It is He who hath made you (His) agents, inheritors of the earth: He hath raised you in ranks, some above others: that He may try you in the gifts He hath given you: for thy Lord is quick in punishment: yet He is indeed Oft-Forgiving, Most Merciful.

---

[24] Reward

Chapter 7
Sürah Al-A'raf (The Heights)
Revealed at Makkah, 206 verses.

In the name of God, Most Gracious, Most Merciful.

1. Alif Lām Mïm Sād.

2. A Book revealed unto thee, so let thy heart be oppressed no more by any difficulty on that account, that with it thou mightest warn (the erring) and teach the believers.

3. Follow (O men!) the revelation given unto you from your Lord, and follow not, as friends or protectors, other than Him. Little it is ye remember of admonition.

4. How many towns have We destroyed (for their sins)? Our punishment took them on a sudden by night or while they slept for their afternoon rest.

5. When (thus) Our punishment took them, no cry did they utter but this: "Indeed we did wrong."

6. Then shall We question those to whom Our message was sent and those by whom We sent it.

7. And verily We shall recount their whole story with knowledge, for We were never absent (at any time or place).

8. The balance that day will be true (to a nicety): those whose scale (of good) will be heavy, will prosper.

9. Those whose scale will be light, will find their souls in perdition[1], for that they wrongfully treated Our Signs.

10. It is We who have placed you with authority on earth, and provided you therein with means for the fulfillment of your life: small are the thanks that ye give!

11. It is We who created you and gave you shape; then We bade the angels bow down to Adam, and they bowed down; not so Iblis; he refused to be of those who bow down.

12. (God) said: "What prevented thee from bowing down when I commanded thee?" He said: "I am better than he: thou didst create me from fire and him from clay."

---

[1] Eternal death, damnation

13. (God) said: "Get thee down from this: it is not for thee to be arrogant here: get out, for thou art of the meanest (of creatures)."

14. He said: "Give me respite till the day they are raised up."

15. (God) said: "Be thou among those who have respite."

16. He said: "Because Thou hast thrown me out of the way, lo! I will lie in wait for them on Thy straight way.

17. "Then will I assault them from before them and behind them from their right and their left: nor wilt Thou find, in most of them, gratitude (for Thy mercies).

18. (God) said: "Get out from this, disgraced and expelled. If any of them follow thee — Hell will I fill with you all.

19. O Adam! dwell thou and thy wife in the Garden, and enjoy (its good things) as ye wish: but approach not this tree, or ye run into harm and transgression."

20. Then began Satan to whisper suggestions to them, bringing openly before their minds all their shame that was hidden from them (before): he said "Your Lord only forbade you this tree, lest ye should become angels or such beings as live forever."

21. And he swore to them both, that he was their sincere adviser.

22. So by deceit he brought about their fall: when they tasted of the tree, their shame became manifest to them, and they began to sew together the leaves of the garden over their bodies. And their Lord called unto them: "Did I not forbid you that tree, and tell you that Satan was an avowed enemy unto you?"

23. They said: "Our Lord! we have wronged our own souls: if Thou forgive us not and bestow not upon us Thy mercy, we shall certainly be lost."

24. (God) said: "Get ye down, with enmity between yourselves. On earth will be your dwelling-place and your means of livelihood, for a time."

25. He said: "Therein shall ye live, and therein shall ye die; but from it shall ye be taken out (at last)."

26. O ye Children of Adam! We have bestowed raiment upon you to cover your shame, as well as to be an adornment to you, but the raiment of righteousness, that is the best. Such are among the Signs of God, that they may receive admonition!

27. O ye Children of Adam! let not Satan seduce you, in the same

manner as he got your parents out of the Garden, stripping them of their raiment, to expose their shame: for he and his tribe watch you from a position where ye cannot see them: We made the evil ones friends (only) to those without faith.

28. When they do aught that is shameful, they say: "We found our fathers doing so"; and "God commanded us thus": say: "Nay, God never commands what is shameful: do ye say of God what ye know not?"

29. Say: "My Lord hath commanded justice; and that ye set your whole selves (to Him) at every time and place of prayer, and call upon Him, making your devotion sincere as in His sight: such as He created you in the beginning, so shall ye return."

30. Some He hath guided: others have (by their choice) deserved the loss of their way: in that they took the evil ones, in preference to God, for their friends and protectors, and think that they receive guidance.

31. O children of Adam! wear your beautiful apparel at every time and place of prayer: eat and drink: but waste not by excess, for God loveth not the wasters.

32. Say: Who hath forbidden the beautiful (gifts) of God, which He hath produced for His servants, and the things, clean and pure, (which He hath provided) for sustenance? Say: they are, in the life of this world, for those who believe, (and) purely for them on the Day of Judgment. Thus do We explain the Signs in detail for those who understand.

33. Say: The things that my Lord hath indeed forbidden are: shameful deeds, whether open or secret; sins and trespasses against truth or reason; assigning of partners to God, for which he hath given no authority; and saying things about God of which ye have no knowledge.

34. To every people is a term appointed: when their term is reached, not an hour can they cause delay, nor (an hour) can they advance (it in anticipation).

35. O ye Children of Adam! whenever there come to you Apostles from amongst you, rehearsing My Signs unto you, those who are righteous and mend (their lives), on them shall be no fear, nor shall they grieve.

111

36. But those who reject Our Signs and treat them with arrogance, they are Companions of the Fire, to dwell therein (forever).

37. Who is more unjust than one who invents a lie against God or rejects His Signs? For such, their portion appointed must reach them from the Book (of decrees); until, when Our messengers (of death) arrive and take their souls, they say: "Where are the things that ye used to invoke besides God?" They will reply, "They have left us in the lurch," and they will bear witness against themselves, that they had rejected God.

38. He will say: "Enter ye in the company of the peoples who passed away before you, men and Jinns, into the Fire. Every time a new people enters, it curses its sister-people (that went before), until they follow each other, all into the Fire. Saith the last about the first: "Our Lord! it is these that misled us: so give them a double penalty in the Fire." He will say: "Doubled for all": but this Ye do not understand.

39. Then the first will say to the last: "See then! no advantage have ye over us; so taste ye of the penalty for all that ye did!"

40. To those who reject Our Signs and treat them with arrogance, no opening will there be of the gates of heaven nor will they enter the Garden, until the camel can pass through the eye of the needle: such is Our reward for those in sin.

41. For them there is Hell, as a couch (below) and folds and folds of covering above: such is Our requital of those who do wrong.

42. But those who believe and work righteousness, no burden do We place on any soul, but that which it can bear, they will be Companions of the Garden, therein to dwell (forever).

43. And We shall remove from their hearts any lurking sense of injury; beneath them will be rivers flowing; and they shall say: "Praise be to God, Who hath guided us to this (felicity): never could we have found guidance, had it not been for the guidance of God: indeed it was the truth that the Apostles of our Lord brought unto us." And they Shall hear the cry: "Behold! the Garden before you! Ye have been made its inheritors, for your deeds (of righteousness)."

44. The Companions of the Garden will call out to the Companions of the Fire: "We have indeed found the promises of our Lord to us true: Have you also found your Lord's promises true?" They shall

say, "Yes"; but a crier shall proclaim between them: "The curse of God is on the wrongdoers;

45. "Those who would hinder (men) from the path of God and would seek in it something crooked: they were those who denied the Hereafter."

46. Between them shall be a veil, and on the heights will be men who would know everyone by his marks: they will call out to the Companions of the Garden, "Peace on you": they will not have entered, but they will have an assurance (thereof.)

47. When their eyes shall be turned towards the Companions of the Fire, they will say: "Our Lord! send us not to the company of the wrongdoers."

48. The men on the heights will call to certain men whom they will know from their marks, saying: "Of what profit to you were your hoards and your arrogant ways?

49. "Behold! are these not the men whom you swore that God with His Mercy would never bless? Enter ye the Garden: no fear shall be on you, nor shall ye grieve."

50. The Companions of the Fire will call to the Companions of the Garden: "Pour down to us water or anything that God doth provide for your sustenance." They will say: "Both these things hath God forbidden to those who rejected Him.

51. "Such as took their religion to be mere amusement and play, and were deceived by the life of the world." That day shall We forget them as they forgot the meeting of this day of theirs, and as they were wont to reject Our Signs.

52. For We had certainly sent unto them a Book, based on knowledge, which We explained in detail, a guide and a mercy to all who believe.

53. Do they just wait for the final fulfillment of the event? On the day the event is finally fulfilled, those who disregarded it before will say: "The Apostles of our Lord did indeed bring true (tidings). Have we no intercessors now to intercede on our behalf? Or could we be sent back? Then should we behave differently from our behavior in the past." In fact they will have lost their souls, and the things they invented will leave them in the lurch.

54. Your Guardian-Lord is God, Who created the heavens and

the earth in six days, and is firmly established on the throne (of authority): He draweth the Night as a veil o'er the Day, each seeking the other in rapid succession: He created the sun, the moon, and the stars, (all) governed by laws under His command. Is it not His to create and to govern? Blessed be God, the Cherisher and Sustainer of the Worlds!

55. Call on your Lord with humility and in private: for God loveth not those who trespass beyond bounds.

56. Do no mischief on the earth, after it hath been set in order, but call on Him with fear and longing (in your hearts): for the mercy of God is (always) near to those who do good.

57. It is He who sendeth the winds like heralds of glad tidings, going before His mercy: when they have carried the heavy-laden clouds, We drive them to a land that is dead, make rain to descend thereon, and produce every kind of harvest therewith: thus shall We raise up the dead: perchance ye may remember.

58. From the land that is clean and good, by the Will of its Cherisher, springs up produce, (rich) after its kind: but from the land that is bad, springs up nothing but that which is niggardly: thus do We explain the Signs by various (symbols) to those who are grateful.

59. We sent Noah to his people. He said: "O my people! worship God! ye have no other god but Him. I fear for you the punishment of a dreadful day!

60. The leaders of his people said: "Ah! we see thee evidently wandering (in mind)."

61. He said: "O my people! no wandering is there in my (mind): on the contrary I am an Apostle from the Lord and Cherisher of the Worlds!

62. "I but fulfil towards you the duties of my Lord's mission: sincere is my advice to you, and I know from God something that ye know not.

63. "Do ye wonder that there hath come to you a message from your Lord, through a man of your own people, to warn you, so that ye may fear God and haply[2] receive his mercy?"

---

[2] Perhaps, maybe

64. But they rejected him and We delivered him, and those with him, in the Ark: But We overwhelmed in the flood those who rejected Our Signs. They were indeed a blind people!

65. To the 'Ad people, (We sent) Hūd, one of their (own) brethren: He said: "O my people! worship God! ye have no other god but Him. Will ye not fear (God)?"

66. The leaders of the Unbelievers among his people said: "Ah! we see thou art an imbecile!" and "we think thou art a liar!"

67. He said: "O my people! I am no imbecile, but (I am) an Apostle from the Lord and Cherisher of the Worlds!

68. "I but fulfil towards you the duties of my Lord's mission: I am to you a sincere and trustworthy adviser.

69. "Do ye wonder that there hath come to you a message from your Lord through a man of your own people, to warn you? Call in remembrance that He made you inheritors after the people of Noah, and gave you a stature tall among the nations. Call in remembrance the benefits (ye have received) from God: that so ye may prosper."

70. They said: "Comest thou to us, that we may worship God alone, and give up the cult of our fathers? Bring us what thou threatenest us with, if so be that thou tellest the truth!"

71. He said: "Punishment and wrath have already come upon you from your Lord: dispute ye with me over names which ye have devised, ye and your fathers, without authority from God? Then wait: I am amongst you, also waiting."

72. We saved him and those who adhered to him, by Our Mercy, and We cut off the roots of those who rejected Our Signs and did not believe.

73. To the Thamūd people (We sent) Saleh, one of their own brethren: he said: "O my people! worship God; ye have no other god but Him. Now hath come unto you a clear (Sign) from your Lord! This she-camel of God is a Sign unto you: so leave her to graze in God's earth, and let her come to no harm, or ye shall be seized with a grievous punishment.

74. "And remember how He made you inheritors after the 'Ad people and gave you habitations in the land: ye build for yourselves palaces and castles in (open) plains, and carve out homes in the mountains; so bring to remembrance the benefits (ye have received)

from God, and refrain from evil and mischief on the earth."

75. The leaders of the arrogant party among his people said to those who were reckoned powerless — those among them who believed: "Know ye indeed that Saleh is an Apostle from his Lord?" They said: "We do indeed believe in the revelation which hath been sent through him."

76. The arrogant party said: "For our part, we reject what ye believe in."

77. Then they hamstrung[3] the she-camel, and insolently defied the order of their Lord, saying: "O Saleh! bring about thy threats, if thou art an apostle (of God)!"

78. So the earthquake took them unawares, and they lay prostrate in their homes in the morning!

79. So Saleh left them, saying: "O my people! I did indeed convey to you the message for which I was sent by my Lord: I gave you good counsel, but ye love not good counsellors!"

80. We also (sent) Lüt: He said to his people: "Do ye commit lewdness[4] such as no people in creation (ever) committed before you?

81. "For ye practice your lusts on men in preference to women: ye are indeed a people transgressing beyond bounds."

82. And his people gave no answer but this: They said, "Drive them out of your city: these are indeed men who want to be clean and pure!"

83. But We saved him and his family, except his wife: she was of those who lagged behind.

84. And We rained down on them a shower (of brimstone): then see what was the end of those who indulged in sin and crime!

85. To the Madyan people We sent Shu'aib, one of their own brethren: he said: "O my people! worship God; Ye have no other god but Him. Now hath come unto you a clear (Sign) from your Lord! Give just measure and weight, nor withhold from the people the things that are their due; and do no mischief on the earth after it has been set in order: that will be best for you, if ye have faith.

86. "And squat not on every road, breathing threats, hindering from the path of God those who believe in Him, and seeking in it something

---

[3] To cripple by cutting the hamstrings (tendons at back of knee).
[4] Indecency, obscenity

crooked; but remember how ye were little, and He gave you increase. And hold in your mind's eye what was the end of those who did mischief.

87. "And if there is a party among you who believes in the message with which I have been sent, and a party which does not believe, hold yourselves in patience until God doth decide between us: for He is the best to decide."

88. The leaders, the arrogant party among his people, said: "O Shu'aib! we shall certainly drive thee out of our city, (thee) and those who believe with thee: or else ye (thou and they) shall have to return to our ways and religion." He said: "What! even though we do detest (them)?

89. "We should indeed invent a lie against God, if we returned to your ways after God hath rescued us therefrom: nor could we by any manner of means return thereto unless it be as in the Will and Plan of God, Our Lord. Our Lord can reach out to the utmost recesses of things by His knowledge. In God is our trust. Our Lord! decide thou between us and our people in truth, for thou art the best to decide."

90. The leaders, the Unbelievers among his people, said, "If ye follow Shu'aib, be sure then ye are ruined!"

91. But the earthquake took them unawares, and they lay prostrate in their homes before the morning!

92. The men who rejected Shu'aib became as if they had never been in the homes where they had flourished: the men who rejected Shu'aib — it was they who were ruined!

93. So Shu'aib left them, saying: "O my people! I did indeed convey to you the messages for which I was sent by my Lord: I gave you good counsel, but how shall I lament over a people who refuse to believe!"

94. Whenever We sent a prophet to a town, We took up its people in suffering and adversity, in order that they might learn humility.

95. Then We changed their suffering into prosperity, until they grew and multiplied, and began to say: "Our fathers (too) were touched by suffering and affluence."...Behold! We called them to account of a sudden, while they realized not (their peril).

96. If the people of the towns had but believed and feared God, We should indeed have opened out to them (all kinds of) blessings

from heaven and earth; but they rejected (the truth), and We brought them to book for their misdeeds.

97. Did the people of the towns feel secure against the coming of Our wrath by night while they were asleep?

98. Or else did they feel secure against its coming in broad daylight while they played about (carefree)?

99. Did they then feel secure against the Plan of God? — But no one can feel secure from the Plan of God, except those (doomed) to ruin!

100. To those who inherit the earth in succession to its (previous) possessors, is it not a guiding (lesson) that, if We so willed, We could punish them (too) for their sins, and seal up their hearts so that they could not hear?

101. Such were the towns whose story We (thus) relate unto thee: there came indeed to them their Apostles with clear (Signs): but they would not believe what they had rejected before. Thus doth God seal up the heart of those who reject faith.

102. Most of them We found not men (true) to their covenant: but most of them We found rebellious and disobedient.

103. Then after them We sent Moses with Our Signs to Pharaoh and his Chiefs, but they wrongfully rejected them: so see what was the end of those who made mischief.

104. Moses said: "O Pharaoh! I am an Apostle from the Lord of the Worlds.

105. "One for whom it is right to say nothing but truth about God. Now have I come unto you (people), from your Lord with a clear (Sign): so let the Children of Israel depart along with me."

106. (Pharaoh) said: "If indeed thou hast come with a Sign, show it forth — if thou tellest the truth."

107. Then (Moses) threw his rod, and behold! it was a serpent, plain (for all to see)!

108. And he drew out his hand and behold! it was white to all beholders!

109. Said the Chiefs of the people of Pharaoh: "This is indeed a sorcerer[5] well-versed.

---

[5] Magician

110. "His plan is to get you out of your land: then what is it ye counsel?"

111. They said: "Keep him and his brother in suspense (for a while); and send to the cities men to collect—

112. and bring up to thee all (our) sorcerers well-versed."

113. So there came the sorcerers to Pharaoh: they said, "Of course we shall have a (suitable) reward if we win!"

114. He said: "Yea, (and more), for ye shall in that case be (raised to posts) nearest (to my person)."

115. They said: "O Moses! wilt thou throw (first), or shall we have the (first) throw?"

116. Said Moses: "Throw ye (first)." So when they threw, they bewitched the eyes of the people, and struck terror into them: for they showed a great (feat of) magic.

117. We put it into Moses's mind by inspiration: "Throw (now) thy rod": and Behold! it swallows up straightway[6] all the falsehoods which they fake[7]!

118. Thus truth was confirmed, and all that they did was made of no effect.

119. So the (great ones) were vanquished there and then, and were made to look small.

120. But the sorcerers fell down prostrate in adoration.

121. Saying: "We believe in the Lord of the Worlds.

122. "The Lord of Moses and Aaron."

123. Said Pharaoh: "Believe ye in Him before I give you permission? Surely this is a trick which ye have planned in the city to drive out its people: but soon shall ye know (the consequences).

124. "Be sure I will cut off your hands and your feet on opposite sides, and I will cause you all to die on the cross."

125. They said: "For us, we are but sent back unto our Lord.

126. "But thou dost wreak[8] thy vengeance on us simply because we believed in the Signs of our Lord when they reached us! Our Lord! pour out on us patience and constancy, and take our souls unto thee

---

[6] (Arch.) Immdediately, at once

[7] Hoax, trick

[8] Give satisfaction to (vengeance)

119

as Muslims (who bow to Thy Will)"!

127. Said the Chiefs of Pharaoh's people: "Wilt thou leave Moses and his people, to spread mischief in the land, and to abandon thee and thy gods?" He said: "Their male children will we slay; (only) their females will we save alive; and we have over them (power) irresistible."

128. Said Moses to his people: "Pray for help from God, and (wait) in patience and constancy: for the earth is God's to give as a heritage to such of His servants as He pleaseth; and the end is (best) for the righteous.

129. They said: "We have had (nothing but) trouble, both before and after thou comest to us." He said: "It may be that your Lord will destroy your enemy and make you inheritors in the earth; that so He may try you by your deeds."

130. We punished the people of Pharaoh with years (of drought) and shortness of crops; that they might receive admonition.

131. But when good (times) came, they said, "This is due to us"; when gripped by calamity, they ascribed it to evil omens connected with Moses and those with him! Behold! in truth the omens of evil are theirs in God's sight, but most of them do not understand!

132. They said (to Moses): "Whatever be the Signs thou bringest, to work therewith the sorcery on us, we shall never believe in thee."

133. So We sent (plagues) on them, wholesale death, Locusts, Lice, Frogs, and Blood: Signs openly Self-explained; but they were steeped in arrogance, a people given to sin.

134. Every time the penalty fell on them, they said: "O Moses! on our behalf call on thy Lord in virtue of His promise to thee: if thou wilt remove the penalty from us we shall truly believe in thee, and we shall send away the Children of Israel with thee."

135. But every time We removed the penalty from them according to a fixed term which they had to fulfil — Behold! they broke their word!

136. So We exacted retribution from them: We drowned them in the sea, because they rejected Our Signs, and failed to take warning from them.

137. And We made a people, considered weak (and of no account), inheritors of lands in both East and West, lands whereon We sent

down Our blessings. The fair promise of thy Lord was fulfilled for the Children of Israel, because they had patience and constancy, and We levelled to the ground the great works and fine buildings which Pharaoh and his people erected (with such pride).

138. We took the Children of Israel (with safety) across the sea. They came upon a people devoted entirely to some idols they had. They said: "O Moses! fashion for us a god like unto the gods they have." He said: "Surely ye are a people without knowledge."

139. "As to these folk, the cult they are in is (but) a fragment of a ruin, and vain is the (worship) which they practice."

140. He said: "Shall I seek for you a god other than the (true) God, when it is God who hath endowed you with gifts above the nations?"

141. And remember, We rescued you from Pharaoh's people, who afflicted you with the worst of penalties, who slew your male children and saved alive your females: in that was a momentous[9] trial from your Lord.

142. We appointed for Moses thirty nights, and completed (the period) with ten (more): thus was completed the term (of communion) with his Lord, forty nights. And Moses had charged his brother Aaron (before he went up): "Act for me amongst my people: do right, and follow not the way of those who do mischief."

143. When Moses came to the place appointed by Us, and his Lord addressed him, he said: "O my Lord! show (Thyself) to me, that I may look upon thee." God said: "By no means canst thou see Me (direct); but look upon the Mount; if it abide in its place then shalt thou see Me." When his Lord manifested His Glory on the Mount, He made it as dust and Moses fell down in a swoon. When he recovered his senses he said: "Glory be to Thee! to Thee I turn in repentance, and I am the first to believe."

144. (God) said: "O Moses! I have chosen thee above (other) men, by the mission I (have given thee) and the words I (have spoken to thee): take then the (revelation) which I give thee, and be of those who give thanks."

145. And We ordained laws for him in the tablets in all matters,

---

[9] Important

both commanding and explaining all things, (and said): "Take and hold these with firmness, and enjoin thy people to hold fast by the best in the precepts[10]: soon shall I show you the homes of the wicked — (how they lie desolate)."

146. Those who behave arrogantly on the earth in defiance of right — them will I turn away from My Signs, they will not believe in them; and if they see the way of right conduct, they will not adopt it as the way; but if they see the way of error that is the way they will adopt; for they rejected Our Signs, and failed to take warning from them.

147. Those who reject Our Signs and the meeting in the Hereafter, vain are their deeds: can they expect to be rewarded except as they have wrought[11]?

148. The people of Moses made in his absence, out of their ornaments, the image of a calf, (for worship): it seemed to low[12]: did they not see that it could neither speak to them nor show them the way? They took it for worship and they did wrong.

149. When they repented, and saw that they had erred, they said: "If our Lord have not mercy upon us and forgive us, we shall indeed be of those who perish."

150. When Moses came back to his people, angry and grieved, he said: "Evil it is that ye have done in my place in my absence: did ye make haste to bring on the judgment of your Lord?" He put down the tablets, seized his brother by (the hair of) his head, and dragged him to him. Aaron said: "Son of my mother! The people did indeed reckon me as naught, and went near to slaying me! Make not the enemies rejoice over my misfortune, nor count thou me amongst the people of sin."

151. Moses prayed: "O my Lord! Forgive me and my brother! Admit us to Thy mercy! For Thou art the Most Merciful of those who show mercy!"

152. Those who took the calf (for worship) will indeed be over-whelmed with wrath from their Lord, and with shame in this life:

---

[10] Moral principles, rules, or teachings

[11] Worked or done.

[12] To moo (like a cow), a lowing sound.

thus do We recompense those who invent (falsehoods).

153. But those who do wrong but repent thereafter and (truly) believe, verily Thy Lord is thereafter Oft-Forgiving, Most Merciful.

154. When the anger of Moses was appeased, he took up the tablets: in the writing thereon was guidance and mercy for such as fear their Lord.

155. And Moses chose seventy of his people for Our place of meeting: when they were seized with violent quaking[13], he prayed: "O my Lord! if it had been Thy Will Thou couldst have destroyed, long before, both them and me: wouldst Thou destroy us for the deeds of the foolish ones among us? This is no more than Thy trial: by it Thou causest whom Thou wilt to stray, and Thou leadest whom Thou wilt into the right path. Thou art our protector: so forgive us and give us Thy mercy; for Thou art the best of those who forgive.

156. "And ordain for us that which is good, in this life and in the Hereafter: for we have turned unto Thee." He said: "With My punishment I visit whom I Will; but My Mercy extendeth to all things. That (Mercy) I shall ordain for those who do right, and practice regular charity, and those who believe in Our Signs;

157. "Those who follow the Apostle, the unlettered Prophet, whom they find mentioned in their own (Scriptures); in the Law[14] and the Gospel[15]; for he commands them what is just and forbids them what is evil: he allows them as lawful what is good (and pure) and prohibits them from what is bad (and impure); He releases them from their heavy burdens and from the yokes[16] that are upon them. So it is those who believe in him, honour him, help him, and follow the light which is sent down with him, it is they who will prosper."

158. Say: "O men! I am sent unto you all, as the Apostle of God, to Whom belongeth the dominion of the heavens and the earth: there is no god but He: it is He that giveth both life and death. So believe in God and His Apostle, the unlettered Prophet, who believe in God and His Words: follow him that (so) ye may be guided."

159. Of the people of Moses there is a section who guide and

---

13 Shaking
14 Torah
15 Injil
16 Servitude, or restrictions

do justice in the light of truth.

160. We divided them into twelve tribes or nations. We directed Moses by inspiration, when his (thirsty) people asked him for water: "Strike the rock with thy staff": out of it there gushed forth twelve springs: each group knew its own place for water. We gave them the shade of clouds, and sent down to them manna and quails,[17] (saying): "Eat of the good things We have provided for you": (but they rebelled): to Us they did no harm, but they harmed their own souls.

161. And remember it was said to them: "Dwell in this town and eat therein as ye wish, but say the word of humility and enter the gate in a posture of humility; We shall forgive you your faults; We shall increase (the portion of) those who do good."

162. But the transgressors among them changed the word from that which had been given them; so We sent on them a plague from heaven, for that they repeatedly transgressed.

163. Ask them concerning the town standing close by the sea. Behold! they transgressed in the matter of the Sabbath. For on the day of their Sabbath their fish did come to them, openly holding up their heads, but on the day they had no Sabbath, they came not: thus did We make a trial of them, for they were given to transgression.

164. When some of them said: "Why do ye preach to a people whom God will destroy or visit with a terrible punishment?" — Said the preachers: "To discharge our duty to your Lord and perchance they may fear Him."

165. When they disregarded the warnings that had been given them, We rescued those who forbade evil; but We visited the wrongdoers with a grievous punishment, because they were given to transgression.

166. When in their insolence they transgressed (all) prohibition, We said to them: "Be ye apes, despised and rejected."

167. Behold! thy Lord did declare that He would send against them, to the Day of Judgment, those who would afflict them with grievous penalty. Thy Lord is quick in retribution, but He is also Oft-Forgiving, Most Merciful.

168. We broke them up into sections on this earth. There are among

---

[17] See footnote on Al-Baqarah 2:57.

them some that are the righteous, and some that are the opposite. We have tried them with both prosperity and adversity: in order that they might turn (to us).

169. After them succeeded an (evil) generation: they inherited the Book, but they chose (for themselves) the vanities of this world, saying (for excuse): "(Everything) will be forgiven us." (Even so), if similar vanities came their way, they would (again) seize them. Was not the covenant of the Book taken from them, that they would not ascribe to God anything but the truth? And they study what is in the Book. But best for the righteous is the home in the Hereafter: will ye not understand?

170. As to those who hold fast by the Book and establish regular prayer; never shall We suffer the reward of the righteous to perish.

171. When We shook the Mount over them, as if it had been a canopy, and they thought it was going to fall on them (We said): "Hold firmly, to what We have given you and bring (ever) to re-membrance what is therein; perchance ye may fear God."

172. When thy Lord drew forth from the Children of Adam, from their loins, their descendants, and made them testify concerning themselves, (saying): "Am I not your Lord (who cherishes and sustains you)?" They said: "Yea! we do testify!" (This), lest ye should say on the Day of Judgment: "Of this we were never mindful."

173. Or lest ye should say: "Our fathers before us may have taken false gods but we are (their) descendants after them: wilt thou then destroy us because of the deeds of men who were futile[18]?"

174. Thus do We explain the Signs in detail! and perchance they may turn (unto Us).

175. Relate to them the story of the man to whom We sent Our Signs, but he passed them by: so Satan followed him up, and he went astray.

176. If it had been Our Will We should have elevated him with Our Signs; but he inclined to the earth, and followed his own vain desires. His similitude is that of a dog: if you attack him, he lolls out his tongue, or if you leave him alone he (still) lolls out his tongue. That is the similitude of those who reject Our Signs; so relate the

---

[18] Useless

story; perchance they may reflect.

177. Evil as an example are people who reject Our Signs and wrong their own souls.

178. Whom God doth guide, he is on the right path: whom He rejects from His guidance, such are the persons who perish.

179. Many are the Jinns and men, We have made for Hell: They have hearts wherewith they understand not, eyes wherewith they see not, and ears wherewith they hear not. They are like cattle, nay more misguided: for they are heedless (of warning).

180. The most beautiful names belong to God: so call on Him by them; but shun such men as use profanity[19] in His names: for what they do, they will soon be requited.

181. Of those We have created are people who direct (others) with truth, and dispense justice therewith.

182. Those who reject Our Signs, We shall gradually visit with punishment, in ways they perceive not.

183. Respite will I grant unto them: for My scheme is strong (and unfailing).

184. Do they not reflect? Their Companion is not seized with madness: he is but a perspicuous[20] warner.

185. Do they see nothing in the government of the heavens and the earth and all that God hath created? (Do they not see) that it may well be that their term is nigh drawing to an end? In what message after this will they then believe?

186. To such as God rejects from His guidance, there can be no guide; He will leave them in their trespasses, wandering in distraction.

187. They ask thee about the (final) Hour, when will be its appointed time? Say: "The knowledge thereof is with my Lord (alone): none but He can reveal as to when it will occur. Heavy were its burden through the heavens and the earth. Only, all of a sudden, will it come to you. They ask thee as if thou wert eager in search thereof: Say: "The knowledge thereof is with God (alone), but most men know not."

188. Say: "I have no power over any good or harm to myself except

---

[19] Irreverence, blasphemy
[20] Plain, easily understood

as God Willeth. If I had knowledge of the unseen, I should have multiplied all good, and no evil should have touched me, I am but a warner, and a bringer of glad tidings to those who have faith."

189. It is He who created you from a single person, and made his mate of like nature, in order that he might dwell with her (in love). When they are united, she bears a light burden and carries it about (unnoticed). When she grows heavy, they both pray to God their Lord, (saying): "If Thou givest us a goodly child, we vow we shall (ever) be grateful."

190. But when He giveth them a goodly child, they ascribe to others a share in the gift they have received: but God is exalted, high above the partners they ascribe to Him.

191. Do they indeed ascribe to Him as partners things that can create nothing, but are themselves created?

192. No aid can they give them, nor can they aid themselves!

193. If ye call them to guidance, they will not obey: for you it is the same whether ye call them or ye hold your peace!

194. Verily those whom ye call upon besides God are servants like unto you: call upon them, and let them listen to your prayer, if ye are (indeed) truthful!

195. Have they feet to walk with? or hands to lay hold with? or eyes to see with? or ears to hear with? Say: "Call your 'god-partners,' scheme (your worst) against me, and give me no respite!

196. "For my Protector is God, Who revealed the Book (from time to time), and He will choose and befriend the righteous.

197. "But those ye call upon besides Him, are unable to help you, and indeed to help themselves."

198. If thou callest them to guidance, they hear not. Thou wilt see them looking at thee, but they see not.

199. Hold to forgiveness; command what is right; but turn away from the ignorant.

200. If a suggestion from Satan assail thy (mind), seek refuge with God; for He heareth and knoweth (all things).

201. Those who fear God, when a thought of evil from Satan assaults them, bring God to remembrance when lo! they see (aright)!

202. But their brethren (the evil ones) plunge them deeper into error, and never relax (their efforts).

203. If thou bring them not a revelation, they say: "Why hast thou not got it together?" Say: "I but follow what is revealed to me from my Lord: This is (nothing but) lights from your Lord, and Guidance, and Mercy, for any who have faith.

204. When the Qur'an is read, listen to it with attention, and hold your peace: that ye may receive Mercy.

205. And do thou (O reader!) bring thy Lord to remembrance in thy (very) soul, with humility and in reverence, without loudness in words, in the mornings and evenings; and be not thou of those who are unheedful.

206. Those who are near to thy Lord, disdain not to do Him worship: they celebrate His praises, and bow down before Him.

Chapter 8
Sürah Al-Anfal (Spoils of War)
Revealed at Madinah, 75 verses.

In the name of God, Most Gracious, Most Merciful.

1. They ask thee concerning (things taken as) spoils of war. Say: "(Such) spoils are at the disposal of God and the Apostle: so fear God, and keep straight the relations between yourselves: obey God and His Apostle, if ye do believe."

2. For, Believers are those who, when God is mentioned, feel a tremor in their hearts, and when they hear His Signs rehearsed, find their faith strengthened, and put (all) their trust in their Lord;

3. Who establish regular prayers and spend (freely) out of the gifts We have given them for sustenance:

4. Such in truth are the Believers: they have grades of dignity with their Lord, and forgiveness, and generous sustenance.

5. Just as thy Lord ordered thee out of thy house in truth even though a party among the Believers disliked it.

6. Disputing with thee concerning the truth after it was made manifest, as if they were being driven to death and they (actually) saw it.

7. Behold! God promised you one of the two (enemy) parties, that it should be yours: ye wished that the one unarmed should be yours, but God willed to justify the truth according to His words, and to cut off the roots of the Unbelievers.

8. That He might justify and prove falsehood false, distasteful though it be to those in guilt.

9. Remember ye implored the assistance of your Lord, and He answered you: "I will assist you with a thousand of the angels, ranks on ranks."

10. God made it but a message of hope, and an assurance to your hearts: (in any case) there is no help except from God: and God is Exalted in Power, Wise.

11. Remember He covered you with a sort of drowsiness, to give you calm as from Himself, and He caused rain to descend on you from heaven, to clean you therewith, to remove from you the stain of Satan, to strengthen your hearts, and to plant your feet firmly therewith.

12. Remember thy Lord inspired the angels (with the message): "I am with you: give firmness to the Believers: I will instil terror into the hearts of the Unbelievers: smite ye above their necks and smite all their finger-tips off them."

13. This because they contended against God and His Apostle: if any contend against God and His Apostle, God is strict in punishment.

14. Thus (will it be said): "Taste ye then of the (punishment): for those who resist God, is the penalty of the Fire."

15. O ye who believe! when ye meet the Unbelievers in hostile array, never turn your backs to them.

16. If any do turn his back to them on such a day unless it be in a stratagem[1] of war, or to retreat to a troop (of his own) He draws on himself the wrath of God, and his abode is Hell — an evil refuge (indeed)!

17. It is not ye who slew them; it was God: when thou threwest (a handful of dust), it was not thy act, but God's: in order that He might test the Believers by a gracious trial from Himself: for God

---

[1] Plan, scheme

is He who heareth and knoweth (all things).

18. That, and also because God is He who makes feeble the plans and stratagems of the Unbelievers.

19. (O Unbelievers!) if ye prayed for victory and judgment, now hath the judgment come to you: if ye desist (from wrong), it will be best for you: if ye return (to the attack) so shall We. Not the least good will your forces be to you even if they were multiplied: for verily God is with those who believe.

20. O ye who believe! obey God and His Apostle, and turn not away from him when ye hear (him speak).

21. Nor be like those who say, "We hear," but listen not:

22. For the worst of beasts in the sight of God are the deaf and the dumb, those who understand not.

23. If God had found in them any good, He would indeed have made them listen; (as it is), if He had made them listen, they would but have turned back and declined (faith).

24. O ye who believe! give your response to God and His Apostle, when He calleth you to that which will give you life; and know that God cometh in between a man and his heart, and that it is He to Whom Ye shall (all) be gathered.

25. And fear tumult or oppression, which affecteth not in particular (only) those of you who do wrong and know that God is strict in punishment.

26. Call to mind when ye were a small (band), despised through the land, and afraid that men might despoil[2] and kidnap you; but He provided a safe asylum for you, strengthened you with His aid, and gave you good things for sustenance: that ye might be grateful.

27. O ye who believe! betray not the trust of God and the Apostle, nor misappropriate knowingly things entrusted to you.

28. And know ye that your possessions and your progeny are but a trial; and that it is God with whom lies your highest reward.

29. O ye who believe! if ye fear God, He will grant you a criterion (to judge between right and wrong), remove from you (all) evil (that may afflict) you, and forgive you: for God is the Lord of grace unbounded.

---

[2] Rob

30. Remember how the Unbelievers plotted against thee, to keep thee in bonds[3], or slay thee, or get thee out (of thy home). They plot and plan, and God too plans, but the best of planners is God.

31. When Our Signs are rehearsed to them, they say: "We have heard this (before): if we wished, we could say (words) like these: these are nothing but tales of the ancients."

32. Remember how they said: "O God! if this is indeed the truth from Thee, rain down on us a shower of stones from the sky, or send us a grievous penalty."

33. But God was not going to send them a penalty whilst thou wast amongst them; nor was He going to send it whilst they could ask for pardon.

34. But what plea have they that God should not punish them, when they keep out (men) from the sacred Mosque — and they are not its guardians? No men can be its guardians except the righteous; but most of them do not understand.

35. Their prayer at the House (of God) is nothing but whistling and clapping of hands: (its only answer can be), "Taste ye the penalty because ye blasphemed."

36. The Unbelievers spend their wealth to hinder (men) from the path of God, and so will they continue to spend; but in the end they will have (only) regrets and sighs; at length they will be overcome: and the Unbelievers will be gathered together to Hell.

37. In order that God may separate the impure from the pure, put the impure, one on another, heap them together, and cast them into Hell. They will be the ones to have lost.

38. Say to the Unbelievers, if (now) they desist (from unbelief), their past would be forgiven them; but if they persist, the punishment of those before them is already (a matter of warning for them).

39. And fight them on until there is no more tumult or oppression, and there prevail justice and faith in God altogether and everywhere; but if they cease, verily God doth see all that they do.

40. If they refuse, be sure that God is your Protector — the Best to protect and the Best to help.

41. And know that out of all the booty that ye may acquire (in

---

[3] "To keep in bonds," that is, to imprison, restraining one's physical freedom.

war), a fifth share is assigned to God, — and to the Apostle, and
to near relatives, orphans, the needy, and the wayfarer, — if ye do
believe in God and in the revelation We sent down to Our servant
on the Day of Testing, — the Day of the Meeting of the two forces.
For God hath power over all things.

42. Remember ye were on the hither side of the valley, and they
on the farther side, and the caravan on lower ground than ye. Even
if ye had made a mutual appointment to meet, ye would certainly
have failed in the appointment: but (thus ye met), that God might
accomplish a matter already enacted; that those who died might die
after a clear Sign (had been given), and those who lived might live
after a clear Sign (had been given). And verily God is He Who heareth
and knoweth (all things).

43. Remember in thy dream God showed them to thee as few:
if He had shown them to thee as many, ye would surely have been
discouraged, and ye would surely have disputed in (your) decision:
but God saved (you): for He knoweth well the (secrets) of (all) hearts.

44. And remember when ye met, He showed them to you as few
in your eyes, and He made you appear as contemptible[4] in their eyes:
That God might accomplish a matter already enacted: for to God do
all questions go back (for decision).

45. O ye who believe! when ye meet a force, be firm, and call
God in remembrance much (and often); that ye may prosper.

46. And obey God and His Apostle; and fall into no disputes, lest
ye lose heart and your power depart; and be patient and persevering:
for God is with those who patiently persevere.

47. And be not like those who started from their homes insolently
and to be seen of men, and to hinder (men) from the path of God:
for God compasseth round about all that they do.

48. Remember Satan made their (sinful) acts seem alluring to them,
and said: "No one among men can overcome you this day, while I
am near to you": but when the two forces came in sight of each other,
he turned on his heels, and said: "Lo! I am clear of you; lo! I see
what ye see not; lo! I fear God; for God is strict in punishment.

49. Lo! the hypocrites say, and those in whose hearts is a disease:

---

[4] Deserving contempt (for being weak and small in numbers).

"These people, — their religion has misled them." But if any trust in God, behold! God is Exalted in might, Wise.

50. If thou couldst see, when the angels take the souls of the Unbelievers (at death), (how) they smite their faces and their backs (saying): "Taste the penalty of the blazing Fire—

51. "Because of (the deeds) which your (own) hands sent forth: for God is never unjust to His servants:

52. "(Deeds) after the manner of the people of Pharaoh and of those before them: they rejected the Signs of God, and God punished them for their crimes: for God is Strong, and Strict in punishment:

53. "Because God will never change the grace which He hath bestowed on a people until they change what is in their (own) souls: and verily God is He Who heareth and knoweth (all things)."

54. "(Deeds) after the manner of the people of Pharaoh and those before them": they treated as false the Signs of their Lord; so We destroyed them for their crimes, and We drowned the people of Pharaoh: for they were all oppressors and wrongdoers.

55. For the worst of beasts in the sight of God are those who reject Him: They will not believe.

56. They are those with whom thou didst make a covenant, but they break their covenant every time and they have not the fear (of God).

57. If ye gain the mastery over them in war, disperse, with them, those who follow them, that they may remember.

58. If thou fearest treachery from any group, throw back (their covenant) to them, (so as to be) on equal terms: for God loveth not the treacherous.

59. Let not the Unbelievers think that they can get the better (of the godly): they will never frustrate (them).

60. Against them make ready your strength to the utmost of your power, including steeds of war, to strike terror into (the hearts of) the enemies, of God and your enemies, and others besides, whom ye may not know, but whom God doth know. Whatever ye shall spend in the cause of God, shall be repaid unto you, and ye shall not be treated unjustly.

61. But if the enemy incline towards peace, do thou (also) incline towards peace, and trust in God: for He is the one that heareth and

knoweth (all things).

62. Should they intend to deceive thee, verily God sufficeth thee: He it is that hath strengthened thee with His aid and with (the company of) the Believers:

63. And (moreover) He hath put affection between their hearts: not if thou hadst spent all that is in the earth, couldst thou have produced that affection, but God hath done it: for He is Exalted in might, Wise.

64. O Apostle! sufficient unto thee is God, (unto thee) and unto those who follow thee among the Believers.

65. O Apostle! rouse the Believers to the fight. If there are twenty amongst you, patient and persevering, they will vanquish two hundred: if a hundred, they will vanquish a thousand of the Unbelievers: for these are a people without understanding.

66. For the present, God hath lightened your (task), for He knoweth that there is a weak spot in you: but (even so), if there are a hundred of you, patient and persevering, they will vanquish two hundred, and if a thousand, they will vanquish two thousand, with the leave of God: for God is with those who patiently persevere.

67. It is not fitting for an Apostle that he should have prisoners of war until he hath thoroughly subdued the land. Ye look for the temporal goods of this world; but God looketh to the Hereafter; and God is Exalted in might, Wise.

68. Had it not been for a previous ordainment[5] from God, a severe penalty would have reached you for the (ransom) that ye took.

69. But (now) enjoy what ye took in war, lawful and good: but fear God: for God is Oft-Forgiving, Most Merciful.

70. O Apostle! say to those who are captives in your hands: "If God findeth any good in your hearts, He will give you something better than what has been taken from you, and He will forgive you: for God Is Oft-Forgiving, Most Merciful."

71. But if they have treacherous designs against thee, (O Apostle!) they have already been in treason against God, and so hath He given (thee) power over them and God is He who hath (full) knowledge and wisdom.

---

[5] Decree, decision

72. Those who believed, and adopted exile, and fought for the faith, with their property and their persons, in the cause of God, as well as those who gave (them) asylum and aid, these are (all) friends and protectors, one of another. As to those who believed but came not into exile, ye owe no duty of protection to them until they seek your aid in religion, it is your duty to help them, except against a people with whom ye have a treaty of mutual alliance: and (remember) God seeth all that ye do.

73. The Unbelievers are protectors, one of another: unless ye do this, (protect each other), there would be tumult and oppression on earth, and great mischief.

74. Those who believe, and adopt exile, and fight for the faith, in the cause of God, as well as those who give (them) asylum and aid, these are (all) in very truth the Believers: for them is the forgiveness of sins and a provision most generous.

75. And those who accept faith subsequently, and adopt exile, and fight for the faith in your company — they are of you. But kindred by blood have prior rights against each other in the Book of God. Verily God is well acquainted with all things.

Chapter 9
Sürah At-Tawbah (Repentance)
Revealed at Madinah, 129 verses.

1. A (declaration) of immunity from God and His Apostle, to those of the pagans with whom ye have contracted mutual alliances: —

2. Go ye, then, for four months, backwards and forwards, (as ye will), throughout the land, but know ye that ye cannot frustrate God (by your falsehood) but that God will cover with shame those who reject Him.

3. And an announcement from God and His Apostle, to the people (assembled) on the Day of the Great Pilgrimage, that God and His Apostle dissolve (treaty) obligations with the pagans. If, then, ye

repent, it were best for you; but if ye turn away, know ye that ye cannot frustrate God. And proclaim a grievous penalty to those who reject faith.

4. (But the treaties are) not dissolved with those pagans with whom ye have entered into alliance and who have not subsequently failed you in aught, nor aided anyone against you. So fulfil your engagements with them to the end of their term: for God loveth the righteous.

5. But when the forbidden months are past, then fight and slay the pagans wherever ye find them and seize them, beleaguer[1] them and lie in wait for them in every stratagem (of war); but if they repent, and establish regular prayers and practice regular charity, then open the way for them: for God is Oft-Forgiving, Most Merciful.

6. If one amongst the pagans ask thee for asylum, grant it to him, so that he may hear the word of God and then escort him to where he can be secure: that is because they are men without knowledge.

7. How can there be a league before God and His Apostle, with the pagans, except those with whom ye made a treaty near the Sacred Mosque? As long as these stand true to you, stand ye true to them: For God doth love the righteous.

8. How (can there be such a league), seeing that if they get an advantage over you, they respect not in you the ties either of kinship or of covenant? With (fair words from) their mouths they entice you, but their hearts are averse from you; and most of them are rebellious and wicked.

9. The Signs of God have they sold for a miserable price, and (many) have they hindered from His way: evil indeed are the deeds they have done.

10. In a Believer they respect not the ties either of kinship or of covenant! It is they who have transgressed all bounds.

11. But (even so), if they repent, establish regular prayers, and practice regular charity, they are your brethren in faith: (thus) do We explain Signs in detail, for those who understand.

12. But if they violate their oaths after their covenant, and taunt you for your faith, fight ye the chiefs of unfaith: for their oaths are nothing to them: that thus they may be restrained.

---

[1] Besiege

13. Will ye not fight people who violated their oaths, plotted to expel the Apostle, and took the aggressive by being the first (to assault) you? Do ye fear them? Nay, it is God whom ye should more justly fear, if ye believe!

14. Fight them, and God will punish them by your hands, cover them with shame, help you (to victory) over them, heal the breasts of Believers,

15. And still[2] the indignation of their hearts. For Allah will turn (in mercy) to whom He will; and Allah is All-Knowing, All-Wise.

16. Or think ye that ye shall be abandoned, as though God did not know those among you who strive with might and main, and take none for friends and protectors except God, His Apostle, and the (community of) Believers? But God is well-acquainted with (all) that ye do.

17. It is not for such as join gods with God, to visit or maintain the mosques of God while they witness against their own souls to infidelity. The works of such bear no fruit: in Fire shall they dwell.

18. The mosques of God shall be visited and maintained by such as believe in God and the Last Day, establish regular prayers, and practice regular charity, and fear none (at all) except God. It is they who are expected to be on true guidance.

19. Do ye make the giving of drink to pilgrims, or the maintenance of the Sacred Mosque, equal to (the pious service of) those who believe in God and the Last Day, and strive with might and main[3] in the cause of God? They are not comparable in the sight of God: and God guides not those who do wrong.

20. Those who believe, and suffer exile and strive with might and main, in God's cause, with their goods and their persons, have the highest rank in the sight of God: They are the people who will achieve (salvation).

21. Their Lord doth give them Glad tidings of a Mercy from Himself, of His good pleasure, and of gardens for them, wherein are delights that endure.

22. They will dwell therein forever. Verily in God's presence is

---

[2] Soothe, pacify.
[3] With all one's power.

a reward, the greatest (of all).

23. O ye who believe! take not for protectors your fathers and your brothers if they love infidelity above faith: if any of you do so, they do wrong.

24. Say: If it be that your fathers, your sons, your brothers, your mates, or your kindred; the wealth that ye have gained; the commerce in which ye fear a decline; or the dwellings in which ye delight, are dearer to you than God, or His Apostle, or the striving in His cause; then wait until God brings about His decision: and God guides not the rebellious.

25. Assuredly God did help you in many battlefields and on the day of Hunain: Behold! your great numbers elated[4] you, but they availed you naught: the land, for all that it is wide, did constrain[5] you, and ye turned back in retreat.

26. But God did pour His calm on the Apostle and on the Believers and sent down forces which ye saw not: He punished the Unbelievers: thus doth He reward those without faith.

27. Again will God, after this, turn (in mercy) to whom He will: for God is Oft-Forgiving, Most Merciful.

28. O ye who believe! truly the pagans are unclean; so let them not, after this year of theirs, approach the Sacred Mosque. And if ye fear poverty, soon will God enrich you, if He wills, out of his bounty, for God is All-Knowing, All-Wise.

29. Fight those who believe not in God nor the Last Day, nor hold that forbidden which hath been forbidden by God and His Apostle, nor acknowledge the religion of truth, (even if they are) of the People of the Book, until they pay the Jizya[6] with willing submission, and feel themselves subdued.

30. The Jews call Uzair a son of God, and the Christians call Christ the son of God. That is a saying from their mouths; (in this) they but imitate what the Unbelievers of old used to say. God's curse be on them: how they are deluded away from the truth!

31. They take their priests and their anchorites[7] to be their lords

---

[4] To make proud.
[5] Confine forcibly, become narrow and difficult.
[6] Poll-tax
[7] Hermits

in derogation[8] of God, and (they take as their Lord) Christ the son of Mary; Yet they were commanded to worship but one God: there is no god but He. Praise and glory to Him: (far is He) from having the partners they associate (with Him).

32. Fain[9] would they extinguish God's light with their mouths, but God will not allow but that His light should be perfected, even though the Unbelievers may detest (it).

33. It is He who hath sent His Apostle with guidance and religion of truth, to proclaim it over all religions, even though the pagans may detest (it).

34. O ye who believe! there are indeed many among the priests and anchorites, who in falsehood devour the substance[10] of men and hinder (them) from the way of God. And there are those who bury gold and silver and spend it not in the way of God: announce unto them a most grievous penalty.

35. On the day when heat will be produced out of that (wealth) in the fire of Hell, and with it will be branded their foreheads, their flanks[11], and their backs, "This is the (treasure) which ye buried for yourselves: taste ye, then, the (treasures) ye buried!"

36. The number of months in the sight of God is twelve (in a year) so ordained by Him the day He created the heavens and the earth; of them four are sacred; that is the straight usage. So wrong not yourselves therein, and fight the pagans all together as they fight you all together. But know that God is with those who restrain themselves.

37. Verily the transposing[12] (of a prohibited month) is an addition to unbelief: the Unbelievers are led to wrong thereby: for they make it lawful one year, and forbidden another year, in order to adjust the number of months forbidden by God and make such forbidden ones lawful. The evil of their course seems pleasing to them. But God guideth not those who reject faith.

38. O ye who believe! what is the matter with you, then, when ye are asked to go forth in the cause of God, ye cling heavily to the

---

[8] Discredit, belittling (His authority, position or majesty)
[9] Gladly
[10] Property, wealth
[11] Sides.
[12] Transfering, interchanging.

earth? Do ye prefer the life of this world to the Hereafter? But little is the comfort of this life, as compared with the Hereafter.

39. Unless ye go forth, He will punish you with a grievous penalty, and put others in your place; but Him ye would not harm in the least. For God hath power over all things.

40. If ye help not (your Leader), (it is no matter): for God did indeed help him: when the Unbelievers drove him out: he had no more than one companion: they two were in the cave, and he said to his companion, "Have no fear, for God is with us": then God sent down His peace upon him, and strengthened him with forces which ye saw not, and humbled to the depths the word of the Unbelievers. But the word of God is exalted to the heights: for God is Exalted in might, Wise.

41. Go ye forth, (whether equipped) lightly or heavily, and strive and struggle, with your goods and your persons, in the cause of God. That is best for you, if ye (but) knew.

42. If there had been immediate gain (in sight), and the journey easy, they would (all) without doubt have followed thee, but the distance was long, (and weighed) on them. They would indeed swear by God, "If we only could, we should certainly have come out with you": they would destroy their own souls; for God doth know that they are certainly lying.

43. God give thee grace! Why didst thou grant them exemption until those who told the truth were seen by thee in a clear light, and thou hadst proved the liars?

44. Those who believe in God and the Last Day ask thee for no exemption from fighting with their goods and persons. And God knoweth well those who do their duty.

45. Only those ask thee for exemption who believe not in God and the Last Day, and whose hearts are in doubt, so that they are tossed in their doubts to and fro.

46. If they had intended to come out, they would certainly have made some preparation therefor; but God was averse to their being sent forth; so He made them lag behind and they were told, "Sit ye among those who sit (inactive)."

47. If they had come out with you, they would not have added to your (strength) but only (made for) disorder, hurrying to and fro

in your midst and sowing sedition[13] among you, and there would have been some among you who would have listened to them. But God knoweth well those who do wrong.

48. Indeed they had plotted sedition before, and upset matters for thee, until the Truth arrived, and the Decree of God became manifest, much to their disgust.

49. Among them is (many) a man who says: "Grant me exemption and draw me not into trial." Have they not fallen into trial already? And indeed Hell surrounds the Unbelievers (on all sides).

50. If good befalls thee, it grieves them; but if a misfortune befalls thee, they say, "We took indeed our precautions beforehand," and they turn away rejoicing.

51. Say: "Nothing will happen to us except what God has decreed for us: He is our Protector": and on God let the Believers put their trust.

52. Say: "Can you expect for us (any fate) other than one of two glorious things (martyrdom or victory)? But we can expect for you either that God will send His punishment from Himself, or by our hands. So wait (expectant); we too will wait with you."

53. Say: "Spend (for the cause) willingly or unwillingly: not from you will it be accepted: for ye are indeed a people rebellious and wicked."

54. The only reasons why their contributions are not accepted are: that they reject God and His Apostle; that they come to prayer without earnestness; and that they offer contributions unwillingly.

55. Let not their wealth nor their (following in) sons dazzle thee: in reality God's plan is to punish them with these things in this life and that their souls may perish in their (very) denial of God.

56. They swear by God that they are indeed of you; but they are not of you; yet they are afraid (to appear in their true colors).

57. If they could find a place to flee to, or caves, or a place of concealment, they would turn straightway thereto, with an obstinate rush.

58. And among them are men who slander thee in the matter of (the distribution of) the alms. If they are given part thereof, they are

---

[13] Rebellion, treason

pleased, but if not, behold! they are indignant!

59. If only they had been content with what God and His Apostle gave them, and had said, "Sufficient unto us is God! God and His Apostle will soon give us of His bounty: to God do we turn our hopes!" (that would have been the right course).

60. Alms are for the poor and the needy, and those employed to administer the (funds); for those whose hearts have been (recently) reconciled (to truth); for those in bondage and in debt; in the cause of God; and for the wayfarer: (thus is it) ordained by God, and God is full of knowledge and wisdom.

61. Among them are men who molest the Prophet and say, "He is (all) ear." Say, "He listens to what is best for you; he believes in God, has faith in the Believers, and is a Mercy to those of you who believe": but those who molest the Apostle will have a grievous penalty.

62. To you they swear by God. In order to please you: but it is more fitting that they should please God and His Apostle if they are Believers.

63. Know they not that for those who oppose God and His apostle, is the fire of Hell? wherein they shall dwell. That is the supreme disgrace.

64. The Hypocrites are afraid lest a Sūrah should be sent down about them, showing them what is (really passing) in their hearts. Say: "Mock ye! but verily God will bring to light all that ye fear (should be revealed)."

65. If thou dost question them, they declare (with emphasis): "We were only talking idly and in play." Say: "Was it at God, and His Signs, and His Apostle, that ye were mocking?"

66. Make ye no excuses: ye have rejected faith after ye had accepted it. If We pardon some of you, We will punish others amongst you, for that they are in sin.

67. The Hypocrites, men and women, (have an understanding) with each other: they enjoin evil, and forbid what is just, and are close with their hands. They have forgotten God; so He hath forgotten them. Verily the Hypocrites are rebellious and perverse.

68. God hath promised the Hypocrites, men and women, and the rejecters of Faith, the fire of Hell: therein shall they dwell: sufficient

is it for them: for them is the curse of God, and an enduring punishment—

69. As in the case of those before you: they were mightier than you in power and more flourishing in wealth and children. They had their enjoyment of their portion: and ye have of yours, as did those before you; and ye indulge in idle talk as they did. They! — Their works are fruitless in this world and in the Hereafter, and they will lose (all spiritual good).

70. Hath not the story reached them of those before them? The people of Noah, and 'Ad, and Thamüd; the people of Abraham, the men of Madyan, and the cities overthrown. To them came their Apostles with Clear Signs. It is not God who wrongs them, but they wrong their own souls.

71. The Believers, men and women, are protectors, one of another: they enjoin what is just, and forbid what is evil: they observe regular prayers, practice regular charity, and obey God and His Apostle. On them will God pour His mercy: for God is Exalted in power, Wise.

72. God hath promised to Believers, men and women, Gardens under which rivers flow, to dwell therein, and beautiful mansions in Gardens of everlasting bliss. But the greatest bliss is the Good Pleasure of God: that is the supreme felicity[14].

73. O Prophet! strive hard against the Unbelievers and the Hypocrites, and be firm against them. Their abode is Hell — an evil refuge indeed.

74. They swear by God that they said nothing (evil), but indeed they uttered blasphemy, and they did it after accepting Islam; and they meditated a plot which they were unable to carry out: this revenge of theirs was (their) only return for the bounty with which God and His Apostle had enriched them! If they repent, it will be best for them; but if they turn back (to their evil ways), God will punish them with a grievous penalty in this life and in the Hereafter: they shall have none on earth to protect or help them.

75. Amongst them are men who made a covenant with God that if He bestowed on them of His bounty, they would give (largely) in charity, and be truly amongst those who are righteous.

76. But when He did bestow of His bounty, they became covetous[15],

---

14 Bliss, delight.
15 Jealous, eagerly desirous

and turned back (from their covenant), averse (from its fulfillment).

77. So He hath put as a consequence hypocrisy into their hearts, (to last) till the Day whereon they shall meet Him: because they broke their covenant with God, and because they lied (again and again).

78. Know they not that God doth know their secret (thoughts) and their secret counsels, and that God knoweth well all things unseen?

79. Those who slander such of the Believers as give themselves freely to (deeds of) charity, as well as such as can find nothing to give except the fruits of their labor, and throw ridicule on them, God will throw back their ridicule on them: and they shall have a grievous penalty.

80. Whether thou ask for their forgiveness or not, (their sin is unforgivable): if thou ask seventy times for their forgiveness, God will not forgive them: because they have rejected God and His Apostle; and God guideth not those who are perversely rebellious.

81. Those who were left behind (in the Tabuk expedition) rejoiced in their inaction behind the back of the Apostle of God: they hated to strive and fight, with their goods and their persons, in the cause of God: they said, "Go not forth in the heat." Say, "The fire of Hell is fiercer in heat." If only they could understand!

82. Let them laugh a little: much will they weep: a recompense for the (evil) that they do.

83. If, then, God bring thee back to any of them, and they ask thy permission to come out (with thee), say: "Never shall ye come out with me, nor fight an enemy with me: for ye preferred to sit inactive on the first occasion: then sit ye (now) with those who lag behind."

84. Nor do thou ever pray for any of them that dies, nor stand at his grave: for they rejected God and His Apostle, and died in a state of perverse rebellion.

85. Nor let their wealth nor their (following in) sons dazzle thee: God's plan is to punish them with these things in this world, and that their souls may perish in their (very) denial of God.

86. When a Sūrah comes down, enjoining them to believe in God and to strive and fight along with His Apostle, those with wealth and influence among them ask thee for exemption, and say: "Leave us (behind): we would be with those who sit (at home)."

87. They prefer to be with (the women), who remain behind (at

home): their hearts are sealed and so they understand not.

88. But the Apostle, and those who believe with him, strive and fight with their wealth and their persons: for them are (all) good things: and it is they who will prosper.

89. God hath prepared for them Gardens under which rivers flow, to dwell therein: that is the supreme felicity.

90. And there were, among the desert Arabs (also), men who made excuses and came to claim exemption; and those who were false to God and His Apostle (merely) sat inactive. Soon will a grievous penalty seize the Unbelievers among them.

91. There is no blame on those who are infirm, or ill, or who find no resources to spend (on the cause), if they are sincere (in duty) to God and His Apostle: no ground (of complaint) can there be against such as do right: and God is Oft-Forgiving, Most Merciful.

92. Nor (is there blame) on those who came to thee to be provided with mounts, and when thou saidst, "I can find no mounts for you," they turned back, their eyes streaming with tears of grief that they had no resources wherewith to provide the expenses.

93. The ground (of complaint) is against such as claim exemption while they are rich. They prefer to stay with the (women) who remain behind: God hath sealed their hearts; so they know not (what they miss).

94. They will present their excuses to you when ye return to them. Say thou: "Present no excuses: we shall not believe you: God hath already informed us of the true state of matters concerning you: it is your actions that God and His Apostle will observe: in the end will ye be brought back to Him who knoweth what is hidden and what is open: then will He show you the truth of all that ye did."

95. They will swear to you by God, when ye return to them, that ye may leave them alone. So leave them alone: For they are an abomination, and Hell is their dwelling place, a fitting recompense for the (evil) that they did.

96. They will swear unto you, that ye may be pleased with them. But if ye are pleased with them, God is not pleased with those who disobey.

97. The Arabs of the desert are the worst in unbelief and hypocrisy, and most fitted to be in ignorance of the command which God hath

sent down to His Apostle: but God is All-Knowing, All-Wise.

98. Some of the desert Arabs look upon their payments as a fine, and watch for disasters for you: on them be the disaster of evil: for God is He that heareth and knoweth (all things).

99. But some of the desert Arabs believe in God and the Last Day, and look on their payments as pious gifts bringing them nearer to God and obtaining the prayers of the Apostle. Aye, indeed they bring them nearer (to Him): soon will God admit them to His Mercy: for God is Oft-Forgiving, Most Merciful.

100. The vanguard (of Islam) — the first of those who forsook (their homes) and of those who gave them aid, and (also) those who follow them in (all) good deeds, well pleased is God with them, as are they with Him: for them hath He prepared Gardens under which rivers flow, to dwell therein forever: that is the supreme felicity.

101. Certain of the desert Arabs round about you are hypocrites, as well as (desert Arabs) among the Madinah folk: they are obstinate in hypocrisy: thou knowest them not: We know them: twice shall We punish them and in addition shall they be sent to a grievous penalty.

102. Others (there are who) have acknowledged their wrong-doings: they have mixed an act that was good with another that was evil. Perhaps God will turn unto them (in mercy): for God is Oft-Forgiving, Most Merciful.

103. Of their goods take alms, that so thou mightest purify and sanctify them; and pray on their behalf. Verily thy prayers are a source of security for them: and God is One Who heareth and knoweth.

104. Know they not that God doth accept repentance from His votaries[16] and receives their gifts of charity, and that God is verily He, the Oft-Returning, Most-Merciful?

105. And say: "Work (righteousness): soon will God observe your work, and His Apostle, and the Believers: soon will ye be brought back to the Knower of what is hidden and what is open: then will He show you the truth of all that ye did."

106. There are (yet) others, held in suspense for the command of God, whether He will punish them, or turn in mercy to them: and God is All-Knowing, Wise.

---

[16] Devoted servants

107. And there are those who put up a mosque by way of mischief and infidelity, to disunite the Believers, and in preparation for one who warred against God and His Apostle aforetime. They will indeed swear that their intention is nothing but good; but God doth declare that they are certainly liars.

108. Never stand thou forth therein. There is a mosque whose foundation was laid from the first day on piety; it is more worthy of thy standing forth (for prayer) therein. In it are men who love to be purified; and God loveth those who make themselves pure.

109. Which then is best? — he that layeth his foundation on piety to God and His good pleasure? — or he that layeth his foundation on an undermined sand-cliff ready to crumble to pieces? And it doth crumble to pieces with him, into the fire of Hell. And God guideth not people that do wrong.

110. The foundation of those who so build is never free from suspicion and shakiness in their hearts, until their hearts are cut to pieces. And God is All-Knowing, Wise.

111. God hath purchased of the Believers their persons and their goods; for theirs (in return) is the Garden (of Paradise): they fight in His cause, and slay and are slain: a promise binding on Him in truth, through the Law, the Gospel, and the Qur'an: and who is more faithful to his covenant than God? Then rejoice in the bargain which ye have concluded: that is the achievement supreme.

112. Those that turn (to God) in repentance; that serve Him, and praise Him; that wander in devotion to the Cause of God; that bow down and prostrate themselves in prayer; that enjoin good and forbid evil; and observe the limits set by God; — (these do rejoice). So proclaim the glad tidings to the Believers.

113. It is not fitting, for the Prophet and those who believe, that they should pray for forgiveness for pagans, even though they be of kin, after it is clear to them that they are companions of the Fire.

114. And Abraham prayed for his father's forgiveness only because of a promise he had made to him. But when it became clear to him that he was an enemy to God, he dissociated himself from him: for Abraham was most tender-hearted, forbearing.

115. And God will not mislead a people after He hath guided them, in order that He may make clear to them what to fear (and avoid)

— for God hath knowledge of all things.

116. Unto God belongeth the dominion of the heavens and the earth. He giveth life and He taketh it. Except for Him ye have no protector nor helper.

117. God turned with favor to the Prophet, the Muhajirs, and the Ansar, who followed Him in a time of distress, after that the hearts of a part of them had nearly swerved (from duty); but He turned to them (also): for He is unto them Most Kind, Most Merciful.

118. (He turned in mercy also) to the three who were left behind: (they felt guilty) to such a degree that the earth seemed constrained to them, for all its spaciousness and their (very) souls seemed straitened to them, and they perceived that there is no fleeing from God and no refuge but to Himself. Then He turned to them, that they might repent: for God is Oft-Returning, Most Merciful.

119. O ye who believe! fear God and be with those who are true (in word and deed).

120. It was not fitting for the people of Madinah and the Bedouin Arabs of the neighborhood, to refuse to follow God's Apostle, nor to prefer their own lives to his: because nothing could they suffer or do, but was reckoned to their credit as a deed of righteousness, whether they suffered thirst, or fatigue, or hunger, in the cause of God, or trod paths to raise the ire[17] of the Unbelievers, or received any injury whatever from an enemy: for God suffereth not the reward to be lost of those who do good—

121. Nor could they spend anything (for the cause), small or great, nor cut across a valley, but the deed is inscribed to their credit; that God might requite their deed with the best (possible reward).

122. Nor should the believers all go forth together: if a contingent[18] from every expedition remained behind, they could devote themselves to studies in religion, and admonish the people when they return to them, that thus they (may learn) to guard themselves (against evil).

123. O ye who believe! fight the Unbelievers who gird[19] you about, and let them find firmness in you; and know that God is with those

---

[17] Displeasure and hatred

[18] A group

[19] Encircle

who fear Him.

124. Whenever there cometh down a Sūrah, some of them say: "Which of you has had his faith increased by it? Yea, those who believe, their faith is increased, and they do rejoice.

125. But those in whose hearts is a disease, it will add doubt to their doubt, and they will die in a state of unbelief.

126. See they not that they are tried every year once or twice? Yet they turn not in repentance, and they take no heed.

127. Whenever there cometh down a Sūrah, they look at each other, (saying), "Doth anyone see you?" Then they turn aside: God hath turned their hearts (from the light); for they are a people that understand not.

128. Now hath come unto you an Apostle from amongst yourselves: it grieves him that ye should perish: ardently anxious is he over you: to the Believers is he most kind and merciful.

129. But if they turn away, Say: "God sufficeth me: there is no god but He: On Him is my trust — He the Lord of the Throne (Of Glory) Supreme!"

Chapter 10
Sūrah Yunus (Jonah)
Revealed at Makkah, 109 verses.

In the name of God, Most Gracious, Most Merciful.

1. Alif Lām Ra. These are the Ayat of the Book of Wisdom.

2. Is it a matter of wonderment to men that We have sent Our inspiration to a man from among themselves? — that he should warn mankind (of their danger), and give the good news to the Believers that they have before their Lord the lofty rank of Truth, (but) say the Unbelievers: "This is indeed an evident sorcerer!"

3. Verily your Lord is God, Who created the heavens and the earth in six Days, and is firmly established on the Throne (of authority), regulating and governing all things. No intercessor (can plead with Him) except after His leave (hath been obtained). This is God your

Lord; Him therefore serve ye: will ye not celebrate His praises?

4. To Him will be your return — of all of you. The promise of God is true and sure. It is He Who beginneth the process of Creation, and repeateth it, that He may reward with justice those who believe and work righteousness, but those who reject Him will have nothing but draughts[1] of boiling fluids, and a Penalty grievous: because they did reject Him.

5. It is He Who made the sun to be a shining glory and the moon to be a light (of beauty), and measured out stages for her: that ye might know the number of years and the count (of time). Nowise did God create this but in truth and righteousness. (Thus) doth He explain his Signs in detail, for those who understand.

6. Verily, in the alternation of the Night and the Day, and in all that God hath created, in the heavens and the earth, are Signs for those who fear Him.

7. Those who rest not their hope on their meeting with Us, but are pleased and satisfied with the life of the present, and those who heed not Our Signs, —

8. Their abode is the Fire, because of the (evil) they earned.

9. Those who believe, and work righteousness, their Lord will guide them because of their faith: beneath them will flow rivers in Gardens of Bliss.

10. (This will be) their cry therein: "Glory to Thee, O God!" and "Peace" will be their greeting therein! And the close of their cry will be: "Praise be to God, the Cherisher and Sustainer of the Worlds!"

11. If God were to hasten for men the ill (they have earned) as they would fain[2] hasten on the good — then would their respite be settled at once. But We leave those who rest not their hope on their meeting with Us, in their trespasses, wandering in distraction to and fro.

12. When trouble toucheth a man, he crieth unto Us (in all postures) lying down on his side, or sitting, or standing. But when We have solved his trouble, he passeth on his way as if he had never cried to Us for a trouble that touched him! Thus do the deeds of transgressors

---

[1] A dose of liquid etc., single act of drinking.

[2] Gladly

seem fair in their eyes!

13. Generations before you We destroyed when they did wrong: their Apostles came to them with Clear Signs, but they would not believe! Thus do We requite those who sin!

14. Then We made you heirs in the land after them, to see how ye would behave!

15. But when Our Clear Signs are rehearsed unto them, those who rest not their hope on their meeting with Us, say: "Bring us a Reading other than this, or change this." Say: "It is not for me, of my own accord, to change it: I follow naught but what is revealed unto me: if I were to disobey my Lord, I should myself fear the Penalty of a Great Day (to come)."

16. Say: "If God had so willed, I should not have rehearsed it to you, nor would He have made it known to you. A whole lifetime before this have I tarried amongst you: will ye not then understand?"

17. Who doth more wrong than such as forge a lie against God, or deny His Signs? But never will prosper those who sin.

18. They serve, besides God, things that hurt them not nor profit them, and they say: "These are our intercessors with God." Say: "Do ye indeed inform God of something He knows not in the heavens or on earth?— Glory to Him! and far is He above the partners they ascribe (to Him)!"

19. Mankind was but one nation, but differed (later). Had it not been for a word that went forth before from thy Lord, their differences would have been settled between them.

20. They say: "Why is not a Sign sent down to him from his Lord?" Say: "The Unseen is only for God (to know). Then wait ye: I too will wait with you."

21. When We make mankind taste of some mercy after adversity hath touched them, Behold! they take to plotting against our Signs! Say: "Swifter to plan is God!" Verily, Our messengers record all the plots that ye make!

22. He it is Who enableth you to traverse through land and sea; so that ye even board ships — they sail with them with a favorable wind, and they rejoice thereat; then comes a stormy wind and the waves come to them from all sides, and they think they are being overwhelmed: they cry unto God, sincerely offering (their) duty unto

Him, saying, "If Thou dost deliver us from this, we shall truly show our gratitude!"

23. But when He delivereth them, Behold! they transgress insolently through the earth in defiance of right! O mankind! your insolence is against your own souls,—an enjoyment of the life of the Present: in the end, to Us is your return, and We shall show you the truth of all that ye did.

24. The likeness of the life of the present is as the rain which We send down from the skies: by its mingling arises the produce of the earth — which provides food for men and animals: (it grows) till the earth is clad with its golden ornaments and is decked[3] out (in beauty): the people to whom it belongs think they have all powers of disposal over it: there reaches it Our command by night or by day, and We make it like a harvest clean-mown, as if it had not flourished only the day before! Thus do We explain the Signs in detail for those who reflect.

25. But God doth call to the Home of Peace: He doth guide whom He pleaseth to a way that is straight.

26. To those who do right is a goodly (reward)—yea, more (than in measure)! No darkness nor shame shall cover their faces! They are Companions of the Garden; they will abide therein (for aye)!

27. But those who have earned evil will have a reward of like evil: ignominy[4] will cover their (faces): no defender will they have from (the wrath of) God: their faces will be covered, as it were, with pieces from the depth of the darkness of Night: they are Companions of the Fire: they will abide therein (for aye)!

28. One Day shall We gather them all together. Then shall We say to those who joined gods (with Us): "To your place! ye and those ye joined as 'partners.'" We shall separate them, and their "partners" shall say: "It was not us that ye worshipped!"

29. "Enough is God for a witness between us and you: we certainly knew nothing of your worship of us!"

30. There will every soul prove (the fruits of) the deeds it sent before: they will be brought back to God their rightful Lord, and their

---

[3] Decorated, adorned, beautified
[4] Disgrace

invented falsehoods will leave them in the lurch.

31. Say: "Who is it that sustains you (in life) from the sky and from the earth? Or who is it that has power over hearing and sight? And who is it that brings out the living from the dead and the dead from the living? And who is it that rules and regulates all affairs?" They will soon say, "God." Say, "Will ye not then show piety (to Him)?"

32. Such is God, your real Cherisher and Sustainer: apart from Truth, what (remains) but error? How then are ye turned away?

33. Thus is the Word of thy Lord proved true against those who rebel: verily they will not believe.

34. Say: "Of your 'partners,' can any originate creation and repeat it?" Say: "It is Allah Who originates creation and repeats it: then how are ye deluded away (from the truth)?"

35. Say: "Of your 'partners' is there any that can give any guidance towards Truth?" Say: "It is God Who gives guidance towards Truth. Is then He Who gives guidance to Truth more worthy to be followed, or he who finds not guidance (himself) unless he is guided? What then is the matter with you? How judge ye?"

36. But most of them follow nothing but fancy: truly fancy can be of no avail against Truth. Verily God is well aware of all that they do.

37. This Qur'an is not such as can be produced by other than God; on the contrary it is a confirmation of (revelations) that went before it, and a fuller explanation of the Book — wherein there is no doubt — from the Lord of the Worlds.

38. Or do they say, "He forged it"? Say: "Bring then a Sürah like unto it, and call (to your aid) anyone you can, besides God, if it be ye speak the truth!"

39. Nay, they charge with falsehood that whose knowledge they cannot compass[5], even before the elucidation[6] thereof hath reached them: thus did those before them make charges of falsehood: but see what was the end of those who did wrong!

40. Of them there are some who believe therein, and some who

---

[5] Grasp or understand mentally.
[6] Clarification or explanation.

do not: and thy Lord knoweth best those who are out for mischief.

41. If they charge thee with falsehood, say: "My work to me, and yours to you! Ye are free from responsibility for what I do, and I for what ye do!"

42. Among them are some who (pretend to) listen to thee: but canst thou make the deaf to hear, — even though they are without understanding?

43. And among them are some who look at thee: but canst thou guide the blind, — even though they will not see?

44. Verily God will not deal unjustly with man in aught: it is man that wrongs his own soul.

45. One day He will gather them together: (it will be) as if they had tarried but an hour of a day: they will recognize each other: assuredly those will be lost who denied the meeting with God and refused to receive true guidance.

46. Whether We show thee (realised in thy lifetime) some part of what We promise them — or We take thy soul (to Our Mercy) (before that), — in any case, to Us is their return: ultimately God is witness to all that they do.

47. To every people (was sent) an Apostle: when their Apostle comes (before them), the matter will be judged between them with justice, and they will not be wronged.

48. They say: "When will this promise come to pass, — if ye speak the truth?"

49. Say: "I have no power over any harm or profit to myself except as God willeth. To every People is a term appointed: when their term is reached, not an hour can they cause delay, nor (an hour) can they advance (it in anticipation[7]).

50. Say: "Do ye see, — if His punishment should come to you by night or by day, what portion of it would the sinners wish to hasten?

51. "Would ye then believe in it at last, when it actually cometh to pass? (It will then be said): 'Ah! now? And ye wanted (aforetime) to hasten it on!'

52. "At length will be said to the wrongdoers: 'Taste ye the enduring punishment! Ye get but the recompense of what ye earned!'"

---

[7] Expectation

53. They seek to be informed by thee: "Is that true?" Say: "Aye! by my Lord! It is the very truth! and ye cannot frustrate it!"

54. Every soul that hath sinned, if it possessed all that is on earth, would fain give it in ransom: they would declare (their) repentance when they see the Penalty: but the judgment between them will be with justice, and no wrong will be done unto them.

55. Is it not (the case) that to God belongeth whatever is in the heavens and on earth? Is it not (the case) that God's promise is assuredly true? Yet most of them understand not.

56. It is He Who giveth life and who taketh it, and to Him shall ye all be brought back.

57. O mankind! there hath come to you a direction from your Lord and a healing for the (diseases) in your hearts, — and for those who believe, a Guidance and a Mercy.

58. Say: "In the Bounty of God, and in His Mercy, — in that let them rejoice": that is better than the (wealth) they hoard.

59. Say: "See ye what things God hath sent down to you for sustenance? Yet ye hold forbidden some things thereof and (some things) lawful." Say: "Hath God indeed permitted you, or do ye invent (things) to attribute to God?"

60. And what think those who invent lies against God, of the Day of Judgment? Verily God is full of Bounty to mankind, but most of them are ungrateful.

61. In whatever business thou mayest be, and whatever portion thou mayest be reciting from the Qur'an, — and whatever deed ye (mankind) may be doing, — We are Witnesses thereof when ye are deeply engrossed therein. Nor is hidden from thy Lord (so much as) the weight of an atom on the earth or in heaven. And not the least and not the greatest of these things but are recorded in a clear Record.

62. Behold! verily on the friends of God there is no fear, nor shall they grieve;

63. Those who believe and (constantly) guard against evil; —

64. For them are Glad Tidings, in the life of the Present and in the Hereafter: no change can there be in the Words of God. This is indeed the supreme Felicity.

65. Let not their speech grieve thee: for all power and honour belong to God: it is He Who heareth and knoweth (all things).

66. Behold! verily to God belong all creatures, in the heavens and on earth. What do they follow who worship as His "partners" other than God? They follow nothing but fancy, and they do nothing but lie.

67. He it is that hath made you the Night that ye may rest therein, and the Day to make things visible (to you). Verily in this are Signs for those who listen (to His Message).

68. They say, "God hath begotten a son!" Glory be to Him! He is Self-Sufficient! His are all things in the heavens and on earth! No warrant[8] have ye for this! Say ye about God what ye know not?

69. Say: "Those who invent a lie against God will never prosper."

70. A little enjoyment in this world! — and, then, to Us will be their return. Then shall We make them taste the severest Penalty for their blasphemies.

71. Relate to them the story of Noah. Behold! he said to his People: "O my People! if it be hard on your (mind) that I should stay (with you) and commemorate the Signs of God—yet I put my trust in God. Get ye then an agreement about your plan and among your Partners, so your plan be not to you dark and dubious[9]. Then pass your sentence on me, and give me no respite.

72. "But if ye turn back, (consider): no reward have I asked of you: my reward is only due from God, and I have been commanded to be of those who submit to God's Will (in Islam)."

73. They rejected him, but We delivered him, and those with him, in the Ark, and We made them inherit (the earth), while We overwhelmed in the Flood those who rejected Our Signs. Then see what was the end of those who were warned (but heeded not)!

74. Then after him We sent (many) apostles to their Peoples: they brought them Clear Signs, but they would not believe what they had already rejected beforehand. Thus do We seal the hearts of the transgressors.

75. Then after them sent We Moses and Aaron to Pharaoh and his chiefs with Our Signs. But they were arrogant: they were a people in sin.

---

[8] Authority
[9] Uncertain, ambiguous.

76. When the Truth did come to them from Us, they said: "This is indeed evident sorcery!"

77. Said Moses: "Say ye (this) about the Truth when it hath (actually) reached you? Is sorcery (like) this? But sorcerers will not prosper."

78. They said: "Hast thou come to us to turn us away from the ways We found our fathers following, — in order that thou and thy brother may have greatness in the land? But not we shall believe in you!"

79. Said Pharaoh: "Bring me every sorcerer well-versed."

80. When the sorcerers came, Moses said to them: "Throw ye what ye (wish) to throw!"

81. When they had had their throw, Moses said: "What ye have brought is sorcery: God will surely make it of no effect: for God prospereth not the work of those who make mischief.

82. "And God by His Words doth prove and establish His truth, however much the Sinners may hate it!"

83. But none believed in Moses except some children of his People, because of the fear of Pharaoh and his chiefs, lest they should persecute them; and certainly Pharaoh was mighty on the earth and one who transgressed all bounds.

84. Moses said: "O my People! if ye do (really) believe in God, then in Him put your trust if ye submit (your will to His)."

85. They said: "In God do we put our trust. Our Lord! make us not a trial for those who practise oppression;

86. "And deliver us by Thy Mercy from those who reject (Thee)."

87. We inspired Moses and his brother with this message: "Provide dwellings for your People in Egypt, make your dwellings into places of worship, and establish regular prayers: and give Glad Tidings to those who believe!"

88. Moses prayed: "Our Lord! Thou hast indeed bestowed on Pharaoh and his Chiefs splendor and wealth in the life of the Present, and so, our Lord, they mislead (men) from Thy Path. Deface, our Lord, the features of their wealth, and send hardness to their hearts, so they will not believe until they see the grievous Penalty."

89. God said: "Accepted is your prayer (O Moses and Aaron)! So stand ye straight, and follow not the path of those who know not."

157

90. We took the Children of Israel across the sea: Pharaoh and his hosts followed them in insolence and spite[10]. At length, when overwhelmed with the flood, he said: "I believe that there is no god except Him Whom the Children of Israel believe in: I am of those who submit (to God in Islam)."

91. (It was said to him): "Ah now! — but a little while before, wast thou in rebellion! — and thou didst mischief (and violence)!

92. "This day shall We save thee in thy body, that thou mayest be a Sign to those who come after thee! But verily, many among mankind are heedless of Our Signs!"

93. We settled the Children of Israel in a beautiful dwelling-place, and provided for them sustenance of the best: it was after knowledge had been granted to them, that they fell into schisms[11]. Verily God will judge between them as to the schisms amongst them, on the Day of Judgment.

94. If thou wert in doubt as to what We have revealed unto thee, then ask those who have been reading the Book from before thee: the Truth hath indeed come to thee from thy Lord: so be in nowise of those in doubt.

95. Nor be of those who reject the Signs of God, or thou shalt be of those who perish.

96. Those against whom the Word of thy Lord hath been verified would not believe —

97. Even if every Sign was brought unto them — until they see (for themselves) the Penalty Grievous.

98. Why was there not a single township (among those We warned), which believed, — so its Faith should have profited it, — except the people of Jonah? When they believed, We removed from them the Penalty of Ignominy[12] in the life of the Present, and permitted them to enjoy (their life) for a while.

99. If it had been thy Lord's Will, they would all have believed, — all who are on earth! Wilt thou then compel mankind, against their will, to believe!

---

[10] Malice, hatred.

[11] To be divided into mutually opposing parties.

[12] Disgrace

100. No soul can believe, except by the Will of God, and He will place Doubt (or obscurity) on those who will not understand.

101. Say: "Behold all that is in the heavens and on earth"; but neither Signs nor Warners profit those who believe not.

102. Do they then expect (anything) but (what happened in) the days of the men who passed away before them? Say: "Wait ye then: for I too, will wait with you."

103. In the end We deliver Our Apostles and those who believe: thus is it fitting on Our part that We should deliver those who believe!

104. Say: "O ye men! if ye are in doubt as to my religion, (behold!) I worship not what ye worship, other than God! But I worship God — Who will take your souls (at death): I am commanded to be (in the ranks) of the Believers.

105. "And further (thus): 'Set thy face towards Religion with true piety, and never in anywise be of the Unbelievers;

106. "Nor call on any, other than God; — such will neither profit thee nor hurt thee: if thou dost, behold! thou shalt certainly be of those who do wrong."

107. If God do touch thee with hurt, there is none can remove it but He: if He do design some benefit for thee, there is none can keep back His favor: He causeth it to reach whomsoever of His servants He pleaseth. And He is the Oft-Forgiving, Most Merciful.

108. Say: "O ye men! now Truth hath reached you from your Lord! Those who receive guidance, do so for the good of their own souls; those who stray, do so to their own loss: and I am not (set) over you to arrange your affairs."

109. Follow thou the inspiration sent unto thee, and be patient and constant, till God doth decide: for He is the Best to decide.

Chapter 11
Sürah Hüd (Hüd)
Revealed at Makkah, 123 verses

In the name of God, Most Gracious, Most Merciful.

1. Alif Lãm Ra. (This is) a Book, with verses basic or fundamental (of established meaning) — further explained in detail — from One Who is Wise and Well-Acquainted (with all things):

2. (It teacheth) that ye should worship none but God. (Say:) "Verily I am (sent) unto you from Him to warn and to bring glad tidings:

3. ("And to preach thus), 'Seek ye the forgiveness of your Lord, and turn to Him in repentance; that He may grant you enjoyment, good (and true), for a term appointed, and bestow His abounding grace on all who abound in merit! But if ye turn away, then I fear for you the Penalty of a Great Day:

4. "'To God is your return, and He hath power over all things.'"

5. Behold! they fold up their hearts, that they may lie hid from Him! Ah! even when they cover themselves with their garments, He knoweth what they conceal, and what they reveal: for He knoweth well the (inmost secrets) of the hearts.

6. There is no moving creature on earth but its sustenance dependeth on God: He knoweth the time and place of its temporary deposit: all is in a clear Record.

7. He it is Who created the heavens and the earth in six Days — and His Throne was over the Waters — that He might try you, which of you is best in conduct. But if thou wert to say to them, "Ye shall indeed be raised up after death," the Unbelievers would be sure to say, "This is nothing but obvious sorcery!"

8. If We delay the Penalty for them for a definite term, they are sure to say, "What keeps it back?" Ah! on the day it (actually) reaches them, nothing will turn it away from them, and they will be completely encircled by that which they used to mock at!

9. If We give man a taste of mercy from Ourselves, and then withdraw it from him, behold! he is in despair and (falls into) blasphemy.

10. But if We give him a taste of (Our) favors after adversity hath touched him, He is sure to say, "All evil has departed from me;"

Behold! he falls into exultation[1] and pride.

11. Not so do those who show patience and constancy, and work righteousness; for them is forgiveness (of sins) and a great reward.

12. Perchance thou mayest (feel the inclination) to give up a part of what is revealed unto thee, and thy heart feeleth straitened lest they say, "Why is not a treasure sent down unto him, or why does not an angel come down with him? But thou art there only to warn! It is God that arrangeth all affairs!

13. Or they may say, "He forged it." Say, "Bring ye then ten Sūrahs forged, like unto it, and call (to your aid) whomsoever ye can, other than God! — if ye speak the truth!

14. "If then they (your false gods) answer not your (call), know ye that this Revelation is sent down (replete[2]) with the knowledge of God, and that there is no god but He! Will ye even then submit (to Islam)?"

15. Those who desire the life of the Present and its glitter — to them We shall pay (the price of) their deeds therein — without diminution[3].

16. They are those for whom there is nothing in the Hereafter but the Fire: vain are the designs they frame therein, and of no effect are the deeds that they do!

17. Can they be (like) those who accept a Clear (Sign) from their Lord, and whom a witness from Himself doth teach, as did the Book of Moses before it — a guide and a mercy? They believe therein; but those of the Sects that reject it — the Fire will be their promised meeting place. Be not then in doubt thereon: for it is the Truth from thy Lord: yet many among men do not believe!

18. Who doth more wrong than those who invent a lie against God? They will be turned back to the presence of their Lord, and the witnesses will say, "These are the ones who lied against their Lord! Behold! the Curse of God is on those who do wrong! —

19. "Those who would hinder (men) from the path of God and would seek in it something crooked: these were they who denied the

---

[1] Rejoice, revel

[2] Satiated, full

[3] Decrease

Hereafter!

20. They will in nowise frustrate (His design) on earth, nor have they protectors besides God! Their Penalty will be doubled! They lost the power to hear, and they did not see!

21. They are the ones who have lost their own souls: and the (fancies) they invented have left them in the lurch!

22. Without a doubt, these are the very ones who will lose most in the Hereafter!

23. But those who believe and work righteousness, and humble themselves before their Lord, — they will be Companions of the Garden, to dwell therein for aye[4]!

24. These two kinds (of men) may be compared to the blind and deaf, and those who can see and hear well. Are they equal when compared? Will ye not then take heed?

25. We sent Noah to his people (with a mission): "I have come to you with a Clear Warning:

26. "That ye serve none but God: verily I do fear for you the Penalty of a Grievous Day."

27. But the Chiefs of the Unbelievers among his people said: "We see (in) thee nothing but a man like ourselves: nor do we see that any follow thee but the meanest among us, in judgment immature: nor do we see in you (all) any merit above us: in fact we think ye are liars!

28. He said: "O my people! see ye if (it be that) I have a Clear Sign from my Lord, and that He hath sent Mercy unto me from His own Presence, but that the Mercy hath been obscured from your sight? Shall we compel you to accept it when ye are averse to it?

29. "And O my People! I ask you for no wealth in return: my reward is from none but God: but I will not drive away (in contempt) those who believe: for verily they are to meet their Lord, and ye I see are the ignorant ones!

30. "And O my People! who would help me against God if I drove them away? Will ye not then take heed?

31. "I tell you not that with me are the Treasures of God, nor do I know what is hidden, nor claim I to be an angel. Nor yet do I say,

---

[4] Forever

of those whom your eyes do despise that God will not grant them (all) that is good: God knoweth best what is in their souls: I should, if I did, indeed be a wrongdoer."

32. They said: "O Noah! thou hast disputed with us, and (much) hast thou prolonged the dispute with us: now bring upon us what thou threatenest us with, if thou speakest the truth!"

33. He said: "Truly, God will bring it on you if He wills, — and then, ye will not be able to frustrate it!

34. "Of no profit will be my counsel to you, much as I desire to give you (good) counsel, if it be that God willeth to leave you astray: He is your Lord! and to Him will ye return!"

35. Or do they say, "He has forged it?" Say: "If I had forged it, on me were my sin! And I am free of the sins of which ye are guilty!

36. It was revealed to Noah: "None of thy people will believe except those who have believed already! So grieve no longer over their (evil) deeds.

37. "But construct an Ark under Our eyes and Our inspiration, and address Me no (further) on behalf of those who are in sin: for they are about to be overwhelmed (in the Flood)."

38. Forthwith he starts constructing the Ark: every time that the Chiefs of his People passed by him they threw ridicule on him. He said: "If ye ridicule us now, we (in our turn) can look down on you with ridicule likewise!

39. "But soon will ye know who it is on whom will descend a Penalty that will cover them with shame — on whom will be unloosed a Penalty lasting."

40. At length, behold! there came Our Command, and the fountains of the earth gushed forth! We said: "Embark therein, of each kind two, male and female, and your family—except those against whom the Word has already gone forth—and the Believers." But only a few believed with him.

41. So he said: "Embark ye on the Ark, in the name of God, whether it move or be at rest! For my Lord is, be sure, Oft-Forgiving, Most Merciful!"

42. So the Ark floated with them on the waves (towering) like mountains, and Noah called out to his son, who had separated himself (from the rest): "O my son! embark with us, and be not with the

Unbelievers!"

43. The son replied: "I will betake myself to some mountain: it will save me from the water." Noah said: "This day nothing can save, from the Command of God, any but those on whom He hath mercy!" — and the waves came between them, and the son was among those overwhelmed in the Flood.

44. Then the word went forth: "O earth! swallow up thy water, and O sky! withhold (thy rain)!" and the water abated, and the matter was ended. The Ark rested on Mount Judi and the word went forth: "Away with those who do wrong!"

45. And Noah called upon his Lord, and said: "O my Lord! surely my son is of my family! and Thy promise is true, and Thou art the Justest of Judges!"

46. He said: "O Noah! he is not of thy family: for his conduct is unrighteous. So ask not of Me that of which thou hast no knowledge! I give thee counsel, lest thou act like the ignorant!"

47. Noah said: "O my Lord! I do seek refuge with Thee, lest I ask Thee for that of which I have no knowledge. And unless Thou forgive me and have Mercy on me, I should indeed be lost!"

48. The word came: "O Noah! come down (from the Ark) with Peace from Us, and blessings on thee and on some of the Peoples (who will spring) from those with thee: but (there will be other) Peoples to whom We shall grant their pleasures (for a time), but in the end will a grievous Penalty reach them from Us."

49. Such are some of the stories of the Unseen, which We have revealed unto thee: before this, neither thou nor thy People knew them. So persevere patiently: for the End is for those who are righteous.

50. To the 'Ad People (We sent) Hüd, one of their own brethren. He said: "O my people! worship God! ye have no other god but Him. (Your other gods) ye do nothing but invent!

51. "O my people! I ask of you no reward for this (Message). My reward is from none but Him Who created me: will ye not then understand?

52. "And O my people! ask forgiveness of your Lord, and turn to Him (in repentance): He will send you the skies pouring abundant rain, and add strength to your strength: so turn ye not back in sin!"

53. They said: "O Hüd! no Clear (Sign) hast thou brought us, and

we are not the ones to desert our gods on thy word! Nor do we believe in thee!

54. "We say nothing but that (perhaps) some of our gods may have seized thee with imbecility." He said: "I call God to witness, and do ye bear witness that I am free from the sin of ascribing, to Him,

55. "Other gods as partners! So scheme (your worst) against me, all of you, and give me no respite.

56. "I put my trust in God, my Lord and your Lord! There is not a moving creature, but He hath grasp of its forelock. Verily, it is my Lord that is on a straight path.

57. "If ye turn away — I (at least) have conveyed the Message with which I was sent to you. My Lord will make another People to succeed you, and you will not harm Him in the least. For my Lord hath care and watch over all things."

58. So when Our Decree issued, We saved Hūd and those who believed with him, by (special) Grace from Ourselves: We saved them from a severe Penalty.

59. Such were the 'Ad people: they rejected the Signs of their Lord and Cherisher; disobeyed His Apostles; and followed the command of every powerful, obstinate transgressor.

60. And they were pursued by a Curse in this Life—and on the Day of Judgment. Ah! behold! for the 'Ad rejected their Lord and Cherisher! Ah! behold! removed (from sight) were 'Ad, the people of Hūd!

61. To the Thamūd People (We sent) Sālih, one of their own brethren. He said: "O my people! worship God: ye have no other god but Him. It is He Who hath produced you from the earth and settled you therein: then ask forgiveness of Him, and turn to Him (in repentance): for my Lord is (always) near, ready to answer."

62. They said: "O Sālih! thou hast been of us!—a center of our hopes hitherto! Dost thou (now) forbid us the worship of what our fathers worshipped? But we are really in suspicious (disquieting) doubt as to that to which thou invitest us."

63. He said: "O my people! Do ye see? — if I have a Clear (Sign) from my Lord and He hath sent Mercy unto me from Himself — who then can help me against God if I were to disobey Him? What

then would ye add to my (portion) but perdition[5]?

64. "And O my people! this she-camel of God is a symbol to you: leave her to feed on God's (free) earth, and inflict no harm on her, or a swift Penalty will seize you!

65. But they did hamstring her. So he said: "Enjoy yourselves in your homes for three days: (then will be your ruin): (Behold) there a promise not to be belied!"

66. When Our Decree issued, We saved Sālih and those who believed with him, by (special) Grace from Ourselves — and from the Ignominy of that Day. For thy Lord — He is the Strong One, and Able to enforce His Will.

67. The (mighty) Blast overtook the wrongdoers, and they lay prostrate in their homes before the morning, —

68. As if they had never dwelt and flourished there. Ah! Behold! for the Thamūd rejected their Lord and Cherisher! Ah! Behold! removed (from sight) were the Thamūd!

69. There came Our Messengers to Abraham with glad tidings. They said, "Peace!" He answered, "Peace!" and hastened to entertain them with a roasted calf.

70. But when he saw their hands went not towards the (meal), he felt some mistrust of them, and conceived a fear of them. They said: "Fear not: we have been sent against the people of Lūt."

71. And his wife was standing (there), and she laughed: but We gave her glad tidings of Isaac, and after him, of Jacob.

72. She said: "Alas for me! Shall I bear a child, seeing I am an old woman, and my husband here is an old man? That would indeed be a wonderful thing!"

73. They said: "Dost thou wonder at God's decree? The grace of God and His blessings on you, O ye people of the house! for He is indeed worthy of all praise, full of all glory!"

74. When fear had passed from (the mind of) Abraham and the glad tidings had reached him, he began to plead with Us for Lūt's people.

75. For Abraham was, without doubt, forbearing (of faults), compassionate, and given to look to God.

---

[5] Death, damnation

76. O Abraham! seek not this. The decree of thy Lord hath gone forth: for them there cometh a Penalty that cannot be turned back!

77. When Our Messengers came to Lüt, he was grieved on their account and felt himself powerless (to protect) them. He said: "This is a distressful day."

78. And his people came rushing towards him, and they had been long in the habit of practicing abominations. He said: "O my people! here are my daughters: they are purer for you (if ye marry)! Now fear God, and cover me not with shame about my guests! Is there not among you a single right-minded man?"

79. They said: "Well dost thou know we have no need of thy daughters: indeed thou knowest quite well what we want!"

80. He said: "Would that I had power to suppress you or that I could betake myself to some powerful support."

81. (The Messengers) said "O Lüt! we are Messengers from thy Lord! By no means shall they reach thee! Now travel with thy family while yet a part of the night remains, and let not any of you look back: but thy wife (will remain behind): to her will happen what happens to the people. Morning is their time appointed: is not the morning nigh?"

82. When Our Decree issued, We turned (the cities) upside down, and rained down on them brimstones hard as baked clay, spread, layer on layer, —

83. Marked as from thy Lord: nor are they ever far from those who do wrong!

84. To the Madyan people (We sent) Shu'aib, one of their own brethren: he said: "O my people! worship God: ye have no other god but Him. And give not short measure or weight: I see you in prosperity, but I fear for you the Penalty of a Day that will compass (you) all round.

85. "And O my people! give just measure and weight, nor withhold from the people the things that are their due: commit not evil in the land with intent to do mischief.

86. "That which is left you by God is best for you, if ye (but) believed! But I am not set over you to keep watch!"

87. They said: "Oh Shu'aib! does thy (religion of) prayer command thee that we leave off the worship which our fathers practiced, or

that we leave off doing what we like with our property? Truly, thou art the one that forbeareth with faults and is right-minded!"

88. He said: "O my people! see ye whether I have a Clear (Sign) from my Lord, and He hath given me sustenance (pure and) good as from Himself? I wish not, in opposition to you, to do that which I forbid you to do. I only desire (your) betterment to the best of my power; and my success (in my task) can only come from God: in Him I trust, and unto Him I look.

89. "And O my people! let not my dissent (from you) cause you to sin, lest ye suffer a fate similar to that of the people of Noah or of Hüd or of Sālih, nor are the people of Lüt far off from you!

90. "But ask forgiveness of your Lord, and turn unto Him (in repentance): for my Lord is indeed Full of mercy and loving-kindness."

91. They said: "O Shu'aib! much of what thou sayest we do not understand! In fact among us we see that thou hast no strength! Were it not for thy family, we should certainly have stoned thee! For thou hast among us no great position!"

92. He said: "O my people! is then my family of more consideration with you than God? For ye cast Him away behind your backs (with contempt). But verily my Lord encompasseth on all sides all that ye do!

93. "And O my people! do whatever ye can: I will do (my part): soon will ye know who it is on whom descends the Penalty of ignominy, and who is a liar! And watch ye! for I too am watching with you!"

94. When Our decree issued, We saved Shu'aib and those who believed with him, by (special) Mercy from Ourselves: but the (mighty) Blast did seize the wrongdoers, and they lay prostrate in their homes by the morning—

95. As if they had never dwelt and flourished there! Ah! behold! how the Madyan were removed (from sight) as were removed the Thamüd!

96. And We sent Moses, with Our Clear (Signs) and an authority manifest,

97. Unto Pharaoh and his Chiefs: but they followed the command of Pharaoh, and the command of Pharaoh was no right (guide).

98. He will go before his people on the Day of Judgment, and lead them into the Fire (as cattle are led to water): but woeful indeed will be the place to which they are led!

99. And they are followed by a curse in this (life) and on the Day of Judgment: and woeful is the gift which shall be given (unto them)!

100. These are some of the stories of communities which We relate unto thee: of them some are standing, and some have been mown down (by the sickle of time).

101. It was not We that wronged them: they wronged their own souls: the deities, other than God, whom they invoked, profited them no whit[6] when there issued the decree of thy Lord: nor did they add aught (to their lot) but perdition!

102. Such is the chastisement of thy Lord when He chastises communities in the midst of their wrong: grievous, indeed, and severe is His chastisement.

103. In that is a Sign for those who fear the Penalty of the Hereafter: that is a Day for which mankind will be gathered together: that will be a Day of Testimony.

104. Nor shall We delay it but for a term appointed.

105. The day it arrives, no soul shall speak except by His leave: of those (gathered) some will be wretched and some will be blessed.

106. Those who are wretched shall be in the Fire: there will be for them therein (nothing but) the heaving of sighs and sobs:

107. They will dwell therein for all the time that the heavens and the earth endure, except as thy Lord willeth: for thy Lord is the (sure) Accomplisher of what He planneth.

108. And those who are blessed shall be in the Garden: they will dwell therein for all the time that the heavens and the earth endure, except as thy Lord willeth: a gift without break.

109. Be not then in doubt as to what these men worship. They worship nothing but what their fathers worshipped before (them): but verily We shall pay them back (in full) their portion without (the least) abatement[7].

110. We certainly gave the Book to Moses, but differences arose

---

[6] Not in the least.
[7] Decrease.

therein: had it not been that a Word had gone forth before from thy Lord, the matter would have been decided between them: but they are in suspicious doubt concerning it.

111. And, of a surety, to all will your Lord pay back (in full the recompense) of their deeds: for He knoweth well all that they do.

112. Therefore stand firm (in the straight path) as thou art commanded — thou and those who with thee turn (unto God); and transgress not (from the Path): for He seeth well all that ye do.

113. And incline not to those who do wrong, or the Fire will seize you; and ye have no protectors other than God, nor shall ye be helped.

114. And establish regular prayers at the two ends of the day and at the approaches of the night: for those things that are good remove those that are evil: be that the word of remembrance to those who remember (their Lord):

115. And be steadfast in patience; for verily God will not suffer the reward of the righteous to perish.

116. Why were there not, among the generations before you, persons possessed of balanced good sense, prohibiting (men) from mischief in the earth — except a few among them whom We saved (from harm)? But the wrongdoers pursued the enjoyment of the good things of life which were given them, and persisted in sin.

117. Nor would thy Lord be the One to destroy communities for a single wrongdoing if its members were likely to mend.

118. If thy Lord had so willed He could have made mankind one People: but they will not cease to dispute,

119. Except those on whom He hath bestowed His Mercy: and for this did He create them: and the Word of thy Lord shall be fulfilled: "I will fill Hell with Jinns and men all together."

120. All that We relate to thee of the stories of the Apostles — with it We make firm thy heart: in them there cometh to thee the Truth, as well as an exhortation and a message of remembrance to those who believe.

121. Say to those who do not believe: "Do whatever ye can: we shall do our part;

122. "And wait ye! we too shall wait."

123. To God do belong the unseen (secrets) of the heavens and the earth, and to Him goeth back every affair (for decision): then

worship Him, and put thy trust in Him: and thy Lord is not unmindful of aught that ye do.

Chapter 12
Sürah Yüsuf (Joseph)
Revealed at Makkah, 111 verses.

In the name of God, Most Gracious, Most Merciful.

1. Alif Lãm Ra. These are the Symbols (or Verses) of the Perspicuous Book.

2. We have sent it down as an Arabic Qur'an, in order that ye may learn wisdom.

3. We do relate unto thee the most beautiful of stories, in that We reveal to thee this (portion of the) Qur'an: before this, thou too wast among those who knew it not.

4. Behold, Joseph said to his father: "O my father! I did see eleven stars and the sun and the moon: I saw them prostrate themselves to me!"

5. Said (the father): "My (dear) little son! relate not thy vision to thy brothers, lest they concoct[1] a plot against thee: for Satan is to man an avowed enemy!

6. "Thus will thy Lord choose thee and teach thee the interpretation of stories (and events) and perfect His favor to thee and to the posterity of Jacob — even as He perfected it to thy fathers Abraham and Isaac aforetime! For God is full of knowledge and wisdom."

7. Verily in Joseph and his brethren are Signs (or Symbols) for Seekers (after Truth).

8. They said: "Truly Joseph and his brother are loved more by our father than we: but we are a goodly body! Really our father is obviously wandering (in his mind)!

9. "Slay ye Joseph or cast him out to some (unknown) land, that so the favor of your father may be given to you alone: (There will

---

[1] Invent, devise

be time enough) for you to be righteous after that!"

10. Said one of them: "Slay not Joseph, but if ye must do something, throw him down to the bottom of the well: he will be picked up by some caravan of travellers."

11. They said: "O our father! why dost thou not trust us with Joseph — seeing we are indeed his sincere well-wishers?

12. "Send him with us tomorrow to enjoy himself and play, and we shall take every care of him."

13. (Jacob) said: "Really it saddens me that ye should take him away: I fear lest the wolf should devour him while ye attend not to him."

14. They said: "If the wolf were to devour him while we are (so large) a party, then should we indeed (first) have perished ourselves!"

15. So they did take him away, and they all agreed to throw him down to the bottom of the well: and We put into his heart (this Message): "Of a surety thou shalt (one day) tell them the truth of this their affair while they know (thee) not."

16. Then they came to their father in the early part of the night, weeping.

17. They said: "Oh our father! we went racing with one another, and left Joseph with our things: and the wolf devoured him... But thou wilt never believe us even though we tell the truth."

18. They stained his shirt with false blood. He said: "Nay, but your minds have made up a tale (that may pass) with you. (For me) patience is most fitting: against that which ye assert, it is God (alone) whose help can be sought"...

19. Then there came a caravan of travellers: they sent their water-carrier (for water), and he let down his bucket (into the well)... He said: "Ah there! Good news! Here is a (fine) young man! So they concealed him as a treasure! But God knoweth well all that they do!

20. The (Brethren) sold him for a miserable price, — for a few dirhams counted out: in such low estimation did they hold him!

21. The man in Egypt who bought him said to his wife: "Make his stay (among us) honourable: maybe he will bring us much good, or we shall adopt him as a son." Thus did we establish Joseph in the land, that We might teach him the interpretation of stories (and events). And God hath full power and control over His affairs; but most among

mankind know it not.

22. When Joseph attained his full manhood, We gave him power and knowledge: thus do We reward those who do right.

23. But she, in whose house he was, sought to seduce him from his (true) self: she fastened the doors, and said: "Now come, thou (dear one)!" He said: "God forbid! truly (thy husband) is my lord! He made my sojourn agreeable! Truly to no good come those who do wrong!"

24. And (with passion) did she desire him, and he would have desired her, but that he saw the evidence of his Lord: thus (did We order) that We might turn away from him (all) evil and shameful deeds: for he was one of Our servants, sincere and purified.

25. So they both raced each other to the door, and she tore his shirt from the back: they both found her lord near the door. She said: "What is the (fitting) punishment for one who formed an evil design against thy wife, but prison or a grievous chastisement?"

26. He said: "It was she that sought to seduce me — from my (true) self." And one of her household saw (this) and bore witness, (thus): — "If it be that his shirt is rent from the front, then is her tale true, and he is a liar!

27. "But if it be that his shirt is torn from the back, then is she the liar, and he is telling the truth!"

28. So when he saw his shirt, — that it was torn at the back, — (her husband) said: "Behold! it is a snare[2] of you women! Truly, mighty is your snare!

29. "O Joseph, pass this over! (O wife), ask forgiveness for thy sin, for truly thou hast been at fault!"

30. Ladies said in the City: "The wife of the (great) 'Aziz is seeking to seduce her slave from his (true) self: truly hath he inspired her with violent love: we see she is evidently going astray."

31. When she heard of their malicious talk, she sent for them and prepared a banquet for them: she gave each of them a knife; and she said (to Joseph), "Come out before them. When they saw him, they did extol him, and (in their amazement) cut their hands: they said "God preserve us! no mortal is this! This is none other than a noble

---

[2] Trap

173

angel!"

32. She said: "There before you is the man about whom ye did blame me! I did seek to seduce him from his (true) self but he did firmly save himself guiltless!... And now, if he doth not my bidding, he shall certainly be cast into prison, and (what is more) be in the company of the vilest[3]!"

33. He said: "O my Lord! the prison is more to my liking than that to which they invite me: unless thou turn away their snare from me, I should (in my youthful folly) feel inclined towards them and join the ranks of the ignorant."

34. So his Lord heard him (in his prayer), and turned away from him their snare: verily He heareth and knoweth (all things).

35. Then it occurred to the men, after they had seen the Signs, (that it was best) to imprison him for a time.

36. Now with him there came into the prison two young men. Said one of them: "I see myself (in a dream) pressing wine." Said the other: "I see myself (in a dream) carrying bread on my head, and birds are eating thereof." "Tell us" (they said) "the truth and meaning thereof: for we see thou art one that doth good (to all)."

37. He said: "Before any food comes (in due course) to feed either of you, I will surely reveal to you the truth and meaning of this ere[4] it come to pass: that is part of the (Duty) which my Lord hath taught me. I have (I assure you) abandoned the ways of a people that believe not in God and that (even) deny the Hereafter.

38. "And I follow the ways of my fathers, — Abraham, Isaac, and Jacob; and never could we attribute any partners whatever to God: that (comes) of the grace of God to us and to mankind: yet most men are not grateful.

39. "O my two companions of the prison! (I ask you): Are many lords differing among themselves better, or God, the One, Supreme and Irresistible?

40. "If not Him, ye worship nothing but names which ye have named, — ye and your fathers, — for which God hath sent you no authority: the Command is for none but God: He hath commanded

---

[3] Meanest people
[4] Before, prior to

that ye worship none but Him: that is the right religion, but Most men understand not...

41. "O my two companions of the prison! as to one of you, he will pour out the wine for his lord to drink: as for the other, he will hang from the cross, and the birds will eat from off his head. (So) hath been decreed that matter whereof ye twain[5] do enquire..."

42. And of the two, to that one whom he considered about to be saved, he said: "Mention me to thy lord." But Satan made him forget to mention him to his lord: and (Joseph) lingered in prison a few (more) years.

43. The king (of Egypt) said: "I do see (in a vision) seven fat kine[6], whom seven lean ones devour, — and seven green ears of corn, and seven (others) withered. O ye chiefs! expound to me my vision if it be that ye can interpret visions."

44. They said: "A confused medley[7] of dreams: and we are not skilled in the interpretation of dreams."

45. But the man who had been released, one of the two (who had been in prison) and who now bethought him after (so long) a space of time, said: "I will tell you the truth of its interpretation: send ye me (therefor)."

46. "O Joseph!" (he said), "O man of truth! expound to us (the dream) of seven fat kine whom seven lean ones devour, and of seven green ears of corn and (seven) others withered: that I may return to the people, and that they may understand."

47. (Joseph) said: "For seven years shall ye diligently sow as is your wont[8]: and the harvests that ye reap, ye shall leave them in the ear, — except a little, of which ye shall eat.

48. "Then will come after that (period) seven dreadful (years), which will devour what ye shall have laid by in advance for them, — (all) except a little which ye shall have (specially) guarded.

49. "Then will come after that (period) a year in which the people will have abundant water, and in which they will press (wine and oil)."

---

[5] Two.

[6] Cows

[7] Mixture

[8] Custom

50. So the king said: "Bring ye him unto me." But when the messenger came to him, (Joseph) said: "Go thou back to thy lord, and ask him, 'What is the state of mind of the ladies who cut their hands?' for my Lord is certainly well aware of their snare."

51. (The king) said (to the ladies): "What was your affair when ye did seek to seduce Joseph from his (true) self?" The ladies said: "God preserve us! no evil know we against him!" Said the 'Aziz's wife: "Now is the truth manifest (to all): it was I who sought to seduce him from his (true) self: he is indeed of those who are (ever) true (and virtuous).

52. "This (say I), in order that he may know that I have never been false to him in his absence, and that God will never guide the snare of the false ones.

53. "Nor do I absolve my own self (of blame): the (human soul) is certainly prone to evil, unless my Lord do bestow His Mercy: but surely certainly my Lord is Oft-Forgiving, Most Merciful."

54. So the king said: "Bring him unto me; I will take him specially to serve about my own person." Therefore when he had spoken to him, he said: "Be assured this day, thou art, before our own Presence, with rank firmly established and fidelity fully proved!"

55. (Joseph) said: "Set me over the storehouses of the land: I will indeed guard them, as one that knows (their importance)."

56. Thus did We give established power to Joseph in the land, to take possession therein as, when, or where he pleased. We bestow of Our mercy on whom We please, and We suffer not, to be lost, the reward of those who do good.

57. But verily the reward of the Hereafter is the best, for those who believe, and are constant in righteousness.

58. Then came Joseph's brethren: they entered his presence, and he knew them, but they knew him not.

59. And when he had furnished them forth with provisions (suitable) for them, he said: "Bring unto me a brother ye have, of the same father as yourselves, (but a different mother): see ye not that I pay out full measure, and that I do provide the best hospitality?

60. "Now if ye bring him not to me, ye shall have no measure (of corn) from me, nor shall ye (even) come near me."

61. They said: "We shall certainly seek to get our wish about him

from his father: indeed we shall do it."

62. And (Joseph) told his servants to put their stock-in-trade (with which they had bartered) into their saddlebags, so they should know it only when they returned to their people, in order that they might come back.

63. Now when they returned to their father, they said: "O our father! no more measure of grain shall we get (unless we take our brother): so send our brother with us, that we may get our measure; and we will indeed take every care of him."

64. He said: "Shall I trust you with him with any result other than when I trusted you with his brother aforetime? But God is the best to take care (of him), and He is the Most Merciful of those who show mercy!"

65. Then when they opened their baggage, they found their stock-in-trade had been returned to them. They said: "O our father! what (more) can we desire? This our stock-in-trade has been returned to us: so we shall get (more) food for our family; we shall take care of our brother; and add (at the same time) a full camel's load (of grain to our provisions): this is but a small quantity."

66. (Jacob) said: "Never will I send him with you until ye swear a solemn oath to me, in God's name, that ye will be sure to bring him back to me unless ye are yourselves hemmed in[9] (and made powerless)." And when they had sworn their solemn oath, he said: "Over all that we say, be God the Witness and Guardian!"

67. Further he said; "O my sons! enter not all by one gate: enter ye by different gates. Not that I can profit you aught against God (with my advice): none can command except God: on Him do I put my trust and let all that trust put their trust on Him."

68. And when they entered in the manner their father had enjoined, it did not profit them in the least against (the Plan of) God: it was but a necessity of Jacob's soul, which he discharged. For he was, by Our instruction, full of knowledge (and experience): but most men know not.

69. Now when they came into Joseph's presence, he received his (full) brother to stay with him. He said (to him): "Behold! I am thy

---

[9] Surrounded

(own) brother; so grieve not at aught of their doings."

70. At length when he had furnished them forth with provisions (suitable) for them, he put the drinking cup into his brother's saddlebag. Then shouted out a Crier: "O ye (in) the Caravan! Behold! ye are thieves, without doubt!"

71. They said, turning towards them: "What is it that ye miss?"

72. They said: "We miss the great beaker[10] of the king; for him who produces it, is (the reward of) a camel-load; I will be bound by it."

73. (The brothers) said: "By God! well ye know that we came not to make mischief in the land, and we are no thieves!"

74. (The Egyptians) said: "What then shall be the penalty of this, if ye are (proved) to have lied?"

75. They said: "The penalty should be that he in whose saddlebag it is found, should be held (as bondman[11]) to atone for the (crime). Thus it is we punish the wrongdoers!"

76. So he began (the search) with their baggage, before (he came to) the baggage of his brother: at length He brought it out of his brother's baggage. Thus did We plan for Joseph. He could not take his brother by the law of the king except that God willed it (so). We raise to degrees (of wisdom) whom We please: but over all endued with knowledge is One, the All-Knowing.

77. They said: "If he steals, there was a brother of his who did steal before (him)." But these things did Joseph keep locked in his heart, revealing not the secrets to them. He (simply) said (to himself): "Ye are the worse situated; and God knoweth best the truth of what ye assert!"

78. They said: "O exalted one! Behold! he has a father, aged and venerable[12], (who will grieve for him): so take one of us in his place: for we see that thou art (gracious) in doing good."

79. He said: "God forbid that we take other than him with whom we found our property: indeed (if we did so), we should be acting wrongfully."

---

[10] A drinking vessel, tumbler
[11] Captive, slave
[12] Honourable, respected, revered

80. Now when they saw no hope of his (yielding), they held a conference in private. The leader among them said: "Know ye not that your father did take an oath from you in God's name, and how, before this, ye did fail in your duty with Joseph? Therefore will I not leave this land until my father permits me, or God commands me; and He is the best to command.

81. "Turn ye back to your father, and say, 'O our father! Behold! thy son committed theft: we bear witness only to what we know, and we could not well guard against the unseen!

82. "'Ask at the town where we have been and the caravan in which we returned, and (you will find) we are indeed telling the truth.'"

83. Jacob said: "Nay, but ye have yourselves contrived a story (good enough) for you. So patience is most fitting (for me). Maybe God will bring them (back) all to me (in the end): for He is indeed full of knowledge and wisdom."

84. And he turned away from them, and said: "How great is my grief for Joseph!" And his eyes became white with sorrow, and he fell into silent melancholy[13].

85. They said: "By God! (never) wilt thou cease to remember Joseph until though reach the last extremity of illness, or until thou die!"

86. He said: "I only complain of my distraction and anguish to God and I know from God that which ye know not...

87. "O my sons! go ye and enquire about Joseph and his brother, and never give up hope of God's Soothing Mercy: truly no one despairs of God's Soothing Mercy, except those who have no faith."

88. Then, when they came (back) into (Joseph's) presence they said: "O exalted one! distress has seized us and our family; we have (now) brought but scanty capital: So pay us full measure, (we pray thee), and treat it as charity to us: for God doth reward the charitable."

89. He said: "Know ye how ye dealt with Joseph, and his brother, not knowing (what ye were doing)?"

90. They said: "Art thou indeed, Joseph?" He said: "I am Joseph, and this is my brother: God has indeed been gracious to us (all): behold, he that is righteous and patient, — never will God suffer the reward

---

[13] Depression and gloom.

to be lost, of those who do right."

91. They said: "By God! indeed has God preferred thee above us, and we certainly have been guilty of sin!"

92. He said: "This day let no reproach be (cast) on you: God will forgive you, and He is the Most Merciful of those who show mercy?

93. "Go with this my shirt, and cast it over the face of my father: he will come to see (clearly). Then come ye (here) to me together with all your family."

94. When the caravan left (Egypt), their father said: "I do indeed scent the presence of Joseph: nay, think me not a dotard[14]."

95. They said: "By God! truly thou art in thine old wandering mind."

96. Then when the bearer of the good news came, he cast (the shirt) over his face, and he forthwith regained clear sight. He said: "Did I not say to you, 'I know from God that which ye know not?'"

97. They said: "O our father! ask for us forgiveness for our sins, for we were truly at fault."

98. He said: "Soon will I ask my Lord for forgiveness for you: for He is indeed Oft-Forgiving, Merciful."

99. Then when they entered the presence of Joseph, he provided a home for his parents with himself, and said: "Enter ye Egypt (all) in safety if it please God."

100. And he raised his parents high on the throne (of dignity), and they fell down in prostration (all) before him. He said: "O my father! this is the fulfillment of my vision of old! God hath made it come true! He was indeed good to me when He took me out of prison and brought you (all here) out of the desert, (even) after Satan had sown enmity between me and my brothers. Verily my Lord understandeth best the mysteries of all that He planneth to do: for verily He is full of knowledge and wisdom.

101. "O my Lord! Thou hast indeed bestowed on me some power, and taught me something of the interpretation of dreams and events, O Thou Creator of the heavens and the earth! Thou art my Protector in this world and in the Hereafter, take thou my soul (at death) as one submitting to Thy Will (as a Muslim), and unite me with the

---

[14] Feeble-minded from age.

righteous."

102. Such is one of the stories of what happened unseen, which
We reveal by inspiration unto thee: nor wast thou (present) with them
when they concerted their plans together in the process of weaving
their plots.

103. Yet no faith will the greater part of mankind have, however
ardently thou dost desire it.

104. And no reward dost thou ask of them for this: it is no less
than a Message for all creatures.

105. And how many Signs in the heavens and the earth do they
pass by? Yet they turn (their faces) away from them!

106. And most of them believe not in God without associating
(others as partners) with Him!

107. Do they then feel secure from the coming against them of
the covering veil of the wrath of God — or of the coming against
them of the (final) Hour all of a sudden while they perceive not?

108. Say thou: "This is my way: I do invite unto God — on evidence
clear as the seeing with one's eyes — I and whoever follows me:
Glory to God! and never will I join gods with God!"

109. Nor did We send before thee (as Apostles) any but men, whom
We did inspire — (men) living in human habitations. Do they not
travel through the earth, and see what was the end of those before
them? But the home of the Hereafter is best, for those who do right.
Will ye not then understand?

110. (Respite will be granted) until, when the Apostles give up
hope (of their people) and (come to) think that they were treated
as liars, there reaches them Our help. And those whom We will are
delivered into safety. But never will be warded off Our punishment
from those who are in sin.

111. There is, in their stories, instruction for men endued with
understanding. It is not a tale invented, but a confirmation of what
went before it — a detailed exposition of all things, and a Guide and
a Mercy to any such as believe.

Chapter 13
Sürah Ar-Ra'd (The Thunder)
Revealed at Makkah, 43 verses.

In the name of God, Most Gracious, Most Merciful.

1. Alif Lām Mim Ra. These are the Signs (or Verses) of the Book: that which hath been revealed unto thee from thy Lord is the Truth; but most men believe not.

2. God is He Who raised the heavens without any pillars that ye can see; then He established Himself on the throne (of authority); He has subjected the sun and the moon (to His law)! Each one runs (its course) for a term appointed. He doth regulate all affairs, explaining the Signs in detail, that ye may believe with certainty in the meeting with your Lord.

3. And it is He Who spread out the earth, and set thereon mountains standing firm, and (flowing) rivers: and fruit of every kind He made in pairs, two and two: He draweth the Night as a veil o'er the Day. Behold, verily in these things there are Signs for those who consider!

4. And in the earth are tracts (diverse though) neighboring, and gardens of vines and fields sown with corn, and palm trees — growing out of single roots or otherwise: watered with the same water, yet some of them We make more excellent than others to eat. Behold, verily in these things there are Signs for those who understand!

5. If thou dost marvel (at their want of faith), strange is their saying: "When we are (actually) dust, shall we indeed then be in a creation renewed?" They are those who deny their Lord! They are those round whose necks will be yokes (of servitude): they will be Companions of the Fire, who dwell therein (for aye)!

6. They ask thee to hasten on the evil in preference to the good: yet have come to pass, before them, (many) exemplary punishments! But verily thy Lord is full of forgiveness for mankind for their wrongdoing: and verily thy Lord is (also) strict in punishment.

7. And the Unbelievers say! "Why is not a Sign sent down to him from his Lord?" But thou art truly a warner and to every people a guide.

8. God doth know what every female (womb) doth bear, by how much the wombs fall short (of their time or number) or do exceed.

Every single thing is before His sight, in (due) proportion.

9. He knoweth the Unseen and that which is open: He is the Great, the Most High.

10. It is the same (to Him) whether any of you conceal his speech or declare it openly; whether he lie hid by night or walk freely by day.

11. For each (such person) there are (angels) in succession, before and behind him: they guard him by command of God. Verily never will God change the condition of a people until they change it themselves (with their own souls). But when (once) God willeth a people's punishment, there can be no turning it back, nor will they find, besides Him, any to protect.

12. It is He Who doth show you the lightning, by way both of fear and of hope: it is He Who doth raise up the clouds, heavy with (fertilizing) rain!

13. Nay, thunder repeateth His praises, and so do the angels, with awe: He flingeth the loud-voiced thunderbolts, and therewith He striketh whomsoever He will... Yet these (are the men) who (dare to) dispute about God, with the strength of His power (supreme)!

14. For Him (alone) is prayer in Truth: any others that they call upon besides Him hear them no more than if they were to stretch forth their hands for water to reach their mouth but it reaches them not: for the prayer of those without faith is nothing but (futile) wandering (in the mind).

15. Whatever beings there are in the heavens and the earth do prostrate themselves to God (acknowledging subjection) — with good will or in spite of themselves: so do their shadows in the mornings and evenings.

16. Say: "Who is the Lord and Sustainer of the heavens and the earth?" Say: "It is God." Say: "Do ye then take (for worship) protectors other than Him, such as have no power either for good or for harm to themselves?" Say: "Are the blind equal with those who see? Or the depths of darkness equal with light?" Or do they assign to God partners who have created (anything) as He has created, so that the creation seemed to them similar? Say: "God is the Creator of all things: He is the One, the Supreme and Irresistible."

17. He sends down water from the skies, and the channels flow,

each according to its measure: but the torrent bears away the foam that mounts up to the surface. Even so, from that (ore[1]) which they heat in the fire, to make ornaments or utensils therewith, there is a scum[2] likewise. Thus doth God (by parables) show forth Truth and Vanity: for the scum disappears like froth cast out; while that which is for the good of mankind remains on the earth. Thus doth God set forth parables.

18. For those who respond to their Lord, are (all) good things. But those who respond not to Him — even if they had all that is in the heavens and on earth, and as much more, (in vain) would they offer it for ransom. For them will the reckoning be terrible: their abode will be Hell — what a bed of misery!

19. Is then one who doth know that that which hath been revealed unto thee from thy Lord is the Truth, like one who is blind? It is those who are endued with understanding that receive admonition —

20. Those who fulfil the Covenant of God and fail not in their plighted word;

21. Those who join together those things which God hath commanded to be joined, hold their Lord in awe, and fear the terrible reckoning;

22. Those who patiently persevere, seeking the countenance of their Lord; establish regular prayers; spend, out of (the gifts) We have bestowed for their sustenance, secretly and openly; and turn off Evil with good: for such there is the final attainment of the (Eternal) Home, —

23. Gardens of perpetual bliss: they shall enter there, as well as the righteous among their fathers, their spouses, and their offspring: and angels shall enter unto them from every gate (with the saLütation):

24. "Peace unto you for that ye persevered in patience! Now how excellent is the final Home!"

25. But those who break the Covenant of God, after having plighted their word thereto and cut asunder those things which God has commanded to be joined, and work mischief in the land — on them

---

[1] Naturally occurring mineral, metal, especially gold.
[2] Impurities that rise to surface of liquid especially in boiling, floating film, refuse

is the Curse; for them is the terrible Home!

26. God doth enlarge, or grant by (strict) measure the Sustenance (which He giveth) to whomso He pleaseth. (The worldly) rejoice in the life of this world: but the life of this world is but little comfort in the Hereafter.

27. The Unbelievers say: "Why is not a Sign sent down to him from his Lord?" Say:"Truly God leaveth, to stray, whom He will; but He guideth to Himself those who turn to Him in penitence[3] —

28. "Those who believe, and whose hearts find satisfaction in the remembrance of God: for without doubt in the remembrance of God do hearts find satisfaction.

29. "For those who believe and work righteousness, is (every) blessedness, and a beautiful place of (final) return."

30. Thus have We sent thee amongst a People before whom (long since) have (other) peoples (gone and) passed away; in order that thou mightest rehearse unto them what We send down unto thee by inspiration; yet do they reject (Him), the Most Gracious! Say: "He is my Lord! There is no god but He! On Him is my trust, and to Him do I turn!"

31. If there were a Qur'an with which mountains were moved, or the earth were cloven asunder, or the dead were made to speak, (this would be the one!) But, truly, the Command is with God in all things! Do not the Believers know, that, had God (so) willed, He could have guided all mankind (to the Right)? But the Unbelievers — never will disaster cease to seize them for their (ill) deeds, or to settle close to their homes, until the Promise of God come to pass, for, verily, God will not fail in His promise.

32. Mocked were (many) Apostles before thee: but I granted respite to the Unbelievers, and finally I punished them; then how (terrible) was My requital!

33. Is then He Who standeth over every soul (and knoweth) all that it doth, (like any others)? And yet they ascribe partners to God. Say: "But name them! Is it that ye will inform Him of something He knoweth not on earth, or is it (just) a show of words?" Nay! to those who believe not, their pretence seems pleasing, but they are

---

[3] Repentance

kept back (thereby) from the Path: and those whom God leaves to stray, no one can guide.

34. For them is a Penalty in the life of this world, but harder, truly, is the Penalty of the Hereafter; and defender have they none against God.

35. The parable of the Garden which the righteous are promised! — beneath it flow rivers: perpetual is the enjoyment thereof and the shade therein: such is the End of the Righteous; and the End of Unbelievers is the Fire.

36. Those to whom We have given the Book rejoice at what hath been revealed unto thee: but there are among the clans those who reject a part thereof. Say: "I am commanded to worship God, and not to join partners with Him. Unto Him do I call, and unto Him is my return."

37. Thus have We revealed it to be a judgment of authority in Arabic. Wert thou to follow their (vain) desires after the knowledge which hath reached thee, then wouldst thou find neither protector nor defender against God.

38. We did send Apostles before thee, and appointed for them wives and children: and it was never the part of an Apostle to bring a Sign except as God permitted (or commanded). For each period is a Book (revealed).

39. God doth blot out or confirm what He pleaseth: with Him is the Mother of the Book.

40. Whether We shall show thee (within thy lifetime) part of what We promised them or take to Ourselves thy soul (before it is all accomplished), thy duty is to (make the Message) reach them: it is Our part to call them to account.

41. See they not that We gradually reduce the land (in their control) from its outlying borders? (Where) God commands, there is none to put back His command: and He is swift in calling to account.

42. Those before them did (also) devise plots; but in all things the master planning is God's. He knoweth the doings of every soul: and soon will the Unbelievers know who gets home in the End.

43. The Unbelievers say: "No Apostle art thou." Say: "Enough for a witness between me and you is God, and such as have knowledge of the Book."

Chapter 14
Sürah Ibrahim (Abraham)
Revealed at Makkah, 52 verses.

In the name of God, Most Gracious, Most Merciful.

1. Alif Lām Ra. A Book which We have revealed unto thee, in order that thou mightest lead mankind out of the depths of darkness into light — by the leave of their Lord — to the Way of (Him) Exalted in Power, Worthy of all Praise! —

2. Of God, to Whom do belong all things in the heavens and on earth! But alas for the Unbelievers for a terrible Penalty (their Unfaith will bring them)! —

3. Those who love the life of this world more than the Hereafter, who hinder (men) from the Path of God and seek therein something crooked: they are astray by a long distance.

4. We sent not an Apostle except (to teach) in the language of his (own) people, in order to make (things) clear to them. Now God leaves straying those whom He pleases and guides whom He pleases: and He is Exalted in Power, Full of Wisdom.

5. We sent Moses with Our Signs (and the command), "Bring out thy people from the depths of darkness into light, and teach them to remember the Days of God." Verily in this there are Signs for such as are firmly patient and constant, — grateful and appreciative.

6. Remember! Moses said to his people: "Call to mind the favor of God to you when He delivered you from the people of Pharaoh: They set you hard tasks and punishments, slaughtered your sons, and let your womenfolk live: therein was a tremendous trial from your Lord."

7. And remember! your Lord caused to be declared (publicly): "If ye are grateful, I will add more (favors) unto you; but if ye show ingratitude, truly My punishment is terrible indeed."

8. And Moses said: "If ye show ingratitude, ye and all on earth together, — yet is God Free of all wants, worthy of all Praise.

9. Has not the story reached you, (O people!), of those who (went) before you? — of the people of Noah, and 'Ad, and Thamūd? — and of those who (came) after them? None knows them but God. To them came Apostles with Clear (Signs); but they put their hands

187

up to their mouths, and said: "We do deny (the mission) on which ye have been sent, and we are really in suspicious (disquieting) doubt as to that to which ye invite us."

10. Their Apostles said: "Is there a doubt about God, the Creator of the heavens and the earth? It is He Who invites you, in order that He may forgive you your sins and give you respite for a term appointed!" They said: "Ah! ye are no more than human, like ourselves! Ye wish to turn us away from the (gods) our fathers used to worship: then bring us some clear authority."

11. Their Apostles said to them: "True, we are human like yourselves, but God doth grant His grace to such of His servants as He pleases. It is not for us to bring you an authority except as God permits. And on God let all men of faith put their trust.

12. "No reason have we why we should not put our trust on God. Indeed He has guided us to the Ways we (follow). We shall certainly bear with patience all the hurt you may cause us: for those who put their trust should put their trust on God."

13. And the Unbelievers said to their Apostles: "Be sure we shall drive you out of our land, or ye shall return to our religion." But their Lord inspired (this Message) to them: "Verily We shall cause the wrongdoers to perish!

14. "And verily We shall cause you to abide in the land, and succeed them. This for such as fear the time when they shall stand before My tribunal[1] — such as fear the punishment denounced."

15. But they sought victory and decision (there and then), and frustration was the lot of every powerful obstinate transgressor.

16. In front of such a one is Hell, and he is given, for drink, boiling fetid[2] water.

17. In gulps[3] will he sip it, but never will he be near swallowing it down his throat: Death will come to him from every quarter, yet will he not die: and in front of him will be a chastisement unrelenting.

18. The parable of those who reject their Lord is that their works are as ashes, on which the wind blows furiously on a tempestuous day: No power have they over aught that they have earned: That is

---

[1] Judgment-seat

[2] Stinking

[3] Large mouthful of a drink

the straying far, far (from the goal).

19. Seest thou not that God created the Heavens and the earth in Truth? If He so will, He can remove you and put (in your place) a new Creation?

20. Nor is that for God any great matter.

21. They will all be marshalled[4] before God together: then will the weak say to those who were arrogant, "For us, we but followed you; can ye then avail us at all against the wrath of God?" They will reply, "If we had received the guidance of God, we should have given it to you: to us it makes no difference (now) whether we rage, or bear (these torments) with patience: for ourselves there is no way of escape."

22. And Satan will say when the matter is decided: "It was God Who gave you a promise of truth: I too promised, but I failed in my promise to you. I had no authority over you except to call you, but ye listened to me: then reproach not me, but reproach your own souls. I cannot listen to your cries, nor can ye listen to mine. I reject your former act in associating me with God. For wrongdoers there must be a grievous Penalty."

23. But those who believe and work righteousness will be admitted to Gardens beneath which rivers flow — to dwell therein for aye with the leave of their Lord: their greeting therein will be: "Peace!"

24. Seest thou not how God sets forth a parable? — A goodly Word like a goodly tree, whose root is firmly fixed, and its branches (reach) to the heavens —

25. It brings forth its fruit at all times, by the leave of its Lord. So God sets forth parables for men, in order that they may receive admonition.

26. And the parable of an evil Word is that of an evil tree. It is torn up by the root, from the surface of the earth: it has no stability.

27. God will establish in strength those who believe, with the Word that stands firm, in this world and in the Hereafter; but God will leave, to stray, those who do wrong: God doeth what He willeth.

28. Hast thou not turned thy vision to those who have changed the favor of God into blasphemy and caused their people to descend to the House of Perdition? —

---

[4] Gathered

29. Into Hell? They will burn therein—an evil place to stay in!

30. And they set up (idols) as equal to God, to mislead (men) from the Path! Say: "Enjoy (your brief power)! But verily ye are making straightway for Hell!"

31. Speak to My servants who have believed, that they may establish regular prayers, and spend (in charity) out of the Sustenance We have given them, secretly and openly, before the coming of a Day in which there will be neither mutual bargaining, nor befriending.

32. It is God Who hath created the heavens and the earth and sendeth down rain from the skies, and with it bringeth out fruits wherewith to feed you; it is He Who hath made the ships subject to you, that they may sail through the sea by His command; and the rivers (also) hath He made subject to you.

33. And He hath made subject to you the sun and the moon, both diligently pursuing their courses: and the Night and the Day hath He (also) made subject to you.

34. And He giveth you of all that ye ask for. But if ye count the favors of God, never will ye be able to number them: verily, man is given up to injustice and ingratitude.

35. Remember Abraham said: "O my Lord! make this city one of peace and security: and preserve me and my sons from worshipping idols.

36. "O my Lord! they have indeed led astray many among mankind: he then who follows my (ways) is of me, and he that disobeys me — but thou art indeed Oft-Forgiving, Most Merciful.

37. "O our Lord! I have made some of my offspring to dwell in a valley without cultivation, by thy Sacred House; in order, O our Lord, that they may establish regular prayer: so fill the hearts of some among men with love towards them, and feed them with fruits: so that they may give thanks.

38. "O our Lord! truly Thou dost know what we conceal and what we reveal: for nothing whatever is hidden from God, whether on earth or in heaven.

39. "Praise be to God, who hath granted unto me in old age Ismail and Isaac: for truly my Lord is He, the Hearer of Prayer!

40. "O my Lord! make me one who establishes regular Prayer, and also (raise such) among my offspring, O our Lord! and accept

Thou my prayer.

41. "O our Lord! cover (us) with Thy Forgiveness — me, my parents, and (all) Believers, on the Day that the Reckoning will be established!"

42. Think not that God doth not heed the deeds of those who do wrong. He but giveth them respite against a Day when the eyes will fixedly stare in horror —

43. They are running forward with necks outstretched, their heads uplifted, their gaze returning not towards them, and their hearts a (gaping) void.

44. So warn mankind of the Day when the Wrath will reach them: then will the wrongdoers say: "Our Lord! respite us (if only) for a short term: we will answer Thy Call, and follow the Apostles!" "What! were ye not wont to swear aforetime that ye should suffer no decline?

45. "And ye dwelt in the dwellings of men who wronged their own souls: ye were clearly shown how We dealt with them; and We put forth many parables in your behalf!"

46. Mighty indeed were the plots which they made, but their plots were (well) within the sight of God, even though they were such as to shake the hills!

47. Never think that God would fail His Apostles in His promise: for God is Exalted in power — the Lord of Retribution.

48. One day the Earth will be changed to a different Earth, and so will be the Heavens, and (men) will be marshalled forth, before God, the One, the Irresistible;

49. And thou wilt see the Sinners that day bound together in fetters —

50. Their garments of liquid pitch[5], and their faces covered with Fire;

51. That God may requite each soul according to its deserts; and verily God is Swift in calling account.

52. Here is a Message for mankind: let them take warning therefrom, and let them know that He is (no other than) One God: let men of understanding take heed.

---

[5] Thick dark inflammable liquid

Chapter 15
Sürah Al-Hijr (The Rocky Tract)
Revealed at Makkah, 99 verses.

In the name of God, Most Gracious, Most Merciful.

1. Alif Läm Ra. These are the Ayat of Revelation — of a Qur'an that makes things clear.

2. Again and again will those who disbelieve wish that they had bowed (to God's Will) in Islam.

3. Leave them alone, to enjoy (the good things of this life) and to please themselves: let (false) Hope amuse them: soon will knowledge (undeceive them).

4. Never did We destroy a population that had not a term decreed and assigned beforehand.

5. Neither can a people anticipate its Term, nor delay it.

6. They say: "O thou to whom the Message is being revealed! Truly thou art mad (or possessed)!

7. "Why bringest thou not angels to us if it be that thou hast the Truth?"

8. We send not the angels down except for just cause: if they came (to the ungodly), behold! no respite would they have!

9. We have, without doubt, sent down the Message; and We will assuredly guard it (from corruption).

10. We did send Apostles before thee amongst the religious sects of old:

11. But never came an Apostle to them but they mocked him.

12. Even so do We let it creep into the hearts of the sinners —

13. That they should not believe in the (Message); but the ways of the ancients have passed away.

14. Even if We opened out to them a gate from heaven, and they were to continue (all day) ascending therein,

15. They would only say: "Our eyes have been intoxicated: nay, we have been bewitched by sorcery."

16. It is We who have set out the Zodiacal Signs[1] in the heavens,

---

[1] Names of groups of fixed stars (or constellations) in the belt of heavens that is divided into 12 equal parts.

and made them fair-seeming to (all) beholders;

17. And (moreover) We have guarded them from every evil spirit accursed:

18. But any that gains a hearing by stealth, is pursued by a flaming fire, bright (to see).

19. And the earth We have spread out (like a carpet); set thereon mountains firm and immovable; and produced therein all kinds of things in due balance.

20. And We have provided therein means of subsistence — for you and for those for whose sustenance ye are not responsible.

21. And there is not a thing but its (sources and) treasures (inexhaustible) are with Us; but We only send down thereof in due and ascertainable measures.

22. And We send the fecundating[2] winds, then cause the rain to descend from the sky, therewith providing you with water (in abundance), though ye are not the guardians of its stores.

23. And verily, it is We Who give life, and Who give death: it is We Who remain Inheritors (after all else passes away).

24. To Us are known those of you who hasten forward, and those who lag behind.

25. Assuredly it is thy Lord who will gather them together: for He is Perfect in Wisdom and Knowledge.

26. We created man from sounding[3] clay, from mud molded into shape;

27. And the Jinn race, We had created before, from the fire of a scorching wind.

28. Behold! thy Lord said to the angels: "I am about to create man, from sounding clay, from mud molded into shape;

29. "When I have fashioned him (in due proportion) and breathed into him of My spirit, fall ye down in obeisance[4] unto him."

30. So the angels prostrated themselves all of them together:

31. Not so Iblis: he refused to be among those who prostrated themselves.

---

[2] Fertilizing

[3] Giving forth sound

[4] Gesture, especially bow or curtsy, expressing submission, respect or saLutation.

32. (God) said: "O Iblis! what is your reason for not being among those who prostrated themselves?"

33. (Iblis) said: "I am not one to prostrate myself to man, whom thou didst create from sounding clay, from mud molded into shape."

34. (God) said: "Then get thee out from here; for thou art rejected, accursed.

35. "And the Curse shall be on thee till the Day of Judgment."

36. (Iblis) said: "O my Lord! give me then respite till the Day the (dead) are raised."

37. (God) said: "Respite is granted thee —

38. "Till the Day of the Time Appointed."

39. (Iblis) said: "O my Lord! because Thou hast put me in the wrong, I will make (wrong) fair-seeming to them on the earth, and I will put them all in the wrong —

40. "Except Thy servants among them, sincere and purified (by Thy grace)."

41. (God) said: "This (Way of My sincere servants) is indeed a Way that leads straight to Me.

42. "For over My servants no authority shalt thou have, except such as put themselves in the wrong and follow thee."

43. And verily, Hell is the promised abode for them all!

44. To it are seven Gates: for each of those Gates is (special) class (of sinners) assigned.

45. The righteous (will be) amid Gardens and fountains (of clear-flowing water).

46. (Their greeting will be): "Enter ye here in Peace and Security."

47. And We shall remove from their hearts any lurking sense of injury: (they will be) brothers (joyfully) facing each other on thrones (of dignity).

48. There no sense of fatigue shall touch them, nor shall they (ever) be asked to leave.

49. Tell My servants that I am indeed the Oft-Forgiving, Most Merciful;

50. And that My Penalty will be indeed the most grievous Penalty.

51. Tell them about the guests of Abraham.

52. When they entered his presence and said, "Peace!" he said, "We feel afraid of you!"

53. They said: "Fear not! We give thee glad tidings of a son endowed with wisdom."

54. He said: "Do ye give me glad tidings that old age has seized me? Of what, then, is your good news?"

55. They said: "We give thee glad tidings in truth: be not then in despair!"

56. He said: "And who despairs of the mercy of his Lord, but such as go astray?"

57. Abraham said: "What then is the business on which ye (have come), O ye messengers (of God)?"

58. They said: "We have been sent to a people (deep) in sin.

59. "Excepting the adherents of Lüt: them we are certainly (charged) to save (from harm) — all —

60. "Except his wife, who, we have ascertained, will be among those who will lag behind."

61. At length when the messengers arrived among the adherents of Lüt,

62. He said: "Ye appear to be uncommon folk."

63. They said: "Yea, we have come to thee to accomplish that of which they doubt.

64. "We have brought to thee that which is inevitably due, and assuredly we tell the truth.

65. "Then travel by night with thy household, when a portion of the night (yet remains), and do thou bring up the rear: let no one amongst you look back, but pass on whither ye are ordered."

66. And We made known this decree to him, that the last remnants of those (sinners) should be cut off by the morning.

67. The inhabitants of the City came in (mad) joy (at news of the young men).

68. Lüt said: "These are my guests: disgrace me not:

69. "But fear God, and shame me not."

70. They said: "Did we not forbid thee (to speak) for all and sundry[5]?"

71. He said: "There are my daughters (to marry). If ye must act (so)."

---

[5] Everyone, collectively and individually.

72. Verily, by thy life (O Prophet), in their wild intoxication, they wander in distraction, to and fro.

73. But the (mighty) Blast overtook them before morning,

74. And We turned (the Cities) upside down, and rained down on them brimstones hard as baked clay.

75. Behold! in this are Signs for those who by tokens do understand.

76. And the (cities were) right on the highroad.

77. Behold! in this is a Sign for those who believe!

78. And the Companions of the Wood were also wrongdoers;

79. So We exacted retribution[6] from them. They were both on an open highway, plain to see.

80. The Companions of the Rocky Tract also rejected the Apostles:

81. We sent them Our Signs, but they persisted in turning away from them.

82. Out of the mountains did they hew[7] (their) edifices[8], (feeling themselves) secure.

83. But the (mighty) Blast seized them of a morning,

84. And of no avail to them was all that they did (with such art and care)!

85. We created not the heavens, the earth, and all between them, but for just ends. And the Hour is surely coming (when this will be manifest). So overlook (any human faults) with gracious forgiveness.

86. For verily it is thy Lord Who is the Master-Creator, knowing all things.

87. And We have bestowed upon thee the Seven Oft-Repeated (verses) and the Grand Qur'an.

88. Strain not thine eyes (wistfully[9]) at what We have bestowed on certain classes of them, nor grieve over them: but lower thy wing (in gentleness) to the Believers.

89. And say: "I am indeed he that warneth openly and without ambiguity" —

90. (Of just such wrath) as We sent down on those who divided

---

[6] Punished them.

[7] Cut, carve

[8] Buildings

[9] Longingly

(Scripture into arbitrary[10] parts) —

91. (So also on such) as have made the Qur'an into shreds[11] (as they please).

92. Therefore, by thy Lord, We will, of a surety, call them to account,

93. For all their deeds.

94. Therefore expound[12] openly what thou art commanded, and turn away from those who join false gods with God.

95. For sufficient are We unto thee against those who scoff[13] —

96. Those who adopt, with God, another god: but soon will they come to know.

97. We do indeed know how thy heart is distressed at what they say.

98. But celebrate the praises of thy Lord, and be of those who prostrate themselves in adoration[14].

99. And serve thy Lord until there come unto thee the Hour that is Certain.

Chapter 16
Sürah An-Nahl (The Bees)
Revealed at Makkah, 128 verses.

In the name of God, Most Gracious, Most Merciful.

1. (Inevitably) cometh (to pass) the Command of God: seek ye not then to hasten it: glory to Him, and far is He above having the partners they ascribe unto Him!

2. He doth send down His angels with inspiration of His Command, to such of His servants as He pleaseth, (saying): "Warn (Man) that there is no god but I: so do your duty unto Me."

3. He has created the heavens and the earth for just ends: far is

---

[10] Based on mere opinion or random choice.
[11] Bits and pieces.
[12] Explain
[13] Ridicule, make fun of.
[14] Worship

He above having the partners they ascribe to Him!

4. He has created man from a sperm drop; and behold this same (man) becomes an open disputer!

5. And cattle He has created for you (men): from them ye derive warmth, and numerous benefits, and of their (meat) ye eat.

6. And ye have a sense of pride and beauty in them as ye drive them home in the evening, and as ye lead them forth to pasture in the morning.

7. And they carry your heavy loads to lands that ye could not (otherwise) reach except with souls distressed: for your Lord is indeed Most Kind, Most Merciful.

8. And (He has created) horses, mules, and donkeys, for you to ride and use for show; and He has created (other) things of what ye have no knowledge.

9. And unto God leads straight the Way, but there are ways that turn aside: if God had willed, He could have guided all of you.

10. It is He Who sends down rain from the sky: from it ye drink, and out of it (grows) the vegetation on which ye feed your cattle.

11. With it He produces for you corn, olives, date-palms, grapes, and every kind of fruit: verily in this is a Sign for those who give thought.

12. He has made subject to you the Night and the Day; the Sun and the Moon; and the Stars are in subjection by His Command: verily in this are Signs for men who are wise.

13. And the things on this earth which He has multiplied in varying colors (and qualities): verily in this is a Sign for men who celebrate the praises of God (in gratitude).

14. It is He Who has made the sea subject, that ye may eat thereof flesh that is fresh and tender, and that ye may extract therefrom ornaments to wear; and thou seest the ships therein that plough the waves, that ye may seek (thus) of the bounty of God and that ye may be grateful.

15. And He has set up on the earth mountains standing firm, lest it should shake with you; and rivers and roads; that ye may guide yourselves,

16. And marks and signposts; and by the stars (men) guide themselves.

17. Is then He Who creates like one that creates not? Will ye not receive admonition[1]?

18. If ye would count up the favors of God, never would ye be able to number them: for God is Oft-Forgiving, Most Merciful.

19. And God doth know what ye conceal, and what ye reveal.

20. Those whom they invoke[2] besides God create nothing and are themselves created.

21. (They are things) dead, lifeless: nor do they know when they will be raised up.

22. Your God is One God: as to those who believe not in the Hereafter, their hearts refuse to know and they are arrogant.

23. Undoubtedly God doth know what they conceal, and what they reveal: verily He loveth not the arrogant.

24. When it is said to them, "What is it that your Lord has revealed?" They say, "Tales of the ancients!"

25. Let them bear, on the Day of Judgment, their own burdens in full, and also (something) of the burdens of those without knowledge, whom they misled. Alas, how grievous the burdens they will bear!

26. Those before them did also plot (against God's Way): but God took their structures from their foundations, and the roof fell down on them from above; and the Wrath seized them from directions they did not perceive.

27. Then, on the Day of Judgment, He will cover them with shame, and say: "Where are My 'partners' concerning whom ye used to dispute (with the godly)?" Those endued with knowledge will say: "This Day, indeed, are the Unbelievers covered with Shame and Misery —

28. "(Namely) those whose lives the angels take in a state of wrongdoing to their own souls. Then would they offer submission (with the pretence[3]), 'We did no evil (knowingly).' (The angels will reply), "Nay, but verily God knoweth all that ye did;

29. "So enter the gates of Hell, to dwell therein. Thus evil indeed is the abode[4] of the arrogant."

---

[1] Warning, counsel

[2] Summon, to call on

[3] False claim

[4] Home or house.

30. To the righteous (when) it is said, "What is it that your Lord has revealed?" they say, "All that is good." To those who do good, there is good in this world, and the Home of the Hereafter is even better. And excellent indeed is the Home of the righteous —

31. Gardens of Eternity which they will enter: beneath them flow (pleasant) rivers: they will have therein all that they wish: thus doth God reward the righteous —

32. (Namely) those whose lives the angels take in a state of purity, saying (to them), "Peace be on you; enter ye the Garden, because of the good which ye did (in the world)."

33. Do the (ungodly) wait until the angels come to them, or there comes the Command of thy Lord (for their doom[5])? So did those who went before them. But God wronged them not: nay, they wronged their own souls.

34. But the evil results of their deeds overtook them, and that very (Wrath) at which they had scoffed[6] hemmed them in[7].

35. The worshippers of false gods say: "If God had so willed, we should not have worshipped aught but Him — neither we nor our fathers — nor should we have prescribed prohibitions other than His." So did those who went before them. But what is the mission of Apostles but to preach the Clear Message?

36. For We assuredly sent amongst every People an Apostle, (with the Command), "Serve God and eschew[8] Evil": of the people were some whom God guided, and some on whom Error became inevitably (established). So travel through the earth, and see what was the end of those who denied (the Truth).

37. If thou art anxious for their guidance, yet God guideth not such as He leaves to stray, and there is none to help them.

38. They swear their strongest oaths by God, that God will not raise up those who die: Nay, but it is a promise (binding) on Him in truth: but most among mankind realize it not.

39. (They must be raised up), in order that He may manifest to them the truth of that wherein they differ, and that the rejecters of

---

[5] Ruin, condemnation
[6] Made fun of
[7] Encircled them
[8] Avoid

Truth may realize that they had indeed (surrendered to) Falsehood.

40. For to anything which We have willed, We but say the Word, "Be," and it is.

41. To those who leave their homes in the cause of God, after suffering oppression — We will assuredly give a goodly home in this world: but truly the reward of the Hereafter will be greater, if they only realized (this)!

42. (They are) those who persevere[9] in patience, and put their trust on their Lord.

43. And before thee also the apostles We sent were but men, to whom We granted inspiration: if ye realize this not, ask of those who possess the Message.

44. (We sent them) with Clear Signs and Books of dark prophecies; and We have sent down unto thee (also) the Message; that thou mayest explain clearly to men what is sent for them, and that they may give thought.

45. Do then those who devise evil (plots) feel secure that God will not cause the earth to swallow them up, or that the Wrath will not seize them from directions they little perceive? —

46. Or that He may not call them to account in the midst of their goings to and fro, without a chance of their frustrating Him?

47. Or that He may not call them to account by a process of slow wastage — for thy Lord is indeed full of kindness and mercy.

48. Do they not look at God's creation, (even) among (inanimate) things — how their (very) shadows turn round, from the right and the left, prostrating themselves to God, and that in the humblest manner?

49. And to God doth obeisance[10] all that is in the heavens and on earth, whether moving (living) creatures or the angels: for none are arrogant (before their Lord).

50. They all revere[11] their Lord, high above them, and they do all that they are commanded.

51. God has said: "Take not (for worship) two gods: for He is just One God: then fear Me (and Me alone)."

---

[9] Persist, remain steadfast

[10] Bow

[11] Adore, worship, honour

52. To Him belongs whatever is in the heavens and on earth, and to Him is duty due always: then will ye fear other than God?

53. And ye have no good thing but is from God: and moreover, when ye are touched by distress, unto Him ye cry with groans;

54. Yet, when He removes the distress from you, behold! some of you turn to other gods to join with their Lord —

55. (As if) to show their ingratitude for the favors We have bestowed on them! Then enjoy (your brief day); but soon will ye know (your folly)!

56. And they (even assign, to things they do not know, a portion out of that which we have bestowed for their sustenance! By God, ye shall certainly be called to account for your false inventions.

57. And they assign daughters for God! Glory be to Him! and for themselves (sons — the issue) they desire!

58. When news is brought to one of them, of (the birth of) a female (child), his face darkens, and he is filled with inward grief!

59. With shame does he hide himself from his people, because of the bad news he has had! Shall he retain it on (sufferance[12] and) contempt, or bury it in the dust? Ah! what an evil (choice) they decide on!

60. To those who believe not in the Hereafter, applies the similitude of evil: to God applies the highest similitude: for He is the Exalted in Power, Full of Wisdom.

61. If God were to punish men for their wrongdoing, He would not leave, on the (earth), a single living creature: but He gives them respite[13] for a stated term: when their term expires, they would not be able to delay (the punishment) for a single hour, just as they would not be able to anticipate[14] it (for a single hour).

62. They attribute to God what they hate (for themselves), and their tongues assert the falsehood that all good things are for themselves: without doubt for them is the Fire, and they will be the first to be hastened on into it!

63. By God, We (also) sent (Our apostles) to peoples before thee; but Satan made, (to the wicked), their own acts seem alluring[15]: he

---

[12] Toleration or permission

[13] Delay, interval (of rest or relief), reprieve.

[14] To cause to happen before its due time.

[15] Charming

is also their patron today, but they shall have a most grievous Penalty.

64. And We sent down the Book to thee for the express purpose, that thou shouldst make clear to them those things in which they differ, and that it should be a guide and a mercy to those who believe.

65. And God sends down rain from the skies, and gives therewith life to the earth after its death: verily in this is a Sign for those who listen.

66. And verily in cattle (too) will ye find an instructive[16] Sign. From what is within their bodies, between excretions[17] and blood, We produce, for your drink, milk, pure and agreeable to those who drink it.

67. And from the fruit of the date palm and the vine[18], ye get out wholesome[19] drink and food: behold, in this also is a Sign for those who are wise.

68. And thy Lord taught the Bee to build its cells in hills, on trees, and in (men's) habitations[20];

69. Then to eat of all the produce (of the earth), and find with skill the spacious paths of its Lord: there issues from within their bodies a drink of varying colors, wherein is healing for men: verily in this is a Sign for those who give thought.

70. It is God who creates you and takes your souls at death; and of you there are some who are sent back to a feeble age, so that they know nothing after having known (much): for God is All-Knowing, All-Powerful.

71. God has bestowed His gifts of sustenance more freely on some of you than on others; those more favored are not going to throw back their gifts to those whom their right hands possess, so as to be equal in that respect. Will they then deny the favors of God?

72. And God has made for you mates (and companions) of your own nature. And made for you, out of them, sons and daughters and grandchildren, and provided for you sustenance of the best; will they then believe in vain things, and be ungrateful for God's favors? —

---

[16] Enlightening
[17] Waste discharged from body especially faeces and urine.
[18] Plant whose fruit is the grape
[19] Healthful.
[20] Dwelling places

73. And worship others than God — such as have no power of providing them, for sustenance, with anything in heavens or earth, and cannot possibly have such power?

74. Invent not similitudes for God: for God knoweth, and ye know not.

75. God sets forth the Parable (of two men: one) a slave under the dominion[21] of another; he has no power of any sort; and (the other) a man on whom We have bestowed goodly favors from Ourselves, and he spends thereof (freely), privately and publicly: are the two equal? (By no means); praise be to God. But most of them understand not.

76. God sets forth (another) Parable of two men: one of them dumb, with no power of any sort; a wearisome burden is he to his master; whichever way he directs him, he brings no good: is such a man equal with one who commands justice, and is on a straight way?

77. To God belongeth the mystery of the heavens and the earth. And the decision of the Hour (of Judgment) is as the twinkling of an eye, or even quicker: for God hath power over all things.

78. It is He Who brought you forth from the wombs of your mothers when ye knew nothing; and He gave you hearing and sight and intelligence and affection: that ye may give thanks (to God).

79. Do they not look at the birds, held poised[22] in the midst of (the air and) the sky? Nothing holds them up but (the power of) God. Verily in this are Signs for those who believe.

80. It is God who made your habitations homes of rest and quiet for you; and made for you out of the skins of animals, (tents for) dwellings, which ye find so light (and handy) when ye travel and when ye stop (in your travels); and out of their wool, and their soft fibers (between wool and hair), and their hair, rich stuff and articles of convenience (to serve you) for a time.

81. It is God who made, out of the things He created some things to give you shade; of the hills He made some for your shelter; He made you garments to protect you from heat, and coats of mail to protect you from your (mutual) violence. Thus does He complete His

---

[21] Control, authority

[22] Held in suspended or supported position, balanced

favors on you, that ye may bow to His will (in Islam).

82. But if they turn away, thy duty is only to preach the clear message.

83. They recognize the favors of God; then they deny them; and most of them are (creatures) ungrateful.

84. One day We shall raise from all peoples a witness: then will no excuse be accepted from Unbelievers, nor will they receive any favors.

85. When the wrongdoers (actually) see the Penalty, then will it in no way be mitigated[23], nor will they then receive respite.

86. When those who gave partners to God will see their "partners," they will say: "Our Lord! these are our 'partners,' those whom we used to invoke besides Thee." But they will throw back their word at them (and say): "Indeed ye are liars!"

87. That day shall they (openly) show (their) submission to God; and all their inventions shall leave them in the lurch[24].

88. Those who reject God and hinder (men) from the path of God, for them will We add Penalty to Penalty; for that they used to spread mischief.

89. One day We shall raise from all peoples a witness against them, from amongst themselves: and We shall bring thee as a witness against these (thy people): and We have sent down to thee the Book explaining all things, a Guide, a Mercy, and glad tidings to Muslims.

90. God commands justice, the doing of good, and liberality to kith and kin[25], and He forbids all shameful deeds, and injustice and rebellion: He instructs you, that ye may receive admonition.

91. Fulfil the covenant of God when ye have entered into it, and break not your oaths after ye have confirmed them; indeed ye have made God your surety; for God knoweth all that ye do.

92. And be not like a woman who breaks into untwisted strands[26] the yarn[27] she has spun, after it has become strong. Nor take your

---

[23] Reduce severity, alleviate pain
[24] Abandon them in difficulty and time of need.
[25] Blood relations
[26] Fibers
[27] Thread

oaths to practice deception between yourselves, lest one party should be more numerous than another: for God will test you by this; and on the Day of Judgment He will certainly make clear to you (the truth of) that wherein ye disagree.

93. If God so willed, He could make you all one people: but He leaves straying whom He pleases, and He guides whom He pleases: but ye shall certainly be called to account for all your actions.

94. And take not your oaths, to practice deception between yourselves, with the result that someone's foot may slip after it was firmly planted; and ye may have to taste the evil (consequences) of having hindered (men) from the path of God, and a mighty Wrath descend on you.

95. Nor sell the covenant of God for a miserable price: for with God is (a prize) far better for you, if ye only knew.

96. What is with you must vanish: what is with God will endure. And We will certainly bestow, on those who patiently persevere, their reward according to the best of their actions.

97. Whoever works righteousness, man or woman, and has faith, verily, to him will We give a new life, a life that is good and pure, and We will bestow on such their reward according to the best of their actions.

98. When thou dost read the Qur'an, seek God's protection from Satan the Rejected One.

99. No authority has he over those who believe and put their trust in their Lord.

100. His authority is over those only, who take him as patron and who join partners with God.

101. When We substitute one revelation for another, and God knows best what He reveals (in stages), they say, "Thou art but a forger": but most of them understand not.

102. Say, the Holy Spirit has brought the revelation from thy Lord in truth, in order to strengthen those who believe, and as a Guide and Glad Tidings to Muslims.

103. We know indeed that they say, "It is a man that teaches him." The tongue of him they wickedly point to is notably foreign, while this is Arabic, pure and clear.

104. Those who believe not in the Signs of God, God will not

guide them, and theirs will be a grievous Penalty.

105. It is those who believe not in the Signs of God, that forge falsehood: it is they who lie!

106. Anyone who, after accepting faith in God, utters unbelief, except under compulsion, his heart remaining firm in faith, but such as open their breast to unbelief, on them is Wrath from God, and theirs will be a dreadful Penalty.

107. This because they love the life of this world better than the Hereafter: and God will not guide those who reject faith.

108. Those are they whose hearts, ears, and eyes God has sealed up, and they take no heed.

109. Without doubt, in the Hereafter they will perish.

110. But verily thy Lord to those who leave their homes after trials and persecutions and who thereafter strive and fight for the faith and patiently persevere, thy Lord, after all this, is Oft-Forgiving, Most Merciful.

111. One day every soul will come up struggling for itself, and every soul will be recompensed (fully) for all its actions, and none will be unjustly dealt with.

112. God sets forth a parable: a city enjoying security and quiet, abundantly supplied with sustenance from every place: yet was it ungrateful for the favors of God: so God made it taste of hunger and terror (in extremes) (closing in on it) like a garment (from every side), because of the (evil) which (its people) wrought.

113. And there came to them an Apostle from among themselves, but they falsely rejected him; so the wrath seized them even in the midst of their iniquities[28].

114. So eat of the sustenance which God has provided for you, lawful and good; and be grateful for the favors of God, if it is He whom ye serve.

115. He has only forbidden you dead meat, and blood, and the flesh of swine, and any (food) over which the name of other than God has been invoked. But if one is forced by necessity, without wilful disobedience, nor transgressing due limits, then God is Oft-Forgiving, Most Merciful.

---

[28] Wickedness, gross injustice

116. But say not, for any false thing that your tongues may put forth, "This is lawful, and this is forbidden," so as to ascribe false things to God. For those who ascribe false things to God, will never prosper.

117. (In such falsehood) is but a paltry profit; but they will have a most grievous Penalty.

118. To the Jews We prohibited such things as We have mentioned to thee before: We did them no wrong, but they were used to doing wrong to themselves.

119. But verily thy Lord, to those who do wrong in ignorance, but who thereafter repent and make amends, thy Lord, after all this, is Oft-Forgiving, Most Merciful.

120. Abraham was indeed a model, devoutly obedient to God, (and) true in faith, and he joined not gods with God:

121. He showed his gratitude for the favors of God, Who chose him, and guided him to a straight way.

122. And We gave him good in this world, and he will be, in the Hereafter, in the ranks of the righteous.

123. So We have taught thee the inspired (message), "Follow the ways of Abraham the true in faith, and he joined not gods with God."

124. The Sabbath was only made (strict) to those who disagreed (as to its observance); but God will judge between them on the Day of Judgment as to their differences.

125. Invite (all) to the way of thy Lord with wisdom and beautiful preaching; and argue with them in ways that are best and most gracious: for thy Lord knoweth best, who have strayed from His Path, and who receive guidance.

126. And if ye do catch them out,[29] catch them out no worse than they catch you out: but if ye show patience, that is indeed the best (course) for those who are patient.

127. And do thou be patient, for thy patience is but from God; nor grieve over them: and distress not thyself because of their plots.

128. For God is with those who restrain themselves, and those who do good.

---

[29] Detect (them) in a mistake, take (them) unawares.

Chapter 17
Sürah Al-Isra (The Night Journey)
Revealed at Makkah, 111 verses.

In the name of God, Most Gracious, Most Merciful.

1. Glory to (God) Who did take His Servant for a Journey by night from the Sacred Mosque to the Farthest Mosque, whose precincts[1] We did Bless — in order that We might show him some of Our Signs: for He is the one Who heareth and seeth (all things).

2. We gave Moses the Book, and made it a Guide to the Children of Israel, (commanding): "Take not other than Me as Disposer of (your) affairs."

3. O ye that are sprung from those whom We carried (in the Ark) with Noah! verily he was a devotee[2] most grateful.

4. And We gave (clear) warning to the Children of Israel in the Book, that twice would they do mischief on the earth and be elated[3] with mighty arrogance (and twice would they be punished)!

5. When the first of the warnings came to pass, We sent against you Our servants given to terrible warfare. They entered the very inmost parts of your homes; and it was a warning (completely) fulfilled.

6. Then did We grant you the Return as against them: We gave you increase in resources and sons, and made you the more numerous in manpower.

7. If ye did well, ye did well for yourselves; if ye did evil, (ye did it) against yourselves; so when the second of the warnings came to pass, (We permitted your enemies) to disfigure[4] your faces, and to enter your Temple as they had entered it before, and to visit with destruction all that fell into their power.

8. It may be that your Lord may (yet) show Mercy unto you; but if ye revert (to your sins), We shall revert (to Our punishments): and We have made Hell a prison for those who reject (all Faith).

9. Verily this Qur'an doth guide to that which is most right (or

---

[1] Surroundings, enclosed space
[2] One devoted most zealously to service of God.
[3] Jubilant
[4] Distort, mar

stable), and giveth the glad tidings to the Believers who work deeds of righteousness, that they shall have a magnificent reward;

10. And to those who believe not in the Hereafter, (it announceth) that We have prepared for them a Penalty grievous (indeed).

11. The prayer that man should make for good, he maketh for evil: for man is given to hasty (deeds).

12. We have made the Night and the Day as two (of Our) Signs: the Sign of the Night have We obscured, while the Sign of the Day We have made to enlighten you; that ye may seek Bounty from your Lord, and that ye may know the number and count of the years: all things have We explained in detail.

13. Every man's fate We have fastened on his own neck: on the Day of Judgment We shall bring out for him a scroll[5], which he will see spread open.

14. (It will be said to him:) "Read thine (own) record: sufficient is thy soul this day to make out an account against thee."

15. Who receiveth guidance, receiveth it for his own benefit: who goeth astray doth so to his own loss: no bearer of burdens can bear the burden of another: nor would We visit with Our Wrath until We had sent an apostle (to give warning).

16. When We decide to destroy a population, We (first) send a definite order to those among them who are given the good things of this life and yet transgress; so that the word is proved true against them: then (it is) We destroy them utterly.

17. How many generations have We destroyed after Noah? And enough is thy Lord to note and see the sins of His servants.

18. If any do wish for the transitory[6] things (of this life), We readily[7] grant them — such things as We will, to such persons as We will: in the end have We provided Hell for them: they will burn therein, disgraced and rejected.

19. Those who do wish for the (things of) the Hereafter, and strive therefor with all due striving, and have Faith — they are the ones whose striving is acceptable (to God).

20. Of the bounties of thy Lord We bestow freely on all — these

---

[5] A roll of paper or parchment

[6] Temporary

[7] Freely, quickly

as well as those: the bounties of thy Lord are not closed (to anyone).

21. See how We have bestowed more on some than on others; but verily the Hereafter is more in rank and gradation and more in excellence.

22. Take not with God another object of worship; or thou (O man!) wilt sit in disgrace and destitution[8].

23. Thy Lord hath decreed that ye worship none but Him, and that ye be kind to parents. Whether one or both of them attain old age in thy life, say not to them a word of contempt, nor repel them, but address them in terms of honour.

24. And, out of kindness, lower to them the wing of humility, and say: "My Lord! bestow on them Thy Mercy even as they cherished me in childhood."

25. Your Lord knoweth best what is in your hearts: if ye do deeds of righteousness, verily He is Most Forgiving to those who turn to Him again and again (in true penitence[9]).

26. And render to the kindred[10] their due rights, as (also) to those in want, and to the wayfarer: but squander not (your wealth) in the manner of a spendthrift[11].

27. Verily spendthrifts are brothers of the Evil Ones; and the Evil One is to his Lord (Himself) ungrateful.

28. And even if thou hast to turn away from them in pursuit of the Mercy from thy Lord which thou dost expect, yet speak to them a word of easy kindness.

29. Make not thy hand tied (like a niggard's) to thy neck, nor stretch it forth to its utmost reach, so that thou become blameworthy and destitute.

30. Verily thy Lord doth provide sustenance in abundance for whom He pleaseth, and He provideth in a just measure: for He doth know and regard all His servants.

31. Kill not your children for fear of want: We shall provide sustenance for them as well as for you: verily the killing of them is a great sin.

---

8 Indigence, privation
9 Repentance
10 Relatives
11 Extravagant.

32. Nor come nigh to adultery: for it is a shameful (deed) and an evil, opening the road (to other evils).

33. Nor take life — which God has made sacred — except for just cause. And if anyone is slain wrongfully, We have given his heir authority (to demand *Qisas* or to forgive): but let him not exceed bounds in the matter of taking life: for he is helped (by the Law).

34. Come not nigh to the orphan's property except to improve it, until he attains the age of full strength; and fulfil (every) engagement, for (every) engagement will be enquired into (on the Day of Reckoning).

35. Give full measure when ye measure, and weigh with a balance that is straight: that is the most fitting and the most advantageous in the final determination.

36. And pursue not that of which thou hast no knowledge; for every act of hearing, or of seeing, or of (feeling in) the heart will be enquired into (on the Day of Reckoning).

37. Nor walk on the earth with insolence: for thou canst not rend the earth asunder, nor reach the mountains in height.

38. Of all such things the evil is hateful in the sight of thy Lord.

39. These are among the (precepts[12] of) wisdom, which thy Lord has revealed to thee. Take not, with God, another object of worship, lest thou shouldst be thrown into Hell, blameworthy and rejected.

40. Has then your Lord, (O Pagans!) preferred for you sons, and taken for Himself daughters among the angels? Truly ye utter a most dreadful saying!

41. We have explained (things) in various (ways) in this Qur'an, in order that they may receive admonition, but it only increases their flight (from the Truth)!

42. Say: if there had been (other) gods with Him — as they say — behold, they would certainly have sought out a way to the Lord of the Throne!

43. Glory to Him! He is high above all that they say! — Exalted and Great (beyond measure)!

44. The seven heavens and the earth, and all beings therein, declare His glory: there is not a thing but celebrates His praise; and yet ye

---

[12] Principles

understand not how they declare His glory! Verily He is Oft-For-bearing, Most Forgiving!

45. When thou dost recite the Qur'an, We put, between thee and those who believe not in the Hereafter, a veil invisible:

46. And We put coverings over their hearts (and minds) lest they should understand the Qur'an, and deafness into their ears: when thou dost commemorate[13] thy Lord — and Him alone — in the Qur'an, they turn on their backs, fleeing (from the Truth).

47. We know best why it is they listen, when they listen to thee; and when they meet in private conference, behold, the wicked say, "Ye follow none other than a man bewitched!"

48. See what similes they strike for thee; but they have gone astray, and never can they find a way.

49. They say: "What! when we are reduced to bones and dust, should we really be raised up (to be) a new creation?"

50. Say: "(Nay!) be ye stones or iron,

51. "Or created matter which, in your minds, is hardest (to be raised up) — (yet shall ye be raised up)!" Then will they say: "Who will cause us to return?" Say: "He Who created you first!" Then will they wag[14] their heads towards thee, and say, "When will that be?" Say, "Maybe it will be quite soon!

52. "It will be on a Day when He will call you, and ye will answer (His call) with (words of) His praise, and ye will think that ye tarried but a little while!"

53. Say to My servants that they should (only) say those things that are best: for Satan doth sow dissensions[15] among them: for Satan is to man an avowed enemy.

54. It is your Lord that knoweth you best: if He please, He granteth you mercy, or if He please, punishment: We have not sent thee to be a disposer of their affairs for them.

55. And it is your Lord that knoweth best all beings that are in the heavens and on earth: We did bestow on some Prophets more (and other) gifts than on others: and We gave to David (the gift of) the Psalms.

---

[13] Glorify
[14] Shake
[15] Conflict, strife

56. Say: "Call on those — besides Him — whom ye fancy: they have neither the power to remove your troubles from you nor to change them."

57. Those whom they call upon do desire (for themselves) means of access to their Lord — even those who are nearest: they hope for His Mercy and fear His Wrath: for the Wrath of thy Lord is something to take heed of.

58. There is not a population but We shall destroy it before the Day of Judgment or punish it with a dreadful Penalty: that is written in the (eternal) Record.

59. And We refrain from sending the Signs, only because the men of former generations treated them as false: We sent the she-camel to the Thamūd to open their eyes, but they treated her wrongfully: We only send the Signs by way of terror (and warning from evil).

60. Behold! We told thee that thy Lord doth encompass mankind round about: We granted the Vision which We showed thee, but as a trial for men — as also the Cursed Tree (mentioned) in the Qur'an: We put terror (and warning) into them, but it only increases their inordinate[16] transgression!

61. Behold! We said to the angels: "Bow down unto Adam": they bowed down except Iblis: he said, "Shall I bow down to one whom Thou didst create from clay?"

62. He said, "Seest Thou? This is the one whom thou hast honoured above me! If Thou wilt but respite me to the Day of Judgment, I will surely bring his descendants under my sway — all but a few!"

63. God said: "Go thy way; if any of them follow thee, verily Hell will be the recompense[17] of you (all) — an ample recompense.

64. "Lead to destruction those whom thou canst among them, with thy (seductive) voice; make assaults on them with thy cavalry and thy infantry; mutually share with them wealth and children; and make promises to them. But Satan promises them nothing but deceit.

65. "As for My servants, no authority shalt thou have over them." Enough is thy Lord for a Disposer of affairs.

66. Your Lord is He that maketh the Ship go smoothly for you through the sea, in order that ye may seek of His Bounty: for He

---

[16] Excessive, extreme

[17] Reward

is unto you Most Merciful.

67. When distress seizes you at sea, those that ye call upon — besides Himself — leave you in the lurch! But when He brings you back safe to land, ye turn away (from Him). Most ungrateful is man!

68. Do ye then feel secure that He will not cause you to be swallowed up beneath the earth when ye are on land, or that He will not send against you a violent tornado (with showers of stones) so that ye shall find no one to carry out your affairs for you?

69. Or do ye feel secure that He will not send you back a second time to sea and send against you a heavy gale[18] to drown you because of your ingratitude, so that ye find no helper therein against Us?

70. We have honoured the sons of Adam; provided them with transport on land and sea; given them for sustenance things good and pure; and conferred on them special favors, above a great part of Our Creation.

71. One day We shall call together all human beings with their (respective) *Imams*[19]: those who are given their record in their right hand will read it (with pleasure), and they will not be dealt with unjustly in the least.

72. But those who were blind in this world will be blind in the Hereafter, and most astray from the Path.

73. And their purpose was to tempt thee away from that which We had revealed unto thee, to substitute in Our name something quite different: (in that case), behold! they would certainly have made thee (their) friend!

74. And had We not given thee strength, thou wouldst nearly have inclined to them a little.

75. In that case We should have made thee taste an equal portion (of punishment) in this life, and an equal portion in death: and moreover thou wouldst have found none to help thee against Us!

76. Their purpose was to scare thee off the land, in order to expel thee; but in that case they would not have stayed (therein) after thee, except for a little while.

77. (This was Our) way with the Apostles We sent before thee:

18 storm

19 The Arabic word *Imam* here may mean a leader, revelation or revealed book, or record of deeds.

thou wilt find no change in Our ways.

78. Establish regular prayers — at the sun's decline till the darkness of the night, and the morning prayer and reading: for the prayer and reading in the morning carry their testimony.

79. And pray in the small watches[20] of the morning: (it would be) an additional prayer (or spiritual profit) for thee: soon will thy Lord raise thee to a station of Praise and Glory!

80. Say: "O my Lord! let my entry be by the Gate of Truth and Honour, and likewise my exit by the Gate of Truth and Honour; and grant me from Thy Presence an authority to aid (me)."

81. And say: "Truth has (now) arrived, and Falsehood perished: for Falsehood is (by its nature) bound to perish."

82. We send down (stage by stage) in the Qur'an that which is a healing and a mercy to those who believe: to the unjust it causes nothing but loss after loss.

83. Yet when We bestow Our favors on man, he turns away and becomes remote on his side (instead of coming to Us), and when Evil seizes him he gives himself up to despair!

84. Say: "Everyone acts according to his own disposition: but your Lord knows best who it is that is best guided on the Way."

85. They ask thee concerning the Spirit (of inspiration). Say: "The Spirit (cometh) by command of my Lord: of knowledge it is only a little that is communicated to you, (O men!)

86. If it were Our Will, We could take away that which We have sent thee by inspiration: then would thou find none to plead thy affair in that matter as against Us —

87. Except for Mercy from thy Lord: for His Bounty is to thee (indeed) great.

88. Say: "If the whole of mankind and Jinns were to gather together to produce the like of this Qur'an, they could not produce the like thereof, even if they backed up each other with help and support.

89. And We have explained to man, in this Qur'an, every kind of similitude: yet the greater part of men refuse (to receive it) except with ingratitude!

90. They say: "We shall not believe in thee, until thou cause spring to gush forth for us from the earth,

---

[20] Early hours of dawn

91. "Or (until) thou have a garden of date trees and vines, and cause rivers to gush forth in their midst, carrying abundant water;

92. "Or thou cause the sky to fall in pieces, as thou sayest (will happen), against us; or thou bring God and the angels before (us) face to face;

93. "Or thou have a house adorned with gold, or thou mount a ladder right into the skies. No, we shall not even believe in thy mounting until thou send down to us a book that we could read." Say: "Glory to my Lord! Am I aught but a man, — an apostle?"

94. What kept men back from Belief when Guidance came to them, was nothing but this: they said, "Has God sent a man like us) to be (His) Apostle?"

95. Say, "If there were settled, on earth, angels walking about in peace and quiet, We should certainly have sent them down from the heavens an angel for an apostle."

96. Say: "Enough is God for a witness between me and you: for He is well-acquainted with His servants, and He sees (all things)."

97. It is he whom God guides, that is on true guidance; but he whom He leaves astray — for such wilt thou find no protector besides Him. On the Day of Judgment We shall gather them together, prone[21] on their faces, blind, dumb, and deaf: their abode will be Hell: every time it shows abatement[22], We shall increase for them the fierceness of the Fire.

98. That is their recompense, because they rejected Our Signs, and said, "When we are reduced to bones and broken dust, should we really be raised up (to be) a new Creation?"

99. See they not that God, Who created the heavens and the earth, has power to create the like of them (anew)? Only He has decreed a term appointed, of which there is no doubt. But the unjust refuse (to receive it) except with ingratitude.

100. Say: "If ye had control of the Treasures of the Mercy of my Lord, behold, ye would keep them back, for fear of spending them: for man is (ever) niggardly!"

101. To Moses We did give nine Clear Signs: ask the Children of Israel: when he came to them, Pharaoh said to him: "O Moses!

---

[21] Prostrate, with face downwards.

[22] Decrease in intensity

I consider thee, indeed, to have been worked upon by sorcery!"

102. Moses said, "Thou knowest well that these things have been sent down by none but the Lord of the heavens and the earth as eye-opening evidence: and I consider thee, indeed, O Pharaoh, to be one doomed to destruction!"

103. So he resolved to remove them from the face of the earth: but We did drown him and all who were with him.

104. And We said thereafter to the Children of Israel, "Dwell securely in the land (of promise)": but when the second of the warnings came to pass, We gathered you together in a mingled crowd.

105. We sent down the (Qur'an) in Truth, and in Truth has it descended: and We sent thee but to give Glad Tidings and to warn (sinners).

106. (It is) a Qur'an which We have divided (into parts from time to time), in order that thou mightest recite it to men at intervals: We have revealed it by stages.

107. Say: "Whether ye believe in it or not, it is true that those who were given knowledge beforehand, when it is recited to them, fall down on their faces in humble prostration,"

108. And they say: "Glory to our Lord! Truly has the promise of our Lord been fulfilled!"

109. They fall down on their faces in tears, and it increases their (earnest) humility.

110. Say: "Call upon God, or call upon *Rahman*[23]: by whatever name ye call upon Him, (it is well): for to Him belong the Most Beautiful Names. Neither speak thy Prayer aloud, nor speak it in a low tone, but seek a middle course between."

111. Say: "Praise be to God Who begets no son, and has no partner in (His) dominion[24]: nor (needs) He any to protect Him from humiliation: Yea, magnify Him for His greatness and glory!"

---

[23] *Rahman* (Arabic), means the Beneficent, the Gracious One. It is one of the 99 Most Beautiful names of God.

[24] Kingdom, power.

Chapter 18
Sūrah Al-Kahf (The Cave)
Revealed at Makkah, 110 verses.

In the name of God, Most Gracious, Most Merciful.

1. Praise be to God, Who hath sent to His Servant the Book, and hath allowed therein no Crookedness:

2. (He hath made it) Straight (and Clear) in order that He may warn (the godless) of a terrible Punishment from Him, and that He may give Glad Tidings to the Believers who work righteous deeds, that they shall have a goodly Reward.

3. Wherein they shall remain forever:

4. Further, that He may warn those (also) who say, "God hath begotten a son":

5. No knowledge have they of such a thing, nor had their fathers. It is a grievous thing that issues from their mouths as a saying. What they say is nothing but falsehood!

6. Thou wouldst only, perchance, fret[1] thyself to death, following after them, in grief, if they believe not in this Message.

7. That which is on earth We have made but as a glittering show for the earth, in order that We may test them — as to which of them are best in conduct.

8. Verily what is on earth We shall make but as dust and dry soil (without growth or herbage).

9. Or dost thou reflect that the Companions of the Cave and of the Inscription were wonders among Our Signs?

10. Behold, the youths betook themselves to the Cave: they said, "Our Lord! bestow on us Mercy from Thyself, and dispose of our affair for us in the right way!

11. Then We drew (a veil) over their ears, for a number of years, in the cave, (so that they heard not):

12. Then We roused them, in order to test which of the two parties was best at calculating the term of years they had tarried!

13. We relate to thee their story in truth: they were youths who believed in their Lord, and We advanced them in guidance:

14. We gave strength to their hearts: Behold, they stood up and

---

[1] Torment or distress yourself with grief.

said: "Our Lord is the Lord of the heavens and of the earth: never shall we call upon any god other than Him: if we did; we should indeed have uttered an enormity[2]!"

15. "These our people have taken for worship gods other than Him: why do they not bring forward an authority clear (and convincing) for what they do? Who doth more wrong than such as invent a falsehood against God?

16. "When ye turn away from them and the things they worship other than God betake yourselves to the Cave: your Lord will shower His mercies on you and dispose of your affair towards comfort and ease."

17. Thou wouldst have seen the sun, when it rose, declining to the right from their Cave, and when it set, turning away from them to the left, while they lay in the open space in the midst of the Cave. Such are among the Signs of God: he whom God guides is rightly guided; but he whom God leaves to stray — for him wilt thou find no protector to lead him to the Right Way.

18. Thou wouldst have deemed them awake, whilst they were asleep, and We turned them on their right and their left sides: their dog stretching forth his two forelegs on the threshold: if thou hadst come up on to them, thou wouldst have certainly turned back from them in flight, and wouldst certainly have been filled with terror of them.

19. Such (being their state), We raised them up (from sleep) that they might question each other. Said one of them, "How long have ye stayed (here)?" They said, "We have stayed (perhaps) a day, or part of a day." (At length) they (all) said, "God (alone) knows best how long ye have stayed here... Now send ye then one of you with this money of yours to the town: let him find out which is the best food (to be had) and bring some to you, that (ye may) satisfy hunger herewith: and let him behave with care and courtesy, and let him not inform anyone about you.

20. "For if they should come upon you, they would stone you or force you to return to their cult[3], and in that case ye would never attain prosperity."

---

[2] A dreadful crime, monstrous wickedness.

[3] System of religious worship, devotion or homage to a person or thing.

21. Thus did We make their case known to the people, that they might know that the promise of God is true, and that there can be no doubt about the Hour of Judgment. Behold they dispute among themselves as to their affair. (Some) said, "Construct a building over them": their Lord knows best about them: those who prevailed over their affair said, "Let us surely build a place of worship over them."

22. (Some) say they were three, the dog being the fourth among them; (others) say they were five, the dog being the sixth — doubtfully guessing at the unknown; (yet others) say they were seven, the dog being the eighth. Say thou: "My Lord knoweth best their number; it is but few that know their (real case)." Enter not, therefore, into controversies concerning them, except on a matter that is clear, nor consult any of them about (the affair of) the Sleepers.

23. Nor say of anything, "I shall be sure to do so and so tomorrow" —

24. Without adding, "So please God!" And call thy Lord to mind when thou forgetest, and say, "I hope that my Lord will guide me ever closer (even) than this to the right road."

25. So they stayed in their Cave three hundred years, and (some) add nine (more).

26. Say: "God knows best how long they stayed: with Him is (the knowledge of) the secrets of the heavens and the earth: how clearly He sees, how finely He hears (everything)! They have no protector other than Him; nor does He share His Command with any person whatsoever.

27. And recite (and teach) what has been revealed to thee of the Book of thy Lord: none can change His Words, and none wilt thou find as a refuge other than Him.

28. And keep thy soul content with those who call on their Lord morning and evening, seeking his Face; and let not thine eyes pass beyond them, seeking the pomp and glitter of this Life; nor obey any whose heart We have permitted to neglect the remembrance of Us, one who follows his own desires, whose case has gone beyond all bounds.

29. Say, "The Truth is from your Lord": let him who will, believe, and let him who will, reject (it): for the wrongdoers We have prepared a Fire whose (smoke and flames), like the wall and roof of a tent,

will hem them in: if they implore relief they will be granted water like melted brass that will scald[4] their faces. How dreadful the drink! How uncomfortable a couch to recline on!

30. As to those who believe and work righteousness, verily We shall not suffer to perish the reward of any who do a (single) righteous deed.

31. For them will be Gardens of Eternity; beneath them rivers will flow; they will be adorned therein with bracelets of gold, and they will wear green garments of fine silk and heavy brocade[5]; they will recline therein on raised thrones. How good the recompense! How beautiful a couch to recline on!

32. Set forth to them the parable of two men: for one of them We provided two gardens of grapevines[6] and surrounded them with date palms: in between the two We placed cornfields.

33. Each of those gardens brought forth its produce, and failed not in the least therein: in the midst of them We caused a river to flow.

34. (Abundant) was the produce this man had: he said to his companion, in the course of a mutual argument: "More wealth have I than you, and more honour and power in (my following of) men."

35. He went into his garden in a state (of mind) unjust to his soul: He said, "I deem not that this will ever perish.

36. "Nor do I deem that the Hour (of Judgment) will (ever) come: even if I am brought back to my Lord, I shall surely find (there) something better in exchange."

37. His companion said to him, in the course of the argument with him: "Dost thou deny Him Who created thee out of dust, then out of a sperm drop, then fashioned thee into a man?

38. "But (I think) for my part that He is God, my Lord, and none shall I associate with my Lord.

39. "Why didst thou not, as thou wentest into thy garden, say: 'God's Will (be done)! There is no power but with God!' If thou dost see me less than thee in wealth and sons,

---

[4] Injure or burn (skin, etc.) with hot liquid or vapor.

[5] Fabric woven with raised patterns of threads of gold or other metal.

[6] Grape plants.

40. "It may be that my Lord will give me something better than thy garden, and that He will send on thy garden thunderbolts (by way of reckoning) from heaven, making it (but) slippery sand! —

41. "Or the water of the garden will run off underground so that thou wilt never be able to find it."

42. So his fruits (and enjoyment) were encompassed (with ruin), and he remained twisting and turning his hands over what he had spent on his property, which had (now) tumbled to pieces to its very foundations, and he could only say, "Woe is me! Would I had never ascribed partners to my Lord and Cherisher!"

43. Nor had he numbers to help him against God, nor was he able to deliver himself.

44. There, the (only) protection comes from God, the True One. He is the Best to reward, and the Best to give success.

45. Set forth to them the similitude of the life of this world: it is like the rain which We send down from the skies: the earth's vegetation absorbs it, but soon it becomes dry stubble[7], which the winds do scatter: it is (only) God Who prevails over all things.

46. Wealth and sons are allurements of the life of this world: but the things that endure, Good Deeds, are best in the sight of thy Lord, as rewards, and best as (the foundation for) hopes.

47. One Day We shall remove the mountains, and thou wilt see the earth as a level stretch, and We shall gather them, all together, nor shall We leave out any one of them.

48. And they will be marshalled[8] before thy Lord in ranks, (with the announcement), "Now have ye come to Us (bare) as We created you first: aye, ye thought We shall not fulfil the appointment made to you to meet (Us)!":

49. And the Book (of Deeds) will be placed (before you); and thou wilt see the sinful in great terror because of what is (recorded) therein; they will say, "Ah! woe to us! What a book is this! It leaves out nothing small or great, but takes account thereof!" They will find all that they did, placed before them: and not one will thy Lord treat with injustice.

---

[7] Cut stalks of cereal plants left sticking up after harvest.
[8] Assembled.

50. Behold! We said to the angels, "Bow down to Adam": they bowed down except Iblis. He was one of the Jinns, and he broke the Command of his Lord. Will ye then take him and his progeny[9] as protectors rather than Me? And they are enemies to you! Evil would be the exchange for the wrongdoers!

51. I called them not to witness the creation of the heavens and the earth, nor (even) their own creation: nor is it for Me to take as helpers such as lead (men) astray!

52. One Day He will say, "Call on those whom ye thought to be My partners," and they will call on them, but they will not listen to them; and We shall make for them a place of common perdition[10].

53. And the Sinful shall see the Fire and apprehend[11] that they have to fall therein; no means will they find to turn away therefrom.

54. We have explained in detail in this Qur'an, for the benefit of mankind, every kind of similitude: but man is, in most things, contentious[12].

55. And what is there to keep back men from believing, now that Guidance has come to them, nor from praying for forgiveness from their Lord, but that (they ask that) the ways of the ancients be repeated with them, or the Wrath be brought to them face to face?

56. We only send the Apostles to give glad tidings and to give warnings: but the Unbelievers dispute with vain argument, in order therewith to weaken the truth, and they treat My Signs as a jest, as also the fact that they are warned!

57. And who doth more wrong than one who is reminded of the Signs of his Lord, but turns away from them, forgetting the (deeds) which his hands have sent forth? Verily We have set veils over their hearts lest they should understand this, and over their ears, deafness. If thou callest them to guidance, even then will they never accept guidance.

58. But your Lord is Most Forgiving, Full of Mercy. If He were to call them (at once) to account for what they have earned, then surely He would have hastened their Punishment: but they have their ap-

---

[9] Offspring
[10] Eternal death, damnation.
[11] Perceive
[12] Quarrelsome

pointed time, beyond which they will find no refuge.

59. Such were the populations We destroyed when they committed iniquities[13]; but We fixed an appointed time for their destruction.

60. Behold, Moses said to his attendant, "I will not give up until I reach the junction of the two seas or (until) I spend years and years in travel."

61. But when they reached the Junction, they forgot (about) their Fish, which took its course through the sea (straight) as in a tunnel.

62. When they had passed on (some distance), Moses said to his attendant: "Bring us our early meal; truly we have suffered much fatigue at this (stage of) our journey."

63. He replied: "Sawest thou (what happened) when we betook ourselves to the rock? I did indeed forget (about) the Fish: none but Satan made me forget to tell (you) about it: it took its course through the sea in a marvelous way!"

64. Moses said: "That was what we were seeking after": so they went back on their footsteps, following (the path they had come).

65. So they found one of Our servants, on whom We had bestowed Mercy from Ourselves and whom We had taught knowledge from Our own presence.

66. Moses said to him: "May I follow thee, on the footing[14] that thou teach me something of the (Higher) Truth which thou hast been taught?"

67. (The other) said: "Verily thou wilt not be able to have patience with me!

68. "And how canst thou have patience about things about which thy understanding is not complete?"

69. Moses said: "Thou wilt find me, if God so will, (truly) patient: nor shall I disobey thee in aught."

70. The other said: "If then thou wouldst follow me, ask me no questions about anything until I myself speak to thee concerning it."

71. So they both proceeded: until, when they were in the boat, he scuttled[15] it. Said Moses: "Hast thou scuttled it in order to drown those in it? Truly a strange thing hast thou done!"

---

[13] Gross injustice

[14] Position, conditions.

[15] Made a hole.

72. He answered: "Did I not tell thee that thou canst have no patience with me?"

73. Moses said: "Rebuke me not for forgetting, nor grieve me by raising difficulties in my case."

74. Then they proceeded: until, when they met a young man, he slew him. Moses said: "Hast thou slain an innocent person who had slain none? Truly a foul (unheard-of) thing hast thou done!"

75. He answered: "Did I not tell thee that thou canst have no patience with me?"

76. (Moses) said: "If ever I ask thee about anything after this, keep me not in thy company: then wouldst thou have received (full) excuse from my side."

77. Then they proceeded: until, when they came to the inhabitants of a town, they asked them for food, but they refused them hospitality. They found there a wall on the point of falling down, but he set it up straight. (Moses) said: "If thou hadst wished, surely thou couldst have exacted some recompense for it!"

78. He answered: "This is the parting between me and thee: now will I tell thee the interpretation of (those things) over which thou wast unable to hold patience.

79. As for the boat, it belonged to certain men in dire[16] want: they plied[17] on the water: I but wished to render it unserviceable, for there was after them a certain king who seized on every boat by force.

80. "As for the youth, his parents were people of Faith, and we feared that he would grieve them by obstinate rebellion and ingratitude (to God and man).

81. "So we desired that their Lord would give them in exchange (a son) better in purity (of conduct) and closer in affection.

82. "As for the wall, it belonged to two youths, orphans, in the Town; there was, beneath it, a buried treasure, to which they were entitled: their father had been a righteous man: so thy Lord desired that they should attain their age of full strength and get out their treasure — a mercy (and favor) from thy Lord. I did it not of my own accord. Such is the interpretation of (those things) over which thou wast unable

---

[16] Urgent

[17] Worked

to hold patience."

83. They ask thee concerning Zul-Qarnain. Say, "I will rehearse to you something of his story."

84. Verily We established his power on earth, and We gave him the ways and the means to all ends.

85. One (such) way he followed,

86. Until, when he reached the setting of the sun, he found it set in a spring of murky water: near it he found a People: We said: "O Zul-Qarnain! (thou hast authority), either to punish them, or to treat them with kindness."

87. He said: "Whoever doth wrong, him shall we punish; then shall he be sent back to his Lord; and He will punish him with a punishment unheard-of (before).

88. "But whoever believes, and works righteousness — he shall have a goodly reward, and easy will be his task as we order it by our command."

89. Then followed he (another) way.

90. Until, when he came to the rising of the sun, he found it rising on a people for whom We had provided no covering protection against the sun.

91. (He left them) as they were: We completely understood what was before him.

92. Then followed he (another) way,

93. Until, when he reached (a tract) between two mountains, he found, beneath, them a people who scarcely understood a word.

94. They said: "O Zul-Qarnain! the Gog and Magog (people) do great mischief on earth: shall we then render thee tribute in order that thou mightest erect a barrier between us and them?"

95. He said: "(The power) in which my Lord has established me is better (than tribute): help me therefore with strength (and labor): I will erect a strong barrier between you and them:

96. "Bring me blocks of iron." At length, when he had filled up the space between the two steep mountain sides, he said, "Blow (with your bellows)." Then, when he had made it (red) as fire, he said: "Bring me, that I may pour over it, molten lead."

97. Thus were they made powerless to scale it or to dig through it.

98. He said: "This is a mercy from my Lord: but when the promise of my Lord comes to pass, He will make it into dust; and the promise of My Lord is true."

99. On that day We shall leave them to surge like waves on one another; the trumpet will be blown, and We shall collect them all together.

100. And We shall present Hell that day for Unbelievers to see, all spread out —

101. (Unbelievers) whose eyes had been under a veil from Remembrance of Me, and who had been unable even to hear.

102. Do the Unbelievers think that they can take my servants as protectors besides Me? Verily We have prepared Hell for the Unbelievers for (their) entertainment.

103. Say: "Shall we tell you of those who lose most in respect of their deeds? —

104. "Those whose efforts have been wasted in this life, while they thought that they were acquiring good by their works?"

105. They are those who deny the Signs of their Lord and the fact of their having to meet Him (in the Hereafter): vain will be their works, nor shall We, on the Day of Judgment, give them any weight.

106. That is their reward, Hell; because they rejected Faith, and took My Signs and My Messengers by way of jest.

107. As to those who believe and work righteous deeds, they have, for their entertainment, the Gardens of Paradise,

108. Wherein they shall dwell (for aye): no change will they wish for themselves.

109. Say: "If the ocean were ink (wherewith to write out) the words of my Lord, sooner would the ocean be exhausted than would the words of my Lord, even if we added another ocean like it, for its aid."

110. Say: "I am but a man like yourselves, (but) the inspiration has come to me, that your God is one God: whoever expects to meet his Lord, let him work righteousness, and in the worship of his Lord, admit no one as partner."

Chapter 19
Sürah Maryam (Mary)
Revealed at Makkah, 98 verses.

In the name of God, Most Gracious, Most Merciful.

1. Kaf. Hã. Ya. 'Ain. Sãd.

2. (This is) a recital[1] of the Mercy of thy Lord to His Servant Zakariya.

3. Behold! he cried to his Lord in secret,

4. Praying: "O my Lord! infirm indeed are my bones, and the hair of my head doth glisten with grey: but never am I unblest, O my Lord, in my prayer to Thee!

5. "Now I fear (what) my relatives (and colleagues) (will do) after me: but my wife is barren: so give me an heir as from Thyself —

6. "(One that) will (truly) represent me, and represent the posterity[2] of Jacob; and make him, O my Lord! one with whom Thou art well-pleased!"

7. (His prayer was answered): "O Zakariya! We give thee good news of a son: his name shall be Yahya: on none by that name have We conferred distinction before."

8. He said: "O my Lord! how shall I have a son, when my wife is barren and I have grown quite decrepit[3] from old age?"

9. He said: "So (it will be): thy Lord saith, 'That is easy for Me: I did indeed create thee before, when thou hadst been nothing!'"

10. (Zakariya) said "O my Lord! give me a Sign." "Thy Sign," was the answer, "shall be that thou shalt speak to no man for three nights, although thou art not dumb."

11. So Zakariya came out to his people from his chamber: he told them by signs to celebrate God's praises in the morning and in the evening.

12. (To his son came the command): "O Yahya! take hold of the Book with might": and We gave him wisdom even as a youth,

13. And pity (for all creatures) as from Us, and purity: he was

---

[1] Report, recount

[2] Offspring

[3] Weak, infirm

devout,

14. And kind to his parents, and he was not overbearing[4] or rebellious.

15. So Peace on him the day he was born, the day that he dies, and the day that he will be raised up to life (again)!

16. Relate in the Book (the story of) Mary, when she withdrew from her family to a place in the East.

17. She placed a screen (to screen herself) from them: then We sent to her Our angel, and he appeared before her as a man in all respects.

18. She said: "I seek refuge from thee to (God) Most Gracious: (come not near) if thou dost fear God."

19. He said: "Nay, I am only a messenger from thy Lord, (to announce) to thee the gift of a holy son."

20. She said: "How shall I have a son, seeing that no man has touched me, and I am not unchaste?"

21. He said: "So (it will be): thy Lord saith, 'That is easy for Me: and (We wish) to appoint him as a Sign unto men and a Mercy from Us': it is a matter (so) decreed."

22. So she conceived him, and she retired with him to a remote place.

23. And the pains of childbirth drove her to the trunk of a palm tree: she cried (in her anguish): "Ah! would that I had died before this! Would that I had been a thing forgotten and out of sight!"

24. But (a voice) cried to her from beneath the (palm tree): "Grieve not! for thy Lord hath provided a rivulet beneath thee;

25. "And shake towards thyself the trunk of the palm tree: it will let fall fresh ripe dates upon thee.

26. "So eat and drink and cool (thine) eye. And if thou dost see any man, say, 'I have vowed a fast to (God) Most Gracious, and this day will I enter into no talk with any human being.'"

27. At length she brought the (babe) to her people, carrying him (in her arms). They said: "O Mary! truly an amazing thing hast thou brought!

28. "O sister of Aaron! thy father was not a man of evil, nor thy

---

[4] Bossy, domineering

mother a woman unchaste!"

29. But she pointed to the babe. They said: "How can we talk to one who is a child in the cradle?"

30. He said: "I am indeed a servant of God: He hath given me revelation and made me a prophet;

31. "And He hath made me Blessed wheresoever I be, and hath enjoined on me Prayer and Charity as long as I live;

32. "(He) hath made me kind to my mother, and not overbearing or miserable;

33. "So Peace is on me the day I was born, the day that I die, and the Day that I shall be raised up to life (again)!"

34. Such (was) Jesus the son of Mary: (it is) a statement of truth, about which they (vainly) dispute.

35. It is not befitting to (the majesty of) God that He should beget a son. Glory be to Him! When He determines a matter, He only says to it, "Be," and it is.

36. Verily, God is my Lord and your Lord: Him therefore serve ye: this is a Way that is straight.

37. But the sects differ among themselves: and woe to the Unbelievers because of the (coming) Judgment of a momentous[5] Day!

38. How plainly will they see and hear, the Day that they will appear before Us! But the unjust today are in error manifest!

39. But warn them of the Day of Distress, when the matter will be determined: for (behold), they are negligent and they do not believe!

40. It is We Who will inherit the earth, and all beings thereon: to Us will they all be returned.

41. Also mention in the Book (the story of) Abraham: he was a man of Truth, a prophet.

42. Behold, he said to his father: "O my father! why worship that which heareth not and seeth not, and can profit thee nothing?

43. "O my father! to me hath come knowledge which hath not reached thee: so follow me: I will guide thee to a Way that is even and straight.

44. "O my father! serve not Satan: for Satan is a rebel against (God) Most Gracious.

---

[5] Very important

45. "O my father! I fear lest a Penalty afflict thee from (God) Most Gracious, so that thou become to Satan a friend."

46. (The father) replied: "Dost thou hate my gods, O Abraham? If thou forbear[6] not I will indeed stone thee: now get away from me for a good long while!"

47. Abraham said: "Peace be on thee: I will pray to my Lord for thy forgiveness: for He is to me Most Gracious.

48. "And I will turn away from you (all) and from those whom ye invoke besides God: I will call on my Lord: Perhaps, by my prayer to my Lord, I shall be not unblest."

49. When he had turned away from them and from those whom they worshipped besides God, We bestowed on him Isaac and Jacob, and each one of them We made a prophet.

50. And We bestowed of Our Mercy on them, and We granted them lofty honour on the tongue of truth.

51. Also mention in the Book (the story of) Moses: for he was specially chosen, and he was an apostle (and) a prophet.

52. And We called him from the right side of Mount (Sinai), and made him draw near to Us, for mystic (converse).

53. And, out of Our Mercy, We gave him his brother Aaron, (also) a prophet.

54. Also mention in the Book (the story of) Ismail: He was (strictly) true to what he promised, and he was an apostle (and) a prophet.

55. He used to enjoin on his people Prayer and Charity, and he was most acceptable in the sight of his Lord.

56. Also mention in the Book the case of Idris: he was a man of truth (and sincerity), (and) a prophet:

57. And We raised him to a lofty station.

58. Those were some of the prophets on whom God did bestow His Grace — of the posterity of Adam, and of those whom We carried (in the Ark) with Noah, and of the posterity of Abraham and Israel — of those whom We guided and chose; whenever the Signs of (God) Most Gracious were rehearsed to them, they would fall down in prostrate adoration and in tears.

59. But after them there followed a posterity who missed prayers

---

[6] Abstain

and followed after lusts: soon, then, will they face Destruction —

60. Except those who repent and believe, and work righteousness: for these will enter the Garden and will not be wronged in the least —

61. Gardens of Eternity, those which (God) Most Gracious has promised to His servants in the Unseen: for His promise must (necessarily) come to pass.

62. They will not there hear any vain discourse, but only saLütations of peace: and they will have therein their sustenance, morning and evening.

63. Such is the Garden which We give as an inheritance to those of Our Servants who guard against evil.

64. (The angels say:) "We descend not but by command of thy Lord: to Him belongeth what is before us, and what is behind us, and what is between: and thy Lord never doth forget" —

65. "Lord of the heavens and of the earth, and of all that is between them: so worship Him, and be constant and patient in His worship: knowest thou of any who is worthy of the same Name as He?"

66. Man says: "What! when I am dead, shall I then be raised up alive?"

67. But does not man call to mind that We created him before out of nothing?

68. So, by thy Lord, without doubt, We shall gather them together, and (also) the Evil Ones (with them); then shall We bring them forth on their knees round about Hell;

69. Then shall We certainly drag out from every sect all those who were worst in obstinate rebellion against (God) Most Gracious.

70. And certainly We know best those who are most worthy of being burned therein.

71. Not one of you but will pass over it: this is, with thy Lord, a Decree which must be accomplished.

72. But We shall save those who guarded against evil, and We shall leave the wrongdoers therein, (humbled) to their knees.

73. When Our Clear Signs are rehearsed to them, the Unbelievers say to those who believe, "Which of the two sides is best in point of position? Which makes the best show in council?"

74. But how many (countless) generations before them have We

destroyed, who were even better in equipment and in glitter to the eye?

75. Say: "If any men go astray, (God) Most Gracious extends (the rope) to them. Until, when they see the warning of God (being fulfilled) — either in punishment or in (the approach of) the Hour — they will at length realize who is worst in position, and (who) weakest in forces!

76. "And God doth advance in guidance those who seek guidance; and the things that endure, Good Deeds, are best in the sight of thy Lord, as rewards, and best in respect of (their) eventual returns."

77. Hast thou then seen the (sort of) man who rejects Our Signs, yet says: "I shall certainly be given wealth and children"?

78. Has he penetrated to the Unseen, or has he taken a contract with (God) Most Gracious?

79. Nay! We shall record what he says, and We shall add and add to his punishment.

80. To Us shall return all that he talks of, and he shall appear before Us bare and alone.

81. And they have taken (for worship) gods other than God, to give them power and glory!

82. Instead, they shall reject their worship, and become adversaries against them.

83. Seest thou not that We have set the Evil Ones on against the Unbelievers, to incite them with fury?

84. So make no haste against them, for We but count out to them a (limited) number (of days).

85. The day We shall gather the righteous to (God) Most Gracious, like a band presented before a king for honours.

86. And We shall drive the sinners to Hell, like thirsty cattle driven down to water —

87. None shall have the power of intercession[7], but such a one as has received permission (or promise from (God) Most Gracious.

88. They say: "(God) Most Gracious has begotten a son!"

89. Indeed ye have put forth a thing most monstrous!

90. As if the skies are ready to burst, the earth to split asunder, and the mountains to fall down in utter ruin,

---

[7] Intervention

91. That they should invoke a son for (God) Most Gracious.

92. For it is not consonant[8] with the majesty of (God) Most Gracious that He should beget a son.

93. Not one of the beings in the heavens and the earth but must come to (God) Most Gracious as a servant.

94. He does take an account of them (all), and hath numbered them (all) exactly.

95. And every one of them will come to him singly on the Day of Judgment.

96. On those who believe and work deeds of righteousness, will (God) Most Gracious bestow Love.

97. So have We made the (Qur'an) easy in thine own tongue, that with it thou mayest give Glad Tidings to the righteous, and warnings to people given to contention[9].

98. But how many (countless) generations before them have We destroyed? Canst thou find a single one of them (now) or hear (so much as) a whisper of them?

Chapter 20
Sūrah Tā-Hā (Tā Hā)
Revealed at Makkah, 135 verses.

In the name of God, Most Gracious, Most Merciful.

1. Tā Hā.

2. We have not sent down the Qur'an to thee to be (an occasion) for thy distress,

3. But only as an admonition to those who fear (God) —

4. A revelation from Him Who created the earth and the heavens on high.

5. (God) Most Gracious is firmly established on the throne (of authority).

---

8 Consistent with
9 Strife

6. To Him belongs what is in the heavens and on earth, and all between them, and all beneath the soil.

7. If thou pronounce the word aloud, (it is no matter): for verily He knoweth what is secret and what is yet more hidden.

8. God! there is no god but He! To Him belong the Most Beautiful Names.

9. Has the story of Moses reached thee?

10. Behold, he saw a fire: so he said to his family, "Tarry[1] ye; I perceive a fire; perhaps I can bring you some burning brand therefrom or find some guidance at the fire."

11. But when he came to the fire, a voice was heard: "O Moses!

12. "Verily I am thy Lord! Therefore (in My presence) put off thy shoes: thou art in the sacred valley Tuwā.

13. "I have chosen thee: listen, then, to the inspiration (sent to thee).

14. "Verily, I am God: there is no god but I: so serve thou Me (only), and establish regular prayer for celebrating My praise.

15. "Verily the Hour is coming — My design[2] is to keep it hidden — for every soul to receive its reward by the measure of its Endeavour.

16. "Therefore let not such as believe not therein but follow their own lusts, divert thee therefrom, lest thou perish!"

17. And what is that in thy right hand, O Moses?"

18. He said, "It is my rod: on it I lean; with it I beat down fodder for my flocks; and in it I find other uses."

19. (God) said, "Throw it, O Moses!"

20. He threw it, and behold! it was a snake, active in motion.

21. (God) said, "Seize it, and fear not: We shall return it at once to its former condition"...

22. Now draw thy hand close to thy side: it shall come forth white (and shining), without harm (or stain) — as another Sign —

23. "In order that We may show thee (two) of Our Greater Signs.

24. "Go thou to Pharaoh, for he had indeed transgressed all bounds."

25. (Moses) said: "O my Lord! expand me my breast;"

---

[1] Stay

[2] Plan

236

26. "Ease my task for me;

27. "And remove the impediment[3] from my speech.

28. "So they may understand what I say:

29. "And give me a Minister from my family,

30. "Aaron, my brother;

31. "Add to my strength through him,

32. "And make him share my task:

33. "That we may celebrate Thy praise without stint[4],

34. "And remember Thee without stint:

35. For Thou art He that (ever) regardeth us."

36. (God) said: "Granted is thy prayer, O Moses!"

37. "And indeed We conferred a favor on thee another time (before).

38. "Behold! We sent to thy mother, by inspiration, the message:

39. ""Throw (the child) into the chest[5], and throw (the chest) into the river: the river will cast him up on the bank, and he will be taken up by one who is an enemy to Me and an enemy to him': but I cast (the garment of) love over thee from Me: and (this) in order that thou mayest be reared under Mine eye.

40. "Behold! thy sister goeth forth and saith, 'Shall I show you one who will nurse and rear the (child)?' So We brought thee back to thy mother, that her eye might be cooled and she should not grieve. Then thou didst slay a man, but We saved thee from trouble, and We tried thee in various ways. Then didst thou tarry a number of years with the people of Midian. Then didst thou come hither as ordained[6], O Moses!

41. "And I have prepared thee for Myself (for service)"...

42. "Go, thou and thy brother, with My Signs, and slacken[7] not, either of you, in keeping Me in remembrance.

43. "Go, both of you, to Pharaoh, for he has indeed transgressed all bounds;

---

[3] Handicap

[4] Without any limitation, unlimited

[5] A cabinet, a strong box

[6] Decreed

[7] Relax

44. "But speak to him mildly; perchance he may take warning or fear (God)."

45. They (Moses and Aaron) said: "Our Lord! we fear lest he hasten with insolence against us, or lest he transgress all bounds."

46. He said: "Fear not: for I am with you: I hear and see (everything).

47. "So go ye both to him, and say, 'Verily we are Apostles sent by thy Lord: send forth, therefore, the Children of Israel with us, and afflict them not: with a Sign, indeed, have we come from thy Lord! And peace to all who follow guidance!

48. "'Verily it has been revealed to us that the Penalty (awaits) those who reject and turn away.'"

49. (When this message was delivered), (Pharaoh) said: "Who, then, O Moses, is the Lord of you two?"

50. He said: "Our Lord is He Who gave to each (created) thing its form and nature, and further, gave (it) guidance."

51. (Pharaoh) said: "What then is the condition of previous generations?"

52. He replied: "The knowledge of that is with my Lord, duly recorded: my Lord never errs, nor forgets —

53. "He Who has made for you the earth like a carpet spread out; has enabled you to go about therein by roads (and channels); and has sent down water from the sky." With it have We produced diverse pairs of plants each separate from the others.

54. Eat (for yourselves) and pasture your cattle: verily, in this are Signs for men endued with understanding.

55. From the (earth) did We create you, and into it shall We return you, and from it shall We bring you out once again.

56. And We showed Pharaoh all Our Signs, but he did reject and refuse.

57. He said: "Hast thou come to drive us out of our land with thy magic, O Moses?

58. "But we can surely produce magic to match thine! So make a tryst[8] between us and thee, which we shall not fail to keep — neither we nor thou — in a place where both shall have even chances."

---

[8] Appointment

59. Moses said: "Your tryst is the Day of the Festival, and let the people be assembled when the sun is well up."

60. So Pharaoh withdrew: he concerted[9] his plan, and then came (back).

61. Moses said to him: "Woe to you! forge not ye a lie against God, lest He destroy you (at once) utterly by chastisement: the forger must suffer frustration!"

62. So they disputed, one with another, over their affair, but they kept their talk secret.

63. They said: "These two are certainly (expert) magicians: their object is to drive you out from your land with their magic, and to do away with your most cherished institutions.

64. "Therefore concert your plan. And then assemble in (serried[10]) ranks: he wins (all along) today who gains the upper hand."

65. They said: "O Moses! whether wilt thou that thou throw (first) or that we be the first to throw?"

66. He said, "Nay, throw ye first!" Then behold their ropes and their rods — so it seemed to him on account of their magic — began to be in lively motion!

67. So Moses conceived in his mind a (sort of) fear.

68. We said: "Fear not! for thou hast indeed the upper hand:

69. "Throw that which is in thy right hand: quickly will it swallow up that which they have faked[11]. What they have faked is but a magician's trick: and the magician thrives not (no matter) where he goes."

70. So the magicians were thrown down to prostration: they said, "We believe in the Lord of Aaron and Moses."

71. (Pharaoh) said: "Believe ye in Him before I give you permission? Surely this must be your leader, who has taught you magic! Be sure I will cut off your hands and feet on opposite sides, and I will have you crucified on trunks of palm trees: So shall ye know for certain, which of us can give the more severe and the more lasting Punishment!"

72. They said: "Never shall we regard thee as more than the Clear

---

[9] Arranged (by cooperation and agreement with his party)

[10] (Rows of soldiers, etc.) Pressed together, close, without gaps

[11] Forged

Signs that have come to us, or than Him Who created us! So decree whatever thou desirest to decree: for thou canst only decree (touching) the life of this world.

73. For us, we have believed in our Lord: may He forgive us our faults, and the magic to which thou didst compel us: for God is Best and Most Abiding."

74. Verily he who comes to his Lord as a sinner (at judgment) — for him is Hell: therein shall he neither die nor live.

75. But such as come to Him as Believers who have worked righteous deeds — for them are ranks exalted —

76. Gardens of Eternity, beneath which flow rivers: they will dwell therein for aye[12]: such is the reward of those who purify themselves (from evil).

77. We sent an inspiration to Moses: "Travel by night with my servants, and strike a dry path for them through the sea, without fear of being overtaken (by Pharaoh), and without (any other) fear."

78. Then Pharaoh pursued them with his forces, but the waters completely overwhelmed them and covered them up.

79. Pharaoh led his people astray instead of leading them aright.

80. O ye Children of Israel! We delivered you from your enemy, and We made a Covenant with you on the side of Mount (Sinai), and We sent down to you Manna[13] and quails:

81. (Saying): "Eat of the good things We have provided for your sustenance, but commit no excess therein, lest My Wrath should justly descend on you: and those on whom descends My Wrath do perish indeed!

82. "But, without doubt, I am (also) He that forgives again and again, to those who repent, believe, and do right — who, in fine are ready to receive true guidance."

83. (When Moses was up on the Mount, God said): "What made thee hasten in advance of thy people, O Moses?"

84. He replied: "Behold, they are close on my footsteps: I hastened to Thee, o my Lord, to please Thee."

85. (God) said: "We have tested thy people in thy absence: the

---

[12] Forever
[13] See Qur'an 2:57 & 7:160

Samiri has led them astray."

86. So Moses returned to his people in a state of indignation and sorrow. He said: "O my people! did not your Lord make a handsome promise to you? Did then the promise seem to you long (in coming)? Or did ye desire that Wrath should descend from your Lord on you, and so ye broke your promise to me?"

87. They said: "We broke not the promise to thee, as far as lay in our power: but we were made to carry the weight of the ornaments of the (whole) people, and we threw them (into the fire), and that was what the Samiri suggested.

88. "Then he brought out (of the fire) before the (people) the image of a calf: it seemed to low[14]: so they said: 'This is your god, and the god of Moses, but (Moses) has forgotten!'"

89. Could they not see that it could not return them a word (for answer), and that it had no power either to harm them or to do them good?

90. Aaron had already, before this, said to them: "O my people! ye are being tested in this: for verily your Lord is (God) Most Gracious: so follow me and obey my command."

91. They had said: "We will not abandon this cult[15], but we will devote ourselves to it until Moses returns to us.

92. (Moses) said: " O Aaron! what kept thee back, when thou sawest them going wrong,

93. "From following me? Didst thou then disobey my order?"

94. (Aaron) replied: "O son of my mother! seize (me not) by my beard nor by (the hair of) my head! Truly I feared lest thou shouldst say, 'Thou hast caused a division among the Children of Israel, and thou didst not respect my word!'"

95. (Moses) said: "What then is thy case, O Samiri?"

96. He replied: "I saw what they saw not: so I took a handful (of dust) from the footprint of the Apostle, and threw it (into the calf): thus did my soul suggest to me."

97. (Moses) said: "Get thee gone! but thy (punishment) in this life will be that thou wilt say, 'Touch me not'; and moreover (for

---

[14] To moo like a cow
[15] System of worship and ceremonies

241

a future penalty) thou hast a promise that will not fail: now look at thy god, of whom thou hast become a devoted worshipper: we will certainly (melt) it in a blazing fire and scatter it broadcast[16] in the sea!"

98. But the God of you all is the One God: there is no god but He: all things He comprehends[17] in His knowledge.

99. Thus do We relate to thee some stories of what happened before: for We have sent thee a Message from Our own Presence.

100. If any do turn away therefrom, verily they will bear a burden on the Day of Judgement;

101. They will abide in this (state): and grievous will the burden be to them on that Day —

102. The Day when the Trumpet will be sounded: that Day, We shall gather the sinful, blear-eyed[18] (with terror),

103. In whispers will they consult each other: "Ye tarried not longer than ten (Days)";

104. We know best what they will say, when their leader most eminent in Conduct will say: "Ye tarried not longer than a day!"

105. They ask thee concerning the mountains: say, "My Lord will uproot them and scatter them as dust;"

106. "He will leave them as plains smooth and level;"

107. Nothing crooked or curved wilt thou see in their place."

108. On that Day will they follow the Caller (straight): no crookedness (can they show) him: all sounds shall humble themselves in the presence of (God) Most Gracious: nothing shalt thou hear but the tramp of their feet (as they march).

109. On that Day shall no intercession avail except for those for whom permission has been granted by (God) Most Gracious and whose word is acceptable to Him.

110. He knows what (appears to His creatures as) before or after or behind them: but they shall not compass it with their knowledge.

111. (All) faces shall be humbled before (Him) — the Living, the Self-Subsisting, Eternal: hopeless indeed will be the man that

---

[16] Scatter widely
[17] Includes, covers
[18] (Eyes) dim-sighted, dull

carries iniquity[19] (on his back).

112. But he who works deeds of righteousness, and has faith, will have no fear of harm nor of any curtailment[20] (of what is his due).

113. Thus have we sent this down — an Arabic Qur'an — and explained therein in detail some of the warnings, in order that they may fear God, or that it may cause their remembrance (of Him).

114. High above all is God, the King, the Truth! Be not in haste with the Qur'an before its revelation to thee is completed, but say, "O my Lord! advance me in knowledge."

115. We had already, beforehand, taken the covenant of Adam, but he forgot: and We found on his part no firm resolve[21].

116. When We said to the angels, "Prostrate yourselves to Adam," they prostrated themselves, but not Iblis: he refused.

117. Then We said: "O Adam! verily, this is an enemy to thee and thy wife: so let him not get you both out of the Garden so that thou art landed in misery.

118. "There is therein (enough provision) for thee not to go hungry nor to go naked,"

119. "Nor to suffer from thirst, nor from the sun's heat."

120. But Satan whispered evil to him: he said, "O Adam! shall I lead thee to the Tree of Eternity and to a kingdom that never decays?"

121. In the result, they both ate of the tree, and so their nakedness appeared to them: they began to sew together, for their covering, leaves from the Garden: thus did Adam disobey His Lord, and allow himself to be seduced.

122. But his Lord chose him (for His Grace): He turned to him, and gave him guidance.

123. He said: "Get ye down, both of you — all together, from the Garden, with enmity one to another; but if, as is sure, there comes to you guidance from Me, whosoever follows My guidance, will not lose his way, nor fall into misery.

124. "But whosoever turns away from My Message, verily for him is a life narrowed down, and We shall raise him up blind on

---

[19] Gross injustice

[20] Reduction

[21] Determination

the Day of Judgment."

125. He will say: "O my Lord! why hast thou raised me up blind, while I had sight (before)?"

126. (God) will say: "Thus didst thou, when Our Signs came unto thee, disregard them: so wilt thou, this day, be disregarded."

127. And thus do We recompense him who transgresses beyond bounds and believes not in the Signs of his Lord: and the Penalty of the Hereafter is far more grievous and more enduring.

128. Is it not a warning to such men (to call to mind) how many generations before them We destroyed, in whose haunts[22] they (now) move? Verily, in this are Signs for men endued with understanding.

129. Had it not been for a Word that went forth before from thy Lord, (their punishment) must necessarily have come; but there is a term appointed (for respite).

130. Therefore be patient with what they say, and celebrate (constantly) the praises of thy Lord before the rising of the sun, and before its setting; yea, celebrate them for part of the hours of the night, and at the sides of the day: that thou mayest have (spiritual) joy.

131. Nor strain thine eyes in longing for the things We have given for enjoyment to parties of them, the splendor of the life of this world, through which We test them: but the provision of thy Lord is better and more enduring.

132. Enjoin prayer on thy people, and be constant therein. We ask thee not to provide sustenance: We provide it for thee. But the (fruit of) the Hereafter is for Righteousness.

133. They say: "Why does he not bring us a Sign from His Lord?" Has not a Clear Sign come to them of all that was in the former Books of Revelation?

134. And if We had inflicted on them a Penalty before this, they would have said: "Our Lord! if only Thou hadst sent us an apostle, we should certainly have followed Thy Signs before we were humbled and put to shame."

135. Say: "Each one (of us), is waiting: wait ye, therefore, and soon shall ye know who it is that is on the straight and even way, and who it is that has received guidance."

---

[22] Place of frequent resort, dwelling places.

Chapter 21
Sūrah Al-Anbiyā (The Prophets)
Revealed at Makkah, 112 verses.

In the name of God, Most Gracious, Most Merciful.

1. Closer and closer to mankind comes their Reckoning: yet they heed not and they turn away.

2. Never comes (aught) to them of a renewed Message from their Lord, but they listen to it as in jest —

3. Their hearts toying as with trifles. The wrongdoers conceal their private counsels, (saying), "Is this (one) more than a man like yourselves? Will ye go to witchcraft with your eyes open?"

4. Say: "My Lord knoweth (every) word (spoken) in the heavens and the earth: He is the One that heareth and knoweth (all things)."

5. "Nay," they say, "(these are) medleys[1] of dreams! — nay, he forged it! — nay, he is (but) a poet! Let him then bring us a Sign like the ones that were sent to (prophets) of old!"

6. (As to those) before them, not one of the populations which We destroyed believed: will these believe?

7. Before thee, also, the Apostles we sent were but men, to whom We granted inspiration: if ye realize this not, ask of those who possess the Message.

8. Nor did We give them bodies that ate no food nor were they exempt from death.

9. In the end We fulfilled to them Our promise, and We saved them and those whom We pleased, but We destroyed those who transgressed beyond bounds.

10. We have revealed for you (O men!) a book in which is a Message for you: will ye not then understand?

11. How many were the populations we utterly destroyed because of their iniquities, setting up in their places other peoples!

12. Yet, when they felt Our Punishment (coming), behold, they (tried to) flee from it.

13. Flee not, but return to the good things of this life which were given you, and to your homes, in order that ye may be called to account.

---

[1] Mixture

14. They said: "Ah! woe to us! We were indeed wrongdoers!"

15. And that cry of theirs ceased not, till We made them as a field that is mown, as ashes silent and quenched.

16. Not for (idle) sport did We create the heavens and the earth and all that is between!

17. If it had been Our wish to take (just) a pastime[2], We should surely have taken it from the things nearest to Us, if We would do (such a thing)!

18. Nay, We hurl the Truth against Falsehood, and it knocks out its brain, and behold, Falsehood doth perish! Ah! woe be to you for the (false) things ye ascribe (to Us).

19. To Him belong all (creatures) in the heavens and on earth: even those who are in His (very) Presence are not too proud to serve Him, nor are they (ever) weary (of His service):

20. They celebrate His praises night and day, nor do they ever flag[3] or intermit[4].

21. Or have they taken (for worship) gods from the earth who can raise (the dead)?

22. If there were, in the heavens and the earth, other gods besides God, there would have been confusion in both! But glory to God, the Lord of the Throne: (high is He) above what they attribute to Him!

23. He cannot be questioned for His acts, but they will be questioned (for theirs).

24. Or have they taken for worship (other) gods besides Him? Say, "Bring your convincing proof: this is the Message of those with me and the Message of those before me." But most of them know not the Truth, and so turn away.

25. Not an apostle did We send before thee without this inspiration sent by Us to him: that there is no god but I; therefore worship and serve Me.

26. And they say: "(God) Most Gracious has begotten offspring." Glory to Him! they are (but) servants raised to honour.

---

[2] Amusement, hobby

[3] Weaken, lose vigor, lag

[4] Discontinue, stop

27. They speak not before He speaks, and they act (in all things) by His command.

28. He knows what is before them, and what is behind them, and they offer no intercession except for those who are acceptable, and they stand in awe and reverence of His (glory).

29. If any of them should say, "I am a god besides Him," such a one We should reward with Hell: thus do We reward those who do wrong.

30. Do not the Unbelievers see that the heavens and the earth were joined together (as one unit of Creation), before We clove[5] them asunder? We made from water every living thing. Will they not then believe?

31. And We have set on the earth mountains standing firm, lest it should shake with them, and We have made therein broad highways (between mountains) for them to pass through: that they may receive guidance.

32. And We have made the heavens as a canopy well guarded: Yet do they turn away from the Signs which these things (point to)!

33. It is He Who created the Night and the Day, and the sun and the moon: all (the celestial[6] bodies) swim along, each in its rounded course.

34. We granted not to any man before thee permanent life (here): if then thou shouldst die, would they live permanently?

35. Every soul shall have a taste of death: and We test you by evil and by good by way of trial: to Us must ye return.

36. When the Unbelievers see thee, they treat thee not except with ridicule. "Is this," (they say), "the one who talks of your gods?" And they blaspheme[7] at the mention of (God) Most Gracious!

37. Man is a creature of haste: soon (enough) will I show you My Signs: then ye will not ask Me to hasten them!

38. They say: "When will this promise come to pass, if ye are telling the truth?"

39. If only the Unbelievers knew (the time) when they will not

---

[5] Split

[6] Astronomical

[7] Profane, mention with disrespect, desecrate

be able to ward off the Fire from their faces, nor yet from their backs, and (when) no help can reach them!

40. Nay, it may come to them all of a sudden and confound[8] them: no power will they have then to avert it, nor will they (then) get respite.

41. Mocked were (many) apostles before thee; but their scoffers were hemmed in by the thing that they mocked.

42. Say, "Who can keep you safe by night and by day from (the Wrath of) (God) Most Gracious?" Yet they turn away from the mention of their Lord.

43. Or have they gods that can guard them from Us? They have no power to aid themselves, nor can they be defended from Us.

44. Nay, We gave the good things of this life to these men and their fathers until the period grew long for them; see they not that we gradually reduce the land (in their control) from its outlying borders? Is it then they who will win?

45. Say, "I do but warn you according to revelation": but the deaf will not hear the call, (even) when they are warned!

46. If but a breath of the Wrath of thy Lord do touch them, they will then say, "Woe to us! we did wrong indeed!"

47. We shall set up scales of justice for the Day of Judgment, so that not a soul will be dealt with unjustly in the least. And if there be (no more than) the weight of a mustard seed, We will bring it (to account): and enough are We to take account.

48. In the past We granted to Moses and Aaron the Criterion[9] (for judgment), and a Light and a Message for those who would do right—

49. Those who fear their Lord in their most secret thoughts, and who hold the Hour (of Judgment) in awe.

50. And this is a blessed Message which We have sent down: will ye then reject it?

51. We bestowed aforetime on Abraham his rectitude[10] of conduct, and well were We acquainted with him.

52. Behold! he said to his father and his people, "What are these images, to which ye are (so assiduously[11]) devoted?"

---

[8] Baffle, daze

[9] Standard (to distinguish between good and evil)

[10] Moral correctness

[11] Persistently and diligently

53. They said, "We found our fathers worshipping them."

54. He said, "Indeed ye have been in manifest error — ye and your fathers."

55. They said, "Have you brought us the Truth, or are you one of those who jest?"

56. He said, "Nay, your Lord is the Lord of the heavens and the earth, He Who created them (from nothing): and I am a witness to this (truth).

57. And by God, I have a plan for your idols after ye go away and turn your backs"...

58. So he broke them to pieces, (all) but the biggest of them, that they might turn (and address themselves) to it.

59. They said, "Who has done this to our gods? He must indeed be some man of impiety!"

60. They said, "We heard a youth talk of them: he is called Abraham."

61. They said, "Then bring him before the eyes of the people, that they may bear witness:"

62. They said, "Art thou the one that did this with our gods, O Abraham?"

63. He said: "Nay, this was done by — this is their biggest one! Ask them, if they can speak intelligently!"

64. So they turned to themselves and said, "Surely ye are the ones in the wrong!"

65. Then were they confounded with shame: (they said), "Thou knowest full well that these (idols) do not speak!"

66. (Abraham) said, "Do ye then worship, besides God, things that can neither be of any good to you nor do you harm?

67. "Fie upon you, and upon the things that ye worship besides God! have ye no sense?"...

68. They said, "Burn him and protect your gods, if ye do (anything at all)!"

69. We said, "O Fire! be thou cool, and (a means of)) safety for Abraham!"

70. Then they sought a stratagem[12] against him: but We made them

---

[12] Plot

the ones that lost most!

71. But We delivered him and (his nephew) Lüt (and directed them) to the land which We have blessed for the nations.

72. And We bestowed on him Isaac and, as an additional gift, (a grandson), Jacob, and We made righteous men of every one (of them).

73. And We made them leaders, guiding (men) by Our Command, and We sent them inspiration to do good deeds, to establish regular prayers, and to practice regular charity; and they constantly served Us (and Us only).

74. And to Lüt, too, we gave Judgment and Knowledge, and We saved him from the town which practiced abominations[13]: truly they were a people given to Evil, a rebellious people.

75. And We admitted him to Our Mercy: for he was one of the Righteous.

76. (Remember) Noah, when he cried (to Us) aforetime: We listened to his (prayer) and delivered him and his family from great distress.

77. We helped him against people who rejected Our Signs: truly they were a people given to Evil: so We drowned them (in the Flood) all together.

78. And remember David and Solomon, when they gave judgment in the matter of the field into which the sheep of certain people had strayed by night: We did witness their judgment.

79. To Solomon We inspired the (right) understanding of the matter: to each (of them) We gave Judgment and Knowledge; it was Our power that made the hills and the birds celebrate Our praises with David: it was We Who did (these things).

80. It was We Who taught him the making of coats of mail[14] for your benefit, to guard you from each other's violence: will ye then be grateful?

81. (It was Our power that made) the violent (unruly) wind flow (tamely) for Solomon, to his order, to the land which We had blessed: for We do know all things.

---

[13] Evil, obscenities

[14] Defensive armour for the body

82. And of the evil ones, were some who dived for him, and did other work besides; and it was We Who guarded them.

83. And (remember) Job when he cried to his Lord, "Truly distress has seized me, but Thou art the Most Merciful of those that are merciful."

84. So We listened to him: We removed the distress that was on him, and We restored his people to him, and doubled their number — as a Grace from Ourselves, and a thing for commemoration[15], for all who serve Us.

85. And (remember) Ismail, Idris, and Zul-kifl, all (men) of constancy and patience;

86. We admitted them to Our Mercy: for they were of the Righteous Ones.

87. And remember Zun-nun, when he departed in wrath: he imagined that We had no power over him! But he cried through the depths of darkness, "There is no god but Thou: Glory to Thee: I was indeed wrong!"

88. So We listened to him: and delivered him from distress: and thus do We deliver those who have faith.

89. And (remember) Zakariya, when he cried to his Lord: "O my Lord! leave me not without offspring, though Thou art the best of inheritors.

90. So We listened to him: and We granted him Yahya: We cured his wife's (barrenness) for him. These (three) were ever quick in emulation[16] in good works: they used to call on Us with love and reverence, and humble themselves before Us.

91. And (remember) her who guarded her chastity: We breathed into her of Our Spirit, and We made her and her son a Sign for all peoples.

92. Verily, this Brotherhood of yours is a single Brotherhood, and I am your Lord and Cherisher: therefore serve Me (and no other).

93. But (later generations) cut off their affair (of unity), one from another: (yet) will they all return to Us.

94. Whoever works any act of righteousness and has Faith — his

---

15 A celebration in memory of

16 Trying to excel others

251

endeavor will not be rejected: We shall record it in his favor.

95. But there is a ban on any population which We have destroyed: that they shall not return.

96. Until the Gog and Magog (people) are let through (their barrier), and they swiftly swarm from every hill.

97. Then will the True Promise draw nigh (of fulfillment): then behold! the eyes of the Unbelievers will fixedly stare in horror: "Ah! woe to us! we were indeed heedless of this; nay, we truly did wrong!"

98. Verily ye, (Unbelievers), and the (false) gods that ye worship besides God, are (but) fuel for Hell! To it will ye (surely) come!

99. If these had been gods, they would not have got there! But each one will abide therein.

100. There, sobbing will be their lot, nor will they there hear (aught else).

101. Those for whom the Good (Record) from Us has gone before, will be removed far therefrom.

102. Not the slightest sound will they hear of Hell: what their souls desired, in that will they dwell.

103. The Great Terror will bring them no grief: but the angels will meet them (with mutual greetings): "This is your Day — (the Day) that ye were promised."

104. The Day that we roll up the heavens like a scroll[17] rolled up for books (completed) — even as We produced the first Creation, so shall We produce a new one: a promise We have undertaken: truly shall We fulfil it.

105. Before this We wrote in the Psalms, after the Message (given to Moses): "My servants, the righteous, shall inherit the earth."

106. Verily in the (Qur'an) is a Message for people who would (truly) worship God.

107. We sent thee not, but as a mercy for all creatures.

108. Say: "What has come to me by inspiration is that your God is One God: will ye therefore bow to His Will (in Islam)?"

109. But if they turn back, say: "I have proclaimed the Message to you all alike and in truth; but I know not whether that which ye are promised is near or far.

---

[17] A roll of paper or parchment

110. "It is He Who knows what is open in speech and what ye hide (in your hearts).

111. "I know not but that it may be a trial for you, and a grant of (worldly) livelihood (to you) for a time.

112. Say: "O my Lord! Judge Thou in truth!" "Our Lord Most Gracious is the One Whose assistance should be sought against the blasphemies ye utter!"

Chapter 22
Sürah Al-Hajj (The Pilgrimage)
Revealed at Madinah, 78 verses.

In the name of God, Most Gracious, Most Merciful.

1. O mankind! fear your Lord! For the convulsion[1] of the Hour (of Judgment) will be a thing terrible!

2. The Day ye shall see it, every mother giving suck shall forget her suckling babe, and every pregnant female shall drop her load (unformed): thou shalt see mankind as in a drunken riot, yet not drunk: but dreadful will be the Wrath of God.

3. And yet among men there are such as dispute about God, without knowledge, and follow every evil one obstinate in rebellion!

4. About the (Evil One) it is decreed that whoever turns to him for friendship, him will he lead astray, and he will guide him to the Penalty of the Fire.

5. O mankind! if ye have a doubt about the Resurrection, (consider) that We created you out of dust, then out of sperm, then out of a leech-like clot, then out of a morsel of flesh, partly formed and partly unformed, in order that We may manifest (Our Power) to you; and We cause whom We will to rest in the wombs for an appointed term, then do We bring you out as babes, then (foster you) that ye may reach your age of full strength; and some of you are called to die,

---

[1] Violent natural disturbance, esp. earthquake

and some are sent back to the feeblest old age, so that they know nothing after having known (much). And (further), thou seest the earth barren and lifeless, but when We pour down rain on it, it is stirred (to life), it swells, and it puts forth every kind of beautiful growth (in pairs).

6. This is so, because God is the Reality: it is He Who gives life to the dead, and it is He Who has power over all things.

7. And verily the Hour will come: there can be no doubt about it, or about (the fact) that God will raise up all who are in the graves.

8. Yet there is among men such a one as disputes about God, without knowledge, without guidance, and without a Book of Enlightenment —

9. (Disdainfully[2]) bending his side, in order to (lead men) astray from the Path of God; for him there is disgrace in this life, and on the Day of Judgment we shall make him taste the Penalty of burning (Fire).

10. (It will be said): "This is because of the deeds which thy hands sent forth, for verily God is not unjust to His servants.

11. There are among men some who serve God, as it were, on the verge: if good befalls them, they are, therewith, well content; but if a trial comes to them, they turn on their faces: they lose both this world and the Hereafter: that is loss for all to see!

12. They call on such deities, besides God, as can neither hurt nor profit them: that is straying far indeed (from the Way)!

13. (Perhaps) they call on one whose hurt is nearer than his profit: evil, indeed, is the patron, and evil the companion (for help)!

14. Verily God will admit those who believe and work righteous deeds, to Gardens, beneath which rivers flow: for God carries out all that He plans.

15. If any think that God will not help him (His Apostle) in this world and the Hereafter, let him stretch out a rope to the ceiling and cut (himself) off: then let him see whether his plan will remove that which enrages (him)!

16. Thus have We sent down Clear Signs; and verily God doth guide whom He will!

---

[2] Scornfully, contemptuously

17. Those who believe (in the Qur'an), those who follow the Jewish (scriptures), and the Sabians, Christians, Magians, and Polytheists — God will judge between them on the Day of Judgment: for God is witness of all things.

18. Seest thou not that to God bow down in worship all things that are in the heavens and on earth — the sun, the moon, the stars; the hills, the trees, the animals; and a great number among mankind? But a great number are (also) such as are fit for Punishment: and such as God shall disgrace — none can raise to honour: for God carries out all that He wills.

19. These two antagonists[3] dispute with each other about their Lord: but those who deny (their Lord) — for them will be cut out a garment of Fire: over their heads will be poured out boiling water.

20. With it will be scalded[4] what is within their bodies, as well as (their) skins.

21. In addition there will be maces[5] of iron (to punish) them.

22. Every time they wish to get away therefrom, from anguish, they will be forced back therein, and (it will be said), "Taste ye the Penalty of Burning!"

23. God will admit those who believe and work righteous deeds, to Gardens beneath which rivers flow: they shall be adorned therein with bracelets of gold and pearls; and their garments there will be of silk.

24. For they have been guided (in this life) to the purest of speeches; they have been guided to the Path of Him Who is worthy of (all) praise.

25. As to those who have rejected (God), and would keep back (men) from the Way of God, and from the Sacred Mosque, which We have made (open) to (all) men — equal is the dweller there and the visitor from the country — and any whose purpose therein is profanity or wrongdoing — them will We cause to taste of a most grievous Penalty.

26. Behold! We gave the site, to Abraham, of the (Sacred) House,

---

3 Adversaries
4 Burn with hot liquid
5 Heavy metal-headed and spiked clubs or sticks.

(saying): "Associate not any thing (in worship) with Me; and sanctify My House for those who compass it round, or stand up, or bow, or prostrate themselves (therein in prayer).

27. "And proclaim the Pilgrimage among men: they will come to thee on foot and (mounted) on every kind of camel, lean on account of journeys through deep and distant mountain highways;

28. "That they may witness the benefits (provided) for them, and celebrate the name of God, through the Days appointed, over the cattle which He has provided for them (for sacrifice): then eat ye thereof and feed the distressed ones in want.

29. "Then let them complete the rites prescribed for them, perform their vows, and (again) circumambulate[6] the Ancient House."

30. Such (is the Pilgrimage): whoever honours the sacred rites of God, for him it is good in the sight of his Lord. Lawful to you (for food in pilgrimage) are cattle except those mentioned to you (as exceptions): but shun the abomination of idols, and shun the word that is false —

31. Being true in faith to God, and never assigning partners to Him: if anyone assigns partners to God, he is as if he had fallen from heaven and been snatched up by birds, or the wind had swooped (like a bird on its prey) and thrown him into a far-distant place.

32. Such (is his state): and whoever holds in honour the Symbols of God, (in the sacrifice of animals), such (honour) should come truly from piety of heart.

33. In them ye have benefits for a term appointed: in the end their place of sacrifice is near the Ancient House.

34. To every people did We appoint rites (of sacrifice), that they might celebrate the name of God over the sustenance He gave them from animals (fit for food), but your God is one God: submit then your wills to Him (in Islam) and give thou the Good News to those who humble themselves —

35. To those whose hearts, when God is mentioned, are filled with fear, who show patient perseverance[7] over their afflictions[8], keep up regular prayer, and spend (in charity) out of what we have bestowed

---

6 Go around, make *tawaf*
7 Steadfastness, patience
8 Hardships, distress

upon them.

36. The sacrificial camels we have made for you as among the Symbols from God: in them is (much) good for you: then pronounce the name of God over them as they line up (for sacrifice): when they are down on their sides (after slaughter), eat ye thereof, and feed such as (beg not but) live in contentment, and such as beg with due humility: thus have we made animals subject to you, that ye may be grateful.

37. It is not their meat nor their blood, that reaches God: it is your piety that reaches Him: He has thus made them subject to you, that ye may glorify God for His guidance to you: and proclaim the Good News to all who do right.

38. Verily God will defend (from ill) those who believe: verily, God loveth not any that is a traitor to faith, or shows ingratitude.

39. To those against whom war is made, permission is given (to fight) because they are wronged — and verily, God is Most powerful for their aid —

40. (They are) those who have been expelled from their homes in defiance[9] of right — (for no cause) except that they say, "Our Lord is God." Did not God check one set of people by means of another, there would surely have been pulled down monasteries, churches, synagogues, and mosques, in which the name of God is commemorated in abundant measure. God will certainly aid those who aid His (cause); for verily God is Full of Strength, Exalted in Might, (Able to enforce His Will).

41. (They are) those who, if We establish them in the land, establish regular prayer and give regular charity, enjoin the right and forbid wrong: with God rests the end (and decision) of (all) affairs.

42. If they treat thy (mission) as false, so did the Peoples before them (with their Prophets) — the People of Noah, and 'Ad, and Thamūd;

43. Those of Abraham and Lūt;

44. And the Companions of the Madyan people: and Moses was rejected (in the same way). But I granted respite to the Unbelievers and (only) after that did I punish them: but how (terrible) was My rejection (of them)!

---

[9] Open resistence

45. How many populations have We destroyed, which were given to wrongdoing! They tumbled down on their roofs. And how many wells are lying idle and neglected, and castles lofty and well-built!

46. Do they not travel through the land, so that their hearts (and minds) may thus learn wisdom and their ears may thus learn to hear? Truly it is not their eyes that are blind but their hearts which are in their breasts.

47. Yet they ask thee to hasten on the Punishment! But God will not fail in His promise. Verily a day in the sight of thy Lord is like a thousand years of your reckoning[10].

48. And to how many populations did I give respite, which were given to wrongdoing? In the end I punished them. To Me is the destination (of all).

49. Say: "O men! I am (sent) to you only to give a clear warning:

50. "Those who believe and work righteousness, for them is forgiveness and a sustenance most generous.

51. "But those who strive against Our Signs, to frustrate them, they will be Companions of the Fire."

52. Never did We send an apostle or a prophet before thee, but, when he framed a desire, Satan threw some (vanity) into his desire: but God will cancel anything (vain) that Satan throws in, and God will confirm (and establish) His Signs: for God is full of knowledge and wisdom:

53. That He may make the suggestions thrown in by Satan, but a trial for those in whose hearts is a disease and who are hardened of heart: verily the wrongdoers are in a schism[11] far (from the Truth):

54. And that those on whom knowledge has been bestowed may learn that the (Qur'an) is the Truth from thy Lord, and that they may believe therein, and their hearts may be made humbly (open) to it: for verily God is the Guide of those who believe, to the Straight Way.

55. Those who reject Faith will not cease to be in doubt concerning (Revelation) until the Hour (of Judgment) comes suddenly upon them, or there comes to them the Penalty of a Day of Disaster.

56. On that Day the Dominion[12] will be that of God: He will judge

---

[10] Calculation

[11] Division of a group into opposing parties.

[12] Authority, sovereignty

between them: so those who believe and work righteous deeds will be in Gardens of Delight.

57. And for those who reject Faith and deny Our Signs, there will be a humiliating Punishment.

58. Those who leave their homes in the cause of God, and are then slain or die — on them will God bestow verily a goodly Provision: truly God is He Who bestows the best Provision.

59. Verily He will admit them to a place with which they shall be well pleased: for God is All-Knowing, Most Forbearing.

60. That (is so). And if one has retaliated to no greater extent than the injury he received, and is again set upon inordinately[13], God will help him: for God is One that blots out (sins) and forgives (again and again).

61. That is because God merges Night into Day, and He merges Day into Night, and verily it is God Who hears and sees (all things).

62. That is because God — He is the Reality: and those besides Him whom they invoke[14] — they are but vain Falsehood: verily God is He, Most High, Most Great.

63. Seest thou not that God sends down rain from the sky, and forthwith the earth becomes clothed with green? For God is He Who understands the finest mysteries, and is well-acquainted (with them).

64. To Him belongs all that is in the heavens and on earth: for verily God — He is Free of all wants, Worthy of all praise.

65. Seest thou not that God has made subject to you (men) all that is on the earth, and the ships that sail through the sea by His command? He withholds the sky (rain) from falling on the earth except by His leave: for God is Most Kind and Most Merciful to man.

66. It is He Who gave you life, will cause you to die, and will again give you life: truly man is a most ungrateful creature!

67. To every People have we appointed rites and ceremonies which they must follow, let them not then dispute with thee on the matter, but do thou invite (them) to thy Lord: for thou art assuredly on the Right Way.

68. If they do wrangle[15] with thee, say, "God knows best what

---

[13] Aggressively, immoderately

[14] Call upon

[15] Dispute, argue

it is ye are doing."

69. "God will judge between you on the Day of Judgment concerning the matters in which ye differ."

70. Knowest thou not that God knows all that is in heaven and on earth? Indeed it is all in a record, and that is easy for God.

71. Yet they worship, besides God, things for which no authority has been sent down to them, and of which they have (really) no knowledge: for those that do wrong there is no helper.

72. When Our Clear Signs are rehearsed[16] to them, thou wilt notice a denial on the faces of the Unbelievers! They nearly attack with violence those who rehearse Our Signs to them. Say, "Shall I tell you of something (far) worse than these Signs? It is the Fire (of Hell)! God has promised it to the Unbelievers! And evil is that destination!"

73. O men! Here is a parable set forth! Listen to it! Those on whom, besides God ye call, cannot create (even) a fly, if they all met together for the purpose! And if the fly should snatch away anything from them, they would have no power to release it from the fly: feeble are those who petition and those whom they petition!

74. No just estimate have they made of God: for God is He Who is strong and able to carry out His Will.

75. God chooses Messengers from angels and from men: for God is He Who hears and sees (all things).

76. He knows what is before them and what is behind them: and to God go back all questions (for decision).

77. O ye who believe! bow down, prostrate yourselves, and adore your Lord; and do good; that ye may prosper.

78. And strive in His cause as ye ought to strive, (with sincerity and under discipline): He has chosen you, and has imposed no difficulties on you in religion; it is the cult[17] of your father Abraham. It is He Who has named you Muslims, both before and in this (Revelation); that the Apostle may be a witness for you, and ye be witnesses for mankind! So establish regular Prayer, give regular Charity, and hold fast to God! He is your Protector — the Best to protect and the Best to help!

---

[16] Recited, repeated
[17] Way

Chapter 23
Sürah Al-Mu'minün (The Believers)
Revealed at Makkah, 118 verses.

In the name of God, Most Gracious, Most Merciful.

1. The Believers must (eventually) win through —

2. Those who humble themselves in their prayers;

3. Who avoid vain talk;

4. Who are active in deeds of charity;

5. Who abstain from sex,

6. Except with those joined to them in the marriage bond, or (the captives) whom their right hands possess — for (in their case) they are free from blame,

7. But those whose desires exceed those limits are transgressors —

8. Those who faithfully observe their trusts and their covenants;

9. And who (strictly) guard their prayers —

10. Those will be the heirs,

11. Who will inherit Paradise: they will dwell therein (forever).

12. Man We did create from a quintessence[1] (of clay);

13. Then We placed him as (a drop of) sperm in a place of rest, firmly fixed;

14. Then We made the sperm into a clot of congealed[2] blood; then of that clot We made a (foetus) lump; then We made out of that lump bones and clothed the bones with flesh; then We developed out of it another creature: so blessed be God, the Best to create!

15. After that, at length, ye will die.

16. Again, on the Day of Judgment, will ye be raised up.

17. And We have made, above you, seven tracts; and We are never unmindful of (Our) Creation.

18. And We send down water from the sky according to (due) measure, and We cause it to soak in the soil; and We certainly are able to drain it off (with ease).

19. With it We grow for you gardens of date palms and vines:

---

[1] Refined extract

[2] Solidified

in them have ye abundant fruits: and of them ye eat (and have enjoyment) —

20. Also a tree springing out of Mount Sinai, which produces oil, and relish for those who use it for food.

21. And in cattle (too) ye have an instructive example: from within their bodies We produce (milk) for you to drink; there are, in them, (besides), numerous (other) benefits for you; and of their (meat) ye eat;

22. And on them, as well as in ships, ye ride.

23. (Further, We sent a long line of prophets for your instruction.) We sent Noah to his people: he said, "O my people! worship God! Ye have no other god but Him: will ye not fear (Him)?"

24. The Chiefs of the Unbelievers among his people said: "He is no more than a man like yourselves: his wish is to assert his superiority over you: if God had wished (to send messengers), He could have sent down angels: never did we hear such a thing (as he says), among our ancestors of old."

25. (And some said:) "He is only a man possessed: wait (and have patience) with him for a time."

26. (Noah) said: "O my Lord! help me; for that they accuse me of falsehood!"

27. So We inspired him (with this message): "Construct the Ark within Our sight and under Our guidance: then when comes Our command, and the fountains of the earth gush forth, take thou on board pairs of every species, male and female, and thy family — except those of them against whom the Word has already gone forth: and address Me not in favor of the wrongdoers; for they shall be drowned (in the Flood).

28. And when thou hast embarked on the Ark — thou and those with thee — say: "Praise be to God, Who has saved us from the people who do wrong."

29. And say: "O my Lord! enable me to disembark with Thy blessing: for Thou art the Best to enable (us) to disembark."

30. Verily in this there are Signs (for men to understand); (thus) do We try (men).

31. Then We raised after them another generation;

32. And We sent to them an apostle from among themselves,

(saying), "Worship God! ye have no other god but Him. Will ye not fear (Him)?"

33. And the Chiefs of his people, who disbelieved and denied the Meeting in the Hereafter, and on whom We had bestowed the good things of this life, said: "He is no more than a man like yourselves; he eats of that of which ye eat, and drinks of what ye drink.

34. "If ye obey a man like yourselves, behold, it is certain ye will be lost.

35. "Does he promise that when ye die and become dust and bones, ye shall be brought forth (again)?

36. "Far, very far is that which ye are promised!

37. "There is nothing but our life in this world! We shall die and we live! But we shall never be raised up again!

38. "He is only a man who invents a lie against God, but we are not the ones to believe in him!"

39. (The prophet) said: "O my Lord! help me: for that they accuse me of falsehood."

40. (God) said: "In but a little while, they are sure to be sorry!"

41. Then the Blast overtook them with justice, and We made them as rubbish of dead leaves (floating on the stream of Time)! So away with the people who do wrong!

42. Then We raised after them other generations.

43. No people can hasten their term, nor can they delay (it).

44. Then sent We Our apostles in succession: every time there came to a people their apostle, they accused him of falsehood: so We made them follow each other (in punishment): We made them as a tale (that is told): so away with a people that will not believe!

45. Then We sent Moses and his brother Aaron, with Our Signs and authority manifest,

46. To Pharaoh and his Chiefs: but these behaved insolently: they were arrogant people.

47. They said: "Shall we believe in two men like ourselves? And their people are subject to us!"

48. So they accused them of falsehood, and they became of those who were destroyed.

49. And We gave Moses the Book, in order that they might receive guidance.

50. And We made the son of Mary and his mother as a Sign: We gave them both shelter on high ground, affording rest and security and furnished with springs.

51. O ye apostles! enjoy (all) things good and pure, and work righteousness: for I am well-acquainted with (all) that ye do.

52. And verily this Brotherhood of yours is a single Brotherhood, and I am your Lord and Cherisher: therefore fear Me (and no other).

53. But people have cut off their affair (of unity), between them, into sects: each party rejoices in that which is with itself.

54. But leave them in their confused ignorance for a time.

55. Do they think that because We have granted them abundance of wealth and sons,

56. We would hasten them on in every good? Nay, they do not understand.

57. Verily those who live in awe for fear of their Lord;

58. Those who believe in the Signs of their Lord;

59. Those who join not (in worship) partners with their Lord;

60. And those who dispense their charity with their hearts full of fear, because they will return to their Lord —

61. It is these who hasten in every good work, and these who are foremost in them.

62. On no soul do We place a burden greater than it can bear: before Us is a record which clearly shows the truth: they will never be wronged.

63. But their hearts are in confused ignorance of this; and there are, besides that, deeds of theirs, which they will (continue) to do —

64. Until, when We seize in Punishment those of them who received the good things of this world, behold, they will groan in supplication!

65. It will be said: "Groan not in supplication this day; for ye shall certainly not be helped by Us.

66. "My Signs used to be rehearsed to you, but ye used to turn back on your heels —

67. "In arrogance: talking nonsense about the (Qur'an), like one telling fables by night."

68. Do they not ponder over the Word (of God), or has anything

(new) come to them that did not come to their fathers of old?

69. Or do they not recognize their Apostle, that they deny him?

70. Or do they say, "He is possessed"? Nay, he has brought them the Truth, but most of them hate the Truth.

71. If the Truth had been in accord with their desires, truly the heavens and the earth, and all beings therein would have been in confusion and corruption! Nay, We have sent them their admonition, but they turn away from their admonition.

72. Or is it that thou askest them for some recompense[3]? But the recompense of thy Lord is best: He is the Best of those who give sustenance.

73. But verily thou callest them to the Straight Way;

74. And verily those who believe not in the Hereafter are deviating from that Way.

75. If We had mercy on them and removed the distress which is on them, they would obstinately persist in their transgression, wandering in distraction to and fro.

76. We inflicted Punishment on them, but they humbled not themselves to their Lord, nor do they submissively entreat (Him)!
—

77. Until We open on them a gate leading to a severe Punishment: then Lo! they will be plunged in despair therein!

78. It is He Who has created for you (the faculties of) hearing, sight, feeling and understanding: little thanks it is ye give!

79. And He has multiplied you through the earth, and to Him shall ye be gathered back.

80. It is He Who gives life and death, and to Him (is due) the alternation of Night and Day: will ye not then understand?

81. On the contrary they say things similar to what the ancients said.

82. They say: "What! when we die and become dust and bones, could we really be raised up again?

83. "Such things have been promised to us and to our fathers before! They are nothing but tales of the ancients!"

84. Say: "To whom belong the earth and all beings therein? (Say) if ye know!"

---
[3] Reward

85. They will say, "To God!" Say: "Yet will ye not receive admonition?"

86. Say: "Who is the Lord of the seven heavens, and the Lord of the Throne (of Glory) Supreme?"

87. They will say, "(They belong) to God." Say: "Will ye not then be filled with awe?"

88. Say: "Who is it in whose hands is the governance of all things — who protects (all), but is not protected (of any)? (Say) if ye know."

89. They will say, "(It belongs) to God." Say: "Then how are ye deluded?"

90. We have sent them the Truth: but they indeed practice Falsehood!

91. No son did God beget, nor is there any god along with Him: (if there were many gods), behold, each god would have taken away what he had created, and some would have lorded it over others! Glory to God! (He is free) from the (sort of) things they attribute to Him!

92. He knows what is hidden and what is open: too high is He for the partners they attribute to Him!

93. Say: "O my Lord! if Thou wilt show me (in my lifetime) that which they are warned against —

94. "Then, O my Lord! put me not amongst the people who do wrong!"

95. And We are certainly able to show thee (in fulfillment) that against which they are warned.

96. Repel evil with that which is best: We are well-acquainted with the things they say.

97. And say: "O my Lord! I seek refuge with Thee from the suggestions of the Evil Ones;

98. "And I seek refuge with Thee, O my Lord! lest they should come near me."

99. (In Falsehood will they be) until, when death comes to one of them, he says: "O my Lord! send me back (to life) —

100. "In order that I may work righteousness in the things I neglected." — "By no means! it is but a word he says," before them is a Partition till the Day they are raised up.

101. Then when the Trumpet is blown, there will be no more relationships between them that day, nor will one ask after another!

102. Then those whose balance (of good deeds) is heavy — they will attain salvation:

103. But those whose balance is light, will be those who have lost their souls; in Hell will they abide.

104. The Fire will burn their faces, and they will therein grin, with their lips displaced.

105. "Were not My Signs rehearsed to you, and ye did but treat them as falsehoods?"

106. They will say: "Our Lord! our misfortune overwhelmed us and we became a people astray!

107. "Our Lord! bring us out of this: if ever we return (to evil), then shall we be wrongdoers indeed!"

108. He will say: "Be ye driven into it (with ignominy[4])! and speak ye not to Me!

109. "A part of My servants there was, who used to pray, 'Our Lord! we believe; then do Thou forgive us, and have mercy upon us: for Thou art the best of those Who show mercy!'

110. "But ye treated them with ridicule, so much so that (ridicule of) them made you forget My Message while ye were laughing at them!

111. "I have rewarded them this day for their patience and constancy: they are indeed the ones that have achieved Bliss..."

112. He will say: "What number of years did ye stay on earth?"

113. They will say: "We stayed a day or part of a day: but ask those who keep account."

114. He will say: "Ye stayed not but a little — if ye had only known!

115. "Did ye then think that We had created you in jest, and that ye would not be brought back to Us (for account)?"

116. Therefore exalted be God, the King, the Reality; there is no god but He, the Lord of the Throne of Honour!

117. If anyone invokes, besides God, any other god, he has no authority therefor; and his reckoning[5] will be only with his Lord! And verily the Unbelievers will fail to win through!

---

4 Disgrace

5 Account

118. So say: "O my Lord! grant thou forgiveness and mercy! for Thou art the Best of those who show mercy!"

Chapter 24
Sürah An-Nur (The Light)
Revealed at Madinah, 64 verses.

In the name of God, Most Gracious, Most Merciful.

1. A Sürah which We have sent down and which We have ordained: in it have We sent down Clear Signs, in order that ye may receive admonition.

2. The woman and the man guilty of adultery or fornication — flog each of them with a hundred stripes: let not compassion move you in their case, in a matter prescribed by God, if ye believe in God and the Last Day: and let a party of the Believers witness their punishment.

3. Let no man guilty of adultery or fornication marry any but a woman similarly guilty, or an Unbeliever: nor let any but such a man or an Unbeliever marry such a woman: to the Believers such a thing is forbidden.

4. And those who launch a charge against chaste women, and produce not four witnesses, (to support their allegation[1]) — flog them with eighty stripes: and reject their evidence ever after: for such men are wicked transgressors —

5. Unless they repent thereafter and mend (their conduct): for God is Oft-Forgiving, Most Merciful.

6. And for those who launch a charge against their spouses, and have (in support) no evidence but their own — their solitary evidence (can be received) if they bear witness four times (with an oath) by God that they are solemnly[2] telling the truth;

7. And the fifth (oath) (should be) that they solemnly invoke the

---

[1] Claim, charge

[2] Earnestly, seriously

curse of God on themselves if they tell a lie.

8. But it would avert the punishment from the wife, if she bears witness four times (with an oath) by God, that (her husband) is telling a lie;

9. And the fifth (oath) should be that she solemnly invokes the wrath of God on herself if (her accuser) is telling the truth.

10. If it were not for God's grace and mercy on you, and that God is Oft-Returning, Full of Wisdom — (ye would be ruined indeed).

11. Those who brought forward the lie are a body among yourselves: think it not to be an evil to you: on the contrary it is good for you: to every man among them (will come the punishment) of the sin that he earned, and to him who took on himself the lead among them, will be a Penalty grievous.

12. Why did not Believers — men and women — when ye heard of the affair — put the best construction[3] on it in their own minds and say, "This (charge) is an obvious lie"?

13. Why did they not bring four witnesses to prove it? When they have not brought the witnesses, such men, in the sight of God, (stand forth) themselves as liars!

14. Were it not for the grace and mercy of God on you, in this world and the Hereafter, a grievous penalty would have seized you in that ye rushed glibly[4] into this affair.

15. Behold, ye received it on your tongues, and said out of your mouths things of which ye had no knowledge; and ye thought it to be a light matter, while it was most serious in the sight of God.

16. And why did ye not, when ye heard it, say — "It is not right of us to speak of this: Glory to God! this is a most serious slander[5]!"

17. God doth admonish you, that ye may never repeat such (conduct), if ye are (true) Believers.

18. And God makes the Signs plain to you: for God is full of knowledge and wisdom.

19. Those who love (to see) scandal published broadcast among the Believers, will have a grievous Penalty in this life and in the

---

[3] Interpretation

[4] Carelessly, rashly

[5] Defamation, libel

Hereafter: God knows, and ye know not.

20. Were it not for the grace and mercy of God on you, and that God is full of kindness and mercy (ye would be ruined indeed).

21. O ye who believe! follow not Satan's footsteps: if any will follow the footsteps of Satan, he will (but) command what is shameful and wrong: and were it not for the grace and mercy of God on you, not one of you would ever have been pure: but God doth purify whom He pleases: and God is One Who hears and knows (all things).

22. Let not those among you who are endued with grace and amplitude[6] of means resolve by oath against helping their kinsmen, those in want, and those who have left their homes in God's cause: let them forgive and overlook: do you not wish that God should forgive you? For God is Oft-Forgiving, Most Merciful.

23. Those who slander chaste women, indiscreet[7] but believing, are cursed in this life and in the Hereafter: for them is a grievous Penalty —

24. On the Day when their tongues, their hands, and their feet will bear witness against them as to their actions.

25. On that Day God will pay them back (all) their just dues, and they will realize that God is the (very) Truth, that makes all things manifest.

26. Women impure are for men impure, and men impure are for women impure; and women of purity are for men of purity, and men of purity are for women of purity: these are not affected by what people say: for them there is forgiveness, and a provision honourable.

27. O ye who believe! enter not houses other than your own, until ye have asked permission and saLüted those in them: that is best for you in order that ye may heed (what is seemly).

28. If ye find no one in the house, enter not until permission is given to you: if ye are asked to go back, go back: that makes for greater purity for yourselves: and God knows well all that ye do.

29. It is no fault on your part to enter houses not used for living in, which serve some (other) use for you: and God has knowledge of what ye reveal and what ye conceal.

---

6 Abundance

7 Tactless

30. Say to the believing men that they should lower their gaze and guard their modesty: that will make for greater purity for them: and God is well acquainted with all that they do.

31. And say to the believing women that they should lower their gaze and guard their modesty; that they should not display their beauty and ornaments except what (must ordinarily) appear thereof; that they should draw their veils over their bosoms and not display their beauty except to their husbands, their fathers, their husbands' fathers, their sons, their husbands' sons, their brothers or their brothers'sons, or their sisters' sons, or their women, or the slaves whom their right hands possess, or male servants free of physical needs, or small children who have no sense of the shame of sex; and that they should not strike their feet in order to draw attention to their hidden ornaments. And O ye Believers! turn ye all together towards God, that ye may attain Bliss.

32. Marry those among you who are single, or the virtuous ones among your slaves, male or female: if they are in poverty, God will give them means out of His grace: for God encompasseth all, and He knoweth all things.

33. Let those who find not the wherewithal[8] for marriage keep themselves chaste, until God gives them means out of His grace. And if any of your slaves ask for a deed in writing (to enable them to earn their freedom for a certain sum), give them such a deed if ye know any good in them; yea, give them something yourselves out of the means which God has given to you. But force not your maids to prostitution when they desire chastity, in order that ye may make a gain in the goods of this life. But if anyone compels them, yet, after such compulsion, is God Oft-Forgiving, Most Merciful (to them).

34. We have already sent down to you verses making things clear, an illustration from (the story of) people who passed away before you, and an admonition for those who fear (God).

35. God is the Light of the heavens and the earth. The parable of His Light is as if there were a Niche and within it a Lamp: the Lamp enclosed in Glass: the Glass as it were a brilliant star: lit from a blessed Tree, an Olive, neither of the East nor of the West, whose

---

8 Money or means

Oil is well-nigh luminous, though fire scarce touched it: Light upon Light! God doth guide whom He will to His Light. God doth set forth Parables for men: and God doth know all things.

36. (Lit is such a light) in houses, which God hath permitted to be raised to honour; for the celebration, in them of His name: in them is He glorified in the mornings and in the evenings, (again and again) —

37. By men whom neither traffic[9] nor merchandise[10] can divert from the Remembrance of God, nor from regular Prayer, nor from the practice of regular Charity: their (only) fear is for the Day when hearts and eyes will be transformed (in a world wholly new) —

38. That God may reward them according to the best of their deeds, and add even more for them out of His Grace: for God doth provide for those whom He will, without measure.

39. But the Unbelievers — their deeds are like a mirage in sandy deserts, which the man parched[11] with thirst mistakes for water; until when he comes up to it, he finds it to be nothing: but he finds God (ever) with him, and God will pay him his account: and God is swift in taking account.

40. Or (the Unbelievers' state) is like the depths of darkness in a vast deep ocean, overwhelmed with billow[12] topped by billow, topped by (dark) clouds: depths of darkness, one above another: if a man stretches out his hand, he can hardly see it! For any to whom God giveth not light, there is no light!

41. Seest thou not that it is God Whose praises all beings in the heavens and on earth do celebrate, and the birds (of the air) with wings outspread? Each one knows its own (mode of) prayer and praise. And God knows well all that they do.

42. Yea, to God belongs the dominion of the heavens and the earth; and to God is the final goal (of all).

43. Seest thou not that God makes the clouds move gently, then joins them together, then makes them into a heap? — then wilt thou

---

9 Business, commerce
10 Goods for sale
11 Hot and dry
12 Waves

see rain issue forth from their midst. And He sends down from the sky mountain masses (of clouds) wherein is hail: He strikes therewith whom He pleases and He turns it away from whom He pleases. The vivid flash of His lightning well-nigh blinds the sight.

44. It is God Who alternates the Night and the Day: verily in these things is an instructive example for those who have vision!

45. And God has created every animal from water: of them there are some that creep on their bellies; some that walk on two legs; and some that walk on four. God creates what He wills: for verily God has power over all things.

46. We have indeed sent down Signs that make things manifest: and God guides whom He wills to a way that is straight.

47. They say, "We believe in God and in the Apostle, and we obey": but even after that, some of them turn away: they are not (really) Believers.

48. When they are summoned to God and His Apostle, in order that He may judge between them, behold some of them decline (to come).

49. But if the right is on their side, they come to him with all submission.

50. Is it that there is a disease in their hearts? Or do they doubt, or are they in fear, that God and His Apostle will deal unjustly with them? Nay, it is they themselves who do wrong.

51. The answer of the Believers, when summoned to God and His Apostle, in order that He may judge between them, is no other than this: they say, "We hear and we obey": it is such as these that will attain felicity[13].

52. It is such as obey God and His Apostle, and fear God and do right, that will win (in the end).

53. They swear their strongest oaths by God that, if only thou wouldst command them, they would leave (their homes). Say: "Swear ye not; obedience is (more) reasonable: verily, God is well-acquainted with all that ye do."

54. Say: "Obey God, and obey the Apostle: but if ye turn away, he is only responsible for the duty placed on him and ye for that placed

---

[13] Bliss

on you. If ye obey him, ye shall be on right guidance. The Apostle's duty is only to preach the clear (Message)."

55. God has promised, to those among you who believe and work righteous deeds, that He will, of a surety, grant them in the land, inheritance (of power), as He granted it to those before them; that He will establish in authority their religion — the one which He has chosen for them; and that He will change (their state), after the fear in which they (lived), to one of security and peace: 'They will worship Me (alone) and not associate aught with Me.' If any do reject faith after this, they are rebellious and wicked.

56. So establish regular Prayer and give regular Charity: and obey the Apostle; that ye may receive mercy.

57. Never think thou that the Unbelievers are going to frustrate (God's Plan) on earth: their abode is the Fire — and it is indeed an evil refuge!

58. O ye who believe! let those whom your right hands possess, and the (children) among you who have not come of age ask your permission (before they come to your presence), on three occasions, before morning prayer; the while ye doff[14] your clothes for the noonday heat; and after the late-night prayer: these are your three times of undress[15]: outside those times it is not wrong for you or for them to move about attending to each other: thus does God make clear the Signs to you: for God is full of knowledge and wisdom.

59. But when the children among you come of age, let them (also) ask for permission, as do those senior to them (in age): thus does God make clear His Signs to you: for God is full of knowledge and wisdom.

60. Such elderly women as are past the prospect of marriage — there is no blame on them if they lay aside their (outer) garments, provided they make not a wanton[16] display of their beauty: but it is best for them to be modest: and God is One Who sees and knows all things.

61. It is no fault in the blind nor in one born lame, nor in one

---

[14] Remove, take off
[15] Privacy
[16] Irresponsible, unchaste

afflicted with illness, nor in yourselves, that ye should eat in your own houses, or those of your fathers, or your mothers, or your brothers, or your sisters, or your father's brothers, or your father's sisters, or your mother's brothers, or your mother's sisters, or in houses of which the keys are in your possession, or in the house of a sincere friend of yours: there is no blame on you, whether ye eat in company or separately. But if ye enter houses, saLüte each other — a greeting or blessing and purity as from God. Thus does God make clear the Signs to you: that ye may understand.

62. Only those are Believers who believe in God and His Apostle: when they are with him on a matter requiring collective action, they do not depart until they have asked for his leave: those who ask for thy leave are those who believe in God and His Apostle; so when they ask for thy leave, for some business of theirs, give leave to those of them whom thou wilt, and ask God for their forgiveness: for God is Oft-Forgiving, Most Merciful.

63. Deem not the summons of the Apostle among yourselves like the summons of one of you to another: God doth know those of you who slip away under shelter of some excuse: then let those beware who withstand[17] the Apostle's order lest some trial befall them, or a grievous Penalty be inflicted on them.

64. Be quite sure that to God doth belong whatever is in the heavens and on earth. Well doth He know what ye are intent upon: and one day they will be brought back to Him, and He will tell them the truth of what they did: for God doth know all things.

---

[17] Resist, oppose

Chapter 25
Sürah Al-Furqãn (The Criterion)
Revealed at Makkah, 77 verses

In the name of God, Most Gracious, Most Merciful.

1. Blessed is He Who sent down the Criterion[1] to His servant, that it may be an admonition to all creatures —

2. He to Whom belongs the dominion of the heavens and the earth: no son has He begotten, nor has He a partner in His dominion: it is He Who created all things, and ordered them in due proportions.

3. Yet have they taken, besides Him, gods that can create nothing but are themselves created; that have no control of hurt or good to themselves; nor can they control Death nor Life nor Resurrection.

4. But the Misbelievers say: "Naught[2] is this but a lie which he has forged, and others have helped him at it." In truth it is they who have put forward an iniquity and a falsehood.

5. And they say: "Tales of the ancients, which he has caused to be written: and they are dictated before him morning and evening."

6. Say: "The (Qur'an) was sent down by Him Who knows the Mystery (that is) in the heavens and the earth: verily He is Oft-Forgiving, Most Merciful."

7. And they say: "What sort of an apostle is this, who eats food, and walks through the streets? Why has not an angel been sent down to him to give admonition with him?

8. "Or (why) has not a treasure been bestowed on him, or why has he (not) a garden for enjoyment?" The wicked say: "Ye follow none other than a man bewitched."

9. See what kinds of comparisons they make for thee! But they have gone astray, and never a way will they be able to find!

10. Blessed is He Who, if that were His Will, could give thee better (things) than those — Gardens beneath which rivers flow; and He could give thee Palaces (secure to dwell in).

11. Nay, they deny the Hour (of the Judgment to come): but We have prepared a Blazing Fire for such as deny the Hour:

---

[1] A standard to judge between good and evil.

[2] Nothing

12. When it sees them from a place far off, they will hear its fury[3] and its raging sigh.

13. And when they are cast, bound together, into a constricted[4] place therein, they will plead for destruction there and then!

14. "This day plead not for a single destruction: plead for destruction oft-repeated!"

15. Say: "Is that best, or the eternal Garden, promised to the righteous? For them, that is a reward as well as a goal (or attainment).

16. "For them there will be therein all that they wish for: they will dwell (there) for aye: a promise to be prayed for from thy Lord."

17. The Day He will gather them together as well as those whom they worship besides God, He will ask: "Was it ye who led these My servants astray, or did they stray from the Path themselves?"

18. They will say: "Glory to Thee! not meet[5] was it for us that we should take for protectors others besides Thee: but Thou didst bestow, on them and their fathers, good things (in life), until they forgot the Message: for they were a people (worthless and) lost.

19. (God will say): "Now have they proved you liars in what ye say: so ye cannot avert (your penalty) nor (get) help." And whoever among you does wrong, him shall We cause to taste of a grievous Penalty.

20. And the apostles whom We sent before thee were all (men) who ate food and walked through the streets: We have made some of you as a trial for others: will ye have patience? For God is One Who sees (all things).

21. Such as fear not the meeting with Us (for Judgment) say: "Why are not the angels sent down to us, or (why) do we not see our Lord?" Indeed they have an arrogant conceit[6] of themselves, and mighty is the insolence of their impiety!

22. The Day they see the angels — no joy will there be to the sinners that Day: the (angels) will say: "There is a barrier forbidden (to you) altogether!"

23. And We shall turn to whatever deeds they did (in this life),

---

[3] Anger

[4] Narrow

[5] Suitable, proper, fit

[6] Personal vanity

and We shall make such deeds as floating dust scattered about.

24. The Companions of the Garden will be well, that Day, in their abode, and have the fairest of places for repose[7].

25. The Day the heaven shall be rent asunder with clouds, and angels shall be sent down, descending (in ranks) —

26. That Day, the dominion as of right and truth, shall be (wholly) for (God) Most Merciful: it will be a day of dire[8] difficulty for the Misbelievers.

27. The Day that the wrongdoer will bite at his hands, He will say, "Oh! would that I had taken a (straight) path with the Apostle!

28. "Ah! woe is me! would that I had never taken such a one for a friend!

29. "He did lead me astray from the Message (of God) after it had come to me! Ah! the Evil One is but a traitor to man!

30. Then the Apostle will say: "O my Lord! truly my people took this Qur'an for just foolish nonsense."

31. Thus have We made for every prophet an enemy among the sinners: but enough is thy Lord to guide and to help.

32. Those who reject Faith say: "Why is not the Qur'an revealed to him all at once?" Thus (is it revealed), that We may strengthen thy heart thereby, and We have rehearsed[9] it to thee in slow, well-arranged stages, gradually.

33. And no question do they bring to thee but We reveal to thee the truth and the best explanation (thereof).

34. Those who will be gathered to Hell (prone[10]) on their faces — they will be in an evil plight, and, as to Path, most astray.

35. Before this, We sent Moses the Book, and appointed his brother Aaron with him as Minister[11];

36. And We commanded: "Go ye both, to the people who have rejected Our Signs": and those (people) We destroyed with utter destruction.

37. And the people of Noah — when they rejected the Apostles,

---

[7] Rest
[8] Dreadful
[9] Recited, repeated
[10] Lying with face downwards.
[11] Helper

We drowned them, and We made them as a Sign for mankind; and We have prepared for (all) wrongdoers a grievous Penalty —

38. As also 'Ād and Thamūd, and the Companions of the Rass, and many a generation between them.

39. To each one We set forth parables and examples; and each one We broke to utter annihilation (for their sins).

40. And the (Unbelievers) must indeed have passed by the town on which was rained a shower of evil: did they not then see it (with their own eyes)? But they fear not the Resurrection.

41. When they see thee, they treat thee no otherwise than in mockery: "Is this the one whom God has sent as an apostle?"

42. "He indeed would well-nigh have misled us from our gods, had it not been that we were constant to them!" Soon will they know, when they see the Penalty, who it is that is most misled in Path!

43. Seest thou such a one as taketh for his god his own passion (or impulse)? Couldst thou be a disposer of affairs for him?

44. Or thinkest thou that most of them listen or understand? They are only like cattle; — nay, they are worse astray in Path.

45. Hast thou not turned thy vision to thy Lord? — how He doth prolong the Shadow! If He willed, He could make it stationary! Then do We make the sun its guide;

46. Then We draw it in towards Ourselves — a contraction by easy stages.

47. And He it is Who makes the Night as a Robe[12] for you; and Sleep as Repose, and makes the Day (as it were) a Resurrection.

48. And He it is Who sends the Winds as heralds[13] of glad tidings, going before His Mercy, and We send down purifying water from the sky —

49. That with it We may give life to a dead land, and slake[14] the thirst of things We have created, cattle and men in great numbers.

50. And We have distributed the (water) amongst them, in order that they may celebrate (Our) praises, but most men are averse (to aught) but (rank[15]) ingratitude.

---

[12] Covering, dress

[13] Couriers, messengers

[14] Satisfy, quench

[15] Gross, virulent, offensive

51. Had it been Our Will, We could have sent a warner to every center of population,

52. Therefore listen not to the Unbelievers, but strive against them with the utmost strenuousness[16], with the (Qur'an).

53. It is He Who has let free the two bodies of flowing water: one palatable[17] and sweet, and the other salt and bitter; yet has He made a barrier between them, a partition that is forbidden to be passed.

54. It is He Who has created man from water: then has He established relationships of lineage[18] and marriage: for thy Lord has power (over all things).

55. Yet do they worship, besides God, things that can neither profit them nor harm them: and the Misbeliever is a helper (of Evil), against his own Lord!

56. But thee We only sent to give glad tidings and admonition.

57. Say: "No reward do I ask of you for it but this: that each one who will may take a (straight) Path to his Lord."

58. And put thy trust in Him Who lives and dies not; and celebrate His praise; and enough is He to be acquainted with the faults of His servants —

59. He Who created the heavens and the earth and all that is between, in six days, and is firmly established on the Throne (of authority): God, Most Gracious: ask thou, then, about Him of any acquainted (with such things).

60. When it is said to them, "Adore[19] ye (God) Most Gracious!", they say, "And what is (God) Most Gracious? Shall we adore that which thou commandest us?" and it increases their flight (from the Truth).

61. Blessed is He Who made Constellations[20] in the skies, and placed therein a Lamp and a Moon giving light;

62. And it is He Who made the Night and the Day to follow each other: for such as have the will to celebrate His praises or to show their gratitude.

---

[16] Vigor and force
[17] Appetizing
[18] Ancestry, parentage
[19] Worship and love
[20] Groups of stars.

63. And the servants of (God) Most Gracious are those who walk on the earth in humility, and when the ignorant address them, they say, "Peace!"

64. Those who spend the night in adoration of their Lord prostrate and standing;

65. Those who say, "Our Lord! avert from us the Wrath of Hell, for its Wrath is indeed an affliction grievous —

66. "Evil indeed is it as an abode, and as a place to rest in;"

67. Those who, when they spend, are not extravagant and not niggardly, but hold a just (balance) between those (extremes);

68. Those who invoke not, with God, any other god, nor slay such life as God has made sacred, except for just cause, not commit fornication[21] — and any that does this (not only) meets punishment

69. (But) the Penalty on the Day of Judgment will be doubled to him, and he will dwell therein in ignominy[22] —

70. Unless he repents, believes, and works righteous deeds, for God will change the evil of such persons into good, and God is Oft-Forgiving, Most Merciful,

71. And whoever repents and does good has truly turned to God with an (acceptable) conversion —

72. Those who witness no falsehood, and, if they pass by futility[23], they pass by it with honourable (avoidance);

73. Those who, when they are admonished with the Signs of their Lord, droop not down at them as if they were deaf or blind:

74. And those who pray, "Our Lord! grant unto us wives and offspring who will be the comfort of our eyes, and give us (the grace) to lead the righteous."

75. Those are the ones who will be rewarded with the highest place in heaven, because of their patient constancy; therein shall they be met with saLütations and peace,

76. Dwelling therein — how beautiful an abode and place of rest!

77. Say (to the rejecters): "My Lord is not uneasy because of you if ye call not on Him, but ye have indeed rejected (Him), and soon will come the inevitable (punishment)!"

---

[21] Adultery

[22] Disgrace

[23] Vain or useless thing or work

Chapter 26
Sürah Ash-Shu'arã (The Poets)
Revealed at Makkah, 227 verses

In the name of God, Most Gracious, Most Merciful.

1. Tã Sïn Mïm.

2. These are Verses of the Book that makes (things) clear.

3. It may be thou frettest[1] thy soul with grief, that they do not become Believers.

4. If (such) were Our Will, We could send down to them from the sky a Sign, to which they would bend their necks in humility.

5. But there comes not to them a newly-revealed message from (God) Most Gracious, but they turn away therefrom.

6. They have indeed rejected (the Message): so they will know soon (enough) the truth of what they mocked at!

7. Do they not look at the earth — how many noble things of all kinds we have produced therein?

8. Verily, in this is a Sign: but most of them do not believe.

9. And verily, thy Lord is He, the Exalted in Might, Most Merciful.

10. Behold, thy Lord called Moses: "Go to the people of iniquity —

11. "The people of Pharaoh: will they not fear God?"

12. He said: "O my Lord! I do fear that they will charge me with falsehood:

13. "My breast will be straitened[2], and my speech may not go (smoothly): so send unto Aaron.

14. "And (further), they have a charge of crime against me; and I fear they may slay me."

15. God said: "By no means! proceed then, both of you, with Our Signs; We are with you, and will listen (to your call).

16. "So go forth, both of you, to Pharaoh, and say: 'We have been sent by the Lord and Cherisher of the Worlds;

17. "'Send thou with us the Children of Israel.'"

18. (Pharaoh) said: "Did we not cherish thee as a child among

---

[1] Worry, grieve

[2] Become narrow

us, and didst thou not stay in our midst many years of thy life?

19. "And thou didst a deed of thine which (thou knowest) thou didst, and thou art an ungrateful (wretch[3])!"

20. Moses said: "I did it then, when I was in error.

21. "So I fled from you (all) when I feared you; but my Lord has (since) invested me with judgment (and wisdom) and appointed me as one of the Apostles.

22. "And this is the favor with which thou dost reproach me — that thou hast enslaved the Children of Israel!"

23. Pharaoh said: "And what is the 'Lord and Cherisher of the Worlds?'"

24. (Moses) said: "The Lord and Cherisher of the heavens and the earth, and all between — if ye want to be quite sure."

25. (Pharaoh) said to those around: "Do ye not listen (to what he says)?"

26. (Moses) said: "Your Lord and the Lord of your fathers from the beginning!"

27. (Pharaoh) said: "Truly your Apostle who has been sent to you is a veritable[4] madman!"

28. (Moses) said: "Lord of the East and the West, and all between! If ye only had sense!"

29. (Pharaoh) said: "If thou dost put forward any god other than me, I will certainly put thee in prison!"

30. (Moses) said: "Even if I showed you something clear (and) convincing?"

31. (Pharaoh) said: "Show it then, if thou tellest the truth!"

32. So (Moses) threw his rod, and behold, it was a serpent, plain (for all to see)!

33. And he drew out his hand, and behold, it was white to all beholders!

34. (Pharaoh) said to the Chiefs around him: "This is indeed a sorcerer[5] well-versed:

35. "His plan is to get you out of your land by his sorcery; then what is it ye counsel?"

---

[3] Miserable person

[4] Truly, absoLütely

[5] Magician

36. They said: "Keep him and his brother in suspense (for a while), and dispatch to the Cities heralds[6] to collect —

37. "And bring up to thee all (our) sorcerers well-versed."

38. So the sorcerers were got together for the appointment of a day well-known,

39. And the people were told: "Are ye (now) assembled? —

40. "That we may follow the sorcerers (in religion) if they win?"

41. So when the sorcerers arrived, they said to Pharaoh: "Of course — shall we have a (suitable) reward if we win?"

42. He said: "Yea, (and more) — for ye shall in that case be (raised to posts) nearest (to my person)."

43. Moses said to them: "Throw ye — that which ye are about to throw!"

44. So they threw their ropes and their rods, and said: "By the might of Pharaoh, it is we who will certainly win!"

45. Then Moses threw his rod, when behold, it straightway swallows up all the falsehoods which they fake[7]!

46. Then did the sorcerers fall down, prostrate in adoration,

47. Saying: "We believe in the Lord of the Worlds,

48. "The Lord of Moses and Aaron."

49. Said (Pharaoh): "Believe ye in him before I give you permission? Surely he is your leader, who has taught you sorcery! But soon shall ye know! "Be sure I will cut off your hands and your feet on opposite sides, and I will cause you all to die on the cross!"

50. They said: "No matter! for us, we shall but return to our Lord!

51. "Only, our desire is that our Lord will forgive us our faults, that we may become foremost among the Believers!"

52. By inspiration We told Moses: "Travel by night with My servants; for surely ye shall be pursued."

53. Then Pharaoh sent heralds to (all) the Cities,

54. (Saying): "These (Israelites) are but a small band,

55. "And they are raging furiously against us;

56. "But we are a multitude amply forewarned."

57. So We expelled them from gardens, springs,

58. Treasures, and every kind of honourable position;

---

[6] Messengers
[7] Forge

59. Thus it was, but We made the Children of Israel inheritors of such things.

60. So they pursued them at sunrise.

61. And when the two bodies saw each other, the people of Moses said: "We are sure to be overtaken."

62. (Moses) said: "By no means! my Lord is with me! Soon will He guide me!

63. Then We told Moses by inspiration: "Strike the sea with thy rod." So it divided, and each separate part became like the huge, firm mass of a mountain.

64. And We made the other party approach thither[8].

65. We delivered Moses and all who were with him;

66. But We drowned the others.

67. Verily in this is a Sign: but most of them do not believe.

68. And verily thy Lord is He, the Exalted in Might, Most Merciful.

69. And rehearse to them (something of) Abraham's story.

70. Behold, he said to his father and his people: "What worship ye?"

71. They said: "We worship idols, and we remain constantly in attendance on them."

72. He said: "Do they listen to you when ye call (on them),

73. "Or do you good or harm?"

74. They said: "Nay, but we found our fathers doing thus (what we do)."

75. He said: "Do ye then see whom ye have been worshipping —

76. "Ye and your fathers before you? —

77. "For they are enemies to me; not so the Lord and Cherisher of the Worlds;

78. "Who created me, and it is He Who guides me;

79. "Who gives me food and drink,

80. "And when I am ill, it is He Who cures me;

81. "Who will cause me to die, and then to live (again);

82. "And Who, I hope, will forgive me my faults on the Day of Judgment...

83. "O my Lord! bestow wisdom on me, and join me with the

---

[8] There

285

righteous;

84. "Grant me honourable mention on the tongue of truth among the latest (generations);

85. "Make me one of the inheritors of the Garden of Bliss;

86. "Forgive my father, for that he is among those astray;

87. "And let me not be in disgrace on the Day when (men) will be raised up —

88. The Day whereon neither wealth nor sons will avail,

89. "But only he (will prosper) that brings to God a sound heart;

90. "To the righteous, the Garden will be brought near,

91. "And to those straying in Evil, the Fire will be placed in full view;

92. "And it shall be said to them: 'Where are the (gods) ye worshipped —

93. "'Besides God? Can they help you or help themselves?'

94. "Then they will be thrown headlong into the (Fire) — they and those straying in Evil,

95. "And the whole hosts of Iblis together.

96. "They will say there in their mutual bickerings[9]:

97. "'By God, we were truly in an error manifest,

98. "'When we held you as equals with the Lord of the Worlds;

99. "'And our seducers[10] were only those who were steeped in guilt.

100. "'Now, then, we have none to intercede (for us),

101. "'Nor a single friend to feel (for us).

102. "'Now if we only had a chance of return, we shall truly be of those who believe!'"

103. Verily in this is a Sign, but most of them do not believe.

104. And verily thy Lord is He, the Exalted in Might, Most Merciful.

105. The people of Noah rejected the Apostles.

106. Behold, their brother Noah said to them: "Will ye not fear (God)?

107. "I am to you an apostle worthy of all trust:

---

[9] Quarrel, wrangle
[10] Tempters

108. "So fear God, and obey me.

109. "No reward do I ask of you for it: my reward is only from the Lord of the Worlds:

110. "So fear God, and obey me."

111. They said: "Shall we believe in thee when it is the meanest[11] that follow thee?"

112. He said: "And what do I know as to what they do?

113. "Their account is only with my Lord, if ye could (but) understand.

114. "I am not one to drive away those who believe.

115. "I am sent only to warn plainly in public."

116. They said: "If thou desist not, O Noah! thou shalt be stoned (to death)."

117. He said: "O my Lord! truly my people have rejected me.

118. "Judge thou, then, between me and them openly, and deliver me and those of the Believers who are with me."

119. So we delivered him and those with him, in the Ark filled (with all creatures).

120. Thereafter We drowned those who remained behind.

121. Verily in this is a Sign: but most of them do not believe.

122. And verily thy Lord is He, the Exalted in Might, Most Merciful.

123. The 'Ād (people) rejected the Apostles.

124. Behold, their brother Hüd said to them: "Will ye not fear (God)?

125. "I am to you an apostle worthy of all trust.

126. "So fear God and obey me.

127. "No reward do I ask of you for it: my reward is only from the Lord of the Worlds.

128. "Do ye build a landmark on every high place to amuse yourselves?

129. "And do ye get for yourselves fine buildings in the hope of living therein (forever)?

130. "And when ye exert your strong hand, do ye do it like men of absoLüte power?

---

[11] People of low classes

131. "Now fear God, and obey me.

132. "Yea, fear Him Who has bestowed on you freely all that ye know.

133. "Freely has He bestowed on you cattle and sons —

134. And Gardens and Springs.

135. "Truly I fear for you the Penalty of a Great Day."

136. They said: "It is the same to us whether thou admonish us or be not among (our) Admonishers[12]!

137. "This is no other than a customary device of the ancients,

138. "And we are not the ones to receive Pains and Penalties!"

139. So they rejected him, and We destroyed them, verily in this is a Sign: but most of them do not believe.

140. And verily thy Lord is He, the Exalted in Might, Most Merciful.

141. The Thamūd (people) rejected the apostles.

142. Behold, their brother Sālih said to them: "Will you fear (God)?

143. "I am to you an apostle worthy of all trust.

144. "So fear God, and obey me.

145. "No reward do I ask of you for it: my reward is only from the Lord of the Worlds.

146. "Will ye be left secure, in (the enjoyment of) all that ye have here? —

147. "Gardens and Springs,

148. "And cornfields and date palms with spathes[13] near breaking with the weight of fruit)?

149. "And ye carve house out of (rocky) mountains with great skill.

150. "But fear God and obey me;

151. "And follow not the bidding of those who are extravagant —

152. "Who make mischief in the land, and mend not (their ways)."

153. They said: "Thou art only one of those bewitched!

154. "Thou art no more than a mortal like us: then bring us a Sign, if thou tellest the truth!"

155. He said: "Here is a she-camel: she has a right of watering, and ye have a right of watering, (severally) on a day appointed.

---

[12] Advisers
[13] Clusters

156. "Touch her not with harm, lest the Penalty of a Great Day seize you."

157. But they hamstrung[14] her: then did they become full of regrets.

158. But the Penalty seized them. Verily in this is a Sign: but most of them do not believe.

159. And verily thy Lord is He, the Exalted in Might, Most Merciful.

160. The people of Lūt rejected the apostles.

161. Behold, their brother Lūt said to them: "Will ye not fear (God)?

162. "I am to you an apostle worthy of all trust.

163. "So fear God and obey me.

164. "No reward do I ask of you for it: my reward is only from the Lord of the Worlds.

165. "Of all the creatures in the world, will ye approach males.

166. "And leave those whom God has created for you to be your mates[15]? Nay, ye are a people transgressing (all limits)!"

167. They said: "If thou desist not, O Lūt! thou wilt assuredly be cast out!"

168. He said: "I do detest your doings."

169. "O my Lord! deliver me and my family from such things as they do!"

170. So We delivered him and his family — all

171. Except an old woman who lingered[16] behind.

172. But the rest We destroyed utterly.

173. We rained down on them a shower (of brimstone): and evil was the shower on those who were admonished (but heeded not)!

174. Verily in this is a Sign: but most of them do not believe.

175. And verily thy Lord is He, the Exalted in Might, Most Merciful.

176. The Companions of the Wood rejected the Apostles.

177. Behold, Shuʿaib said to them: "Will ye not fear (God)?

178. "I am to you an apostle worthy of all trust.

179. "So fear God and obey me.

180. "No reward do I ask of you for it: my reward is only from

---

[14] Crippled her
[15] Companions
[16] Remained

the the Lord of the Worlds.

181. "Give just measure, and cause no loss (to others by fraud).

182. "And weigh with scales true and upright.

183. "And withhold not things justly due to men, nor do evil in the land, working mischief.

184. "And fear Him Who created you and (Who created) the generations before (you).

185. They said: "Thou art only one of those bewitched!

186. "Thou art no more than a mortal like us, and indeed we think thou art a liar!

187. "Now cause a piece of the sky to fall on us, if thou art truthful!"

188. He said: "My Lord knows best what ye do."

189. But they rejected him. Then the punishment of a day of overshadowing gloom seized them, and that was the Penalty of a Great Day.

190. Verily in that is a Sign: but most of them do not believe.

191. And verily thy Lord is He, The Exalted in Might, Most Merciful.

192. Verily this is a Revelation from the Lord of the Worlds:

193. With it came down the Spirit of Faith and Truth —

194. To thy heart and mind that thou mayest admonish

195. In the perspicuous[17] Arabic tongue.

196. Without doubt it is (announced) in the mystic Books of former peoples.

197. Is it not a Sign to them that the learned of the Children of Israel knew it (as true)?

198. Had We revealed it to any of the non-Arabs,

199. And had he recited it to them, they would not have believed in it.

200. Thus have We caused it to enter the hearts of the Sinners.

201. They will not believe in it until they see the grievous Penalty;

202. But the (Penalty) will come to them of a sudden, while they perceive it not;

203. Then they will say: "Shall we be respited?"

204. Do they then ask for Our Penalty to be hastened on?

---

[17] Clear, plain, easily understood

205. Seest thou? If We do let them enjoy (this life) for a few years,

206. Yet there comes to them at length the (Punishment) which they were promised!

207. It will profit them not that they enjoyed (this life)!

208. Never did We destroy a population, but had its warners —

209. By way of reminder; and We never are unjust.

210. No evil ones have brought down this (Revelation):

211. It would neither suit them, nor would they be able (to produce it).

212. Indeed they have been removed far from even (a chance of) hearing it.

213. So call not on any other god with God, or thou wilt be among those under the Penalty.

214. And admonish thy nearest kinsmen,

215. And lower thy wing to the Believers who follow thee.

216. Then if they disobey thee, say: "I am free (of responsibility) for what ye do!"

217. And put thy trust on the Exalted in Might, the Merciful —

218. Who seeth thee standing forth (in prayer),

219. And thy movements among those who prostrate themselves.

220. For it is He Who heareth and knoweth all things.

221. Shall I inform you, (O people!), on whom it is that the evil ones descend?

222. They descend on every lying, wicked person,

223. (Into whose ears) they pour hearsay[18] vanities[19], and most of them are liars.

224. And the Poets — it is those straying in Evil, who follow them:

225. Seest thou not that they wander distracted in every valley?

226. And that they say what they practice not? —

227. Except those who believe, work righteousness, engage much in the remembrance of God, and defend themselves only after they are unjustly attacked. And soon will the unjust assailants know what vicissitudes[20] their affairs will take!

---

[18] Gossip

[19] Useless things

[20] Change of circumstances

Chapter 27
Sürah An-Naml (The Ant)
Revealed at Makkah, 93 verses

In the name of God, Most Gracious, Most Merciful.

1. Tä Sïn. These are verses of the Qur'an — a Book that makes (things) clear;

2. A Guide; and Glad Tidings for the Believers —

3. Those who establish regular prayers and give in regular charity, and also have (full) assurance of the Hereafter.

4. As to those who believe not in the Hereafter, We have made their deeds pleasing in their eyes; and so they wander about in distraction.

5. Such are they for whom a grievous Penalty is (waiting): and in the Hereafter theirs will be the greatest loss.

6. As to thee, the Qur'an is bestowed upon thee from the presence of One Who is Wise and All-Knowing.

7. Behold! Moses said to his family: "I perceive a fire; soon will I bring you from there some information, or I will bring you a burning brand to light our fuel, that ye may warm yourselves."

8. But when he came to the (Fire), a voice was heard: "Blessed are those in the Fire and those around: and Glory to God, the Lord of the Worlds!

9. "O Moses! verily, I am God, the Exalted in Might, the Wise!...

10. "Now do thou throw thy rod!" But when he saw it moving (of its own accord) as if it had been a snake, he turned back in retreat, and retraced not his steps: "O Moses (it was said), "Fear not: truly, in My presence, those called as apostles have no fear —

11. "But if any have done wrong and have thereafter substituted good to take the place of evil, truly, I am Oft-Forgiving, Most Merciful.

12. "Now put thy hand into thy bosom, and it will come forth white without stain (or harm): (these are) among the nine Signs (thou wilt take) to Pharaoh and his people: for they are a people rebellious in transgression.

13. But when our Signs came to them, that should have opened their eyes, they said: "This is sorcery manifest!"

14. And they rejected those Signs in iniquity and arrogance, though

their souls were convinced thereof: so see what was the end of those who acted corruptly!

15. We gave (in the past) knowledge to David and Solomon: and they both said: "Praise be to God, Who has favored us above many of His servants who believe!"

16. And Solomon was David's heir. He said: "O ye people! we have been taught the speech of Birds, and on us has been bestowed (a little) of all things: this is indeed Grace manifest (from God)."

17. And before Solomon were marshalled[1] his hosts[2] — of Jinns and men and birds, and they were all kept in order and ranks.

18. At length, when they came to a (lowly) valley of ants, one of the ants said: "O ye ants, get into your habitations, lest Solomon and his hosts crush you (under foot) without knowing it."

19. So he smiled, amused at her speech; and he said: "O my Lord! so order me that I may be grateful for Thy favors, which Thou hast bestowed on me and on my parents, and that I may work the righteousness that will please Thee: and admit me, by Thy Grace, to the ranks of Thy righteous Servants."

20. And he took a muster[3] of the Birds; and he said: "Why is it I see not the hoopoe? Or is he among the absentees?

21. "I will certainly punish him with a severe Penalty, or execute him, unless he bring me a clear reason (for absence)."

22. But the hoopoe tarried not far: he (came up and) said: "I have compassed (territory) which thou hast not compassed, and I have come to thee from Saba with tidings[4] true.

23. "I found (there) a woman ruling over them and provided with every requisite[5]; and she has a magnificent throne.

24. "I found her and her people worshipping the sun besides God: Satan has made their deeds seem pleasing in their eyes, and has kept them away from the Path — so they receive no guidance —

25. "(Kept them away from the Path), that they should not worship God, Who brings to light what is hidden in the heavens and the earth,

---

[1] Gathered

[2] Armies

[3] Inspection, to check numbers.

[4] News

[5] Thing needed for success

and knows what ye hide and what ye reveal.

26. "God! — there is no god but He! — Lord of the Throne Supreme!"

27. (Solomon) said: "Soon shall we see whether thou hast told the truth or lied!

28. "Go thou, with this letter of mine, and deliver it to them: then draw back from them, and (wait to) see what answer they return" ...

29. (The Queen) said: "Ye chiefs! here is — delivered to me — a letter worthy of respect.

30. "It is from Solomon, and is (as follows): 'In the name of God, Most Gracious, Most Merciful:

31. "'Be ye not arrogant against me but come to me in submission to the true Religion.'"

32. She said: "Ye Chiefs! advise me in (this) my affair: no affair have I decided except in your presence."

33. They said: "We are endued[6] with strength, and given to vehement[7] war: but the command is with thee; so consider what thou wilt command."

34. She said: "Kings, when they enter a country, despoil[8] it, and make the noblest of its people its meanest: thus do they behave.

35. "But I am going to send him a present, and (wait) to see with what (answer) return (my) ambassadors."

36. Now when (the embassy) came to Solomon, he said: "Will ye give me abundance in wealth? But that which God has given me is better than that which He has given you! Nay it is ye who rejoice in your gift!

37. "Go back to them, and be sure we shall come to them with such hosts as they will never be able to meet: we shall expel them from there in disgrace, and they will feel humbled (indeed)."

38. He said (to his own men): "Ye Chiefs! which of you can bring me her throne before they come to me in submission?"

39. Said an Ifrit[9], of the Jinns: "I will bring it to thee before thou rise from thy Council: indeed I have full strength for the purpose,

---

[6] Possess
[7] Fierce
[8] Plunder
[9] A large, powerful jinn.

and may be trusted."

40. Said one who had knowledge of the Book: "I will bring it to thee within the twinkling of an eye!" Then when (Solomon) saw it placed firmly before him, he said: "This is by the grace of my Lord! — to test me whether I am grateful or ungrateful! And if any is grateful, truly his gratitude is (a gain) for his own soul; but if any is ungrateful, truly my Lord is Free of All Needs, Supreme in Honour!"

41. He said: "Transform her throne out of all recognition by her: let us see whether she is guided (to the truth) or is one of those who receive no guidance."

42. So when she arrived, she was asked, "Is this thy throne?" She said, "It was just like this; and knowledge was bestowed on us in advance of this, and we have submitted to God (in Islam)."

43. And he diverted her from the worship of others besides God: for she was (sprung) of a people that had no faith.

44. She was asked to enter that lofty Palace: but when she saw it, she thought it was a lake of water, and she (tucked up her skirts), uncovering her legs. He said. "This is but a palace paved smooth with slabs of glass." She said: "O my Lord! I have indeed wronged my soul: I do (now) submit (in Islam), with Solomon, to the Lord of the Worlds."

45. We sent (aforetime), to the Thamūd, their brother Sālih, saying, "Serve God": but behold, they became two factions[10] quarrelling with each other.

46. He said: "O my people! why ask ye to hasten on the evil in preference to the good? If only ye ask God for forgiveness, ye may hope to receive mercy."

47. They said: "Ill omen[11] do we augur[12] from thee and those that are with thee." He said: "Your ill omen is with God; yea, ye are a people under trial."

48. There were in the City nine men of a family who made mischief in the land, and would not reform.

49. They said: "Swear a mutual oath by God that we shall make

---

[10] Groups

[11] Sign, forewarning

[12] Predict, foretell

a secret night attack on him and his people, and that we shall then say to his heir (when he seeks vengeance): 'We were not present at the slaughter of his people, and we are positively telling the truth.'"

50. They plotted and planned, but We too planned, even while they perceived it not.

51. Then see what was the end of their plot! — this, that we destroyed them and their people, all (of them).

52. Now such were their houses — in utter ruin — because they practiced wrongdoing. Verily in this is a Sign for people of knowledge.

53. And We saved those who believed and practiced righteousness.

54. We also sent Lüt (as an apostle): "behold," he said to his people, "Do ye do what is shameful though ye see (its iniquity[13])?

55. "Would ye really approach men in your lusts rather than women? Nay, ye are a people (grossly) ignorant!"

56. But his people gave no other answer but this: they said, "Drive out the followers of Lüt from your city: these are indeed men who want to be clean and pure!"

57. But We saved him and his family, except his wife: her We destined[14] to be of those who lagged behind.

58. And We rained down on them a shower (of brimstone): and evil was the shower on those who were admonished (but heeded not)!

59. Say: Praise be to God, and Peace on His servants whom He has chosen (for his Message). (Who) is better? — God or the false gods they associate with Him?

60. Or, who has created the heaven and the earth, and who sends you down rain from the sky? Yea, with it We cause to grow well-planted orchards[15] full of beauty and delight: it is not in your power to cause the growth of the trees in them. (Can there be another) god besides God? Nay, they are a people who swerve from justice.

61. Or, who has made the earth firm to live in; made rivers in its midst; set thereon mountains immovable; and made a separating bar between the two bodies of flowing water? (Can there be another) god besides God? Nay, most of them know not.

62. Or, who listens to the (soul) distressed when it calls on Him,

---

[13] Wickedness

[14] Decreed, fated

[15] Enclosure with fruit trees.

and who relieves its suffering, and makes you (mankind) inheritors of the earth? (Can there be another) god besides God? Little it is that ye heed!

63. Or, who guides you through the depths of darkness on land and sea, and who sends the winds as heralds of glad tidings, going before His mercy? (Can there be another) god besides God? — High is God above what they associate with Him!

64. Or, who originates Creation, then repeats it, and who gives you sustenance from heaven and earth? (Can there be another) god besides God? Say, "Bring forth your argument, if ye are telling the truth!"

65. Say: None in the heavens or on earth, except God, knows what is hidden: nor can they perceive when they shall be raised up (for Judgment).

66. Still less can their knowledge comprehend[16] the Hereafter: nay, they are in doubt and uncertainty thereanent[17]; nay, they are blind thereunto[18]!

67. The Unbelievers say: "What! when we become dust,— we and our fathers — shall we really be raised (from the dead)?

68. "It is true we were promised this — we and our fathers before (us): these are nothing but tales of the ancients."

69. Say: "Go ye through the earth and see what has been the end of those guilty (of sin)."

70. But grieve not over them, nor distress thyself because of their plots.

71. They also say: "When will this promise (come to pass)? (Say) if ye are truthful."

72. Say: "It may be that some of the events which ye wish to hasten on may be (close) in your pursuit!"

73. But verily thy Lord is full of grace to mankind: yet most of them are ungrateful.

74. And verily thy Lord knoweth all that their hearts do hide, as well as all that they reveal.

75. Nor is there aught of the Unseen, in heaven or earth, but is

---

[16] Grasp

[17] About that matter.

[18] To it.

(recorded) in a clear record.

76. Verily this Qur'an doth explain to the Children of Israel most of the matters in which they disagree.

77. And it certainly is a Guide and Mercy to those who believe.

78. Verily thy Lord will decide between them by His Decree: and He is Exalted in Might, All-Knowing.

79. So put thy trust in God: for thou art on (the Path of) manifest Truth.

80. Truly thou canst not cause the Dead to listen, nor canst thou cause the Deaf to hear the call, (especially) when they turn back in retreat.

81. Nor canst thou be a guide to the Blind, (to prevent them) from straying; only those wilt thou get to listen who believe in Our Signs, and they will bow in Islam.

82. And when the Word is fulfilled against them (the unjust), We shall produce from the earth a beast to (face) them: he will speak to them, for that mankind did not believe with assurance in Our Signs.

83. One Day We shall gather together from every people a troop of those who reject Our Signs, and they shall be kept in ranks —

84. Until, when they come (before the Judgment Seat), God will say: "Did ye reject My Signs, though ye comprehended them not in knowledge, or what was it ye did?"

85. And the Word will be fulfilled against them, because of their wrongdoing, and they will be unable to speak (in plea[19]).

86. See they not that We have made the Night for them to rest in and the Day to give them light? Verily in this are Signs for any people that believe!

87. And the Day that the Trumpet will be sounded — then will be smitten[20] with terror those who are in the heavens, and those who are on earth, except such as God will please (to exempt): and all shall come to His (Presence) as beings conscious of their lowliness.

88. Thou seest the mountains and thinkest them firmly fixed: but they shall pass away as the clouds pass away: (such is) the artistry of God, Who disposes of all things in perfect order: for He is well-

---

[19] In defense.
[20] Stricken

acquainted with all that ye do.

89. If any do good, good will (accrue[21]) to them therefrom; and they will be secure from terror that Day.

90. And if any do evil, their faces will be thrown headlong[22] into the Fire: "Do ye receive a reward other than that which ye have earned by your deeds?"

91. For me, I have been commanded to serve the Lord of this City, Him Who has sanctified[23] it and to Whom (belong) all things: and I am commanded to be of those who bow in Islam to God's Will —

92. And to rehearse[24] the Qur'an: and if any accept guidance, they do it for the good of their own souls, and if any stray, say: "I am only a Warner."

93. And say: "Praise be to God, Who will soon show you His Signs, so that ye shall know them"; and thy Lord is not unmindful of all that ye do.

Chapter 28
Sürah Al-Qasas (The Narrations)
Revealed at Makkah, 88 verses

In the name of God, Most Gracious, Most Merciful.

1. Tä Sïn Mïm

2. We rehearse[1] to thee some of the story of Moses and Pharaoh in Truth, for people who believe.

4. Truly Pharaoh elated[2] himself in the land and broke up its people into sections, depressing[3] a small group among them: their sons he

---

[21] Result

[22] Head foremost.

[23] Blessed

[24] Recite

[1] Recount, relate

[2] Jubilant and arrogant

[3] Oppressing

slew but he kept alive their females: for he was indeed a maker of mischief.

5. And We wished to be gracious to those who were being depressed in the land, to make them leaders (in faith) and make them heirs,

6. To establish a firm place for them in the land, and to show Pharaoh, Haman, and their hosts, at their hands, the very things against which they were taking precautions.

7. So We sent this inspiration to the mother of Moses: "Suckle (thy child), but when thou hast fears about him, cast him into the river, but fear not nor grieve: for We shall restore him to thee, and We shall make him one of Our apostles."

8. Then the people of Pharaoh picked him up (from the river): (it was intended) that (Moses) should be to them an adversary and a cause of sorrow: for Pharaoh and Haman and (all) their hosts were men of sin.

9. The wife of Pharaoh said: "(Here is) a joy of the eye, for me and for thee: slay him not. It may be that he will be of use to us, or we may adopt him as a son." And they perceived not (what they were doing)!

10. But there came to be a void in the heart of the mother of Moses: she was going almost to disclose his (case), had We not strengthened her heart (with faith), so that she might remain a (firm) believer.

11. And she said to the sister of (Moses), "Follow him." So she (the sister) watched him in the character of a stranger, and they knew not.

12. And We ordained that he refused suck at first, until (his sister came up and) said: "Shall I point out to you the people of a house that will nourish and bring him up for you and be sincerely attached to him?" ...

13. Thus did We restore him to his mother, that her eye might be comforted, that she might not grieve, and that she might know that the promise of God is true: but most of them do not understand.

14. When he reached full age, and was firmly established (in life), We bestowed on him wisdom and knowledge: for thus do We reward those who do good.

15. And he entered the City at a time when its people were not

watching: and he found there two men fighting — one of his own religion, and the other, of his foes. Now the man of his own religion appealed to him against his foe, and Moses struck him with his fist and made an end of him. He said: "This is a work of Evil (Satan): for he is an enemy that manifestly misleads!"

16. He prayed: "O my Lord! I have indeed wronged my soul! Do Thou then forgive me!" So (God) forgave him: for He is the Oft-Forgiving, Most Merciful.

17. He said: "O my Lord! for that Thou hast bestowed Thy Grace on me, never shall I be a help to those who sin!"

18. So he saw the morning in the City, looking about, in a state of fear, when behold, the man who had, the day before, sought his help called aloud for his help (again). Moses said to him: "Thou art truly, it is clear, a quarrelsome fellow!"

19. Then, when he decided to lay hold of the man who was an enemy to both of them, that man said: "O Moses! is it thy intention to slay me as thou slewest a man yesterday? Thy intention is none other than to become a powerful violent man in the land, and not to be one who sets things right!"

20. And there came a man, running, from the furthest end of the City. He said: "O Moses! the Chiefs are taking counsel together about thee, to slay thee: so get thee away, for I do give thee sincere advice."

21. He therefore got away therefrom, looking about, in a state of fear. He prayed: "O my Lord! save me from people given to wrong-doing."

22. Then when he turned his face towards (the land of) Madyan, he said: "I do hope that my Lord will show me the smooth and straight Path."

23. And when he arrived at the watering (place) in Madyan, he found there a group of men watering (their flocks), and besides them he found two women who were keeping back (their flocks). He said: "What is the matter with you?" They said: "We cannot water (our flocks) until the shepherds take back (their flocks): and our father is a very old man."

24. So he watered (their flocks) for them; then he turned back to the shade, and said: "O my Lord! truly am I in (desperate) need of any good that thou dost send me!" ...

25. Afterwards one of the (damsels[4]) came (back) to him, walking bashfully[5]. She said: "My father invites thee that he may reward thee for having watered (our flocks) for us." So when he came to him and narrated the story, he said: "Fear thou not: (well) hast thou escaped from unjust people."

26. Said one of the (damsels): "O my (dear) father! engage him on wages: truly the best of men for thee to employ is the (man) who is strong and trusty"...

27. He said: "I intend to wed one of these my daughters to thee, on condition that thou serve me for eight years; but if thou complete ten years, it will be (grace[6]) from thee. But I intend not to place thee under a difficulty: thou wilt find me, indeed, if God wills, one of the righteous."

28. He said: "Be that (the agreement) between me and thee: whichever of the two terms I fulfil, let there be no ill-will to me. Be God a witness to what we say."

29. Now when Moses had fulfilled the term, and was travelling with his family, he perceived a fire in the direction of Mount Tür. He said to his family: "Tarry[7] ye; I perceive a fire; I hope to bring you from there some information, or a burning firebrand[8], that ye may warm yourselves."

30. But when he came to the (Fire), a voice was heard from the right bank of the valley, from a tree in hallowed[9] ground: "O Moses! verily I am God, the Lord of the Worlds...

31. "Now do thou throw thy rod!" But when he saw it moving (of its own accord) as if it had been a snake, he turned back in retreat and retraced not his steps: "O Moses!" (It was said), "Draw near, and fear not: for thou art of those who are secure.

32. "Move thy hand into thy bosom, and it will come forth white without stain (or harm), and draw thy hand close to thy side (to guard)

---

[4] Young woman
[5] Modestly, shyly.
[6] Favor
[7] Stay, wait
[8] Piece of burning wood
[9] Sacred

against fear. Those are the two credentials[10] from thy Lord to Pharaoh and his Chiefs: for truly they are a people rebellious and wicked."

33. He said: "O my Lord! I have slain a man among them, and I fear lest they slay me.

34. "And my brother Aaron — he is more eloquent in speech than I: so send him with me as a helper, to confirm (and strengthen) me; for I fear that they may accuse me of falsehood."

35. He said: "We will certainly strengthen thy arm through thy brother, and invest you both with authority, so they shall not be able to touch you: with Our Signs shall ye triumph — you two as well as those who follow you."

36. When Moses came to them with Our Clear Signs, they said: "This is nothing but sorcery faked[11] up: never did we hear the like among our fathers of old!"

37. Moses said: "My Lord knows best who it is that comes with guidance from Him and whose End will be best in the Hereafter: certain it is that the wrongdoers will not prosper."

38. Pharaoh said: "O Chiefs! no god do I know for you but myself: therefore, O Haman! light me a (kiln[12] to bake bricks) out of clay, and build me a lofty palace, that I may mount up to the god of Moses: but as far as I am concerned, I think (Moses) is a liar!"

39. And he was arrogant and insolent in the land, beyond reason — he and his hosts: they thought that they would not have to return to Us!

40. So We seized him and his hosts, and We flung them into the sea: now behold what was the End of those who did wrong!

41. And We made them (but) leaders inviting to the Fire; and on the Day of Judgment no help shall they find.

42. In this world We made a Curse to follow them: and on the Day of Judgment they will be among the loathed (and despised).

43. We did reveal to Moses the Book after We had destroyed the earlier generations, (to give) insight to men and Guidance and Mercy, that they might receive admonition.

---

10 Evidence or a clear proof.

11 Forged, artifical

12 Furnace or oven.

44. Thou wast not on the Western Side when We decreed the commission[13] to Moses, nor wast thou a witness (of those events).

45. But We raised up (new) generations, and long were the ages that passed over them; but thou wast not a dweller among the people of Madyan, rehearsing Our Signs to them; but it is We Who send apostles (with inspiration).

46. Nor wast thou at the side of (the Mountain of) Tür when We called (to Moses), yet (art thou sent) as a Mercy from thy Lord, to give warning to a people to whom no warner had come before thee: in order that they may receive admonition.

47. If (We had) not (sent thee to the Quraish) — in case a calamity should seize them for (the deeds) that their hands have sent forth, they might say: "Our Lord! why didst Thou not send us an apostle? We should then have followed the Signs and been amongst those who believe!"

48. But (now), when the Truth has come to them from Ourselves, they say, "Why are not (Signs) sent to him, like those which were sent to Moses?" Do they not then reject (the Signs) which were formerly sent to Moses? They say: "Two kinds of sorcery, each assisting the other!" And they say: "For us, we reject all (such things)!"

49. Say: "Then bring ye a Book from God, which is a better Guide than either of them, that I may follow it! (Do), if ye are truthful!"

50. But if they hearken[14] not to thee, know that they only follow their own lusts: and who is more astray than one who follows his own lusts, devoid of guidance from God? For God guides not people given to wrongdoing.

51. Now have We caused the word to reach them themselves, in order that they may receive admonition.

52. Those to whom We sent the Book before this — they do believe in this (Revelation);

53. And when it is recited to them, they say: "We believe therein, for it is the Truth from our Lord: indeed we have been Muslims (bowing to God's Will) from before this."

---

[13] Appointment as a messenger.
[14] Respond, listen

54. Twice will they be given their reward, for that they have persevered[15], that they avert Evil with Good, and that they spend (in charity) out of what We have given them.

55. And when they hear vain talk, they turn away therefrom and say: "To us our deeds, and to you yours; peace be to you: we seek not the ignorant."

56. It is true thou wilt not be able to guide everyone whom thou lovest: but God guides those whom He will and He knows best those who receive guidance.

57. They say: "If we were to follow the guidance with thee, we should be snatched away from our land." Have We not established for them a secure Sanctuary[16], to which are brought as tribute fruits of all kinds? — a provision from Ourselves? But most of them understand not.

58. And how many populations We destroyed, which exulted[17] in their life (of ease and plenty)! Now those habitations of theirs, after them, are deserted — all but a (miserable) few! and We are their heirs!

59. Nor was thy Lord the one to destroy a population until He had sent to its Center an apostle, rehearsing to them Our Signs: nor are We going to destroy a population except when its members practice iniquity[18].

60. The (material) things which ye are given are but the conveniences[19] of this life and the glitter thereof; but that which is with God is better and more enduring: will ye not then be wise?

61. Are (these two) alike? — one to whom We have made a goodly promise, and who is going to reach its (fulfillment), and one to whom we have given the good things of this life, but who, on the Day of Judgment, is to be among those brought up (for punishment)?

62. That Day (God) will call to them, and say: "Where are my 'partners'? — whom ye imagined (to be such)?"

---

[15] Remained constant, steadfast

[16] Haven, refuge

[17] Behaved arrogantly

[18] Wickedness, wrong

[19] Comforts

63. Those against whom the charge will be proved, will say: "Our Lord! these are the ones whom we led astray: we led them astray, as we were astray ourselves: we free ourselves (from them) in Thy presence! It was not us they worshipped."

64. It will be said (to them): "Call upon your 'partners' (for help)": they will call upon them, but they will not listen to them; and they will see the Penalty (before them); (how they will wish) 'If only they had been open to guidance!'

65. That Day (God) will call to them, and say: "What was the answer ye gave to the Apostles?"

66. Then the (whole) story that day will seem obscure[20] to them (like light to the blind) and they will not be able (even) to question each other.

67. But any that (in this life) had repented, believed, and worked righteousness, will have hopes to be among those who achieve salvation.

68. Thy Lord does create and choose as He pleases: no choice have they (in the matter): Glory to God! and far is He above the partners they ascribe[21] (to Him)!

69. And thy Lord knows all that their hearts conceal and all that they reveal.

70. And He is God: there is no god but He. To Him be praise, at the first and at the last: for Him is the Command, and to Him shall ye (all) be brought back.

71. Say: See ye? If God were to make the Night perpetual[22] over you to the Day of Judgment, what god is there other than God, who can give you enlightenment[23]? Will ye not then hearken?

72. Say: See ye? If God were to make the Day perpetual over you to the Day of Judgment, what god is there other than God, who can give you a Night in which ye can rest? Will ye not then see?

73. It is out of His Mercy that He has made for you Night and Day — that ye may rest therein, and that ye may seek of His Grace

---

[20] Dim, unfamiliar
[21] Assign
[22] Eternal, constant.
[23] Information and knowledge.

— and in order that ye may be grateful.

74. The Day that He will call on them, He will say: "Where are My 'partners' whom ye imagined (to be such)?"

75. And from each people shall We draw a witness, and We shall say: "Produce your Proof": then shall they know that the Truth is in God (alone), and the (lies) which they invented will leave them in the lurch[24]."

76. Qārūn was doubtless, of the people of Moses; but he acted insolently[25] towards them: such were the treasures We had bestowed on him, that their very keys would have been a burden to a body of strong men: Behold, his people said to him: "Exult[26] not, for God loveth not those who exult (in riches).

77. "But seek, with the (wealth) which God has bestowed on thee, the Home of the Hereafter, nor forget thy portion in this world: but do thou good, as God has been good to thee, and seek not (occasions for) mischief in the land: for God loves not those who do mischief."

78. He said: "This has been given to me because of a certain knowledge which I have." Did he not know that God had destroyed, before him (whole) generations — which were superior to him in strength and greater in amount (of riches) they had collected? But the wicked are not called (immediately) to account for their sins.

79. So he went forth among his people in the (pride of his worldly) glitter. Said those whose aim is the Life of this World: "Oh that we had the like of what Qārūn has got! For he is truly a lord of mighty good fortune."

80. But those who had been granted (true) knowledge said: "Alas for you! the reward of God (in the Hereafter) is best for those who believe and work righteousness: but this none shall attain, save those who steadfastly persevere (in good)."

81. Then We caused the earth to swallow him up and his house; and he had not (the least little) party to help him against God, nor could he defend himself.

82. And those who had envied his position the day before began

---

[24] A most difficult position
[25] Rudely, arrogantly
[26] Be not proud

to say on the morrow: "Ah! it is indeed God Who enlarges the provision or restricts it, to any of His servants He pleases! Had it not been that God was gracious to us, He could have caused the earth to swallow us up! Ah! those who reject God will assuredly never prosper."

83. That House of the Hereafter We shall give to those who intend not high-handedness or mischief on earth: and the End is (best) for the righteous.

84. If any does good, the reward to him is better than his deed; but if any does evil, the doers of evil are only punished (to the extent) of their deeds.

85. Verily He Who ordained the Qur'an for thee, will bring thee back to the Place of Return. Say: "My Lord knows best who it is that brings true guidance, and who is in manifest error."

86. And thou hadst not expected that the Book would be sent to thee except as a Mercy from thy Lord: therefore lend not thou support in any way to those who reject (God's Message).

87. And let nothing keep thee back from the Signs of God after they have been revealed to thee: and invite (men) to thy Lord, and be not of the company of those who join gods with God.

88. And call not, besides God, on another god. There is no god but He. Everything (that exists) will perish except His own Face. To Him belongs the Command, and to him will ye (all) be brought back.

Chapter 29
Sürah Al 'Ankabüt (The Spider)
Revealed at Makkah, 69 verses

In the name of God, Most Gracious, Most Merciful.

1. Alif Lãm Mïm.

2. Do men think that they will be left alone on saying, "We believe," and that they will not be tested?

3. We did test those before them, and God will certainly know those who are true from those who are false.

4. Do those who practice evil think that they will get the better of us? Evil is their judgment!

5. For those whose hopes are in the meeting with God (in the Hereafter, let them strive); for the Term (appointed) by God is surely coming: and He hears and knows (all things).

6. And if any strive (with might and main), they do so for their own souls: for God is free of all needs from all creation.

7. Those who believe and work righteous deeds, from them shall We blot out all evil (that may be) in them, and We shall reward them according to the best of their deeds.

8. We have enjoined on man kindness to parents: but if they (either of them) strive (to force) thee to join with Me (in worship) anything of which thou hast no knowledge, obey them not. Ye have (all) to return to Me, and I will tell you (the truth) of all that ye did.

9. And those who believe and work righteous deeds, them shall We admit to the company of the Righteous.

10. Then there are among men such as say, "We believe in God"; but when they suffer affliction[1] in (the cause of) God, they treat men's oppression as if it were the Wrath of God! and if help comes (to thee) from thy Lord, they are sure to say, "We have (always) been with you!" Does not God know best all that is in the hearts of all Creation?

11. And God most certainly knows those who believe, and as certainly those who are Hypocrites.

12. And the Unbelievers say to those who believe: "Follow our path, and we will bear (the consequences) of your faults." Never in the least will they bear their faults: in fact they are liars!

13. They will bear their own burdens, and (other) burdens along with their own, and on the Day of Judgement they will be called to account for their falsehoods.

14. We (once) sent Noah to his people, and he tarried[2] among them a thousand years less fifty: but the Deluge[3] overwhelmed[4] them while they (persisted in) sin.

15. But We saved him and the Companions of the Ark, and We made the (Ark) a Sign for all Peoples!

---

[1] Hardship, injury
[2] Lived
[3] Flood
[4] Drowned

16. And (We also saved) Abraham: Behold, he said to his people, "Serve God and fear Him: that will be best for you — if ye understand!

17. "For ye do worship idols besides God, and ye invent falsehood. The things that ye worship besides God have no power to give you sustenance: then seek ye sustenance from God, serve Him, and be grateful to Him: to Him will be your return.

18. "And if ye reject (the Message), so did generations before you: and the duty of the apostle is only to preach publicly (and clearly)."

19. See they not how God originates creation, then repeats it: truly that is easy for God.

20. Say: "Travel through the earth and see how God did originate creation: so will God produce a later creation: for God has power over all things.

21. "He punishes whom He pleases, and He grants mercy to whom He pleases, and towards Him are ye turned.

22. "Not on earth nor in heaven will ye be able (fleeing) to frustrate (His plan), nor have ye, besides God, any protector or helper."

23. Those who reject the Signs of God and the Meeting with Him (in the Hereafter) — it is they who shall despair of My mercy: it is they who will (suffer) a most grievous Penalty.

24. So naught[5] was the answer of (Abraham's) people except that they said: "Slay him or burn him." But God did save him from the Fire: verily in this are Signs for people who believe.

25. And He said: "For you, ye have taken (for worship) idols besides God, out of mutual love and regard between yourselves in this life; but on the Day of Judgement ye shall disown each other and curse each other: and your abode will be the Fire, and ye shall have none to help.

26. But Lüt had faith in Him: he said: "I will leave home for the sake of my Lord: for He is Exalted in Might, and Wise."

27. And We gave (Abraham) Isaac and Jacob, and ordained among his progeny[6] Prophethood and Revelation, and We granted him his reward in this life; and he was in the Hereafter (of the company) of the Righteous.

---

[5] Nothing
[6] Offspring

28. And (remember) Lūt; "Behold," he said to his people: "Ye do commit lewdness[7], such as no people in Creation (ever) committed before you.

29. "Do ye indeed approach men, and cut off the highway? — And practice wickedness (even) in your councils?" But his people gave no answer but this: they said: "Bring us the Wrath of God if thou tellest the truth."

30. He said: "O my Lord! Help Thou me against people who do mischief!"

31. When Our Messengers came to Abraham with the good news, they said: "We are indeed going to destroy the people of this township: for truly they are (addicted to) crime."

32. He said: "But there is Lūt there." They said: "Well do we know who is there: we will certainly save him and his following, except his wife: she is of those who lag behind!"

33. And when Our Messengers came to Lūt, he was grieved on their account, and felt himself powerless (to protect) them: but they said "Fear thou not, nor grieve: we are (here) to save thee and thy following, except thy wife: she is of those who lag behind.

34. "For we are going to bring down on the people of this township a Punishment from heaven, because they have been wickedly rebellious."

35. And We have left thereof an evident Sign, for any people who (care to) understand.

36. To the Madyan (people) (We sent) their brother Shu'aib. Then he said: "O my people! Serve God, and fear the Last Day: nor commit evil on the earth, with intent to do mischief."

37. But they rejected him: then the mighty Blast seized them, and they lay prostrate in their homes by the morning.

38. Remember also the 'Ād and the Thamūd (people): clearly will appear to you from (the traces of) their buildings (their fate): the Evil One made their deeds alluring to them, and kept them back from the Path, though they were gifted with Intelligence and Skill.

39. (Remember also) Qārūn, Pharaoh, and Hāmān: there came to

---

[7] Indecency, obscenity

them Moses with Clear Signs, but they behaved with insolence on the earth; yet they could not overreach[8] (Us).

40. Each one of them We seized for his crime: of them, against some We sent a violent tornado (with showers of stones); some were caught by a (mighty) Blast; some We caused the earth to swallow up; and some We drowned (in the waters): it was not God Who injured (or oppressed) them: they injured (and oppressed) their own souls.

41. The parable of those who take protectors other than God is that of the Spider, who builds (to itself) a house; but truly the flimsiest[9] of houses is the Spider's house, if they but knew.

42. Verily God doth know of (everything) whatever that they call upon besides Him: and He is Exalted (in power), Wise.

43. And such are the Parables We set forth for mankind, but only those understand them who have Knowledge.

44. God created the heavens and the earth in true (proportions): verily in that is a Sign for those who believe.

45. Recite what is sent of the Book by inspiration to thee, and establish Regular Prayer: for Prayer restrains from shameful and unjust deeds; and remembrance of God is the greatest (thing in life) without doubt. And God knows the (deeds) that ye do.

46. And dispute ye not with the People of the Book, except with means better (than mere disputation[10]), unless it be with those of them who inflict wrong (and injury): but say, "We believe in the Revelation which has come down to us and in that which came down to you; Our God and your God is one; and it is to Him we bow (in Islam)."

47. And thus (it is) that We have sent down the Book to thee. So the People of the Book believe therein, as also do some of these (pagan Arabs): and none but Unbelievers reject Our Signs.

48. And thou wast not (able) to recite a Book, before this (Book came), nor art thou (able) to transcribe[11] it with thy right hand: in that case, indeed, would the talkers of vanities[12] have doubted.

49. Nay, here are Signs self-evident in the hearts of those endowed

---

[8] outwit, outstrip
[9] Weakest
[10] Argumentation
[11] Write down
[12] Unrealities, futilities

with knowledge: and none but the unjust reject Our Signs.

50. Yet they say: "Why are not Signs sent down to him from his Lord?" Say: "The Signs are indeed with God: and I am indeed a clear Warner."

51. And is it not enough for them that We have sent down to thee the Book which is rehearsed to them? Verily, in it is Mercy and a Reminder to those who believe.

52. Say: "Enough is God for a Witness between me and you: He knows what is in the heavens and on earth. And it is those who believe in vanities and reject God, that will perish (in the end)."

53. They ask thee to hasten on the Punishment (for them): had it not been for a term (of respite) appointed, the Punishment would certainly have come to them: and it will certainly reach them, — of a sudden, while they perceive not!

54. They ask thee to hasten on the Punishment but, of a surety, Hell will encompass the rejecters of Faith! —

55. On the Day that the Punishment shall cover them from above them and from below them, and (a Voice) shall say: "Taste ye (the fruits) of your deeds!"

56. O My servants who believe! truly, spacious is My Earth: therefore serve ye Me — (and Me alone)!

57. Every soul shall have a taste of death: in the end to Us shall ye be brought back.

58. But those who believe and work deeds of righteousness — to them shall We give a Home in Heaven, — lofty mansions beneath which flow rivers, — to dwell therein for aye[13]; — an excellent reward for those who do (good)! —

59. Those who persevere in patience, and put their trust in their Lord and Cherisher.

60. How many are the creatures that carry not their own sustenance? It is God Who feeds (both) them and you: for He hears and knows (all things).

61. If indeed thou ask them who has created the heavens and the earth and subjected the sun and the moon (to His Law); they will certainly reply, "God." How are they then deluded away (from the

---

[13] Forever

truth)?

62. God enlarges the sustenance (which He gives) to whichever of His servants He pleases; and He (similarly) grants by (strict) measure, (as He pleases): for God has full knowledge of all things.

63. And if indeed thou ask them who it is that sends down rain from the sky, and gives life therewith to the earth after its death, they will certainly reply, "God!" Say, "Praise be to God!" But most of them understand not.

64. What is the life of this world but amusement and play? But verily the Home in the Hereafter, that is life indeed, if they but knew.

65. Now, if they embark on a boat, they call on God, making their devotion sincerely (and exclusively) to Him; but when He has delivered them safely to (dry) land, behold, they give a share (of their worship to others)!

66. Disdaining[14] ungratefully Our gifts and giving themselves up to (worldly) enjoyment! But soon will they know.

67. Do they not then see that We have made a Sanctuary[15] secure, and that men are being snatched away from all around them? Then, do they believe in that which is vain, and reject the Grace of God?

68. And who does more wrong than he who invents a lie against God or rejects the Truth when it reaches Him? Is there not a home in Hell for those who reject Faith?

69. And those who strive in Our (Cause), We will certainly guide them to Our Paths: for verily God is with those who do right.

Chapter 30
Sürah Ar-Rüm (The Romans)
Revealed at Makkah, 60 verses

In the name of God, Most Gracious, Most Merciful.

1. Alif Lām Mïm.

2. The Roman Empire has been defeated —

3. In a land close by; but they, (even) after (this) defeat of theirs,

---

[14] Rejecting contemptuously

[15] A sacred place, place of refuge

will soon be victorious —

4. Within a few years. With God is the Decision, in the Past and in the Future: on that Day shall the Believers rejoice —

5. With the help of God. He helps whom He will, and He is Exalted in Might, Most Merciful.

6. (It is) the promise of God. Never does God depart from His promise: but most men understand not.

7. They know but the outer (things) in the life of this world, but of the End of things they are heedless.

8. Do they not reflect in their own minds? Not but for just ends and for a term appointed, did God create the heavens and the earth, and all between them: yet are there truly many among men who deny the meeting with their Lord (at the Resurrection)!

9. Do they not travel through the earth, and see what was the End of those before them? They were superior to them in strength: they tilled the soil and populated it in greater numbers than these have done: there came to them their apostles with Clear (Signs), (which they rejected, to their own destruction): it was not God Who wronged them but they wronged their own souls.

10. In the long run evil in the extreme will be the End of those who do evil; for that they rejected the Signs of God, and held them up to ridicule.

11. It is God Who begins (the process of) creation; then repeats it; then shall ye be brought back to Him.

12. On the Day that the Hour will be established, the guilty will be struck dumb with despair.

13. No intercessor will they have among their "Partners," and they will (themselves) reject their "Partners."

14. On the Day that the Hour will be established, — that Day shall (all men) be sorted out.

15. Then those who have believed and worked righteous deeds, shall be made happy in a Mead[1] of Delight.

16. And those who have rejected Faith and falsely denied Our Signs and the meeting of the Hereafter, such shall be brought forth to Punishment.

---

[1] Meadow

17. So (give) glory to God, when ye reach eventide[2] and when ye rise in the morning;

18. Yea, To Him be praise, in the heavens and on earth; and in the late afternoon and when the day begins to decline.

19. It is He Who brings out the living from the dead, and brings out the dead from the living, and Who gives life to the earth after it is dead: and thus shall ye be brought out (from the dead).

20. Among His Signs is this, that He created you from dust; and then — Behold, ye are men scattered (far and wide)!

21. And among His Signs is this, that He created for you mates[3] from among yourselves, that ye may dwell in tranquillity[4] with them, and He has put love and mercy between your (hearts); verily in that are Signs for those who reflect.

22. And among His Signs is the creation of the heavens and the earth, and the variations in your languages and your colors: verily in that are Signs for those who know.

23. And among His Signs is the sleep that ye take by night and by day, and the quest[5] that ye (make for livelihood) out of His Bounty[6]: verily in that are Signs for those who hearken.

24. And among His Signs, He shows you the lightning, by way both of fear and of hope, and He sends down rain from the sky and with it gives life to the earth after it is dead: verily in that are Signs for those who are wise.

25. And among His Signs is this, that heaven and earth stand by His Command: then when He calls you, by a single call, from the earth, behold, ye (straightway) come forth.

26. To Him belongs every being that is in the heavens and on earth: all are devoutly[7] obedient to Him.

27. It is He Who begins (the process of) creation; then repeats it; and for Him it is most easy. To Him belongs the loftiest similitude (we can think of) in the heavens and the earth: for He is Exalted in

---

[2] Evening time

[3] Spouses, companions

[4] Peace and calm

[5] Search

[6] Grace, blessings

[7] Earnestly

Might, Full of Wisdom.

28. He does propound[8] to you a similitude from your own (experience): do ye have partners among those whom your right hands possess, to share as equals in the wealth We have bestowed on you? Do ye fear them as ye fear each other? Thus do We explain the Signs in detail to a people that understand.

29. Nay, the wrongdoers (merely) follow their own lusts, being devoid of knowledge. But who will guide those whom God leaves astray? To them there will be no helpers.

30. So set thou thy face steadily and truly to the Faith: (Establish) God's handiwork according to the pattern on which He has made mankind: no change (let there be) in the work (wrought[9]) by God: that is the standard Religion: but most among mankind understand not.

31. Turn ye back in repentance to Him, and fear Him: establish regular prayers, and be not ye among those who join gods with God, —

32. Those who split up their Religion, and become (mere) Sects, — each party rejoicing in that which is with itself!

33. When trouble touches men, they cry to their Lord, turning back to Him in repentance: but when He gives them a taste of Mercy as from Himself, behold, some of them pay part-worship to other gods besides their Lord —

34. (As if) to show their ingratitude for the (favors) We have bestowed on them! Then enjoy (your brief day); but soon will ye know (your folly).

35. Or have We sent down authority to them, which points out to them the things to which they pay part-worship?

36. When We give men a taste of Mercy, they exult[10] threat: and when some evil afflicts them because of what their (own) hands have sent forth, behold, they are in despair!

37. See they not that God enlarges the provision and restricts it, to whomsoever He pleases? Verily in that are Signs for those who

---

[8] Propose for consideration
[9] Done
[10] Glorify, become proud

believe.

38. So give what is due to kindred[11], the needy, and the wayfarer[12]. That is best for those who seek the Countenance, of God, and it is they who will prosper.

39. That which ye lay out for increase through the property of (other) people, will have no increase with God: but that which ye lay out for charity, seeking the Countenance of God, (will increase): it is these who will get a recompense multiplied.

40. It is God Who has created you: further, He has provided for your sustenance; then He will cause you to die; and again He will give you life. Are there any of your (false) "Partners" who can do any single one of these things? Glory to Him! and High is He above the partners they attribute (to Him)!

41. Mischief has appeared on land and sea because of (the meed[13]) that the hands of men have earned, that (God) may give them a taste of some of their deeds: in order that they may turn back (from Evil).

42. Say: "Travel through the earth and see what was the End of those before (you): most of them worshipped others besides God."

43. But set thou thy face to the right Religion, before there come from God the Day which there is no chance of averting: on that Day shall men be divided (in two).

44. Those who reject Faith will suffer from that rejection: and those who work righteousness will spread their couch (of repose) for themselves (in heaven):

45. That He may reward those who believe and work righteous deeds, out of His Bounty: for He loves not those who reject Faith.

46. Among His Signs is this, that He sends the Winds, as heralds[14] of Glad Tidings, giving you a taste of His (Grace and) Mercy — that the ships may sail (majestically) by His Command and that ye may seek of His Bounty: in order that ye may be grateful.

47. We did indeed send, before thee, apostles to their (respective) peoples, and they came to them with Clear Signs: then, to those who

---

[11] Relatives
[12] Traveller
[13] Reward
[14] Messengers

transgressed, We meted[15] out Retribution[16]: and it was due from us to aid those who believed.

48. It is God Who sends the Winds, and they raise the Clouds: then does He spread them in the sky as He wills, and break them into fragments, until thou seest raindrops issue from the midst thereof: then when He has made them reach such of His servants as He Wills, behold, they do rejoice!

49. Even though, before they received (the rain) — just before this — they were dumb with despair!

50. Then contemplate[17] (O man!) the memorials of God's Mercy! — how He gives life to the earth after its death: verily the same will give life to the men who are dead: for He has power over all things.

51. And if We (but) send a Wind from which they see (their tilth[18]) turn yellow, behold, they become, thereafter, ungrateful (Unbelievers)!

52. So verily thou canst not make the dead to hear, nor canst thou make the deaf to hear the call, when they show their backs and turn away.

53. Nor canst thou lead back the blind from their straying: only those wilt thou make to hear, who believe in Our Signs and submit (their wills in Islam).

54. It is God Who created you in a state of (helpless) weakness, then gave (you) strength after weakness, then, after strength, gave (you) weakness and a hoary[19] head: He creates as He wills, and it is He Who has all knowledge and power.

55. On the Day that the Hour (of reckoning) will be established, the transgressors will swear that they tarried not but an hour: thus were they used to being deluded!

56. But those endued with knowledge and faith will say: "Indeed ye did tarry, within God's Decree, to the Day of Resurrection, and this is the Day of Resurrection: but ye — ye were not aware!"

---

[15] Apportion, allot
[16] Punishment
[17] Consider
[18] Cultivation
[19] Gray

57. So on that Day no excuse of theirs will avail the Transgressors, nor will they be invited (then) to seek grace (by repentance).

58. Verily We have propounded for men, in this Qur'an, every kind of Parable: but if thou bring to them any Sign, the Unbelievers are sure to say, "Ye do nothing but talk vanities[20]."

59. Thus does God seal up the hearts of those who understand not.

60. So patiently persevere: for verily the promise of God is true: nor let those shake thy firmness, who have (themselves) no certainty of faith.

Chapter 31
Sūrah Luqmān (Luqmān the Wise)
Revealed at Makkah, 34 verses

In the name of God, Most Gracious, Most Merciful.

1. Alif Lām Mïm.

2. These are Verses of the Wise Book —

3. A Guide and a Mercy to the Doers of Good —

4. Those who establish regular Prayer, and give regular Charity, and have (in their hearts) the assurance of the Hereafter.

5. These are on (true) guidance from their Lord; and these are the ones who will prosper.

6. But there are, among men, those who purchase idle tales, without knowledge (or meaning), to mislead (men) from the Path of God and throw ridicule (on the Path): for such there will be a humiliating Penalty.

7. When Our Signs are rehearsed to such a one, he turns away in arrogance, as if he heard them not, as if there were deafness in both his ears: announce to him a grievous Penalty.

8. For those who believe and work righteous deeds, there will be Gardens of Bliss —

9. To dwell therein. The promise of God is true: and He is Exalted

---

[20] Vain things

in Power, Wise.

10. He created the heavens without any pillars that ye can see; He set on the earth mountains standing firm, lest it should shake with you; and He scattered through it beasts of all kinds. We send down rain from the sky, and produce on the earth every kind of noble creature, in pairs.

11. Such is the Creation of God: now show Me what is there that others besides Him have created: nay, but the transgressors are in manifest error.

12. We bestowed (in the past) wisdom on Luqmān: "Show (thy) gratitude to God." Any who is (so) grateful does so to the profit of his own soul: but if any is ungrateful, verily God is free of all wants, worthy of all praise.

13. Behold, Luqmān said to his son by way of instruction: "O my son! Join not in worship (others) with God: for false worship is indeed the highest wrongdoing."

14. And We have enjoined on man (to be good) to his parents: in travail upon travail[1] did his mother bear him, and in years twain[2] was his weaning[3]: (hear the command), "Show gratitude to Me and to thy parents: to Me is (thy final) Goal.

15. "But if they strive to make thee join in worship with Me things of which thou hast no knowledge, obey them not; yet bear them company in this life with justice (and consideration), and follow the way of those who turn to Me (in love): in the End the return of you all is to Me, and I will tell you the truth (and meaning) of all that ye did."

16. "O my son!" (said Luqmān), "If there be (but) the weight of a mustard- seed and it were (hidden) in a rock, or (anywhere) in the heavens or on earth, God will bring it forth: for God understands the finest mysteries[4], (and) is well-acquainted (with them).

17. "O my son! establish regular prayer, enjoin what is just, and forbid what is wrong: and bear with patient constancy whate'er betide[5]

---

[1] Distress, hardship

[2] Two

[3] To accustom infant to food other than milk.

[4] Secrets

[5] Happen

thee; for this is firmness (of purpose) in (the conduct of) affairs.

18. "And swell not thy cheek (for pride) at men, nor walk in insolence[6] through the earth; for God loveth not any arrogant boaster.

19. "And be moderate in thy pace[7], and lower thy voice; for the harshest of sounds without doubt is the braying of the ass."

20. Do ye not see that God has subjected to your (use) all things in the heavens and on earth, and has made His bounties flow to you in exceeding measure, (both) seen and unseen? Yet there are among men those who dispute about God, without knowledge and without guidance, and without a Book to enlighten them!

21. When they are told to follow the (revelation) that God has sent down, they say: "Nay, we shall follow the ways that we found our fathers (following)." What! even if it is Satan beckoning[8] them to the Penalty of the (Blazing) Fire!

22. Whoever submits his whole self to God, and is a doer of good, has grasped indeed the most trustworthy handhold: and with God rests the End and Decision of (all) affairs.

23. But if any reject Faith, let not his rejection grieve thee: to Us is their return, and We shall tell them the truth of their deeds: for God knows well all that is in (men's) hearts.

24. We grant them their pleasure for a little while: in the end shall We drive them to a chastisement[9] unrelenting[10].

25. If thou ask them, who it is that created the heavens and the earth, they will certainly say, "God." Say: "Praise be to God!" But most of them understand not.

26. To God, belong all things in heaven and earth: verily God is He (that is) free of all wants, worthy of all praise.

27. And if all the trees on earth were pens and the ocean (were ink), with seven oceans behind it to add to its (supply), yet would not the Words of God be exhausted (in the writing): for God is Exalted in Power, Full of Wisdom.

---

[6] Impertinence, arrogance
[7] Manner of walking, gait
[8] Inviting them
[9] Punishment
[10] Incessant

28. And your creation or your resurrection is in no wise but as an individual soul: for God is He Who hears and sees (all things).

29. Seest thou not that God merges Night into Day and He merges Day into Night; that He has subjected the sun and the moon (to His Law), each running its course for a term appointed: and that God is well acquainted with all that ye do?

30. That is because God is the (only) Reality, and because whatever else they invoke besides Him is Falsehood; and because God — He is the Most High, Most Great.

31. Seest thou not that the ships sail through the Ocean by the grace of God? — that He may show you of His Signs? Verily in this are Signs for all who constantly persevere and give thanks.

32. When a wave covers them like the canopy (of clouds), they call to God, offering Him sincere devotion. But when He has delivered them safely to land, there are among them those that halt between (right and wrong). But none reject Our Signs except only a perfidious[11] ungrateful (wretch[12])!

33. O mankind! do your duty to your Lord, and fear (the coming of a Day when no father can avail aught for his son, nor a son avail aught for his father. Verily, the promise of God is true: let not then this present life deceive you nor let the Chief Deceiver deceive you about God.

34. Verily the knowledge of the Hour is with God (alone). It is He Who sends down rain, and He Who knows what is in the wombs. Nor does anyone know what it is that he will earn on the morrow: nor does anyone know in what land he is to die. Verily with God is full knowledge and He is acquainted (with all things).

---

[11] Treacherous, disloyal
[12] Miserable person.

Chapter 32
Sürah As-Sajdah (The Prostration)
Revealed at Makkah, 30 verses

In the name of God, Most Gracious, Most Merciful.

1. Alif Lãm Mïm.

2. (This is) the revelation of the Book in which there is no doubt — from the Lord of the Worlds.

3. Or do they say, "He has forged it"? Nay, it is the Truth from thy Lord, that thou mayest admonish a people to whom no warner has come before thee: in order that they may receive guidance.

4. It is God Who has created the heavens and the earth, and all between them, in six Days, and is firmly established on the Throne (of authority): ye have none, besides Him, to protect or intercede (for you): will ye not then receive admonition?

5. He rules (all) affairs from the heavens to the earth: in the end will (all affairs) go up to Him, on a Day, the space[1] whereof will be (as) a thousand years of your reckoning.

6. Such is He, the knower of all things, hidden and open, the Exalted (in power), the Merciful;

7. He Who has made everything which He has created most Good. He began the creation of man with (nothing more than) clay,

8. And made his progeny[2] from a quintessence[3] of the nature of a fluid despised:

9. But He fashioned him in due proportion, and breathed into him something of His spirit. And He gave you (the faculties of) hearing and sight and feeling (and understanding): little thanks do ye give!

10. And they say: "What! when we lie, hidden and lost, in the earth, shall we indeed be in a creation renewed?" Nay, they deny the meeting with their Lord!

11. Say: "The Angel of Death, put in charge of you, will (duly) take your souls: then shall ye be brought back to your Lord."

12. If only thou couldst see when the guilty ones will bend low

---

[1] Length, range
[2] Descendants, offspring
[3] Finest extract

their heads before their Lord, (saying:) "Our Lord! We have seen and we have heard: now then send us back (to the world): we will work righteousness: for we do indeed (now) believe."

13. If We had so willed, We could certainly have brought every soul its true guidance: but the Word from Me will come true. "I will fill Hell with Jinns and men all together."

14. "Taste ye then — for ye forgot the meeting of this day of yours, and We too will forget you — taste ye the Penalty of Eternity for your (evil) deeds!"

15. Only those believe in Our Signs who, when they are recited to them, fall down in adoration[4], and celebrate the praises of their Lord, nor are they (ever) puffed[5] up with pride.

16. Their limbs do forsake[6] their beds of sleep, the while they call on their Lord, in Fear and Hope: and they spend (in charity) out of the sustenance which We have bestowed on them.

17. Now no person knows what delights of the eye are kept hidden (in reserve) for them — as a reward for their (good) Deeds.

18. Is then the man who believes no better than the man who is rebellious and wicked? Not equal are they.

19. For those who believe and do righteous deeds, are Gardens as hospitable homes, for their (good) deeds.

20. As to those who are rebellious and wicked, their abode will be the Fire: every time they wish to get away therefrom, they will be forced thereinto, and it will be said to them: "Taste ye the Penalty of the Fire, the which ye were wont to reject as false."

21. And indeed We will make them taste of the Penalty of this (life) prior[7] to the supreme Penalty, in order that they may (repent and) return.

22. And who does more wrong than one to whom are recited the Signs of his Lord, and who then turns away therefrom? Verily from those who transgress We shall exact[8] (due) Retribution[9].

---

[4] Worship

[5] Swollen

[6] Leave

[7] Before

[8] Claim, demand

[9] Punishment

23. We did indeed aforetime[10] give the Book to Moses: be not then in doubt of its reaching (thee): and We made it a guide to the Children of Israel.

24. And We appointed, from among them, Leaders, giving guidance under Our command, so long as they persevered with patience and continued to have faith in Our Signs.

25. Verily thy Lord will judge between them on the Day of Judgement, in the matters wherein they differ (among themselves).

26. Does it not teach them a lesson, how many generations We destroyed before them, in whose dwellings they (now) go to and fro? Verily in that are Signs: do they not then listen?

27. And do they not see that We do drive Rain to parched[11] soil (bare of herbage[12]), and produce therewith crops, providing food for their cattle and themselves? Have they not the vision[13]?

28. They say: "When will this decision be, if ye are telling the truth?"

29. Say: "On the Day of Decision, no profit will it be to Unbelievers if they (then) believe! Nor will they be granted a respite[14]."

30. So turn away from them, and wait: they too are waiting.

Chapter 33
Sūrah Al-Ahzāb (The Confederates)
Revealed at Madinah, 73 verses

In the name of God, Most Gracious, Most Merciful.

1. O Prophet! Fear God, and hearken[1] not to the Unbelievers and the Hypocrites: verily God is full of knowledge and wisdom.

2. But follow that which comes to thee by inspiration from thy Lord: for God is well acquainted with (all) that ye do.

---

[10] Before this
[11] Dry and hot.
[12] Plants or growth
[13] Insight
[14] Delay
[1] Listen

3. And put thy trust in God, and enough is God, as a Disposer of affairs.

4. God has not made for any man two hearts in his (one) body: nor has He made your wives whom ye divorce by *Zihar*[2] your mothers: nor has He made your adopted sons your sons. Such is (only) your (manner of) speech by your mouths. But God tells (you) the Truth, and He shows the (right) Way.

5. Call them by (the names) of their fathers: that is juster in the sight of God, but if ye know not their father's (names, call them) your Brothers in faith, or your *mawlas*[3]. But there is no blame on you if ye make a mistake therein: (what counts is) the intention of your hearts: and God is Oft-Returning, Most Merciful.

6. The Prophet is closer to the Believers than their own selves, and his wives are their mothers. Blood-relations among each other have closer personal ties, in the Decree of God, than (the Brotherhood of) Believers and Muhajirs: nevertheless do ye what is just to your closest friends: such is the writing in the Decree (of God).

7. And remember We took from the Prophets their Covenant as (We did) from thee: from Noah, Abraham, Moses, and Jesus the son of Mary: We took from them a solemn Covenant[4]:

8. That (God) may question the (Custodians) of Truth concerning the Truth they (were charged with): and He has prepared for the Unbelievers a grievous Penalty.

9. O ye who believe! Remember the Grace of God, (bestowed) on you, when there came down on you hosts (to overwhelm you): but We sent against them a hurricane[5] and forces that ye saw not. But God sees (clearly) all that ye do.

10. Behold! they came on you from above you and from below you, and behold, the eyes became dim and the hearts gaped up to the throats, and ye imagined various (vain) thoughts about God!

11. In that situation were the Believers tried: they were shaken

---

[2] *Zihar:* An evil Arab custom. A husband would pronounce words implying that his wife was like his mother. After that she could not demand her rights as wife, nor could she contract another marriage.

[3] *Mawlas*: Freedmen

[4] Pledge, vow

[5] Storm

as by a tremendous[6] shaking.

12. And behold! the Hypocrites and those in whose hearts is a disease (even) say: "God and His Apostle promised us nothing but delusion[7]!"

13. Behold! a party among them said: "Ye men of Yathrib! Ye cannot stand (the attack)! Therefore go back!" and a band of them ask for leave of the Prophet, saying, "Truly our houses are bare and exposed," though they were not exposed: they intended nothing but to run away.

14. And if an entry had been effected to them from the sides of the (City), and they had been incited to sedition[8] they would certainly have brought it to pass, with none but a brief delay!

15. And yet they had already covenanted with God not to turn their backs, and a covenant with God must (surely) be answered for.

16. Say: "Running away will not profit you if ye are running away from death or slaughter[9]; and even if (ye do escape), no more than a brief (respite) will ye be allowed to enjoy!"

17. Say: "Who is it that can screen you from God if it be His wish to give you Punishment or to give you Mercy?" Nor will they find for themselves, besides God, any protector or helper.

18. Verily God knows those among you who keep back (men) and those who say to their brethren, "Come along to us," but come not to the fight except for just a little while,

19. Covetous[10] over you. Then when fear comes, thou wilt see them looking to thee, their eyes revolving, like (those of) one over whom hovers[11] death: but when the fear is past, they will smite[12] you with sharp tongues, covetous of goods. Such men have no faith, and so God has made their deeds of none effect: and that is easy for God.

20. They think that the Confederates[13] have not withdrawn; and

---

[6] Huge, dreadful

[7] Illusion

[8] Rebellion

[9] Massacre

[10] Jealous

[11] Hangs around

[12] Strike

[13] Allies

if the Confederates should come (again), they would wish they were in the deserts (wandering) among the Bedouins, and seeking news about you (from a safe distance); and if they were in your midst, they would fight but little.

21. Ye have indeed in the Apostle of God a beautiful pattern of (conduct) for anyone whose hope is in God and the Final Day, and who engages much in the praise of God.

22. When the Believers saw the Confederate forces, they said: "This is what God and His Apostle had promised us, and God and His Apostle told us what was true." And it only added to their faith and their zeal in obedience.

23. Among the Believers are men who have been true to their Covenant with God: of them some have completed their vow to (the extreme), and some (still) wait: but they have never changed (their determination) in the least:

24. That God may reward the men of Truth for their Truth and punish the Hypocrites if that be His Will, or turn to them in Mercy: for God is Oft-Forgiving, Most Merciful.

25. And God turned back the Unbelievers for (all) their fury[14]: no advantage did they gain, and enough is God for the Believers in their fight. And God is full of Strength, Able to enforce His Will.

26. And those of the people of the Book who aided them — God did take them down from their strongholds[15] and cast terror into their hearts, (so that) some ye slew, and some ye made prisoners.

27. And He made you heirs of their lands, their houses, and their goods, and of a land which ye had not frequented (before). And God has power over all things.

28. O Prophet! say to thy Consorts[16]: "If it be that ye desire the life of this world, and its glitter, — then come! I will provide for your enjoyment and set you free in a handsome manner."

29. But if ye seek God and His Apostle, and the Home of the Hereafter, verily God has prepared for the well-doers amongst you a great reward.

---

[14] Anger, fierceness

[15] Fortresses

[16] Wives

30. O Consorts of the Prophet! if any of you were guilty of evident unseemly conduct, the Punishment would be doubled to her, and that is easy for God.

31. But any of you that is devout in the service of God and His Apostle, and works righteousness — to her shall We grant her reward twice: and We have prepared for her a generous Sustenance.

32. O Consorts of the Prophet! ye are not like any of the (other) women: if ye do fear (God), be not too complaisant[17] of speech, lest one in whose heart is a disease should be moved with desire: but speak ye a speech (that is) just.

33. And stay quietly in your houses, and make not a dazzling[18] display, like that of the former Times of Ignorance; and establish regular Prayer and give regular Charity; and obey God and His Apostle. And God only wishes to remove all abomination[19] from you, ye Members of the Family, and to make you pure and spotless.

34. And recite what is rehearsed to you in your homes, of the Signs of God and His wisdom: for God understands the finest mysteries and is well-acquainted (with them).

35. For Muslim men and women — for believing men and women, for devout men and women, for true men and women, for men and women who are patient and constant, for men and women who humble themselves, for men and women who give in charity, for men and women who fast (and deny themselves), for men and women who guard their chastity, and for men and women who engage much in God's praise — for them has God prepared forgiveness and great reward.

36. It is not fitting for a Believer, man or woman, when a matter has been decided by God and His Apostle, to have any option about their decision: if anyone disobeys God and His Apostle, he is indeed on a clearly wrong Path.

37. Behold! thou didst say to one who had received the grace of God and thy favor: "Retain thou (in wedlock) thy wife, and fear God." But thou didst hide in thy heart that which God was about to make

---

[17] Polite, soft-spoken
[18] Bright, confusing
[19] Evil

manifest: thou didst fear the people, but it is more fitting that thou shouldst fear God. Then when Zaid had dissolved (his marriage) with her, with the necessary (formality), We joined her in marriage to thee: in order that (in future) there may be no difficulty to the Believers in (the matter of) marriage with the wives of their adopted sons, when the latter have dissolved with the necessary (formality) (their marriage) with them, and God's command must be fulfilled.

38. There can be no difficulty to the Prophet in what God has indicated to him as a duty. It was the practice (approved) of God amongst those of old that have passed away, and the command of God is a decree determined.

39. (It is the practice of those) who preach the Messages of God, and fear Him, and fear none but God, and enough is God to call (men) to account.

40. Muhammad is not the father of any of your men, but (he is) the Apostle of God, and the Seal of the Prophets: and God has full knowledge of all things.

41. O ye who believe! celebrate the praises of God and do so often;

42. And glorify Him morning and evening.

43. He it is Who sends blessings on you, as do His angels, that He may bring you out from the depths of Darkness into Light: and He is Full of Mercy to the Believers.

44. Their saLütation on the Day they meet Him will be "Peace!": and He has prepared for them a generous Reward.

45. O Prophet! Truly We have sent thee as a Witness, a Bearer of Glad Tidings, and a Warner —

46. And as one who invites to God's (Grace) by His leave, and as a Lamp spreading Light.

47. Then give the glad tidings to the Believers, that they shall have from God a very great Bounty.

48. And obey not (the behests[20]) of the Unbelievers and the Hypocrites, and heed not their annoyances[21], but put thy trust in God, for enough is God as a Disposer of affairs.

49. O ye who believe! when ye marry believing women, and then

---

[20] Commands

[21] Provocations

divorce them before ye have touched them, no period of '*Iddah* have ye to count in respect of them: so give them a present, and set them free in a handsome manner.

50. O Prophet! We have made lawful to thee thy wives to whom thou hast paid their dowers; and those whom thy right hand possesses out of the prisoners of war whom God has assigned to thee; and daughters of thy paternal uncles and aunts, and daughters of thy maternal uncles and aunts, who migrated (from Mecca) with thee; and any believing woman who dedicates her soul to the Prophet if the Prophet wishes to wed her — this only for thee, and not for the Believers (at large); We know what We have appointed for them as to their wives and the captives whom their right hands possess — in order that there should be no difficulty for Thee. And God is Oft-Forgiving, Most Merciful.

51. Thou mayest defer (the turn of) any of them that thou pleasest, and thou mayest receive any thou pleasest: and there is no blame on thee if thou invite one whose (turn) thou hadst set aside. This were nigher[22] to the cooling of their eyes, the prevention of their grief, and their satisfaction — that of all of them — with that which thou hast to give them: and God knows (all) that is in your hearts: and God is All-Knowing, Most Forbearing.

52. It is not lawful for thee (to marry more) women after this, nor to change them for (other) wives, even though their beauty attract thee, except any thy right hand should possess (as handmaidens): and God doth watch over all things.

53. O ye who Believe! enter not the Prophet's houses — until leave is given you — for a meal, (and then) not (so early as) to wait for its preparation: but when ye are invited, enter; and when ye have taken your meal, disperse, without seeking familiar talk. Such (behavior) annoys the Prophet: He is ashamed to dismiss you, but God is not ashamed (to tell you) the truth. And when ye ask (his ladies) for anything ye want, ask them from before a screen: that makes for greater purity for your hearts and for theirs. Nor is it right for you that ye should annoy God's Apostle, or that ye should marry his widows after him at any time. Truly such a thing is in God's sight an enormity[23].

---

[22] (Arch.) Nearer. Here it means most proper or suitable.
[23] Dreadful sin or crime

54. Whether ye reveal anything or conceal it, verily God has full knowledge of all things.

55. There is no blame (on these ladies if they appear) before their fathers or their sons, their brothers, or their brothers' sons, or their sisters' sons, or their women, or the (slaves) whom their right hands possess. And (ladies), fear God: for God is Witness to all things.

56. God and His angels send blessings on the Prophet: O ye that believe! send ye blessings on him, and saLüte him with all respect.

57. Those who annoy[24] God and his Apostle — God has cursed them in this world and in the Hereafter, and has prepared for them a humiliating Punishment.

58. And those who annoy believing men and women undeservedly[25], bear (on themselves) a calumny[26] and a glaring sin.

59. O Prophet! Tell thy wives and daughters, and the believing women, that they should cast their outer garments over their persons (when abroad[27]): that is most convenient, that they should be known (as such) and not molested[28]: and God is Oft-Forgiving, Most Merciful.

60. Truly, if the Hypocrites, and those in whose hearts is a disease, and those who stir up sedition in the City, desist not, We shall certainly stir thee up against them: then will they not be able to stay in it as thy neighbors for any length of time:

61. They shall have a curse on them: wherever they are found, they shall be seized and slain (without mercy).

62. (Such was) the practice (approved) of God among those who lived aforetime: no change wilt thou find in the practice (approved) of God.

63. Men ask thee concerning the Hour: say, "The knowledge thereof is with God (alone)": and what will make thee understand? — perchance the Hour is nigh!

64. Verily God has cursed the Unbelievers and prepared for them a Blazing Fire —

---

[24] Vex, cause pain

[25] Without just cause or reason

[26] Slander

[27] Outside their houses

[28] Harassed

65. To dwell therein forever: no protector will they find, nor helper.

66. The Day that their faces will be turned upside down in the Fire, they will say: "Woe to us! would that we had obeyed God and obeyed the Apostle!"

67. And they would say: "Our Lord! we obeyed our chiefs and our great ones, and they misled us as to the (right) path.

68. "Our Lord! give them Double Penalty and curse them with a very great Curse!"

69. O ye who believe! be ye not like those who vexed and insulted Moses, but God cleared him of the (calumnies) they had uttered: and he was honourable in God's sight.

70. O ye who believe! fear God, and (always) say a word directed to the Right:

71. That He may make your conduct whole and sound and forgive you your sins: he that obeys God and His Apostle has already attained the highest Achievement.

72. We did indeed offer the Trust to the Heavens and the Earth and the Mountains: but they refused to undertake it, being afraid thereof: but man undertook it — he was indeed unjust and foolish —

73. (With the result) that God has to punish the Hypocrites, men and women, and the Unbelievers, men and women, and God turns in Mercy to the Believers, men and women: for God is Oft-Forgiving, Most Merciful.

Chapter 34
Sürah Saba (Sheba)
Revealed at Makkah, 54 verses

In the name of God, Most Gracious, Most Merciful.

1. Praise be to God, to Whom belong all things in the heavens and on earth: to Him be Praise in the Hereafter: and He is full of Wisdom, acquainted with all things.

2. He knows all that goes into the earth, and all that comes out thereof; all that comes down from the sky and all that ascends thereto:

and He is the Most Merciful, the Oft-Forgiving.

3. The Unbelievers say, "Never to us will come the Hour": say, "Nay! but most surely, by my Lord, it will come upon you — by Him Who knows the unseen — from Whom is not hidden the least little atom in the Heavens or on earth: nor is there anything less than that, or greater, but is in the Record Perspicuous[1]:

4. That He may reward those who believe and work deeds of righteousness: for such is Forgiveness and a Sustenance Most Generous."

5. But those who strive against Our Signs, to frustrate[2] them — for such will be a Penalty — a Punishment most humiliating.

6. And those to whom knowledge has come see that the (Revelation) sent down to thee from thy Lord — that is the Truth, and that it guides to the Path of the Exalted (in Might), Worthy of all praise.

7. The Unbelievers say (in ridicule[3]): "Shall we point out to you a man that will tell you, when ye are all scattered to pieces in disintegration[4], that ye shall (then be raised) in a New Creation?

8. "Has he invented a falsehood against God, or has a spirit (seized) him?" — Nay, it is those who believe not in the Hereafter, that are in (real) Penalty, and in farthest Error.

9. See they not what is before them and behind them, of the sky and the earth? If We wished, We could cause the earth to swallow them up, or cause a piece of the sky to fall upon them. Verily in this is a Sign for every devotee[5] that turns to God (in repentance).

10. We bestowed Grace aforetime on David from Ourselves: "O ye Mountains! sing ye back the Praises of God with him! and ye birds (also)! and We made the iron soft for him —

11. (Commanding), "Make thou coats of mail, balancing well the rings of chain armor, and work ye righteousness; for be sure I see (clearly) all that ye do."

---

[1] Easily understood and expressed.

[2] To thwart, baffle

[3] In jest

[4] Crumbled to dust

[5] Worshipper

12. And to Solomon (We made) the Wind (obedient): its early morning (stride) was a month's (journey), and its evening (stride) was a month's (journey); and We made a Font[6] of molten brass to flow for him; and there were Jinns that worked in front of him, by the leave of his Lord, and if any of them turned aside from Our command, We made Him taste of the Penalty of the Blazing Fire.

13. They worked for him as he desired, (making) Arches, Images, Basins as large as Reservoirs, and (cooking) Cauldrons[7] fixed (in their places): "Work ye, sons of David, with thanks! But few of My servants are grateful!"

14. Then, when We decreed (Solomon's) death, nothing showed them his death except a little worm of the earth, which kept (slowly) gnawing[8] away at his staff: so when he fell down, the Jinns saw plainly that if they had known the unseen, they would not have tarried[9] in the humiliating Penalty (of their Task).

15. There was, for Saba', aforetime, a Sign in their homeland — two Gardens to the right and to the left. Eat of the Sustenance (provided) by your Lord, and be grateful to Him: a territory fair and happy, and a Lord Oft-Forgiving!

16. But they turned away (from God), and We sent against them the flood (released) from the Dams, and We converted their two Garden (rows) into "gardens" producing bitter fruit, and tamarisks[10], and some few (stunted[11]) Lote trees.

17. That was the Requital[12] We gave them because they ungratefully rejected Faith: and never do We give (such) requital except to such as are ungrateful rejecters.

18. Between them and the Cities on which We had poured Our blessings, We had placed Cities in prominent positions, and between them We had appointed stages of journey in due proportion: "Travel therein, secure, by night and by day."

---

6 Fountain

7 Large boiling-vessel.

8 Eating away

9 Remained

10 A kind of ever green shrub.

11 Retarded

12 Punishment

19. But they said: "Our Lord! place longer distances between our journey-stages." But they wronged themselves (therein). At length We made them as a tale (that is told), and We dispersed them all in scattered fragments. Verily in this are Signs for every (soul that is) patiently constant and grateful.

20. And on them did Satan prove true his idea, and they followed him, all but a Party that believed.

21. But he had no authority over them — except that We might test the man who believes in the Hereafter from him who is in doubt concerning it: and thy Lord doth watch over all things.

22. Say: "Call upon other (gods) whom ye fancy[13], besides God: they have no power — not the weight of an atom — in the heavens or on earth; no (sort of) share have they therein, nor is any of them a helper to God.

23. "No intercession can avail in His Presence except for those for whom He has granted permission. So far (is this the case) that, when terror is removed from their hearts (at the Day of Judgement, then) will they say, 'What is it that your Lord commanded?' They will say, 'That which is true and just; and He is the Most High, Most Great.'"

24. Say: "Who gives you sustenance, from the heavens and the earth?" Say: "It is God, and certain it is that either we or ye are on right guidance or in manifest error!"

25. Say: "Ye shall not be questioned as to our sins, nor shall we be questioned as to what ye do."

26. Say: "Our Lord will gather us together and will in the end decide the matter between us (and you) in truth and justice: and He is the One to decide, the One Who knows all."

27. Say: "Show me those whom ye have joined with Him as partners: by no means (can ye). Nay, He is God, the Exalted in Power, the Wise."

28. We have not sent thee but as a universal (Messenger) to men, giving them glad tidings, and warning them (against sin), but most men understand not.

29. They say: "When will this promise (come to pass) if ye are

---

[13] Imagine

telling the truth?"

30. Say: "The appointment to you is for a Day, which ye cannot put back for an hour nor put forward."

31. The Unbelievers say: "We shall neither believe in this scripture nor in (any) that (came) before it." Couldst thou but see when the wrongdoers will be made to stand before their Lord, throwing back the word (of blame) on one another! Those who had been despised[14] will say to the arrogant ones: "Had it not been for you, we should certainly have been Believers!"

32. The arrogant ones will say to those who had been despised: "Was it we who kept you back from Guidance after it reached you? Nay, rather, it was ye who transgressed."

33. Those who had been despised will say to the arrogant ones: "Nay! it was a plot (of yours) by day and by night. Behold! ye (constantly) ordered us to be ungrateful to God and to attribute equals to Him!" They will declare (their) repentance when they see the Penalty: We shall put yokes on the necks of the Unbelievers: it would only be a requital for their (ill) deeds.

34. Never did We send a Warner to a population, but the wealthy ones among them said: "We believe not in the (Message) with which ye have been sent."

35. They said: "We have more in wealth and in sons, and we cannot be punished."

36. Say: "Verily my Lord enlarges and restricts the provision to whom He pleases, but most men understand not."

37. It is not your wealth nor your sons, that will bring you nearer to Us in degree: but only those who believe and work Righteousness — these are the ones for whom there is a multiplied Reward for their deeds, while secure they (reside) in the dwellings on high!

38. Those who strive against Our Signs, to frustrate them, will be given over into Punishment.

39. Say: "Verily my Lord enlarges and restricts the Sustenance to such of His servants as He pleases: and nothing do ye spend in the least (in His cause) but He replaces it: for He is the Best of those Who grant Sustenance.

---

[14] Considered weak and looked down upon

40. One day He will gather them all together, and say to the angels, "Was it you that these men used to worship?"

41. They will say, "Glory to Thee! Our (tie) is with Thee — as Protector — not with them. Nay, but they worshipped the Jinns: most of them believed in them."

42. So on that day no power shall they have over each other, for profit or harm: and We shall say to the wrongdoers, "Taste ye the penalty of the Fire — the which ye were wont to deny!"

43. When Our Clear Signs are rehearsed to them, they say, "This is only a man who wishes to hinder you from the (worship) which your fathers practiced." And they say, "This is only a falsehood invented!" And the Unbelievers say of the Truth when it comes to them, "This is nothing but evident magic!"

44. But We had not given them Books which they could study, nor sent apostles to them before thee as Warners.

45. And their predecessors rejected (the Truth); these have not received a tenth of what We had granted to those: yet when they rejected My apostles, how (terrible) was My rejection (of them)!

46. Say: "I do admonish you on one point: that ye do stand up before God — (it may be) in pairs, or (it may be) singly — and reflect (within yourselves): your Companion is not possessed: he is no less than a Warner to you, in face of a terrible Penalty."

47. Say: "No reward do I ask of you: it is (all) in your interest: my reward is only due from God: and He is Witness to all things."

48. Say: "Verily my Lord doth cast the (mantle[15] of) Truth (over His servants) — He that has full knowledge of (all) that is hidden."

49. Say: "The Truth has arrived, and Falsehood neither creates anything new, nor restores anything."

50. Say: "If I am astray, I only stray to the loss of my own soul: but if I receive guidance, it is because of the inspiration of my Lord to me: it is He Who hears all things, and is (ever) near."

51. If thou couldst but see when they will quake[16] with terror: but then there will be no escape (for them), and they will be seized from a position (quite) near.

---

[15] Cloak, covering
[16] Tremble

52. And they will say, "We do believe (now) in the (truth)": but how could they receive (faith) from a position (so) far off—

53. Seeing that they did reject faith (entirely) before, and that they (continually) cast (slanders[17]) on the Unseen from a position far off?

54. And between them and their desires, is placed a barrier, as was done in the past with their partisans: for they were indeed in suspicious (disquieting) doubt.

Chapter 35
Sūrah Al-Fātir (The Originator of Creation)
Revealed at Makkah, 45 verses

In the name of God, Most Gracious, Most Merciful.

1. Praise be to God, Who created (out of nothing) the heavens and the earth, Who made the angels messengers with wings — two, or three, or four (Pairs): He adds to Creation as He pleases: for God has power over all things.

2. What God out of His Mercy doth bestow on mankind there is none can withhold: what He doth withhold, there is none can grant, apart from Him: and He is the Exalted in Power, Full of Wisdom.

3. O men! call to mind the grace of God unto you! Is there a Creator, other than God, to give you Sustenance from heaven or earth? There is no god but He: how then are ye deluded away from the Truth?

4. And if they reject thee, so were apostles rejected before thee: to God go back for decision all affairs.

5. O men! certainly the promise of God is true. Let not then this present life deceive you, nor let the Chief Deceiver deceive you about God.

6. Verily Satan is an enemy to you: so treat him as an enemy. He only invites his adherents, that they may become Companions of the Blazing Fire.

7. For those who reject God, is a terrible Penalty: but for those

---

[17] Utter or circulate false reports about.

who believe and work righteous deeds, is Forgiveness, and a magnificent Reward.

8. Is he, then, to whom the evil of his conduct is made alluring[1], so that he looks upon it as good (equal to one who is rightly guided)? For God leaves to stray whom He wills, and guides whom He wills. So let not thy soul go out in (vainly) sighing after them: for God knows well all that they do!

9. It is God Who sends forth the Winds, so that they raise up the Clouds, and We drive them to a Land that is dead, and revive the earth therewith after its death: even so (will be) the Resurrection!

10. If any do seek for glory and power — to God belong all glory and power. To Him mount up (all) Words of Purity: it is He Who exalts each Deed of Righteousness. Those that lay Plots of Evil — for them is a Penalty terrible; and the plotting of such will be void[2] (of result).

11. And God did create you from dust; then from a sperm drop; then He made you in pairs. And no female conceives, or lays down (her load), but with His knowledge. Nor is a man long-lived granted length of days, nor is a part cut off from his life, but is in a Decree (ordained). All this is easy for God.

12. Nor are the two bodies of flowing water alike — the one palatable, sweet, and pleasant to drink, and the other, salty and bitter. Yet from each (kind of water) do ye eat flesh fresh and tender, and ye extract ornaments to wear; and thou seest the ships therein that plough the waves, that ye may seek (thus) of the Bounty of God that ye may be grateful.

13. He merges Night into Day, and He merges Day into Night, and He has subjected the sun and the moon (to His Law): each one runs its course for a term appointed. Such is God your Lord: to Him belongs all Dominion[3]. And those whom ye invoke besides Him have not the least power.

14. If ye invoke them, they will not listen to your call, and if they were to listen, they cannot answer your (prayer). On the Day of Judgement they will reject your "Partnership." And none (O man!)

---

[1] Appealing

[2] Null, invalid

[3] Sovereignty, power

can tell thee (the Truth) like the One Who is acquainted with all things.

15. O ye men! it is ye that have need of God: but God is the One Free of all wants, Worthy of all praise.

16. If He so pleased, He could blot you out and bring in a New Creation:

17. Nor is that (at all) difficult for God.

18. Nor can a bearer of burdens bear another's burden. If one heavily laden should call another to (bear) his load, not the least portion of it can be carried (by the other), even though he be nearly related. Thou canst but admonish such as fear their Lord unseen and establish regular Prayer and whoever purifies himself does so for the benefit of his own soul; and the destination (of all) is to God.

19. The blind and the seeing are not alike;

20. Nor are the depths of Darkness and the Light;

21. Nor are the (chilly) shade and the (genial[4]) heat of the sun:

22. Nor are alike those that are living and those that are dead. God can make any that He wills to hear; but thou canst not make those to hear who are (buried) in graves.

23. Thou art no other than a warner.

24. Verily We have sent thee in truth, as a bearer of glad tidings, and as a warner: and there never was a people, without a warner having lived among them (in the past).

25. And if they reject thee, so did their predecessors[5], to whom came their Apostles with Clear Signs, Books of Dark Prophecies, and the Book of Enlightenment.

26. In the end did I punish those who rejected Faith: and how (terrible) was My rejection (of them)!

27. Seest thou not that God sends down rain from the sky? With it We then bring out produce of various colors. And in the mountains are tracts white and red, of various shades of color, and black intense in hue[6].

28. And so amongst men and crawling creatures and cattle, are they of various colors. Those truly fear God, among His Servants, who have knowledge: for God is Exalted in Might, Oft-Forgiving.

---

[4] Pleasant

[5] Forefathers, those who lived before them.

[6] Color

29. Those who rehearse[7] the Book of God, establish regular Prayer and spend (in Charity) out of what We have provided for them, secretly and openly, hope for a Commerce[8] that will never fail:

30. For He will pay them their meed[9], nay, He will give them (even) more out of His Bounty; for He is Oft-Forgiving, Most Ready to appreciate (service).

31. That which We have revealed to thee of the Book is the Truth — confirming what was (revealed) before it: for God is assuredly — with respect to his servants — well acquainted and fully-Observant.

32. Then We have given the Book for inheritance to such of Our servants as We have chosen: but there are among them some who wrong their own souls; some who follow a middle course; and some who are, by God's leave, foremost in good deeds; that is the highest Grace.

33. Gardens of Eternity will they enter: therein will they be adorned[10] with bracelets of gold and pearls; and their garments there will be of silk.

34. And they will say: "Praise be to God, Who has removed from us (all) sorrow: for Our Lord is indeed Oft-Forgiving, ready to appreciate (service):

35. "Who has, out of His bounty, settled us in a Home that will last: no toil[11] nor sense of weariness[12] shall touch us therein."

36. But those who reject (God) — for them will be the Fire of Hell: no term shall be determined for them, so they should die, nor shall its Penalty be lightened for them: thus do We reward every ungrateful one!

37. Therein will they cry aloud (for assistance): "Our Lord! bring us out: we shall work righteousness, not the (deeds) we used to do!" Did we not give you long enough life so that he that would should receive admonition? And (moreover) the warner came to you. So taste ye (the fruit of your deeds): for the wrongdoers there is no helper."

---

[7] Study, recite

[8] Trade

[9] Merited reward they rightly deserve.

[10] Decorated

[11] Hard labor

[12] Boredom, fatigue

38. Verily God knows (all) the hidden things of the heavens and the earth: verily He has full knowledge of all that is in (men's) hearts.

39. He it is that has made you inheritors in the earth: if, then, any do reject (God), their rejection (works) against themselves: their rejection but adds to the odium[13] for the Unbelievers in the sight of their Lord: their rejection but adds to (their own) undoing.

40. Say: "Have ye seen (these) 'partners' of yours whom ye call upon besides God?" Show me what it is they have created in the (wide) earth. Or have they a share in the heavens? Or have We given them a Book from which they (can derive) clear (evidence)? — Nay, the wrongdoers promise each other nothing but delusions[14].

41. It is God Who sustains the heavens and the earth, lest they cease (to function): and if they should fail, there is none — not one — can sustain them thereafter: verily He is Most Forbearing, Oft-Forgiving.

42. They swore their strongest oaths by God that if a warner came to them, they would follow his guidance better than any (other) of the Peoples: but when a warner came to them, it has only increased their flight (from righteousness) —

43. On account of their arrogance in the land and their plotting of Evil. But the plotting of Evil will hem in[15] only the authors thereof. Now are they but looking for the way the ancients were dealt with? But no change wilt thou find in God's way (of dealing): no turning off wilt thou find in God's way (of dealing).

44. Do they not travel through the earth, and see what was the end of those before them — though they were superior to them in strength? Nor is God to be frustrated[16] by anything whatever in the heavens or on earth: for He is All-Knowing, All-Powerful.

45. If God were to punish men according to what they deserve, He would not leave on the back of the (earth) a single living creature: but He gives them respite for a stated Term: when their Term expires, verily God has in his sight all His servants.

---

[13] Widespread dislike or hatred
[14] Deceptions
[15] Encircle
[16] Thwarted, upset, baffled

Chapter 36
Sūrah Yā-Sīn (Yā Sīn)
Revealed at Makkah, 83 verses

In the name of God, Most Gracious, Most Merciful.

1. Yā Sīn.

2. By the Qur'an, full of Wisdom —

3. Thou art indeed one of the apostles.

4. On a Straight Way.

5. It is a Revelation sent down by (Him) the Exalted in Might, Most Merciful.

6. In order that thou mayest admonish a people, whose fathers had received no admonition, and who therefore remain heedless (of the Signs of God).

7. The Word is proved true against the greater part of them; for they do not believe.

8. We have put yokes[1] round their necks right up to their chins, so that their heads are forced up (and they cannot see).

9. And We have put a bar[2] in front of them and a bar behind them, and further, We have covered them up; so that they cannot see.

10. The same is it to them whether thou admonish them or thou do not admonish them: they will not believe.

11. Thou canst but admonish: such a one as follows the Message and fears the (Lord) Most Gracious, unseen: give such a one, therefore, good tidings, of Forgiveness and a Reward most generous.

12. Verily We shall give life to the dead, and We record that which they sent before and that which they leave behind, and of all things have We taken account in a clear Book (of evidence).

13. Set forth to them, by way of a parable, the (story of) the Companions of the City. Behold, there came Apostles to it.

14. When We (first) sent to them two apostles, they rejected them: but We strengthened them with a third: they said, "Truly, we have been sent on a mission to you."

15. The (people) said: "Ye are only men like ourselves; and (God)

---

[1] Yoke: A device usually consisting of a crosspiece and fitting an animal's neck.
[2] An immaterial barrier or obstacle.

Most Gracious sends no sort of revelation: Ye do nothing but lie."

16. They said: "Our Lord doth know that we have been sent on a mission to you:

17. "And Our duty is only to proclaim the clear Message."

18. The (people) said: "For us, we augur[3] an evil omen[4] from you: if ye desist not, we will certainly stone you, and a grievous punishment indeed will be inflicted on you by us."

19. They said: "Your evil omens are with yourselves: (deem[5] ye this an evil omen), if ye are admonished? Nay, but ye are a people transgressing[6] all bounds!"

20. Then there came running, from the farthest part of the City, a man, saying, "O my people! obey the Apostles:

21. "Obey those who ask no reward of you (for themselves), and who have themselves received Guidance.

22. "It would not be reasonable in me if I did not serve Him Who created me, and to Whom ye shall (all) be brought back.

23. "Shall I take (other) gods besides Him? If (God) Most Gracious should intend some adversity[7] for me, of no use whatever will be their intercession for me, nor can they deliver me.

24. "I would indeed, if I were to do so, be in manifest Error.

25. "For me, I have faith in the Lord of you (all): Listen, then, to me!"

26. It was said: "Enter thou the Garden." He said "Ah me! would that my People knew (what I know)! —

27. "For that my Lord has granted me Forgiveness and has enrolled[8] me among those held in honour!"

28. And We sent not down against his People, after Him, any hosts[9] from heaven, nor was it needful for Us so to do.

29. It was no more than a single mighty Blast[10], and behold! they

---

[3] Predict, foretell.
[4] An event suggesting something good or evil.
[5] Consider
[6] Violating bounds or laws of reason, morality, or decency.
[7] Hardship
[8] Enlisted, included.
[9] Armies.
[10] A loud thunder, explosion, burst

were (like ashes) quenched[11] and silent.

30. Ah! alas for (My) servants! There comes not an apostle to them but they mock[12] Him!

31. See they not how many generations before them We destroyed? Not to them will they return:

32. But each one of them all — will be brought before Us (for judgment).

33. A Sign for them is the earth that is dead; We do give it life, and produce grain therefrom, of which ye do eat.

34. And We produce therein orchards with date palms and Vines, and We cause springs to gush forth therein.

35. That they may enjoy the fruits of this (artistry): it was not their hands that made this: will they not then give thanks?

36. Glory to God, Who created in pairs all things that the earth produces, as well as their own (human) kind and (other) things of which they have no knowledge.

37. And a Sign for them is the Night: We withdraw therefrom the Day, and behold they are plunged in darkness;

38. And the Sun runs his course for a period determined for him: that is the decree of (Him), the exalted in Might, the All-Knowing.

39. And the Moon — We have measured for her mansions[13] (to traverse[14]) till she returns like the old (and withered) lower part of date-stalk[15].

40. It is not permitted to the Sun to catch up the Moon, nor can the Night outstrip[16] the Day: each (just) swims along in (its own) orbit[17] (according to Law).

41. And a Sign for them is that We bore their race (through the flood) in the loaded Ark[18];

---

[11] Extinguished, dead.

[12] Make fun of.

[13] Twenty-eight divisions of the sky occupied by the moon in successive days of a month.

[14] To travel.

[15] Main stem of palm tree, or a slender attachment of it.

[16] Surpass

[17] Circuit, course

[18] Boat, or the ship in which the Prophet Noah (pbuh) and his followers were saved.

42. And We have created for them similar (vessels[19]) on which they ride.

43. If it were Our Will, We could drown them; then would there be no helper (to hear their cry), nor could they be delivered.

44. Except by way of Mercy from Us, and by way of (worldly) convenience (to serve them) for a time.

45. When they are told, "Fear ye that which is before you and that which will be after you, in order that ye may receive Mercy," (they turn back).

46. Not a Sign comes to them from among the Signs of their Lord, but they turn away therefrom.

47. And when they are told, "Spend ye of (the bounties[20]) with which God has provided you," the Unbelievers say to those who believe: "Shall we then feed those whom, if God had so willed, He would have fed, (Himself)? — Ye are in nothing but manifest error."

48. Further, they say, "When will this promise (come to pass), if what ye say is true?"

49. They will not (have to) wait for aught[21] but a single Blast: it will seize them while they are yet disputing among themselves!

50. No (chance) will they then have, by will, to dispose (of their affairs), nor to return to their own people!

51. The trumpet shall be sounded, when behold! from the sepulchres[22] (men) will rush forth to their Lord!

52. They will say: "Ah! woe unto us! Who hath raised us up from our beds of repose[23]? ... (A voice will say:) "This is what (God) Most Gracious had promised, and true was the word of the Apostles!"

53. It will be no more than a single Blast, when lo! they will all be brought up before Us!

54. Then, on that Day, not a soul will be wronged in the least, and ye shall but be repaid the meeds[24] of your past Deeds.

55. Verily the Companions of the Garden shall that Day have joy

---

[19] Ships

[20] Blessings.

[21] Anything

[22] Tombs, especially cut in rock or built of stone or brick.

[23] Rest

[24] The merited reward

in all that they do;

56. They and their associates will be in groves[25] of (cool) shade, reclining on thrones (of dignity);

57. (Every) fruit (enjoyment) will be there for them; they shall have whatever they call for;

58. "Peace! — a Word (of saLütation) from a Lord Most Merciful!

59. And O ye in sin! get ye apart this Day!

60. "Did I not enjoin on you, O ye children of Adam, that ye should not worship Satan; for that he was to you an enemy avowed[26]? —

61. "And that ye should worship Me, (for that) this was the Straight Way?

62. "But he did lead astray a great multitude[27] of you. Did ye not, then, understand?

63. "This is the Hell of which ye were (repeatedly) warned!

64. "Embrace ye the (Fire) this Day, for that ye (persistently) rejected (Truth)."

65. That Day shall We set a seal on their mouths. But their hands will speak to Us, and their feet bear witness, to all that they did.

66. If it had been Our Will, We could surely have blotted out[28] their eyes; then should they have run about groping for the Path, but how could they have seen?

67. And if it had been Our Will, We could have transformed[29] them (to remain) in their places; then should they have been unable to move about, nor could they have returned (after error).

68. If We grant long life to any, We cause him to be reversed in nature: will they not then understand?

69. We have not instructed the (Prophet) in Poetry, nor is it meet[30] for Him: this is no less than a Message and a Qur'an making things clear:

70. That it may give admonition to any (who are) alive, and that

---

[25] A small wood, a group of trees.

[26] Self-proclaimed

[27] Crowd, a great many people.

[28] Destroyed

[29] Change them utterly in their form, outward appearance, character, disposition.

[30] Suitable, fit, proper

the charge[31] may be proved against those who reject (Truth).

71. See they not that it is We Who have created for them — among the things which Our hands have fashioned — cattle, which are under their dominion? —

72. And that We have subjected them to their (use)? Of them some do carry them and some they eat:

73. And they have (other) profits from them (besides), and they get (milk) to drink. Will they not then be grateful?

74. Yet they take (for worship) gods other than God, (hoping) that they might be helped!

75. They have not the power to help them: but they will be brought up (before Our Judgment-Seat) as a troop[32] (to be condemned[33]).

76. Let not their speech, then, grieve thee. Verily We know what they hide as well as what they disclose.

77. Doth not man see that it is We Who created Him from sperm? Yet behold! He (stands forth) as an open adversary[34]!

78. And he makes comparisons for us, and forgets his own (Origin and) Creation: He says, "Who can give life to (dry) bones and decomposed[35] ones (at that)?"

79. Say, "He will give them life Who created them for the first time! For He is well-versed[36] in every kind of creation! —

80. "The same Who produces for you fire out of the green tree, when behold! Ye kindle[37] therewith (your own fires)!

81. "Is not He Who created the heavens and the earth able to create the like thereof?" — Yea, indeed! for He is the Creator Supreme, of skill and knowledge (infinite)!

82. Verily, when He intends a thing, His command is, "Be," and it is!

83. So glory to Him in Whose hands is the dominion of all things; and to Him will ye be all brought back.

---

[31] Accusation, indictment

[32] A band, group of people

[33] Sentenced

[34] Rival, antagonist, disputant

[35] Rotten

[36] Skillful

[37] To light

Chapter 37
Sūrah As-Saffat (Those Ranged in Ranks)
Revealed at Makkah, 182 verses

In the name of God, Most Gracious, Most Merciful.

1. By those who range themselves in ranks.

2. And so are strong in repelling (evil),

3. And thus proclaim the message (of God)!

4. Verily, verily, your God is One! —

5. Lord of the heavens and of the earth, and all between them, and Lord of every point at the rising of the sun!

6. We have indeed decked[1] the lower heaven with beauty (in) the stars —

7. (For beauty) and for guard against all obstinate rebellious evil spirits.

8. (So) they should not strain their ears in the direction of the Exalted Assembly but be cast away from every side.

9. Repulsed, for they are under a perpetual[2] penalty.

10. Except such as snatch away something by stealth, and they are pursued by a flaming fire, of piercing brightness.

11. Just ask their opinion: are they the more difficult to create, or the (other) beings We have created? Them have We created out of a sticky clay!

12. Truly dost thou marvel[3], while they ridicule,

13. And, when they are admonished, pay no heed —

14. And, when they see a Sign, turn it to mockery[4],

15. And say, "This is nothing but evident sorcery[5]!

16. "What! when we die, and become dust and bones, shall we (then) be raised up (again)?

17. "And also our fathers of old?"

18. Say thou: "Yea, and ye shall then be humiliated (on account of your evil)."

---

[1] Beautified.

[2] Eternal, lasting.

[3] To be amazed

[4] Joke, ridicule.

[5] Magic

19. Then it will be a single (compelling) cry; and behold, they will begin to see!

20. They will say, "Ah! woe to us! This is the Day of Judgement!"

21. (A voice will say,) "This is the Day of Sorting Out, whose truth ye (once) denied!"

22. "Bring ye up," it shall be said, "The wrongdoers and their wives, and the things they worshipped —

23. "Besides God, and lead them to the Way to the (Fierce) Fire!

24. "But stop them, for they must be asked:

25. "'What is the matter with you that ye help not each other?'"

26. Nay, but that day they shall submit (to Judgment);

27. And they will turn to one another, and question one another.

28. They will say: "It was ye who used to come to us from the right hand (of power and authority)!"

29. They will reply: "Nay, ye yourselves had no faith!

30. "Nor had we any authority over you. Nay, it was ye who were a people in obstinate rebellion!

31. "So now has been proved true, against us, the Word of our Lord that we shall indeed (have to) taste (the punishment of our sins):

32. "We led you astray: for truly we were ourselves astray."

33. Truly, that day, they will (all) share in the Penalty.

34. Verily that is how We shall deal with Sinners.

35. For they, when they were told that there is no god except God, would puff[6] themselves up with Pride.

36. And say: "What! shall we give up our gods for the sake of a Poet possessed[7]?"

37. Nay! He has come with the (very) Truth, and he confirms (the Message of) the Apostles (before Him).

38. Ye shall indeed taste of the Grievous Penalty —

39. But it will be no more than the retribution[8] of (the Evil) that ye have wrought[9] —

40. But the sincere (and devoted) servants of God —

41. For them is a Sustenance determined,

---

[6] To be swollen (with pride).

[7] Mad, possessed (of madness).

[8] Punishment

[9] Worked, practiced or did.

42. Fruits (Delights), and they (shall enjoy) honour and dignity,

43. In Gardens of Felicity[10],

44. Facing each other on Thrones (of dignity):

45. Round will be passed to them a Cup from a clear-flowing fountain,

46. Crystal-white, of a taste delicious to those who drink (thereof),

47. Free from headiness[11]; nor will they suffer intoxication therefrom.

48. And beside them will be chaste women; restraining their glances, with big eyes (of wonder and beauty).

49. As if they were (delicate) eggs closely guarded.

50. Then they will turn to one another and question one another.

51. One of them will start the talk and say: "I had an intimate companion (on the earth),

52. "Who used to say, 'What! art thou amongst those who bear witness to the truth (of the Message)?

53. "'When we die and become dust and bones, shall we indeed receive rewards and punishments?'"

54. (A voice) said: "Would ye like to look down?"

55. He looked down and saw him in the midst of the Fire.

56. He said: "By God! thou wast little short of bringing me to perdition[12]!

57. "Had it not been for the Grace of my Lord, I should certainly have been among those brought (there)!

58. "Is it (the case) that we shall not die,

59. "Except our first death, and that we shall not be punished?"

60. Verily this is the supreme achievement!

61. For the like of this let all strive, who wish to strive.

62. Is that the better entertainment or the Tree of Zaqqum[13]?

63. For We have truly made it (as) a trial for the wrongdoers.

64. For it is a tree that springs out of the bottom of Hellfire:

65. The shoots of its fruit-stalks are like the heads of devils:

66. Truly they will eat thereof and fill their bellies therewith.

---

[10] Bliss, happiness.

[11] Violence or recklessness (caused by liquor).

[12] Eternal death

[13] Compare this bitter tree of Hell with the one mentioned in 17:60.

67. Then on top of that they will be given a mixture made of boiling water.

68. Then shall their return be to the (Blazing) Fire.

69. Truly they found their fathers on the wrong Path;

70. So they (too) were rushed down on their footsteps!

71. And truly before them, many of the ancients went astray —

72. But We sent aforetime, among them, (apostles) to admonish them —

73. Then see what was the end of those who were admonished (but heeded not) —

74. Except the sincere (and devoted) servants of God.

75. (In the days of old), Noah cried to Us, and We are the Best to hear prayer.

76. And We delivered him and his people from the Great Calamity.

77. And made his progeny[14] to endure (on this earth);

78. And We left (this blessing) for him among generations to come in later times:

79. "Peace and saLütation to Noah among the nations!"

80. Thus indeed do We reward those who do right.

81. For he was one of Our believing Servants.

82. Then the rest We overwhelmed[15] in the Flood.

83. Verily among those who followed his Way was Abraham.

84. Behold, He approached his Lord with a sound heart.

85. Behold, he said to his father and to his people, "What is that which ye worship?

86. "Is it a Falsehood — gods other than God — that ye desire?

87. "Then what is your idea about the Lord of the Worlds?"

88. Then did he cast a glance at the stars.

89. And he said, "I am indeed sick (at heart)!"

90. So they turned away from him, and departed.

91. Then did he turn to their gods and said, "Will ye not eat (of the offerings before you)?...

92. "What is the matter with you that ye speak not (intelligently)?"

93. Then did he turn upon them, striking (them) with the right hand.

---

14 Offspring
15 Engulfed, drowned.

94. Then came (the worshippers) with hurried steps and faced (him).

95. He said: "Worship ye that which ye have (yourselves) carved[16]?

96. "But God has created you and your handiwork!"

97. They said: "Build him a furnace, and throw him into the Blazing Fire!"

98. (This failing), they then sought a stratagem[17] against him, but We made them the ones most humiliated!

99. He said: "I will go to my Lord! He will surely guide me!

100. "O my Lord! grant me a righteous (son)!"

101. So We gave him the good news of a boy ready to suffer and forbear.

102. Then, when (the son) reached (the age of) (serious) work with him, he said: "O my son! I see in vision[18] that I offer thee in sacrifice: now see what is thy view!" (The son) said: "O my father! do as thou art commanded: thou will find me, if God so wills, one practicing Patience and Constancy!"

103. So when they had both submitted their wills (to God), and He had laid him prostrate on his forehead (for sacrifice),

104. We called out to him, "O Abraham!

105. "Thou hast already fulfilled the vision!" — thus indeed do We reward those who do right.

106. For this was obviously a trial —

107. And We ransomed[19] him with a momentous[20] sacrifice:

108. And We left (this blessing) for him among generations (to come) in later times:

109. "Peace and saLütation to Abraham!"

110. Thus indeed do We reward those who do right.

111. For he was one of Our believing Servants.

112. And We gave him the good news of Isaac — a prophet — one of the Righteous.

113. We blessed him and Isaac: but of their progeny are (some)

---

[16] Produced by a process of cutting (stone or wood etc.)

[17] Plot, plan

[18] Dream

[19] Redeem, deliver and replace.

[20] Most significant

that do right, and (some) that obviously do wrong, to their own souls.

114. Again, (of old,) We bestowed Our favor on Moses and Aaron.

115. And We delivered them and their people from (their) Great Calamity;

116. And We helped them, so they overcame (their troubles);

117. And We gave them the Book which helps to make things clear;

118. And We guided them to the Straight Way.

119. And We left (this blessing) for them among generations (to come) in later times:

120. "Peace and saLütation to Moses and Aaron!"

121. Thus indeed do We reward those who do right.

122. For they were two of Our believing Servants.

123. So also was Elias among those sent (by us).

124. Behold, he said to his people, "Will ye not fear (God)?

125. "Will ye call upon Ba'l and forsake the Best of Creators —

126. "God, your Lord and Cherisher and the Lord and Cherisher of your fathers of old?"

127. But they rejected him, and they will certainly be called up (for punishment) —

128. Except the sincere and devoted Servants of God (among them).

129. And We left (this blessing) for him among generations (to come) in later times:

130. "Peace and saLütation to such as Elias!"

131. Thus indeed do We reward those who do right.

132. For He was one of Our believing Servants.

133. So also was Lüt among those sent (by us).

134. Behold, We delivered him and his adherents, all

135. Except an old woman who was among those who lagged behind:

136. Then We destroyed the rest.

137. Verily, ye pass by their (sites), by day —

138. And by night: will ye not understand?

139. So also was Jonah among those sent (by us).

140. When he ran away (like slave from captivity) to the ship (fully) laden,

141. He (agreed to) cast lots, and he was condemned:

142. Then the big Fish did swallow him, and he had done acts worthy of blame.

143. Had it not been that he (repented and) glorified God,

144. He would certainly have remained inside the Fish till the Day of Resurrection.

145. But We cast him forth on the naked shore in a state of sickness,

146. And We caused to grow over him, a spreading plant of the Gourd kind,

147. And We sent him (on a mission) to a hundred thousand (men) or more.

148. And they believed; so We permitted them to enjoy (their life) for a while.

149. Now ask them their opinion: is it that thy Lord has (only) daughters, and they have sons? —

150. Or that We created the angels female, and they are witnesses (thereto)?

151. Is it not that they say, from their own invention,

152. "God has begotten children"? But they are liars!

153. Did He (then) choose daughters rather than sons?

154. What is the matter with you? How judge ye?

155. Will ye not then receive admonition?

156. Or have ye an authority manifest?

157. Then bring ye your Book (of authority) if ye be truthful!

158. And they have invented a blood-relationship between Him and the Jinns: but the Jinns know (quite well) that they have indeed to appear (before His Judgment-Seat)!

159. Glory to God! (He is free) from the things they ascribe (to Him)!

160. Not (so do) the servants of God, sincere and devoted.

161. For, verily, neither ye nor those ye worship —

162. Can lead (any) into temptation concerning God,

163. Except such as are (themselves) going to the blazing Fire!

164. (Those ranged in ranks say): "Not one of us but has a place appointed,

165. "And we are verily ranged in ranks (for service):

166. "And we are verily those who declare (God's) glory!"

167. And there were those who said,

168. "If only we had had before us a message from those of old.

169. "We should certainly have been servants of God, sincere (and devoted)!"

170. But (now that the Qur'an has come), they reject it: but soon will they know!

171. Already has Our Word been passed before (this) to Our Servants sent (by Us),

172. That they would certainly be assisted,

173. And that Our forces — they surely must conquer.

174. So turn thou away from them for a little while,

175. And watch them (how they fare), and they soon shall see (how thou farest)!

176. Do they wish (indeed) to hurry on Our Punishment?

177. But when it descends into the open space before them, evil will be the morning for those who were warned (and heeded not)!

178. So turn thou away from them for a little while,

179. And watch (how they fare) and they soon shall see (how thou farest)!

180. Glory to thy Lord, the Lord of Honour and Power! (He is free) from what they ascribe (to Him)!

181. And Peace on the Apostles!

182. And praise to God, the Lord and Cherisher of the Worlds.

Chapter 38
Sūrah Sād (Sād)
Revealed at Makkah, 88 verses

In the name of God, Most Gracious, Most Merciful.

1. Sād: By the Qur'an, full of Admonition: (this is the Truth).

2. But the Unbelievers (are steeped) in Self-glory and Separatism.

3. How many generations before them did We destroy? In the end they cried (for mercy) — when there was no longer time for being saved!

4. So they wonder that a Warner has come to them from among themselves! And the Unbelievers say, "This is a sorcerer telling lies!

5. "Has he made the gods (all) into one God? Truly this is a wonderful thing!"

6. And the leaders among them go away (impatiently), (saying), "Walk ye away, and remain constant to your gods! For this is truly a thing designed (against you)!

7. "We never heard (the like) of this among the people of these latter days: this is nothing but a made-up tale!

8. "What! Has the Message been sent to him — (of all persons) among us?" ... But they are in doubt concerning My (own) Message! Nay, they have not yet tasted My Punishment!

9. Or have they the Treasures of the Mercy of thy Lord — the Exalted in Power, the Grantor of Bounties without measure!

10. Or have they the dominion of the heavens and the earth and all between? If so, let them mount up with the ropes and means (to reach that end)!

11. But there — will be put to flight even a host of confederates[1].

12. Before them (were many who) rejected apostles — the People of Noah, and 'Ād, and Pharaoh the Lord of Stakes[2].

13. And Thamūd, and the People of Lūt, and the Companions of the Wood; such were the Confederates.

14. Not one (of them) but rejected the Apostles, but My Punishment came justly and inevitably[3] (on them).

15. These (to day) only wait for a single mighty Blast, which (when it comes) will brook[4] no delay.

16. They say: "Our Lord! Hasten to us our sentence (even) before the Day of Account!"

17. Have patience at what they say, and remember Our Servant David, the man of strength: for he ever turned (to God).

18. It was We that made the hills declare, in unison[5] with him,

---

[1] Allies.

[2] Pegs, poles (with which armies pitched their tents), hence Lord of many armies.

[3] Certainly, unavoidably.

[4] Tolerate, give no respite.

[5] Agreement, coinciding (in pitch), concord

Our Praises, at eventide[6] and at break of day.

19. And the birds gathered (in assemblies): all with him did turn (to God).

20. We strengthened his kingdom, and gave him wisdom and sound judgment in speech and decision.

21. Has the Story of the Disputants reached thee? Behold, they climbed over the wall of the private chamber;

22. When they entered the presence of David, and he was terrified of them, they said: "Fear not: We are two disputants, one of whom has wronged the other: decide now between us with truth, and treat us not with injustice, but guide us to the even Path.

23. "This man is my brother; he has nine and ninety ewes[7], and I have (but) one: Yet he says, 'Commit her to my care,' and is (moreover) harsh to me in speech."

24. (David) said: "He has undoubtedly wronged thee in demanding thy (single) ewe to be added to his (flock of) ewes: truly many are the Partners (in business) who wrong each other: not so do those who believe and work deeds of righteousness, and how few are they?" ... And David gathered that We had tried him: he asked forgiveness of his Lord, fell down, bowing (in prostration), and turned (to God in repentance).

25. So We forgave him this (lapse[8]): he enjoyed, indeed, a Near Approach to Us, and a beautiful place of (final) Return.

26. O David! We did indeed make thee a vicegerent on earth: so judge thou between men in truth (and justice): nor follow thou the lusts (of thy heart), for they will mislead thee from the Path of God: for those who wander astray from the Path of God, is a Penalty Grievous, for that they forget the Day of Account.

27. Not without purpose did We create heaven and earth and all between! That were the thought of Unbelievers! But woe to the Unbelievers because of the Fire (of Hell)!

28. Shall We treat those who believe and work deeds of righteousness, the same as those who do mischief on earth? Shall We treat

---

[6] Evening
[7] Female sheep
[8] Oversight, omission

those who guard against evil, the same as those who turn aside from the right?

29. (Here is) a Book which We have sent down unto thee, full of blessings, that they may meditate[9] on its Signs, and that men of understanding may receive admonition.

30. To David We gave Solomon (for a son) — how excellent in Our service! Ever did he turn (to Us)!

31. Behold, there were brought before him, at eventide, coursers[10] of the highest breeding; and swift of foot;

32. And he said, "Truly do I love the love of Good, with a view to the glory of my Lord," — until (the sun) was hidden in the veil (of Night):

33. "Bring them back to me." Then began he to pass his hand over (their) legs and their necks.

34. And We did try Solomon: We placed on his throne a body (without life): but he did turn (to Us in true devotion):

35. He said, "O my Lord! Forgive me, and grant me a Kingdom, which, (it may be), suits not another after me: for Thou art the Grantor of Bounties (without measure)."

36. Then We subjected the Wind to his power, to flow gently to his order, whithersoever[11] he willed —

37. As also the evil ones, (including) every kind of builder and diver —

38. As also others bound together in fetters.

39. "Such are Our Bounties: whether thou bestow them (on others) or withhold them, no account will be asked."

40. And he enjoyed, indeed, a near approach to Us, and a beautiful place of (final) Return.

41. Commemorate Our servant Job, behold he cried to his Lord: "The Evil One has afflicted me with distress and suffering"!

42. (The command was given:) "Strike with thy foot: here is (water) wherein to wash, cool and refreshing, and (water) to drink."

43. And We gave him (back) his people, and doubled their number

---

[9] Think, study

[10] Swift horses

[11] Wherever

— as a Grace from Ourselves, and a thing for commemoration[12], for all who have Understanding.

44. "And take in thy hand a little grass, and strike therewith: and break not (thy oath)." Truly We found him full of patience and constancy: how excellent in Our service! Ever did he turn (to Us)!

45. And commemorate Our servants Abraham, Isaac, and Jacob, possessors of Power and Vision.

46. Verily We did chose them for a special (purpose) — proclaiming the Message of the Hereafter.

47. They were, in Our sight, truly, of the company of the Elect and the Good.

48. And commemorate Ismail, Elisha, and Zul-Kifl: each of them was of the company of the Good.

49. This is a message (of admonition): and verily, for the Righteous, is a beautiful place of (final) Return) —

50. Gardens of Eternity, whose doors will (ever) be open to them;

51. Therein will they recline (at ease); therein can they call (at pleasure) for fruit in abundance, and (delicious) drink;

52. And beside them will be chaste women restraining their glances, (companions) of equal age.

53. Such is the promise made to you for the Day of Account!

54. Truly such will be Our Bounty (to you); it will never fail —

55. Yea, such! But — for the wrongdoers will be an evil place of (final) Return!

56. Hell! — they will burn therein — an evil bed (indeed, to lie on)! —

57. Yea, such! — then shall they taste it — a boiling fluid, and a fluid dark, murky[13], intensely cold! —

58. And other Penalties of a similar kind, to match them!

59. Here is a troop[14] rushing headlong with you! No welcome for them! Truly, they shall burn in the Fire!

60. (The followers shall cry to the misleaders:) "Nay, ye (too)! No welcome for you! It is ye who have brought this upon us! Now

---

[12] Celebrating the memory
[13] Thick, dirty
[14] A band, group.

evil is (this) place to stay in!"

61. They will say: "Our Lord! Whoever brought this upon us, add to him a double Penalty in the Fire!"

62. And they will say: "What has happened to us that we see not men whom we used to number among the bad ones?

63. "Did we treat them (as such) in ridicule or have (our) eyes failed to perceive them?"

64. Truly that is just and fitting, the mutual recriminations[15] of the People of the Fire!

65. Say: "Truly am I a Warner: no god is there but the One God, Supreme and Irresistible —

66. "The Lord of the heavens and the earth, and all between — Exalted in Might, able to enforce His will, forgiving again and again."

67. Say: "That is a message supreme (above all) —

68. "From which ye do turn away!

69. "No knowledge have I of the Chiefs on high, when they discuss (matters) among themselves.

70. "Only this has been revealed to me: that I am to give warning plainly and publicly."

71. Behold, thy Lord said to the angels: "I am about to create man from clay:

72. "When I have fashioned him (in due proportion) and breathed into him of My spirit, fall ye down in obeisance[16] unto him."

73. So the angels prostrated themselves, all of them together;

74. Not so Iblis: he was haughty, and became one of those who reject Faith.

75. (God) said: "O Iblis! what prevents thee from prostrating thyself to one whom I have created with My hands? Art thou haughty? Or art thou one of the high (and mighty) ones?"

76. (Iblis) said: "I am better than he: Thou createdst me from fire, and him Thou createdst from clay."

77. (God) said: "Then get thee out from here: for thou art rejected, accursed.

78. "And My Curse shall be on thee till the Day of Judgement."

---

[15] Retort Accusation, countercharge

[16] Gesture especially a bow or curtsy, expressing submission, respect or saLutation.

79. (Iblis) said: "O my Lord! give me then respite[17] till the Day the (dead) are raised."

80. (God) said: "Respite then is granted thee —

81. "Till the day of the Time Appointed."

82. (Iblis) said: "Then, by Thy power, I will put them all in the wrong —

83. "Except Thy Servants amongst them, sincere and purified (by Thy grace)."

84. (God) said: "Then it is just and fitting — and I say what is just and fitting —

85. "That I will certainly fill Hell with thee and those that follow thee — every one."

86. Say: "No reward do I ask of you for this (Qur'an), nor am I a pretender.

87. "This is no less than a Message to (all) the Worlds.

88. "And ye shall certainly know the truth of it (all) after a while."

Chapter 39
Sürah Az-Zumar (The Crowds)
Revealed at Makkah, 75 verses

In the name of God, Most Gracious, Most Merciful.

1. The revelation of this Book is from God, the Exalted in Power, Full of Wisdom.

2. Verily it is We Who have revealed the Book to thee in Truth: so serve God, offering Him sincere devotion.

3. Is it not to God that sincere devotion is due? But those who take for protectors other than God (say): "We only serve them in order that they may bring us nearer to God." Truly God will judge between them in that wherein they differ. But God guides not such as are false and ungrateful.

4. Had God wished to take to Himself a son, He could have chosen

---

[17] Delay

whom He pleased out of those whom He doth create: but Glory be to Him! (He is above such things.) He is God, the One, the Irresistible.

5. He created the heavens and the earth in true (proportions): He makes the Night overlap the Day, and the Day overlap the Night: He has subjected the sun and the moon (to His law) each one follows a course for a time appointed. Is not He the Exalted in Power — He Who forgives again and again?

6. He created you (all) from a single person: then created, of like nature, his mate; and He sent down for you eight head of cattle in pairs: He makes you, in the wombs of your mothers, in stages, one after another, in three veils of darkness. Such is God, your Lord and Cherisher: to Him belongs (all) dominion. There is no god but He: then how are ye turned away (from your true Center)?

7. If ye reject (God), truly God has no need of you; but He liketh not ingratitude from His servants: if ye are grateful, He is pleased with you. No bearer of burdens can bear the burden of another. In the end, to your Lord is your return, when He will tell you the truth of all that ye did (in this life). For He knoweth well all that is in (men's) hearts.

8. When some trouble toucheth man, he crieth unto his Lord, turning to Him in repentance: but when He bestoweth a favor upon him as from Himself, (man) doth forget what he cried and prayed for before, and he doth set up rivals unto God, thus misleading others from God's Path. Say "Enjoy thy blasphemy[1] for a little while: verily thou art (one) of the Companions of the Fire!"

9. Is one who worships devoutly during the hours of the night prostrating himself or standing (in adoration[2]), who takes heed of the Hereafter, and who places his hope in the Mercy of his Lord — (like one who does not)? Say: "Are those equal, those who know and those who do not know? It is those who are endued[3] with understanding that receive admonition."

10. Say: "O ye my servants who believe! Fear your Lord: good is (the reward) for those who do good in this world. Spacious is God's

---

[1] Profanity, disbelief and disrespect

[2] Worship

[3] Furnished with, given

earth! Those who patiently persevere will truly receive a reward without measure!"

11. Say: "Verily, I am commanded to serve God with sincere devotion;

12. "And I am commanded to be the first of those who bow to God in Islam."

13. Say: "I would, if I disobeyed my Lord, indeed have fear of the Penalty of a Mighty Day."

14. Say: "It is God I serve, with my sincere (and exclusive) devotion:

15. "Serve ye what ye will besides Him." Say: "Truly, those in loss are those who lose their own souls and their People on the Day of Judgement: Ah! that is indeed the (real and) evident Loss!"

16. They shall have layers of fire above them, and layers (of fire) below them: with this doth God warn off His servants: "O my servants! Then fear ye Me!"

17. Those who eschew[4] evil — and fall not into its worship — and turn to God (in repentance) — for them is Good News: so announce the Good News to My Servants —

18. Those who listen to the Word, and follow the best (meaning) in it: those are the ones whom God has guided, and those are the ones endued with understanding.

19. Is, then, one against whom the decree of Punishment is justly due (equal to one who eschews evil)? Wouldst thou, then, deliver one (who is) in the Fire?

20. But it is for those who fear their Lord, that lofty mansions, one above another, have been built: beneath them flow rivers (of delight): (such is) the promise of God: never doth God fail in (His) promise.

21. Seest thou not that God sends down rain from the sky, and leads it through springs in the earth? Then He causes to grow, therewith, produce of various colors: then it withers; thou wilt see it grow yellow; then He makes it dry up and crumble away. Truly, in this, is a Message of remembrance to men of understanding.

22. Is one whose heart God has opened to Islam, so that he has

---

[4] Avoid

received enlightenment from God, (no better than one hard-hearted)? Woe to those whose hearts are hardened against celebrating the praises of God! They are manifestly wandering (in error)!

23. God has revealed (from time to time) the most beautiful message in the form of a Book, consistent with itself, (yet) repeating (its teaching in various aspects): the skins of those who fear their Lord tremble thereat; then their skins and their hearts do soften to the celebration of God's praises. Such is the guidance of God: He guides therewith whom He pleases, but such as God leaves to stray, can have none to guide.

24. Is, then, one who has to fear the brunt[5] of the Penalty on the Day of Judgement (and receive it) on his face, (like one guarded therefrom)? It will be said to the wrongdoers: "Taste ye (the fruits of) what ye earned!"

25. Those before them (also) rejected (revelation), and so the Punishment came to them from directions they did not perceive.

26. So God gave them a taste of humiliation in the present life, but greater is the Punishment of the Hereafter, if they only knew!

27. We have put forth for men, in this Qur'an every kind of Parable, in order that they may receive admonition.

28. (It is) a Qur'an in Arabic, without any crookedness (therein): in order that they may guard against Evil.

29. God puts forth a Parable — a man belonging to many partners at variance[6] with each other, and a man belonging entirely to one master: are those two equal in comparison? Praise be to God! But most of them have no knowledge.

30. Truly thou wilt die (one day) and truly they (too) will die (one day).

31. In the end will ye (all), on the Day of Judgement, settle your disputes in the presence of your Lord.

32. Who, then, doth more wrong than one who utters a lie concerning God, and rejects the truth when it comes to him? Is there not in Hell an abode for blasphemers[7]?

---

[5] Chief stress or force of

[6] In disagreement.

[7] Disbelievers who utter profanities against God.

33. And he who brings the Truth and he who confirms (and supports) it — such are the men who do right.

34. They shall have all that they wish for, in the presence of their Lord: such is the reward of those who do good:

35. So that God will turn off from them (even) the worst in their deeds and give them their reward according to the best of what they have done.

36. Is not God enough for His servant? But they try to frighten thee with other (gods) besides Him! For such as God leaves to stray, there can be no guide.

37. And such as God doth guide there can be none to lead astray. Is not God Exalted in Power, (able to enforce His Will), Lord of Retribution[8]?

38. If indeed thou ask them who it is that created the heavens and the earth, they would be sure to say, "God." Say: "See ye then? The things that ye invoke besides God, can they, if God wills some Penalty for me, remove His Penalty? Or if He wills some Grace for me, can they keep back His Grace?" Say: "Sufficient is God for me! In Him trust those who put their trust."

39. Say: "O my people! Do whatever ye can: I will do (my part): but soon will ye know —

40. "Who it is to whom come a Penalty of ignominy[9], and on whom descends a Penalty that abides[10]."

41. Verily We have revealed the Book to thee in Truth, for (instructing) mankind. He, then, that receives guidance benefits his own soul: but he that strays injures his own soul. Nor art thou set over them to dispose of their affairs.

42. It is God that takes the souls (of men) at death: and those that die not (He takes) during their sleep: those on whom He has passed the decree of death, He keeps back (from returning to life), but the rest He sends (to their bodies) for a term appointed. Verily in this are Signs for those who reflect.

43. What! Do they take for intercessors others besides God? Say:

---

[8] Punishment

[9] Disgrace

[10] Lasts, endures

"Even if they have no power whatever and no intelligence?"

44. Say: "To God belongs exclusively (the right to grant) Intercession: to Him belongs the dominion of the heavens and the earth: in the End, it is to Him that ye shall be brought back."

45. When God, the One and Only is mentioned, the hearts of those who believe not in the Hereafter are filled with disgust and horror; but when (gods) other than He are mentioned, behold, they are filled with joy!

46. Say: "O God! Creator of the heavens and the earth! Knower of all that is hidden and open! It is Thou that wilt judge between Thy Servants in those matters about which they have differed."

47. Even if the wrongdoers had all that there is on earth, and as much more, (in vain) would they offer it for ransom[11] from the pain of the Penalty on the Day of Judgement: but something will confront them from God, which they could never have counted upon!

48. For the evils of their Deeds will confront them, and they will be (completely) encircled by that which they used to mock[12] at!

49. Now, when trouble touches man, he cries to Us; but when We bestow a favor upon him as from Ourselves, he says, "This has been given to me because of a certain knowledge (I have)!" Nay, but this is but a trial, but most of them understand not!

50. Thus did the (generations) before them say! But all that they did was of no profit to them.

51. Nay, the evil results of their deeds overtook them. And the wrongdoers of this (generation) — the evil results of their deeds will soon overtake them (too), and they will never be able to frustrate[13] (Our Plan)!

52. Know they not that God enlarges the provision or restricts it, for any He pleases? Verily, in this are Signs for those who believe!

53. Say: "O my Servants who have transgressed against their souls! Despair not of the Mercy of God: for God forgives all sins: for He is Oft-Forgiving, Most Merciful.

54. "Turn ye to your Lord (in repentance) and bow to His (Will),

---

[11] In exchange
[12] Make fun of
[13] Defeat, thwart

before the Penalty comes on you: after that ye shall not be helped.

55. "And follow the Best of (the courses) revealed to you from your Lord, before the Penalty comes on you — of a sudden, while ye perceive not! —

56. "Lest the soul should (then) say: Ah! woe is me! — in that I neglected (my duty) towards God, and was but among those who mocked!' —

57. "Or (lest) it should say: 'If only God had guided me, I should certainly have been among the righteous!' —

58. "Or (lest) it should say when it (actually) sees the Penalty: 'If only I had another chance I should certainly be among those who do good!'

59. "(The reply will be) 'Nay, but there came to thee My Signs and thou didst reject them: thou wast haughty, and became one of those who reject Faith!' "

60. On the Day of Judgement wilt thou see those who told lies against God; their faces will be turned black; is there not in Hell an abode for the Haughty[14]?

61. But God will deliver the righteous to their place of salvation: no evil shall touch them, nor shall they grieve.

62. God is the Creator of all things, and He is the Guardian and Disposer of all affairs.

63. To Him belong the keys of the heavens and the earth: and those who reject the Signs of God, it is they who will be in loss.

64. Say: "Is it someone other than God that ye order me to worship, O ye ignorant ones?"

65. But it has already been revealed to thee — as it was to those before thee — "If thou wert to join (gods with God), truly fruitless will be thy work (in life), and thou wilt surely be in the ranks of those who lose (all spiritual good)."

66. Nay, but worship God, and be of those who give thanks.

67. No just estimate have they made of God, such as is due to Him: on the Day of Judgement the whole of the earth will be but His handful, and the heavens will be rolled up in His right hand: Glory to Him! High is He above the Partners they attribute to Him!

---

[14] Proud, arrogant

68. The Trumpet will (just) be sounded, when all that are in the heavens and on earth will swoon[15], except such as it will please God (to exempt). Then will a second one be sounded, when behold, they will be standing and looking on!

69. And the Earth will shine with the glory of its Lord: the Record (of Deeds) will be placed (open); the Prophets and the witnesses will be brought forward: and a just decision pronounced between them; and they will not be wronged (in the least).

70. And to every soul will be paid in full (the fruit) of its deeds; and (God) knoweth best all that they do.

71. The Unbelievers will be led to Hell in crowds; until, when they arrive there, its gates will be opened, and its Keepers will say, "Did not Apostles come to you from among yourselves, rehearsing[16] to you the Signs of your Lord, and warning you of the meeting of this Day of yours?" The answer will be: "True: but the Decree of Punishment has been proved true against the Unbelievers!"

72. (To them) will be said: "Enter ye the gates of Hell, to dwell therein: and evil is (this) abode of the arrogant!"

73. And those who feared their Lord will be led to the Garden in crowds: until behold, they arrive there; its gates will be opened: and its Keepers will say: "Peace be upon you! Well have ye done! Enter ye here, to dwell therein."

74. They will say: "Praise be to God, Who has truly fulfilled His promise to us, and has given us (this) land in heritage: we can dwell in the Garden as we will: how excellent a reward for those who work (righteousness)!"

75. And thou wilt see the angels surrounding the Throne (Divine) on all sides, singing Glory and Praise to their Lord. The Decision between them (at Judgment) will be in (perfect) justice. And the cry (on all sides) will be, "Praise be to God, the Lord of the Worlds!"

---

[15] Faint, collapse
[16] Reciting

Chapter 40
Sūrah Ghāfir (The Forgiver)
Revealed at Makkah, 85 verses

In the name of God, Most Gracious, Most Merciful.

1. Hā Mīm.

2. The revelation of this Book is from God, Exalted in Power, Full of Knowledge —

3. Who forgiveth Sin, accepteth Repentance, is strict in Punishment, and hath a long reach (in all things). There is no god but He: to Him is the Final Goal.

4. None can dispute about the Signs of God but the Unbelievers. Let not, then, their strutting[1] about through the land deceive thee!

5. But (there were people) before them, who denied (the Signs) — the People of Noah, and the confederates (of Evil) after them; and every People plotted against their prophet, to seize him, and disputed by means of vanities, therewith to condemn the truth; but it was I that seized them! And how (terrible), was My Requital[2] !

6. Thus was the Decree of thy Lord proved true against the Unbelievers; that truly they are Companions of Fire!

7. Those who sustain the Throne (of God) and those around it sing Glory and Praise to their Lord; believe in Him; and implore forgiveness for those who believe: "Our Lord! Thy reach is over all things, in Mercy and Knowledge. Forgive, then, those who turn in repentance, and follow Thy Path: and preserve them from the Penalty of the Blazing Fire!

8. "And grant, our Lord! That they enter the Gardens of Eternity, which Thou hast promised to them, and to the righteous among their fathers, their wives, and their posterity[3]! For Thou art (He), the Exalted in Might, Full of Wisdom.

9. "And preserve them from (all) ills; and any whom thou dost preserve from ills that Day — on them wilt Thou have bestowed Mercy indeed: and that will be truly (for them) the highest Achievement.

---

[1] Walking with pompous or affected stiff erect gait.
[2] Punishment
[3] Offspring

10. The Unbelievers will be addressed: "Greater was the aversion[4] of God to you than (is) your aversion to yourselves, seeing that ye were called to the Faith and ye used to refuse."

11. They will say: "Our Lord! twice hast Thou made us without life, and twice hast Thou given us Life! Now have we recognized our sins: is there any way out (of this)?"

12. (The answer will be:) "This is because, when God was invoked[5] as the only (object of worship), ye did reject Faith, but when partners were joined to Him, ye believed! The command is with God, Most High, Most Great!"

13. He it is Who showeth you His Signs and sendeth down sustenance for you from the sky: but only those receive admonition who turn (to God).

14. Call ye, then, upon God with sincere devotion to Him, even though the Unbelievers may detest it.

15. Raised high above ranks (or degrees), (He is) the Lord of the Throne (of authority): by His command doth He send the spirit (of inspiration) to any of His servants He pleases, that it may warn (men) of the Day of Mutual Meeting —

16. The Day whereon they will (all) come forth: Not a single thing concerning them is hidden from God. Whose will be the dominion[6] that Day? That of God, the One, the Irresistible!

17. That Day will every soul be requited[7] for what it earned; no injustice will there be that Day, for God is Swift in taking account.

18. Warn them of the Day that is (ever) drawing near, when the hearts will (come) right up to the throats to choke (them); no intimate friend nor intercessor will the wrongdoers have, who could be listened to.

19. (God) knows of (the tricks) that deceive with the eyes, and all that the hearts (of men) conceal.

20. And God will judge with (Justice and) Truth: but those whom (men) invoke besides Him, will not (be in a position) to judge at all.

---

4 Repugnance, disgust
5 Called upon
6 Authority, sovereignty
7 Rewarded or punished

Verily it is God (alone) Who hears and sees (all things).

21. Do they not travel through the earth and see what was the End of those before them? They were even superior to them in strength, and in the traces[8] (they have left) in the land: but God did call them to account for their sins, and none had they to defend them against God.

22. That was because there came to them their apostles with Clear (Signs), but they rejected them: So God called them to account: for He is full of Strength, Strict in Punishment.

23. Of old We sent Moses, with Our Signs and Authority manifest,

24. To Pharaoh, Haman, and Qārūn; but they called (him) "a sorcerer[9] telling lies!"...

25. Now, when he came to them in Truth, from Us, they said, "Slay the sons of those who believe with him, and keep alive their females," but the plots of Unbelievers (end) in nothing but errors (and delusions)!"...

26. Said Pharaoh: "Leave me to slay Moses; and let him call on his Lord! What I fear is lest he should change your religion, or lest he should cause mischief to appear in the land!"

27. Moses said: "I have indeed called upon my Lord and your Lord (for protection) from every arrogant one who believes not in the Day of Account!"

28. A believer, a man from among the people of Pharaoh, who had concealed his faith, said: "Will ye slay a man because he says, 'My Lord is God'? — when he has indeed come to you with Clear (Signs) from your Lord? And if he be a liar on him is (the sin of) his lie: but, if he is telling the Truth, then will fall on you something of the (calamity[10]) of which he warns you: truly God guides not one who transgresses and lies!

29. "O my people! yours is the dominion this day: ye have the upper hand in the land: but who will help us from the Punishment of God, should it befall us?" Pharaoh said: "I but point out to you that which I see (myself); nor do I guide you but to the Path of Right!"

---

8 Remains, relics

9 Magician

10 Catastrophe, disaster

30. Then said the man who believed: "O my People! truly I do fear for you something like the Day (of disaster) of the Confederates (in sin)! —

31. "Something like the fate of the people of Noah, the 'Ād, and the Thamūd, and those who came after them: but God never wishes injustice to His Servants.

32. "And, O my People! I fear for you a Day when there will be mutual calling (and wailing)

33. A day when ye shall turn your backs and flee: no defender shall ye have from God: any whom God leaves to stray, there is none to guide...

34. "And to you there came Joseph in times gone by, with Clear Signs, but ye ceased not to doubt of the (mission) for which he had come: at length, when he died, ye said: 'No apostle will God send after him.' Thus doth God leave to stray such as transgress and live in doubt, —

35. "(Such) as dispute about the Signs of God, without any authority that hath reached them. Grievous and odious[11] (is such conduct) in the sight of God and of the Believers. Thus doth God seal up every heart — of arrogant and obstinate transgressors."

36. Pharaoh said: "O Haman! Build me a lofty palace, that I may attain the ways and means —

37. "The ways and means of (reaching) the heavens, and that I may mount up to the God of Moses; but as far as I am concerned, I think (Moses) is a liar!" Thus was made alluring[12], in Pharaoh's eyes, the evil of his deeds, and he was hindered from the Path; and the plot of Pharaoh led to nothing but perdition[13] (for him).

38. The man who believed said further: "O my People! follow me: I will lead you to the Path of Right.

39. "O my people! This life of the present is nothing but (temporary) convenience: it is the Hereafter that is the Home that will last.

40. "He that works evil will not be requited but by the like thereof:

---

[11] Detestable, loathsome.

[12] Attractive, appealing

[13] Eternal death, damnation

and he that works a righteous deed — whether man or woman — and is a Believer — such will enter the Garden (of Bliss): therein will they have abundance without measure.

41. "And O my People! how (strange) it is for me to call you to Salvation while ye call me to the Fire!

42. "Ye do call upon me to blaspheme[14] against God, and to join with Him Partners of whom I have no knowledge; and I call you to the Exalted in Power, Who forgives again and again!"

43. "Without doubt ye do call me to one who is not fit to be called to, whether in this world, or in the Hereafter; our Return will be to God; and the Transgressors will be Companions of the Fire!

44. "Soon will ye remember what I say to you (now), my (own) affair I commit to God: for God (ever) watches over His Servants."

45. Then God saved him from (every) ill that they plotted (against him), but the brunt[15] of the Penalty encompassed[16] on all sides the People of Pharaoh.

46. In front of the Fire will they be brought, morning and evening: and (the Sentence will be) on the Day that Judgment will be established: "Cast ye the People of Pharaoh into the severest Penalty!"

47. Behold, they will dispute with each other in the Fire! The weak ones (who followed) will say to those who had been arrogant, "We but followed you: can ye then take (on yourselves) from us some share of the Fire?"

48. Those who had been arrogant will say: "We are all in this (Fire)! Truly, God has judged between (His) Servants!"

49. Those in the Fire will say to the Keepers of Hell: "Pray to your Lord to lighten us the Penalty for a Day (at least)!"

50. They will say: "Did there not come to you your apostles with Clear Signs?" They will say, "Yes." They will reply, "Then pray (as ye like) but the Prayer of those without Faith is nothing but (futile[17] wandering) in (mazes[18] of) error!"

---

14 To speak profanely, curse or swear
15 Force or impact.
16 Encircled
17 Vain, useless.
18 Web, network.

51. We will, without doubt, help Our apostles and those who believe (both) in this world's life and on the Day when the Witnesses will stand forth —

52. The Day when no profit will it be to wrongdoers to present their excuses, but they will (only) have the Curse and the Home of Misery.

53. We did aforetime give Moses the (Book of) Guidance, and We gave the Book in inheritance to the Children of Israel —

54. A Guide and a Message to men of understanding.

55. Patiently, then, persevere: for the Promise of God is true: and ask forgiveness for thy fault, and celebrate the Praises of thy Lord in the evening and in the morning.

56. Those who dispute about the Signs of God without any authority bestowed on them — there is nothing in their breasts but (the quest of) greatness, which they shall never attain to: seek refuge, then, in God: it is He Who hears and sees (all things).

57. Assuredly the creation of the heavens and the earth is a greater (matter) than the creation of men: Yet most men understand not.

58. Not equal are the blind and those who (clearly) see: nor are (equal) those who believe and work deeds of righteousness, and those who do evil. Little do ye learn by admonition!

59. The Hour will certainly come: therein is no doubt: yet most men believe not.

60. And your Lord says: "Call on Me; I will answer your (Prayer): But those who are too arrogant to serve Me will surely find themselves in Hell — in humiliation!"

61. It is God Who has made the Night for you, that ye may rest therein, and the Day, as that which helps (you) to see. Verily God is Full of Grace and Bounty to men: yet most men give no thanks.

62. Such is God, your Lord, the Creator of all things, there is no god but He: then how ye are deluded away from the Truth!

63. Thus are deluded those who are wont[19] to reject the Signs of God.

64. It is God Who has made for you the earth as a resting place,

---

[19] Accustomed to.

and the sky as a canopy,[20] and has given you shapes — and made your shapes beautiful — and has provided for you Sustenance, of things pure and good — such is God your Lord. So Glory to God, the Lord of the Worlds!

65. He is the living (One): There is no god but He: Call upon Him, giving Him sincere devotion. Praise be to God, Lord of the Worlds!

66. Say: "I have been forbidden to invoke those whom ye invoke besides God, seeing that the Clear Signs have come to me from my Lord: and I have been commanded to bow (in Islam) to the Lord of the Worlds."

67. It is He Who has created you from dust, then from a sperm drop, then from a leech-like clot; then does He get you out (into the light) as a child: then lets you (grow and) reach your age of full strength; then lets you become old, though of you there are some who die before; and lets you reach a term appointed: in order that ye may learn wisdom.

68. It is He Who gives Life and Death; and when He decides upon an affair, He says to it, "Be," and it is.

69. Seest thou not those that dispute concerning the Signs of God? How are they turned away (from Reality)? —

70. Those who reject the Book and the (revelations) with which We sent Our apostles: But soon shall they know —

71. When the yokes (shall be) round their necks, and the chains; they shall be dragged along —

72. In the boiling fetid[21] fluid, then in the Fire shall they be burned;

73. Then shall it be said to them: "Where are the (deities) to which ye gave part-worship —

74. "In derogation[22] of God?" They will reply: "They have left us in the lurch: nay, we invoked not, of old, anything (that had real existence)." Thus does God leave the Unbelievers to stray.

75. "That was because ye were wont to rejoice on the earth in things other than the Truth, and that ye were wont to be insolent.

76. "Enter ye the gates of Hell, to dwell therein: and evil is (this) abode of the arrogant!"

---

[20] Covering, an overhanging shelter.

[21] Stinking.

[22] Lessening or impairing authority.

77. So persevere in patience! For the Promise of God is true: and whether We show thee (in this life) some part of what We promise them, or We take thy soul (to Our Mercy) (before that), (in any case) it is to Us that they shall (all) return.

78. We did aforetime send apostles before thee: of them there are some whose story We have related to thee, and some whose story We have not related to thee. It was not (possible) for any apostle to bring a Sign except by the leave of God: but when the Command of God issued, the matter was decided in truth and justice, and there perished, there and then, those who stood on Falsehoods.

79. It is God Who made cattle for you, that ye may use some for riding and some for food;

80. And there are (other) advantages in them for you (besides); that ye may through them attain to any need (there may be) in your hearts; and on them and on ships ye are carried.

81. And He shows you always His Signs; then which of the Signs of God will ye deny?

82. Do they not travel through the earth and see what was the end of those before them? They were more numerous than these and superior in strength and in the traces (they have left) in the land: yet all that they accomplished was of no profit to them.

83. For when their Apostles came to them with Clear Signs, they exulted[23] in such knowledge (and skill) as they had; but that very (Wrath) at which they were wont to scoff[24] hemmed[25] them in.

84. But when they saw Our Punishment, they said: "We believe in God — the One God — and we reject the partners we used to join with Him."

85. But their professing the Faith when they (actually) saw Our Punishment was not going to profit them. (Such has been) God's way of dealing with His servants (from the most ancient times). And even thus did the rejecters of God perish (utterly)!

---

[23] Were proud of
[24] Make fun of
[25] Encircled them.

Chapter 41
Sūrah Fussilat (Explained)
Revealed at Makkah, 54 verses

In the name of God, Most Gracious, Most Merciful.

1. Hā Mïm.

2. A revelation from (God), Most Gracious, Most Merciful —

3. A Book, whereof the verses are explained in detail — a Qur'an in Arabic, for people who understand —

4. Giving Good News and Admonition: yet most of them turn away, and so they hear not.

5. They say: "Our hearts are under veils, (concealed) from that to which thou dost invite us, and in ours ears is a deafness, and between us and thee is a screen: so do thou (what thou wilt); for us, we shall do (what we will!)"

6. Say thou: "I am but a man like you: it is revealed to me by inspiration, that your God is One God: so stand true to Him, and ask for His forgiveness." And woe to those who join gods with God —

7. Those who practice not Regular Charity, and who even deny the Hereafter.

8. For those who believe and work deeds of righteousness is a reward that will never fail.

9. Say: Is it that ye deny Him Who created the earth in two Days? And do ye join equals with Him? He is the Lord of (all) the Worlds.

10. He set on the (earth), mountains standing firm, high above it, and bestowed blessings on the earth, and measured therein all things to give them nourishment in due proportion, in four Days, in accordance with (the needs of) those who seek (sustenance).

11. Moreover He comprehended[1] in His design the sky, and it had been (as) smoke: He said to it and to the earth: "Come ye together, willingly or unwillingly." They said: "We do come (together), in willing obedience."

12. So He completed them as seven firmaments[2] in two Days and

---

[1] Included
[2] Groups of stars.

He assigned[3] to each heaven its duty and command. And We adorned the lower heaven with lights, and (provided it) with guard. Such is the Decree of (Him) the Exalted in Might, Full of knowledge.

13. But if they turn away, say thou: "I have warned you of a stunning[4] Punishment (as of thunder and lightning) like that which (overtook) the 'Ād and the Thamūd!"

14. Behold, the Apostles came to them, from before them and behind them, (preaching): "Serve none but God." They said, "If our Lord had so pleased, He would certainly have sent down angels (to preach): now we reject your mission (altogether)."

15. Now the 'Ād behaved arrogantly through the land, against (all) truth and reason, and said: "Who is superior to us in strength?" What! did they not see that God, Who created them, was superior to them in strength? But they continued to reject Our Signs!

16. So We sent against them a furious Wind through days of disaster, that We might give them a taste of a Penalty of humiliation in this Life; but the Penalty of the Hereafter will be more humiliating still: and they will find no help.

17. As to the Thamūd, We gave them guidance, but they preferred blindness (of heart) to Guidance; so the stunning Punishment of humiliation seized them, because of what they had earned.

18. But We delivered those who believed and practiced righteousness.

19. On the Day that the enemies of God will be gathered together to the Fire, they will be marched in ranks.

20. At length, when they reach the (Fire), their hearing, their sight, and their skins will bear witness against them, as to (all) their deeds.

21. They will say to their skins: "Why bear ye witness against us?" They will say: "God hath given us speech, (He) Who giveth speech to everything: He created you for the first time, and unto Him were ye to return.

22. "Ye did not seek to hide yourselves, lest your hearing, your sight, and your skins should bear witness against you! But ye did think that God knew not many of the things that ye used to do!

---

[3] Alloted
[4] Shocking, startling

23. "But this thought of yours which ye did entertain concerning your Lord, hath brought you to destruction, and (now) have ye become of those utterly lost!"

24. If, then, they have patience, the Fire will be a Home for them! And if they beg to be received into favor, into favor will they not (then) be received.

25. And We have destined[5] for them intimate companions (of like nature), Who made alluring to them what was before them and behind them; and the sentence among the previous generations of Jinns and men, who have passed away, is proved against them; for they are utterly lost.

26. The Unbelievers say: "Listen not to this Qur'an, but talk at random in the midst of its (reading), that ye may gain the upper hand!"

27. But We will certainly give the Unbelievers a taste of a severe Penalty, and We will requite them for the worst of their deeds.

28. Such is the requital of the enemies of God — the Fire: therein will be for them the Eternal Home: a (fit) requital, for that they were wont[6] to reject Our Signs.

29. And the Unbelievers will say: "Our Lord! show us those, among Jinns and men, who misled us: we shall crush them beneath our feet, so that they become the vilest[7] (before all)."

30. In the case of those who say, "Our Lord is God," and, further, stand straight and steadfast, the angels descend on them (from time to time): "Fear ye not!" (they suggest), "nor grieve! but receive the Glad Tidings of the Garden (of Bliss), the which ye were promised!

31. "We are your protectors in this life and in the Hereafter: therein shall ye have all that your souls shall desire; therein shall ye have all that ye ask for! —

32. "A hospitable[8] gift from One Oft-Forgiving, Most Merciful!"

33. Who is better in speech than one who calls (men) to God, works righteousness, and says, "I am of those who bow in Islam?"

34. Nor can Goodness and Evil be equal. Repel (Evil) with what is better: then will he between whom and thee was hatred become

---

[5] Appointed, decreed
[6] Accustomed to
[7] Lowest
[8] Generous

as it were thy friend and intimate!

35. And no one will be granted such goodness except those who exercise patience and self-restraint, none but persons of the greatest good fortune.

36. And if (at any time) an incitement to discord[9] is made to thee by the Evil One, seek refuge in God. He is the One Who hears and knows all things.

37. Among His Signs are the Night and the Day, and the sun and the moon. Adore[10] not the Sun and the Moon, but adore God Who created them, if it is Him ye wish to serve.

38. But if they (Unbelievers) are arrogant, (no matter): for in the presence of thy Lord are those who celebrate His praises by night and by day. And they never flag[11] (nor feel themselves above it).

39. And among His Signs is this: thou seest the earth barren and desolate; but when We send down rain to it, it is stirred to life and yields increase. Truly, He Who gives life to the (dead) earth can surely give life to (men) who are dead. For He has power over all things.

40. Those who pervert[12] the Truth in Our Signs are not hidden from Us. Which is better? — he that is cast into the Fire, or he that comes safe through, on the Day of Judgement? Do what ye will: Verily He seeth (clearly) all that ye do.

41. Those who reject the Message when it comes to them (are not hidden from Us); and indeed it is a Book of exalted power.

42. No falsehood can approach it from before or behind it: it is sent down by One Full of Wisdom, Worthy of all Praise.

43. Nothing is said to thee that was not said to the apostles before thee: That thy Lord has at His command (all) Forgiveness as well as a most Grievous Penalty.

44. Had We sent this as a Qur'an (in a language) other than Arabic, they would have said: "Why are not its verses explained in detail? What! (a Book) not in Arabic? and (a Messenger) an Arab?" Say: "It is a guide and a healing to those who believe; and for those who believe not, there is a deafness in their ears, and it is blindness in

---

[9] Strife, lack of harmony
[10] Worship
[11] Slack
[12] Corrupt, distort

their (eyes); they are (as it were) being called from a place far distant!"

45. We certainly gave Moses the Book aforetime: but dispute arose therein. Had it not been for a word that went forth before from thy Lord, (their differences) would have been settled between them: but they remained in suspicious disquieting[13] doubt thereon.

46. Whoever works righteousness benefits his own soul; whoever works evil, it is against his own soul: nor is thy Lord ever unjust (in the least) to His servants.

47. To Him is referred the Knowledge of the Hour (of Judgment: He knows all): no date fruit comes out of its sheath, nor does a female conceive (within her womb) nor bring forth (young), but by His Knowledge. The Day that (God) will propound[14] to them the (question), "Where are the partners (ye attributed) to Me?" They will say, "We do assure thee not one of us can bear witness!"

48. The (deities) they used to invoke aforetime will leave them in the lurch[15], and they will perceive that they have no way of escape.

49. Man does not weary of asking for good (things), but if ill touches him, he gives up all hope (and) is lost in despair.

50. When We give him a taste of some mercy from Ourselves, after some adversity has touched him, he is sure to say, "This is due to my (merit): I think not that the Hour (of Judgment) will (ever) be established; but if I am brought back to my Lord, I have (much) good (stored) in His sight!" But We will show the Unbelievers the truth of all that they did, and We shall give them the taste of a severe Penalty.

51. When We bestow favors on man, he turns away, and gets himself remote on his side (instead of coming to Us); and when Evil seizes him, (he comes) full of prolonged prayer!

52. Say: "See ye if the (Revelation) is (really) from God, and yet do ye reject it? Who is more astray than one who is in schism[16] far (from any purpose)?"

53. Soon will We show them Our Signs in the (furthest) regions (of the earth), and in their own souls, until it becomes manifest to

---

[13] Upsetting, distressing

[14] Propose, offer for consideration.

[15] Most difficult time

[16] Division of a group into mutually opposing parties.

them that this is the Truth. Is it not enough that thy Lord doth witness all things?

54. Ah indeed! are they in doubt concerning the Meeting with their Lord? Ah indeed! it is He that doth encompass all things!

Chapter 42
Sūrah Ash-Shūrā (The Consultation)
Revealed at Makkah, 53 verses

In the name of God, Most Gracious, Most Merciful.

1. Hā Mīm;

2. 'Ain Sīn Qāf.

3. Thus doth (He) send Inspiration to thee as (He did) to those before thee — God, Exalted in Power, Full of Wisdom.

4. To Him belongs all that is in the heavens and on earth: and He is Most High, Most Great.

5. The heavens are almost rent asunder from above them (by His Glory): and the angels celebrate the Praises of their Lord, and pray for forgiveness for (all) beings on earth: Behold! Verily God is He, the Oft-Forgiving, Most Merciful.

6. And those who take as protectors others besides Him — God doth watch over them; and thou art not the disposer of their affairs.

7. Thus have We sent by inspiration to thee an Arabic Qur'an: that thou mayest warn the Mother of Cities[1] and all around her — and warn (them) of the Day of Assembly, of which there is no doubt: (when) some will be in the Garden, and some in the Blazing Fire.

8. If God had so willed, He could have made them a single people; but He admits whom He will to His Mercy; and the wrongdoers will have no protector nor helper.

9. What! Have they taken (for worship) protectors besides Him? But it is God, He is the Protector, and it is He Who gives life to the dead: it is He Who has power over all things.

---

[1] Makkah

10. Whatever it be wherein ye differ, the decision thereof is with God: Such is God my Lord: in Him I trust, and to Him I turn.

11. (He is) the Creator of the heavens and the earth: He has made for you pairs from among yourselves, and pairs among cattle: by this means does He multiply you: there is nothing whatever like unto Him, and He is the One that hears and sees (all things).

12. To Him belong the keys of the heavens and the earth: He enlarges and restricts the Sustenance to whom He will: for He knows full well all things.

13. The same religion has He established for you as that which He enjoined[2] on Noah — the which We have sent by inspiration to thee — and that which We enjoined on Abraham, Moses, and Jesus: Namely, that ye should remain steadfast in Religion, and make no divisions therein: to those who worship other things than God, hard is the (way) to which thou callest them. God chooses to Himself those whom He pleases, and guides to Himself those who turn (to Him).

14. And they became divided only after knowledge reached them — through selfish envy as between themselves. Had it not been for a Word that went forth before from thy Lord, (tending[3]) to a term appointed, the matter would have been settled between them: but truly those who have inherited the Book after them are in suspicious (disquieting) doubt concerning it.

15. Now then, for that (reason), call (them to the Faith), and stand steadfast as thou art commanded, nor follow thou their vain desires; but say: "I believe in the Book which God has sent down; and I am commanded to judge justly between you. God is Our Lord and your Lord. For us (is the responsibility for) Our deeds, and for you for your deeds. There is no contention[4] between us and you. God will bring us together, and to Him is (Our) final goal.

16. But those who dispute concerning God after He has been accepted, futile[5] is their dispute in the sight of their Lord: on them is Wrath, and for them will be a Penalty Terrible.

17. It is God Who has sent down the Book in truth, and the Balance

---

[2] Commanded, prescribed
[3] To be moving or directed to.
[4] Strife, controversy
[5] Vain, useless

(by which to weigh conduct). And what will make thee realize that perhaps the Hour is close at hand?

18. Only those wish to hasten it who believe not in it: those who believe hold it in awe, and know that it is the Truth. Behold, verily those that dispute concerning the Hour are far astray.

19. Gracious is God to His servants: He gives Sustenance to whom He pleases: and He has Power and can carry out His Will.

20. To any that desires the tilth[6] of the Hereafter, We give increase in his tilth; and to any that desires the tilth of this world, We grant somewhat thereof, but he has no share or lot in the Hereafter.

21. What! have they partners (in godhead), who have established for them some religion without the permission of God? Had it not been for the Decree of Judgement, the matter would have been decided between them (at once): but verily the wrongdoers will have a grievous Penalty.

22. Thou wilt see the wrongdoers in fear on account of what they have earned, and (the burden of) that must (necessarily) fall on them. But those who believe and work righteous deeds will be in the luxuriant[7] prolific meads[8] of the Gardens: they shall have before their Lord, all that they wish for: that will indeed be the magnificent Bounty (of God).

23. That is (the Bounty) whereof God gives Glad Tidings to His Servants who believe and do righteous deeds. Say: "No reward do I ask of you for this except the love of those near of kin." And if anyone earns any good, We shall give Him an increase of good in respect thereof: for God is Oft-Forgiving, Most Ready to appreciate (service).

24. What! do they say, "He has forged[9] a falsehood against God?" But if God willed, He could seal up thy heart. And God blots out Vanity, and proves the Truth by His Words. For He knows well the secrets of all hearts.

25. He is the One that accepts repentance from His Servants and forgives sins: and He knows all that ye do.

---

[6] Cultivation, reward

[7] Lush and profuse

[8] Meadow, a well-watered grassy land.

[9] Fabricated

26. And He listens to those who believe and do deeds of righteousness, and gives them increase of His Bounty: but for the Unbelievers there is a terrible Penalty.

27. If God were to enlarge the provision for His Servants, they would indeed transgress beyond all bounds through the earth; but He sends (it) down in due measure as He pleases: for He is with His Servants Well-Acquainted, Watchful.

28. He is the One that sends down rain (even) after (men) have given up all hope, and scatters His Mercy (far and wide). And He is the Protector, Worthy Of all Praise.

29. And among His Signs is the creation of the heavens and the earth, and the living creatures that He has scattered through them: and He has power to gather them together when He wills.

30. Whatever misfortune happens to you, is because of the things your hands have wrought[10], and for many (of them) He grants forgiveness.

31. Nor can ye frustrate[11] (aught), (fleeing) through the earth; nor have ye, besides God, anyone to protect or to help.

32. And among His Signs are the ships, smooth-running through the ocean, (tall) as mountains.

33. If it be His Will, He can still the Wind: then would they become motionless on the back of the (ocean). Verily in this are Signs for everyone who patiently perseveres and is grateful.

34. Or He can cause them to perish because of the (evil) which (the men) have earned: but much doth He forgive.

35. But let those know, who dispute about Our Signs, that there is for them no way of escape.

36. Whatever ye are given (here) is (but) a convenience of this Life: but that which is with God is better and more lasting: (it is) for those who believe and put their trust in their Lord;

37. Those who avoid the greater crimes and shameful deeds, and, when they are angry even then forgive;

38. Those who hearken to their Lord, and establish regular prayer; who (conduct) their affairs by mutual Consultation; who spend out

---

[10] Done

[11] Frustrate, baffle

of what We bestow on them for Sustenance;

39. And those who, when an oppressive wrong is inflicted on them, (are not cowed[12] but) help and defend themselves.

40. The recompense[13] for an injury is an injury equal thereto (in degree): but if a person forgives and makes reconciliation[14], his reward is due from God: for (God) loveth not those who do wrong.

41. But indeed if any do help and defend themselves after a wrong (done) to them, against such there is no cause of blame.

48. If then they turn away, We have not sent thee as a guard over them. Thy duty is but to convey (the Message). And truly, when We give man a taste of Mercy from Ourselves, He doth exult[15] thereat[16], but when some ill happens to him, on account of the deeds which His hands have sent forth, truly then is man ungrateful!

49. To God belongs the dominion of the heavens and the earth. He creates what He wills (and plans). He bestows[17] (children) male or female according to His Will (and Plan).

50. Or He bestows both males and females, and He leaves barren whom He will: for He is Full of knowledge and power.

51. It is not fitting for a man that God should speak to him except by inspiration, or from behind a veil, or by the sending of a Messenger to reveal, with God's permission, what God wills: for He is Most High, Most Wise.

52. And thus have We, by Our command, sent inspiration to thee: thou knewest not (before) what was Revelation, and what was Faith; but We have made the (Qur'an) a Light, wherewith We guide such of Our servants as We will; and verily thou dost guide (men) to the Straight Way —

53. The Way of God, to whom belongs whatever is in the heavens and whatever is on earth: Behold (how) all affairs tend towards God!

---

[12] Intimidated, to subdue the spirit

[13] Compensation, amends

[14] Heal and settle, make friendly (after estrangement).

[15] Becomes happy and proud.

[16] On that account, because of it

[17] Grants

Chapter 43
Sürah Az-Zukhruf (Ornaments of Gold)
Revealed at Makkah, 89 verses

In the name of God, Most Gracious, Most Merciful.

1. Hā Mïm.

2. By the Book that makes things clear —

3. We have made it a Qur'an in Arabic, that ye may be able to understand (and learn wisdom).

4. And verily, it is in the Mother of the Book, in Our Presence, high (in dignity), full of wisdom.

5. Shall We then take away the Message from you and repel (you), for that ye are a people transgressing[1] beyond bounds?

6. But how many were the prophets We sent amongst the peoples of old?

7. And never came there a prophet to them but they mocked[2] him.

8. So We destroyed (them) — stronger in power than these — and (thus) has passed on the Parable of the peoples of old.

9. If thou wert to question them, 'Who created the heavens and the earth?' They would be sure to reply, 'They were created by (Him), the Exalted in Power, Full of knowledge' —

10. (Yea, the same that) has made for you the earth (like a carpet) spread out, and has made for you roads (and channels) therein, in order that ye may find guidance (on the way);

11. That sends down (from time to time rain from the sky in due measure; and We raise to life therewith a land that is dead; even so will ye be raised (from the dead) —

12. That has created pairs in all things, and has made for you ships and cattle on which ye ride,

13. In order that ye may sit firm and square on their backs, and when so seated, ye may celebrate the (kind) favor of your Lord, and say, "Glory to Him Who has subjected these to Our (use), for We could never have accomplished this (by ourselves).

14. "And to Our Lord, surely, must We turn back!"

---

[1] Trespassing

[2] Made fun of him

15. Yet they attribute to some of His servants a share with Him (in His godhead)! Truly is man a blasphemous ingrate[3] avowed[4]!

16. What! Has He taken Daughters out of what He Himself creates, and granted to you sons for choice?

17. When news is brought to one of them of (the birth of) what he sets up as a likeness to (God) Most Gracious, his face darkens, and he is filled with inward grief!

18. Is then one brought up among trinkets[5], and unable to give a clear account in a dispute (to be associated with God)?

19. And they make into females angels who themselves serve God. Did they witness their creation? Their evidence will be recorded, and they will be called to account!

20. ("Ah!") they say, "If it had been the will of (God) Most Gracious, We should not have worshipped such (deities)!" Of that they have no knowledge! They do nothing but lie!

21. What! have We given them a Book before this, to which they are holding fast?

22. Nay! they say: "We found Our fathers following a certain religion, and We do guide ourselves by their footsteps."

23. Just in the same way, whenever We sent a Warner before thee to any people, the wealthy ones among them said: "We found Our fathers following a certain religion, and We will certainly follow in their footsteps."

24. He said: "What! even if I brought you better guidance than that which ye found your fathers following?" They said: "For us, We deny that ye (prophets) are sent (on a mission at all)."

25. So We exacted[6] retribution[7] from them: now see what was the end of those who rejected (Truth)!

26. Behold! Abraham said to his father and his people: "I do indeed clear myself of what ye worship:

27. "(I worship) only Him Who made me, and He will certainly guide me."

---

[3] Ungrateful

[4] Confessed, admitted

[5] Trifling ornaments, small fancy articles

[6] Inflicted

[7] Punishment

391

28. And he left it as a Word to endure among those who came after him, that they may turn back (to God).

29. Yea, I have given the good things of this life to these (men) and their fathers, until the Truth has come to them, and an Apostle making things clear.

30. But when the Truth came to them, they said: "This is sorcery[8], and We do reject it."

31. Also, they say: "Why is not this Qur'an sent down to some leading man in either of the two (Chief) cities?"

32. Is it they who would portion out the Mercy of thy Lord? It is We Who portion out between them their livelihood in the life of this world: and We raise some of them above others in ranks, so that some may command work from others. But the Mercy of thy Lord is better than the (wealth) which they amass[9].

33. And were it not that (all) men might become of one (evil) way of life, We would provide, for everyone that blasphemes against (God) Most Gracious, silver roofs for their houses and (silver) stairways on which to go up.

34. And (silver) doors to their houses, and thrones (of silver) on which they could recline,

35. And also adornments[10] of gold. But all this were nothing but conveniences[11] of the present life: the Hereafter, in the sight of thy Lord, is for the Righteous.

36. If anyone withdraws himself from remembrance of (God) Most Gracious, We appoint for him an evil one, to be an intimate companion to him.

37. Such (evil ones) really hinder them from the Path, but they think that they are being guided aright!

38. At length, when (such a one) comes to Us, he says (to his evil companion): "Would that between me and thee were the distance of East and West!" Ah! Evil is the companion (indeed)!

39. When ye have done wrong, it will avail you nothing, that day,

---

[8] Magic

[9] Collect, hoard

[10] Ornaments, decorations

[11] Things or articles for daily use

that ye shall be partners in punishment!

40. Canst thou then make the deaf to hear, or give direction to the blind or to such as (wander) in manifest error?

41. Even if We take thee away, We shall be sure to exact retribution from them.

42. Or We shall show thee that (accomplished) which We have promised them: for verily We shall prevail over them.

43. So hold thou fast to the Revelation sent down to thee: verily thou art on Straight Way.

44. The (Qur'an) is indeed the Message, for thee and for thy people; and soon shall ye (all) be brought to account.

45. And question thou Our apostles whom We sent before thee; did We appoint any deities other than (God) Most Gracious, to be worshipped?

46. We did send Moses aforetime, with Our Signs, to Pharaoh and his Chiefs: he said, "I am an apostle of the Lord of the Worlds."

47. But when he came to them with Our Signs, behold, they ridiculed them.

48. We showed them Sign after Sign, each greater then its fellow, and We seized them with Punishment, in order that they might turn (to Us).

49. And they said, "O thou Sorcerer! invoke thy Lord for us according to His covenant[12] with thee; for We shall truly accept guidance."

50. But when We removed the Penalty from them, behold, they broke their word.

51. And Pharaoh proclaimed among his people, saying: "O my people! does not the dominion of Egypt belong to me, (witness) these streams flowing underneath my (palace)? What! see ye not then?

52. "Am I not better than this (Moses), who is a contemptible[13] wretch[14] and can scarcely express himself clearly?

53. "Then why are not gold bracelets bestowed on him or (why) come (not) with him angels accompanying him in procession?"

---

[12] A solemn promise
[13] Insignificant
[14] Unfortunate, miserable person

54. Thus did he make fools of his people, and they obeyed him: Truly were they a people rebellious (against God).

55. When at length they provoked Us, We exacted retribution from them, and We drowned them all —

56. And We made them (a people) of the Past and an Example to later ages.

57. When (Jesus) the son of Mary is held up as an example, behold, thy people raise a clamor[15] thereat (in ridicule)!

58. And they say, "Are Our gods best, or He?" This they set forth to thee, only by way of disputation[16]: yea, they are a contentious[17] people.

59. He was no more than a servant: We granted Our favor to him, and We made him an example to the Children of Israel.

60. And if it were Our Will, We could make angels from amongst you, succeeding each other on the earth.

61. And (Jesus) shall be a Sign (for the coming of) the Hour (of Judgment): therefore have no doubt about the (Hour), but follow ye Me: this is a Straight Way.

62. Let not the Evil One hinder you: for he is to you an enemy avowed.

63. When Jesus came with Clear Signs, he said: "Now have I come to you with Wisdom, and in order to make clear to you some of the (points) on which ye dispute: therefore fear God and obey me.

64. "For God; He is my Lord and your Lord: so worship ye Him: this is a Straight Way."

65. But sects from among themselves fell into disagreement: then woe to the wrongdoers, from the Penalty of a Grievous Day!

66. Do they only wait for the Hour — that it should come on them all of a sudden, while they perceive not?

67. Friends on that Day will be foes, one to another, except the Righteous.

68. My devotees[18]! no fear shall be on you that Day, nor shall ye grieve —

---

15 Uproar

16 Debate, discussion

17 Quarrelsome

18 Devoted servants

69. (Being) those who have believed in Our Signs and bowed (their wills to Ours) in Islam.

70. Enter ye the Garden, ye and your wives, in (beauty and) rejoicing.

71. To them will be passed round, dishes and goblets[19] of gold: there will be there all that the souls could desire, all that the eyes could delight in: and ye shall abide therein (for aye[20]).

72. Such will be the Garden of which ye are made heirs for your (good) deeds (in life).

73. Ye shall have therein abundance of fruit, from which ye shall have satisfaction.

74. The Sinners will be in the Punishment of Hell, to dwell therein (for aye):

75. Nowise[21] will the (punishment) be lightened for them, and in despair will they be there overwhelmed[22].

76. Nowise shall We be unjust to them: but it is they who have been unjust themselves.

77. They will cry: "O Malik[23]! would that thy Lord put an end to us!" He will say, "Nay, but ye shall abide!"

78. Verily We have brought the truth to you: but most of you have a hatred for Truth.

79. What! have they settled some Plan (among themselves)? But it is We who settle things.

80. Or do they think that We hear not their secrets and their private counsels? Indeed (We do), and Our Messengers are by them, to record.

81. Say: "If (God) Most Gracious had a son, I would be the first to worship."

82. Glory to the Lord of the heavens and the earth, the Lord of the Throne (of Authority)! (He is free) from the things they attribute (to Him)!

83. So leave them to babble[24] and play (with vanities) until they

---

[19] Drinking cups
[20] Forever
[21] In no way, by no means
[22] Engulfed, drowned
[23] Malik: The angel in charge of Hell.
[24] Chatter, to talk nonsense

meet that Day of theirs, which they have been promised.

84. It is He Who is God in heaven and God on earth; and He is full of Wisdom and Knowledge.

85. And blessed is He to Whom belongs the dominion of the heavens and the earth, and all between them: with Him is the knowledge of the Hour (of Judgment): And to Him shall ye be brought back.

86. And those whom they invoke besides God have no power of intercession — only he who bears witness to the Truth, and they know (him).

87. If thou ask them, who created them, they will certainly say, God: how then are they deluded away (from the Truth)?

88. (God has knowledge) of the (Prophet's) cry, "O my Lord! truly these are a people who will not believe!"

89. But turn away from them, and say "Peace!" but soon shall they know!

Chapter 44
Sūrah Ad-Dukhān (The Smoke)
Revealed at Makkah, 59 verses

In the name of God, Most Gracious, Most Merciful.

1. Hā Mïm.

2. By the Book that makes things clear —

3. We sent it down during a Blessed Night: for We (ever) wish to warn (against Evil).

4. In that (night) is made distinct every affair of wisdom,

5. By command, from Our presence. For We (ever) send (revelations),

6. As a Mercy from thy Lord: for He hears and knows (all things);

7. The Lord of the heavens and the earth and all between them, if ye (but) have an assured faith.

8. There is no god but He: it is He Who gives life and gives death — the Lord and Cherisher to you and your earliest ancestors.

9. Yet they play about in doubt.

10. Then watch thou for the Day that the sky will bring forth a kind of smoke (or mist) plainly visible,

11. Enveloping the people: this will be a Penalty Grievous.

12. (They will say:) "Our Lord! remove the Penalty from us for We do really believe!"

13. How shall the Message be (effectual) for them, seeing that an Apostle explaining things clearly has (already) come to them —

14. Yet they turn away from him and say: "Tutored (by others), a man possessed[1]!"

15. We shall indeed remove the Penalty for a while, (but) truly ye will revert (to your ways).

16. One day We shall seize you with a mighty onslaught[2] We will indeed (then) exact Retribution[3]!

17. We did, before them, try the people of Pharaoh: there came to them an apostle most honourable,

18. Saying: "Restore to me the servants of God: I am to you an apostle worthy of all trust;

19. "And be not arrogant as against God: for I come to you with authority manifest[4].

20. "For me, I have sought Safety with my Lord and your Lord, against your injuring me.

21. "If ye believe me not, at least keep yourselves away from me."

22. (But they were aggressive): then he cried to his Lord: "These are indeed a people given to sin."

23. (The reply came): "March forth with My servants by night: for ye are sure to be pursued.

24. "And leave the sea as a furrow[5] (divided). For they are a host (destined) to be drowned."

25. How many were the gardens and springs they left behind.

26. And corn fields and noble buildings.

27. And wealth (and conveniences of life), wherein they had taken such delight!

28. Thus (was their end)! And We made other people inherit (those things)!

---

[1] Mad

[2] Raid, fierce attack

[3] Punishment

[4] Obvious, clear

[5] A trench, hollow between ridges, channel

29. And neither heaven nor earth shed a tear over them: nor were they given a respite[6] (again).

30. We did deliver aforetime the Children of Israel from humiliating Punishment,

31. Inflicted by Pharaoh, for he was arrogant (even) among inordinate[7] transgressors[8].

32. And We chose them aforetime above the nations, knowingly,

33. And granted them Signs in which there was a manifest trial.

34. As to these (Quraish), they say forsooth[9]:

35. "There is nothing beyond our first death, and we shall not be raised again.

36. "Then bring (back) our forefathers if what ye say is true!"

37. What! are they better than the people of Tubba[10] and those who were before them? We destroyed them because they were guilty of sin.

38. We created not the heavens, the earth, and all between them, merely in (idle) sport:

39. We created them not except for just ends: but most of them do not understand.

40. Verily the Day of Sorting Out is the time appointed for all of them —

41. The Day when no protector can avail his client in aught, and no help can they receive.

42. Except such as receive God's Mercy: for He is exalted in Might, Most Merciful.

43. Verily the tree of Zaqqūm

44. Will be the food of the Sinful —

45. Like molten brass; it will boil in their insides,

46. Like the boiling of scalding[11] water.

47. (A voice will cry:) "Seize ye him and drag him into the midst of the Blazing Fire!

---

6 Delay (or opportunity)

7 Immoderate, excessive

8 Those who violate and go beyond bounds of law, decency, etc.,

9 (Used ironically or in a derogatory sense) Truly, no doubt

10 Family name of ancient Himyar kings of Yemen.

11 Boiling

48. "Then pour over his head the Penalty of Boiling Water;

49. "Taste thou (this)! Truly wast thou Mighty, full of honour!

50. "Truly this is what ye used to doubt!"

51. As to the Righteous (they will be) in a position of Security,

52. Among Gardens and Springs;

53. Dressed in fine silk and in rich brocade[12], they will face each other;

54. So; and We shall join them to Companions with beautiful, big, and lustrous[13] eyes.

55. There can they call for every kind of fruit in peace and security;

56. Nor will they there taste Death, except the first Death; and He will preserve them from the Penalty of the Blazing Fire —

57. As a Bounty from thy Lord! That will be the supreme achievement!

58. Verily, We have made this (Qur'an) easy, in thy tongue, in order that they may give heed[14].

59. So wait thou and watch; for they (too) are waiting.

Chapter 45
Sūrah Al-Jāthiyah (The Kneeling Down)
Revealed at Makkah, 37 verses

In the name of God, Most Gracious, Most Merciful.

1. Hā Mīm.

2. The revelation of the Book is from God, the Exalted in power, Full of Wisdom.

3. Verily in the heavens and the earth, are Signs for those who believe.

4. And in the creation of yourselves and the fact that animals are scattered (through the earth), are Signs for those of assured Faith.

---

12 Thick silk
13 Shiny
14 Bear in mind

5. And in the alternation[1] of Night and Day, and the fact that God sends down Sustenance from the sky, and revives[2] therewith the earth after its death, and the change of the winds, are Signs for those that are wise.

6. Such are the Signs of God, which We rehearse[3] to thee in truth: then in what exposition[4] will they believe after (rejecting) God and His Signs?

7. Woe to each sinful dealer in Falsehoods:

8. He hears the Signs of God rehearsed to him, yet is obstinate[5] and lofty[6], as if he had not heard them: then announce to him a Penalty Grievous!

9. And when he learns something of Our Signs, he takes them in jest: for such there will be a humiliating Penalty.

10. In front of them is Hell: and of no profit to them is anything they may have earned, nor any protectors they may have taken to themselves besides God: for them is a tremendous[7] Penalty.

11. This is (true) Guidance: and for those who reject the Signs of their Lord, is a grievous Penalty of abomination.

12. It is God Who has subjected[8] the sea to you, that ships may sail through it by His command, that ye may seek of His Bounty, and that ye may be grateful.

13. And He has subjected to you, as from Him, all that is in the heavens and on earth: behold, in that are Signs indeed for those who reflect[9].

14. Tell those who believe, to forgive those who do not look forward to the Days of God: it is for Him to recompense[10] (for good or ill) each People according to what they have earned.

---

[1] Succession
[2] Gives life
[3] Recount, repeat
[4] Explanation, discourse
[5] Stubborn
[6] Arrogant, proud
[7] Great, dreadful
[8] Pressed into your service
[9] Think, ponder
[10] Reward

15. If anyone does a righteous deed, it enures[11] to the benefit of his own soul; if he does evil, it works against (His own soul). In the end will ye (all) be brought back to your Lord.

16. We did aforetime grant to the Children of Israel the Book, the Power of Command, and Prophethood; We gave them, for Sustenance, things good and pure; and We favored them above the nations.

17. And We granted them Clear Signs in affairs (of Religion): it was only after knowledge had been granted to them that they fell into schisms[12], through insolent envy[13] among themselves. Verily thy Lord will judge between them on the Day of Judgement as to those matters in which they set up differences.

18. Then We put thee on the (right) Way of Religion: so follow thou that (Way), and follow not the desires of those who know not.

19. They will be of no use to thee in the sight of God: it is only wrongdoers (that stand as) protectors, one to another: but God is the Protector of the Righteous.

20. These are clear evidences[14] to men, and a Guidance and Mercy to those of assured Faith.

21. What! do those who seek after evil ways think that We shall hold them equal with those who believe and do righteous deeds — that equal will be their Life and their death? Ill is the judgment that they make.

22. God created the heavens and the earth for just ends, and in order that each soul may find the recompense of what it has earned, and none of them be wronged.

23. Then seest thou such a one as takes as his god his own vain desire? God has, knowing (him as such), left him astray, and sealed his hearing and his heart (and understanding), and put a cover on his sight. Who, then, will guide him after God (has withdrawn Guidance)? Will ye not then receive admonition[15]?

24. And they say: "What is there but our life in this world? We

---

[11] Takes effect

[12] Became divided into mutually hostile parties.

[13] Rivalry

[14] Proofs, eye-opening evidence

[15] Warning, advice

401

shall die and we live, and nothing but Time can destroy us." But of that they have no knowledge: they merely conjecture[16]:

25. And when Our Clear Signs are rehearsed[17] to them, their argument is nothing but this: they say, "Bring (back) our forefathers, if what ye say is true!"

26. Say: "It is God Who gives you life, then gives you death; then He will gather you together for the Day of Judgement about which there is no doubt": but most men do not understand.

27. To God belongs the dominion of the heavens and the earth, and the Day that the Hour of Judgment is established — that Day will the dealers in Falsehood perish!

28. And thou wilt see every sect bowing the knee: every sect will be called to its Record: "This Day shall ye be recompensed[18] for all that ye did!

29. "This Our Record speaks about you with truth: for We were wont[19] to put on record all that ye did."

30. Then, as to those who believed and did righteous deeds, their Lord will admit them to His Mercy: that will be the Achievement for all to see.

31. But as to those who reject God, (to them will be said): "Were not Our Signs rehearsed to you? But ye were arrogant, and were a people given to sin!

32. "And when it was said that the promise of God was true, and that the Hour — there was no doubt about its (coming), ye used to say, 'We know not what is the Hour: we only think it is an idea, and we have no firm assurance.'"

33. Then will appear to them the evil (fruits) of what they did, and they will be completely encircled by that which they used to mock[20] at!

34. It will also be said: "This Day We will forget you as ye forgot the meeting of this Day of yours! And your abode[21] is the Fire, and

---

[16] Guess, surmise, assume
[17] Recited
[18] Rewarded
[19] Accustomed to
[20] Laugh at, make fun of
[21] Home

no helpers have ye!

35. "This, because ye used to take the Signs of God in jest, and the life of the world deceived you." (From) that Day, therefore, they shall not be taken out thence[22], nor shall they be received into Grace.

36. Then Praise be to God, Lord of the heavens and Lord of the earth, Lord and Cherisher of all the Worlds!

37. To Him be Glory throughout the heavens and the earth: and He is Exalted in Power, Full of Wisdom!

Chapter 46
Sūrah Al-Ahqāf (Winding Sand-tracts)
Revealed at Makkah, 35 verses

In the name of God, Most Gracious, Most Merciful.

1. Hā Mīm.

2. The revelation of the Book is from God the Exalted in Power, Full of Wisdom.

3. We created not the heavens and the earth and all between them but for just ends[1], and for a term appointed[2]: but those who reject Faith turn away from that whereof[3] they are warned.

4. Say: "Do ye see what it is ye invoke besides God? Show me what it is they have created on earth, or have they a share in the heavens? Bring me a Book (revealed) before this, or any remnant[4] of knowledge (ye may have), if ye are telling the truth!"

5. And who is more astray than one who invokes, besides God, such as will not answer him to the Day of Judgement, and who (in fact) are unconscious of their call (to them)?

6. And when mankind are gathered together (at the Resurrection), they will be hostile to them and reject their worship (altogether)!

---

[22] From there
[1] Purpose
[2] Fixed period of time
[3] About or against which
[4] Surviving trace of

7. When Our Clear Signs are rehearsed to them, the Unbelievers say, of the Truth when it comes to them: "This is evident sorcery!"

8. Or do they say, "He has forged it"? Say: "Had I forged it, then can ye obtain no single (blessing) for me from God. He knows best of that whereof ye talk (so glibly[5])! Enough is He for a witness between me and you! And He is Oft-Forgiving, Most Merciful."

9. Say: "I am no bringer of newfangled[6] doctrine[7] among the apostles, nor do I know what will be done with me or with you. I follow but that which is revealed to me by inspiration: I am but a Warner open and clear."

10. Say: "See ye? If (this teaching) be from God, and ye reject it, and a witness from among the Children of Israel testifies to its similarity (with earlier scriptures[8]), and has believed while ye are arrogant, (how unjust ye are!) truly, God guides not a people unjust."

11. The Unbelievers say of those who believe: "If (this Message) were a good thing, (such men) would not have gone to it first, before us!" and seeing that they guide not themselves thereby, they will say, "This is an (old), old falsehood!"

12. And before this, was the Book of Moses as a guide and a mercy; and this Book confirms (it) in the Arabic tongue; to admonish the unjust, and as Glad Tidings[9] to those who do right.

13. Verily those who say, "Our Lord is God," and remain firm (on that Path) — on them shall be no fear, nor shall they grieve.

14. Such shall be Companions of the Garden, dwelling therein (for aye[10]): a recompense for their (good) deeds.

15. We have enjoined[11] on man kindness to his parents: in pain did his mother bear him, and in pain did she give him birth. The carrying of the (child) to his weaning[12] is (a period of) thirty months. At length, when he reaches the age of full strength and attains forty years, he

---

[5] Readily, carelessly

[6] Different from the old

[7] Faith, religion, creed

[8] Revealed Books

[9] Happy news

[10] Forever

[11] Commanded, prescribed

[12] To accustom an infant to food other than milk.

says, "O my Lord! grant me that I may be grateful for Thy favor which Thou hast bestowed upon me, and upon both my parents, and that I may work righteousness such as Thou mayest approve; and be gracious to me in my issue[13]. Truly have I turned to Thee and truly do I bow (to Thee) in Islam."

16. Such are they from whom We shall accept the best of their deeds and pass by their ill deeds: (they shall be) among the Companions of the Garden: a promise of truth, which was made to them (in this life).

17. But (there is one) who says to his parents, "Fie[14] on you! Do ye hold out the promise to me that I shall be raised up, even though generations have passed before me (without rising again)?" And they two seek God's aid, (and rebuke[15] the son): "Woe to thee! have Faith! For the promise of God is true." But he says, "This is nothing but tales of the ancients!"

18. Such are they against whom is proved the Sentence among the previous generations of Jinns and men, that have passed away; for they will be (utterly[16]) lost.

19. And to all are (assigned[17]) degrees according to the deeds which they (have done), and in order that (God) may recompense their deeds, and no injustice be done to them.

20. And on the Day that the Unbelievers will be placed before the Fire, (it will be said to them): "Ye received your good things in the life of the world, and ye took your pleasure out of them: but today shall ye be recompensed with a Penalty of humiliation: for that ye were arrogant on earth without just cause, and that ye (ever) transgressed."

21. Mention (Hūd) one of 'Ād's (own) brethren: behold, he warned his people about the winding Sand-tracts: but there have been Warners before him and after him: "Worship ye none other than God: truly I fear for you the Penalty of a Mighty Day."

---

13 Offspring
14 An expression of disgust
15 Admonish, reprimand
16 Completely
17 Allotted

22. They said: "Hast thou come in order to turn us aside[18] from Our gods? Then bring upon us the (calamity) with which thou dost threaten us, if thou art telling the truth!"

23. He said: "The Knowledge (of when it will come) is only with God: I proclaim to you the mission on which I have been sent: but I see that ye are a people in ignorance!"...

24. Then, when they saw the (Penalty in the shape of) a cloud traversing[19] the sky, coming to meet their valleys, they said, "This cloud will give us rain!" "Nay, it is the (calamity) ye were asking to be hastened! — a wind wherein is a Grievous Penalty!

25. "Everything will it destroy by the command of its Lord!" Then by the morning they — nothing was to be seen but (the ruins of) their houses! Thus do We recompense those given to sin!

26. And We had firmly established them in a (prosperity and) power which We have not given to you (ye Quraish!) and We had endowed them with (faculties[20] of) hearing, seeing, heart and intellect: but of no profit to them were their (faculties of) hearing, sight, and heart and intellect, when they went on rejecting the Signs of God; and they were (completely) encircled by that which they used to mock at!

27. We destroyed aforetime populations round about you; and We have shown the Signs in various ways, that they may turn (to Us).

28. Why then was no help forthcoming to them from those whom they worshipped as gods, besides God, as a means of access (to God)? Nay, they left them in the lurch[21]: but that was their Falsehood and their invention[22].

29. Behold, We turned towards thee a company of Jinns (quietly) listening to the Qur'an: when they stood in the presence thereof, they said, "Listen in silence!" When the (reading) was finished, they returned to their people, to warn (them of their sins).

30. They said, "O our people! We have heard a Book revealed after Moses, confirming what came before it: it guides (men) to the Truth and to a Straight Path.

---

[18] Away from

[19] Crossing

[20] Abilities

[21] Most difficult time or turn

[22] Fabrication

31. "O our people, hearken[23] to the one who invites (you) to God, and believe in him: He will forgive you your faults, and deliver you from a Penalty Grievous.

32. "If any does not hearken to the one who invites (Us) to God, he cannot frustrate[24] (God's Plan) on earth, and no protectors can he have besides God: such men (wander) in manifest error."

33. See they not that God, Who created the heavens and the earth, and never wearied[25] with their creation, is able to give life to the dead? Yea, verily He has power over all things.

34. And on the Day that the Unbelievers will be placed before the Fire, (they will be asked,) "Is this not the Truth? " They will say, "Yea, by our Lord!" (One will say:) "Then taste ye the Penalty, for that ye were wont[26] to deny (Truth)!"

35. Therefore patiently persevere[27], as did (all) apostles of inflexible[28] purpose; and be in no haste about the (Unbelievers). On the Day that they see the (Punishment) promised them, (it will be) as if they had not tarried[29] more than an hour in a single day. (Thine but) to proclaim the Message: but shall any be destroyed except those who transgress[30]?

Chapter 47
Sūrah Muhammad (Muhammad the Prophet)
Revealed at Madinah, 38 verses

In the name of God, Most Gracious, Most Merciful.

1. Those who reject God and hinder (men) from the Path of God — their deeds will God render astray (from their mark).

2. But those who believe and work deeds of righteousness, and

---

[23] Listen

[24] Thwart, defeat

[25] Exhausted

[26] Used to, were accustomed to

[27] Be steadfast, constant

[28] Strong

[29] Stayed

[30] Violate the bounds of law and decency.

believe in the (Revelation) sent down to Muhammad — for it is the Truth from their Lord, He will remove from them their ills and improve their condition.

3. This because those who reject God follow vanities[1], while those who believe follow the Truth from their Lord: Thus does God set forth for men their lessons by similitudes[2].

4. Therefore, when ye meet the Unbelievers (in fight), smite[3] at their necks; at length, when ye have thoroughly subdued[4] them, bind a bond[5] firmly (on them): thereafter (is the time for) either generosity or ransom[6]: Until the war lays down its burdens[7]. Thus (are ye commanded): but if it had been God's Will, He could certainly have exacted retribution[8] from them (Himself); but (He lets you fight) in order to test you, some with others. But those who are slain[9] in the way of God, He will never let their deeds be lost.

5. Soon will He guide them and improve their condition,

6. And admit them to the Garden which He has announced for them.

7. O ye who believe! if ye will aid (the cause of) God, He will aid you, and plant your feet firmly.

8. But those who reject (God), for them is destruction, and (God) will render their deeds astray (from their mark)[10].

9. That is because they hate the Revelation of God; so He has made their deeds fruitless.

10. Do they not travel through the earth, and see what was the End of those before them (who did evil)? God brought utter[11] destruction on them, and similar (fates await) those who reject God.

11. That is because God is the Protector of those who believe,

---

[1] Falsehood, baseless things or ideas
[2] Parables
[3] Strike
[4] Defeated, brought them under control
[5] Tie, i.e., bind them and make them prisoners.
[6] Payment in return for their freedom.
[7] That is, until the war comes to an end.
[8] Punishment
[9] Killed
[10] Their works will produce no results.
[11] Complete

but those who reject God have no protector.

12. Verily God will admit those who believe and do righteous deeds, to Gardens beneath which rivers flow; while those who reject God will enjoy (this world) and eat as cattle eat; and the Fire will be their abode.

13. And how many cities, with more power than thy city which has driven thee out, have We destroyed (for their sins)? And there was none to aid them.

14. Is then one who is on a clear (Path) from his Lord, no better than one to whom the evil of his conduct seems pleasing, and such as follow their own lusts[12]?

15. (Here is) a Parable of the Garden which the righteous are promised: in it are rivers of water incorruptible[13]: rivers of milk of which the taste never changes; rivers of wine, a joy to those who drink; and rivers of honey pure and clear. In it there are for them all kinds of fruits, and Grace[14] from their Lord. (Can those in such Bliss[15]) be compared to such as shall dwell forever in the Fire, and be given, to drink, boiling water, so that it cuts up their bowels (to pieces)?

16. And among them are men who listen to thee, but in the end, when they go out from thee, they say to those who have received Knowledge: "What is it he said just then?" Such are men whose hearts God has sealed, and who follow their own lusts.

17. But to those who receive Guidance, He increases (the light of) Guidance, and bestows on them their Piety and Restraint[16] (from evil).

18. Do they then only wait for the Hour, that it should come on them of a sudden? But already have come some tokens[17] thereof, and when it (actually) is on them, how can they benefit then by their admonition[18]?

---

[12] Desires

[13] That which does not change or become bad.

[14] Mercy

[15] Happiness and contentment.

[16] The strength to keep away from

[17] Signs

[18] Advice, reminder

19. Know, therefore, that there is no god but God, and ask forgiveness for thy fault, and for the men and women who believe: for God knows how ye move about and how ye dwell in your homes.

20. Those who believe say, "Why is not a Sürah sent down (for us)?" But when a Sura of basic or categorical[19] meaning is revealed, and fighting is mentioned therein, thou wilt see those in whose hearts is a disease looking at thee with a look of one in swoon[20] at the approach of death: but more fitting for them —

21. Were it to obey and say what is just, and when a matter is resolved[21] on, it were best for them if they were true to God.

22. Then, is it to be expected of you, if ye were put in authority, that ye will do mischief in the land, and break your ties of kith and kin[22]?

23. Such are the men whom God has cursed for He has made them deaf and blinded their sight.

24. Do they not then earnestly[23] seek to understand the Qur'an, or are their hearts locked up by them?

25. Those who turn back as apostates[24] after Guidance was clearly shown to them, the Evil One has instigated[25] them and buoyed[26] them up with false hopes.

26. This, because they said to those who hate what God has revealed, "We will obey you in part of (this) matter"; but God knows their (inner) secrets.

27. But how (will it be) when the angels take their souls at death, and smite their faces and their backs?

28. This because they followed that which called forth the Wrath of God, and they hated God's good pleasure; so He made their deeds of no effect.

29. Or do those in whose hearts is a disease, think that God will

---

[19] Decisive
[20] Fainting
[21] Settled, decided
[22] Blood relations
[23] Seriously
[24] Abandoning faith, turning back after accepting guidance.
[25] Urged on, incited
[26] Encouraged, kept afloat
[27] Malice, animosity, spite

not bring to light all their rancor[27]?

30. Had We so willed, We could have shown them up to thee, and thou shouldst have known them by their marks: but surely thou wilt know them by the tone of their speech! And God knows all that ye do.

31. And We shall try you until We test those among you who strive their utmost and persevere[28] in patience; and We shall try your reported (mettle[29]).

32. Those who reject God, hinder (men) from the Path of God, and resist the Apostle, after Guidance has been clearly shown to them, will not injure God in the least, but He will make their deeds of no effect.

33. O ye who believe! obey God, and obey the Apostle, and make not vain[30] your deeds!

34. Those who reject God, and hinder (men) from the Path of God, then die rejecting God, God will not forgive them.

35. Be not weary and faint-hearted crying for peace. When ye should be Uppermost: for God is with you, and will never put you in loss for your (good) deeds.

36. The life of this world is but play and amusement: and if ye believe and guard against evil, He will grant you your recompense, and will not ask you (to give up) your possessions[31].

37. If He were to ask you for all of them, and press you, ye would covetously[32] withhold, and He would bring out all your ill-feeling.

38. Behold, ye are those invited to spend (of your substance[33]) in the way of God: but among you are some that are niggardly[34]. But any who are niggardly are so at the expense of their own souls. But God is free of all wants, and it is ye that are needy. If ye turn back (from the Path), He will substitute[35] in your stead[36] another people; then they would not be like you!

---

[28] Are constant

[29] Courage and constancy, fortitude

[30] Worthless

[31] Wealth, property

[32] Eagerly

[33] Wealth

[34] Miserly, stingy

[35] Replace with

[36] In your place

Chapter 48
Sūrah Al-Fath (The Victory)
Revealed at Madinah, 29 verses

In the name of God, Most Gracious, Most Merciful.

1. Verily We have granted thee a manifest[1] Victory:

2. That God may forgive thee thy faults of the past and those to follow; fulfil His favor to thee; and guide thee on the Straight Way;

3. And that God may help thee with powerful help.

4. It is He who sent down Tranquillity[2] into the hearts of the Believers, that they may add Faith to their Faith; for to God belong the Forces of the heavens and the earth; and God is full of Knowledge and Wisdom —

5. That He may admit the men and women who believe, to Gardens beneath[3] which rivers flow, to dwell therein for aye[4], and remove their ills from them — and that is, in the sight of God, the highest achievement (for man) —

6. And that He may punish the Hypocrites[5], men and women, and the Polytheists[6], men and women, who imagine an evil opinion of God. On them is a round of Evil: the Wrath of God is on them: He has cursed them and got Hell ready for them: and evil is it for a destination.

7. For to God belong the Forces of the heavens and the earth; and God is Exalted in Power, Full of Wisdom.

8. We have truly sent thee as a witness, as a bringer of Glad Tidings[7], and as a Warner:

9. In order that ye (o men) may believe in God and His Apostle, that ye may assist and honour Him, and celebrate His praises morning and evening.

---

[1] Clear, obvious

[2] Calm, serenity

[3] Under

[4] Forever

[5] Those who pretend they are Muslims, but in reality are not.

[6] Those who worship false gods or idols besides One True God.

[7] Happy news.

10. Verily those who plight[8] their fealty[9] to thee do no less than plight their fealty to God: the Hand of God is over their hands: Then anyone who violates His oath, does so to the harm of his own soul, and anyone who fulfills what he has covenanted[10] with God, God will soon grant him a great Reward.

11. The desert Arabs who lagged[11] behind will say to thee: "We were engaged in (looking after) our flocks and herds, and our families; do thou then ask forgiveness for us." They say with their tongues what is not in their hearts. Say: "Who then has any power at all (to intervene[12]) on your behalf with God, if His will is to give you some loss or to give you some profit? but God is well acquainted with all that ye do.

12. "Nay, ye thought that the Apostle and the Believers would never return to their families; this seemed pleasing in your hearts, and ye conceived an evil thought, for ye are a people lost (in wickedness)."

13. And if any believe not in God and His Apostle, We have prepared, for those who reject God, a Blazing Fire!

14. To God belongs the dominion[13] of the heavens and the earth: He forgives whom He wills, and He punishes whom He wills: but God is Oft-Forgiving, Most Merciful.

15. Those who lagged behind (will say), when ye (are free to) march and take booty[14] (in war): "Permit us to follow you." They wish to change God's decree[15]: Say: "Not thus will ye follow us: God has already declared (this) beforehand": then they will say, "but ye are jealous of us." Nay, but little do they understand (such things).

16. Say to the desert Arabs who lagged behind: "Ye shall be summoned (to fight) against a people given to vehement[16] war: then

---

8 Pledge their faith, promise
9 Allegiance, loyalty, devotion
10 Solemnly promised
11 Lingered
12 Intercede
13 Sovereignty, kingdom
14 Spoils of war.
15 Decision
16 Fierce

413

shall ye fight, or they shall submit. Then if ye show obedience, God will grant you a goodly reward, but if ye turn back as ye did before, He will punish you with a grievous Penalty."

17. No blame is there on the blind, nor is there blame on the lame, nor on one ill (if he joins not the war): but he that obeys God and His Apostle, (God) will admit him to Gardens beneath which rivers flow; and he who turns back, (God) will punish him with a grievous Penalty.

18. God's Good Pleasure was on the Believers when they swore Fealty to thee under the Tree: He knew what was in their hearts, and He sent down tranquillity to them, and He rewarded them with a speedy Victory;

19. And many gains will they acquire (besides): and God is Exalted in Power, Full of Wisdom.

20. God has promised you many gains that ye shall acquire, and He has given you these beforehand; and He has restrained the hands of men from you; that it may be a Sign for the Believers, and that He may guide you to a Straight Path;

21. And other gains (there are), which are not within your power, but which God has compassed[17]: and God has power over all things.

22. If the Unbelievers should fight you, they would certainly turn their backs; then would they find neither protector nor helper.

23. (Such has been) the practice (approved) of God already in the past: no change wilt thou find in the practice (approved) of God.

24. And it is He who has restrained their hands from you and your hands from them in the midst of Makkah, after that He gave you the victory over them. And God sees well all that ye do.

25. They are the ones who denied revelation and hindered you from the Sacred Mosque and the sacrificial animals, detained from reaching their place of sacrifice. Had there not been believing men and believing women whom ye did not know that ye were trampling[18] down and on whose account a crime would have accrued[19] to you without (your) knowledge. (God would have allowed you to force

---

[17] Has them within His knowledge and power.

[18] Tread underfoot, press down or crush

[19] Collected (against you), will have afflicted

your way, but He held back your hands) that He may admit to His mercy whom He will. If they had been apart[20], We should certainly have punished the Unbelievers among them with a grievous punishment.

26. While the Unbelievers got up in their hearts heat and cant[21] — the heat and cant of Ignorance — God sent down His tranquillity to His Apostle and to the Believers, and made them stick close to the command of self-restraint; and well were they entitled[22] to it and worthy of it. And God has full knowledge of all things.

27. Truly did God fulfil the vision for His Apostle: Ye shall enter the Sacred Mosque, if God wills, with minds secure, heads shaved, hair cut short, and without fear. For He knew what ye knew not, and He granted, besides this, a speedy victory.

28. It is He who has sent His Apostle with Guidance and the Religion of Truth, to proclaim it over all religion: and enough is God for a Witness.

29. Muhammad is the Apostle of God; and those who are with him are strong against Unbelievers, (but) compassionate amongst each other. Thou wilt see them bow and prostrate themselves (in prayer), seeking Grace from God and (His) Good Pleasure. On their faces are their marks, (being) the traces of their prostration. This is their similitude in the Torah; and their similitude in the Gospel is: like a seed which sends forth its blade[23], then makes it strong; it then becomes thick, and it stands on its own stem, (filling) the sowers with wonder and delight. As a result, it fills the Unbelievers with rage at them. God has promised those among them who believe and do righteous deeds Forgiveness, and a great Reward.

---

[20] Separate from others
[21] Hypocrisy, insincere use of words implying piety.
[22] Qualified for it.
[23] A flat spear-shaped leaf of grass and cereals.

Chapter 49
Sürah Al-Hujurat (The Inner Apartments)
Revealed at Madinah, 18 verses

In the name of God, Most Gracious, Most Merciful.

1. O ye who believe! put not yourselves forward before God and His Apostle: But fear God: for God is He Who hears and knows all things.

2. O ye who believe! raise not your voices above the voice of the Prophet, nor speak aloud to him in talk, as ye may speak aloud to one another, lest your deeds become vain and ye perceive not.

3. Those that lower their voice in the presence of God's Apostle — their hearts has God tested for piety: for them is Forgiveness and a great Reward.

4. Those who shout out to thee from without the Inner Apartments — most of them lack understanding.

5. If only they had patience until thou couldst come out to them, it would be best for them: but God is Oft-Forgiving, Most Merciful.

6. O ye who believe! if a wicked person comes to you with any news, ascertain the truth, lest ye harm people unwittingly[1], and afterwards become full of repentance for what ye have done.

7. And know that among you is God's Apostle: were he, in many matters, to follow your (wishes), ye would certainly fall into misfortune: but God has endeared the Faith to you, and has made it beautiful in your hearts, and He has made hateful to you unbelief, wickedness, and rebellion: such indeed are those who walk in righteousness —

8. A grace and favor from God; and God is full of Knowledge and Wisdom.

9. If two parties among the Believers fall into a quarrel make ye peace between them: but if one of them transgresses beyond bounds against the other, then fight ye (all) against the one that transgresses until it complies with the command of God; but if it complies, then make peace between them with justice, and be fair: for God loves those who are fair (and just).

---

[1] Unknowingly

10. The Believers are but a single Brotherhood: So make peace and reconciliation between your two (contending[2]) brothers: And fear God, that ye may receive Mercy.

11. O ye who believe! let not some men among you laugh at others: it may be that the (latter) are better than the (former): Nor let some women laugh at others: it may be that the (latter) are better than the (former): nor defame[3] nor be sarcastic[4] to each other, nor call each other by (offensive[5]) nicknames[6]: Ill-seeming is a name connoting[7] wickedness, (to be used of one) after he has believed: And those who do not desist[8] are (indeed) doing wrong.

12. O ye who believe! avoid suspicion as much (as possible): for suspicion in some cases is a sin: and spy not on each other, nor speak ill of each other behind their backs. Would any of you like to eat the flesh of his dead brother? Nay, ye would abhor[9] it...but fear God: for God is Oft-Returning, Most Merciful.

13. O mankind! We created you from a single (pair) of a male and a female, and made you into nations and tribes, that ye may know each other (not that ye may despise[10] each other). Verily the most honoured of you in the sight of God is (he who is) the most righteous of you. And God has full knowledge and is well acquainted (with all things).

14. The desert Arabs say, "We believe." Say, "Ye have no faith; but ye (only) say, 'We have submitted our wills to God.' For not yet has Faith entered your hearts. But if ye obey God and His Apostle, He will not belittle[11] aught of your deeds: for God is Oft-Forgiving, Most Merciful."

---

[2] Disputing, at odds

[3] Slander

[4] Scornful

[5] Insulting

[6] A name jokingly or admiringly or contemptuously added to or used in place of a person's proper name.

[7] Suggesting or indicating

[8] Refrain

[9] Hate, despise

[10] Hate

[11] Decrease, diminish

15. Only those are Believers who have believed in God and His Apostle, and have never since doubted, but have striven with their belongings and their persons in the Cause of God: Such are the sincere ones.

16. Say: "What! Will ye instruct God about your Religion?" but God knows all that is in the heavens and on earth: He has full knowledge of all things.

17. They impress on thee as a favor that they have embraced Islam. Say, "Count not your Islam as a favor upon me: Nay, God has conferred[12] a favor upon you that He has guided you to the Faith, if ye be true and sincere.

18. "Verily God knows the secrets of the heavens and the earth: and God sees well all that ye do."

Chapter 50
Sūrah Qāf (Qaf)
Revealed at Makkah, 45 verses

In the name of God, Most Gracious, Most Merciful.

1. Qāf. By the Glorious Qur'an (Thou art God's Apostle).

2. But they wonder that there has come to them a Warner from among themselves. So the Unbelievers say: "This is a wonderful thing!

3. "What! when we die and become dust, (shall we live again?). That is a (sort of) Return far (from our understanding)."

4. We already know how much of them the earth takes away: with Us is a Record guarding (the full account).

5. But they deny the truth when it comes to them: So they are in a confused state.

6. Do they not look at the sky above them? How We have made it and adorned[1] it, and there are no flaws[2] in it?

---

[12] Bestowed
[1] Beautified
[2] Defects

7. And the earth—We have spread it out, and set thereon mountains standing firm, and produced therein every kind of beautiful growth (in pairs) —

8. To be observed and commemorated[3] by every devotee[4] turning (to God).

9. And We send down from the sky Rain charged[5] with blessing, and We produce therewith Gardens and Grain for harvests;

10. And tall (and stately[6]) palm trees, with shoots[7] of fruit stalks[8], piled one over another —

11. As sustenance for (God's) Servants; and We give (new) life therewith to land that is dead: Thus will be the Resurrection.

12. Before them was denied (the Hereafter) by the people of Noah[9], the Companions of the Rass[10], the Thamüd,

13. The 'Ãd, Pharaoh, the Brethren of Lüt,

14. The Companions of the Wood, and the people of Tubba[11]; each one (of them) rejected the Apostles, and My warning was duly fulfilled (in them).

15. Were We then weary with the first Creation, that they should be in confused doubt about a new Creation?

16. It was We who created man and We know what dark suggestions his soul makes to him: for We are nearer to him than (his) jugular[12] vein.

17. Behold, two (guardian angels) appointed to learn (his doings) learn (and note them), one sitting on the right and one on the left.

18. Not a word does he utter but there is a sentinel[13] by him, ready (to note it).

---

[3] Remembered, celebrated

[4] Devoted worshipper or servant

[5] Full of, saturated with

[6] Grand, imposing

[7] Buds, blossom, sprout

[8] Offshoot, small branch

[9] See Qur'an 11:25-48, 71:1-28

[10] See Qur'an 25:38. According to some they were the people of Madian to whom Prophet Shuaib was sent to warn.

[11] See also Qur'an 44:37

[12] Life-vein.

[13] A watcher

19. And the stupor[14] of death will bring truth (before his eyes): "This was the thing which thou wast trying to escape!"

20. And the Trumpet shall be blown: that will be the Day whereof warning (had been given).

21. And there will come forth every soul: with each will be an (angel) to drive, and an (angel) to bear witness.

22. (It will be said:) "Thou wast heedless of this; now have We removed thy veil, and sharp is thy sight this Day!"

23. And his companion will say: "Here is (his record) ready with me!"

24. (The sentence will be:) "Throw, throw into Hell every contumacious[15] Rejecter (of God)! —

25. "Who forbade what was good, transgressed all bounds, cast doubts and suspicions;

26. "Who set up another god besides God: throw him into a severe Penalty."

27. His companion will say: "Our Lord! I did not make him transgress, but he was (himself) far astray."

28. He will say: "Dispute not with each other in My Presence: I had already in advance sent you Warning.

29. "The Word changes not before Me, and I do not the least injustice to My Servants."

30. One day We will ask Hell, "Art thou filled to the full?" It will say, "are there any more (to come)?"

31. And the Garden will be brought nigh[16] to the righteous — no more a thing distant.

32. (A voice will say:) "This is what was promised for you — for everyone who turned (to God) in sincere repentance, who kept (his law).

33. "Who feared (God) Most Gracious unseen, and brought a heart turned in devotion (to Him):

34. "Enter ye therein in Peace and Security; this is a Day of Eternal Life!"

---

[14] Helpless amazement, dazed state
[15] Stubbornly or willfully disobedient, rebellious
[16] Near

35. There will be for them therein all that they wish — and more besides in Our Presence.

36. But how many generations before them did We destroy (for their Sins) — stronger in power than they? Then did they wander through the land: Was there any place of escape (for them)?

37. Verily in this is a Message for any that has a heart and understanding or who gives ear and earnestly[17] witnesses (the truth).

38. We created the heavens and the earth and all between them in Six Days, nor did any sense of weariness touch Us.

39. Bear, then with patience, all that they say, and celebrate the praises of thy Lord, before the rising of the sun and before (its) setting,

40. And during part of the night, (also,) celebrate His praises, and (so likewise) after the postures of adoration[18].

41. And listen for the Day when the Caller will call out from a place quite near —

42. The Day when they will hear a (mighty) Blast[19] in (very) truth): that will be the Day of Resurrection.

43. Verily it is We Who give Life and Death; and to Us is the Final Goal —

44. The Day when the Earth will be rent asunder, from (men) hurrying out: that will be a gathering together — quite easy for Us.

45. We know best what they say; and thou art not one to overawe[20] them by force. So admonish[21] with the Qur'an such as fear My Warning!

---

[17] Seriously

[18] That is, after the regular prayer.

[19] Loud sound

[20] Compel by force, daunt by arousing fear or reverence.

[21] Warn

Chapter 51
Sūrah Adh-Dhariyat (The Winds That Scatter)
Revealed at Makkah, 60 verses

In the name of God, Most Gracious, Most Merciful.

1. By the (Winds) that scatter broadcast[1];

2. And those that lift and bear away heavy weights;

3. And those that flow with ease and gentleness;

4. And those that distribute and apportion[2] by command —

5. Verily that which ye are promised is true;

6. And verily Judgment and Justice must indeed come to pass.

7. By the Sky with (its) numerous Paths,

8. Truly ye are in a doctrine[3] discordant[4],

9. Through which are deluded[5] (away from the Truth) such as would be deluded.

10. Woe to the falsehood-mongers —

11. Those who (flounder[6]) heedless in a flood of confusion:

12. They ask, "When will be the Day of Judgment and Justice?"

13. (It will be) a Day when they will be tried (and tested) over the Fire!

14. "Taste ye your trial! this is what ye used to ask to be hastened!"

15. As to the Righteous, they will be in the midst of Gardens and Springs,

16. Taking joy in the things which their Lord gives them, because, before then, they lived a good life.

17. They were in the habit of sleeping but little by night,

18. And in the hours of early dawn, they (were found) praying for Forgiveness;

19. And in their wealth and possessions (was remembered) the right of the (needy), him who asked, and him who (for some reason) was prevented (from asking).

---

[1] Scatter or spread freely.

[2] Give as due share

[3] Creed, beliefs

[4] Not in harmony, disagreeing, conflicting

[5] Deceived

[6] Struggle and plunge (as) in mud or when wading, manage badly or with difficulty.

20. On the earth are Signs for those of assured Faith,

21. As also in your own selves: will ye not then see?

22. And in heaven is your Sustenance, as (also) that which ye are promised.

23. Then, by the Lord of heaven and earth, this is the very Truth, as much as the fact that ye can speak intelligently to each other.

24. Has the story reached thee, of the honoured guests of Abraham?

25. Behold, they entered His presence, and said: "Peace!" He said, "Peace!" (and thought, "These seem) unusual people."

26. Then he turned quickly to his household, brought out a fatted calf.

27. And placed it before them...He said, "Will ye not eat?"

28. (When they did not eat), he conceived a fear of them. They said, "Fear not," and they gave him glad tidings of a son endowed with knowledge.

29. But his wife came forward (laughing) aloud: she smote her forehead and said: "A barren old woman!"

30. They said, "Even so has thy Lord spoken: and He is full of Wisdom and Knowledge."

31. (Abraham) said: "And what, O ye Messengers, is your errand[7] (now)?"

32. They said, "We have been sent to a people (deep) in sin —

33. "To bring on, on them (a shower of) stones of clay (brimstone[8]),

34. "Marked as from thy Lord for those who trespass[9] beyond bounds."

35. Then We evacuated[10] those of the Believers who were there.

36. But We found not there any just (Muslim) persons except in one house:

37. And We left there Sign for such as fear the Grievous Penalty.

38. And in Moses (was another Sign): Behold, We sent him to Pharaoh, with authority manifest[11].

39. But (Pharaoh) turned back with his Chiefs, and said, "A

---

[7] Purpose or mission.

[8] Sulphur

[9] Transgress, violate or infringe upon.

[10] Vacated

[11] Clear, obvious

sorcerer, or one possessed!"

40. So We took him and his forces, and threw them into the sea: and his was the blame.

41. And in the 'Ād (people) (was another Sign): Behold, We sent against them the devastating[12] Wind:

42. It left nothing whatever that it came up against, but reduced it to ruin and rottenness.

43. And in the Thamūd (was another Sign): Behold, they were told, "Enjoy (your brief day) for a little while!"

44. But they insolently[13] defied[14] the command of their Lord: so the stunning[15] noise (of an earthquake) seized them, even while they were looking on.

45. Then they could not even stand (on their feet), nor could they help themselves.

46. So were the people of Noah before them: for they wickedly transgressed.

47. With the power and skill did We construct the Firmament[16]: for it is We Who create the vastness of Space.

48. And We have spread out the (spacious) earth: how excellently We do spread out!

49. And of everything We have created pairs: that ye may receive instruction.

50. Hasten ye then (at once) to God: I am from Him a warner to you, clear and open!

51. And make not another an object of worship with God: I am from Him a Warner to you, clear and open!

52. Similarly, no apostle came to the Peoples before them, but they said (of him) in like manner, "A sorcerer, or one possessed!"

53. Is this the legacy[17] they have transmitted, one to another? Nay, they are themselves a people transgressing beyond bounds!

54. So turn away from them: not thine is the blame.

---

[12] Disastrous

[13] Rudely, arrogantly

[14] Resisted, spurned

[15] Shocking

[16] Vault of heaven with its clouds and stars.

[17] Heritage, tradition

55. But teach (thy Message): for teaching benefits the Believers.

56. I have only created Jinns and men, that they may serve Me.

57. No sustenance do I require of them nor do I require that they should feed Me.

58. For God is He Who gives (all) Sustenance, Lord of Power, Steadfast (forever).

59. For the wrongdoers, their portion is like unto the portion of their fellows (of earlier generations): then let them not ask Me to hasten (that portion)!

60. Woe, then, to the Unbelievers, on account of that Day of theirs which they have been promised!

Chapter 52
Sürah At-Tür (The Mount)
Revealed at Makkah, 49 verses

In the name of God, Most Gracious, Most Merciful.

1. By the Mount (of Revelation);

2. By a Decree Inscribed[1]

3. In a Scroll[2] unfolded;

4. By the much-frequented Fane[3];

5. By the Canopy Raised High;

6. And by the Ocean filled with Swell[4] —

7. Verily, the Doom[5] of thy Lord will indeed come to pass —

8. There is none can avert it —

9. On the Day when the Firmament will be in dreadful commotion[6].

10. And the mountain will fly hither and thither.

11. Then woe that Day to those that treat (truth) as Falsehood —

12. That play (and paddle) in shallow trifles.

---

[1] Recorded, written

[2] A roll of paper or parchment

[3] Temple, house of worship

[4] A series of long unbroken waves.

[5] (Arch.) Sentence, decision, condemnation

[6] Disturbance

13. That Day shall they be thrust down to the Fire of Hell, irresistibly.

14. "This," it will be said, "is the Fire — which ye were wont to deny!

15. "Is this then a fake, or is it ye that do not see?

16. "Burn ye therein: the same is it to you whether ye bear it with patience, or not: Ye but receive the recompense of your (own) deeds."

17. As to the Righteous, they will be in Gardens, and in Happiness —

18. Enjoying the (Bliss) which their Lord hath bestowed on them, and their Lord shall deliver them from the Penalty of the Fire.

19. (To them will be said:) "Eat and drink ye, with profit and health, because of your (good) deeds."

20. They will recline (with ease) on Thrones (of dignity) arranged in ranks; and We shall join them to Companions, with beautiful, big and lustrous eyes.

21. And those who believe and whose families follow them in Faith — to them shall We join their families: nor shall We deprive them (of the fruit) of aught of their works: (Yet) is each individual in pledge for his deeds.

22. And We shall bestow on them, of fruit and meat, anything they shall desire.

23. They shall there exchange, one with another, a (loving) cup free of frivolity[7], free of all taint[8] of ill.

24. Round about them will serve, (devoted) to them, youths (handsome) as Pearls well-guarded.

25. They will advance to each other, engaging in mutual enquiry.

26. They will say: "Aforetime, We were not without fear for the sake of our people.

27. "But God has been good to us, and has delivered us from the Penalty of the Scorching Wind.

28. "Truly we did call unto Him from of old: truly it is He, the Beneficent, the Merciful."

29. Therefore proclaim thou the praises (of thy Lord): For by the

---

[7] Silliness, nonsense

[8] Stain

Grace of thy Lord, thou art no (vulgar[9]) soothsayer[10], nor art thou one possessed.

30. Or do they say — "A Poet! we await for him some calamity (hatched[11]) by Time!"

31. Say thou: "Await ye! I too will wait along with you!"

32. Is it that their faculties of understanding urge them to this, or are they but a people transgressing beyond bounds?

33. Or do they say, "He fabricated the (Message)"? Nay, they have no faith!

34. Let them then produce a recital[12] like unto it — if (it be) they speak the Truth!

35. Were they created of nothing, or were they themselves the creators?

36. Or did they create the heavens and the earth? Nay, they have no firm belief.

37. Or are the Treasures of thy Lord with them, or are they the managers (of affairs)?

38. Or have they a ladder, by which they can (climb up to heaven and) listen (to its secrets)? Then let (such a) listener of theirs produce a manifest proof.

39. Or has He only daughters and ye have sons?

40. Or is it that thou dost ask for a reward, so that they are burdened with a load of debt? —

41. Or that the Unseen is in their hands, and they write it down?

42. Or do they intend a plot (against thee)? But those who defy God are themselves involved in a Plot!

43. Or have they a god other then God? Exalted is God far above the things they associate with Him!

44. Were they to see a piece of the sky falling (on them), they would (only) say: "Clouds gathered in heaps!"

45. So leave them alone until they encounter that Day of theirs,

---

9 Common, coarse

10 Foreteller, diviner

11 Produced, brought about by

12 A book, a narration

wherein they shall (perforce[13]) swoon[14] (with terror) —

46. The Day when their plotting will avail them nothing and no help shall be Given them.

47. And verily, for those who do wrong, there is another punishment besides this: but most of them understand not.

48. Now await in patience the command of thy Lord: for verily thou art in our eyes: and celebrate the praises of thy Lord the while thou standest forth.

49. And for part of the night also praise thou Him — and at the retreat of the stars!

Chapter 53
Sürah An-Najm (The Star)
Revealed at Makkah, 62 verses

In the name of God, Most Gracious, Most Merciful.

1. By the Star when it goes down —

2. Your Companion is neither astray nor being misled,

3. Nor does he say (aught[1]) of (his own) Desire.

4. It is no less than inspiration sent down to him:

5. He was taught by one Mighty in Power,

6. Endued with Wisdom: For he appeared (in stately form)

7. While he was in the highest part of the horizon:

8. Then he approached and came closer,

9. And was at a distance of but two bow-lengths or (even) nearer;

10. So did (God) convey the inspiration to His Servant — (conveyed) what He (meant) to convey.

11. The (Prophet's) (mind and) heart in no way falsified that which he saw.

12. Will ye then dispute with him concerning what he saw?

13. For indeed he saw him at a second descent.

14. Near the Lote-tree beyond which none may pass:

---

[13] Necessarily, unavoidably
[14] Pass out, faint
[1] Anything

15. Near it is the Garden of Abode.

16. Behold, the Lote-tree was shrouded (in mystery unspeakable!)

17. (His) sight never swerved, nor did it go wrong!

18. For truly did he see, of the Signs of his Lord, the Greatest!

19. Have ye seen Lāt, and 'Uzza,

20. And another, the third (goddess), Manat?

21. What! for you the male sex, and for Him, the female?

22. Behold, such would be indeed a division most unfair!

23. These are nothing but names which ye have devised— ye and your fathers — for which God has sent down no authority (whatever). They follow nothing but conjecture[2] and what their own souls desire! — even though there has already come to them Guidance from their Lord!

24. Nay, shall man have (just) anything he hankers[3] after?

25. But it is to God that the End and the Beginning (of all things) belong.

26. How-many-so-ever be the angels in the heavens, their intercession will avail nothing except after God has given leave for whom He pleases and that he is acceptable to Him.

27. Those who believe not in the Hereafter, name the angels with female names.

28. But they have no knowledge therein. They follow nothing but conjecture; and conjecture avails nothing against Truth.

29. Therefore shun[4] those who turn away from Our Message and desire nothing but the life of this world.

30. That is as far as knowledge will reach them. Verily thy Lord knoweth best those who stray from His path, and He knoweth best those who receive guidance.

31. Yea, to God belongs all that is in the heavens and on earth; so that He rewards those who do evil, according to their deeds, and He rewards those who do good, with what is best.

32. Those who avoid great sins and shameful deeds. Only (falling into) small faults, verily thy Lord is ample in forgiveness. He knows

---

[2] Guesswork
[3] Crave or long for
[4] Avoid

429

you well when He brings you out of the earth, and when ye are hidden in your mother's wombs, therefore justify not yourselves. He knows best who it is that guards against evil.

33. Seest thou one who turns back,

34. Gives a little, then hardens (his heart)?

35. What! has he knowledge of the Unseen so that he can see?

36. Nay, is he not acquainted with what is in the Books of Moses —

37. And of Abraham who fulfilled his engagements? —

38. Namely, that no bearer of burdens can bear the burden of another;

39. That man can have nothing but what he strives for;

40. That (the fruit of) his striving will soon come in sight;

41. Then will he be rewarded with a reward complete;

42. That to thy Lord is the final Goal;

43. That it is He who granteth Laughter and Tears;

44. That it is He who granteth Death and Life;

45. That He did create in pairs — male and female.

46. From a seed when lodged (in its place);

47. That He hath promised a Second Creation (Raising of the Dead)

48. That it is He Who giveth wealth and satisfaction;

49. That He is the Lord of Sirius (the Mighty Star);

50. And that it is He Who destroyed the (powerful) ancient 'Ād (people),

51. And the Thamūd, nor gave them a lease[5] of perpetual[6] life.

52. And before them, the people of Noah, for that they were (all) most unjust and most insolent transgressors.

53. And He destroyed the Overthrown Cities (of Sodom and Gomorrah),

54. So that (ruins unknown) have covered them up.

55. Then which of the gifts of thy Lord, (O man,) wilt thou dispute about?

56. This is a Warner, of the (series of) Warners of old!

57. The (Judgment) ever approaching draws nigh:

58. No (soul) but God can lay it bare.

---

[5] Contract

[6] Eternal, endless

59. Do ye then wonder at this recital?

60. And will ye laugh and not weep —

61. Wasting your time in vanities[7]?

62. But fall ye down in prostration to God, and adore (Him)!

Chapter 54
Sürah Al-Qamar (The Moon)
Revealed at Makkah, 55 verses

In the name of God, Most Gracious, Most Merciful.

1. The Hour (of Judgment) is nigh[1], and the moon is cleft asunder[2].

2. But if they see a Sign, they turn away, and say, "This is (but) transient[3] magic."

3. They reject (the warning) and follow their (own) lusts but every matter has its appointed time.

4. There have already come to them Recitals[4] wherein there is (enough) to check (them),

5. Mature wisdom — but (the preaching of) Warners profits them not.

6. Therefore, (O Prophet,) turn away from them. The day that the Caller will call (them) to a terrible affair,

7. They will come forth — their eyes humbled — from (their) graves, (torpid[5]) like locusts scattered abroad,

8. Hastening, with eyes transfixed[6], towards the Caller! "Hard is this Day!" the Unbelievers will say.

9. Before them the People of Noah rejected (their apostle): they rejected Our servant, and said, "Here is one possessed!" and he was

---

[7] Useless things

[1] Near

[2] Split

[3] Momentary, of short duration, quickly passing away

[4] A detailed account of a number of connected incidents, a narrative.

[5] Sluggish, sleepy, listless

[6] Root (a person) to the spot (because of horror), paralyse faculties of.

driven out.

10. Then he called on his Lord: "I am one overcome: do thou then help (me)!"

11. So We opened the gates of heaven, with water pouring forth.

12. And We caused the earth to gush forth with springs, so the waters met (and rose) to the extent decreed.

13. But We bore him on an (Ark) made of broad planks[7] and caulked[8] with palm-fibre:

14. She floats under Our eyes (and care): a recompense to one who had been rejected (with scorn)!

15. And We have left this as a Sign (for all time): then is there any that will receive admonition[9]?

16. But how (terrible) was My Penalty and My Warning?

17. And We have indeed made the Qur'an easy to understand and remember: then is there any that will receive admonition?

18. The 'Ād (people) (too) rejected (Truth): then how terrible was my Penalty and my Warning!

19. For We sent against them a furious wind, on a Day of violent Disaster,

20. Plucking out men as if they were roots of palm trees torn up (from the ground).

21. Yea, how (terrible) was my Penalty and my Warning!

22. But We have indeed made the Qur'an easy to understand and remember: then is there any that will receive admonition?

23. The Thamūd (also) rejected (their) Warners.

24. For they said: "What! a man! a solitary one from among ourselves! shall we follow such a one? Truly should we then be straying in mind, and mad!

25. "Is it that the Message is sent to him, of all people amongst us? Nay, he is a liar, an insolent one!"

26. Ah! they will know on the morrow, which is the liar, the insolent one!

27. For We will send the she-camel by way of trial for them. So

---

[7] Long wide piece of timber

[8] Stop up seams of ship with waterproofing material, etc.

[9] Warning, counsel

watch them, (O Saleh), and possess thyself in patience!

28. And tell them that the water is to be divided between them: each one's right to drink being brought forward (by suitable turns).

29. But they called to their companion, and he took a sword in hand, and hamstrung[10] (her).

30. Ah! how (terrible) was My Penalty and My Warning!

31. For We sent against them a single Mighty Blast, and they became like the dry stubble[11] used by one who pens[12] cattle.

32. And We have indeed made the Qur'an easy to understand and remember: then is there any that will receive admonition?

33. The People of Lūt rejected (his) Warning.

34. We sent against them a violent tornado[13] with showers of stones, (which destroyed them), except Lūt's household: them We delivered by early Dawn —

35. As a Grace from Us: Thus do We reward those who give thanks.

36. And (Lūt) did warn them of Our Punishment, but they disputed about the Warning.

37. And they even sought to snatch away his guests from him, but We blinded their eyes. (They heard:) "Now taste ye My Wrath and My Warning."

38. Early on the morrow an abiding Punishment seized them:

39. "So taste ye My Wrath and My Warning."

40. And We have indeed made the Qur'an easy to understand and remember: then is there any that will receive admonition?

41. To the people of Pharaoh, too, aforetime[14], came Warners (from God).

42. The (people) rejected all Our Signs; but We seized them with such Penalty (as comes) from One Exalted in Power, able to carry out His Will.

43. Are your Unbelievers, (O Quraish), better than they? or have ye an immunity[15] in the Sacred Books?

---

[10] Crippled

[11] Cut stalks of cereal plants left sticking up after harvest

[12] Enclose, shut in (cattle etc.) in pen or a small enclosure.

[13] A violent storm of whirling winds.

[14] Previously

[15] Exemption

44. Or do they say: "We acting together can defend ourselves?"

45. Soon will their multitude be put to flight, and they will show their backs.

46. Nay, the Hour (of Judgment) is the time promised them (for their full recompense): And that Hour will be Most grievous and most bitter.

47. Truly those in sin are the ones straying in mind, and mad.

48. The day they will be dragged through the Fire on their faces, (they will hear:) "Tastes ye the touch of Hell!"

49. Verily, all things have We created in proportion and measure.

50. And Our command is but a single (Act) — like the twinkling of an eye.

51. And (oft) in the past, have We destroyed gangs like unto you: Then is there any that will receive admonition?

52. All that they do is noted in (their) Books (of Deeds):

53. Every matter, small and great, is on record.

54. As to the Righteous, they will be in the midst of Gardens and Rivers.

55. In an Assembly of Truth, in the Presence of a Sovereign Omnipotent[16].

Chapter 55
Sürah Ar-Rahman (God Most Gracious)
Revealed at Makkah, 78 verses

In the name of God, Most Gracious, Most Merciful.

1. (God) Most Gracious!

2. It is He Who has taught the Qur'an.

3. He has created man:

4. He has taught him speech (and Intelligence)

5. The sun and the moon follow courses (exactly) computed[1];

6. And the herbs and the trees — both (alike) bow in adoration.

---

[16] All-Powerful, supreme
[1] Reckoned, calculated

7. And the Firmament has He raised high, and He has set up the balance (of Justice),

8. In order that ye may not transgress (due) balance.

9. So establish weight with justice and fall not short in the balance.

10. It is He Who has spread out the earth for (His) creatures:

11. Therein is fruit and date palms, producing spathes[2] (enclosing dates):

12. Also corn with (its) leaves and stalk for fodder, and sweet-smelling plants.

13. Then which of the favors of your Lord will ye deny?

14. He created man from sounding clay like unto pottery

15. And He created Jinns from fire free of smoke:

16. Then which of the favors of your Lord will ye deny?

17. (He is) Lord of the two Easts and Lord of the two Wests:

18. Then which of the favors of your Lord will ye deny?

19. He has let free the two bodies of flowing water, meeting together:

20. Between them is a Barrier which they do not transgress:

21. Then which of the favors of your Lord will ye deny?

22. Out of them come Pearls and Coral[3]:

23. Then which of the favors of your Lord will ye deny?

24. And His are the Ships sailing smoothly through the seas, lofty as mountains:

25. Then which of the favors of your Lord will ye deny?

26. All that is on earth will perish;

27. But will abide[4] (forever) the Face of thy Lord, full of Majesty[5], Bounty[6] and Honour.

28. Then which of the favors of your Lord will ye deny?

29. Of Him seeks (its needs) every creature in the heavens and on earth: every day in (new) Splendor doth He (shine)!

30. Then which of the favors of your Lord will ye deny?

---

[2] Large bract or pair of bracts enveloping flower-cluster

[3] A substance composed of calcium carbonate (red, pink, white etc.) secreted by marine polyps for support and habitation.

[4] Endure

[5] Magnificence, glory

[6] Munificence, benevolence

31. Soon shall We settle your affairs, O both ye worlds!

32. Then which of the favors of your Lord will ye deny?

33. O ye assembly of Jinns and men! if it be ye can pass beyond the zones of the heavens and the earth, pass ye! Not without authority shall ye be able to pass!

34. Then which of the favors of your Lord will ye deny?

35. On you will be sent (O ye evil ones twain[7]!) a flame of fire (to burn) and a smoke (to choke): No defence will ye have:

36. Then which of the favors of your Lord will ye deny?

37. When the sky is rent asunder, and it becomes red like ointment:

38. Then which of the favors of your Lord will ye deny?

39. On that day no question will be asked of man or Jinn as to his sin.

40. Then which of the favors of your Lord will ye deny?

41. (For) the sinners will be known by their Marks: and they will be seized by their forelocks and their feet.

42. Then which of the favors of your Lord will ye deny?

43. This is the Hell which the Sinners deny.

44. In its midst and in the midst of boiling hot water will they wander round!

45. Then which of the favors of your Lord will ye deny?

46. But for such as fear the time when they will stand before (the Judgment Seat of) their Lord, there will be two Gardens —

47. Then which of the favors of your Lord will ye deny?

48. Containing all kinds (of trees and delights) —

49. Then which of the favors of your Lord will ye deny?

50. In them (each) will be two Springs flowing (free);

51. Then which of the favors of your Lord will ye deny?

52. In them will be Fruits of every kind, two and two.

53. Then which of the favors of your Lord will ye deny?

54. They will recline on Carpets, whose inner linings will be of rich brocade[8]: the Fruit of the Gardens will be Near (and easy of reach).

55. Then which of the favors of your Lord will ye deny?

56. In them will be (Maidens), Chaste, restraining their glances,

---

[7] Two (persons or things)

[8] Fabric woven with raised patterns (of added metal threads).

whom no man or Jinn before them has touched —

57. Then which of the favors of your Lord will ye deny?

58. Like unto rubies and coral.

59. Then which of the favors of your Lord will ye deny?

60. Is there any Reward for Good — other than Good?

61. Then which of the favors of your Lord will ye deny?

62. And besides these two, there are two other Gardens —

63. Then which of the favors of your Lord will ye deny?

64. Dark green in color (from plentiful watering).

65. Then which of the favors of your Lord will ye deny?

66. In them (each) will be two springs pouring forth water in continuous abundance:

67. Then which of the favors of your Lord will ye deny?

68. In them will be Fruits, and dates and pomegranates:

69. Then which of the favors of your Lord will ye deny?

70. In them will be fair (Companions), good, beautiful —

71. Then which of the favors of your Lord will ye deny?

72. Companions restrained (as to their glances), in (goodly) pavilions[9] —

73. Then which of the favors of your Lord will ye deny?

74. Whom no man or Jinn before them has touched —

75. Then which of the favors of your Lord will ye deny?

76. Reclining on green cushions and rich carpets of beauty.

77. Then which of the favors of your Lord will ye deny?

78. Blessed be the name of thy Lord, full of Majesty, Bounty and Honour.

Chapter 56
Sürah Al-Waqi'ah (The Inevitable Event)
Revealed at Makkah, 96 verses

In the name of God, Most Gracious, Most Merciful.

1. When the event inevitable cometh to pass.

2. Then will no (soul) entertain falsehood concerning its coming.

---

[9] Large peaked Tents

3. (Many) will it bring low, (many) will it exalt[1];

4. When the earth shall be shaken to its depths,

5. And the mountains shall be crumbled to atoms,

6. Becoming dust scattered abroad,

7. And ye shall be sorted out into three classes.

8. Then (there will be) the Companions of the Right Hand — What will be the Companions of the Right Hand?

9. And the Companions of the Left Hand — What will be the Companions of the Left Hand?

10. And those Foremost (in Faith) will be Foremost (in the Hereafter).

11. These will be those Nearest to God:

12. In Gardens of Bliss:

13. A number of people from those of old,

14. And a few from those of later times.

15. (They will be) on Thrones encrusted[2] (with gold and precious stones).

16. Reclining on them, facing each other.

17. Round about them will (serve) youths of perpetual (freshness).

18. With goblets[3], (shining) beakers[4], and cups (filled) out of clear-flowing fountains:

19. No after-ache[5] will they receive therefrom, nor will they suffer intoxication[6]:

20. And with fruits, any that they may select;

21. And the flesh of fowls, any that they may desire.

22. And (there will be) Companions with beautiful, big, and lustrous eyes —

23. Like unto Pearls well-guarded.

24. A Reward for the Deeds of their past (life).

25. No frivolity[7] will they hear therein nor any taint[8] of ill —

---

[1] Raise high, elevate

[2] Overlaid with ornamental layer (or crust) of precious material.

[3] Drinking cups

[4] Large drinking cup

[5] Hangover, unpleasant after-effects of something

[6] Drunkenness

[7] Silliness

[8] Stain

26. Only the saying, "Peace! Peace."

27. The Companions of the Right Hand — What will be the Companions of the Right Hand?

28. (They will be) among Lote trees without thorns,

29. Among Talh[9] trees with flowers (or fruits) piled one above another —

30. In shade long-extended,

31. By water flowing constantly,

32. And fruit in abundance,

33. Whose season is not limited nor (supply) forbidden,

34. And on Thrones (of Dignity), raised high.

35. We have created (their Companions) of special creation.

36. And made them virgin-pure (and undefiled[10]) —

37. Beloved (by nature), equal in age —

38. For the Companions of the Right Hand.

39. A (goodly) number from those of old,

40. And a (goodly) number from those of later times.

41. The Companions of the Left Hand, — What will be the Companions of the Left Hand?

42. (They will be) in the midst of a fierce Blast of Fire and in Boiling Water,

43. And in the shades of Black Smoke:

44. Nothing (will there be) to refresh, nor to please:

45. For that they were wont[11] to be indulged[12], before that, in wealth (and luxury).

46. And persisted obstinately in wickedness supreme!

47. And they used to say, "What! when we die and become dust and bones, shall we then indeed be raised up again? —

48. "(We) and our fathers of old?"

49. Say: "Yea, those of old and those of later times,

50. "All will certainly be gathered together for the meeting appointed for a Day well-known.

---

[9] Banana tree, or a special kind of acacia tree, which flowers profusely, the flowers appearing in tiers one above another.

[10] Clean and pure

[11] Accustomed to, used to

[12] All their desires were granted

51. "Then will ye truly — O ye that go wrong, and treat (Truth) as Falsehood!

52. "Ye will surely taste of the Tree of Zaqqūm.

53. "Then will ye fill your insides therewith,

54. "And drink boiling water on top of it:

55. "Indeed ye shall drink like diseased camels raging[13] with thirst!

56. Such will be their entertainment on the Day of Requital[14]!

57. It is We Who have created you: why will ye not witness the Truth?

58. Do ye then see? — the (human seed) — that ye throw out, —

59. Is it ye who create it, or are We the Creators?

60. We have decreed Death to be your common lot, and We are not to be frustrated[15]

61. From changing your Forms and creating you (again) in (Forms) that ye know not.

62. And ye certainly know already the first form of creation: why then do ye not celebrate His praises?

63. See ye the seed that ye sow in the ground?

64. Is it ye that cause it to grow, or are We the Cause?

65. Were it Our Will, We could crumble it to dry powder, and ye would be left in wonderment,

66. (Saying), "We are indeed left with debts (for nothing):

67. "Indeed are we shut out (of the fruits of our labor)."

68. See ye the water which ye drink?

69. Do ye bring it down (in rain) from the cloud, or do We?

70. Were it Our Will, We could make it salt (and unpalatable[16]): then why do ye not give thanks?

71. See ye the Fire which ye kindle?

72. Is it ye who grow the tree which feeds the Fire, or do We grow it?

73. We have made it a memorial (of our handiwork), and an article of comfort and convenience for the denizens[17] of deserts.

---

[13] Seething, roaring, violent
[14] Reward or punishment
[15] Thwart, prevent, or baffle
[16] Unpleasant to the taste
[17] Dwellers, residents

74. Then celebrate with praises the name of thy Lord, the Supreme:

75. Furthermore I call to witness the setting of the Stars —

76. And that is indeed a mighty adjuration[18] if ye but knew —

77. That this is indeed a Qur'an most honourable,

78. In a Book well-guarded,

79. Which none shall touch but those who are clean:

80. A Revelation from the Lord of the Worlds.

81. Is it such a Message that ye would hold in light esteem?

82. And have ye made it your livelihood that ye should declare it false?

83. Then why do ye not (intervene) when (the soul of the dying man) reaches the throat —

84. And ye the while (sit) looking on —

85. But We are nearer to him than ye, and yet see not —

86. Then why do you not — if you are exempt from (future) account —

87. Call back the soul, if ye are true (in your claim of Independence)?

88. Thus, then, if he be of those Nearest to God,

89. (There is for him) Rest and Satisfaction, and a Garden of Delights.

90. And if he be of the Companions of the Right Hand,

91. (For him is the salutation), "Peace be unto thee," from the Companions of the Right Hand.

92. And if he be of those who treat (truth) as Falsehood, who go wrong,

93. For him is Entertainment with Boiling Water.

94. And burning in Hell-Fire.

95. Verily, this is the very Truth and Certainty.

96. So celebrate with praises the name of thy Lord, the Supreme.

---

18 Oath

Chapter 57
Sürah Al-Hadïd (The Iron)
Revealed at Madinah, 29 verses

In the name of God, Most Gracious, Most Merciful.

1. Whatever is in the heavens and on earth, let it declare the Praises and Glory of God: for He is the Exalted in Might, the Wise.

2. To Him belongs the dominion[1] of the heavens and the earth; it is He Who gives life and Death; and He has Power over all things.

3. He is the First and the Last, the Evident and the Immanent[2]: and He has full knowledge of all things.

4. He it is Who created the heavens and the earth in six Days, and is moreover firmly established on the Throne (of authority). He knows what enters within the earth and what comes forth out of it, what comes down from heaven and what mounts up to it. And He is with you wheresoever ye may be. And God sees well all that ye do.

5. To Him belongs the dominion of the heavens and the earth: and all affairs are referred back to God.

6. He merges Night into Day, and He merges Day into Night; and He has full knowledge of the secrets of (all) hearts.

7. Believe in God and His Apostle, and spend (in charity) out of the (substance[3]) whereof He has made you heirs. For, those of you who believe and spend (in charity) — for them is a great Reward.

8. What cause have ye why ye should not believe in God? — And the Apostle invites you to believe in your Lord, and has indeed taken your Covenant, if ye are men of faith.

9. He is the One Who sends to His Servants manifest Signs, that He may lead you from the depths of Darkness into the Light. And verily, God is to you Most Kind and Merciful.

10. And what cause have ye why ye should not spend in the cause of God? — For to God belongs the heritage of the heavens and the earth. Not equal among you are those who spent (freely) and fought,

---

[1] Sovereignty, power
[2] Indwelling, inherent (in), permanently pervading the universe
[3] Riches

before the Victory, (with those who did so later). Those are higher in rank than those who spent (freely) and fought afterwards. But to all has God promised a goodly (reward), and God is well-acquainted with all that ye do.

11. Who is he that will loan to God a beautiful Loan? For (God) will increase it manifold to his credit, and he will have (besides) a liberal reward.

12. One Day shalt thou see the believing men and the believing women — how their Light runs forward before them and by their right hands: (their greeting will be): "Good News for you this Day! Gardens beneath which flow rivers! To dwell therein for aye[4]! This is indeed the highest Achievement!"

13. One day will the Hypocrites — men and women — say to the Believers: "Wait for us! let us borrow (a light) from your Light!" It will be said: "Turn ye back to your rear[5]! then seek a light (where ye can)!" So a wall will be put up betwixt[6] them, with a gate therein. Within it will be Mercy throughout, and without it, all alongside, will be (Wrath and) Punishment!

14. (Those without) will call out, "Were we not with you?" (The others) will reply, "True! but ye led yourselves into temptation[7]; ye looked forward (to our ruin); ye doubted (God's promise); and (your false) desires deceived you; until there issued the Command of God. And the Deceiver deceived you in respect of God.

15. "This Day shall no ransom be accepted of you, nor of those who rejected God. Your abode is the Fire: That is the proper place to claim you: and an evil refuge it is !"

16. Has not the time arrived for the Believers that their hearts in all humility should engage in the remembrance of God and of the truth which has been revealed (to them) and that they should not become like those to whom was given Revelation aforetime, but long ages passed over them and their hearts grew hard? For many among them are rebellious transgressors.

---

[4] Ever
[5] Back part (of a thing)
[6] Between
[7] (Incitement to) sin

17. Know ye (all) that God giveth life to the earth after its death! Already have We shown the Signs plainly to you, that ye may learn wisdom.

18. For those who give in Charity, men and women, and loan to God a Beautiful Loan, it shall be increased manifold (to their credit), and they shall have (besides) a liberal reward.

19. And those who believe in God and His Apostles — they are the Sincere (Lovers of truth), and the Witnesses (who testify), in the eyes of their Lord: they shall have their Reward and their Light, but those who reject God and deny Our Signs — they are the Companions of Hell-Fire.

20. Know ye (all), that the life of this world is but play and amusement, pomp and mutual boasting and multiplying, (in rivalry) among yourselves, riches and children: Here is a similitude[8]: How rain and the growth which it brings forth, delight (the hearts of) the tillers; soon it withers; thou wilt see it grow yellow; then it becomes dry and crumbles away. But in the Hereafter is a Penalty severe (for the devotees of wrong), and Forgiveness from God and (His) Good Pleasure (for the devotees of God). And what is the life of this world, but goods and chattels[9] of deception?

21. Be ye foremost (in seeking) forgiveness from your Lord, and a Garden (of Bliss), the width whereof is as the width of heaven and earth, prepared for those who believe in God and His apostles: that is the Grace of God, which He bestows on whom He pleases: and God is the Lord of Grace abounding[10].

22. No misfortune can happen on earth or in your souls but is recorded in a decree before We bring it into existence: that is truly easy for God:

23. In order that ye may not despair over matters that pass you by, nor exult[11] over favors bestowed upon you. For God loveth not any vainglorious[12] boaster —

---

[8] Likeness, parable
[9] Movable possessions
[10] Plentiful, abundant
[11] Feel proud, happy
[12] Boastful, extremely vain

24. Such persons as are covetous[13] and commend covetousness to men. And if any turn back (from God's Way), verily God is free of all needs, worthy of all praise.

25. We sent aforetime our apostles with Clear Signs and sent down with them the Book and the Balance (of Right and Wrong), that men may stand forth in justice; and We sent down Iron, in which is (material for) mighty war, as well as many benefits for mankind, that God may test who it is that will help, unseen, Him and His apostles; for God is Full of Strength, exalted in Might (and able to enforce His will).

26. And We sent Noah and Abraham, and established in their line Prophethood and Revelation: and some of them were on right guidance, but many of them became rebellious transgressors.

27. Then, in their wake, We followed them up with (others of) Our apostles: We sent after them Jesus the son of Mary, and bestowed on him the Gospel; and We ordained in the hearts of those who followed him Compassion and Mercy. But the monasticism which they invented for themselves, We did not prescribe for them: (We commanded) only the seeking for the Good pleasure of God; but that they did not foster[14] as they should have done. Yet We bestowed, on those among them who believed, their (due) reward, but many of them are rebellious transgressors.

28. O ye that believe! fear God, and believe in His apostle, and He will bestow on you a double portion of His Mercy: He will provide for you a light by which ye shall walk (straight in your path), and He will forgive you (your past): For God is Oft-Forgiving. Most Merciful:

29. That the People of the Book may know that they have no power whatever over the Grace of God, that (His) Grace is (entirely) in His hand, to bestow it on whomsoever He wills. For God is the Lord of Grace abounding.

---

[13] Miserly
[14] Promote, cherish

Chapter 58
Sürah Al-Mujadilah (The Woman who Pleads)
Revealed at Madinah, 22 verses

In the name of God, Most Gracious, Most Merciful.

1. God has indeed heard (and accepted) the statement of the woman who pleads with thee concerning her husband and carries her complaint (in prayer) to God: and God (always) hears the arguments between both sides among you: for God hears and sees (all things).

2. If any men among you divorce their wives by *Zihar* (calling them mothers), they cannot be their mothers: none can be their mothers except those who gave them birth. And in fact they use words (both) iniquitous[1] and false: but truly God is one that blots out (sins), and forgives (again and again).

3. But those who divorce their wives by *Zihar*, then wish to go back on the words they uttered, (it is ordained that such a one) should free a slave before they touch each other: this are ye admonished to perform: and God is well-acquainted with (all) that ye do.

4. And if any has not (the wherewithal[2]), he should fast for two months consecutively[3] before they touch each other. But if any is unable to do so, he should feed sixty indigent[4] ones. This, that ye may show your faith in God and His Apostle. Those are limits (set by) God. For those who Reject (Him), there is a grievous Penalty.

5. Those who resist God and His Apostle will be humbled to dust, as were those before them: for We have already sent down clear Signs. And the Unbelievers (will have) a humiliating Penalty,

6. On the Day that God will raise them all up (again) and show them the truth (and meaning) of their conduct. God has reckoned its (value), though they may have forgotten it: for God is Witness to all things.

7. Seest thou not that God doth know (all) that is in the heavens and on earth? There is not a secret consultation between three, but He makes the fourth among them, nor between five but He makes

---

[1] Grossly unjust, evil
[2] Means or money
[3] Continuously, one after the other
[4] Needy

the sixth, nor between fewer nor more, but He is in their midst wheresoever they be: in the end will He tell them the truth of their conduct, on the Day of Judgment for God has full knowledge of all things.

8. Turnest thou not thy sight towards those who were forbidden secret counsels yet revert to that which they were forbidden (to do)? And they hold secret counsels among themselves for iniquity[5] and hostility, and disobedience to the Apostle. And when they come to thee, they salute thee, not as God salutes thee, (but in crooked ways): and they say to themselves, "Why does not God punish us for our words?" Enough for them is Hell: in it will they burn, and evil is that destination!

9. O ye who believe! when ye hold secret counsel, do it not for iniquity and hostility, and disobedience to the Prophet; but do it for righteousness and self-restraint; and fear God, to whom ye shall be brought back.

10. Secret counsels are only (inspired) by the Evil One, in order that he may cause grief to the Believers; but he cannot harm them in the least, except as God permits; and on God let the Believers put their trust.

11. O ye who believe! When ye are told to make room in the assemblies, (spread out and) make room: (Ample) room will God provide for you. And when ye are told to rise up, rise up: God will raise up, to (suitable) ranks (and degrees), those of you who believe and who have been granted Knowledge: and God is well-acquainted with all ye do.

12. O ye who believe! When ye consult the Apostle in private, spend something in charity before your private consultation. That will be best for you, and most conducive[6] to purity (of conduct). But if ye find not (the wherewithal), God is Oft-Forgiving, Most Merciful.

13. Is it that ye are afraid of spending sums in charity before your private consultation (with him)? If, then ye do not so, and God forgives you, then (at least) establish regular prayer; practice regular charity; and obey God and His Apostle: and God is well-acquainted with all

---

[5] Injustice, wrongdoing
[6] Helpful

that ye do.

14. Turnest thou not thy attention to those who turn (in friendship) to such as have the Wrath of God upon them? They are neither of you nor of them, and they swear to falsehood knowingly.

15. God has prepared for them a severe Penalty: evil indeed are their deeds.

16. They have made their oaths a screen (for their misdeeds): thus they obstruct (men) from the Path of God: therefore shall they have a humiliating Penalty.

17. Of no profit whatever to them, against God, will be their riches nor their sons: they will be Companions of the Fire, to dwell therein (for aye)!

18. One day will God raise them all up (for Judgment): then will they swear to Him as they swear to you: and they think that they have something (to stand upon): No, indeed! they are but liars!

19. The Evil One has got the better of them: So he has made them lose the remembrance of God. They are the Party of the Evil One. Truly, it is the Party of the Evil One that will perish!

20. Those who resist God and His Apostle will be among those most humiliated.

21. God has decreed: "It is I and My Apostle who must prevail": For God is One full of strength, able to enforce His Will.

22. Thou wilt not find any people who believe in God and the Last Day, loving those who resist God and His Apostle, even though they were their fathers or their sons, or their brothers, or their kindred[7]. For such He has written Faith in their hearts, and strengthened them with a spirit from Himself. And He will admit them to Gardens beneath which Rivers flow, to dwell therein (forever). God will be well pleased with them, and they with Him. They are the Party of God. Truly it is the Party of God, that will achieve Felicity[8].

---

[7] Relatives
[8] Bliss, happiness.

Chapter 59
Sürah Al-Hashr (The Gathering)
Revealed at Madinah, 24 verses

In the name of God, Most Gracious, Most Merciful.

1. Whatever is in the heavens and on earth, let it declare the Praises and Glory of God: for He is the Exalted in Might, the Wise.

2. It is He who got out the Unbelievers among the People of the Book from their homes at the first gathering (of the forces). Little did ye think that they would get out: and they thought that their fortresses would defend them from God! but the (wrath of) God came to them from quarters from which they little expected (it), and cast terror into their hearts, so that they destroyed their dwellings by their own hands and the hands of the Believers. Take warning, then, O ye with eyes (to see)!

3. And had it not been that God has decreed banishment for them, He would certainly have punished them in this world: and in the Hereafter they shall (certainly) have the Punishment of the Fire.

4. That is because they resisted God and His Apostle: and if anyone resists God, verily God is severe in Punishment.

5. Whether ye cut down (O ye Muslims!) the tender palm trees, or ye left them standing on their roots, it was by leave of God, and in order that He might cover with shame the rebellious transgressors.

6. What God has bestowed on His Apostle (and taken away) from them — for this ye made no expedition with either cavalry or camelry: but God gives power to His apostles over any He pleases: and God has power over all things.

7. What God has bestowed on His Apostle (and taken away) from the people of the townships, belongs to God, to His Apostle and to kindred[1] and orphans, the needy and the wayfarer[2]; in order that it may not (merely) make a circuit[3] between the wealth among you. So take what the Apostle assigns to you, and deny yourselves that which he withholds[4] from you. And fear God; for God is strict in

---

[1] Relatives
[2] Traveller
[3] Circulation
[4] Restrains

Punishment.

8. (Some part is due) to the indigent[5] Muhajirs, those who were expelled from their homes and their property, while seeking Grace from God and (His) Good pleasure, and aiding God and His Apostle: such are indeed the sincere ones —

9. But those who, before them, had homes (in Madinah) and had adopted the Faith, show their affection to such as came to them for refuge, and entertain no desire, in their hearts for things given to the (latter), but give them preference over themselves, even though poverty was their (own lot). And those saved from the covetousness of their own souls, they are the ones that achieve prosperity.

10. And those who came after them say: "Our Lord! Forgive us, and our brethren who came before us into the Faith, and leave not, in our hearts, rancor[6] (or sense of injury) against those who have believed. Our Lord! Thou art indeed Full of Kindness, Most Merciful."

11. Hast thou not observed the Hypocrites say to their misbelieving brethren among the People of the Book? — "If ye are expelled, We too will go out with you, and we will never hearken[7] to anyone in your affair; and if ye are attacked (in fight) we will help you." But God is witness that they are indeed liars.

12. If they are expelled, never will they go out with them; and if they are attacked (in fight), they will never help them; and if they do help them, they will turn their backs; so they will receive no help.

13. Of a truth ye are stronger (than they) because of the terror in their hearts, (sent) by God. This is because they are men devoid of understanding.

14. They will not fight you (even) together, except in fortified townships, or from behind walls. Strong is their fighting (spirit) amongst themselves: thou wouldst think they were united, but their hearts are divided: that is because they are a people devoid of wisdom.

15. Like those who lately preceded them, they have tasted the evil result of their conduct, and (in the Hereafter there is) for them

---

[5] Needy, poor
[6] Hostility, malice
[7] Listen to, obey

a grievous Penalty —

16. (Their allies deceived them), like the Evil One, when he says to man, "Deny God"; but when (man) denies God, (the Evil One) says, "I am free of thee: I do fear God, the Lord of the Worlds!"

17. The end of both will be that they will go into the Fire, dwelling therein forever. Such is the reward of wrongdoers.

18. O ye who believe! Fear God, and let every soul look to what (provision) he has sent forth for the morrow[8]. Yea, fear God: for God is well-acquainted with (all) they ye do.

19. And be ye not like those who forget God; and He made them forget their own souls! Such are the rebellious transgressors!

20. Not equal are the Companions of the Fire and the Companions of the Garden: it is the Companions of the Garden that will achieve Felicity[9].

21. Had We sent down this Qur'an on a mountain verily, thou would have seen it humble itself and cleave asunder for fear of God, such are the similitudes which We propound[10] to men, that they may reflect[11].

22. God is He, than Whom there is no other god — Who knows (all things) both secret and open; He, Most Gracious, Most Merciful.

23. God is He, than Whom there is no other god — the Sovereign, the Holy One, the Source of Peace (and Perfection). The Guardian of Faith, the Preserver of Safety, the Exalted in Might, the Irresistible, the Supreme: Glory to God! (high is He) above the partners they attribute to Him.

24. He is God, the Creator, the Evolver, the Bestower of Forms (or colors). To Him belong the Most Beautiful Names: Whatever is in the heavens and on earth, doth declare His Praises and Glory: and He is the exalted in Might, the Wise.

---

[8] Tomorrow, i.e., for the life to come
[9] Bliss, happiness
[10] Offer for consideration, propose
[11] Ponder

Chapter 60
Sūrah Al-Mumtahinah
(The Woman To Be Examined)
Revealed at Madinah, 13 verses

In the name of God, Most Gracious, Most Merciful.

1. O ye who believe! take not My enemies and yours as friends (or protectors) — offering them (your) love, even though they have rejected the Truth that has come to you, and have (on the contrary) driven out the Prophet and yourselves (from your homes), (simply) because ye believe in God your Lord! If ye have come out to strive in My Way and to seek My Good Pleasure, (take them not as friends), holding secret converse[1] of love (and friendship) with them: for I know full well all that ye conceal and all that ye reveal. And any of you that does this has strayed from the Straight Path.

2. If they were to get the better of you, they would behave to you as enemies, and stretch forth their hands and their tongues against you for evil; and they desire that ye should reject the Truth.

3. Of no profit to you will be your relatives and your children on the Day of Judgment: He will judge between you: for God sees well all that ye do.

4. There is for you an excellent example (to follow) in Abraham and those with him, when they said to their people: "We are clear of you and of whatever ye worship besides God: we have rejected you, and there has arisen between us and you, enmity and hatred forever — unless ye believe in God and Him alone": But not when Abraham said to his father: "I will pray for forgiveness for thee, though I have no power (to get) aught on thy behalf from God." (They prayed): "Our Lord! in Thee do we trust and to Thee do we turn in repentance: to Thee is (our) final Goal.

5. "Our Lord! Make us not a (test and) trial for the Unbelievers, but forgive us, our Lord! For Thou art the Exalted in Might, the Wise."

6. There was indeed in them an excellent example for you to follow — for those whose hope is in God and in the Last Day. But if any turn away, truly God is Free of all Wants, Worthy of all Praise.

---

[1] (Arch.) Conversation

452

7. It may be that God will grant love (and friendship) between you and those whom ye (now) hold as enemies: for God has power (over all things); and God is Oft-Forgiving, Most Merciful.

8. God forbids you not, with regard to those who fight you not for (your) Faith nor drive you out of your homes, from dealing kindly and justly with them: for God loveth those who are just.

9. God only forbids you, with regard to those who fight you for (your) Faith, and drive you out of your homes, and support (others) in driving you out, from turning to them (for friendship and protection). It is such as turn to them (in these circumstances), that do wrong.

10. O ye who believe! when there come to you believing women refugees, examine (and test) them: God knows best as to their Faith: if ye ascertain that they are Believers, then send them not back to the Unbelievers. They are not lawful (wives) for the Unbelievers, nor are the (Unbelievers) lawful (husbands) for them. But pay the Unbelievers what they have spent (on their dower). And there will be no blame on you if ye marry them on payment of their dower to them. But hold not to the guardianship of unbelieving women: ask for what ye have spent on their dowers, and let the (Unbelievers) ask for what they have spent (on the dowers of women who come over to you). Such is the command of God: He judges (with justice) between you: and God is Full of Knowledge and Wisdom.

11. And if any of your wives deserts you to the Unbelievers, and ye have an accession[2] (by the coming over of a woman from the other side), then pay to those whose wives have deserted the equivalent of what they had spent (on their (dower). And fear God, in Whom ye believe.

12. O Prophet! when believing women come to thee to take the oath of fealty[3] to thee, that they will not associate in worship any other thing whatever with God, that they will not steal, that they will not commit adultery (or fornication), that they will not kill their children, that they will not utter slander, intentionally forging falsehood, and that they will not disobey thee in any just matter — then do thou receive their fealty, and pray to God for the forgiveness (of

---

[2] Addition, being added, or thing added
[3] Allegiance, fidelity

their sins): for God is Oft-Forgiving, Most Merciful.

13. O ye who believe! turn not (for friendship) to people on whom is the Wrath of God. Of the Hereafter they are already in despair, just as the Unbelievers are in despair about those (buried) in graves.

Chapter 61
Sürah As-Saff (The Battle Array)
Revealed at Madinah, 14 verses

In the name of God, Most Gracious, Most Merciful.

1. Whatever is in the heavens and on earth, let it declare the Praises and Glory of God: for He is the Exalted in Might, the Wise.

2. O ye who believe! why say ye that which ye do not?

3. Grievously odious[1] is it in the sight of God that ye say that which ye do not.

4. Truly God loves those who fight in His Cause in battle array, as if they were a solid cemented structure.

5. And remember, Moses said to his people: "O my people! why do ye vex[2] and insult me, though ye know that I am the apostle of God (sent) to you?" Then when they went wrong, God let their hearts go wrong: for God guides not those who are rebellious transgressors.

6. And remember, Jesus, the son of Mary, said: "O Children of Israel! I am the apostle of God (sent) to you confirming the Law (which came) before me, and giving glad Tidings of an Apostle to come after me, whose name shall be Ahmad." But when he came to them with Clear Signs, they said, "This is evident sorcery!"

7. Who doth greater wrong than one who invents falsehood against God, even as he is being invited to Islam? And God guides not those who do wrong.

8. Their intention is to extinguish God's Light (by blowing) with their mouths: but God will complete (the revelation of) His Light, even though the Unbelievers may detest (it).

9. It is He Who has sent His Apostle with Guidance and the Religion

---

[1] Disgusting, abhorent, loathsome
[2] Annoy

of Truth, that he may proclaim it over all religion, even though the Pagans may detest (it).

10. O ye who believe! shall I lead you to a bargain that will save you from a grievous Penalty? —

11. That ye believe in God and His Apostle, and that ye strive (your utmost) in the Cause of God, with your property and your persons: that will be best for you, if ye but knew!

12. He will forgive you your sins, and admit you to Gardens beneath which rivers flow, and to beautiful mansions[3] in Gardens of Eternity: that is indeed the supreme Achievement.

13. And another (favor will He bestow), which ye do love — help from God and a speedy victory: so give the Glad Tidings to the Believers.

14. O ye who believe! be ye helpers of God: as said Jesus, the son of Mary, to the Disciples, "Who will be my helpers to (the work of) God?" Said the Disciples, "We are God's helpers!" Then a portion of the Children of Israel believed, and a portion disbelieved: but We gave power to those who believed against their enemies, and they became the ones that prevailed.

Chapter 62
Sürah Al-Jumu'ah (Friday)
Revealed at Madinah, 11 verses

In the name of God, Most Gracious, Most Merciful.

1. Whatever is in the heavens and on earth, doth declare the Praises and Glory of God — the Sovereign, the Holy One, the Exalted in Might, the Wise.

2. It is He Who has sent amongst the Unlettered an apostle from among themselves, to rehearse[1] to them His Signs, to sanctify[2] them, and to instruct them in Scripture and Wisdom — although they had

---

[3] Large residences
[1] Recite
[2] Purify, bless

been, before, in manifest error; —

3. As well as (to confer all these benefits upon) others of them, who have not already joined them: and He is Exalted in Might, Wise.

4. Such is the Bounty of God, which He bestows on whom He will: and God is the Lord of the highest bounty.

5. The similitude of those who were charged with the (obligations of the) Mosaic Law, but who subsequently failed in those (obligations), is that of a donkey which carries huge tomes[3] (but understands them not). Evil is the similitude of people who falsify the Signs of God: and God guides not people who do wrong.

6. Say: "O ye that stand on Judaism! if ye think that ye are friends to God, to the exclusion of (other) men, then express your desire for Death, if ye are truthful!"

7. But never will they express their desire (for Death), because of the (deeds) their hands have sent on before them! And God knows well those that do wrong!

8. Say: "The Death from which ye flee will truly overtake you: then will ye be sent back to the Knower of things secret and open: and He will tell you (the truth of) the things that ye did!"

9. O ye who believe! when the call is proclaimed to prayer on Friday (the Day of Assembly), hasten earnestly to the Remembrance of God, and leave off business (and traffic[4]): that is best for you if ye but knew!

10. And when the Prayer is finished, then may ye disperse through the land, and seek of the Bounty of God: and celebrate the Praises of God often (and without stint[5]): that ye may prosper.

11. But when they see some bargain or some amusement, they disperse headlong[6] to it, and leave thee standing. Say: "The (blessing) from the Presence of God is better than any amusement or bargain! And God is the Best to provide (for all needs)."

---

[3] Books, volumes (of book), esp. large heavy ones.

[4] Trade

[5] Limitation

[6] Impetuously

Chapter 63
Sūrah Al-Munāfiqūn (The Hypocrites)
Revealed at Madinah, 11 verses

In the name of God, Most Gracious, Most Merciful.

1. When the Hypocrites come to thee, they say, "We bear witness that thou art indeed the Apostle of God." Yea, God knoweth that thou art indeed His Apostle, and God beareth witness that the Hypocrites are indeed liars.

2. They have made their oaths a screen[1] (for their misdeeds): thus they obstruct (men) from the Path of God: truly evil are their deeds.

3. That is because they believed, then they rejected Faith: so a seal was set on their hearts: therefore they understand not.

4. When thou lookest at them, their exteriors please thee; and when they speak, thou listenest to their words. They are as (worthless as hollow) pieces of timber propped up, (unable to stand on their own). They think that every cry is against them. They are the enemies; so beware of them. The curse of God be on them! How are they deluded (away from the Truth)!

5. And when it is said to them, "Come, the Apostle of God will pray for your forgiveness," they turn aside their heads, and thou wouldst see them turning away their faces in arrogance.

6. It is equal to them whether thou pray for their forgiveness or not. God will not forgive them. Truly God guides not rebellious transgressors.

7. They are the ones who say, "Spend nothing on those who are with God's Apostle, to the end that they may disperse (and quit Madinah). But to God belong the treasures of the heavens and the earth; but the Hypocrites understand not.

8. They say, "If we return to Madinah, surely the more honourable (element) will expel therefrom the meaner." But honour belongs to God and His Apostle, and to the Believers; but the Hypocrites know not.

9. O ye who believe! let not your riches or your children divert you from the remembrance of God. If any act thus, the loss is their

---

[1] Cover, mask

own.

10. And spend something (in charity) out of the substance which We have bestowed on you, before death should come to any of you and he should say, "O my Lord! why didst thou not give me respite[2] for a little while? I should then have given (largely) in charity, and I should have been one of the doers of good."

11. But to no soul will God grant respite when the time appointed (for it) has come: and God is well-acquainted with (all) that ye do.

Chapter 64
Sūrah At-Taghābun (The Mutual Loss and Gain)
Revealed at Madinah, 18 verses

In the name of God, Most Gracious, Most Merciful.

1. Whatever is in the heavens and on earth, doth declare the Praises and Glory of God: to Him belongs Dominion, and to Him belongs Praise: and He has power over all things.

2. It is He Who has created you; and of you are some that are Unbelievers, and some that are Believers: and God sees well all that ye do.

3. He has created the heavens and the earth in just proportions, and has given you shape, and made your shapes beautiful: and to Him is the final Goal.

4. He knows what is in the heavens and on earth: and He knows what ye conceal and what ye reveal: yes, God knows well the (secrets) of (all) hearts.

5. Has not the story reached you, of those who rejected Faith aforetime? So they tasted the evil result of their conduct; and they had a grievous Penalty.

6. That was because there came to them apostles with Clear Signs, but they said: "Shall (mere) human beings direct us?" So they rejected (the Message) and turned away. But God can do without (them): and God is free of all needs, worthy of all praise.

7. The Unbelievers think that they will not be raised up (for Judgment). Say: "Yea, by my Lord, ye shall surely be raised up: then

---

[2] Delay

shall ye be told (the truth) of all that ye did. And that is easy for God."

8. Believe, therefore, in God and His Apostle, and in the Light which We have sent down. And God is well-acquainted with all that ye do.

9. The Day that He assembles you (all) for a day of Assembly — that will be a day of mutual loss and gain (among you). And those who believe in God and work righteousness — He will remove from them their ills, and He will admit them to Gardens beneath which rivers flow, to dwell therein forever: that will be the Supreme Achievement.

10. But those who reject Faith and treat Our Signs as falsehoods, they will be Companions of the Fire, to dwell therein for aye: and evil is that Goal.

11. No kind of calamity can occur, except by the leave of God: and if anyone believes in God, (God) guides his heart (aright): for God knows all things.

12. So obey God, and obey His Apostle; but if ye turn back, the duty of Our Apostle is but to proclaim (the Message) clearly and openly.

13. God! there is no god but He: and on God, therefore, let the Believers put their trust.

14. O ye who believe! truly, among your wives and your children are (some that are) enemies to yourselves: so beware of them! But if ye forgive and overlook, and cover up (their faults), verily God is Oft-Forgiving, Most Merciful.

15. Your riches and your children may be but a trial: but in the Presence of God, is the highest Reward.

16. So fear God as much as ye can; listen and obey; and spend in charity for the benefit of your own souls: and those saved from the covetousness of their own souls — they are the ones that achieve prosperity.

17. If ye loan to God a beautiful loan, He will double it to your (credit), and He will grant you forgiveness: for God is most Ready to appreciate (service), Most Forbearing —

18. Knower of what is hidden and what is open, exalted in Might, Full of Wisdom.

Chapter 65
Sürah At-Talaq (The Divorce)
Revealed at Madinah, 12 verses

In the name of God, Most Gracious, Most Merciful.

1. O Prophet! when ye do divorce women, divorce them at their prescribed periods, and count (accurately) their prescribed periods: and fear God your Lord: and turn them not out of their houses, nor shall they (themselves) leave, except in case they are guilty of some open lewdness[1]. Those are limits set by God: and any who transgresses the limits of God, does verily wrong his (own) soul: thou knowest not if perchance[2] God will bring about thereafter some new situation.

2. Thus when they fulfil their term appointed, either take them back on equitable[3] terms or part with them on equitable terms; and take for witness two persons from among you, endued with justice, and establish the evidence (as) before God. Such is the admonition given to him who believes in God and the Last Day. And for those who fear God, He (ever) prepares a way out,

3. And He provides for him from (sources) he never could imagine. And if anyone puts his trust in God, sufficient is (God) for him. For God will surely accomplish His purpose: verily, for all things has God appointed a due proportion.

4. Such of your women as have passed the age of monthly courses, for them the prescribed period, if ye have any doubt, is three months, and for those who have no courses (it is the same): for those who carry (life within their wombs), their period is until they deliver their burdens: and for those who fear God, He will make their path easy.

5. That is the Command of God, which He has sent down to you: and if anyone fears God, He will remove his ills from him and will enlarge His reward.

6. Let the women live (in 'iddah) in the same style as ye live, according to your means: annoy them not, so as to restrict them. And if they carry (life in their wombs), then spend (your substance) on

---

[1] Indecency, obscenity
[2] (Arch.) By chance, maybe
[3] Just

460

them until they deliver their burden: and if they suckle your (offspring), give them their recompense: and take mutual counsel together, according to what is just and reasonable. And if ye find yourselves in difficulties, let another woman suckle (the child) on the (father's) behalf.

7. Let the man of means spend according to his means: and the man whose resources are restricted, let him spend according to what God has given him. God puts no burden on any person beyond what He has given him. After a difficulty, God will soon grant relief.

8. How many populations that insolently opposed the command of their Lord and of His apostles, did We not then call to account — to severe account? — and We imposed on them an exemplary Punishment.

9. Then did they taste the evil result of their conduct, and the End of their conduct was Perdition[4].

10. God has prepared for them a severe Punishment (in the Hereafter). Therefore fear God, O ye men of understanding — who have believed! — for God hath indeed sent down to you a Message, —

11. An Apostle, who rehearses to you the Signs of God containing clear explanations, that he may lead forth those who believe and do righteous deeds from the depths of Darkness into Light. And those who believe in God and work righteousness, He will admit to Gardens beneath which rivers flow, to dwell therein forever: God has indeed granted for them a most excellent provision.

12. God is He Who created seven Firmaments and of the earth a similar number. Through the midst of them (all) descends His Command: that ye may know that God has power over all things, and that God comprehends all things in (His) Knowledge.

Chapter 66
Sürah At-Tahrïm (Prohibition)
Revealed at Madinah, 12 verses

In the name of God, Most Gracious, Most Merciful.

1. O Prophet! why holdest thou to be forbidden that which God

---

[4] Ruin

has made lawful to thee? Thou seekest to please thy consorts[1]. But God is Oft-Forgiving, Most Merciful.

2. God has already ordained[2] for you, (O men), the dissolution[3] of your oaths (in some cases): and God is your Protector, and He is Full of Knowledge and Wisdom.

3. When the Prophet disclosed a matter in confidence to one of his consorts, and she then divulged[4] it (to another), and God made it known to him, he confirmed part thereof and repudiated[5] a part. Then when he told her thereof, she said, "Who told thee this?" He said, "He told me Who knows and is well-acquainted (with all things)."

4. If ye two turn in repentance to Him, your hearts are indeed so inclined; but if ye back up each other against him, truly God is his Protector, and Gabriel, and (every) righteous one among those who believe — and furthermore, the angels — will back (him) up.

5. It may be, if he divorced you (all), that God will give him in exchange Consorts better than you — who submit (their wills), who believe, who are devout, who turn to God in repentance, who worship (in humility), who travel (for faith) and fast — previously married or virgins.

6. O ye who believe! save yourselves and your families from a Fire whose fuel is Men and Stones, over which are (appointed) angels stern (and) severe, who flinch[6] not (from executing) the Commands they receive from God, but do (precisely) what they are commanded.

7. (They will say), "O ye Unbelievers! make no excuses this day! Ye are being but requited for all that ye did!"

8. O ye who believe! turn to God with sincere repentance: in the hope that your Lord will remove from you your ills and admit you to Gardens beneath which Rivers flow — the Day that God will not permit to be humiliated the Prophet and those who believe with him. Their Light will run forward before them and by their right hands, while they say, "Our Lord! perfect our Light for us, and grant us

---

[1] Wives

[2] Prescribed

[3] Undoing or relaxing of

[4] Disclosed

[5] Disown, reject

[6] Draw back (from duty)

Forgiveness; for Thou has power over all things."

9. O Prophet! strive hard against the Unbelievers and the Hypocrites, and be firm against them. Their abode is Hell — an evil refuge (indeed).

10. God sets forth, for an example to the Unbelievers, the wife of Noah and the wife of Lüt: they were (respectively) under two of Our righteous servants, but they were false to their (husbands), and they profited nothing before God on their account, but were told: "Enter ye the Fire along with (others) that enter!"

11. And God sets forth, as an example to those who believe, the wife of Pharaoh: Behold, she said: "O my Lord! build for me, in nearness to Thee, a mansion in the Garden, and save me from Pharaoh and his doings, and save me from those that do wrong";

12. And Mary the daughter of 'Imran, who guarded her chastity; and We breathed into her (body) of Our spirit; and she testified to the truth of the words of her Lord and of His Revelations, and was one of the devout (servants).

Chapter 67
Sürah Al-Mulk (The Dominion)
Revealed at Makkah, 30 verses

In the name of God, Most Gracious, Most Merciful.

1. Blessed be He in Whose hands is Dominion: and He over all things Hath Power —

2. He Who created Death and Life, that He may try which of you is best in deed: and He is the Exalted in Might, Oft-Forgiving; —

3. He Who created the seven heavens one above another; no want of proportion wilt thou see in the Creation of (God) Most Gracious, so turn thy vision again: Seest thou any flaw?

4. Again turn thy vision a second time; (thy) vision will come back to thee dull and discomfited[1], in a state worn out.

5. And We have, (from of old), adorned the lowest heaven with

---

[1] Baffled, confused, (arch) defeated

Lamps, and We have made such (Lamps) (as) missiles[2] to drive away the Evil Ones, and have prepared for them the Penalty of the Blazing Fire.

6. For those who reject their Lord (and Cherisher) is the Penalty of Hell: and evil is (such) destination.

7. When they are cast therein, they will hear the (terrible) drawing in of its breath even as it blazes forth.

8. Almost bursting with fury: every time a Group is cast therein, its Keepers will ask, "Did no Warner come to you?"

9. They will say: "Yes indeed: a Warner did come to us, but we rejected him and said, 'God never sent down any (Message): ye are in nothing but an egregious[3] delusion!'"

10. They will further say: "Had we but listened or used our intelligence, we should not (now) be among the Companions of the Blazing Fire!"

11. They will then confess their sins: but far will be (Forgiveness) from the Companions of the Blazing Fire!

12. As for those who fear their Lord unseen, for them is Forgiveness and a great Reward.

13. And whether ye hide your word or publish it, He certainly has (full) knowledge, of the secrets of (all) hearts.

14. Should He not know — He that created? And He is the One that understands the finest mysteries (and) is well-acquainted (with them).

15. It is He Who has made the earth manageable for you, so traverse[4] ye through its tracts and enjoy of the Sustenance which He furnishes: but unto Him is the Resurrection.

16. Do ye feel secure that He Who is in heaven will not cause you to be swallowed up by the earth when it shakes (as in an earthquake)?

17. Or do ye feel secure that He Who is in Heaven will not send against you a violent tornado (with showers of stones), so that ye shall know how (terrible) was My warning?

---

[2] (Object or weapon) for throwing at a target
[3] Deplorable, outrageous
[4] Travel

18. But indeed men before them rejected (My warning): then how (terrible) was My rejection (of them)?

19. Do they not observe the birds above them, spreading their wings and folding them in? None can uphold them except (God) Most Gracious: truly it is He that watches over all things.

20. Nay, who is there that can help you, (even as) an army, besides (God) Most Merciful? In nothing but delusion are the Unbelievers.

21. Or who is there that can provide you with Sustenance if He were to withhold[5] His provision? Nay, they obstinately persist in insolent impiety and flight (from the Truth).

22. Is then one who walks headlong, with his face grovelling[6], better guided — or one who walks evenly on a Straight Way?

23. Say: "It is He Who has created you (and made you grow), and made for you the faculties of hearing, seeing, feeling and understanding: little thanks it is ye give."

24. Say: "It is He Who has multiplied you through the earth, and to Him shall ye be gathered together."

25. They ask: When will this promise be (fulfilled)? If ye are telling the truth.

26. Say: "As to the knowledge of the time, it is with God alone: I am (sent) only to warn plainly in public."

27. At length, when they see it close at hand, grieved will be the faces of the Unbelievers, and it will be said (to them): "This is (the promise fulfilled), which ye were calling for!"

28. Say: "See ye? — if God were to destroy me, and those with me, or if He bestows His Mercy on us — yet who can deliver the Unbelievers from a grievous Penalty?"

29. Say: "He is (God) Most Gracious: we have believed in Him, and on Him have we put our trust: so soon will ye know which (of us) it is that is in manifest error."

30. Say: "See ye? — if your stream be some morning lost (in the underground earth), who then can supply you with clear-flowing water?"

---

[5] Hold back
[6] Prone, with face downwards

Chapter 68
Sürah Al-Qalam (The Pen)
Revealed at Makkah, 52 verses

In the name of God, Most Gracious, Most Merciful,

1. Nün. By the Pen and by the (Record) which (men) write —
2. Thou art not, by the grace of thy Lord, mad or possessed.
3. Nay, verily for thee is a Reward unfailing:
4. And thou (standest) on an exalted standard of character.
5. Soon wilt thou see and they will see,
6. Which of you is afflicted with madness.
7. Verily it is thy Lord that knoweth best, which (among men) hath strayed from His Path: and He knoweth best those who receive (True) Guidance.
8. So hearken not to those who deny (the Truth).
9. Their desire is that thou shouldst be pliant[1]; so would they be pliant.
10. Heed not the type of despicable man — ready with oaths.
11. A slanderer, going about with calumnies[2].
12. (Habitually) hindering (all) good, transgressing beyond bounds, deep in sin.
13. Violent (and cruel) — with all that, base-born —
14. Because he possesses wealth and (numerous) sons.
15. When to him are rehearsed Our Signs, "Tales of the Ancients," he cries.
16. Soon shall We brand[3] (the beast) on the snout[4]!
17. Verily We have tried them as We tried the people of the Garden when they resolved to gather the fruits of the (garden) in the morning.
18. But made no reservation, ("If it be God's Will").
19. So there came, on the (garden) a visitation from thy Lord, (which swept away) all around, while they were asleep.
20. So the (garden) became, by the morning, like a dark and

---

[1] Bending easily, yielding, compliant
[2] Slanderous reports, malicious misrepresentation, false charge
[3] Burn with hot iron to apply mark (of ownership).
[4] Projecting nose of an animal, (derogatory) human nose

desolate[5] spot, (whose fruit had been gathered).

21. As the morning broke, they called out, one to another —

22. "Go ye to your tilth (betimes) in morning, if ye would gather the fruits."

23. So they departed, conversing in secret low tones, (saying) —

24. "Let not a single indigent person break in upon you into the (garden) this day."

25. And they opened the morning, strong in an (unjust) resolve.

26. But when they saw the (garden), they said: "We have surely lost our way:

27. "Indeed we are shut out (of the fruits of our labor)!"

28. Said one of them, more just (than the rest): "Did I not say to you, 'Why not glorify (God)?' "

29. They said: "Glory to our Lord! Verily we have been doing wrong!"

30. Then they turned, one against another, in reproach.

31. They said: "Alas for us! We have indeed transgressed!

32. "It may be that our Lord will give us in exchange a better (garden) than this: for we do turn to Him (in repentance)!"

33. Such is the Punishment (in this life); but greater is the Punishment in the Hereafter — if only they knew!

34. Verily, for the righteous are Gardens of Delight, in the Presence of their Lord.

35. Shall We then treat the People of Faith like the People of Sin?

36. What is the matter with you? How judge ye?

37. Or have ye a Book through which ye learn —

38. That ye shall have through it whatever ye choose?

39. Or have ye Covenants with Us on oath, reaching to the Day of Judgment (providing) that ye shall have whatever ye shall demand?

40. Ask thou of them, which of them will stand surety of that!

41. Or have they some "partners" (in Godhead)? Then let them produce their "partners," if they are truthful!

42. The Day that the shin[6] shall be laid bare, and they shall be summoned to bow in adoration, but they shall not be able —

---

[5] Deserted
[6] Front of leg below knee

43. Their eyes will be cast down—ignominy[7] will cover them; seeing that they had been summoned aforetime to bow in adoration[8], while they were whole, (and had refused).

44. Then leave Me alone with such as reject this message: by degrees shall We punish them from directions they perceive not.

45. A (long) respite will I grant them: truly powerful is My plan.

46. Or is it that thou dost ask them for a reward, so that they are burdened with a load of debt? —

47. Or that the Unseen is in their hands, so that they can write it down?

48. So wait with patience for the command of thy Lord, and be not like the Companion of the Fish — when he cried out in agony.

49. Had not Grace from His Lord reached him, he would indeed have been cast off on the naked shore, in disgrace.

50. Thus did his Lord choose him and make him of the Company of the Righteous.

51. And the Unbelievers would almost trip[9] thee up with their eyes when they hear the message; and they say: "Surely he is possessed!"

52. But it is nothing less than a Message to all the worlds.

Chapter 69
Sürah Al-Hãqqah (The Sure Reality)
Revealed at Makkah, 52 verses

In the name of God, Most Gracious, Most Merciful.

1. The Sure Reality!

2. What is the Sure Reality?

3. And what will make thee realize what the Sure Reality is?

4. The Thamüd and the 'Ãd people (branded) as false the Stunning Calamity!

5. But the Thamüd — they were destroyed by a terrible storm of thunder and lightning!

6. And the 'Ãd — they were destroyed by a furious wind, ex-

---

7 Disgrace
8 Worship
9 Stumble, slip

ceedingly violent;

7. He made it rage against them seven nights and eight days in succession: So that thou couldst see the (whole) people lying prostrate in its (path), as if they had been roots of hollow palm trees tumbled down!

8. Then seest thou any of them left surviving?

9. And Pharaoh, and those before him, and the Cities overthrown, committed habitual Sin.

10. And disobeyed (each) the Apostle of their Lord; so He punished them with an abundant Penalty.

11. We, when the water (of Noah's flood) overflowed beyond its limits, carried you (mankind), in the floating (Ark).

12. That We might make it a message unto you, and that ears (that should hear the tale and) retain its memory should bear its (lessons) in remembrance.

13. Then, when one Blast is sounded on the Trumpet,

14. And the earth is moved, and its mountains, and they are crushed to powder at one stroke, —

15. On that Day shall the (Great) Event come to pass,

16. And the sky will be rent asunder, for it will that Day be flimsy[1],

17. And the angels will be on its sides, and eight will, that Day, bear the Throne of thy Lord above them.

18. That Day shall ye be brought to Judgment: not an act of yours that ye hide will be hidden.

19. Then He that will be given his Record in his right hand will say: "Ah here! read ye my Record!

20. "I did really understand that my Account would (one Day) reach me!"

21. And he will be in a life of Bliss,

22. In a Garden on high,

23. The Fruits whereof (will hang in bunches) low and near.

24. "Eat ye and drink ye, with full satisfaction; because of the (good) that ye sent before you in the days that are gone!"

25. And he that will be given his Record in his left hand, will say: "Ah! would that my record had not been given to me!

---

[1] Weak

26. "And that I had never realized how my account (stood)!

27. "Ah! would that (Death) had made an end of me!

28. "Of no profit to me has been my wealth!

29. "My power has perished from me!"...

30. (The stern command will say): "Seize ye him, and bind ye him,

31. "And burn ye him in the Blazing Fire.

32. "Further, make him march in a chain, whereof the length is seventy cubits[2]!

33. "This was he that would not believe in God Most High,

34. "And would not encourage the feeding of the indigent!

35. "So no friend hath he here this Day.

36. "Nor hath he any food except the corruption from the washing of wounds,

37. "Which none do eat but those in sin."

38. So I do call to witness what ye see

39. And what ye see not,

40. That this is verily the word of an honoured apostle;

41. It is not the word of a poet: little it is ye believe!

42. Nor is it the word of a soothsayer[3]: little admonition it is ye receive.

43. (This is) a Message sent down from the Lord of the Worlds.

44. And if the apostle were to invent any sayings in Our name,

45. We should certainly seize him by his right hand,

46. And We should certainly then cut off the artery of his heart:

47. Nor could any of you withhold him (from Our wrath).

48. But verily this is a Message for the God-fearing.

49. And We certainly know that there are amongst you those that reject (it)

50. But truly (Revelation) is a cause of sorrow for the Unbelievers.

51. But verily it is Truth of assured certainty.

52. So glorify the name of thy Lord Most High.

---

[2] Ancient measure of length, approximately equal to length of forearm.

[3] Diviner

Chapter 70
Sürah Al-Maʻarij (The Ways of Ascent)
Revealed at Makkah, 44 verses

In the name of God, Most Gracious, Most Merciful.

1. A questioner asked about a Penalty to befall —

2. The Unbelievers, the which there is none to ward off —

3. (A Penalty) from God, Lord of the Ways of Ascent.

4. The angels and the spirit ascend unto Him in a Day the measure whereof is (as) fifty thousand years:

5. Therefore do thou hold Patience — a Patience of beautiful (contentment).

6. They see the (Day) indeed as a far-off (event):

7. But We see it (quite) near.

8. The Day that the sky will be like molten brass,

9. And the mountains will be like wool,

10. And no friend will ask after a friend,

11. Though they will be put in sight of each other — the sinner's desire will be: Would that he could redeem himself from the Penalty of that Day by (sacrificing) his children,

12. His wife and his brother,

13. His kindred who sheltered him,

14. And all, all that is on earth — so it could deliver him:

15. By no means! for it would be the Fire of Hell! —

16. Plucking out (his being) right to the skull! —

17. Inviting (all) such as turn their backs and turn away their faces (from the Right).

18. And collect (wealth) and hide it (from use)!

19. Truly man was created very impatient —

20. Fretful when evil touches him;

21. And niggardly when good reaches him —

22. Not so those devoted to Prayer —

23. Those who remain steadfast to their prayer;

24. And those in whose wealth is a recognised right

25. For the (needy) who asks and him who is prevented (for some reason from asking);

26. And those who hold to the truth of the Day of Judgment;

27. And those who fear the displeasure of their Lord —

28. For their Lord's displeasure is the opposite of Peace and Tranquillity —

29. And those who guard their chastity,

30. Except with their wives and the (captives) whom their right hands possess, — for (then) they are not to be blamed,

31. But those who trespass beyond this are transgressors —

32. And those who respect their trusts and covenants;

33. And those who stand firm in their testimonies;

34. And those who guard (the sacredness) of their worship —

35. Such will be the honoured ones in the Gardens (of Bliss).

36. Now what is the matter with the Unbelievers that they rush madly before thee —

37. From the right and from the left, in crowds?

38. Does every man of them long to enter the Garden of Bliss?

39. By no means! For We have created them out of the (base matter) they know!

40. Now I do call to witness the Lord of all points in the East and the West that We can certainly —

41. Substitute for them better (men) than they; and We are not to be defeated (in Our Plan).

42. So leave them to plunge in vain talk and play about, until they encounter that Day of theirs which they have been promised! —

43. The Day whereon they will issue from their sepulchres[1] in sudden haste as if they were rushing to a goal-post (fixed for them) —

44. Their eyes lowered in dejection — ignominy covering them (all over)! Such is the Day the which they are promised!

Chapter 71
Sürah Nüh (Noah)
Revealed at Makkah, 28 verses

In the name of God, Most Gracious, Most Merciful.

1. We sent Noah to his People (with the Command): "Do thou

---

[1] Tombs, burial vault or cave

warn thy People before there comes to them a grievous Penalty."

2. He said: "O my People! I am to you a Warner, clear and open:

3. "That ye should worship God, fear Him and obey me:

4. "So He may forgive you your sins and give you respite for a stated Term: for when the Term given by God is accomplished, it cannot be put forward: if ye only knew."

5. He said: "O my Lord! I have called to my People night and day:

6. "But my call only increases (their) flight (from the Right).

7. "And every time I have called to them, that Thou mightest forgive them, they have (only) thrust their fingers into their ears, covered themselves up with their garments, grown obstinate, and given themselves up to arrogance.

8. "So I have called to them aloud;

9. "Further I have spoken to them in public and secretly in private,

10. "Saying, 'Ask forgiveness from your Lord; for He is Oft-Forgiving;

11. "'He will send rain to you in abundance;

12. "'Give you increase in wealth and sons; and bestow on you Gardens and bestow on you rivers (of flowing water).

13. "'What is the matter with you, that ye place not your hope for kindness and long-suffering in God —

14. "'Seeing that it is He that has created you in diverse stages?

15. "'See ye not how God has created the seven heavens one above another,

16. "'And made the moon a light in their midst, and made the sun as a (Glorious) Lamp?

17. "'And God has produced you from the earth growing (gradually),

18. "'And in the End He will return you into the (earth), and raise you forth (again at the Resurrection[1])?

19. "'And God has made the earth for you as a carpet (spread out),

20. "'That ye may go about therein, in spacious roads.'"

21. Noah said: "O my Lord! They have disobeyed me, but they

---

[1] Rising again of dead on the Day of Judgment.

follow (men) whose wealth and children give them no increase but only Loss.

22. "And they have devised a tremendous[2] Plot.

23. "And they have said (to each other), 'Abandon not your gods: Abandon neither Wadd nor Suwaʻ, neither Yaguth nor Yaʻuq, nor Nasr'[3] —

24. "They have already misled many; and grant Thou no increase to the wrongdoers but in straying (from their mark)."

25. Because of their sins they were drowned (in the flood), and were made to enter the Fire (of Punishment): and they found — in lieu of God — none to help them.

26. And Noah, said: "O my Lord! Leave not of the Unbelievers, a single one on earth!

27. "For, if Thou dost leave (any of) them, they will but mislead Thy devotees, and they will breed none but wicked ungrateful ones.

28. "O my Lord! Forgive me, my parents, all who enter my house in Faith, and (all) believing men and believing women: and to the wrongdoers grant Thou no increase but in perdition[4]!"

Chapter 72
Sürah Al-Jinn (The Spirits)
Revealed at Makkah, 28 verses

In the name of God, Most Gracious, Most Merciful.

1. Say: It has been revealed to me that a company of Jinns listened (to the Qurʼan). They said, 'We have really heard a wonderful Recital!

2. 'It gives guidance to the Right, and we have believed therein: we shall not join (in worship) any (gods) with our Lord.

3. 'And Exalted is the Majesty of our Lord: He has taken neither a wife nor a son.

---

[2] Immense

[3] The names of their five false gods. Of these Wadd was depicted in the shape of a man (manly power), Suwaʻ in that of a woman (beauty), Yaghuth in that of a lion (brute strength), Yaʻuq in that of a horse (swiftness), and Nasr in that of an eagle (sharp sight or insight).

[4] Ruin

4. 'There were some foolish ones among us, who used to utter extravagant[1] lies against God;

5. 'But we do think that no man or spirit should say aught that is untrue against God.

6. 'True, there were persons among mankind who took shelter with persons among the Jinns, but they increased them in folly.

7. 'And they (came to) think as ye thought, that God would not raise up any one (to Judgment).

8. 'And we pried[2] into the secrets of heaven; but we found it filled with stern guards and flaming fires.

9. 'We used, indeed, to sit there in (hidden) stations, to (steal) a hearing; but any who listen now will find a flaming fire watching him in ambush[3].

10. 'And we understand not whether ill is intended to those on earth, or whether their Lord (really) intends to guide them to right conduct.

11. 'There are among us some that are righteous, and some the contrary: we follow divergent[4] paths.

12. 'But we think that we can by no means frustrate God throughout the earth, nor can we frustrate Him by flight.

13. 'And as for us, since we have listened to the Guidance, we have accepted it: and any who believes in his Lord has no fear, either of a short (account) or of any injustice.

14. 'Amongst us are some that submit their wills (to God), and some that swerve from justice. Now those who submit their wills — they have sought out (the path) of right conduct:

15. 'But those who swerve — they are (but) fuel for Hell-fire' —

16. (And God's Message is): "If they (the Pagans) had (only) remained on the (right) Way, We should certainly have bestowed on them Rain in abundance.

17. "That We might try them by that (means). But if any turns away from the remembrance of his Lord, He will cause him to undergo a severe Penalty.

---

[1] Immoderate, extreme

[2] Look or peer inquisitively, inquire impertinently into (affairs, etc.)

[3] Hiding

[4] Separate, different

18. "And the places of worship are for God (alone): So invoke not any one along with God;

19. "Yet when the Devotee⁵ of God stands forth to invoke Him, they just make round him a dense crowd."

20. Say: "I do no more than invoke my Lord, and I join not with Him any (false god)."

21. Say: "It is not in my power to cause you harm, or to bring you to right conduct."

22. Say: "No one can deliver me from God (If I were to disobey Him), nor should I find refuge except in Him,

23. "Unless I proclaim what I receive from God and His Messages: for any that disobey God and His Apostle — for them is Hell: they shall dwell therein forever."

24. At length, when they see (with their own eyes) that which they are promised — then will they know who it is that is weakest in (his) helper and least important in point of numbers.

25. Say: "I know not whether the (Punishment) which ye are promised is near, or whether my Lord will appoint for it a distant term.

26. "He (alone) knows the Unseen, nor does He make any one acquainted with His Mysteries —

27. "Except an apostle whom He has chosen: and then He makes a band of watchers march before him and behind him,

28. "That He may know that they have (truly) brought and delivered the Messages of their Lord: and He surrounds (all the mysteries) that are with them, and takes account of every single thing."

Chapter 73
Sūrah Al-Muzammil (Folded in Garments)
Revealed at Makkah, 20 verses

In the name of God, Most Gracious, Most Merciful.

1. O thou folded in garments!

2. Stand (to prayer) by night, but not all night —

---

⁵ Devoted servant

3. Half of it — or a little less,

4. Or a little more; and recite the Qur'an in slow, measured rhythmic tones.

5. Soon shall We send down to thee a weighty Message.

6. Truly the rising by night is most potent[1] for governing (the soul), and most suitable for (framing) the Word (of Prayer and Praise).

7. True, there is for thee by day prolonged occupation with ordinary duties:

8. But keep in remembrance the name of thy Lord and devote thyself to Him wholeheartedly.

9. (He is) Lord of the East and the West: there is no god but He: take Him therefore for (thy) Disposer of Affairs.

10. And have patience with what they say, and leave them with noble (dignity).

11. And leave Me (alone to deal with) those in possession of the good things of life, who (yet) deny the Truth; and bear with them for a little while.

12. With Us are Fetters (to bind them), and a Fire (to burn them),

13. And a Food that chokes, and a Penalty Grievous.

14. One Day the earth and the mountains will be in violent commotion[2]. And the mountains will be as a heap of sand poured out and flowing down.

15. We have sent to you, (O men!) an apostle, to be a witness concerning you, even as We sent an apostle to Pharaoh.

16. But Pharaoh disobeyed the apostle; so We seized him with a heavy Punishment.

17. Then how shall ye, if ye deny (God), guard yourselves against a Day that will make children hoary-headed[3]? —

18. Whereon the sky will be cleft asunder? His Promise needs must be accomplished.

19. Verily this is an admonition: therefore, whoso will, let him take a (straight) path to his Lord!

20. Thy Lord doth know that thou standest forth (to prayer) nigh two-thirds of the night, or half the night, or a third of the night, and

---

[1] Powerful, effective

[2] Turmoil

[3] Gray-headed

so doth a party of those with thee. But God doth appoint night and day in due measure. He knoweth that ye are unable to keep count thereof. So He hath turned to you (in mercy): read ye, therefore, of the Qur'an as much as may be easy for you. He knoweth that there may be (some) among you in ill-health; others travelling through the land, seeking of God's bounty; yet others fighting in God's Cause, read ye, therefore, as much of the Qur'an as may be easy (for you); and establish regular Prayer and give regular Charity; and loan to God a Beautiful Loan. And whatever good ye send forth for your souls ye shall find it in God's Presence — yea, better and greater, in Reward and seek ye the Grace of God: for God is Oft-Forgiving, Most Merciful.

Chapter 74
Sürah Al-Mudathir (One Wrapped Up)
Revealed at Makkah, 56 verses

In the name of God, Most Gracious, Most Merciful.

1. O thou wrapped up (in a mantle)!
2. Arise and deliver thy warning!
3. And thy Lord do thou magnify!
4. And thy garments keep free from stain!
5. And all abomination[1] shun!
6. Nor expect, in giving, any increase (for thyself)!
7. But, for thy Lord's (Cause), be patient and constant!
8. Finally, when the Trumpet is sounded,
9. That will be — that Day — a Day of Distress —
10. Far from easy for those without Faith.
11. Leave Me alone, (to deal) with the (creature) whom I created (bare and) alone! —
12. To whom I granted resources in abundance,
13. And sons to be by his side! —
14. To whom I made (life) smooth and comfortable!
15. Yet is he greedy — that I should add (yet more) —

---

[1] Loathsome evil

16. By no means! For to Our Signs he has been refractory[2]!

17. Soon will I visit him with a mount of calamities!

18. For he thought and he plotted; —

19. And woe to him! How he plotted! —

20. Yea, Woe to him; how he plotted! —

21. Then he looked round;

22. Then he frowned and he scowled;

23. Then he turned back and was haughty;

24. Then said he: "This is nothing but magic, derived from of old;

25. "This is nothing but the word of a mortal!"

26. Soon will I cast him into Hell-Fire!

27. And what will explain to thee what Hell-Fire is?

28. Naught[3] doth it permit to endure, and naught doth it leave alone!

29. Darkening and changing the color of man!

30. Over it are Nineteen.

31. And We have set none but angels as Guardians of the Fire; and We have fixed their number only as a trial for Unbelievers — in order that the People of the Book may arrive at certainty, and the Believers may increase in Faith — and that no doubts may be left for the People of the Book and the Believers, and that those in whose hearts is a disease and the Unbelievers may say, "What symbol doth God intend by this?" Thus doth God leave to stray whom He pleaseth, and guide whom He pleaseth; and none can know the forces of thy Lord, except He. And this is no other than a warning to mankind.

32. Nay, verily: By the Moon,

33. And by the Night as it retreateth,

34. And by the Dawn as it shineth forth —

35. This is but one of the mighty (portents),

36. A warning to mankind —

37. To any of you that chooses to press forward, or to follow behind

38. Every soul will be (held) in pledge for its deeds.

39. Except the Companions of the Right Hand.

---

[2] Stubborn, rebellious

[3] Nothing

40. (They will be) in Gardens (of Delight); they will question each other,

41. And (ask) of the Sinners:

42. "What led you into Hell-Fire?"

43. They will say: "We were not of those who prayed;"

44. "Nor were we of those who fed the indigent;"

45. "But we used to talk vanities[4] with vain talkers;

46. "And we used to deny the Day of Judgment,"

47. "Until there came to us (the Hour) that is certain."

48. Then will no intercession[5] of (any) intercessors profit them.

49. Then what is the matter with them that they turn away from admonition? —

50. As if they were affrighted[6] asses,

51. Fleeing from a lion!

52. Forsooth[7], each one of them wants to be given scrolls (of revelation) spread out!

53. By no means! But they fear not the Hereafter,

54. Nay, this surely is an admonition:

55. Let any who will, keep it in remembrance!

56. But none will keep it in remembrance except as God wills: He is the Lord of Righteousness, and the Lord of Forgiveness.

Chapter 75
Sūrah Al-Qiyamah (The Resurrection)
Revealed at Makkah, 40 verses

In the name of God, Most Gracious, Most Merciful.

1. I do call to witness the Resurrection Day;

2. And I do call to witness the self-reproaching spirit: (eschew[1] Evil).

3. Does man think that We cannot assemble his bones?

---

4 Gossip, idle talk
5 Mediation
6 Frightened
7 (Archaic, ironical, or derogatory) Truly, in truth
1 Avoid

4. Nay, We are able to put together in perfect order the very tips of his fingers.

5. But man wishes to do wrong (even) in the time in front of him.

6. He questions: "When is the Day of Resurrection?"

7. At length, when the sight is dazed,

8. And the moon is buried in darkness.

9. And the sun and moon are joined together —

10. That Day will Man say: "Where is the refuge?"

11. By no means! No place of safety!

12. Before thy Lord (alone), that Day will be the place of rest.

13. That Day will Man be told (all) that he put forward, and all that he put back.

14. Nay, man will be evidence against himself,

15. Even though he were to put up his excuses.

16. Move not thy tongue concerning the (Qur'an) to make haste therewith.

17. It is for Us to collect it and to promulgate[2] it:

18. But when We have promulgated it, follow thou its recital (as promulgated):

19. Nay more, it is for Us to explain it (and make it clear):

20. Nay, (ye men!) but ye love the fleeting[3] life,

21. And leave alone the Hereafter.

22. Some faces, that Day, will beam (in brightness and beauty) —

23. Looking towards their Lord;

24. And some faces, that Day, will be sad and dismal[4],

25. In the thought that some back-breaking calamity was about to be inflicted on them;

26. Yea, when (the soul) reaches to the collar bone (in its exit),

27. And there will be a cry, "Who is a magician (to restore him)?"

28. And he will conclude that it was (the Time) of Parting;

29. And one leg will be joined with another:

30. That Day the Drive will be (all) to thy Lord!

31. So he gave nothing in charity, nor did he pray! —

---

[2] Proclaim, explain

[3] Transitory, passing

[4] Gloomy

32. But on the contrary, he rejected Truth and turned away!

33. Then did he stalk[5] to his family in full conceit[6]!

34. Woe to thee, (O men!), yea, woe!

35. Again, Woe to thee, (O men!), yea, woe!

36. Does man think that he will be left uncontrolled, (without purpose)?

37. Was he not a drop of sperm emitted[7] (in lowly form)?

38. Then did he become a leech-like clot; then did (God) make and fashion (him) in due proportion.

39. And of him He made two sexes, male and female.

40. Has not He, (the same), the power to give life to the dead?

Chapter 76
Sūrah Al-Insan (The Man)
Revealed at Madinah, 31 verses

In the name of God, Most Gracious, Most Merciful.

1. Has there not been over Man a long period of Time, when he was nothing — (not even) mentioned?

2. Verily We created Man from a drop of mingled sperm, in order to try him: So We gave him (the gifts), of Hearing and Sight.

3. We showed him the Way: whether he be grateful or ungrateful (rests on his will).

4. For the Rejecters we have prepared chains, yokes[1], and a blazing Fire.

5. As to the Righteous, they shall drink of a Cup (of Wine) mixed with Kafur[2] —

6. A Fountain where the Devotees of God do drink, making it flow in unstinted[3] abundance.

7. They perform (their) vows, and they fear a Day whose evil flies

---

[5] Walk in stately or imposing manner, stride
[6] Vanity
[7] Discharged
[1] Wooden cross-piece fastened over necks of two oxen, etc.
[2] Literally, camphor, it is a fountain in Paradise.
[3] Unlimited

far and wide.

8. And they feed, for the love of God, the indigent, the orphan, and the captive —

9. (Saying),"We feed you for the sake of God alone: no reward do we desire from you, nor thanks."

10. "We only fear a Day of distressful Wrath from the side of our Lord."

11. But God will deliver them from the evil of that Day, and will shed over them a Light of Beauty and (blissful) Joy.

12. And because they were patient and constant, He will reward them with a Garden and (garments of) silk.

13. Reclining in the (Garden) on raised thrones, they will see there neither the sun's (excessive heat) nor (the moon's) excessive cold.

14. And the shades of the (Garden) will come low over them, and the bunches (of fruit), there, will hang low in humility.

15. And amongst them will be passed round vessels of silver and goblets of crystal —

16. Crystal-clear, made of silver: they will determine the measure thereof (according to their wishes).

17. And they will be given to drink there of a Cup (of Wine) mixed with Zanjabil[4] —

18. A fountain there, called Salsabil[5].

19. And round about them will (serve) youths of perpetual (freshness): If thou seest them, thou wouldst think them scattered Pearls.

20. And when thou lookest, it is there thou wilt see a Bliss and a Realm Magnificent.

21. Upon them will be green garments of fine silk and heavy brocade, and they will be adorned with bracelets of silver; and their Lord will give to them to drink of a wine pure and holy.

22. "Verily this is a Reward for you, and your Endeavor is accepted and recognised."

23. It is We Who have sent down the Qur'an to thee by stages.

24. Therefore be patient with constancy to the Command of thy

---

[4] Literally means ginger.

[5] Salsabil means "Seek the way."

Lord, and hearken not to the sinner or the ingrate[6] among them.

25. And celebrate the name of thy Lord morning and evening,

26. And part of the night, prostrate thyself to Him; and glorify Him a long night through.

27. As to these, they love the fleeting life, and put away behind them a Day (that will be) hard.

28. It is We Who created them, and We have made their joints strong; but, when We will, We can substitute the like of them by a complete change.

29. This is an admonition: Whosoever will, let him take a (straight) Path to his Lord.

30. But ye will not, except as God wills; for God is full of Knowledge and Wisdom.

31. He will admit to His Mercy whom He will; But the wrongdoers, — for them has He prepared a grievous Penalty.

Chapter 77
Sūrah Al-Mursalat (Those Sent Forth)
Revealed at Makkah, 50 verses

In the name of God, Most Gracious, Most Merciful.

1. By the (Winds) sent forth one after another (to man's profit);

2. Which then blow violently in tempestuous[1] Gusts[2],

3. And scatter (things) far and wide;

4. Then separate them, one from another,

5. Then spread abroad a Message,

6. Whether of Justification or of Warning —

7. Assuredly, what ye are promised must come to pass.

8. Then when the stars become dim;

9. When the heaven is cleft asunder;

10. When the mountains are scattered (to the winds) as dust;

11. And when the apostles are (all) appointed a time (to collect) —

---

[6] Ungrateful
[1] Fierce, stormy
[2] Blasts

12. For what Day are these (portents[3]) deferred?

13. For the Day of Sorting out.

14. And what will explain to thee what is the Day of Sorting out?

15. Ah woe, that Day, to the Rejecters of Truth!

16. Did We not destroy the men of old (for their evil)?

17. So shall We make later (generations) follow them.

18. Thus do We deal with men of sin.

19. Ah woe, that Day, to the Rejecters of Truth!

20. Have We not created you from a fluid (held) despicable[4]? —

21. The which We placed in a place of rest, firmly fixed,

22. For a period (of gestation[5]), determined (according to need)?

23. For We do determine (according to need); for We are the best to determine (things).

24. Ah woe, that Day! to the Rejecters of Truth!

25. Have We not made the earth (as a place) to draw together

26. The living and the dead,

27. And made therein mountains standing firm, lofty (in stature); and provided for you water sweet (and wholesome)?

28. Ah woe, that Day, to the Rejecters of Truth!

29. (It will be said:) "Depart ye to that which ye used to reject as false!

30. "Depart ye to a Shadow (of smoke ascending) in three columns,

31. "(Which yields) no shade of coolness, and is of no use against the fierce Blaze.

32. "Indeed it throws about sparks (huge) as Forts,

33. "As if there were (a string of) yellow camels (marching swiftly)."

34. Ah woe, that Day, to the Rejecters of Truth!

35. That will be a Day when they shall not be able to speak.

36. Nor will it be open to them to put forth pleas.

37. Ah woe, that Day, to the Rejecters of Truth!

38. That will be a Day of Sorting out! We shall gather you together and those before (you)!

---

[3] Omen, significant sign of something to come

[4] Abhorrent

[5] The period of carrying or being carried in the womb between conception and birth.

39. Now, if ye have a trick (or plot), use it against Me!

40. Ah woe, that Day, to the Rejecters of Truth!

41. As to the Righteous, they shall be amidst (cool) shades and springs (of water).

42. And (they shall have) fruits, — all they desire.

43. "Eat ye and drink ye to your heart's content: for that ye worked (Righteousness).

44. Thus do We certainly reward the Doers of Good.

45. Ah woe, that Day, to the Rejecters of Truth!

46. (O ye unjust!) Eat ye and enjoy yourselves (but) a little while, for that ye are Sinners.

47. Ah woe, that Day, to the Rejecters of Truth!

48. And when it is said to them, "Prostrate yourselves!" they do not so.

49. Ah woe, that Day, to the Rejecters of Truth!

50. Then what Message, after that, will they believe in?

Chapter 78
Sürah An-Naba (The Great News)
Revealed at Makkah, 40 verses

In the name of God, Most Gracious, Most Merciful.

1. Concerning what are they disputing?

2. Concerning the Great News,

3. About which they cannot agree.

4. Verily, they shall soon (come to) know!

5. Verily, verily they shall soon (come to) know!

6. Have We not made the earth as a wide expanse[1],

7. And the mountains as pegs?

8. And (have We not) created you in pairs,

9. And made your sleep for rest,

10. And made the night as a covering,

11. And made the day as a means of subsistence?

12. And (have We not) built over you the seven firmaments,

13. And placed (therein) a Light of Splendor?

---

[1] Wide area or extent

14. And do We not send down from the clouds water in abundance,

15. That We may produce therewith corn and vegetables,

16. And gardens of luxurious[2] growth?

17. Verily the Day of Sorting out is a thing appointed,

18. The Day that the Trumpet shall be sounded, and ye shall come forth in crowds;

19. And the heavens shall be opened as if there were doors,

20. And the mountains shall vanish, as if they were a mirage[3].

21. Truly Hell is as a place of ambush,

22. For the transgressors a place of destination:

23. They will dwell therein for ages.

24. Nothing cool shall they taste therein, nor any drink,

25. Save a boiling fluid and a fluid, dark, murky[4], intensely cold,

26. A fitting recompense (for them).

27. For that they used not to fear any account (for their deeds),

28. But they (impudently[5]) treated Our Signs as false.

29. And all things have We preserved on record.

30. "So taste ye (the fruits of your deeds); for no increase shall We grant you, except in Punishment."

31. Verily for the Righteous there will be a fulfilment of (the heart's) desires;

32. Gardens enclosed, and grapevines;

33. Companions of equal age;

34. And a cup full (to the brim[6]).

35. No vanity shall they hear therein, nor Untruth —

36. Recompense from thy Lord, a gift, (amply) sufficient,

37. (From) the Lord of the heavens and the earth, and all between, (God) Most Gracious: None shall have power to argue with Him.

38. The Day that the Spirit and the angels will stand forth in ranks, none shall speak except any who is permitted by (God) Most Gracious, and He will say what is right.

---

[2] Lavish, rich

[3] Optical illusion caused by atmospheric conditions, esp. appearance of sheet of water in desert or hot road, illusory thing.

[4] Muddy

[5] Arrogantly, insolently

[6] Brink

39. That Day will be the sure Reality: Therefore, whoso will, let him take a (straight) return to his Lord!

40. Verily, We have warned you of a Penalty near, the Day when man will see (the deeds) which his hands have sent forth, and the Unbeliever will say, "Woe unto me! Would that I were (mere) dust!"

Chapter 79
Sūrah An-Nazi'at (Those who Tear Out)
Revealed at Makkah, 46 verses

In the name of God, Most Gracious, Most Merciful.

1. By the (angels) who tear out (the souls of the wicked) with violence;

2. By those who gently draw out (the souls of the blessed);

3. And by those who glide along (on errands[7] of mercy),

4. Then press forward as in a race,

5. Then arrange to do (the Commands of their Lord) —

6. One Day everything that can be in commotion[8] will be in violent commotion,

7. Followed by oft-repeated (commotions):

8. Hearts that Day will be in agitation;

9. Cast down will be (their owners') eyes.

10. They say (now): "What! shall we indeed be returned to (our) former state?

11. "What! — when we shall have become rotten bones?"

12. They say: "It would, in that case, be a return with loss!"

13. But verily, it will be but a single (Compelling) Cry,

14. When, behold, they will be in the (full) awakening (to Judgment).

15. Has the story of Moses reached thee?

16. Behold, thy Lord did call to him in the sacred valley of Tuwa: —

17. "Go thou to Pharaoh for he has indeed transgressed all bounds.

---

[7] Short journey to carry or deliver something.

[8] Turmoil, disturbance

18. "And say to him, 'Wouldst thou that thou shouldst be purified (from sin)? —

19. "'And that I guide thee to thy Lord, so thou shouldst fear Him?'"

20. Then did (Moses) show him the Great Sign.

21. But (Pharaoh) rejected it and disobeyed (guidance);

22. Further, he turned his back, striving hard (against God).

23. Then he collected (his men) and made a proclamation,

24. Saying, "I am your Lord, Most High."

25. But God did punish him, (and made an) example of him — in the Hereafter, as in this life.

26. Verily in this is an instructive warning for whosoever feareth (God).

27. What! Are ye the more difficult to create or the heaven (above)? (God) hath constructed it:

28. On high hath He raised its canopy, and He hath given it order and perfection.

29. Its night doth He endow with darkness, and its splendor doth He bring out (with light).

30. And the earth, moreover, hath He extended (to a wide expanse);

31. He draweth out therefrom its moisture and its pasture;

32. And the mountains hath He firmly fixed —

33. For use and convenience to you and your cattle.

34. Therefore, when there comes the great, overwhelming (Event) —

35. The Day when man shall remember (all) that he strove for,

36. And Hell-Fire shall be placed in full view for (all) to see —

37. Then, for such as had transgressed all bounds,

38. And had preferred the life of this world,

39. The Abode will be Hell-Fire;

40. And for such as had entertained the fear of standing before their Lord's (tribunal[9]) and had restrained (their) soul from lower desires,

41. Their abode will be the Garden.

42. They ask thee about the Hour — 'When will be its appointed time?'

---

[9] Judgment-seat.

43. Wherein art thou (concerned) with the declaration thereof?

44. With thy Lord is the Limit fixed therefor.

45. Thou art but a Warner for such as fear it.

46. The Day they see it, (it will be) as if they had tarried[10] but a single evening, or (at most till) the following morn!

Chapter 80
Sürah 'Abasa (He Frowned)
Revealed at Makkah, 42 verses

In the name of God, Most Gracious, Most Merciful.

1. (The Prophet) frowned and turned away,

2. Because there came to him the blind man (interrupting).

3. But what could tell thee but that perchance he might grow (in spiritual understanding)?

4. Or that he might receive admonition, and the teaching might profit him?

5. As to one who regards Himself as self-sufficient,

6. To him dost thou attend;

7. Though it is no blame to thee if he grow not (in spiritual understanding).

8. But as to him who came to thee striving earnestly,

9. And with fear (in his heart),

10. Of him wast thou unmindful.

11. By no means (should it be so)! For it is indeed a Message of instruction:

12. Therefore let whoso will, keep it in remembrance.

13. (It is) in Books held (greatly) in honour,

14. Exalted (in dignity), kept pure and holy,

15. (Written) by the hands of scribes —

16. Honourable and Pious and Just.

17. Woe to man! What hath made him reject God?

18. From what stuff hath He created him?

19. From a sperm drop: He hath created him, and then mouldeth

---

[10] Remained, lived

490

him in due proportions;

20. Then doth He make His path smooth for him;

21. Then He causeth him to die, and putteth him in his grave;

22. Then, when it is His Will, He will raise him up (again).

23. By no means hath he fulfilled what God hath commanded him.

24. Then let man look at his food, (and how We provide it):

25. For that We pour forth water in abundance,

26. And We split the earth in fragments,

27. And produce therein corn,

28. And Grapes and nutritious plants,

29. And Olives and Dates,

30. And enclosed Gardens, dense with lofty trees,

31. And fruits and fodder —

32. For use and convenience to you and your cattle.

33. At length, when there comes the Deafening Noise —

34. That Day shall a man flee from his own brother,

35. And from his mother and his father,

36. And from his wife and his children.

37. Each one of them, that Day, will have enough concern (of his own) to make him indifferent to the others.

38. Some faces that Day will be beaming,

39. Laughing, rejoicing.

40. And other faces that Day will be dust-stained,

41. Blackness will cover them:

42. Such will be the Rejecters of God, the doers of iniquity[11].

Chapter 81
Sürah At-Takwir (The Folding Up)
Revealed at Makkah, 29 verses

In the name of God, Most Gracious, Most Merciful.

1. When the sun (with its spacious light) is folded up;

2. When the stars fall, losing their lustre[12];

3. When the mountains vanish (like a mirage);

---

[11] Evil, gross injustice

[12] Brilliance, shining light

4. When the she-camels, ten months with young, are left untended;

5. When the wild beasts are herded together (in the human habitations[13]);

6. When the oceans boil over with a swell;

7. When the souls are sorted out, (being joined, like with like);

8. When the female (infant), buried alive, is questioned —

9. For what crime she was killed;

10. When the scrolls are laid open;

11. When the world on High is unveiled;

12. When the Blazing Fire is kindled to fierce heat;

13. And when the Garden is brought near —

14. (Then) shall each soul know what it has put forward.

15. So verily I call to witness the planets — that recede,

16. Go straight, or hide;

17. And the Night as it dissipates[14];

18. And the Dawn as it breathes away the darkness —

19. Verily this is the word of a most honourable Messenger,

20. Endued with Power, with rank before the Lord of the Throne,

21. With authority there, (and) faithful to his trust.

22. And (O people!) your companion is not one possessed;

23. And without doubt he saw him in the clear horizon.

24. Neither doth he withhold grudgingly a knowledge of the Unseen.

25. Nor is it the word of an evil spirit accursed.

26. Then whither go ye?

27. Verily this is no less than a Message to (all) the Worlds:

28. (With profit) to whoever among you wills to go straight:

29. But ye shall not will except as God wills — the Cherisher of the Worlds.

---

[13] Living places
[14] Disappear

Chapter 82
Sūrah Al-Infitar (The Cleaving Asunder)
Revealed at Makkah, 19 verses

In the name of God, Most Gracious, Most Merciful.

1. When the Sky is cleft asunder;

2. When the Stars are scattered;

3. When the Oceans are suffered[15] to burst forth;

4. And when the Graves are turned upside down —

5. (Then) shall each soul know what it hath sent forward and (what it hath) kept back.

6. O man! What has seduced[16] thee from thy Lord Most Beneficent? —

7. Him Who created thee, fashioned thee in due proportion, and gave thee a just bias[17];

8. In whatever Form He wills, does He put thee together.

9. Nay! but ye do reject Right and Judgment!

10. But verily over you (are appointed angels) to protect you —

11. Kind and honourable — writing down (your deeds):

12. They know (and understand) all that ye do.

13. As for the Righteous, they will be in bliss;

14. And the Wicked — they will be in the Fire,

15. Which they will enter on the Day of Judgment,

16. And they will not be able to keep away therefrom.

17. And what will explain to thee what the Day of Judgment is?

18. Again, what will explain to thee what the Day of Judgment is?

19. (It will be) the Day when no soul shall have power (to do) aught[18] for another: For the command, that Day, will be (wholly) with God.

---

[15] Allowed

[16] Lead astray, tempted to sin or crime.

[17] Leaning, disposition

[18] Anything

Chapter 83
Sürah Al-Mutaffifin (The Dealers in Fraud)
Revealed at Makkah, 36 verses

In the name of God, Most Gracious, Most Merciful.

1. Woe to those that deal in fraud —

2. Those who, when they have to receive by measure from men, exact full measure,

3. But when they have to give by measure or weight to men, give less than due.

4. Do they not think that they will be called to account? —

5. On a Mighty Day,

6. A Day when (all) mankind will stand before the Lord of the Worlds?

7. Nay! Surely the record of the wicked is (preserved) in *Sijjin*[19].

8. And what will explain to thee what *Sijjin* is?

9. (There is) a Register (fully) inscribed[20].

10. Woe, that Day, to those that deny —

11. Those that deny the Day of Judgment.

12. And none can deny it but the Transgressor beyond bounds the Sinner!

13. When Our Signs are rehearsed to him, he says, "Tales of the ancients!"

14. By no means! but on their hearts is the stain of the (ill) which they do!

15. Verily, from (the Light of) their Lord, that Day, will they be veiled.

16. Further, they will enter the Fire of Hell.

17. Further, it will be said to them: "This is the (reality) which ye rejected as false!

18. Nay, verily the record of the Righteous is (preserved) in '*Illiyin*[21].

19. And what will explain to thee what '*Illiyun* is?

---

[19] From the root *sijn*, a prison, *sijjin* is a dungeon or a prison where the wicked are confined.

[20] In which records are preserved, written down

[21] *Illiyun or illiyin* literally, means "high places."

20. (There is) a Register (fully) inscribed,

21. To which bear witness those Nearest (to God).

22. Truly the Righteous will be in Bliss:

23. On Thrones (of Dignity) will they command a sight (of all things):

24. Thou wilt recognise in their faces the beaming brightness of Bliss.

25. Their thirst will be slaked[22] with Pure Wine sealed:

26. The seal thereof will be Musk: And for this let those aspire, who have aspirations:

27. With it will be (given) a mixture of *Tasnim*[23]:

28. A spring, from (the waters) whereof drink those nearest to God.

29. Those in sin used to laugh at those who believed,

30. And whenever they passed by them, used to wink at each other (in mockery[24]);

31. And when they returned to their own people, they would return jesting;

32. And whenever they saw them, they would say, "Behold! These are the people truly astray!"

33. But they had not been sent as keepers over them!

34. But on this Day the Believers will laugh at the Unbelievers:

35. On Thrones (of Dignity) they will command (a sight) (of all things).

36. Will not the Unbelievers have been paid back for what they did?

Chapter 84
Sürah Al-Inshiqaq (The Rending Asunder)
Revealed at Makkah, 25 verses

In the name of God, Most Gracious, Most Merciful.

1. When the sky is rent asunder,

---

[22] Quenched, satisfied

[23] The name of a heavenly fountain, literally it indicates height, fulness, opulence.

[24] Jest

2. And hearkens to (the Command of) its Lord, and it must needs (do so) —

3. And when the earth is flattened out,

4. And casts forth what is within it and becomes (clean) empty,

5. And hearkens to (the Command of) its Lord — and it must needs (do so) — (then will come Home the full reality).

6. O thou man! Verily thou art ever toiling on towards thy Lord — painfully toiling — but thou shalt meet Him.

7. Then he who is given his Record in his right hand,

8. Soon will his account be taken by an easy reckoning,

9. And he will turn to his people, rejoicing!

10. But he who is given his Record behind his back —

11. Soon will he cry for perdition[25],

12. And he will enter a Blazing Fire.

13. Truly, did he go about among his people, rejoicing!

14. Truly, did he think that he would not have to return (to Us)!

15. Nay, nay! for his Lord was (ever) watchful of him!

16. So I do call to witness the ruddy[26] glow of Sunset;

17. The Night and its Homing;

18. And the Moon in her fullness:

19. Ye shall surely travel from stage to stage.

20. What then is the matter with them, that they believe not? —

21. And when the Qur'an is read to them, they fall not prostrate,

22. But on the contrary the Unbelievers reject (it).

23. But God has full knowledge of what they secrete[27] (in their breasts)

24. So announce to them a Penalty Grievous,

25. Except to those who believe and work righteous deeds: For them is a Reward that will never fail.

---

[25] Eternal death

[26] Reddish

[27] Hide

Chapter 85
Sürah Al-Buruj (The Zodiacal Signs)
Revealed at Makkah, 22 verses

In the name of God, Most Gracious, Most Merciful.

1. By the sky, (displaying) the Zodiacal Signs[28];

2. By the promised Day (of Judgment);

3. By one that witnesses, and the subject of the witness —

4. Woe to the makers of the pit (of fire),

5. Fire supplied (abundantly) with fuel:

6. Behold! They sat over against the (fire),

7. And they witnessed (all) that they were doing against the Believers.

8. And they ill-treated them for no other reason than that they believed in God, Exalted in Power, Worthy of all Praise! —

9. Him to Whom belongs the dominion of the heavens and the earth! And God is Witness to all things.

10. Those who persecute (or draw into temptation) the Believers, men and women, and do not turn in repentance, will have the Penalty of Hell: They will have the Penalty of the Burning Fire.

11. For those who believe and do righteous deeds, will be Gardens; beneath which rivers flow: That is the great Salvation, (the fulfilment of all desires),

12. Truly strong is the Grip (and Power) of thy Lord.

13. It is He Who creates from the very beginning, and He can restore (life).

14. And He is the Oft-Forgiving, Full of Loving-Kindness,

15. Lord of the Throne of Glory,

16. Doer (without let[29]) of all that He intends.

17. Has the story reached thee, of the forces —

18. Of Pharaoh and the Thamüd?

19. And yet the Unbelievers (persist) in rejecting (the Truth)!

20. But God doth encompass them from behind!

21. Nay, this is a Glorious Qur'an,

22. (Inscribed) in a Tablet Preserved!

---

[28] See 15:16

[29] (Archaic) Hindrance, stoppage

Chapter 86
Sürah At-Tariq (The Night Star)
Revealed at Makkah, 17 verses

In the name of God, Most Gracious, Most Merciful.

1. By the Sky and the Night-Visitant[30] (therein) —

2. And what will explain to thee what the Night-Visitant is? —

3. (It is) the Star of piercing brightness —

4. There is no soul but has a protector over it.

5. Now let man but think from what he is created!

6. He is created from a drop emitted[31] —

7. Proceeding from between the backbone and the ribs:

8. Surely (God) is able to bring him back (to life)!

9. The Day that (all) things secret will be tested,

10. (Man) will have no power, and no helper.

11. By the Firmament which returns (in its round),

12. And by the Earth which opens out (for the gushing of springs or the sprouting of vegetation) —

13. Behold this is the Word that distinguishes (Good from Evil):

14. It is not a thing for amusement.

15. As for them, they are but plotting a scheme,

16. And I am planning a scheme.

17. Therefore grant a delay to the Unbelievers: Give respite to them gently (for awhile).

Chapter 87
Sürah Al-A'la (The Most High)
Revealed at Makkah, 19 verses

In the name of God, Most Gracious, Most Merciful.

1. Glorify the name of thy Guardian-Lord Most High,

2. Who hath created, and further, given order and proportion;

3. Who hath ordained laws. And granted guidance;

---

[30] Visitant (archaic): visitor, esp. a supernatural one.

[31] Discharged

4. And Who bringeth out the (green and luscious[32]) pasture,

5. And then doth make it (but) swarthy[33] stubble[34].

6. By degrees shall We teach thee to declare (the Message), so thou shalt not forget,

7. Except as God wills: For He knoweth what is manifest and what is hidden.

8. And We will make it easy for thee (to follow) the simple (Path).

9. Therefore give admonition in case the admonition profits (the hearer).

10. The admonition will be received by those who fear (God):

11. But it will be avoided by those most unfortunate ones,

12. Who will enter the Great Fire,

13. In which they will then neither die nor live.

14. But those will prosper who purify themselves,

15. And glorify the name of their Guardian-Lord, and (lift their hearts) in prayer.

16. Nay (behold), ye prefer the life of this world;

17. But the Hereafter is better and more enduring.

18. And this is in the Books of the earliest (Revelations) —

19. The Books of Abraham and Moses.

Chapter 88
Sūrah Al-Ghāshiah (The Overwhelming Event)
Revealed at Makkah, 26 verses

In the name of God, Most Gracious, Most Merciful.

1. Has the story reached thee of the overwhelming[35] (Event)?

2. Some faces, that Day, will be humiliated,

3. Labouring (hard), weary —

4. The while they enter the Blazing Fire —

5. The while they are given, to drink, of a boiling hot spring,

---

[32] Richly sweet in taste or smell
[33] Dark
[34] Cut stalks of cereal plants left sticking up after harvest
[35] Bringing to sudden ruin or destruction, overpowering

6. No food will there be for them but a bitter *Dari*[36]

7. Which will neither nourish nor satisfy hunger.

8. (Other) faces that Day will be joyful,

9. Pleased with their striving, —

10. In a Garden on high,

11. Where they shall hear no (word) of vanity:

12. Therein will be a bubbling spring:

13. Therein will be Thrones (of dignity), raised on high,

14. Goblets placed (ready),

15. And cushions set in rows,

16. And rich carpets (all) spread out.

17. Do they not look at the Camels, how they are made? —

18. And at the Sky, how it is raised high? —

19. And at the Mountains, how they are fixed firm? —

20. And at the Earth, how it is spread out?

21. Therefore do thou give admonition, for thou art one to admonish.

22. Thou art not one to manage (men's) affairs.

23. But if any turn away and reject God, —

24. God will punish him with a mighty Punishment.

25. For to Us will be their return;

26. Then it will be for Us to call them to account.

Chapter 89
Sūrah Al-Fajr (The Dawn)
Revealed at Makkah, 30 verses

In the name of God, Most Gracious, Most Merciful.

1. By the break of Day;

2. By the Nights twice five;

3. By the even and odd (contrasted);

4. And by the Night when it passeth away; —

5. Is there (not) in these an adjuration[37] (or evidence) for those who understand?

---

[36] A plant, bitter and thorny, loathsome in smell and appearance.

[37] Request earnestly, appeal

6. Seest thou not how thy Lord dealt with the 'Ād (people) —

7. Of the (city of) Iram, with lofty pillars,

8. The like of which were not produced in (all) the land?

9. And with the Thamūd (people), who cut out (huge) rocks in the valley? —

10. And with Pharaoh, lord of stakes[38]?

11. (All) these transgressed beyond bounds in the lands,

12. And heaped therein mischief (on mischief).

13. Therefore did thy Lord pour on them a scourge[39] of diverse chastisements:

14. For thy Lord is (as a Guardian) on a watchtower.

15. Now, as for man, when his Lord trieth him, giving him honour and gifts, then saith he, (puffed[40] up), "My Lord hath honoured me."

16. But when He trieth him, restricting his subsistence[41] for him, then saith he (in despair), "My Lord hath humiliated me!"

17. Nay, nay! but ye honour not the orphans!

18. Nor do ye encourage one another to feed the poor! —

19. And ye devour inheritance — all with greed,

20. And ye love wealth with inordinate[42] love!

21. Nay! When the earth is pounded to powder,

22. And thy Lord cometh, and His angels, rank upon rank,

23. And Hell, that Day, is brought (face to face) — on that Day will man remember, but how will that remembrance profit him?

24. He will say: "Ah! Would that I had sent forth (good deeds) for (this) my (Future) Life!"

25. For, that Day, His Chastisement will be such as none (else) can inflict,

26. And His bonds will be such as none (other) can bind.

27. (To the righteous soul will be said:) "O (thou) soul, in (complete) rest and satisfaction!

28. "Come back thou to thy Lord — well pleased (thyself), and well-pleasing unto Him!

---

[38] Poles. See also 38:12

[39] Whip for punishment

[40] Swollen (with pride)

[41] Sustenance

[42] Immoderate, excessive

29. "Enter thou, then, among My devotees!

30. "Yea, enter thou My Heaven!

Chapter 90
Sürah Al-Balad (The City)
Revealed at Makkah, 20 verses

In the name of God, Most Gracious, Most Merciful.

1. I do call to witness this City —

2. And thou art a freeman of this City —

3. And (the mystic ties of) parent and child —

4. Verily We have created man into toil and struggle.

5. Thinketh he, that none hath power over him?

6. He may say (boastfully): Wealth have I squandered[43] in abundance!

7. Thinketh he that none beholdeth him?

8. Have We not made for him a pair of eyes? —

9. And a tongue, and a pair of lips? —

10. And shown him the two highways?

11. But he hath made no haste on the path that is steep.

12. And what will explain to thee the path that is steep? —

13. (It is:) freeing the bondman;

14. Or the giving of food in a day of privation

15. To the orphan with claims of relationship,

16. Or to the indigent[44] (down) in the dust.

17. Then will he be of those who believe, and enjoin patience, (constancy, and self-restraint), and enjoin deeds of kindness and compassion.

18. Such are the Companions of the Right Hand.

19. But those who reject Our Signs, they are the (unhappy) Companions of the Left Hand.

20. On them will be Fire vaulted[45] over (all round).

---

[43] Consumed, spent, misused

[44] Destitute, needy

[45] Closed in upon them in arched, vault-like, covering

Chapter 91
Sūrah Ash-Shams (The Sun)
Revealed at Makkah, 15 verses

In the name of God, Most Gracious, Most Merciful.

1. By the Sun and his (glorious) splendour;
2. By the Moon as she follows him;
3. By the Day as it shows up (the Sun's) glory;
4. By the Night as it conceals it;
5. By the Firmament and its (wonderful) structure;
6. By the Earth and its (wide) expanse:
7. By the Soul, and the proportion and order given to it;
8. And its enlightenment as to its wrong and its right —
9. Truly he succeeds that purifies it,
10. And he fails that corrupts it!

11. The Thamūd (people) rejected (their prophet) through their inordinate wrongdoing,

12. Behold, the most wicked man among them was deputed (for impiety).

13. But the Apostle of God said to them: "It is a she-camel of God! And (bar[46] her not from) having her drink!"

14. Then they rejected him (as a false prophet), and they hamstrung[47] her. So their Lord, on account of their crime, obliterated[48] their traces and made them equal (in destruction, high and low)!

15. And for Him is no fear of its consequences.

Chapter 92
Sūrah Al-Layl (The Night)
Revealed at Makkah, 21 verses

In the name of God, Most Gracious, Most Merciful.

1. By the Night as it conceals (the light);
2. By the Day as it appears in glory;

---

[46] Prevent
[47] Crippled
[48] Wiped out

503

3. By (the mystery of) the creation of male and female —

4. Verily, (the ends) ye strive for are diverse.

5. So he who gives (in charity) and fears (God),

6. And (in all sincerity) testifies to the Best —

7. We will indeed make smooth for him the path to Bliss.

8. But he who is a greedy miser and thinks himself self-sufficient,

9. And gives the lie to the Best —

10. We will indeed make smooth for him the path to Misery;

11. Nor will his wealth profit him when he falls headlong (into the Pit).

12. Verily We take upon Ourselves to guide,

13. And verily unto Us (belong) the End and the Beginning.

14. Therefore do I warn you of a Fire blazing fiercely;

15. None shall reach it but those most unfortunate ones

16. Who give the lie to Truth and turn their backs.

17. But those most devoted to God shall be removed far from it —

18. Those who spend their wealth for increase in self-purification,

19. And have in their minds no favor from anyone for which a reward is expected in return,

20. But only the desire to seek for the Countenance of their Lord Most High;

21. And soon will they attain (complete) satisfaction.

Chapter 93
Sürah Ad-Duha (The Glorious Morning Light)
Revealed at Makkah, 11 verses

In the name of God, Most Gracious, Most Merciful.

1. By the Glorious Morning Light,

2. And by the Night when it is still —

3. Thy Guardian-Lord hath not forsaken thee, nor is He displeased.

4. And verily the Hereafter will be better for thee than the present.

5. And soon will thy Guardian-Lord give thee (that wherewith) thou shalt be well-pleased.

6. Did He not find thee an orphan and give thee shelter (and care)?

7. And He found thee wandering, and He gave thee guidance.
8. And He found thee in need, and made thee independent.
9. Therefore, treat not the orphan with harshness,
10. Nor repulse the petitioner (unheard);
11. But the bounty of the Lord — rehearse and proclaim!

Chapter 94
Sūrah Al-Sharh (The Expansion of the Breast)
Revealed at Makkah, 8 verses

In the name of God, Most Gracious, Most Merciful.
1. Have We not expanded thee thy breast?
2. And removed from thee thy burden
3. The which did gall[49] thy back? —
4. And raised high the esteem (in which) thou (art held)?
5. So, verily, with every difficulty, there is relief:
6. Verily, with every difficulty there is relief.
7. Therefore, when thou art free (from thine immediate task), still labor hard,
8. And to thy Lord turn (all) thy attention.

Chapter 95
Sūrah At-Tīn (The Fig)
Revealed at Makkah, 8 verses

In the name of God, Most Gracious, Most Merciful.
1. By the Fig and the Olive,
2. And the Mount of Sinai,
3. And this City of security —
4. We have indeed created man in the best of moulds,
5. Then do We abase him (to be) the lowest of the low —
6. Except such as believe and do righteous deeds: For they shall have a reward unfailing.

---
[49] Rub sore, injure by rubbing, mental soreness

7. Then what can, after this, contradict thee, as to the Judgment (to come)?

8. Is not God the wisest of Judges?

Chapter 96
Sürah Al-'Alaq (The Clinging Clot)
Revealed at Makkah, 19 verses

In the name of God, Most Gracious, Most Merciful.

1. Proclaim! (or read!) in the name of thy Lord and Cherisher, Who created —

2. Created man, out of a (mere) clot of congealed[50] blood:

3. Proclaim! And thy Lord is Most Bountiful[51] —

4. He Who taught (the use of) the Pen —

5. Taught man that which he knew not.

6. Nay, but man doth transgress all bounds,

7. In that he looketh upon himself as self-sufficient.

8. Verily, to thy Lord is the return (of all).

9. Seest thou one who forbids —

10. A votary[52] when he (turns) to pray?

11. Seest thou if he is on (the road of) Guidance? —

12. Or enjoins Righteousness?

13. Seest thou if he denies (Truth) and turns away?

14. Knoweth he not that God doth see?

15. Let him beware! If he desist not, We will drag him by the forelock —

16. A lying, sinful forelock!

17. Then, let him call (for help) to his council (of comrades):

18. We will call on the angels of punishment (to deal with him)!

19. Nay, heed him not: But bow down in adoration, and bring thyself the closer (to God)!

---

[50] Thick, solidified

[51] Generous

[52] One devoted to service of God

Chapter 97
Sūrah Al-Qadr (The Night of Power)
Revealed at Makkah, 5 verses

In the name of God, Most Gracious, Most Merciful.

1. We have indeed revealed this (Message) in the Night of Power:

2. And what will explain to thee what the Night of Power is?

3. The Night of Power is better than a thousand months.

4. Therein come down the angels and the Spirit by God's permission, on every errand:

5. Peace!...This until the rise of morn!

Chapter 98
Sūrah Al-Bayyinah (The Clear Evidence)
Revealed at Madinah, 8 verses

In the name of God, Most Gracious, Most Merciful.

1. Those who reject (Truth), among the People of the Book and among the Polytheists[53], were not going to depart (from their ways) until there should come to them Clear Evidence —

2. An apostle from God, rehearsing scriptures kept pure and Holy:

3. Wherein are laws (or decrees) right and straight.

4. Nor did the People of the Book make schisms[54], until after there came to them Clear Evidence.

5. And they have been commanded no more than this: To worship God, offering Him sincere devotion, being true (in faith); to establish regular prayer; and to practise regular charity; and that is the Religion Right and Straight.

6. Those who reject (Truth), among the People of the Book and among the Polytheists, will be in Hell-Fire, to dwell therein (for aye). They are the worst of creatures.

7. Those who have faith and do righteous deeds — they are the best of creatures.

---

[53] Idolaters, those who associate false gods with One True God.
[54] Division into mutual opposing parties.

8. Their reward is with God: Gardens of Eternity[55], beneath which rivers flow; they will dwell therein forever; God well pleased with them, and they with Him: all this for such as fear their Lord and Cherisher.

Chapter 99
Sürah Az-Zalzalah (The Earthquake)
Revealed at Madinah, 8 verses

In the name of God, Most Gracious, Most Merciful.

1. When the earth is shaken to her (utmost) convulsion[56],
2. And the earth throws up her burdens (from within),
3. And man cries (distressed): 'What is the matter with her?' —
4. On that Day will she declare her tidings:
5. For that thy Lord will have given her inspiration.
6. On that Day will men proceed in companies sorted out, to be shown the deeds that they (had done).
7. Then shall anyone who has done an atom's weight of good, see it!
8. And anyone who has done an atom's weight of evil, shall see it.

Chapter 100
Sürah Al-'Adiyat (Those that Run)
Revealed at Makkah, 11 verses

In the name of God, Most Gracious, Most Merciful.

1. By the (Steeds[57]) that run, with panting (breath),
2. And strike sparks of fire,
3. And push home the charge in the morning,
4. And raise the dust in clouds the while,
5. And penetrate forthwith into the midst (of the foe) en masse[58] —

---

[55] Eternal, perpetuity
[56] Violent irregular movement due to involuntary contraction.
[57] War horses
[58] All together

6. Truly man is, to his Lord, ungrateful;

7. And to that (fact) he bears witness (by his deeds);

8. And violent is he in his love of wealth.

9. Does he not know — when that which is in the graves is scattered abroad,

10. And that which is (locked up) in (human) breasts is made manifest —

11. That their Lord had been Well-acquainted with them, (even to) that Day?

Chapter 101
Sürah Al-Qari'ah (The Calamity)
Revealed at Makkah, 11 verses

In the name of God, Most Gracious, Most Merciful.

1. The (Day) of Noise and Clamor[59]:

2. What is the (Day) of Noise and Clamor?

3. And what will explain to thee what the (Day) of Noise and Clamor is?

4. (It is) a Day whereon men will be like moths[60] scattered about,

5. And the mountains will be like carded[61] wool.

6. Then, he whose balance (of good deeds) will be (found) heavy,

7. Will be in a life of good pleasure and satisfaction.

8. But he whose balance (of good deeds) will be (found) light —

9. Will have his home in a (bottomless) Pit.

10. And what will explain to thee what this is?

11. (It is) a Fire Blazing fiercely!

---

[59] Shouting, confused noise, loud appeal
[60] Small night insects
[61] Cleansed, combed fibres of wool

Chapter 102
Sürah At-Takathur (The Piling Up)
Revealed at Makkah, 8 verses

In the name of God, Most Gracious, Most Merciful.

1. The mutual rivalry for piling up (the good things of this world) diverts you (from the more serious things),

2. Until ye visit the graves.

3. But nay, ye soon shall know (the reality).

4. Again, ye soon shall know!

5. Nay, were ye to know with certainty of mind, (ye would beware!)

6. Ye shall certainly see Hell-Fire!

7. Again, ye shall see it with certainty of sight!

8. Then, shall ye be questioned that Day about the joy (ye indulged in!)

Chapter 103
Sürah 'Al-Asr (The Time Through the Ages)
Revealed at Makkah, 3 verses

In the name of God, Most Gracious, Most Merciful.

1. By (the Token of) Time (through the ages),

2. Verily Man is in loss,

3. Except such as have Faith, and do righteous deeds, and (join together) in the mutual teaching of Truth, and of Patience and Constancy.

Chapter 104
Sürah Al-Humazah (The Scandal Monger)
Revealed at Makkah, 9 verses

In the name of God, Most Gracious, Most Merciful.

1. Woe to every (kind of) scandalmonger and backbiter,

2. Who pileth up wealth and layeth it by,

3. Thinking that his wealth would make him last forever!

4. By no means! He will be sure to be thrown into that which breaks to pieces.

5. And what will explain to thee that which breaks to pieces?

6. (It is) the Fire of (the Wrath of) God kindled (to a blaze),

7. The which doth mount (right) to the Hearts:

8. It shall be made into a vault[62] over them,

9. In columns outstretched.

Chapter 105
Sūrah Al-Fīl (The Elephant)
Revealed at Makkah, 5 verses

In the name of God, Most Gracious, Most Merciful.

1. Seest thou not how thy Lord dealt with the Companions of the Elephant?

2. Did He not make their treacherous plan go astray?

3. And He sent against them Flights of Birds,

4. Striking them with stones of baked clay.

5. Then did He make them like an empty field of stalks[63] and straw, (of which the corn) has been eaten up.

Chapter 106
Sūrah Quraish (The Quraysh)
Revealed at Makkah, 4 verses

In the name of God, Most Gracious, Most Merciful.

1. For the covenants (of security and safeguard enjoyed) by the Quraish,

2. Their covenants (covering) journeys by winter and summer —

3. Let them adore the Lord of this House,

4. Who provides them with food against hunger, and with security against fear (of danger).

---

[62] An arched roof

[63] Stems

Chapter 107
Sürah Al-Ma'un (The Neighborly Needs)
Revealed at Makkah, 7 verses

In the name of God, Most Gracious, Most Merciful.

1. Seest thou one who denies the Judgment (to come)?
2. Then such is the (man) who repulses[64] the orphan (with harshness),
3. And encourages not the feeding of the indigent.
4. So woe to the worshippers
5. Who are neglectful of their prayers,
6. Those who (want but) to be seen (of men),
7. But refuse (to supply) (even) neighborly needs.

Chapter 108
Sürah Al-Kauthar (The Abundance)
Revealed at Makkah, 3 verses

In the name of God, Most Gracious, Most Merciful.

1. To thee have We granted the Fount[65] (of Abundance).
2. Therefore to thy Lord turn in Prayer and Sacrifice.
3. For he who hateth thee, he will be cut off (from Future Hope).

Chapter 109
Sürah Al-Käfirün (The Disbelievers)
Revealed at Makkah, 6 verses

In the name of God, Most Gracious, Most Merciful.

1. Say : O ye that reject Faith!
2. I worship not that which ye worship,
3. Nor will ye worship that which I worship.

---

[64] Drive back, repel
[65] Fountain

4. And I will not worship that which ye have been wont[66] to worship,

5. Nor will ye worship that which I worship.

6. To you be your Way, and to me mine.

Chapter 110
Sūrah An-Nasr (The Help)
Revealed at Madinah, 3 verses

In the name of God, Most Gracious, Most Merciful.

1. When comes the Help of God, and Victory,

2. And thou dost see the people enter God's Religion in crowds,

3. Celebrate the praises of thy Lord, and pray for His Forgiveness: For He is Oft-Returning (in Grace and Mercy).

Chapter 111
Sūrah Abu Lahab (The Father of Flame)
Revealed at Makkah, 5 verses

In the name of God, Most Gracious, Most Merciful.

1. Perish the hands of the Father of Flame! Perish he!

2. No profit to him from all his wealth, and all his gains!

3. Burnt soon will he be in a Fire of Blazing Flame!

4. His wife shall carry the (crackling) wood — As fuel! —

5. A twisted rope of palm-leaf fibre round her (own) neck!

Chapter 112
Sūrah Al-Ikhlās (The Purity of Faith)
Revealed at Makkah, 4 verses

In the name of God, Most Gracious, Most Merciful.

1. Say: He is God, the One and Only;

---

[66] Accustomed to.

2. God, the Eternal, Absolute;
3. He begetteth not, nor is He begotten;
4. And there is none like unto Him.

Chapter 113
Sürah Al-Falaq (The Daybreak)
Revealed at Makkah, 5 verses

In the name of God, Most Gracious, Most Merciful.
1. Say: I seek refuge with the Lord of the Dawn,
2. From the mischief of created things;
3. From the mischief of Darkness as it overspreads;
4. From the mischief of those who practise Secret Arts;
5. And from the mischief of the envious one as he practises envy.

Chapter 114
Sürah An-Nas (The Mankind)
Revealed at Makkah, 6 verses

In the name of God, Most Gracious, Most Merciful.
1. Say: I seek refuge with the Lord and Cherisher of Mankind,
2. The King (or Ruler) of Mankind,
3. The God (or Judge) of Mankind —
4. From the mischief of the Whisperer (of Evil), who withdraws (after his whisper) —
5. (The same) who whispers into the hearts of Mankind —
6. Among Jinns and among men.

INDEX

Aaron, 6:84; 20:29-36, 90-94.

'Abasa, S. 80.

Ablutions, 4:43; 5:6.

Abraham, fulfilled God's Commands, 2:124;
 and Ka'bah, 2:125-127; 3:96,97;
 religion of, 2:130,135;
 not Jew nor Christian, 3:67;
 nor Pagan, 3:95;
 rejects worship of heavenly bodies, 4:75-79;
 argues with sceptic, 2:258;
 argues with his father against idolatry, 4:74; 19:41-50;
 argues with his people against idols, 21:51-71; 26:70-82;
        29:16-18,24-25; 37:83-98;
 on life to the dead, 2:260;
 preaches to his people, 6:80-83;
 prays for father, 9:113-114; 26:86;
 sacrifice of son, 37:99-111;
 Angels visit him to announce son, 11:69-73: 15:51-56;
 2:24-30; pleads for Lut's people, 11:74-76;
 his prayer, 14:35-41; 26:83-87;
 a model, 16:120-123;
 safe in fire, 21:69;
 Book of, 53:37; 87:19;
 his example in dealing with Unbelievers, 60:4-6.

Abu Lahab (Father of Flame), 111:1-5;

'Ād people, 7:65-72, 11:50-60; 25:38; 26:123-140; 29:38; 41:15-
 16; 46:21-26; 2:41-42; 54:18-21; 69:4-8; 89:6-14.

Adam, creation, 2:30-34;
 fall, 2:35-39; 7:19-25;
 two sons (Abel and Cain), 5:27-31;
 tempted by Satan, 20:120-121.

'Ādiyat, S. 100.

Adjurations, Oaths and, in Qur'an,

Admonition, 87:9-13: 88:21-26.

Adultery, 17:32; 26:2-3, 4-10.

Ahmad, coming prophesied, 61:6.

Ahqaf, S. 46.

Ahzab. S. 33.

'A'ishah, 26:11; 46:1.

Akala, 5:66; 13:35.

A'la. S. 87.

'Alaq, S. 96.

Al-i-'Imran, S. 3.

An'am, S. 6.

Anbiya', S. 21.

Anfal. S. 8.

Angels, plea to God, 2:30-34;
        Gabriel and Michael, 2:97-98;
        not sent except for just cause, 15:7-8;
        sent for warning to men, 16:2;
        the impious and the angels, 25:21-22;
        on the Day of Judgement, 25:25;
        as messengers with wings, 35:1;
        pray for forgiveness for all on earth, 42:5;
        unbelievers give female names to, 53:27;
        and the Spirit ascend to God, 70:4;
        on errands of justice and mercy, 79:1-5;
        to protect men, 82:10-12;
        recording angels, 50:17-18.

Animals, form communities, 6:38;
        serve man, 16:5-8;
        dumb animals, duty to, 76:8.

'Ankabut, S. 29.

Ansar, 8:72; 59:9; 63:7.

Apes, transgressors become as, 2:65; 7:166.

Apostates, 47:25.

A'raf, S. 7.

'Asr, S. 103.

Assemblies, gradations of Muslim, 62:9.

Ayat, see Signs of God.

'Aziz, an attribute of God, 22:40; title of Egyptian nobleman,
        12:30.

Badr (battle of), 3:13;
        lessons of, 8:5-19, 42-48;

Bakkah (Makkah), 3:96.

Balad, S. 90.

Balance, 43:17; 55:7-9; 57:25; 101:6-9.

Bani Isra'il, see Isra', S. 17.

Banu Nadir, 59:2-6.

Baptism of God, 2:138.

Baqarah, S. 2.

Bara'ah, see Tawbah, S. 9.

Barzakh, 23:100; 15:53; 55:20.

Bayyinah, S. 98.

Beast (of the last Days), 27:82.

Believers, fear God, 3:102;

    to fear nothing else, 10:62;

    hold together, 3:103;

    enjoin right and forbid wrong, 3:104,110;

    protected from harm, 3:111; 5:101;

    protected by angels, 41:30-31;

    warned against Unbelievers, 3:118-120,196; 9:23-24;
        60:13;

    their lives sacred, 4:92-93;

    not to slight those who salute, 4:94;

    those who strive and fight, 4:95; 9:20-21, 88-89;

    if weak and oppressed, 4:97-100;

    not sit where God's Signs are ridiculed, 4:140; 6:68;

    to prefer Believers for friends, 4:144; 5:57-58;

    witnesses to fair dealing, 5:8;

    duties to God, 5:35: 66:8;

    not to ask inquisitive questions, 5:101-102;

    grades of dignity, 8:4;

    described, 8:2-4; 9:71, 111-112; 10:104-106; 13:20-24,
        28-29; 23:1-11, 57-61; 28:53-55; 32:15-17; 42:36-
        39; 49:7,11;

    to be firm, 7:45;

    to obey and not lose heart, 8:46;

    not to be weary and faint-hearted, 47:35;

    affection between their hearts, 8:63;

    to conquer against odds, 8:65-66;

    adopt exile, fight for God (Muhajir), 8:72, 74-75;

    help and give asylum (Ansar), 8:72;

    ask for no exemption from danger, 9:43-45;

    protect each other, 9:71;

    rejoice in their (spiritual) bargain, 9:111; 61:10-11;

    to be with those true in word and deed, 9:119;

to study and teach, 9:122;
will be established in strength, 14:27;
to practise prayer and charity, 14:31;
to say what is best, 17:53-55;
to be heirs, to inherit Paradise, 23:10-11;
promise to, 29:55-57;
manners, 29:62-63;
evil will be blotted out from, 29:7;
their ills removed, 47:2;
conduct, 33:69-71; 48:29;
prayer for them by those around Throne of God, 40:7-9;
not to despair or exult, 57:23;
to make peace, 49:9;
to avoid suspicion and spying, 49:12;
to remember God in humility, 57:16;
sincere lovers of truth and witnesses, 57:19;
receive special Mercy, Light, and Forgiveness, 57:28;
do what they say, 61:2-3;
helpers to God's work, 61:14;
trust in God, 44:13;
persecuted, but will reach Salvation, 85:6-11.

Bequests, 2:180.
Birds, 67:19.
Blasphemy, monstrous, to attribute begotten son to God, 19:88-92.
Book, (Revelation), is guidance sure, 2:2;
to be studied, 2:121;
Qur'an, verses fundamental and allegorical, 3:7;
Qur'an, light and guide, 5:15-16;
People of the, 3:64-80,98-99,113-115,187,199; 4:47,153-161;
appeal to People of the, 5:59-60,68;
their hypocrisy, 5:61-63;
forgiven if they had stood fast to their lights, 5:66;
know but refuse to believe, 6:20;
mother or foundation of the, 3:7; 13:39; 43:4;
for each period, 13:38;
on a blessed Night, 44:3-4;
from God, 46:2.
See also Qur'an, Revelation.
Booty, 48:15; see also Spoils of War.

Brotherhood, one, of the Righteous, 21:92;
        of the Prophets, 23:52-54.
Burdens of others, none can bear, 6:164; 17:15; 29:12-13; 35:18;
        39:7; 53:38;
        unbelievers will bear double, 16:25;
        no soul has burdens greater than it can bear, 2:286; 7:42;
        23:62.
Buruj, S. 85.
Cave of Thawr, 9:40.
Cave, Companions of the, 18:9-22, 25-26.
Certainty, three kinds, 49:51; 102:5.
Certainty, 56:95.
Charity, 2:110,177,179,195,215,219,254,261-274; 3:134; 30:39;
        57:18; 63:10; 64:16-17;
        objects of, 2:273; 9:60;
        meaning of, 61:19.
Children, 2:233; 42:49-50.
Christ, see Jesus. Christians, 2:138-140; 5:14;
        who became Muslims, 28:53; 29:47;
        nearest in love to Islam, 5:82-85.
Cities overthrown, 69:9;
Cleanliness, 4:43; 5:6.
Commerce that will never fail, 35:29.
Confederates, S.33, 33:9-20, 22-27.
Consultation, mutual, 42:38;
Courtesy, 4:86.
Covetousness,3:180; 4:32; 57:24.
Cowardice, 3:122.
Creation,
        begins and repeated, 10:4; 27:64; 29:19-20;
        a new, 8:5; 14:48; 17:49, 98; 21:104, 35:16;
        for just ends, 15:85; 16:3; 44:39; 45:22; 46:3;
        doth obeisance to God, 16:48-50;
        not for sport, 21:16-17;
        of man, 23:12-14;
        in six Days, 7:54,32:4; 57:4;
        variety in, 35:27-28;
        God commands 'Be' and it is, 2:117;16:40,36:82;40:68;
            54:50;
        in true proportions, 39:5;

519

of heaven and earth greater than creation of man,
40:57,79:27;
purpose of, 51:56-58.
Criterion, 2:53, 8:29; 21:48-50; 25:1.
Dahr, see Insan, S.76;
Time, 76:1.
Dari', 88:6.
David, 6:84; 21:78-80; 34:10-11; 38:17-26;
fights Goliath, 2:251.
Day, 7:54; 22:47; 32:4-5; 41:12; 70:4;
Dead will be raised to life, 6:36.
Death, by God's leave, 3:145;
inevitable, 3:185; 4:78;
confusion of the wicked, 6:93-94;
angels reproach Unbelievers, 8:50-54;
in death the transgressor will not die, 14:17; 20:74; 87:13;
for wrongdoers, 16:28-29;
for righteous, 16:30-32;
taste of, 3:185; 21:35; 29:57;
first, 37:59;
not the end of all things, 14:24-26;
and changed form thereafter, 56:60-61;
scene at, 56:83-87; 75:26-29;
sincere men flee not from death, 62:6-8.
Degrees, according to good and evil done, 6:132.
Despair, deprecated, 3:139, 146;
not of the Mercy of God, 39:53.
Desert Arabs, 9:90-99, 101-106; 48:11-12,16; 49:14.
Desertion in fight, 4:89-91.
Determinism, 81:28-29
Dhariyat, S.51.
Dhu al Kifl, 21:85; 38:48.
Dhu al Nun, 21:87-88, 68:48-50;
see also Jonah.
Dhu al Qarnain, 18:83-98;
Differences, decision with God, 42:10.
Difficulty, there is relief with every, 94:5-8.
Discipline, 3:152; 61:4.
Discord, incited by Evil, 41:36.
Disease in the hearts of Hypocrites and Unbelievers, 2:10; 5:52;

8:49; 9:125; 22:53; 24:50; 33:12, 32, 60; 47:20, 29; 74:31.

Disputations deprecated, 29:46.

Distribution of Charity, 2:177.

Distribution of property taken from the enemy; anfal, if after
        fighting, 8:41, fay, if without fighting, 59:7-8;

Divorce, 2:228-232, 236-237, 241; 65:1-7; see also 4:35.
        See also Zihar.

Dower, 2:229, 236-237; 4:4, 19-21, 25.

Duha, S. 93.

Dukhan, S. 44.

"Earn" (kasaba), 31:34.

Earth, will be changed to a different Earth, 14:48;
        prepared for God's creatures, 15:19-20; 26:7; 77:25-28;
        spacious is God's Earth, 29:56.
        manageable for man, 67:15;
        convulsion of, a symbol, 99:1-6.

Eating (akala) or enjoyment, 5:66; 77:43, 46;

Elephant, Companions of the, 105:1-5.

Elias (Elijah), 6:85; 37:123-132.

Elisha, 6:86; 38:48.

Evidence, re transactions, 2:282-283;
        re bequests, 5:106-108;
        re charges against chaste women, 24:4-10.

Evil, 4:51-55, 123; 10:27-30; 26:221-226; 42:36-39;
        comes from ourselves but good from God, 4:79:
        makes fools of men, 6:71;
        recompensed justly, 6:160;
        not external, but a taint of the soul, 15:15-16;
        will destroy Evil, 19:83;
        will come to evil end, 30:10;
        deceives evil, 59:15-17;
        repel evil with good, 13:22; 23:96; 41:34.

Evil Spirit, rejected, accursed, 3:36; 15:17; 16:98.

Excess forbidden, in food, 5:87;
        in religion, 4:171; 5:77-81.

Eyes, ears, and skins will bear witness against sinners, 41:20-23.

Ezekiel, 21:85.

'Face' of God, 2:112, 272, 6:52; 13:22; 18:28; 28:88; 30:39; 60:27;

Faith, rejecters of, 2:6-7, 165-167; 3:4, 10, 12, 21-22, 90-91,
116, 181-184; 4:136, 137, 167-168;

ransom not accepted, 5:36-37;
follow ancestral ways, 5:104;
destroyed, 6:6;
ask for angel to be sent down, 6:8-9;
lie against their own souls, 6:24;
will see Truth in Hereafter, 6:28-30;
will be in confusion, 6:110;
hearts inclined to deceit, 6:113;
taste evil result of conduct, 64:5-6;
their way and worship repudiated, 109:1-6;
signs of, 2:165, 285;
sellers of, 3:77, 177;
strengthened in danger and disaster, 3:173;
and righteousness, 5:69;
followed by unbelief, 16:106-109;
seven jewels of, 23:9;
and charity, 57:7-11.
Fajr, S. 89.
Falaq, S. 113.
False gods, 7:194-198; 16:20-21; 21:22, 24; 34:22-27; 41:47-48;
46:5-6; 53:19-24; 71:23-24.
Falsehood perishes, 21:18;
deludes, 51:8-11.
Famines in Makkah, 23:75; 44:10;
Fasting, 2:184-185, 187.
Fate, man's fate on his own neck, 17:13.
Fath, S. 48.
Fatihah, S. 1.
Fatir, S. 35.
Fear of God, what is, 2:2; 98:8;
as He should be feared, 3:102;
command to People of the Book and Muslims, 4:131;
piety and restraint (Taqwa), 47:17:
unseen, 67:12;
of His displeasure, 70:27;
righteousness, 74:56.
Fear as motive for reclamation, 2:74, 39:16;
in signs of God, 17:59,
Fear no evil, 3:175.
Fear, none for the Righteous, 2:38;

or for Believers, 2:62;
  or those who submit to God, 2:112;
  or who spend for God, 2:262, 274;
  or who believe and do good, 2:277; 5:69;
  or who believe and amend, 6:48; 7:35;
  or for friends of God, 10:62;
  or for God's devotees, 43:68;
  or for those who remain firm in God, 46:13.
Fear of men, 4:77.
Fig, S. 95.
Fighting, in cause of God, 2:190-193; 4:84;
  prescribed, 2:216; 2:244;
  in Prohibited month, 2:217;
  by Children of Israel, 2:246-251;
  in cause of God and oppressed men and women, 4:74-76;
  till no more, 8:39;
  against odds, 8:65;
  in case of, 9:5-6, 12, 13-16;
  those who believe not, and reject Truth, 9:29;
  with firmness, 9:123;
  permitted to those who are wronged, 22:39-41;
  when, and till when, 47:4;
  and the faint-hearted, 47:20;
  exemptions from, 48:17.
Fil, S. 105.
Fire, parable, 2:17-18;
  mystic Fire of Moses, 20:10;
  God's gift, 56:72-73.
Fire, see Hell.
Food, lawful and unlawful, 2:168, 172-173; 5:1, 3, 5, 87-88;
  6:118-119, 121, 145-146; 16:114-118;
  less important than righteousness, 5:93.
Forbidden, conduct, 6:151-152; 7:33;
  not things clean and pure, 7:32.
Forgiveness, 2:109; 4:48, 110, 116; 7:199; 39:53; 42:5; 45:14;
  53:32; 57:21;
  duty of Believers, 42:37, 40; 45:14;
  forgiveness, by Believers, for people of the Book, 2:109;
  words for, 2:109;
  by God, for sins other than joining gods with God, 4:48,

110, 116;

    hold to, and command the right, 7:199;

    God forgives all sins, 39:53;

    angels pray for forgiveness of all beings on earth, 42:5;

    forgive, even when angry, 42:37;

    and reconciliation, 42:40;

    Believers to forgive those who do not look forward to the
            days of God, 45:14;

    God forgives those who avoid great sins and shameful
            deeds, 53:32;

    be foremost in seeking, 57:21.

Fraud, 83:1-6.

Free will, in God's Plan, 6:107;

    no compulsion to believe, 10:99;

    Truth offered, to be accepted or rejected, 18:29;

    limited by God's Will, 74:56; 76:29-31; 81:28-29;

    just bias, 82:7;

Friday Prayers, 62:9-11.

Friends, 3:28.

Fruits and eating, metaphorical meaning of, 43:73; 47:15; 77:42-43.

Furqan, S. 25.

Gabriel, 2:97, 98; 26:193; 66:4; 81:19-21.

Gambling, 2:219; 5:90; Game, not to be killed in Sacred Precincts,
    5:94-96.

Ghashiyah, S. 88.

Glad Tidings to men, 2:25; 5:19; 16:89; 48:8.

God, Cherisher, 1:2; 6:164;

    Guardian Lord, 2:21-22;

    as a Guardian on a Watchtower, 89:14;

    protector, 2:257: 3:150; 22:78;

    sets guardians over man, 6:61;

    Helper, 3:150; 4:45; 11:51;

    help of, how to be celebrated, 110:1-3;

    refuge to Him from all ills and mischiefs, 93:1-5; 94:1-6;

    Creator of all, 2:29, 117; 6:73;

    creates and sustains all, 7:54; 11:6-7; 13:16-17; 21:30-33;
            66:2-3;

    created all nature, 25:61-62;

    to Him belongs the heritage of the heavens and the earth,
            3:180; 15:23; 19:40;

gives Sustenance, 29:60-62; 51:58;

Lord of Bounties, 3:174;

His Bounties open to all, 17:20-21;

Most Bountiful, 96:3;

Merciful, 6:26; 5:74; 6:12,54,133;

Most Kind, 9:117-118;

Full of loving kindness, 85:14;

Beneficent, 52:28;

His love bestowed on the Righteous, 19:96;

Forgiving, 4:25,26; 5:74; 15:49; 16:119; 39:53; 85:14;

guides, 6:71,88; 92:12;

ordains laws and grants guidance, 87:3;

calls to Home of Peace, 10:25;

His favours, Gardens and Fruits, 6:141;

cattle, 6:142;

mercy after adversity, 10:21;

traverse through land and sea, 10:22;

in life and death, 10:31,56; 22:6;

Cherisher and Sustainer, 10:32;

direction, healing, guidance, mercy, 10:57;

gifts from heaven and earth, 14:32-33;

numberless, 14:34; 16:18;

cattle and things ye know not, 16:5-8;

rain, corn, and fruit, 16:10-11;

night and day, sun, moon, and stars, gifts from heaven and earth, 16:12-13;

sea and ships, 16:14; 17:66;

mountains, rivers, roads, 16:15-16;

cattle and fruits, 16:66-67;

the Bee, 16:68-69;

bestowed variously; be grateful, 16:71-73;

in our birth, our faculties and affections, 16:77-78;

in our homes and in the service of animals, 16:80-81;

subjection of earth and sea, 22:65;

blessings from heaven and earth, 23:17-22;

long line of prophets, 23:23;

faculties, and progeny, 23:78-79;

shadows and the sun, 25:45-46;

night and day, sleep, 25:47;

wind and rain, 25:48-50;

bodies of water, 25:53;

man's creation, lineage and marriage, 25:54;

creation of heavens and earth and man's benefits, 27:60-61;

listens to the soul and makes man inherit the earth, 27:62;

guides through darkness, winds as heralds, 27:63;

originates and repeats creation, gives sustenance, 27:64;

feeds creation, 29:60-62;

sends rain and revives the earth, 29:63;

made heaven and earth with all its produce, 31:10;

subjected all things to your use, 31:20; 36:71-73; 45:12-13;

His Mercy, gifts none can withhold, 35:2-3;

life, grain, fruits, and springs, 36:33-35;

earth and the heavens, 41:10-12; 51:47-48;

accepts repentance and forgives, 42:25;

listens and gives increase, 42:26-28;

heavens and earth, rain and life, 43:9-11;

creation in pairs, ships and cattle, 43:12-13: 51:49;

created man and taught him speech, 55:3-4;

set up justice, 55:7-9;

spread out earth, with fruit, corn, and plants, 55:10-12;

two bodies of water, 55:19-20;

pearls and coral, 55:22;

ships, 55:24;

grants the need of every creature, 55:29;

settles their affairs, 55:31;

stream and flowing water, 67:30;

given heaven's canopy its order and perfection, 79:27-28; night, its darkness and splendour, 79:29;

expanse of the earth, its moisture, pasture, and mountains, 79:30-33;

orphan's shelter, 93:6;

wanderer's guide, 99:7;

satisfies need, 93:8;

expanded thy breast, 94:1;

removed thy burden, 94:2;

raised high thy esteem, 94:4;

present everywhere, 2:115; 7:7;

gave you life, 2:28; 6:122;

gives life and death, 3:156; 4:95; 15:23;

takes the souls of men, 39:42;
to Him go back all questions for decision, 3:109, 128;
to Him tend all affairs, 42:53;
to Him is the Goal, 53:42;
to Him is the return of all, 96:8;
Unity, 2:163; 6:19; 16:22; 23:91-92; 37:1-5; 38:65-68;
      92:1-4;
One, not one in a Trinity, 5:72;
nor one of two, 16:51;
no begotten son, 2:116; 6:100; 10:68; 19:35; 23:91;
nor consort nor daughters, 6:100-101; 16:57; 37:149-157;
      43:16-19;
no partners, 6:22-23, 136-137,163;
Wise, 4:26: 6:18;
best Disposer of Affairs, 3:173; 73:9;
Most High, Great, 4:34; 87:1;
Irresistible, 6:18, 61;
Doer of all He intends, 85:16;
power, 2:284; 3:29; 6:12-13, 65; 10:55; 16:77-81: 53:42-
      54; 85:12-16;
Self-Sufficient, 6:133;
Ready to appreciate service, 141:5; 35:30; 64:7;
Most Forbearing, 2:225, 235, 263; 3:155; 5:101; 22:59;
      64:17;
Wisest of Judges, 95:8;
Justice, 21:47;
never unjust, 4:40;
Best of Planners, 3:54: 13:42;
will separate evil from good, 3:179;
His Wrath, 1:7; 7:97-99;
quick in retribution, but forgiving and merciful, 7:167;
      13:6;
Swift in taking account, 24:39;
Best to decide, 10:109;
Best of those who show mercy, 13:109, 118;
Most Merciful of those who show mercy, 7:151; 12:64, 92;
      21:83;
decision with Him. 42:10;
Exalted in power, Wise, 31:9; 99:1;
Free of all wants, 31:26: 35:15;

Worthy of all praise, 31:26;

Ample in forgiveness, 63:32;

Living, 2:255; 40:65;

Eternal, 2:255: 20:111;

His Artistry, 27:88;

His Face will abide forever, 55:27;

all will perish except His own Self, 28:88;

His knowledge, 2:284; 3:5, 29; 6:3, 117; 13:8-10; 16:23; 21:4; 31:34; 34:2; 64:4;

His dominion, 3:189; 4:126; 5:120; 67:1;

Command rests with Him, 6:57; 13:41;

Lord of the Throne of Glory Supreme, 9:129; 23:86; 40:15; 85:15;

Lord of the Throne of Honour, 23:16;

Lord of the mystery of heaven and earth, 16:77;

Lord of Power, 51:58;

Lord of the two Easts and the two Wests, 55:17; 70:40; 73:9;

Lord of the Dawn, 93:1;

Lord of the Ways of Ascent, 70:3;

in heaven and on earth, 43:84;

To Him belong the End and the Beginning, 92:13;

listens to prayer, 2:186;

sends calm or tranquillity, 3:154; 9:26; 43:4, 18, 26;

purges, 3:141, 154;

tests, 3:142, 154, 166; 6:53; 29:2-5; 67:2;

sees all, 3:163;

sufficeth, 3:173; 8:64; 39:36; 65:3;

will lighten difficulties, 4:28;

sanctifies, 4:49;

recognises all good, 4:147;

will accept from the Good the best of their deeds, and pass by their ill deeds, 29:7; 46:16;

removes affliction, 6:17;

delivers from dangers, 6:63-64;

sends revelations, 6:91;

orders all things, 6:95-99;

gives Light to men, 6:122;

His Light will be perfected, 9:32-33; 61:8;

is the Light of heavens and earth, 24:35-36;

changes not His Grace unless people change themselves, 7:53; 13:11;

will not mislead, 9:115;

suffers not reward to be lost, 9:120-121; 11:115;

sufferers in His Cause to be rewarded, 16:41-42;

doth provide without measure, 24:38;

witnesses all things, 10:61;

understands the finest mysteries, 67:14;

will show them the truth of their conduct, 58:6;

nature of, 2:255; 3:2-3, 6, 18; 6:95-103; 25:2-3, 6; 32:2-9; 40:2-3;43:84-85;57:1-6;59:22-24;92:1-4;94:1-3;

close to man, 2:186;

ever near, 34:50;

near to man, 50:16; 56:85;

compasses mankind round about, 17:60;

with you wherever ye may be, 57:4;

only reality, 6:62; 31:30;

the Truth, 20:114;

to Him belong the Forces of heavens and earth, 47:7;

decrees unalterable, 6:34; 18:27;

His word finds fulfilment. 6:115;

no vision can grasp Him, 6:103;

most beautiful names, 7:180; 17:110; 20:8; 59:24;

worship of, 2:114, 152;

to be worshipped and trusted, 11:123;

sincere devotion due to Him, 39:9, 11; 40:14;

we trust in Him, 67:29;

His promise is true, 4:122; 14:47;

seek His Face, 6:52; 18:28;

dedicate life to Him, 6:162;

call on Him humbly, with fear and longing, 7:55-56;

forget Him not, 59:19;

to God, turn thy attention, 94:8;

all Creation speaks of Him, 13:12-13; 17:44; 24:41-46; 57:1;

praise and glory to Him, 1:1; 17:111; 30:17-19, 34:1; 37:180-182;45:36-37;55:78; 56:74, 96;59:1; 61:1;62:1; 64:1; 87:1;

and His Signs, 10:3-6; 13:2-4; See Signs of God;

His Command must come to pass, 16:1;

His command is but a single Act, 54:50;
all good from Him, 16:53;
what He commands, 16:90-91;
what is with Him will endure, 16:96;
His words inexhaustible, 18:109; 31:27;
rejecters of, will not injure God, 47:32;
rejecter of, described, 50:24-26;
who are His servants, 25:63-76;
those most devoted to God, 92:17-21;
claim to exclusive friendship of, condemned, 62:6;
"so please God," 18:23-24.

Goliath, 2:249-251.

Good, rewarded double, 4:40;
    rewarded ten times, 6:160;
    increased progressively, 42:23.

Good and Evil, 4:79, 85.

Good for evil, 23:96; 28:54; 41:34;

Gospel, 5:47.

Hadid, S. 57.

Hajj, see Pilgrimage.

Hajj, S. 22.

Haman, 28:6, 38; 29:39; 40:36-37.

Hā Mīm, S. 41.

Hands and Feet will bear witness against sinners, 36:65.

Haqqah, S. 69.

Harūt, 2:102.

Hashr, S. 59.

Heaven, as gardens, in nearness to God, rivers flowing, eternal
    home, 3:15, 198;
    Companions pure and holy, cool shades, 4:57;
    for righteous deeds, 4:124;
        truthful to profit from truth; gardens with flowing
    rivers; eternal home; God well pleased with them, and they
        with God; the great Salvation, 5:119;
    no lurking sense of injury in hearts, 7:43;
    mercy from God, Good Pleasure, Gardens, eternity, 9:21
    22;
    Gardens, mansions, Good Pleasure of God, 9:72;
    Gardens, fountains, peace and security, no lurking sense of
        injury, nor fatigue, 15:45-48;

Gardens of Eternity, rivers, adornments, thrones, 18:31;
22:23;

Gardens of Eternity, no vain discourse, peace, sustenance,
19:61-63;

Gardens as hospitable homes, 32:19;

Gardens of eternity; adornments; sorrow removed; no toil
or weariness, 35:33-35;

joy; associates; cool shade; thrones; all they call for;
peace, 36:55-58;

. fruits; honour and dignity; gardens; thrones; cup; chaste
women; 37:41-49;

final return, gardens of eternity, ease, fruit and drink,
chaste women; 38:49-52;

lofty mansions, rivers, 39:20;

garden, peace, eternity, angels singing, 39:73-75;

meads of gardens; all they wish for; Bounty, 42:22;

no fear nor grief; Gardens; rejoicing; dishes and goblets of
gold; eternity; satisfaction, 43:68-73;

security, gardens and springs, adornments, companions,
fruit, no further death; supreme achievement,
44:51-57;

parable of garden, rivers, Grace from God, 47:15;

Garden; peace and security; more than all they wish; In Our
Presence, 50:31-35;

Garden, happiness, food and drink; thrones of dignity;
companions; families; service, 52:17-24;

Gardens and Rivers; Assembly of Truth; Presence of
Sovereign Omnipotent, 54:54-55;

Gardens, Springs, Fruits, Carpets, Chaste Companions,
55:46-77;

nearest to God; Gardens; Thrones; Service; Fruits and
Meat; Companions; no frivolity nor taint of ill;
Peace, 56:11-38;

nearest to God; Rest and Satisfaction; Garden of Delights;
Companions: Salutation of Peace, 56:88-91;

Light runs before them; Gardens; Eternity; Highest
Achievement, 57:12;

Bliss; Garden; Fruits, 69:21-24;

Cup; Fountain of Abundance, 76:5-6;

Garden; adornments; Thrones; No Excess of Heat or Cold;

531

Shades; Cup; Fountain; Service; Realm Magnificent, 76:5-22;

Fulfilment of heart's desires; Gardens; Companions; Cup; no vanity or Untruth, 78:31-35;

Garden, 79:41;

Thrones; In their faces the Beaming Brightness of Bliss, Pure Wine; Spring, 88:22-28;

Joy; Striving; Garden; no Vanity; Spring; Throne; Cushions; Carpets, 88:8. 16;

Rest and Satisfaction; coming back to God; well-pleased and well-pleasing to Him; among God's Devotees; God's Heaven, 89:27-30;

Gardens of Eternity; Rivers; God well-pleased with them, and they with Him, 98:8;

salutation in, 10:10; 15:46; 56:91;

"My Heaven," said by God, 89:30;

Hell, skins roasted and renewed, 4:56;

of no profit are hoards and arrogant ways, 7:48;

for such as took religion to be amusement, and were deceived by the life of the world, 7:51;

filled with jinns and men, 11:119;

drink, boiling fetid water, 14:16-17;

Death will come, but will not die, 14:17;

fetters, liquid pitch, faces covered with Fire, 14:49-50;

garment of Fire, boiling water, maces of iron, 22:19-22;

Blazing fire, furious, 25:11-12;

Sinners bound together; will plead for destruction, but the destruction will be oft-repeated, 25:13-14;

Punishment to cover them from above and below, 25:55;

Fire, wicked forced into it every time they wish to get away, 32:20;

men repeatedly warned; 36:63;

Tree of Zaqqum, and boiling water, 3:62-67; 44:43-48; 55:52-55; to burn in Hell and taste of boiling fluid; and other Penalties, 38:55-58;

Unbelievers led in crowds, previously warned; abode of the arrogant; 39:71-72;

dispute and self-recrimination, 40:47-50;

to dwell for aye; punishment not lightened; overwhelming despair, 43:74;

God not unjust; sinners unjust themselves, 43:76;
capacity unlimited, 50:30;
Sinners known by their marks, 55:41;
Hell, which they denied; boiling water, 55:43-44;
Blast of Fire. Boiling Water, Shades of Black Smoke,
       56:42-44; drawing in its breath, bursting with
       fury, 67:6-8;
record in left hand, vain regrets, 69:25-29;
seize him, bind him, burn him, make him march in a chain,
       69:30-37;
naught doth it permit to endure, and naught doth it leave
       alone, 74:26-29;
Over it are Nineteen, 74:30-31;
a place of ambush; destination for transgressors; to dwell
       therein for ages; taste there nothing cool nor
       drink, save boiling fluid, or intensely cold, 78:21-
       25;
Day when hellfire shall be placed in full view, 79:35-39;
stain on sinners' hearts; Light of God veiled from them,
       enter the Fire, 83:14-16;
faces humiliated, enter the Fire; drink boiling water; food
       bitter Dari', 88:2-7;
brought face to face; will then remember; chastisement
       and bonds, 89:23-26;
bottomless Pit; fire blazing fiercely, 2:9-11;
That which Breaks to Pieces; wrath of God, 104:4-9;
they will neither die nor live, 20:74; 87:13;
to it are seven Gates, 15:44;
is it enternal? 6:128; 11:107.
who will pass over it? 19:71; 102:6.
Hereafter, not a falsehood, 6:31;
       man must meet God, 6:31;
       Home in the, 6:32;
       Wrath of God, 6:40-41; 12:107;
       Home of Peace, 6:127;
       wrongdoers will not prosper, 6:135.
       prophets and those to whom Message was sent will be
           questioned, 7:6;
       deeds will be balanced, 7:8-9;
       no intercession for those who disregarded Hereafter, 7:53;,

Fire and Garden endure, except as God wills, 11:107-108;
the arrogant and the weak in the, 14:21;
wrongdoers will ask for respite, 14:44-46;
Home of the, 28:83; 29:64;
better than silver and gold, 43:33-35;
denied by men, 50:12-14;
better than the present, 93:4.
Hijr, see Rocky Tract.
Hijr, S. 15.
Houses, manners about entering, 24:27-29.
Hüd,   7:65-72; 11:50-60; 26:123-140; 46:21.26.
Hüd, S. 11.
Hujurat, S. 49.
Humazah, S. 104.
Humility, 4:42-43; 7:161; 57:16;
shadows show humility to God, 13:15: 74:14.
Hunayn, 9:25.   '
Hür, companions in heaven, 44:54, 52:20.
Hypocrites, do not believe in God and the Last Day, 2:8;
deceive themselves, 2:9;
disease in their hearts, 2:10;
make mischief, 2:11-12;
fools and mockers, 2:13-15;
barter guidance for error, 2:16;
deaf, dumb, and blind, 2:17-18;
in terror and darkness, 2:19-20;
dazzling speech; led by arrogance, 2:204-206;
refuse to fight, 3:167-168;
resort to evil, turn away from Revelation; come when
seized by misfortune; to be kept clear of and
admonished, 4:60-63;
tarry behind in misfortune; wish to share good
fortune, 4:70-73;
thrown out of the way; reject Faith; renegades; to be seized
and slain, 4:88-89;
wait events; think of overreaching God; distracted in mind,
4:41-143;
in lowest depths of Fire; no helper, 4:145;
afraid of being found out, 9:64-65;
understanding with each other; perverse; curse of God,

9:67-69;
>not to be taken as friends, 58:14-19;
>liars and deceivers, cowards, 59:11-14;
>liars; screen misdeeds with oaths, 63:1-4.

Iblis, (see also Satan), 2:34, 7:11-18; 15:31-44; 17:61-65; 18:50;
20:116-123; 38:71-85.

Ibrahim, see Abraham.

Ibrahim, S. 14.

'lddah, 2:228, 231-232, 234-235; 33:49; 65:4, 6-7.

Idris, 19:56-57; 21:85.

lkhlas, S. 112.

'llliyun, 83:18-21.

Immorality, 4:15-18.

'lmran, family of, 3:35.

lnfitar, S. 82.

Inheritance, 2:180, 240; 4:7-9, 11-12, 19, 33, 176; 5:105-108.

Injury, forgiveness or self-defence, 42:39-43.

Insan, see Dahr, S. 76.

1nshiqaq, S. 84.

1nshirah, see Sharh, S. 94.

Inspiration, 17:85-87; 40:15; 42:3, 7, 51-53.

Intercession, 6:51, 70; 10:3; 19:87; 39:44; 43:86; 53:26.

Intoxicants, see Wine.

Iqra', see Alaq, S. 96.

Iram, 89:7.

Isaac, 6:84; 21:72; 37:112-113.

Islam, described, 3:110; 42:15;
>to be first to bow in, 6:14, 163; 39:12;
>vanguard of, 9:100;
>heart opened to, 39:22;
>a favour and privilege, 49:17.

Isma'il, 2:125-129; 6:86; 19:54-55; 21:85.

Isra', S. 17.

Israel, Children of, 2:40-86;
>favours, 2:47-53; 2:60, 122; 45:16-17;
>contumacy, 2:54-59, 61, 63-74; 5:71; 7:138-141;
>their relations with Muslims, 2:75-79;
>their arrogance, 2:80, 88, 91;
>their Covenants, 2:83-86, 93, 100; 5:12, 13, 70;
>their love of this life, 2:96;

ask for a king, 2:246-251;
divided and rebellious, 7:161-171;
twice warned,   17:4-8;
delivered from enemy, 20:80-82;
given Book and leaders, 32:23-25; 40:53-54;
the learned among them knew the Qur'an to be true, 26:197

Jacob, 2:132-133; 6:84; 19:49, 21:72.

Jathiyah, S. 45.

Jesus, a righteous prophet, 6:85;
birth, 3:45-47; 19:22-23;
messenger to Israel, 3:49-51;
disciples, 3:52-53;   5:111-115;
taken up, 3:55-58; 4:157-159;
like Adam, 3:59;
not crucified, 4:157;
no more than messenger, 4:171; 5:75; 43:59, 63-64;
not God, 5:17,72;
sent with Gospel, 5:46;
not son of God, 9:30;
Message and miracles, 5:113; 19:30-33;
prays for Table of viands, 5:114;
taught no false worship, 5:116-118;
disciples declare themselves Muslims, 5:111;
mission limited, 13:38;
followers have compassion and mercy, 51:27;
disciples as God's helpers, 61:14;
as a Sign, 23:50; 43:61;
prophesied Ahmad, 61:6.

Jews, will listen to falsehood, 5:41-42;
utter blasphemy, 5:64;
enmity to Islam, 5:82;
and Christians. 2:140; 4:153-161, 171; 5:18;
See also Israel, Children of.

Jihad, 9:20. See also Fighting; Striving.

Jinn, S. 72.

Jinns, 6:100; 15:27; 34:41; 46:29-32; 55:15; 72:1-15.

Job, 6:84; 21:83-84; 38:41-44.

John (the Baptist), see Yahya.

Jonah (or Jonas, or Yunus), 4:163; 6:86; 10:98, 37:139-148; (Dhu al Nun) 21:87; 68:48-50; (Companion of the Fish).

Joseph, 6:84;

his story, 12:4-101;

his vision, 12:4-6;

jealousy of his brothers, 12:7-10;

their plot, 12:11-18;

sold by his brethren, 12:19-20;

bought by 'Aziz of Egypt, 12:21;

tempted by 'Aziz's wife, 12:22-29;

her ruse, 12:30-34;

in prison, 12:35-42;

interprets King's vision, 12:43-54;

established in power, 12:55-57;

his dealings with his brethren, 12:58-93;

reunion of whole family, 12:94-101.

Judgement, must come, 6:51; 6:128; 34:3-5; 40:59; 51:5-6, 12-14;

52:7-10; 56:1-7; 64:7-10; 95:7;

will come suddenly, 7:187; 36:48-50;

as the twinkling of an eye, 16:77; 54:50;

Hour known to God alone, 93:63; 67:26; 79:42-46;

is near, 54:1-5; 78:40;

men will be sorted out into three classes, 56:7-56;

Foremost in Faith, nearest to God, 56:11-26;

Companions of Right Hand, 56:27-40;

Companions of left Hand, 56:41-56;

Lesser Judgement, 75:22-30; 78:40;

the Great News, 78:1-5;

deniers of, 107:1-7.

Judgement Day, full recompense only then, 3:185;

earth changed, and men gathered; Book of Deeds, 18:47-49;

men surge like waves; trumpet blown; Unbelievers will see and hear, 18:99-101;

sectarian differences to be solved; Distress for lack of Faith, 19:37-39;

rejecters of the message will bear a grievous burden, 20:100-101.

trumpet will sound; sinful in terror; interval will seem short, 20:102-104;

they will follow the Caller; trump of their feet; all sounds humbled; 20:108;

no Intercession except by permission, 20:109;

no fear for the righteous, 20:112;

rejecters will be raised up blind, 20:124-127;

scales of Justice, 21:47;

True Promise will approach fulfilment; sobs of Unbelievers; the Good will suffer no grief, 21:97-103;

heavens will be rolled up like a scroll; new creation,
21:104;

terrible convulsion; men in drunken riot; Wrath of God,
22:1-2;

trumpet is blown; Balance of Good Deeds, heavy or light,
23:101-104;

Voice of Judgement, 23:105-111;

Time will seem short, 23:112-115;

false worship will be exposed, 25:17-19;

heavens rent asunder; angels sent down; Dominion wholly
for God, 25:25-26;

wrongdoer's regrets, 25:27-30;

terror for evildoers, not for doer of good, 27:83-90;

guilty in despair, no Intercessor, 30:12-13;

justice done, 36:51-54;

joy and peace for the Good, 36:55-58;

Day of Sorting Out, 30:14-16; 37:20-21;

Wrongdoers questioned; recriminations, 37:22-23;

contrast between the righteous, with sound hearts and those
straying in evil, 37:88-102;

Wrongdoers' arrogances, 37:33-36;

retribution for evil, 37:37-39;

felicity for servants of God, 37:40-61;

Tree of Zaqqum, 37:62-68;

wrongdoers rushed on their fathers' footsteps, 37:69-74;

trumpet; all in heaven and earth will swoon; second trumpet, renewed Earth will shine with God's Glory;
recompense, 39:67-70;

no intercession; justice and truth, 40:18-20;

sudden; friends will be foes, except the righteous, 43:66-
67; no fear on God's devotees, 43:68-69;

dealers in falsehood to perish; righteous to obtain Mercy,
45:27-35;

not to be averted; Fire for the false and the triflers,

52:7-16;

wrongdoers swoon in terror, 52:45-47;

Caller to a terrible affair, 54:6-8;

no defence for the evil; known by their Marks, 55:35-44;

mutual gain and loss, 64:9-10;

Shin to be laid bare, 68:42-43;

trumpet; Great Event; Angels will bear the Throne; nothing hidden; Good and Evil recompensed, 69:13-37;

sky like molten brass; no friend will ask after friend; no deliverance for evil, 70:8,18;

wicked will issue from sepulchres in haste, 70:43-44;

Will know reality, not known whether near or far, 72:24-25; children hoary-headed; sky cleft asunder, 73:17-18;

trumpet; Day of Distress for those without Faith, 74:8-10;

stars become dim; messengers collect; sorting out, 77:7-15;

woe to Rejecters of Truth, 77:29-50;

sorting out; Trumpet; heavens opened; mountains vanish; 78:17-20;

Spirit and Angels stand forth; Day of Reality, 78:38-40;

commotion and agitation, 79:6-9;

single Cry, 79:13-14;

Deafening Noise; no one for another; some Faces beaming; some dust stained, 80:33-42;

sun, stars, mountains, outer nature change; souls sorted out; World on High unveiled, 81:1-14;

sky cleft asunder: stars and Oceans scattered; Graves turned upside down; each soul will know its deeds, 82:1-5;

no soul can do aught for another, 82:17-19;

sky and earth changed; man ever toiling on towards his Lord; Record of Good or Ill, 84:1-15;

things secret tested, 86:9-10;

Overwhelming Event; Faces humiliated and Faces joyful, 88:1-16;

Earth pounded to powder; Lord cometh; hell and heaven shown, 89:21-30;

Earth in convulsion; man in distress; sorted out, 99:1-8;

Contents of graves scattered abroad; of human breasts

made manifest; Lord well acquainted, 100:9-11;
Noise and Clamour; Good and Evil rewarded, 101:1-11.

Judi, Mount, 11:44.

Jumu'ah, S. 62.

Justice, 4:58, 65, 105, 135; 7:29; 16:90; 57:25;

Ka'bah, built by Abraham, 2:125-127;
no killing of game, 5:94-96;
asylum of security for men, 5:97.

Kafirün, S. 109.

Kafür, cup mixed with, 76:5.

Kahf, S. 18.

Karma or Determinism, 53:31.

Kauthar (Fount of Abundance), 108:1-2;

Kawthar, S. 108.

Keys of heavens and earth, 39:63; 42:12.

Khandaq, battle, 33:9-20.

Kindred, rights of, 2:83, 177; 4:7-9, 36; 8:41; 16:90; 17:26;
24:22; 42:23.

Knowledge (Certainty) 69:51; 102:5-7;
of five things, with God alone, 31:34.

Lahab, see Masad, S. III.

Languages, variations in man's — and colours, 30:22.

Lat, 53:19.

Latif, 22:63; 42:19.

Layl, S. 92.

"Leaves to stray," 14:4; 16:93; 39:23.

Life of this world, 6:32; 57:20.

Life sacred, 17:33.

Light, manifest, 4:174;
and Darkness, 6:1;
parable of, 24:35-36;
goes before and with Believers, 57:12-15; 66:8;
provided by God, that Believers may walk straight, 57:28;
of God, veiled from unbelievers, 88:15.

Loan, beautiful, to God, 2:245, 57:11, 18; 64:17; 78:20.

Loss (spiritual), 39:15.

Lote tree, 34:16; 53:14-18; 56:28.

Luqman, 31:12;
his teaching, 31:12-19.

Luqman, S. 31.

Lüt (Lot), 6:86; 7:80-84; 11:77-83; 15:57-77; 21:74-75; 26:160-
175; 27:54-58; 29:26, 28-31; 37:133-138; 51:31-37; 54:33-
39;
    his wife disobedient, 11:81; 15:60; 66:10.
Ma'arij, S. 70.
Madyan, 7:85-93, 11:84-95; 29:36-37.
Magians (Majus), 12:17.
Ma'idah, S. 5.
Makkah, Bakkah, 3:96;
    mystic relation to Prophet, 90:1-4;
    city of security, 95:3;
Man, vicegerent on earth, 2:30; 6:165;
    tested by God, 2:155; 3:186; 47:31; 57:25;
    things men covet, 3:14;
    duty, 4:1-36; 17:23-39; 29:8-9; 30:38; 3:33; 46:14; 70:22-
        35;
    created from clay, for a term, 6:2; 15:26;
    called to account, 6:44;
    will return to God, 6:60, 72; 10:45-46;
    confusion of the wicked at death, 6:93-94;
    plots against own soul, 6:123; 10:44;
    personal responsibility, 6:164;
    ungrateful, 7:10; 36:45-47; 74:15-25; 100:1-8;
    warned against Satan, 7:27;
    knows of God, but misled by Evil, 7:172-175;
    and family life, 7:189-190;
    limited Free Will, 10:99;
    behaviour in and out of trouble, 10:12; 11:9-11; 16:53-55;
        17:67-70; 29:10, 65-66; 30:33-34; 31:32; 39:8,
        49; 41:49-51; 42:48; 89:15-16;
    God's spirit breathed into him, 15:29;
    lowly in origin, but blessed with favours, 16:4-8; 32:7-9;
        35:11; 36:77-78; 76:1-3; 77:20-24; 80:17-32;
        86:5-8;   96:2-5;
    prays for evil, 17:11;
    is given to hasty deeds, 17:11; 16:37;
    his fate fastened round his neck, 17:13;
    to be judged by his record, 17:71;
    his physical growth, 22:5; 23:12-14; 40:67;
    death and resurrection, 23:15-16;

tongues, hands, and feet will bear witness against men, 24:24; made from water, 25:54;

relationships of lineage and marriage, 25:54;

should submit Self to God, 31:22;

not two hearts in one breast, 39:4;

to worship God, 39:64-66;

misfortunes, due to his deeds, 42:30;

angels note his doings, 50:17-18, 23;

his growth and activity depend on God, 56:57-74;

to be created again after death in new forms, 56:60-61;

riches and family may be a trial, 64:14-15;

created and provided for by God, 67:23-24; 74:12-15;

is impatient, 70:19-21;

who will be honoured ones among men, 70:22-35;

evidence against himself, 75:14-15;

his arrogance, 75:31-40; 90:5-7;

loves the fleeting world, 76:27;

seduced from God, 82:6-12;

painfully toiling on to God, 84:6;

travels from stage to stage, 84:16-19;

guilty of sins, 89:17-20;

created into toil and struggle, 90:4;

gifted with faculties, 90:8-10;

strives for diverse ends, 92:4-11;

created in best of moulds, 95:4;

abased unless he believes and does righteousness, 95:5-6;

transgresses all bounds, 96:6-14.

Manat, 53:20.

Mankind, one nation, 2:213; 10:19;

created from single pair, 4:1; 39:6; 49:13;

transgress insolently, 10:23;

heed not, though Reckoning near, 21:1-3;

pattern according to which God has made mankind, 30:30;

honour depends on righteousness, 49:13.

Manners, about entering houses, 24:27-29;

in the home, 24:58-61;

in the Prophet's presence, 29:62-63; 49:1-5;

in the Prophet's houses, 33:53

to bless and salute the Prophet, 33:56;

not to annoy Prophet or believing men or women, 33:57-

58; require verification of news before belief,
49:6;
among the community, 49:11;
in assemblies, 58:11.
Marriage, to unbelievers or slaves, 2:221;
to how many, lawful, 4:3;
dower not to be taken back (in case of divorce), 4:20-21;
prohibited degrees, 4:22-24;
if no means to wed free believing women, 4:25;
if breach feared, two arbiters to be appointed, 4:35;
if wife fears cruelty or desertion, amicable settlement,
4:128;
turn not away from a woman, 4:129;
with chaste ones among People of the Book, 5:6;
of adulterers, 24:3;
to those who are poor, 24:32;
those who cannot afford marriage, to keep themselves
chaste until God gives them means, 24:33;
Prophet's Consorts, 33:28-29, 50-52;
without cohabitation, no 'Iddah on divorce, 33:49;
conditions for the Prophet, 33:50-52;
Martyrs, not dead, 2:154; 3:169;
rejoice in glory, 3:170-171;
receive forgiveness and mercy, 3:157-158.
will receive best Provision, 22:58-59.
Marüt, 2:102.
Mary (mother of Jesus), birth, 3:35-37;
annunciation of Jesus, 3:42-51; 4:156; 19:16-21;
in child birth, 19:23-26;
brought the babe to her people, 19:27-33;
guarded her chastity, 21:91; 66:12.
Maryam, S. 19.
Masad, S.   111.
Ma'un, S.   107.
Measure and weight, give full, 17:35; 83:1-3.
Miracles, see Signs of God.
Mi'raj,   17:1.
Mischief on land and sea, 30:41;
of created things, 93:1-5; 94:4-6.
Misers condemned, 17:29, 47:38

Monasticism disapproved, 57:27;

Months, number of, 9:35-37.

Moses, and his people, 2:51-61;

 advises Israelites, 5:23-29;

 guided by God, 6:84;

 and Pharaoh, 7:103-137; 10:75-92; 11:96-99; 17:101-103;

  20:42- 53, 56-79; 23:45-49; 25:35-36; 26:10-69;

  28:4-21, 31-42; 11:23-46; 43:45-56; 51:38-40;

  79:15-26;

 resists idol worship, 7:138-141;

 sees the Glory on the Mount, 7:142-145;

 reproves his people for calf-worship, and prays for them,

  7:148-156;

 his people, 7:159-162;

 his Book, doubts and differences, 11:110;

 to teach his people gratitude, 14:5-8;

 nine Clear Signs, 7:133; 17:101;

 to the junction of the two Seas, 18:60-82.

 his call, 19:51-51; 20:9-56; 28:29-35;

 his childhood, mother, and sister, 20:38-40; 28:7-13;

 converts Egyptian magicians, 20:70-73; 26:46-52;

 indignant at calf-worship, 20:86-98;

 and the mystic Fire, 27:7-14; 28:29-35;

 his mishap in the City, 28:14-21;

 in Madyan, 28:22-28;

 guided to straight way, 37:114-122;

 Books of, 53:36; 87:19;

 vexed by his people, 61:5.

Mosque (of Quba), 9:107-108;

Mosques, 9:17-19, 28.

Mountains, 20:105-107; 21:31; 31:10; 59:21; 73:14; 101:5.

Muddaththtir, S. 74.

Muhajirs, 59:8-9; 63:7;

Muhammad, his mission, 7:158; 48:8-9;

 respect due to messenger, 2:104; 4:46;

 no more than a messenger, 3:144;

 gentle, 3:159;

 sent as favour to Believers, 3:164; 4:170;

 and to People of the Book, 5:21;

 a mercy to Believers, 9:61;

mercy to all creatures, 21:107;

as a mercy from God, 28:46-47; 33:45-48; 36:6; 42:48; 72:20-23, 27-28; 76:24-26.

his work, 3:164; 4:70-71; 6:107, 7:156-151; 10:2; 52:29-34; 74:1-7;

not mad or possessed, 7:184; 68:2; 81:22;

warner, 7:184, 188; 15:89; 53:56-62;

anxious for the Believers, 11:128;

brings Message as revealed, 10:15-16;

his teaching, 11:2-4; 12:108; 34:46-50;

to deliver revelation entirely as it comes to him, 11:12-14; 46:9;

God is witness to his mission, 13:43; 29:52; 46:8;

heart distressed for men, 15:97; 16:127; 18:6; 25:30;

to invite and argue, in ways most gracious, 16:125-128;

inspired, 18:110; 63:2-18;

mocked, 25:41-42; 34:7-8;

asks no reward, 25:57; 34:47; 38:86; 42:23;

his duty, 27:91-93; 30:30;

his household (consorts), 33:28-34, 50-53, 55, 59; 64:1, 3-6;

close to Believers, 33:6;

beautiful pattern of conduct, 33:21;

seal of the Prophets, 33:40;

universal Messenger to men, 34:28;

fealty to him is fealty to God, 48:10, 18;

Messenger of God, 48:29;

resist him not, 58:20-22;

Foretold by Jesus, 61:6;

Foretold by Moses, 46:10.

his Religion to prevail over all religion, 61:9;

unlettered, 7:157; 62:2;

leads from darkness to light, 65:11;

to strive hard, 66:9;

exalted standard of character, 68:4;

not a poet or soothsayer, 69:40-43;

devoted to prayer, 73:1-8, 20: 74:3;

witness, 73:15-16;

and the blind man, 80:1-10;

saw the Angel of Revelation, 53:4-18; 81:22-25;

to adore God and bring himself closer to Him, 96:19;
rehearsing scriptures, 98:2.

Muhammad, S. 47.

Mujadilah, S. 58.

Mulk, S. 67;

Mu'min, see Ghafir S. 40.

Mu'minun, S. 23.

Mumtahinah, S. 60.

Munafiqun, S. 63.

Murder 2:178-179; 5:35.

Mursalat, S. 77.

Muslim men and women, befitting conduct, 33:35-36.

Muzzammil, S. 73.

Naba', S. 78.

Nadir Banu, Jews, 59:2, 7, 11;

Nahl, S. 16.

Najm, S. 53.

Names, most beautiful, of God, 7:180, 17:110; 20:8; 59:24.

Naml, S. 27.

Nas, S. 114.

Nasr, 71:23;

Nasr, S. 110.

Nature declares God's praises, 24:41-44; 50:6-11;
shows God's goodness, and that His Promise is true, 78:6-
16.

Nazi'at, S. 79.

"Neither die nor live", 20:74; 87:13.

New Moon, 2:189.

News, to be tested, 4:89.

Night as a symbol, 79:29; 92:1; 93:2.

Night of Power 97:1-5.

Nisa', S. 4.

Noah, 6:84;7:59-64; 10:71-73; 11:25-49;21:76-77;23:23-30; 25:37;
26:105-122; 29:14-15;37:75-82; 51:46; 54:9-15; 69:11-
12; 71:1-28;
unrighteous son not saved, 11:45-47;
wife unrighteous, 66:10.

Nüh, S. 71.

Nür, S. 24.

Oaths, 2:224-227; 5:92; 16:94; 24:22, 53; 66:2; 68:10.

Obedience, 3:132; 4:59, 64, 66, 80-81; 5:95; 14:12; 8:20-25, 46; 24:51-12, 54; 47:33; 64:11-12.

Obligations to be fulfilled, 5:1.

Olive, as a symbol, 23:20; 24:35; 95:1;

Orphans, 2:220; 4:2, 6, 10, 127; 17:34;
       guardians of, 4:6.

Pairs, in all creatures, 13:3; 31:10; 36:36; 42:11; 43:12; 51:49;
       53:45.

Parables, man who kindled a fire, 2:17-18;
       rain-laden cloud, 2:19-20;
       goat herd, 2:171;
       hamlet in ruins, 2:259;
       grain of corn, 2:261;
       hard, barren rock, 2:264;
       fertile garden, 2:265-266;
       rope, 3:103;
       frosty wind, 3:117;
       dog who lolls out his tongue, 7:176;
       undermined sandcliff, 9:109-110;
       rain and storm, 10:24;
       blind and deaf, 11:24;
       garden of joy, 13:35;
       ashes blown about by wind, 14:18;
       goodly trees, with roots, branches, and fruit, 14:24-25;
       evil tree, 14:26;
       slave versus man liberally favoured, 16:75;
       dumb man versus one who commands justice, 16:76;
       woman who untwists her yarn, 16:92;
       City favoured but ungrateful, 16:112-113;
       two men, one proud of his possessions and the other
           absorbed in God, 18:32-44;
       this life like rain, pleasant but transitory, 18:45-46;
       fall from Unity, like being snatched up by birds or carried
           off by winds, 22:31;
       a fly, 22:73;
       Light, 24:31-36;
       mirage, 24:39;
       depths of darkness, 24:40;
       spider, 29:41;
       partners, 30:28;

Companions of the City, 36:13-32;
one master and several masters, 39:29;
Garden promised to the Righteous with four kinds of
       rivers, 47:15;
seed growing, 48:29;
rain and physical growth, 57:20;
mountain that humbles itself; 59:21;
donkey, 62:51;
if stream of water be lost, 67:30;
People of the Garden, 68:17-33.
Parents, kindness to, 17:23; 29:8; 31:14; 46:15-18.
'Partners' of God, a falsehood, 10:34-35, 66; 16:86; 28:62-64,71-
      75; 30:40; 42:21.
Passion or Impulse, worship of, 25:43;
Path, see Way.
Patience and perseverance, 2:45, 153; 3:186, 200; 10:109; 11:115;
      16:126-127; 20:130-132; 40:55, 77; 46:35; 50:39; 70:5;
      73:10-11.
"Peace," the greeting of the Righteous, 7:46; 10:10; 14:23; 36:58.
Peace, incline towards, 8:61.
Peace, Salam, meaning, 19:62.
Peace, Sakinah, Tranquillity, 11:26, 40; 48:4, 18, 26.
Pearls, well-guarded, 52:24; 56:23;
Pen, 68:1; 96:4-5.
Penalty for sin, 3:188; 6:15-16; 10:50-53; 11:101-104; 13:34;
      16:88; 46:20; 70:1-3.
Persecution with Fire, 85:1-11.
Personal responsibility, 4:164; 10:30; 14:51; 53:38-41.
Pharaoh, cruelty, 2:49;
drowned, 2:50;
people of, 14:41-42;
dealings with Moses, 7:103-137; 10:75-92; see Moses;
body saved, 10:90-92;
denies God, 28:38; 79:24;
a man from his People confesses Faith, 40:28-44;
arrogant to the Israelites, 44:17-33;
wife righteous, 66:11;
sin and disobedience, 69:9; 73:16; 85:17-20; 89:10-14.
Pilgrimage, 2:158, 196-203; 3:97; 5:2; 22:26-33.
Piling up (the good things of this world), 102:1-4.

Pledge, everyone in pledge for his deeds, 52:21; 74:38.

Pleiades, 53:1; 86:1.

Plotters, 16:45-47.

Poets, 26:224-227; 36:69; 69:41.

Prayer, 1:1-7; 2:238-239; 3:8, 26-27, 147, 191-194; 4:43; 5:6;
    11:114; 17:78-81; 23:118; 50:39-40; 52:48-49; 73:1-8, 20;
    be steadfast in, 2:110;
    during travel, or in danger, 4:101-104;
    for Unbelievers, 9:113-114;
    due to God alone, 13:14-15.

Prayers, the five canonical, 11:144; 17:78-79; 20:130; 30:17-18;
why all prayers not answered, 42:27.

Precautions in danger, 4:71.

Priests and anchorites, 9:31, 34.

Prisoners of war, 8:67-71.

Prohibited Degrees in marriage, 4:22-24.

Property, 2:188; 4:5, 29;
    to be distributed equitably, 59:7-9.

Prophets, 2:253;
    continuous line, 3:33-34; 4:163-165; 5:19; 6:84-90; 23:23-
    50; 57:26-27;
    covenants from, 3:81; 33:7-8;
    never false to their trusts, 3:161;
    rejected, 3:184; 6:34; 25:37; 34:45; 51:52-55;
    slain, 3:183;
    all to be believed in, 4:150-152;
    to give account, 5:109;
    mocked, 6:10; 13:32; 15:11; 21:41;
    why sent, 6:48, 131; 14:4-6;
    had enemies, 6:112; 25:31;
    rehearse God's Signs, 7:35-36;
    sent to every people, 10:47; 16:36;
    had families, 13:38;
    human, but guided, 14:10-12; 16:43-44; 17:94-95; 21:7-8;
        25:7-8, 20.
    persecuted and threatened, 14:13;
    witnesses against their people, 16:89;
    and Messengers, meaning, 19:51.
    one brotherhood, 23:52-54;
    some named, some not, 40:78.

Prophet's Consorts, extra responsibilities and duties, 33:28-34.
     who are to be, 33:50-52.
     respect due to them, 33:53-55.
     respect due to Prophet's Consorts and believing men and
        women, 33:56-58.
     Prophet's wives and daughters and all believing women to
        be modest, 33:59-62.
Prosperity (spiritual), 87:4-15;
     success, 91:9-10.
Publicity versus secrecy, 4:148.
Punishment, for man's arrogance and rebellion, 96:15-18;
     abiding — for wilful rebellion, but not after repentance, nor
        for minor sins, 79:37-39.

Qadir, 4:149.
Qadr, S. 97.
Qaf, S. 50.
Qalam, S. 68.
Qamar, S. 54.
Qari'ah, S. 101.
Qarun, 28:76-82; 29:39.
Qasas, S. 28.
Qiblah, 2:142-145, 149-150.
Qiyamah, S. 75.
Quba', (Mosque), 11:107-108.
Qur'an, inspired Message, 4:82; 6:19;
     cannot be produced by other than divine agency, 2:23;
        10:38; 11:13; 17:89;
     verses, fundamental and allegorical, 3:7; 11:1;
     God is witness, 6:19;
     God's revelation, 6:92; 7:105-107; 27:6; 45:2;
     follow it and do right, 6:155;
     respect and attention due to, 7:204-206;
     Book of Wisdom, 10:1; 31:2; 36:2;
     in Arabic, 12:2; 13:37; 41:44; 42:7; 43:30;
     described, 13:31, 36-37; 14:1; 56:77-80;
     makes things clear, 15:1; 25:33; 26:2; 27:1; 28:2; 36:69-
        70; 43:2;
     not to be made into shreds, 15:91;
     purpose of revelation, 16:64-65;
     language pure Arabic, 16:103;

good news and warning, 17:9-10;
and the Unbelievers, 17:45-47;
healing and mercy, 17:82;
explains similitudes, 17:89; 18:54; 39:27;
no crookedness therein, 18:1-2;
teaching, 18:2-4; 19:97; 20:2-7; 26:210-220;
easy, 19:97; 44:58; 54:17, 22, 32, 40;
revealed in stages, 17:106; 25:32; 76:23; 87:6-7;
"my people took it for nonsense", 25:30;
solves Israel's controversies, 27:76;
recite Qur'an, 73:4; and pray, 29:45;
carries own evidence, 29:47-49, 51;
guide and mercy, 31:3;
Truth from God, 32:3; 35:31;
beautiful Message consistent with itself, 39:23;
instructs mankind, 39:41; 80:11-12;
no falsehood can approach it, 41:42.
same Message to earlier prophets, 41:43; 43:44-45;
not sent to worldly leaders, 43:31-32;
seek earnestly to understand, 47:24;
admonish with, 50:45;
taught by God, 55:1-2;
to be received with humility, 59:21;
how to be read and studied, 2:121; 75:16-18;
in books of honour and dignity; 80:13-16;
Message to all the Worlds, 81:26-29;
Unbelievers reject it, 84:20-25;
Tablet Preserved, 85:21-22;
See also Book, and Revelation.
Quraysh, S. 106.
Quraysh, unbelieving, 54:43-46, 51;
appeal to, 106:1-4;
Qurayzah Tribe, 33:26-27.
Ra'd, S. 13.
Rahman, S. 55.
Raiment of righteousness is best, 7:26.
Rain, God's gift, 56:68-70.
Ramadan, 2:185.
Ransom, sought in vain by sinners, 3:91; 10:54; 13:18.
Rass, Companions of the, 25:38; 50:12.

Reality, the sure, 69:1-3.

Record, 50:4; 69:19, 25; 83:7-9, 18-21; 84:7-15.

Religion, no compulsion in, 2:256;
    of Islam, 3:19-20, 83-84;
    no excesses in, 4:171; 5:77-81;
    perfected, 5:3;
    not play and amusement, 6:70;
    do not divide and make sects, 6:159; 30:32;
    universal, 13:19-22;
    no difficulties imposed in, 22:78;
    standard religion is to establish pattern according to which God has made man, 30:30;
    same for all prophets, 42:13-15;
    ancestral, 43:22-24;
    right way of, 45:18.

Remembrance of God, what is, 63:9.

Repentance, with amendment, accepted, 6:54; 42:25.

Respite for Evil, 3:178; 10:11; 12:110; 14:42-43, 44; 29:53-55; 86:15-17.

Resurrection, 16:38-40; 17:49-52; 19:66-72; 22:5; 46:33-34; 50:3,20-29,41-44; 75:1-15; 79:10-12; 86:5-8.

Retaliation disapproved, 5:45.

Revelation, doubts solved, 2:23;
    of Moses and Jesus, 2:87;
    abrogated or forgotten, 2:106;
    guidance, 3:73;
    to Prophet and those before him, 5:48;
    Word that distinguishes Good from Evil, 86:11-14;
    do not entertain doubt about, 6:114; 11:17;
    purpose of, 7:2, 203;
    in stages, 16:101;
    through the Holy Spirit, 16:102-103; 26:192-199;
    to be proclaimed, 96:1;
    nature of, 41:2-4, 6-8; 69:50-51; 81:15-21;
        See also Book, and Qur'an.

Revile not false gods, 6:108.

Reward, without measure, 3:27; 39:10;
    better than deed deserves, 27:84; 30:39;
    according to best of deeds, and more, 24:38; 29:7; 39:35;
    for good, no reward other than good, 55:60;

Righteous, company of the, 4:69;
     shall inherit the earth, 21:105;
     described, 51:15-19; 76:5-12.
Righteousness, 2:177, 207-208, 212; 3:16-17, 92, 133-135, 191-
     195; 4:36, 125; 5:93; 7:42-43; 16:97;
     steep path of, 90:11-18.
Rocky Tract, Companions of, 15:80-85.
Roman Empire, 30:2-5;
Rum, S. 30.
Saba', S. 34.
Saba', 27:22; 34:15-21;
Sabbath, transgressors of, 7:163-166;
     made strict, 16:124.
Sabians, 2:26; 5:69; 22:17.
Sacrifice, 22:34-37.
Sād, S.38.
Safa and Marwah, 2:158.
Saff, S. 61.
Saffat, S. 37.
Sajdah, S. 32.
Sālih, 7:73-79: 11:61-68; 26:141-159: 27:45-53.
Salsabil, 16:18.
Salvation, 5:119; 25:15; 78:31.
Samiriy, 20:85, 95-97.
Satan, (see also Iblis),   2:36; 4:117-120; 24:21;
          excites enmity and hatred, 5:91;
          resist his suggestions, 7:200-201;
          deceives, 8:48;
          reproaches own followers, 14:22;
          evil spirit, rejected, accursed, 3:36; 15:17, 34; 16:98;
          has no authority over Believers, 16:99-100;
          suggests vanity, 22:52-53;
          is an enemy, 35:6; 36:60.
Scandal, 24:19; 104:1.
Scriptures, people of the, 2:62;
          kept pure and holy, 98:2.
Secrecy, when permissible, 4:114;
          in counsels, disapproved, 58:7-10, 12-13.
Sects and divisions disapproved, 30:32; 42:13-14; 43:64-65;
               45:17, 28.

Seed, grows by God's providence, 56:63-67.

Seven Tracts or Firmaments, 2:29; 23:17; 65:12; 67:3; 71:15;

Shadow, allegory, 25:45.

Shameful things to be shunned, 7:28.

Shams, S. 91.

She-camel as a Symbol to Thamūd, 7:73; 17:59; 26:155-158.

Ship, sailing of, as a Sign, 2:164; 14:32; 16:14; 17:66; 22:65;
          31:31; 35:12; 42:32-33; 45:12; 55:24.

Shu'ara', S. 26.

Shu'ayb, 7:85-93; 11:84-95; 29:36-37.

Shura, S. 42.

Siege of Madinah, 33:9-27.

Signs of God, demanded by those without knowledge, clear to those
          with Faith, 2:118;

          in the creation of the heavens and the earth, 2:164; 3:190;

made clear, that men may consider, 2:219-220;

          sign of authority to the prophet Samuel, 2:248;

          denial of, 3:11, 108;

          rejecters, deaf and dumb, in darkness, 6:39,

          in all things, 6:95-99;

          wicked demand special Signs, 6:124;

          rejecters make excuse, 6:156-158;

          consequences of rejection, 7:36-41, 146-147;

          rejecters wrong their own souls, 7:177;

          rejecters get respite, 7:182;

          rejecters lose guidance, 6:186.

          day and night as Signs, 17:12;

          in nature and all creation, 10:5-6; 30:20-27; 45:3-6;

          self evident Signs, the Book, 29:49-51;

          winds and ships, 30:46; 42:32-35;

          ships, 31:31;

          the Night, sun and moon, 36:37-40;

          the Ark through the Flood, and similar ships, 36:41-44;

          in this life, 39:59;

          rejecters are deluded, 40:63;

          rain and revived Earth, 41:39-40;

          in the farthest regions of the earth, and in their own souls,
                   41:53;

          rejected or taken in jest, 45:8-9;

          on earth, in your own selves, and in heaven, 51:20-23;

creation of man from Seed, 56:57-59;
death, 56:60-62;
seed in the ground, 56:63-67;
water, 56:68-70;
fire, 56:71-73;
mocked, 68:15.
camels, sky, mountains, earth, 88:17-20;
forces of nature, 89:1-5;
no special Sign (miracle) given, 6:109; 10:20; 8:7; 17:59;
    21:5-6;
Sijjin, 88:7-9.
Sin, 4:30-32, 36-39, 107-112, 116; 7:100-102; 10:54; 74:43-48;
wrongdoers will be cut off, 6:45;
to be eschewed, 6:120;
causes destruction, 7:4-5; 77:16-19;
will not prosper, 10:17;
and Faith have different goals, 68:35-41;
God forgives all sins, 39:53;
Sinai, 19:52; 95:2;
Sinners, 23:63-77; 26:200-209; 83:29-36;
their hearing, sight, and skins will bear witness, 41:20-23;
different witnesses against them, 85:3.
Sirius (Dog Star), 86:1;
Slander, 11:79; 24:23; 68:11-12.
Solomon, 2:102; 6:84; 21:79, 81-82; 27:15-44; 34:12-14; 38:30-40;
and the ants, 27:18-19;
and the Hoopoe, 27:22-26;
and the Queen of Saba, 27:22-44.
Son, adopted, 33:4-5.
Soul, burden not greater than it can bear, 2:286; 7:42; 23:62;
responsibility, 3:30; 74:38;
justly dealt with, 16:111;
taste of death, 21:35;
human, three stages of development, 75:2;
enters heaven, not body, 89:27-30.
Spendthrifts condemned, 17:26-29; 25:67.
Spirit, the, 70:4; 78.38; 97:4.
the Holy, God strengthened Jesus with, 2:87, 253;
God's, breathed into man, 15:29;
of inspiration, 17:85-86;

God strengthens Believers with, 58:22;

Spoils of war, 8:1, 41;

Star, adjuration by, 53:1; 86:1-4.

Stars, 7:54; 16:12, 16; 22:18; 37:6-10; 67:5; 77:8; 81:2; 82:2.

Straight Way, 1:6; 6:153; etc.

Striving, 9:20, 81; 22:78; 25:52; 29:69; 61:11;

Suffering, adversity, and prosperity, 7:94-96.

Sun, 91:1.

Superstitions, 5:103; 6:138-140, 143-144.

Sürah, revelation increases faith, 9:124-127;

Sustenance, literal and figurative, 10:59; 16:73; 19:62; 42:12;
        51:57-58; 67:21.

Suwa', 71:23;

Taghabun, S. 64.

Ta Ha, S. 20.

Tahrim, S. 66.

Takathur, S. 102.

Takwir, S. 81.

Talaq, S. 65.

Talh (tree), 56:29.

Talüt, 2:247-249.

Taqwa, 2:2; 59:18-19.

Tariq, S. 86.

Tasnim, 83:27-28.

Tatfif, see Mutaffifin, S. 83.

Tawbah, S. 9.

Term appointed, for every people, 7:34; 10:49; 15:4-5; 16:61;
        20:129.

Testing, by God, 3:154; 34:21;

Thamüd, 7:73-79; 11:61-68; 25:38; 26:141-159; 27:45-53; 29:38;
        41:17; 51:43-45; 54:23-31; 69:4-8; 85:17-20; 89:9-14;
        91:11-15;

Theft, punishment, 5:38-39.

Tin, S. 95.

Traffic and Trade, 4:29

Transition between second and third person, 84:20;
        between "We" and "Me", see "We" and "Me."

Travel through the earth, 6:11; 22:46; 27:69; 29:20-22; 30:9,42;
        35:44; 40:21, 82; 47:10;

Treasures of God, 6:50; 6:59; 11:31; 15:21.

Treaties, 11:1-4, 7-10;
Trench (or Ditch), Battle of the, 24:55; S. 33; 33:9-11.
Trials, 2:214-218.
Trumpet, on Day of Judgement, 6:73; 23:101; 39:68; 69:13.
Trust offered to Heavens. Earth, and Mountains, undertaken by
      Man, 33:72-73;
Trusts, 4:58; 8:27.
Truth, 23:70-71, 90;
      Rejecters of, 77:1-50; 98:1-6.
Tubba', 44:37;
Tur, S. 52.
Uhud, lessons of, 3:121-128, 140-180;
Ummah, 2:143-144.
'Umrah, 2:196;
Unbelievers, plot in vain, 8:30;
      despise revelation, 8:31;
      challenge a Penalty, 8:32-35;
      prayers empty, 8:35;
      spend for wrong purposes, 8:36;
      past forgiven; if they repent, 8:38; 9:11;
      break covenants, 8:56;
      will not frustrate the godly, 8:60-61;
      protect each other, 8:73;
      described, 9:73-78; 14:3:
      will wish they had believed, 15:2;
      will bear double burdens, 16:25;
      to be covered with shame, 16:27;
      dispute vainly, 18:56-57;
      their efforts wasted, 18:102-106;
      their arrogance, 19:73-82; 35:43;
      deeds like mirage, 24:39;
      as in depths of darkness, 24:40;
      mutual recriminations at Judgement, 34:31-33;
      self-glory and separatism, 38:2-14;
      dispute about the Signs of God, 40:4-6;
      hate Truth, 43:78;
      will turn back from fight, 48:22-23;
      their high-handedness, 48:25-26;
      vain fancies, 52:35-44;
      give them not friendship but kind and just dealing, 60:1-9;

rush madly, 70:36-39.

Unity, 2:163; 6:19; 92:1-4.

Usury, 2:275-276; 2:278-280; 3:130.

'Uzayr, 9:30.

'Uzza, 53:19.

Vain discourse to be avoided, 6:68.

Vicegerent, God's, on earth, 2:30.

Victory, uses of, 48:1-3;
    through help of God, 61:13.

Virtues, see Righteousness, and Believers.

Wadd, 71:23;

"Wait ye, we too shall wait," 9:52; 10:102; 11:122; 20:135: 44:59;
    52:31.

Waqi'ah, S. 56.

War against God, 5:33-34.

Warning before destruction, 17:16;
    given in three ways, 39:16.

Waste not, 6:141; 7:31.

Water, animals created from, 21:30, 24:45; 25:54;
    two bodies of flowing water, 25:53; 18:60; 35:12; 55:19-
    20;
    God's throne over the waters, 11:7;
    circulation of, 23:18.

Way, the, 1:6; 42:52-53; 90:10-18; etc.

Wealth, hoarding condemned, 104:2-3;

"We" and "Me": transition between the first person plural and
singular in reference to God, 23:8; 2:150-151; 31:10, 11;
    68:44; 70:40;

Wicked, their faces headlong in the fire, 27:90; 67:22;

Widows, 2:234-235, 240.

Will of God, 10:99-100; 30:5; 81:29; 82:8.

Will of man, 24:62;
    Free Will versus Determinism, 81:28-29; 82:7;

Winds, like heralds of glad tidings, 7:57-58; 15:22; 30:46, 48, 51;
    mystic symbolism, 77:1-6.

Wine, 2:219; 5:90;
    heavenly wine, 47:15; 76:21; 83:25;

Witnesses, among men, 2:143; 22:78;
    at Judgement, 85:3.

Woman, wronged, plea accepted, 58:1-2.

Women, 2:222-223; 4:15, 19-22, 34, 127;
       to be reverenced, 4:l;
       false charges against, 24:4-5, 11-20; 24:23-26;
       modesty, 24:30-31;
       believing, refugees, 60:10-12;
       the four perfect, 66:11.
Wood, Companions of the, 15:78; 26:176-191.
World, this, but play and amusement, 6:32; 29:64; 47:36; 57:20;
       deceives men, 6:130;
       not to be preferred, 9:38-39; 13:26; 28:60-61;
       gets its reward, but not in Hereafter, 11:15-17; 17:18;
           42:20;
       man loves, 75:20-21; 76:27.
Worship, true worship and charity, 107:2-7;
Writing, for contracts, 2:282.
Wrongdoers, 11:18-22, 101-104, 116-117; 39:47;
       See also Unbelievers.
Yaghuth, 71:23;
Yahya, (John the Baptist), birth, 3:39; 6:85;
       his character and position, 19:12-15;
       reverenced God, 21:90.
Ya Sin, S. 36.
Ya'uq, 71:23;
Yunus, S. 10; see also Jonah.
Yusuf, S. 12. see also Joseph.
Zayd the freedman, 33:37-38;
Zakariya, 3:37-41; 6:85; 19:2-11; 21:90.
Zakah, (Regular Charity), 2:43, 110, 177, 277; 4:162; 5:55. Zanjabil,
       76:17.
Zaqqum, 17:60; 37:62-66; 44:43-46; 56:52.
Zaynab, daughter of Jahsh, 33:28, 37-38, 50.
Zaynab, daughter of Khuzaymah, 33:28, 50.
Zihar, 33:4; 58:2-4.
Zalzalah, S. 99.
Zodiacal Signs, 15:16.
Zukhruf, S. 49.
Zumar, S. 39.